water

GOVERNMENT IN OUR REPUBLIC

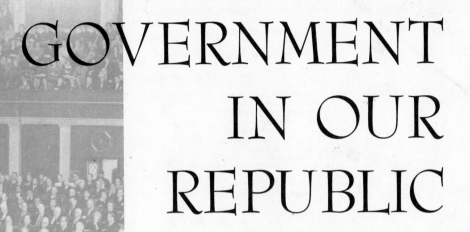

GOVERNMENT
IN OUR
REPUBLIC

STUART GERRY BROWN

Maxwell Professor of American Civilization
Maxwell School of Citizenship and Public Affairs
Syracuse University

CHARLES L. PELTIER

Late Head of Social Studies
Newton High School
Newtonville, Massachusetts

New York   **THE MACMILLAN COMPANY**

CHARTS BY VAUGHN GRAY

PHOTOGRAPH ACKNOWLEDGMENTS

Association of Better Business Bureaus, Inc.: 364, Checking advertisements
Brown Brothers: 160, T. Roosevelt
Caterpillar Tractor Company: 307, Road builder; 327, Road smoother
Department of Tourism, St. Thomas: 347, V.I. Government House
A. Devaney, Inc.: 82, Voters (Joseph Scaylea); 410, Newspaper stand; 447, Barbecue (Joseph Scaylea); 602, Receiving Social Security check (David W. Carson)
Federal Aviation Agency: 194, Air traffic control
Harris and Ewing: 168, Coolidge addressing Congress; 169, Fireside chat of F. D. Roosevelt
ILO Photo: 550, Eye examination
ILGWU: 550, Union sculpture class; 551, Union recreation (Justice)
League of Women Voters, New York City: 364, Getting out the vote
Library of Congress: 1, 47, John Hancock's Defiance; 49, 353, Parade of the Stamp Act; 150, Library of Congress
Monkmeyer: 388, Jury (Brooks); 447, Speaker (Meisel)
N.B.C. Photo: 463, 1952 Convention
New York City Department of Personnel: 326, Policeman; 327, Fire scene
New York State Citizens Committee for the Public Schools: 364, Parents Association
Charles Pfizer and Company: 9, Druggist
Puerto Rico News Service: 346, Governor Muñoz Marin, Puerto Rico House of Representatives, Supreme Court Building
Remington Rand Division of Sperry Rand Corporation: 9, Typist
Republican National Committee: 150, Senator campaigning, Senator giving out policy; 446, Women workers; 462, Staff, TV set up, Rostrum at Cow Palace; 463, Senator, Candidate group interview
Standard Oil Company, (N.J.): 8, Cowboys, Service center, Country store; 194, Truck; 306, Bookmobile, High school band, Swimming; 327, School bus interior; 389, Mailman at meeting, Counting ballots; 447, Caucus; 602, Boy in high school
TVA: 194, Lineman
Trust Territory Photo: 346, Pacific Trust—Copra; 347, Samoa—Government House, Village
United Nations: 365, Audience at UN
United Press International Photo: title page, Eisenhower addressing Congress; 82, Voters
United States Department of Agriculture: 307, Farmers Grange (Soil Conservation Service); 583, Spraying Boise National Park (Forest Service), Group planning
U.S. Department of The Air Force: 692, Pentagon; 693, Ground Observer Corps
U.S. Department of The Army: 693, Maneuvers on Iwo Jima, Anti-Aircraft at Camp Gorden
U.S. Department of Commerce: 410, Census taker (Bureau of Census), Univac; 499, Set of standards (Bureau of Standards)
U.S. Department of Defense: 692, Marines hitting beach (Photo courtesy Leatherneck Magazine)
U.S. Department of Health, Education and Welfare: 499, National Cancer Institute (Public Health Service); 602, Scientist (National Institutes of Health)
U.S. Department of Labor: 550, Consumer Price Index
U.S. Department of The Interior: 94, Horseshoe Dam and Quincey Valley Farms (Bureau of Reclamation); 95, Fish samples (Fish and Wildlife Service—Rex Gary Schmidt), Washington National Park (National Park Service)
U.S. Department of The Navy: 692, Navy jets
U.S. Department of State: 169, Eisenhower signing law; 640, Herter and Foreign Ministers, Foreign Service Institute class; 640-641, Pipes in Pakistan, Wheat loading in Tunisia, Malaria Laboratory in the Philippines (Canlas) (International Cooperation Administration)
U.S. Department of The Treasury: 499, Amellia Island Light (Coast Guard Official Photo)
Wide World Photo: 82, 18-year-olds; 150, Congressional Conference; 151, Representative and mail from home; 169, Truman reviewing troops; 388, Voters in Wisconsin; 551, Across the bargaining board

CONTENTS

v

UNIT THREE - YOU AND YOUR GOVERNMENT

CHARTS

PREFACE

Our purpose in this book is to give an accurate, readable, and comprehensive account of the American governments—local, state, and national—in a book suitable for a one-unit senior high school course. At the same time, and equally important, we have tried to give both student and teacher continuing opportunities to deal with ideas, to grapple with the substance of government as what a great but highly diverse people do for themselves through their public agencies. This means that we stressed variety of interests, conflict of purposes—what James Madison called "factions." We have tried throughout to show how reasonable compromises, measured against the public interest, make free government possible (and peaceful) among us within our fifty states.

We have emphasized the problems of responsible citizenship by showing what decisions are actually made by the citizen (or should be made), and how they are made. And, finally, we have asked the student to consider seriously how, as a citizen, he intends to face his own future in America and the future of America in the world.

What began several years ago as a pleasant and rewarding collaboration between Charles Peltier, Head of the Newton, Massachusetts, High School Social Studies Department and me was tragically ended by the untimely death of Dr. Peltier in the spring of 1959. I should like to record here my sense of personal loss, and my great debt for the imaginative work he had nearly completed on the book. I am grateful to Mrs. Charles Peltier for her careful reading of the proofs.

I am indebted to a number of friends for advice and favors. In particular Dean Ralph Kharas and Mr. Richard T. Mosher have helped me with the chapters on the courts and law enforcement and Professor Roscoe C. Martin has given useful advice on local government. My research assistants, Donald G. Baker and Robert L. Piper, have cheerfully run a thousand errands and I am most grateful. Mrs. Dorothy Arnof of The Macmillan Company has made such thoughtful and meticulous contributions to the book that she has far exceeded any "line of duty" for an editor, and I am deeply grateful.

And I should like to say here, what she knows from long hours of work, that my wife's help has been indispensable. It was she who encouraged me at the outset to undertake this book. Her criticism, through all stages of preparation, has been thoughtful and perceptive, and her assistance in proofreading (as in all my writings) has been skillful as well as generous.

STUART GERRY BROWN

Maxwell Graduate School of Citizenship and Public Affairs
Syracuse University
January 31, 1960

The unanimous Declaration of the thirteen united States

When in the Course of human events, it becomes necessary for one people to dissolve the political bands which have connected them with another, and to assume among the Powers of the earth, the separate and equal station to which the Laws of Nature and of Nature's God entitle them, a decent respect to the opinions of mankind requires that they should declare the causes which impel them to the separation.

We hold these truths to be self-evident, that all men are created equal, and that they are endowed by their Creator with certain unalienable Rights, that among these are Life, Liberty and the pursuit of Happiness. That to secure these rights, Governments are instituted among Men, deriving their just powers from the consent of the governed. That whenever any Form of Government becomes destructive of these ends, it is the Right of the People to alter or to abolish it, and to institute new Government, laying its foundation on such principles and organizing its powers in such form, as to them shall seem most likely to effect their Safety and Happiness, Prudence, indeed, will dictate that Governments long established should not be changed for light and transient causes; and accordingly all experience hath shown, that mankind are more disposed to suffer, while evils are sufferable, than to right themselves by abolishing the forms to which they are accustomed. But when a long train of abuses and usurpations, pursuing invariably the same Object evinces a design to reduce them under absolute Despotism, it is their right, it is their duty, to throw off such Government, and to provide new Guards for their future security. . . .

We, therefore, the Representatives of the United States of America, in General Congress, Assembled, appealing to the Supreme Judge of the world for the rectitude of our intentions, do, in the Name, and by Authority of the good People of these colonies, solemnly publish and declare, That these United Colonies are, and of Right ought to be Free and Independent States; that they are Absolved from all Allegiance to the British Crown, and that all political connection between them and the State of Great Britain, is and ought to be totally dissolved; and that as Free and Independent States, they have full Power to levy War, conclude Peace, contract Alliances, establish Commerce, and do all other Acts and Things which Independent States may of right do. And for the support of this Declaration, with a firm reliance on the Protection of Divine Providence, we mutually pledge to each other our Lives, our Fortunes and our Sacred Honor.

THE MEANING OF DEMOCRACY

Unit I

CHAPTER 1

We the People

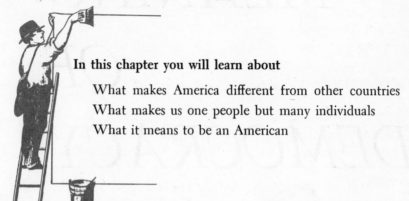

In this chapter you will learn about

What makes America different from other countries

What makes us one people but many individuals

What it means to be an American

"We the people of the United States. . . ." With this phrase begins the Constitution of the United States of America. This Constitution, as you know from your study of American history, defines the rules and establishes the principles by which we, the people, govern ourselves. To understand our government, therefore, you must first know who "we, the people" are, what we have in common with each other, what distinguishes us, and what any of us mean when we speak of "our country."

THE NATION AND ITS PEOPLE

It is often said about the United States that it is *unique* among the nations of the world and that it is an experiment. Later we shall examine the statement that America is an experiment. Let us see now what we mean by the uniqueness of the United States.

What Is a "People"?

In some sense, every country is unique. The word *unique* comes from the Latin word *unus* ("one") and means "one of a kind," "different," or "unlike the other." You can see right away that England is different from France, and Argentina is different from Pakistan. There are many ways in which they differ from one another. Consider language. The people of England speak a language quite unlike that of the people of France. Likewise the man from Argentina could not be expected, without studying it, to understand the speech of the people of Pakistan. There are also many other differences which distinguish these people from one another—differences of custom, government, tastes in food, education, music, and literature. If you were suddenly and surprisingly transported to one of these countries, it would not take you too long to find out which of the four you were in.

This does not mean that all Frenchmen or all Englishmen are exactly alike in custom, taste in food, amount and kind of education, manner of speech, and other ways. But all Frenchmen are enough like each other so that a stranger would know at once they belonged to the same country. The French people have inhabited the same land in Europe for many centuries. They speak the same language, and they share many customs and traditions. In other words, the French people have a common *culture* which makes them unique, or one of a kind, and hence like each other in many ways. At the same time, they remain different from people who are not French. It is because of this uniqueness of what we call French culture that tourists visit France.

These things are true of many of the other countries of the world. We can speak with clear meaning of the Germans, the English, or the Chinese and call each a *homogeneous* people. By this we mean one-ness or likeness, or that the people of that nation tend to be alike.

AMERICA—UNIQUE AMONG NATIONS

Open your telephone book at random. You will find names indicating American beginnings in many different countries. A recent issue of the Boston telephone book, for example, lists six Wangs, 224 LeBlancs, 76 Schmidts, 67 Swensons, and over 2,800 Sullivans. If you lived in France and opened the Paris telephone book, almost all the names you would see in it would be French.

Our ancestors represent nearly every one of the older countries and cultures of the world. If you look at an account of the Olympic games, the only way you can tell which competitors are the Americans is by the designation "United States of America." Three of our best swimmers in the 1952 Olympics were named Cleveland, Konno, and Oyakawa, all from the Ohio State University. The names of the American athletes are as many and as various as the nations competing.

In one sense, the only Americans are the American Indians. Only the Indians, as the Europeans found them here, are like the French or the Chinese, for example, in having inhabited the same land and inherited the same customs and traditions over centuries of time. But in a broader sense, all the people who have come here from all the countries of the world are Americans. Though our common language is English, only some of our people have English ancestors. Think back to the days of your own grandfathers and to the days of their fathers and grandfathers, and you will find that the Americans are indeed one people from many. In a song about "Our Football Team," Irving Caesar, the well-known composer of popular songs, summed it up:

> Some parents came from Hungary, from Poland and Rumania,
> From Switzerland, from Portugal and Spain—
> From Austria and Italy, from Greece and Lithuania,
> From Holland, and from France, and the Ukraine—
> From England, Ireland, Germany, they sought our hospitality
> And found a welcome on our friendly shores,
> From Finland and Batavia, Peru and Scandinavia,
> In millions they came through our open doors—
> Their fatherlands and motherlands included many other lands,
> Before through storm and gale they sailed away,
> So on our team we have their sons
> To kick the goals and make the runs,
> And that's what matters in the U.S.A.
> *—Reprinted by permission of Irving Caesar*

There is no American people in the same sense that there is a French or a Chinese people. This is one of the important elements in America's uniqueness. We are set off from most countries precisely because we are not homogeneous. We do *not* all have the same inheritance in language, customs, and tradition as do so many of the nations of the world. Other countries are unique because of their **oneness;** the United States is unique because of its *manyness.* Our taste in food is as varied as chop suey, waffles, spaghetti, roast beef, ragout, frankfurters, and kreplech. The great religions of the world are represented in our temples, meeting houses, cathedrals, churches, and synagogues. In the reading rooms of our metropolitan libraries you will find people reading such papers as *The Hellenic World, Il Progresso Italo Americano, Kuryer Codzienny,* and the *Irish World.* Yet each of us, different as he is in all these ways, is an American. We are all Americans.

We have seen that as Americans we are a people of many different backgrounds. As free individuals, however, we also possess many individual differences. The conditions of American life bring about still others. Americans follow thousands of different occupations. Some of us work on farms; some in factories. Some are engaged in business; others in the professions. Many of us are housewives.

4

The parts of the country in which we live also distinguish Americans. Some Americans live in the South. This background produces certain differences which distinguish them from people who live in the Midwest, the Far West, or along the Atlantic seaboard. In certain ways New Englanders can be distinguished from Texans or Californians.

But people who live in the same region—or even next door to each other—can differ greatly among themselves in national origins, in religion, in occupation, in political beliefs, in income, in ambitions, and in many other ways. They do not even all talk the same way. "We the people," in spite of being one people, are individuals, distinguished and divided in many ways.

Our Different National Backgrounds

We have already discussed our differing national backgrounds. A few of us had American Indians as ancestors. But most of our ancestors came here in just the last few hundred years, from Europe, Asia, and Africa. There are in our country citizens who themselves came or whose ancestors came from almost every part of the world, although far more have come from certain countries and regions than from others. Before 1680, nine-tenths of the colonists were of English stock. Consequently, our land became an English-speaking nation. But from 1680 until after the War Between the States, the majority of the new arrivals came from France, Germany, Ireland, Scotland, Switzerland, and Africa. At the time of the American Revolution, one-third of the people living in the colonies were of foreign birth.

5

These people brought some of their political attitudes with them. The stamp of their differences was placed on many early American communities. Some of the conflicts of the old world still exist here today.

Of the non-English-speaking peoples who came to the new world, the largest group has been the Germans. Germans came to Pennsylvania in colonial days, some for religious freedom, others to seek their fortunes. In the middle of the nineteenth century, when crops failed in Germany, and people lost their farms and possessions, many Germans came to America. They settled in such cities as Milwaukee, St. Louis, Buffalo, Cincinnati, and Chicago.

Toward the end of the nineteenth century and in the years just before World War I, large numbers of people came from Italy and from eastern Europe, especially from Poland, Hungary, Czechoslovakia, and Rumania. Many of these people came to work in American factories, where they could earn high wages. For this reason, large groups of Italians, Poles, and Czechs live in industrial cities such as Detroit, Cleveland, Pittsburgh, Akron, New York, Syracuse, Toledo, and Chicago. As early as 1890, New York City had half as many Italians as Naples, twice as many Irish as Dublin, and two and one-half times as many Poles as Warsaw. The city then contained as many Germans as Hamburg, but not so many Poles and Canadians as Chicago.

America has always attracted Scandinavian farmers. Many Norwegians, Swedes, and Danes came to the United States to obtain good cheap land and to carry on farming. Scandinavian-Americans form a very important part of the population in the rich dairy and farm lands of Wisconsin, Minnesota, and the Dakotas, as well as in other parts of the country.

The Asians who came to the United States across the Pacific settled in greatest numbers on the West Coast. There they found many descendants of Spaniards and Mexicans, as well as adventurous Easterners who had traveled across the continent as pioneers. Japanese-American farmers, who specialize in growing fruit and vegetables, have helped to make California into a wonderful garden. Chinese businessmen and artisans have contributed to the rapid growth of cities like San Francisco and Los Angeles. Both of these nationality groups came to the United States chiefly in the latter part of the nineteenth century and the early years of the twentieth century. Both have had a long struggle to win full acceptance in the new world. Both have recently won for themselves the right to become citizens by naturalization.

Our Different Religions

Just as people brought with them to America their customs and attitudes, so they brought their various religious beliefs. Many continued to worship God as their forefathers had. Others worshiped in new ways, as their consciences dictated. As you know, many of the early colonists of New England were Puritans. Having been persecuted in Europe, they came to build their own communities and churches in America. But since the New England Puritans were themselves intolerant, some among them left the Massachusetts Bay settlements and followed Roger Williams to Rhode Island. Others, seeking greater opportunities, followed Thomas Hooker to Connecticut to start independent churches. Quakers and other new Protestant groups who were also persecuted in Europe came to Pennsylvania. Others went to Maryland, which had been settled originally by English Catholics.

Later groups of immigrants brought their religions with them. There are hundreds of thousands of American Baptists, Roman Catholics, Greek Orthodox, Lutherans, Methodists, Presbyterians, and Episcopalians. Jews came to our shores from many countries. Although there were some Jewish merchants in Rhode Island, New York, and Pennsylvania in colonial days, Jews did not come in large numbers until the end of the nineteenth century. More than 70,000 Americans practice Buddhism. There are few Zoroastrians or Shintoists (one is an ancient Persian and the other a nationalist Japanese religion) in America, but every other living and organized religion in the world is well represented on the North American continent!

The basic American principle is that each man shall be free to choose his own religion and to practice it according to the dictates of his own conscience. No government may tell him that he *must* worship or how to run his church. Nor may anyone be forced to pay money for the support of a church. Therefore, while many people continued to follow the religion of their ancestors, others broke away and started new denominations of their own. Thus over a million Latter-Day Saints or Mormons practice their faith in Utah and elsewhere, and the followers of Mary Baker Eddy have made Christian Science an important religious body.

Our Different Occupations

One of the most important differences among Americans is the matter of occupation. It is almost impossible to determine exactly the number of American occupations. You might be able to distinguish 238 basic occupations, which could be further divided into thousands, each different from the others.

Take farming as an example. Newspapers sometimes speak loosely of a "farm vote." But such a phrase merely covers up the fact that there are many different kinds of farmers in America, and that they do not all have the same interest. Thus there are dairy farmers in upstate New York, Wisconsin, or Minnesota. There are grain farmers in Iowa, Kansas, Nebraska, and the Dakotas. There are fruit farmers in Washington, Oregon, California, Florida, Louisiana, and Georgia. There are cotton farmers in Texas, Oklahoma, Wyoming, and Florida. In most of the 50 states there are at least some farmers

7

THE MANY PUBLICS OF AMERICA·

Not only is our country unique in its size, but it is also unique in the many different publics who live here whose opinions diverge and conflict in as many ways as they correspond. *Compromise,* by which our government is able to give all of them some of what they want, is a striking feature of our uniqueness.

The publics include the owner of a large ranch in the Southwest, the cowboys he employs, and the small farmer in the East. They may all share some views, but will certainly also have different ones.

The gas station owner and the small grocer, independent businessmen, have views which coincide and conflict—as do those of their customers.

The pharmacist and the stenographer also expect some of the same things from government, but want different things in other areas.

The miracle of our government is that it manages to reconcile these widespread points of view—and many, many others—to keep our country free.

9

who belong in each of these classifications. If you motor through upstate New York you will see fields of wheat, while in "industrial" Massachusetts you will find acres and acres of fruit trees and tobacco.

Even farmers who work in the same part of the country and in the same kind of production do not have identical interests. There are farmers who own and operate thousands of acres with hundreds of employees. There are still millions of one-family farms. And there are more millions of agricultural workers who do not own their land but "hire out" to others. To satisfy all these diverse groups is almost an impossible task. When we remember that the farmers are also divided by cultural and regional differences, it seems something of a miracle that the United States is able to satisfy any of the farmers at all.

There is as much diversity in other principal occupations. A packing-house worker in Chicago or Omaha differs in many respects from an assembly-line automobile worker in Detroit, or a mill worker in Lowell. A medical specialist in Rochester, Minnesota, is likely to have quite different interests and needs from a general practitioner in a small town anywhere. A vice-president in charge of production for a great steel corporation will have quite different interests from your local hardware dealer, even though both are businessmen. Even teachers are divided. Some may be college professors; others may teach first grade in a small country school.

Our Different Incomes

Income also divides Americans into many groups. Some people are very rich; other people are very poor. Most people belong somewhere in the middle.

Sometimes the income groups follow occupations; sometimes they cut across these. Persons who earn over $25,000 per year form one economic group, but they may be doctors, baseball players, farmers, lawyers, actors, disc jockeys, or production managers. At the same time, not *all* doctors, baseball players, farmers, lawyers, actors, disc jockeys, or production managers belong to that economic group. A good many other occupations never yield such a high income. You may remember also, from your United States history, times when people who wanted a cheaper currency made up an economic group; and there is a group described by President Franklin D. Roosevelt as "ill-fed, ill-housed, and ill-clothed."

The typical American, however, is neither rich nor poor, except in the sense that he is extremely wealthy by comparison with the typical citizen of practically all other lands. But our economic differences are not brought about by the extremes of rich and poor. On the contrary, most of the economic differences which do separate us are caused by the different ways in which we make our living.

Our economic differences are not by any means fixed or rigid. Each person is concerned with earning what he can. No man needs to stay poor because his father was poor. On the other hand, very few people can seriously expect to become millionaires if they start with nothing. Yet no profession or school is closed to an able person because he is poor, and no rich person can expect any special privilege because he is wealthy. The different ways in which we earn our living and our dependence on these ways divide us in a far more important sense than the dollar and cents differences of our incomes.

The Importance of These Differences for Government

Many, if not all, of these differences of national background, customs, religion, region of the country, occupation, and income affect our political attitudes and activities. We may join and take an active part in the political program of some special-interest group working for those measures which we think will improve, or protect, our own special position. Such groups include the AFL-CIO (American Federation of Labor-Congress of Industrial Organizations, a group of labor unions), the American Farm Bureau Federation, the NAM (National Association of Manufacturers), the American Soy Bean Association, the National Federation of Small Business, the National Education Association, the National Association for the Advancement of Colored People, the Association of Catholic Trade Unionists, the Automobile Association of America, and many others. Each group, and through the groups each individual, tries to influence the actions of our government.

We also express these differences in the way we vote for our Congressmen, our governors, and our President. The people we vote for belong to a **political party.** The **platform** or program of that party seems to us, the voters, to represent our own particular interests better than do proposals of the other party. Yet, on a national level, neither of the two major parties, the Republican or the Democratic, appeals only to interests of one group. Actually, the great contribution of these parties has been to lessen our differences and to unify our people. The search for the common interests of large numbers of people has been their business since they began. If you examine the national platform of either party in any election, you will find it includes some statement intended to appeal to each of the larger groups of our people—the workers, farmers, businessmen, professional people, youth, and housewives.

Our differences are important, therefore, because they affect the way we vote, the opinions we express, and the actions we expect of our government. It is, as we shall see in the next chapter, the job of government to find us ways of getting along in spite of our differences.

How, then, is America unique? In general, we can say that America is unique just because people of so many different customs, beliefs, and back-

11

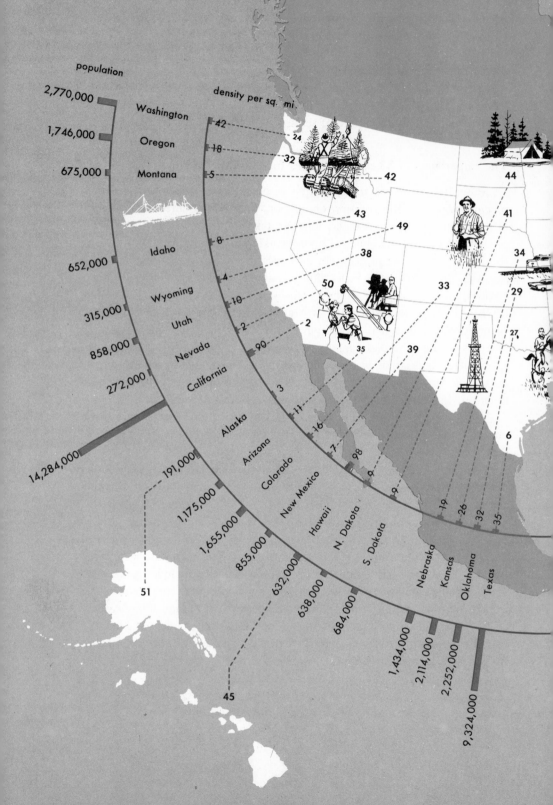

population

2,770,000   Washington

1,746,000   Oregon

675,000   Montana

density per sq. mi.

42 ---- 24

18 ---- 32

5 ---- 42

43

49

652,000   Idaho

8

44

38

Wyoming

4

315,000   Utah

10 ---- 50

858,000   Nevada

2 ---- 2

272,000   California

90

35

39

41

34

29

27

14,284,000

3

11

16

Alaska

7

Arizona

98

191,000

Colorado

9

1,175,000

New Mexico

9

1,655,000

Hawaii

6

855,000

N. Dakota

51

632,000

S. Dakota

19

638,000

26

684,000

32

35

45

1,434,000

2,114,000

2,252,000

9,324,000

Nebraska

Kansas

Oklahoma

Texas

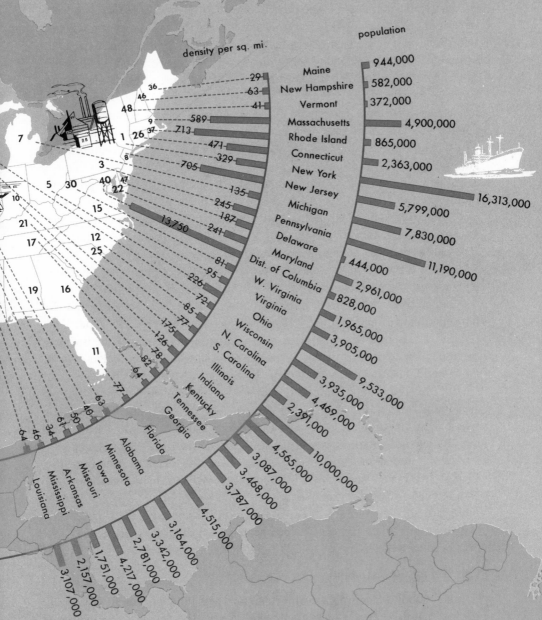

Population Distribution

Rank in population is indicated by the numerals within the state borders and the District of Columbia

density per sq. mi.

population

State	density	population	rank
Maine	29	944,000	36
New Hampshire	63	582,000	46
Vermont	41	372,000	48
Massachusetts	589	4,900,000	9
Rhode Island	713	865,000	37
Connecticut	471	2,363,000	26
New York	329	16,313,000	1
New Jersey	705	5,799,000	8
Michigan	135	7,830,000	7
Pennsylvania	245	11,190,000	3
Delaware	187	444,000	47
Maryland	241	2,961,000	22
Dist. of Columbia	13,750	828,000	40
W. Virginia	81	1,965,000	30
Virginia	95	3,905,000	15
Ohio	226	9,533,000	5
Wisconsin	72	3,935,000	12
N. Carolina	85	4,469,000	10
S. Carolina	77	2,391,000	25
Illinois	175	10,000,000	4
Indiana	126	4,565,000	11
Kentucky	78	3,087,000	17
Tennessee	82	3,468,000	16
Georgia	64	3,787,000	19
Florida	77	4,515,000	21
Alabama	63	3,164,000	20
Minnesota	50	3,342,000	18
Iowa	46	2,781,000	34
Missouri	61	4,217,000	13
Arkansas	34	1,751,000	46
Mississippi	46	2,157,000	24
Louisiana	64	3,107,000	23

13

grounds live here together, sharing the same government and the same country. But there are other reasons for this uniqueness as well.

The Bigness of America

One thing that makes America unique is its *bigness*. America is a very large country in land surface. Look at any map of the world and you will see that very few countries cover as much territory. The United States stretches across an entire continent—2,800 miles from east to west and 1,600 miles from north to south, with an additional 586,400 square miles in Alaska and 6,454 in Hawaii, to say nothing of our overseas territories. This big land area has a great variety of geographic features: lakes as big as oceans, vast, dry deserts, wall-like mountain ridges, and some of the longest rivers in the world. The climate ranges from long, icy winters in the north to long, semi-tropical growing seasons in the south.

America is also big in the richness of its resources. America produces more coal and oil than any other country. Its rivers and mineral fuels generate more than a hundred million watts of electricity. Its vast forests produce more than eight hundred varieties of wood. Almost every mineral and raw material needed for the complex processes of modern industry can be found within the borders of our country. The millions of acres of fertile farmland grow almost every variety of food, and much more than we can consume.

Out of these rich natural resources, American workers and businessmen have produced about half of the world's wealth—products in goods and services. From bars of pig iron to television sets, from oranges to washing machines, the American people—7 percent of the world's population—make, grow, build, and sell more goods than all the rest of the world together.

But the 180 million American people also buy and use as much as the remaining two and one-half billion people in the world. Forty-five million telephones, fifty million cars, and almost forty million electric refrigerators are in use. And these staggering figures increase every year. This bigness of resources, production, and consumption gives the average American the highest living standard known. In a day or two, an American worker can earn enough to buy, for example, a small radio set. In other countries, people must save all their earnings for weeks or months before buying a radio.

No such bigness has ever before been imagined. No other people have ever been so well off.

Our Unique Responsibilities

Our unique bigness and wealth have made us unique in another respect. As the guardians of so much wealth and power, the American people have a unique responsibility to all of mankind. We have the responsibility of using wisely and for peace the goods we have inherited and the goods we have produced. Most of us know this, and we have done much to meet the challenge. No people have given more generously to the relief of disaster in other lands than have Americans. If an earthquake shakes Japan or Greece, we rush our aid to the scene. If, behind the Iron Curtain, the flooding of the Danube River brings suffering to the people of satellite countries, American relief is forthcoming. After World War II we came forward with billions of dollars for the reconstruction of war-torn regions. No country has contributed more to the work of the World Health Organization, a United Nations agency charged with the aiding of undeveloped nations in improving health. It may be that we have not always acted as wisely, or as charitably, or as generously as we might have. It is also true that our great wealth has aroused the envy of many poorer peoples, and that our generosity is sometimes misunderstood. But since we are now one of the great powers of the globe, and a leader of the free world, we can expect our responsibilities to become greater rather than smaller.

What Is an American?

The American people are not homogeneous in their national and cultural heritage. But that makes it still more remarkable that somehow over 180 million persons, descended from the people of almost every land and nation of the earth, do constitute *one* people. The boys with the Polish, Greek, Japanese, English, or Scandinavian names who wear the jersey of the United States at the Olympic Games are not Poles, Greeks, Japanese, Englishmen, or Scandinavians. They are Americans. It is the same with the telephone book, with the Wangs, LeBlancs, Schmidts, Swensons, and Sullivans. Only the names come from everywhere and anywhere. The people who answer to them are Americans. What, then, is an American?

In the eighteenth century, about the time of the American Revolution, an American farmer who had come from France to settle in the colonies was the first person to make a serious answer to this question, What is an American? His name was Michel Guillaume de Crèvecoeur. But his French name and heritage did not prevent him from feeling in his heart that he was an American. Here is what Crèvecoeur had to say:

What then is the American, this new man? He is either a European, or the descendant of a European, hence that strange mixture of blood, which you will find in no other country. I could point out to you a family whose grandfather was an Englishman, whose wife was Dutch, whose son married a French woman, and whose present four sons have now four wives of different nations. *He* is an American, who, leaving behind him all his ancient prejudices and manners, receives new ones from the new mode of life he has embraced, the new government he obeys, and the new rank he holds. . . . Here individuals of all nations are melted into a new race of men, whose labours and posterity will one day cause great changes in

15

the world. . . . The American ought therefore to love his country much better than that wherein either he or his forefathers were born. Here the rewards of his industry follow with equal steps the progress of his labour; his labour is founded on the basis of nature, self-interest; can it want a stronger allurement? Wives and children, who before in vain demanded of him a morsel of bread, now fat and frolicsome, gladly help their father to clear those fields whence exuberant crops are to arise to feed and clothe them all; without any part being claimed, either by a despotic prince, a rich abbot, or a mighty lord. Here religion demands but little of him; a small voluntary salary to the minister, and gratitude to God; can he refuse these? The American is a new man, who acts upon new principles; he must therefore entertain new ideas, and form new opinions. From voluntary idleness, servile dependence, penury, and useless labour, he has passed to toils of a very different nature, rewarded by ample subsistence—This is an American.

To twentieth-century ears, some of this sounds a bit quaint. Many of us do own and farm land, but we are no longer typically a nation of farmers. No longer is the poverty and the oppression of feudal Europe fresh in our memories. We are accustomed to the opportunity for a high standard of living and to freedom from oppression of tyrants. The point of Crèvecoeur's statement, however, is still true. We are one people. We do work usefully and receive just rewards from our labor. Religion in America is free. We give thanks to God for our good fortune, and we are free to give our voluntary contribution to any church—or to no church. The fields have been cleared, but the spirit of the men who cleared them is still alive and gives to America her great and special vitality.

THE GROWTH OF AMERICA

The oneness of America as a nation and the uniqueness of her people and country were not simply here all at once but grew out of America's history. Crèvecoeur's statement tells us much about the pioneering spirit of the early Americans. But since Crèvecoeur's time many events have taken place that we need to know about in order to understand modern America.

The Industrial Revolution

One very far-reaching change that has affected our ways of living since the days of Crèvecoeur was a result of the **industrial revolution**. This revolution began in England toward the end of the eighteenth century. Machines gradually replaced simple tools. Factories began to produce cotton and wool cloth, pots and pans, shoes, furniture, and other goods—the goods that people had formerly made for themselves or that craftsmen had made painstakingly and slowly by hand.

The money wages offered by the factory owners lured thousands of men, women, and children from the farms to the new factory towns to work by the hour in the shops and mills. But the coming of the machines and factories did not mean the same things to both the owners and the workers. To the owners and managers, these changes meant the chance to win wealth and influence. To the workers, they too often meant long hours, wretched working conditions, and even whippings for women and children who did not work fast enough. The English workers tried to fight back by forming trade unions (which were illegal at first) and by creating political organizations. In 1848, when Karl Marx and Friedrich Engels wrote their **Communist Manifesto** (see Chap. 26)—calling upon the workers of the world to unite— working conditions were desperately bad not only in England but all over Europe. To many it seemed true, as Marx said, that the workers had nothing to lose but their chains and their poverty.

Such were conditions in Europe. But what of America?

In American factories, wages were also low and working hours were as long as twelve or fourteen hours a day. Nevertheless, the American worker was much better off than his contemporary in Europe.

Alexis de Tocqueville, a Frenchman who traveled through America in the 1830's, commented on this situation:

> These manufacturing speculators are extremely numerous; their interests differ; they cannot therefore easily concert or combine their exertions. On the other hand, the workmen have always some sure resources which enable them to refuse to work when they cannot get what they conceive to be the fair price for their labor. In the constant struggle for wages that is going on between these two classes, their strength is divided and success alternates from one to the other.
>
> It is even probable that in the end the interest of the working class will prevail, for the high wages which they have already obtained make them every day less dependent on their masters, and as they grow more independent, they have greater facilities for obtaining a further increase of wages.

The "sure resources" to which de Tocqueville referred were political liberty and the natural resources in land, timber, water, and minerals which made the new world so much richer than the old. These resources were there for anyone who had the courage and the willingness to go after them. Many Americans took Horace Greeley's famous advice, "Go west, young man, and grow up with the country." They left settled communities and safe jobs in the East to build new homes, farms, and businesses for themselves in the

17

European laborer, on the other hand, had to be satisfied with
ıd, since there was nowhere else for him to go and no free land
:s for him to develop.

ı the farm and the frontier forced Americans to become self-reliant,
:nt, willing to take a chance. These qualities carried over into the
new fields of business. The American workman held on to his self-respect.
There were some periods of bitter economic depression when many were
without work and more had too few of the good things of life. But because
of the same "sure resources" of which de Tocqueville spoke, the Americans
survived these disasters and continued to improve their standard of living.
Industrial expansion, the growth of cities and towns, and the effective use of
mass production gave America the unique bigness and wealth it has today.

The Increase in Population

In 1790 the new United States was less than one-third the size it is now.
But the growth of population is even more startling. In 1790, there were
fewer than four million people in America—less than half of the population
of New York City today! By 1850, there were 23 million Americans; by 1880,
50 million; by 1920, 105 million. Today, more than 180 million people live
in the United States. In the old world, the industrial revolution caused discontent and class struggle. Our land became, in the nineteenth century more
than ever, the land of opportunity for the downtrodden everywhere. These
people came to our shores by the hundred thousands. In one year 1,879,789
immigrants arrived. They came to acquire land, to earn better wages, and—
most important of all—to win for their children and grandchildren the
chance to advance themselves in the new world.

But the population not only increased, it also changed in character. In
Crèvecoeur's time almost all the Americans had come from the countries
of northern Europe, especially from England. While immigration from these
countries continued and increased in the nineteenth century, more immigrants started to come from southern and eastern Europe than from the
northern countries. Thousands more came from the Far East. Americans, as
Crèvecoeur foretold, were formed out of the mixture of all the races and
creeds of men while the land, as the poet Archibald MacLeish has put it,
"lay waiting for her westward people."

Growth of Equality

Part of the American experiment—an experiment in freedom and equality
(which we shall discuss in the next chapter)—rested on the conviction that,
as Jefferson put it, the many are not born with saddles on their backs, and
the few, booted and spurred, born to ride them. All people, in other words,
are worth whatever they can make of themselves, not what their birth decrees
for them. But while this equality was one of the ideals of the American

18

nation, it was achieved only slowly and gradually. For example, already in Crèvecoeur's time there were a great many Negroes in our land. They were, with few exceptions, slaves. They did not share in the opportunities of the new country. Great changes, however, have taken place in the life and condition of the Negro since that time. Negroes were brought to our shores from Africa as slaves; their descendants are free men and citizens. Many Negroes worked their way up in a wide variety of occupations. For instance, Dr. Charles R. Drew became one of our country's outstanding authorities on blood; Ralph Bunche won the Nobel Peace Prize; and Roy Campanella was three times voted the most valuable player in the National League. Crèvecoeur would be greatly impressed by the change in the condition of Negroes from the early days of our country to today. Certainly he would have been impressed by the activities of these men—having to do with blood banks, United Nations negotiations in the Near East, and the great American game of baseball.

The immigrants from across the seas, speaking strange languages and following unfamiliar customs, were at first set apart from their other American neighbors. But gradually, as their children and grandchildren were born here, as they learned to speak English, and as their customs became familiar, their neighbors looked upon them as equals.

Thus the nation grew. It grew in bigness, in wealth, in population, and gradually it began to realize its ideals.

SUMMARY

We have seen in this chapter that America is unique because our people spring from a great variety of national and racial origins. Our forefathers came to the new world from all the countries of the old and brought with them no uniform tradition of customs, habits, or opinion. We have seen how our different national and racial origins account in part for the diversity in our habits, customs, and beliefs, even today. We noted other differences due to the regions in which we live and our varied occupations and incomes. In spite of this "manyness"—this diversity in our culture—we have emerged as *one* people. We are all Americans, working and worshiping freely together, for our own and the common good.

Two great forces which tend to bring our differing interest groups together are the major political parties. Both parties try to appeal to all groups and have not normally been content to promote only one sort of interest. The problem of American democratic government is to find workable compromises or solutions for these differences, making "one people" out of many individuals.

How to Study

As a student, you devote many hours to study. Why not get the most out of the time you put in? Here are some suggestions for improving your study techniques which, if followed as you read each chapter in the text, should help you become a better student. Using Chapter 1 which you have just finished as an example, consider how you might have read it for greater profit.

First look at the chapter organization. Notice that Chapter 1 is subdivided into main heads. The main heading on page 3 is "America—Unique Among Nations." It is subdivided into smaller headings: Our Different National Backgrounds, Our Different Religions, Our Different Occupations, Our Different Incomes, The Importance of These Differences for Government, Our Unique Responsibilities, and What Is an American? Since these headings are signposts that direct you to the main ideas in the chapter, you should look at them before you read each chapter. Next look at the illustrations; they also give you some idea of the content, and they will help you to watch for significant ideas when you read the chapter.

After reading the chapter, turn back again to the headings. Just a re-reading of them gives you a quick review of the content. If you discover that you cannot supply details under any one of the subheads, re-read that section. The summary at the end should also be considered carefully, for it will help you to organize your thoughts about the meaning of the chapter.

The pictures and captions also deserve another examination. In Chapter 1, pp. 12–13, is a map of the United States, showing not only population figures, but also where each state ranks in order of population. The map is decorated with drawings indicating something about the occupations of various regions. Consider your own state and where it fits into this over-all picture. Be sure you understand the statistics on the map. Make a few comparisons between your state and one adjoining it—or one far removed from it. Use the map to illustrate the various points made in this chapter—about our differences and our uniqueness, our bigness and our one-ness.

The cartoon on p. 5 should also be examined carefully, showing as it does a political cartoonist's view of "We the People." What is the artist trying to say? Does the cartoon sum up the situation as you understand it after reading this chapter?

The story on pp. 8–9, told in pictures and captions, should also be an integral part of your reading of the chapter. Note how it picks up and illustrates concretely the ideas discussed in the chapter.

Each chapter in the book should be read and thought about in the same way. What you get out of your reading depends on what you put into it. Your reading experience can open a new world of interest in what goes on around you, and an understanding of events in the news, of the fascinatingly intricate workings of your government, and of people around you.

Now you are ready to start in on the activities which appear at the end of each chapter in this book. Some of these everyone should do; others may be assigned by the teacher to individual students. However they are handled, they will help you to get the most out of the book—enable you to have a real grasp of the subject of government: what it is, how it came about, what it means to you personally, and what you personally can do about it.

The first group of questions, "Know What You Read," will give you a good review of the material in the chapter. You should answer all these questions, preferably in your notebook.

The next section, "What Do You Think?" will suggest many fruitful subjects for debate and/or discussion among the class members. By answering them, you can develop your ability to think and speak about government, to plan debates and panel discussions. The topics suggested may lead you to related questions, all showing your understanding of the wide range of the subject of the chapter.

"Problems and Projects for You," the next section at each chapter end, is for further enrichment. Some of these are simple, involving discussion with your classmates after a little investigation. Others require deeper research and study. For the artists of the class, this section provides suggestions for possible drawings. Everyone should do at least one of this group—and possibly more—with your teacher assigning or helping you choose your subject.

The words under "Extend Your Vocabulary" are all used in the chapter. Some of them you may know in another context. The important thing now is to learn the meaning within the framework of the chapter. Your reading outside—in newspapers, magazines, and books—will become more interesting and significant if you extend the definitions of the words to the new meanings.

Every group of chapter activities ends with "Your Notebook: The Government of—." You must realize that there are in the United States almost as many kinds of local governments as there are communities—villages, towns, townships, cities. This section will provide you with your own self-written textbook on the problems and government of your community. By keeping your notebook conscientiously up to date, you will discover a new face to your community, and will begin taking an active part in it.

At the end of each unit, a group of activities is included to help you "dig out" the significance of the unit and the relation to it of the document with which it is introduced. The document is one with which you are probably familiar. Nevertheless, the new context of this book will throw a spotlight on it, illuminating it in a new way and revealing new depths of meaning.

· The list of books at each unit end suggests places to find more information in which you may be interested. Some of the books listed are also referred to in "What Do You Think?" or "Problems and Projects for You" sections.

A word of caution—and suggestion. When you are asked, in these questions and activities, to "compare" something with something else, be sure to show both likeness and differences. When you are asked to interpret a statement or express your own opinion, give careful thought to why your answer is what it is. Make your answer as forceful as you can. And do not forget the rules of good spoken and written English which you have been learning in your language arts courses throughout high school. What you say is of primary importance; how you say it makes the difference between an uninterested, unimpressed audience—and an audience alertly attentive to (though not necessarily in agreement with) your ideas.

KNOW WHAT YOU READ

1. Several writers have referred to the people of the United States as "one people from many." Is this a good description of Americans? Why do you think so?
2. Explain the statement that "The United States is unique because its people are so different."
3. Why did our country become an English-speaking nation?
4. From what countries of the world have immigrants come in greatest numbers?
5. In what way did freedom to worship affect the development of religion in the United States?
6. In what ways do our people differ in occupation? How do people in the same occupation differ?
7. In what income group does the "typical American" belong?
8. What effect do all these differences have on politics and political beliefs in the United States?
9. In what way do the major political parties tend to lessen the differences among the people in the United States?
10. Summarize the differences that divide the people of the United States and the likenesses that unite them.
11. Why is our *standard of living* so high? How does it compare with that of the rest of the world?
12. What responsibilities do we have because of our great wealth?
13. Why were American workingmen in the early nineteenth century better off than were the workingmen in Europe?
14. Compare our country's population today with that of 1790. How do you explain this great growth?

WHAT DO YOU THINK?

1. Do you agree with your authors' claim that our country, because of its great wealth, has a unique responsibility to all mankind?
2. Is it true that equality is an American ideal? Defend your answer.
3. Would you favor a separate political party for organized labor? Another party for the farmers? Or a combined farmer-labor party? Why? Why don't we have such parties now?
4. Joseph Goebbels, Hitler's propaganda minister, stated that it would be easy to divide our people in wartime because we were a nation of so many different groups. Why might this have seemed to be a reasonable assumption? Why was he wrong?

PROBLEMS AND PROJECTS FOR YOU

1. Report to the class on "American beginnings as shown in our telephone book."
2. You have read an eighteenth century answer to the question, "What is an American?" Write in 300 to 400 words your own twentieth century answer.
3. On an outline map, indicate places from which our people came and places where they settled in notable numbers.
4. Write a paper, or report to the class, on the topic, "Effects of the Frontier on the American People." (Standard for this topic is the work of Frederick Jackson Turner. Or see Chapter 37, The Frontier Heritage, in Billington's *Westward Expansion.*)
5. Make a list of all the organizations and institutions in your own community which provide equality of opportunity to all who wish to make use of it.
6. Report to the class on the coming to America of any one of the many national-origins groups which have migrated to our country, and on its contributions to our culture. (One of the best-known references which will help you is Wittke's *We Who Made America.*)
7. On which issues would the various publics shown in the picture story, pp. 8–9, agree, and on which would they differ? How could the platform of a political party hope to appeal to all of the publics? Give reasons for your answers.
8. It is often argued that we need a "realistic" division of political parties in the United States, that the two major parties are too much alike. Conduct a panel discussion on the real differences between the two parties and the reasons for their similarities.
9. Make a chart to show income groups in the United States.
10. Study the national platform of either of the major parties for a current or recent election. To what extent is it true that ". . . it includes some statement intended to appeal to each of the larger groups of our people . . ."? Report your conclusions, giving specific illustrations.

EXTEND YOUR VOCABULARY

Explain each of these words or phrases from this chapter. Do you know a different definition of any of them?

a people	industrial revolution	wealth
homogeneous	standard of living	culture
unique	economic differences	

YOUR NOTEBOOK: THE GOVERNMENT OF ——

Set up this heading in your notebook, filling in the name of your community.
Under that heading, write in answers to the questions at each chapter end.
1. What different nationalities are found in your community? (You might look in the telephone book, or examine the names to be found in the athletic team lineups of your school.)
2. List the names of religious groups with churches in your community.
3. List here all the occupations with which you come in contact in three days (e.g., postman, bus driver, librarian, etc.). Compare your list with that of two friends. Write here the total number of occupations observed by the three of you.
4. Write a short paragraph summarizing the income differences of the people of your community.
5. Study the map, pp. 12–13. Where does your state stand in rank in population? Has the population decreased or increased since the last census? Why?

READ MORE ABOUT IT

At the end of each chapter is included a list of books or magazine articles pertinent to the subject of the chapter, with brief descriptions of each when it first appears. (Some references are given more than once.) Some of the readings will be readily available; others may be more difficult to find. Those of you who choose one such reading will be rewarded by interesting sidelights on each subject. In addition to readings suggested here, daily newspapers are an invaluable source of interesting information about your government.

BROGAN, DENIS W., *The American Character*. Knopf, 1944.
Wise comment, spiced with humor.
BURNS, JAMES M., and PELTASON, JACK W., *Government by the People*. Prentice-Hall, 1954. Chap. 1.
Deals simply and interestingly with all phases of the federal government.
COMMAGER, HENRY STEELE, *The American Mind*. Yale University Press, 1950.
Advanced but interesting, especially last chapter on the 20th century.
JESSUP, J. K., "Western Man and the American Idea." *Life*, November 5, 1951. 96–116.
Very readable.
LERNER, MAX, *America as a Civilization*. Simon and Schuster, 1957. Chaps. I, II, III.
Difficult but very rewarding.
DE TOCQUEVILLE, ALEXIS, *Democracy in America*. ed. Henry Steele Commager, Oxford University Press, 1947.
A readable classic; also available in a two-volume paperback edition (Vintage Books, Inc.).

CHAPTER 2

The Democratic Way of Life

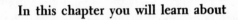

In this chapter you will learn about

The United States as an experiment

The meaning of government

The "consent of the governed"

The rights of minorities

Equality of opportunity

Rules of democracy

The method of compromise

Democracy and self-discipline

America, as we have seen in Chapter 1, is unique among nations because people of many backgrounds, customs, and beliefs are united as one people of a very large and rich nation. We also referred to its being an *experiment*. To make an experiment is to test or try something. What the Founding Fathers tried was to set up a new kind of government, with a written Constitution. They planned a government to which the people themselves would *agree* to give authority, instead of a government which resulted from someone's seizing the power (as had so many eighteenth-century governments). They wanted a government which would somehow protect the freedom and rights of the *individual* without undermining the safety and welfare of the *community* as a whole. What did this mean in the eighteenth century? What does it mean today?

25

AMERICA—AN EXPERIMENT IN FREEDOM

Calling America an experiment is closely related to calling it unique, especially in its wealth and responsibilities. To manage our enormous wealth wisely requires big government. No *free* country has ever maintained so large or so complicated a government as that of the United States. What began in our country as an experiment in free government on a small scale has remained in our time still an experiment, but on a large scale.

The United States of 1789, which adopted the Constitution, was a nation of fewer than four million people. Most of these people lived along the Atlantic seaboard, although some were beginning to settle along the Great Lakes, the Ohio River, and near the Mississippi. Most Americans were then independent farmers. Only one person in 25 lived in a large town or city, and no city contained more than 42,000 people. The new nation was 3,000 miles away from the politics and wars of Europe; it wished above all to be left alone by other nations, so that its citizens could live and prosper in peace. Here in America democracy was established as an experiment in freedom, in the belief that human beings can manage their own affairs without bosses, or only under bosses of their own choosing. What is remarkable is that this small, weak country not only survived to grow big and powerful but also continued to protect the freedom on which the experiment was based.

In what sense can we refer to our government today as an experiment? It is not hard to see why the establishment of a free government under a written Constitution was an experiment in the eighteenth century. Why is it proper still to use that term in talking about the American free government more than a century and a half later? The answer to this question is not easy. It lies in the very nature of government itself.

THE NATURE OF GOVERNMENT

What is government? *To govern* means "to steer" or "to direct something." Ancient writers often compared the state to a ship, and the governor or ruler to the captain who steers his ship safely through stormy seas. Government, in order to steer or direct, must establish relationship with the people who are ruled. We can, therefore, distinguish different governments from each other by asking who does the ruling and who is ruled. In a **democracy**, at least theoretically, the people rule themselves. In practice, of course, "the people" means adult citizens. In any case, the power to rule is more widely distributed among the people of a democracy than under any other form of government.

There is a much more important and fundamental way of distinguishing governments, however, and that is by asking *how*, or in what way, the ruler or rulers govern. Ruling is really nothing more than telling other people what to do and then making sure they do it. One way of "telling" is to threaten, or to use force. The other way is to persuade, or to get the ruled to agree to what needs to be done and to do it voluntarily. The vital question of government is whether authority, or rule, is forced upon the people or whether the people agree to give the government authority.

The government of the People's Democratic Republic of China, no matter how fine the name may sound, is a **dictatorship**. The government of Great Britain is a **constitutional monarchy**. Both governments control the lives and activities of the people within their borders. Here the likeness ends. In the People's Democratic Republic, the people are not consulted. Their leaders make decisions for them and they cannot get rid of their leaders (except by rebellion) if they dislike what these leaders do. But in Great Britain, the government depends on the consent of the governed: the people.

In Great Britain, the people agreed to be governed by the kind of laws and institutions they have, with the power of governing in the hands of elected representatives. While they hold office the representatives may exercise very great power. They determine war or peace, questions of government or private ownership of big business, or the taxes to be paid by the "loyal subjects" of the monarch. If, however, the people are displeased with their representatives, they may vote them out of office. The British monarch has no real power. He or she has a strong hold on the loyalties of the people but performs only ceremonial duties. The real power of government, as in our country, rests in the people's elected representatives.

When the American colonists revolted against their distant English rulers, one big complaint was that they had no real voice in choosing their government. The English people living at home had some voice in the election of British lawmakers, but there was no such right for Englishmen living in the colonies. Thus, in the slogan of the American colonists, "Taxation without representation is tyranny," the key word is **representation**. Some colonists were annoyed by the taxes themselves; most objected to the fact that the taxes were imposed under laws which they had no part in making.

Government by Force and by Consent

The colonists stated their convictions about the government in the preamble to the Declaration of Independence. This preamble fired the imagination of mankind and has remained a stirring statement of principle although the colonists' specific complaints have long since been forgotten.

When in the course of human events, it becomes necessary for one people to dissolve the political bands, which have connected them with another, and to assume among the Powers of the earth, the separate and equal station to which the Laws of Nature and of Nature's God entitle them, a decent respect to the opinions of mankind requires that they should declare the causes which impel them to the separation.

We hold these truths to be self-evident, that all men are created equal, that they are endowed by their Creator with certain unalienable Rights, that among these are Life, Liberty and the Pursuit of Happiness. That to secure these rights, Governments are instituted among Men, deriving their just powers from the consent of the governed. That whenever any form of Government becomes destructive of these ends, it is the Right of the People to alter or to abolish it, and to institute new Government, laying its foundation on such principles and organizing its powers in such form, as to them shall seem most likely to effect their Safety and Happiness. Prudence, indeed, will dictate that Governments long established should not be changed for light and transient causes; and accordingly all experience hath shown, that mankind are more disposed to suffer, while evils are sufferable, than to right themselves by abolishing the forms to which they are accustomed. But when a long train of abuses and usurpations, pursuing invariably the same Object evinces a design to reduce them under absolute Despotism, it is their right, it is their duty, to throw off such Government, and to provide new Guards for their future security.

The fundamental principle of American government is in the clause which says that the "just powers" of government are derived from the "consent of the governed."

This principle of the consent of the governed distinguishes our experiment from a dictatorship, such as Germany in the time of Adolf Hitler. Hitler came to power in 1933, when Germany was a free republic. Its president legally appointed Hitler to be Chancellor, chief minister of state. Once Hitler was in power, however, he abolished free elections—the means by which the people give their consent. His political party used armed force to suppress other parties. Hitler then built up and transformed the German army into an instrument of his own personal power. The republic was destroyed, and the people lost their power to remove their leaders and to choose new ones. Then, as happens in a dictatorship, the people lost all their other liberties. There were "elections" and the people could "vote"—that is, mark ballots—but they had no right to make choices. There was only one candidate for each office, so that the people had to vote for the man they were told to elect. They could not choose one candidate in preference to another.

INVITATION FROM AMERICA
News Item—Russia has accepted a United States invitation to send Soviet observers to this country to watch the windup of the Presidential campaign.

Reg Manning
McNaught Syndicate, Inc.

The Union of Soviet Socialist Republics (modern Communist Russia) is also a dictatorship. The Soviet rulers hold their power by a combination of military authority and a secret police force. As in Hitler's Germany, there is only one party, in this case the Communist Party. The Communist Party in the U.S.S.R. is more like a military organization than like the Republican or Democratic party in our own country. Through the Party organization, the leaders control the government, the army, and the secret police. Although a written Constitution exists and even guarantees freedom of speech and press, the people cannot form new political groups or say "no" to their government. The Soviet Constitution is thus a kind of "window dressing" for the dictatorship.

If the Premier, or chief of the Soviet state, wishes to get something done, he has only to give an order. If the other top leaders in the Party agree, the army, the police, the Party, and the lesser officials of government will immediately carry it out. No other group of government officials and no body of the people can stop the action. When, according to Communist doctrine, private property was abolished, the land was taken away from the farmers, and they were forced to work for the state on collective government-owned farms. The leaders decided on this action without consulting the farmers or the people in general.

29

The Principle of Consent

We have seen that in a dictatorship the ruler's power is absolute and unlimited. Contrast the situation in Soviet Russia today, for example, with the case of the American President. In 1952, the United States was involved in a war in Korea. We were anxious to rearm fully, since the world faced the possible outbreak of another great war. But the workers in the steel industry went on strike. Because the production of steel is absolutely necessary for the building up of military strength, President Truman knew that the strike had to be ended quickly. He made serious efforts to persuade the managers of the steel companies and the leaders of the unions to end the dispute and assure the country that steel would again be produced. When these efforts failed, President Truman felt that he must take some drastic action. Since the law gave him no power to compel the companies and the unions to sign an agreement, he issued an order by which the national government took over the steel mills to operate them until the unions and management could settle their differences. In this way, the mills could be kept busy producing steel, and national security would not be endangered while the dispute dragged on. The steel companies immediately protested the order and began an action in the courts. While they waited for their suit to be settled, they complied with the President's order, as did the unions, and steel production went on.

Very soon, the case came before the Supreme Court and a decision was handed down. The Court ruled that the Constitution gives the President no authority to act as he had done in seizing the steel industry. Promptly the President ordered the mills returned to their private owners in an orderly manner. Why did he do so? It was not only contrary to his will, but also contrary to what he believed to be in the best interest of the United States. As President, he was the highest officer of the land and commander-in-chief of the armed forces. The Supreme Court had no army or air force—no visible instrument of power with which it could have challenged a contrary decision by the nation's chief executive. The Court was simply nine men, some of whom had been appointed by President Truman. It was merely the duty of the Court to decide whether or not the people of the United States, through their written Constitution, had ever given their highest officer the power to act as he did in seizing the steel mills. The judges did not agree; six thought the President had exercised a power not granted to him by the Constitution, while three believed that he had acted legally. When the majority opinion was announced, however, the President immediately accepted it.

Why was this so? The answer lies in the **principle of consent**. The people of the United States gave their consent to the management of their affairs by an orderly process of law. The law, under the Constitution, is interpreted by the courts and must be obeyed by everyone, including the President. If, as in this case, there is no law to justify a presidential action, and if a large enough number of our people and their representatives want the President to have that power, they may grant it to him. This might be done by an appropriate act of Congress, or possibly by an amendment to the Constitution itself. For example, Congress once voted to give President Franklin D. Roosevelt the power to change the amount of gold in the dollar. Congress might have refused him this power.

Again, the authority of the Congress to pass laws taxing income and of the President and the Treasury to collect income taxes grows out of an amendment to the Constitution (Amendment XVI, p. 65). Eighteen years earlier the Supreme Court had ruled that our government had no authority to collect such a tax. Thus it became necessary to change the Constitution itself to make the levy of an income tax legal. Through the proper consent-giving process, this was done.

Limitations on Power Under Government by Consent

Neither the President of the United States nor any other official has the power to do whatever he wishes, even when he is acting for the public good. He may do only what a written constitution, state or federal, says he may do, or what laws made under these constitutions say he may do. In 1950, President Truman, without waiting for a vote of Congress or a court decision, ordered American fighting men to go to Korea and to resist the North Korean Communists. His power to do this was not challenged, since the Constitution of the United States makes the President the commander-in-chief of the armed forces, with power to use these forces—according to law or treaty. In the case of the Korean War, President Truman directed American forces to be used *for* the United Nations in a police action *of* the United Nations in accordance with the treaty (1946) which authorized American membership *in* the United Nations.

For over 150 years, the American people have been willing to leave this power of commanding the armed forces in the President's hands. It would be possible to take that power away from the President, or to give him, in time of emergency, additional power, for example, the power to seize privately owned businesses. But the President cannot simply take power or decide to change the law himself, and compel the American people to accept the change. Thus the government of the United States operates only by consent of the governed. This consent is expressed through amendments to the Constitution, or through the vote of a majority of our duly elected representatives.

Majority Consent and the Rights of Minorities

It should be pointed out that "consent of the people" does not necessarily mean all of our people agree either with the laws or with the choice of candidates for office. Consent in our democracy is of two kinds. First, we speak of **majority consent**. This means that officials are elected and laws adopted by the votes of majorities. Whenever there is a majority, there is also a minority of people who don't agree. Thus we must also have **minority consent**. This means that those who disagree must consent to obey the laws passed by the majority and also the orders of elected leaders so long as the right of the minority to try to change the majority by peaceful persuasion is protected by government.

This principle makes American democracy an experiment. In other words, as long as the people of our country continue to try to solve their problems and govern themselves by agreement, they are taking a risk. The risk is that consent may not be obtained and that the government will collapse. Think what would happen if all the people refused to vote in a presidential election!

Most Americans today, even if they do not think about it seriously, do accept the principle of consent. We assume our government will act only in ways which we have authorized either through elections or through the votes of our elected representatives. Many years of experience with free government reduce the danger of failing, but each year brings new and bigger problems which are continually harder to solve. Thus there is no end to the risk.

THE PRINCIPLES OF AMERICAN DEMOCRACY

What are the principles which have led the American people to continue their experiment in the belief that it will succeed? These principles are found in the famous sentence of the Declaration of Independence which speaks of "self-evident truths." The "truths" are that "all men are created equal," that they have "certain unalienable Rights," and that "among these are Life, Liberty and the Pursuit of Happiness."

Equality of Opportunity

The first one of these "truths" may raise questions in our minds. Surely all men are not actually equal. Some are tall; some are short; some are strong; some are weak; some are very intelligent or talented; others less so. The list of inequalities could be made much longer. Yet we Americans believe very deeply in equality. Our system takes it for granted that we are equal, since every man's vote counts the same as every other man's. Every person is entitled to the same treatment before the law.

Why is this so? The answer is that our belief in equality rests on a deep faith: faith in the dignity of each individual human being. If we are Jews or Christians, we believe that all human beings are children of God. We all share the conviction that in spirit all men are brothers. For this reason, all human beings are entitled to equal respect because they are human. We put our belief in human equality into practice by creating a system of government which gives us **equality of opportunity**. We want each American to have the same opportunity as every other to demonstrate his ability and his character. We may not always achieve this, but it is our goal.

Examples of the working out of equality of opportunity are not hard to find. Persons in your own community who started in life with the handicap of poverty or little education have become successful and respected because they had the necessary ability and will power and have worked hard. In your own school, you have the opportunity to get an education. Whether you graduate at the top of your class or near the bottom will depend on both your ability and your character. The same is true of your opportunity to become soloist in the glee club, play the lead in the senior play, or become star passer on your football team. In setting up schools for you, the people of your state and community have not tried to guarantee success to all of you, but they have tried to provide you with the opportunity to *achieve* something. The rest is up to you.

In general, American schools have been so successful in granting equal opportunity to all the children of all the people that a former president of Harvard University, James B. Conant, has called them the "engine of democracy." In adult life as well, we have, as a nation, made great progress in offering to our people the opportunity to advance themselves as far as they are qualified to go. It is a continuing challenge to all of us to make such opportunity ever greater and more nearly equal. Well as we have done, we are still obviously far short of perfection.

Unalienable Rights

This equality of opportunity rests upon certain other convictions about human beings and government. These are contained in the rights of which the Declaration of Independence spoke. If we are all created equal, then each of us must be free to pursue his own happiness—in his own way. Each of us now strives to become what he wishes to be, and by his own work and efforts. A man's career, his beliefs, and his manner of life are to a great extent matters of choice. It is partly accident but largely choice which results in the great variety of occupations and interests of the American people, as we considered in Chapter 1. If we lived in a dictatorship, on the other hand, we would be shaped and molded by some outside authority. Then those of us who wished to try to become newspaper reporters or automobile mechanics and to buy small homes of our own might find ourselves forced to work in a government mine or factory or on a collective farm thousands of miles away.

Such action is contrary to our American belief that there is something worth while in every person which makes him uniquely valuable both to himself and to his community. This is why Americans believe that every individual has the right to make important decisions for himself. There is only one course for a people who believe so strongly in this dignity of the individual: it is the experiment which the founders of the United States undertook— government by consent of the governed.

Theory and practice—our goals and what actually happens—are not easy to bring together. Our very belief in the dignity of the individual creates endless conflict. Since each individual is "as good as" every other, there are endless differences in thinking, speaking, and acting. Each man has a sacred right to be as different from every other as he wishes. This does not mean that some men will not (or should not) try to change other men's ways of thinking and acting. But to do so they must use persuasion, not force. Government must protect the right of even the most radical agitators to address the people and try to persuade them so long as they do not advocate violence.

Thus the government has the problem of permitting individual differences, defending them by the force of law, and still getting things done reasonably well. This is not easy. Since differences among free individuals are the result of their very freedom and individuality, there can be no end to the problem of protecting differences and still getting things done. Government by consent involves continuously meeting new problems. The government of the United States is, therefore, truly an experiment; indeed, it could be nothing else and remain free.

THE RULES OF AMERICAN DEMOCRACY

People who believe in our system of government believe that every individual has a worth and dignity precisely because *he is human*; they believe that all human beings are equal and that they have certain unalienable rights. So fundamental are these principles that to change or deny any one of them is to invite tyranny.

Before our legislators or other authorized representatives could actually begin to enact laws which would carry out these principles, however, it was necessary to recognize certain "rules of democracy." These rules of democracy must not be confused with the **laws** made by a democratic legislature. The rules are the *means* by which the laws are made and enforced. The rules are seldom changed, although new laws may be passed from year to year.

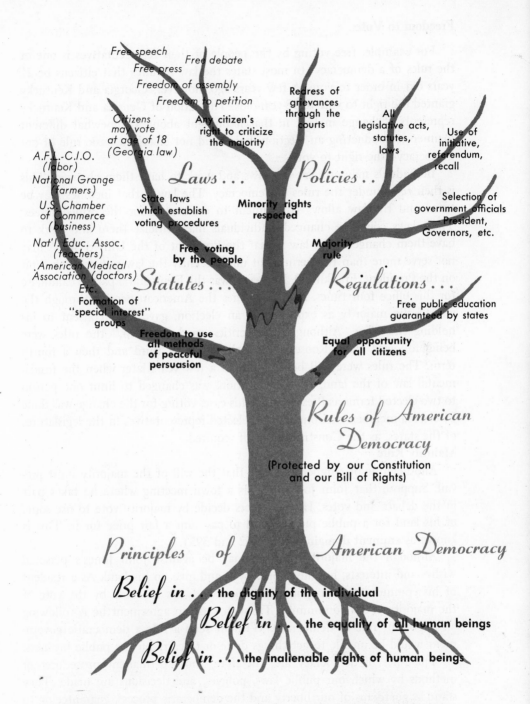

Free speech
Free debate
Free press
Freedom of assembly
Freedom to petition

Redress of
grievances
through the
courts

Citizens
may vote
at age of 18
(Georgia law)

Any citizen's
right to criticize
the majority

All
legislative acts,
statutes,
laws

Use of
initiative,
referendum,
recall

A.F.L.-C.I.O.
(labor)
National Grange
(farmers)
U.S. Chamber
of Commerce
(business)
Nat'l. Educ. Assoc.
(teachers)
American Medical
Association (doctors)
Etc.

Laws . . .

Policies . .

State laws
which establish
voting procedures

**Minority rights
respected**

Selection of
government officials
— President,
Governors, etc.

**Free voting
by the people**

**Majority
rule**

Statutes . . .

Regulations . . .

Formation of
"special interest"
groups

Free public education
guaranteed by states

**Freedom to use
all methods
of peaceful
persuasion**

**Equal opportunity
for all citizens**

*Rules of American
Democracy*

(Protected by our Constitution
and our Bill of Rights)

Principles   of   American Democracy

Belief in . . . the dignity of the individual

Belief in . . . the equality of all human beings

Belief in . . . the inalienable rights of human beings

All of our laws, statutes, policies, and regulations have their roots in the three great
principles of American democracy. It is often a long journey, however, from fundamental
principle to law or policy. This chart illustrates the distinction between democratic principles
and rules. It also shows how our laws and privileges are related to the rules (see text,
pp. 34–36).

Freedom to Vote

For example, free voting by the people or their representatives is one of the rules of a democracy. In most states the law requires that citizens be 21 years old in order to vote. A few years ago, however, Georgia and Kentucky granted the right to vote to 18-year-olds. The action of Georgia and Kentucky represents a change in law, in that it brought about a somewhat different manner of conducting an election; but it did not change a basic rule of our democracy—the right to vote.

Individuals may criticize our laws and work to have them changed. This is their *right* under the **rules** of democracy. The law is that incomes may be taxed and the law allows government to draft men for the armed forces. These laws could be changed. Individuals may criticize them and work to have them changed. The law is that the President of the United States may not serve more than two terms. But until recently the law put no such limit on the President. Franklin D. Roosevelt was the Democratic party's candidate for this office four times, and four times the American people, through the will of the majority as expressed in an election, gave their consent to his holding the office. Although some critics cried "dictator," the rules were being followed when Roosevelt was elected for a third and then a fourth term. The rules were still being followed a few years later when the fundamental law of the land, the Constitution, was changed to limit one person to two elected terms as President. In this case, voting for the change was done by elected members of Congress and elected representatives in the legislatures of the states, as the Constitution itself required.

Majority Rule

Another rule of democracy states that the will of the majority must prevail. Suppose that John Jones attends a town meeting where he takes part in the debate and votes. His neighbors decide by majority vote to use some of his land for a public purpose and to pay him a fair price for it. This is known as **eminent domain** (see pp. 62 and 395).

Although the majority decision may be against John Jones's personal wishes and interests, he must abide by it and give up his land. As a resident of his community he has, in effect, agreed always to abide by the vote of the majority of his community. Through such an agreement he is following an important rule of democracy. Without such a rule a democratic government would be unable to get things done or to carry on the public business.

The rules of democracy are, therefore, those permanent procedures or methods by which our public laws, policies, and decisions are made. They stand as guardians of our liberty and the democratic process, guaranteeing to us that the government carries out the expressed wishes of our people. (See drawing, p. 35, for relation between the principles of democracy, the rules, and the laws.)

Compulsion and the Democratic Process

We have seen that there are two basically different ways in which people can be governed—by force and by consent. But even government by consent involves some compulsion. For example, in the circumstances described above, Mr. Jones could be forced against his will to accept a fair price for his land so that the community might have a new school. Again, whenever the people of a community vote taxes to run their government, they are also voting to compel one another to pay those taxes. Government cannot operate without the power to compel the governed to do those things that must be done. What is important is whether the governed have a voice in granting that power to their government, or whether the power is arbitrarily imposed by government on the governed.

The more complex society is, the more difficult it becomes to manage its affairs through consent. In a small community like John Jones's, all the people may come together in a town hall, argue about each issue, and then express their consent by voting. But our entire population of over 180 million people cannot meet together and decide every issue in person. Other ways had to be found to do this. Much of our history is the story of how we found new ways in which a growing population could work out its differences by consent.

DEMOCRACY—THE COMPROMISE OF DIFFERENCES

The broad survey made in Chapter 1 (pp. 3–11) of the many differences which divide Americans shows that there is no possible way in which the American government could fully satisfy all its citizens. Our system can never be perfect from the point of view of the individual. Something is always happening—laws and regulations are being passed, policies are being adopted, decisions are being made—which some of us do not like. What we actually do is **compromise**—that is, agree to accept less than we think we deserve, so that all of us may get something, as the chart, p. 38, suggests. Willing acceptance of less than we think we should have is the continuing price of freedom, since if a few of us were to get all we wish, most of us would get very little or none. We would lose our freedom.

Although we must accept these policies, decisions, laws, and regulations, our freedom of speech enables us to express our disagreement and to try to persuade others that we are right and they are wrong. Our dissatisfaction must never be so serious, however, that any significant number of us revolts against the government. With the single major exception of the War Between the States, we have avoided such a disrupting event. Thus we find

Compromise

Compromises are made in the family

Compromises are made in local political affairs

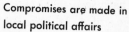

tax dollars

John wants the family car to drive his gang to the game every Saturday during the football season.

These people want better schools, as good as the best in the state, and are willing to pay higher taxes for such schools.

A

Mary also wants the car to drive her friends to the games each Saturday.

These people want lower taxes. They do not want to pay the higher taxes which new schools would make necessary.

B

Compromise:

Neither gets what he wants, but each gets something. Each has the family car on alternate Saturdays.

Compromise:

Neither group gets what it wants. Better schools are voted, but not so good as group A wanted. Group B does not get its tax reduction but does not have to pay the higher taxes which would have been necessary to pay for the schools group A wanted.

that today both farmers and city dwellers may be dissatisfied with the government's support of the farmer's income. The farmer wants higher price supports. The consumer wants lower food prices. Both labor leaders and industrial leaders may be dissatisfied with the government's labor policy. Each groups wants more benefits for itself and perhaps less for the other fellow. A great many people criticize our foreign policy from all points of view. Yet every one of these dissatisfied persons must accept these policies, although they represent less than what each believes he is entitled to have. But in spite of all the criticism, some of it loud and sharp, very little, if anything, is heard about revolt, overthrow of government, burning the capital, or withdrawing from the Union.

The fundamental **procedure** of democracy and the living process of American government is, therefore, the principle of compromise. Under democracy, government reflects the expressed will of the majority. It is continually modified, however, by the will of individuals and groups belonging to the minorities. The modifications, the give-and-take necessary to get laws passed and administered, reflect the practice of compromise which keeps our democracy alive.

The majority itself is endlessly changing its membership. The make-up of the majority varies, slowly or rapidly, as people's opinions change. What was once a minority view may now be the view of the majority. Thus social security, long advocated by minorities, has become law, and neither political party would think of repealing it. On the other hand, some things that were once popular have become unpopular. We have amended the Constitution to wipe out an amendment made only fourteen years earlier (see pp. 66 and 67). We can change, and have changed, almost everything except the method (rules) by which we decide which changes to make in establishing and enforcing our laws and policies. Thus there is only one broad limit to the power of the majority. The majority may not alter the rules of democracy by which it came into existence, or prevent opposing groups from using every means of persuasion to change policies and replace representatives of the old majority in the government by their own spokesmen.

Pressure Groups and the Principle of Compromise

James Madison, in *The Federalist* (papers written in the winter of 1787–1788 by Madison, Hamilton, and John Jay to persuade the people of New York to ratify the Constitution), says that society is filled with factions. (Instead of "factions" we would today refer to "pressure groups" or "special-interest groups.") Conflicts and abuses of privileges or rights result from the existence and activities of these factions. Many people believe, Madison reports, that society can be well ordered and peaceful only if these factions are controlled or suppressed. This would bring about order, but, says Madison, at the price of freedom. Factions, he points out, however dangerous they may be, are rooted in freedom, for freedom itself can have no meaning unless it means that people are free to have *different* opinions and *different* interests. Factions, or interest groups, are organized by people to express such differences.

In one sense, therefore, as Madison shows us, democracy is the method by which the desires of interest groups and pressure groups are constantly adjusted to one another. In our democracy, this is done by working out possible compromises. Some American businesses, for example, compete with foreign businesses whose costs are lower. Since American bicycles (or pottery) cost more to produce than the British (or Japanese), American manufacturers wish the government to "protect" them by putting a high tariff (tax) on the imported products of these foreign competitors. Other American businesses, however, are anxious to sell their products abroad. For instance, American automobile manufacturers with mass production methods can produce big cars more cheaply than European makers can. Therefore, they want American tariffs to remain low, since they are not afraid of foreign competition in this country. They want, in turn, the foreign countries to let our autos into their countries at a low tariff.

Thus different American businesses differ on tariff policy, and no policy will entirely suit all of them. What we actually get is a compromise: one group gets some protection, but not as much as it wishes; the other has to be satisfied with somewhat higher tariffs than it had hoped for. Neither gets all it wishes. The laws and policies of a democracy are thus a result of a compromise between the wishes of groups with different interests.

Self-Discipline: The Lifeblood of Democracy

We have seen thus far that the continuing "stuff" or content of democracy is a series of temporary laws and policies—on terms of office and voting requirements, on taxes and the draft, and other matters. These temporary decisions are made under relatively permanent rules. Accepting and abiding by the rules is not a simple matter. Indeed, it is easier to obey the law than to submit to the rules of democracy. This submission to the rules requires a self-discipline much greater than that required in non-democratic systems. T. V. Smith, university professor and former member of Congress, has called this the "discipline of democracy"—the *permanent* condition of accepting less than you think you deserve. In accepting less, you compromise your own wishes with the wishes of others, who also are getting less than they think they deserve. In this way, all may be more or less satisfied. Compromise thus lies at the very heart of the democratic process.

Compromise in a democracy, however, is not only a matter of compromising interests. Democracy permits us as individuals to hold absolute and unchanging beliefs, but insists that we must not expect to impose such beliefs on others. In a democracy, we cannot allow any one group to dominate, whether this group is a political party, a church, or a sect of any kind. If such domination were allowed to develop, groups or views which differed from it could be suppressed. That is why the Communist is out of place in America. Instead of self-discipline, he would force a discipline on others; in place of loyalty to the principle of difference, he would compel others to accept his beliefs. In place of temporary majorities, he would have rule by a permanent minority, backed up by a secret police. The Communist sees no place for compromise because he believes that there can be no compromise between absolute right and wrong, and he is sure that he is absolutely right and everyone else is absolutely wrong. We can see the results of this attitude in the dictator-ruled countries of the world. A democracy alone allows its members to express opposing opinions.

Only if we can be loyal to the right of others to differ from us can we as a people keep and cherish the most diverse faiths. Under democracy, we are free to persuade, but not free to use force. We may by speech and example convince our neighbor that he should come into our church, political party, trade association, or labor union; but we may not force him to do so. We must respect his right to belong to a completely different church, party, association, or union, as well as his right to try to convince us that we are wrong. We must do so even though we believe strongly that our answers are the right ones. This involves more than being tolerant. It means that we must give to others the right to be themselves so that we may have the right to be ourselves.

Such a principle does not mean that in a democracy all kinds of beliefs and all actions are allowed. We do have laws, agreed upon by our elected representatives, against robbery, murder, urging the violent overthrow of the government, speeding on our highways, swindling, and other deeds of force, violence, and fraud. Such laws are necessary, of course, since a few people think so little of their fellow men that they are willing to deprive them of their rights to life, property, and a peaceful existence. Democracy does not mean lawlessness or indifference. It does need citizens who are well educated and well informed and who think as much of their fellow men as of themselves, because democracy, unlike other ways of government, rests finally upon the character of the individual citizen. We who believe in democracy must believe that the nature of the individual is such that he *can* practice self-control in the interests of his own well-being and the welfare of his community. We take a calculated risk that if they are free enough, men *will* control their own wishes, and by means of the law control those who are unwilling to abide by the rules of democracy. Thus order may continue to grow out of confusion.

Perhaps we can now answer the question raised at the beginning of this book: What is an American? An American is one who makes endless compromises with other persons whose beliefs, customs, traditions, prejudices, and interests are different from his own. He does so because he believes, as they too must believe, that freedom for oneself must mean freedom for others. He knows that freedom leads to conflict, and that conflicts can be settled only by force or by compromise. The American chooses compromise, knowing it to be the more difficult but more fruitful way of settling conflict. Finally, the American is one who believes that human beings, regardless of their origins, beliefs, and interests, are able to manage their own affairs in such a way as to promote "Life, Liberty and the Pursuit of Happiness."

SUMMARY

People who believe in our way of life and our form of government believe that all human beings are equal and that they have certain unalienable rights. We put this belief into practice by creating a system of government which gives every American equality of opportunity.

We have seen that *to govern* means "to steer or direct something." This steering or directing can be based on either force or consent. From its beginning, America has been made up of people with many differing backgrounds and interests who have tried to govern themselves by consent. The Americans of 1776 took the calculated risk of trying to build a great nation on the principle that all "just powers" of government belong to government only by the "consent of the governed."

Consent in our democracy is of two kinds: majority consent and minority consent. This means that our officials are elected and our laws are adopted by the votes of majorities. The minority who do not agree must consent to obey the laws passed by the majority so long as their right to change the majority by peaceful persuasion is protected.

This principle makes America an experiment, since government by consent always involves taking a risk—the risk that consent might not be obtained; government would then collapse. Government by consent is truly a *continuing* experiment, for each year brings newer and bigger problems.

There are so many differences among Americans (Chap. 1, pp. 3–11) that there is no possible way in which the American government could fully satisfy all of its citizens. What we actually do is *compromise*—that is, agree to accept less than we think we deserve so that all of us may get something. This demands of each American a self-discipline much greater than that required in non-democratic systems. Willing acceptance of less than we think we deserve (compromise) is a continuing price of freedom and lies at the heart of the democratic process.

KNOW WHAT YOU READ

1. What is the meaning of the word *govern?*
2. When we speak of "government by the people," which people do we mean?
3. What are some fundamental differences between the governments of Great Britain and Red China?
4. According to this text, the "fundamental principle of American government" is stated in the preamble to the Declaration of Independence. What is that principle? What does it mean?
5. In the section Government by Force and by Consent, you should note carefully these phrases or clauses:
   (a) the people give their consent
   (b) power to remove their leaders
   (c) right to make choices
   (d) form new political groups
   (e) say "no" to their government
   Use each of these, carefully and thoughtfully, to explain the differences between dictator government and our own kind of government.
6. Read again the story of President Truman and the steel strike on pp. 30–31.
   (a) For what purpose is the story included?
   (b) Why did the President return the steel mills to their owners?
   (c) How might the American people have given this seizure power to their President?
7. Why did President Truman believe that he had the power to send American fighting forces into Korea. Was he right in so thinking?
8. Review carefully everything you studied in this chapter, and explain just what you understand by *government by consent*. What, specifically, do we mean by *majority consent? Minority consent?*
9. In our democracy, officials are elected and laws adopted by votes of majorities. Is this fair to minority groups? How are the rights of minorities protected under our system of government?
10. In a government by consent, can people be forced to do things they don't want to do? Explain.
11. Equality as an ideal does not mean equality in size, strength, intelligence, or talent. What does it mean? Why do people in general agree with this meaning?
12. What is meant by "the dignity of the individual"?
13. There is a difference among the *principles* of democracy, the *rules* of democracy, and the *laws* of democracy. Explain the difference.
14. In a democracy as large and complex as ours, "pressure groups" or "special-interest groups" are necessary to carry on the public business. Why is this so?
15. What did T. V. Smith mean by the "discipline of democracy"?

43

16. Why does the Communist not approve of compromise as a way of getting things done?
17. Why does your text refer to the continuing "stuff" or content of democracy as a series of "temporary" laws and policies?
18. If you really believe in democracy, what must you believe about people in general?
19. What, according to our text, is an American?

WHAT DO YOU THINK?

1. Many schools have student councils, student legislatures, student senates, student courts, etc. Few if any have student government, i.e., government of the students, *by* the students, for the students. Why is this so? How much government *by* students is possible?
2. Some of you may think this chapter is too idealistic. What do you think? Why? Be specific.
3. Are there cases in which we should *not* make compromises? If so, what are they?
4. You must have heard this many times: "I'm as good as he is." How does the meaning change if one says, "He's as good as I am."
5. Only two states give the right to vote to 18-year-olds. Most reserve the voting privilege for those 21 and over. Is this a denial of equality of opportunity. Why have most states preferred the age of 21?

PROBLEMS AND PROJECTS FOR YOU

1. Using a good United States history book, review the compromises that went into the making of the Constitution. Report to the class on these, showing in each case just why each was truly a compromise. Point out clearly just what interest groups were involved. What did each want? Why did it seem important to that group? Finally, how did each group accept less than it wanted?
2. Do the same for any other major compromise of our country's history.
3. Many Americans, starting out with apparent handicaps, have taken advantage of the opportunities our society has offered them and have made good. Make a list of persons who have done this in the last fifty years.
4. Some people claim that the British system of government is more democratic that ours. Study their system and prepare a statement of your own conclusion.

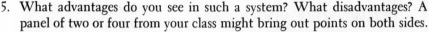

By the Associated Press

New York

In the fall of 1949 little Ivan Ivanovitch enrolled in the first grade of a Leningrad public school. Next summer, having completed seven years of general education, he will arrive at a fork in his educational path.

Unlike his American counterpart, young Johnny Johnson, Ivan will not have the privilege of deciding which fork to take.

Ivan will be told. What he is told will depend on whether he is assessed as a promising natural scientist or engineer or just as a technician or skilled laborer.

What Ivan would like to do will not make much difference. Soviet schools are run for the ...

5. What advantages do you see in such a system? What disadvantages? A panel of two or four from your class might bring out points on both sides.

6. Make a study of a recent or current political-party platform to try to find the compromises which go into the making of a platform. (This will probably be best done as a group study.)

7. In 1949 the Armed Forces Information and Education Division of the Department of Defense asked the National Council for the Social Studies (an organization of teachers) for a description of the good democratic citizen. The Council set up a committee which reported in 1950. The report listed twenty-four characteristics of a good citizen. Each of the twenty-four characteristics was broken down into more specific items. Below is given number 4 of the characteristics, with six specific items under it. Organize a panel discussion to analyze and give views on any three of the items (a) through (f) which go with the characteristic.

> The good citizen understands and accepts the following democratic principles as guides in evaluating his own behavior and the policies and practices of other persons and groups, and judges his own behavior and the behavior of others by them:
> (a) That each individual possesses dignity and worth as a person and is entitled to consideration as a person;
> (b) That governments exist by the consent of the governed;
> (c) That each citizen has certain civil rights guaranteed by the Constitution;
> (d) That government is by law, not by men;
> (e) That in a large nation with diverse social and economic interests, compromise is frequently necessary;
> (f) That since the people are intelligent enough to govern themselves, they do not need protection by censorship—hence free speech, a free press, and academic freedom are necessary.

8. If you like to draw, try making an original cartoon or poster expressing some idea related to (a), (b), or (e) above.

9. Study the cartoon, p. 29. What does the artist imply about important differences between government in the Soviet Union and the United States?

45

10. Some people think that only publicly controlled educational institutions promote equality of educational opportunity. Use college catalogs available in your guidance office or library—or any other source—to discover how privately-owned schools and colleges try to promote equality of opportunity through scholarship programs. Report your findings.
11. That which is majority opinion today may not be majority opinion one year from today. Why is this so?

EXTEND YOUR VOCABULARY

rights of the individual
experiment
experiment in freedom
democracy
dictatorship
constitutional monarchy
consent of the governed
principle of consent
majority consent
minority consent

equality of opportunity
dignity of the individual
principles of democracy
rules of democracy
majority rule
pressure group
interest group
tariff
principle of compromise
discipline of democracy

YOUR NOTEBOOK: THE GOVERNMENT OF ——

1. What scholarships are provided by individuals or organizations in your community to help those who might otherwise be unable to complete their education?
2. What percent of the children who enter the first grade in your school system finally graduate from high school (or other secondary school)? What are the chief reasons why many do not graduate?
3. What local differences of opinion or of objectives have been settled by compromise within the last year or two? What were the differences? What was the settlement? (For example, in one local situation some of the people were in favor of water meters; others were opposed. Temporary settlement: the community will have water meters, but installation is postponed for a year.)
4. Study the drawing, Compromise, on p. 38. What local issue in your community has been similarly solved? What personal issue in your own family.

READ MORE ABOUT IT

BECKER, CARL L., *The Declaration of Independence*. Knopf, 1942.
  On the origins of the ideas in the Declaration. Also available in paperback edition (Vintage Books).
BURNS, JAMES M., and PELTASON, JACK W., *Government by the People*. Prentice-Hall, 1954. Chap. 2.
IRISH, MARIAN D., and PROTHRO, JAMES W., *The Politics of American Democracy*. Prentice-Hall, 1959. Chap. 2.
  Interesting study of politics in a democracy.
LERNER, MAX, *America as a Civilization*. Simon and Schuster, 1957. Chap. VI.
MILL, J. S., *Representative Government*. Everyman's Library.
  An inexpensive readily available edition of this classic.
RANNEY, AUSTIN, *The Governing of Men*. Holt, 1958. Chaps. 4 and 9.
  A thoughtful and reliable study.
RANNEY, AUSTIN, and KENDALL, WILLMOORE, *Democracy and the American Party System*. Harcourt, Brace, 1956. Chaps. 1–3.
  A good discussion of the way the party system operates in our country.
SMITH, T. V., *The Democratic Way of Life*. University of Chicago Press, 1926.
  Easy and interesting essay on compromise and freedom.

THINK ABOUT

THE MEANING
OF DEMOCRACY

At the beginning of this unit is reproduced a facsimile of the Declaration of Independence, with the Preamble and conclusion surprinted on it. Although you have undoubtedly read these before, read them again carefully, in the light of Chapters 1 and 2 of this book.

1. Why do you think the Declaration was chosen as the *key* document for a unit entitled "The Meaning of Democracy"?
2. Do you think "these truths" are "self-evident"?
3. Your authors call America "an experiment in freedom and equality." Does the Declaration present a "blueprint" for that experiment? Explain your answers, using quotations from the Declaration to illustrate.
4. A list of grievances formed the middle section of the Declaration. They were the facts the colonists "submitted to a candid world." Read the list and choose three grievances to illustrate from history.
5. How pertinent does the Declaration seem to problems of today's world?

47

PREAMBLE

We the People of the United States, in Order to form a more perfect Union, establish Justice, insure domestic Tranquility, provide for the common defence, promote the general Welfare, and secure the Blessings of Liberty to ourselves and our Posterity, do ordain and establish this Constitution for the United States of America.

THE NATURE

OF OUR

GOVERNMENT

Unit II

The Constitution of the United States of America

ARTICLE I

Section 1

All legislative Powers herein granted shall be vested in a Congress of the United States, which shall consist of a Senate and House of Representatives.

Section 2

1. The House of Representatives shall be composed of Members chosen every second Year by the People of the several States, and the Electors in each State shall have the Qualifications requisite for Electors of the most numerous Branch of the State Legislature.

2. No Person shall be a Representative who shall not have attained to the Age of twenty five Years, and been seven Years a Citizen of the United States, and who shall not, when elected, be an Inhabitant of that State in which he shall be chosen.

3. Representatives and direct Taxes shall be apportioned among the several States which may be included within this Union, according to their respective Numbers, [which shall be determined by adding to the whole Number of free Persons, including those bound to Service for a Term of Years, and excluding Indians not taxed, three fifths of all other Persons.] The actual Enumeration shall be made within three Years after the first Meeting of the Congress of the United States, and within every subsequent Term of ten Years, in such Manner as they shall by Law direct. The Number of Representatives shall not exceed one for every thirty Thousand, but each State shall have at Least one Representative; [and until such enumeration shall be made, the State of New Hampshire shall be entitled to chuse three, Massachusetts eight, Rhode-Island and Providence Plantations one, Connecticut five, New-York six, New Jersey four, Pennsylvania eight, Delaware one, Maryland six, Virginia ten, North Carolina five, South Carolina five, and Georgia three.]

4. When vacancies happen in the Representation from any State, the Executive Authority thereof shall issue Writs of Election to fill such Vacancies.

5. The House of Representatives shall chuse their Speaker and other Officers; and shall have the sole Power of Impeachment.

Section 3

1. The Senate of the United States shall be composed of two Senators from each State, [chosen by the Legislature thereof,] for six Years; and each Senator shall have one Vote.

EXPLANATORY NOTES

All italic clauses in brackets in Constitution are now obsolete.

Notice that Article I grants all federal legislative powers to Congress. Note also the little word **herein**. *That word means that the Congress shall* **not have all legislative powers whatever, but only such legislative power as is granted by the Constitution.** *This article contains the Great Compromise (see Chap. 3, pp. 71–72).*

1) "Electors" means voters, that is, those who are qualified to vote under state and federal laws. See p. 77.

2) Most states require a representative to live not only in the state but in the district he represents.

3) Indians who choose to remain on reservations without paying taxes may not vote. [The remainder of this bracketed clause is obsolete.] The first census under this clause was taken in 1790; a new census has been taken every ten years since then. In 1902, a special Bureau of the Census in the Department of Commerce was established for this purpose. At present there is a Representative for about every 413,000 people.

4) This means that the governor calls a special election unless a vacancy occurs at a time very close to the time of a regularly scheduled election.

5) The Speaker and other officers are discussed on pp. 120–122. "Impeachment" means bringing charges against someone. In 1868 the House voted to impeach President Johnson. He was tried by the Senate and acquitted.

1) See Amendment XVII, Sec. 1, p. 65.

50

2. Immediately after they shall be assembled in Consequence of the first Election, they shall be divided as equally as may be into three Classes. [The. Seats of the Senators of the first Class shall be vacated at the Expiration of the second Year, of the second Class at the Expiration of the fourth Year, and of the third Class at the Expiration of the sixth Year,] so that one third may be chosen every second Year; [and if Vacancies happen by Resignation, or otherwise, during the Recess of the Legislature of any State, the Executive thereof may make temporary Appointments until the next Meeting of the Legislature, which shall then fill such Vacancies.]

3. No Person shall be a Senator who shall not have attained to the Age of thirty Years, and been nine Years a Citizen of the United States, and who shall not, when elected, be an Inhabitant of that State for which he shall be chosen.

4. The Vice President of the United States shall be President of the Senate, but shall have no Vote, unless they be equally divided.

5. The Senate shall chuse their other Officers, and also a President pro tempore, in the Absence of the Vice President, or when he shall exercise the Office of President of the United States.

6. The Senate shall have the sole Power to try all Impeachments. When sitting for that Purpose, they shall be on Oath or Affirmation. When the President of the United States is tried the Chief Justice shall preside: And no Person shall be convicted without the Concurrence of two thirds of the Members present.

7. Judgment in Cases of Impeachment shall not extend further than to removal from Office, and disqualification to hold and enjoy any Office of honor, Trust or Profit under the United States: but the Party convicted shall nevertheless be liable and subject to Indictment, Trial, Judgment and Punishment, according to Law.

Section 4

1. The Times, Places and Manner of holding Elections for Senators and Representatives, shall be prescribed in each State by the Legislature thereof; but the Congress may at any time by Law make or alter such Regulations, except as to the Places of chusing Senators.

2. [The Congress shall assemble at least once in every Year, and such Meeting shall be on the first Monday in December, unless they shall by Law appoint a different Day.]

2) Thus the Senate is a continuing body, two-thirds of its members always having had previous experience. See Amendment XVII, Sec. 2, pp. 65–66.

4) The only constitutional duty of the Vice-President is stated here (see p. 127).

5) See pp. 127–128 for discussion of the officers of the Senate.

6) See Art. I, Sec. 2, Cl. 5, for origin of impeachment proceedings.

7) Impeachment applies only to a person's qualification to hold office. He may later be tried as a criminal in criminal court on the same charges.

1) Congress prescribes by law that elections of members of the House of Representatives and one-third of the Senators shall be held on the first Tuesday after the first Monday in November of every even-numbered year; and that presidential elections shall be held every four years on the same day as elections to Congress.

See Amendment XX, Sec. 2. Congress now convenes on the third day of January.

Section 5

1. Each House shall be the Judge of the Elections, Returns and Qualifications of its own Members, and a Majority of each shall constitute a Quorum to do Business; but a smaller Number may adjourn from day to day, and may be authorized to compel the Attendance of absent Members, in such Manner, and under such Penalties as each House may provide.

2. Each House may determine the Rules of its Proceedings, punish its Members for disorderly Behaviour, and, with the Concurrence of two thirds, expel a Member.

3. Each House shall keep a Journal of its Proceedings, and from time to time publish the same, excepting such Parts as may in their Judgment require Secrecy; and the Yeas and Nays of the Members of either House on any question shall, at the Desire of one fifth of those Present, be entered on the Journal.

4. Neither House, during the Session of Congress, shall, without the Consent of the other, adjourn for more than three days, nor to any other Place than that in which the two Houses shall be sitting.

1) To "adjourn from day to day" means to keep the chamber in session each day for discussion of business even if not enough members are present for a vote.

2) See pp. 120–125 for discussion of House rules and pp. 125–131 for Senate rules.

*3) The journal is the **Congressional Record** (see p. 116). Secret meetings of the House, Senate, or any of their committees are called "executive sessions."*

Section 6

1. The Senators and Representatives shall receive a Compensation for their Services, to be ascertained by Law, and paid out of the Treasury of the United States. They shall in all Cases, except Treason, Felony and Breach of the Peace, be privileged from Arrest during their Attendance at the Session of their respective Houses, and in going to and returning from the same; and for any Speech or Debate in either House, they shall not be questioned in any other Place.

2. No Senator or Representative shall, during the Time for which he was elected, be appointed to any civil Office under the Authority of the United States, which shall have been created, or the Emoluments whereof shall have been encreased during such time; and no Person holding any Office under the United States, shall be a Member of either House during his Continuance in Office.

1) Present salary for Representatives and Senators is $22,500 plus money for certain expenses (see pp. 115). These "privileges" are to make sure that members of Congress are not prevented from attending sessions, and to enable them to feel free to say anything they wish in debate (see pp. 114–116).

2) This measure is intended to prevent corruption of public officials.

Section 7

1. All Bills for raising Revenue shall originate in the House of Representatives; but the Senate may propose or concur with Amendments as on other Bills.

2. Every Bill which shall have passed the House of Representatives and the Senate, shall, before it becomes a Law, be presented to the President of the United States; If he approve he shall sign it, but if not he shall return it, with his Objections to that House in which it shall have originated, who shall enter the Objections at large on their Journal, and

1) The idea that all revenue bills should originate in the House was inherited from the English House of Commons. It was felt that control of money should be kept as close as possible to the people as a protection against tyrants.

proceed to reconsider it. If after such Reconsideration two thirds of that House shall agree to pass the Bill, it shall be sent, together with the Objections, to the other House, by which it shall likewise be reconsidered, and if approved by two thirds of that House, it shall become a Law. But in all such Cases the Votes of both Houses shall be determined by Yeas and Nays, and the Names of the Persons voting for and against the Bill shall be entered on the Journal of each House respectively. If any Bill shall not be returned by the President within ten Days (Sundays excepted) after it shall have been presented to him, the Same shall be a Law, in like Manner as if he had signed it, unless the Congress by their Adjournment prevent its Return, in which Case it shall not be a Law.

3. Every Order, Resolution, or Vote to which the Concurrence of the Senate and House of Representatives may be necessary (except on a question of Adjournment) shall be presented to the President of the United States; and before the Same shall take Effect, shall be approved by him, or being disapproved by him, shall be repassed by two thirds of the Senate and House of Representatives, according to the Rules and Limitations prescribed in the Case of a Bill.

Section 8

1. The Congress shall have Power to lay and collect Taxes, Duties, Imposts and Excises, to pay the Debts and provide for the common Defence and general Welfare of the United States; but all Duties, Imposts and Excises shall be uniform throughout the United States;

2. To borrow Money on the credit of the United States;

3. To regulate Commerce with foreign Nations, and among the several States, and with the Indian Tribes;

4. To establish an uniform Rule of Naturalization, and uniform Laws on the subject of Bankruptcies throughout the United States;

2) When a bill is passed by Congress on a date less than ten days before it adjourns, the President may exercise the "pocket veto" if he does not approve of the bill. This means that he may simply ignore it ("put it in his pocket") and the bill will not become law.

3) This applies only to laws enacted by Congress; it does not apply to expressions of opinions, like the 1954 declaration that Formosa must be defended.

Section 8 is the basis of national law (see pp. 96–97). Acts of Congress must be based on one or more of these powers (see p. 93). The Supreme Court over the years has tended to interpret them more liberally, so that many laws are based on "implied" powers (see pp. 193–94).

1) In 1895 the Supreme Court declared a personal income tax was unconstitutional because of this clause. In 1913 Amendment XVI was adopted, giving Congress the power to collect taxes on personal income. "General welfare" has been interpreted very broadly in recent years; for example, the Social Security System (pp. 599–600) would formerly have been thought unconstitutional because of government interference in private life.

2) Our 285-odd billion-dollar national debt is based on this power. Laws of Congress enable the Treasury to sell bonds (promises to pay with interest) "on the credit of the United States."

3) The "commerce clause" is the source of many laws that do not appear to be strictly commercial. Thus laws regulating not only things like railroad rates but also television broadcasts, and even the laws against kidnaping, are based on the power of Congress to make laws respecting matters which cross state lines.

53

5. To coin Money, regulate the Value thereof, and of foreign Coin, and fix the Standard of Weights and Measures;

6. To provide for the Punishment of counterfeiting the Securities and current Coin of the United States;

7. To establish Post Offices and post Roads;

8. To promote the Progress of Science and useful Arts, by securing for limited Times to Authors and Inventors the exclusive Right to their respective Writings and Discoveries;

9. To constitute Tribunals inferior to the supreme Court;

10. To define and punish Piracies and Felonies committed on the high Seas, and Offences against the Law of Nations;

11. To declare War, grant Letters of Marque and Reprisal, and make Rules concerning Captures on Land and Water;

12. To raise and support Armies, but no Appropriation of Money to that Use shall be for a longer Term than two Years;

13. To provide and maintain a Navy;

14. To make Rules for the Government and Regulation of the land and naval Forces;

15. To provide for calling forth the Militia to execute the Laws of the Union, suppress Insurrections and repel Invasions;

16. To provide for organizing, arming, and disciplining, the Militia, and for governing such Part of them as may be employed in the Service of the United States reserving to the States respectively, the Appointment of the Officers, and the Authority of training the Militia according to the discipline prescribed by Congress;

17. To exercise exclusive Legislation in all Cases whatsoever, over such District (not exceeding ten Miles square) as may, by Cession of particular States, and the Acceptance of Congress, become the Seat of the Government of the United States, and to exercise like Authority over all Places purchased by the Consent of the Legislature of the State in which the Same shall be, for the Erection of Forts, Magazines, Arsenals, dock-Yards, and other needful Buildings;— And

18. To make all Laws which shall be necessary and proper for carrying into Execution the foregoing Powers, and all other Powers vested by this Constitution in the Government of the United States, or in any Department or Officer thereof.

5) This is the basis for the Bureau of the Mint in the Treasury Department (see p. 520).
See pp. 256–257.

8) This reference concerns the issuance of patents (see pp. 513–514), trademarks (p. 54), and copyrights (pp. 116–117).

9) The whole federal judiciary system (pp. 222–237) is based on this clause.

10) "Law of Nations" means treaties, international agreements, and conventions recognized by the United States.

11) The President is commander-in-chief of our armed forces, but he must have authority from Congress to wage war except when the United States is attacked. "Letters of Marque and Reprisal" are obsolete; they were papers issued to private citizens in wartime, authorizing them to arm merchant vessels and engage an enemy.

12, 13, 14) These made certain that the military was under civilian control. See Chapter 27, p. 680.

15, 16) These clauses give Congress power over the National Guard. See Art. II, Sec. 2, Cl. 1.

17) This clause is the legal basis for the District of Columbia and for other federal property (see p. 349).

18) This is known as the "elastic clause" because it is used to imply powers which are not specifically mentioned in Section 8. The Supreme Court has consistently ruled, however, that all congressional actions based on an implied power must have a basis in one of the enumerated powers of Section 8.

Section 9

1. [The Migration or Importation of such Persons as any of the States now existing shall think proper to admit, shall not be prohibited by the Congress prior to the Year one thousand eight hundred and eight, but a Tax or duty may be imposed on such Importation, not exceeding ten dollars for each Person.]

2. The Privilege of the Writ of Habeas Corpus shall not be suspended, unless when in Cases of Rebellion or Invasion the public Safety may require it.

3. No Bill of Attainder or ex post facto Law shall be passed.

1) See Amendment XIII, p. 64.

2) "Habeas Corpus" is a legal paper issued by a judge, requiring a jailer to release a prisoner unless he is formally charged with or convicted of a specific crime (see pp. 249 and 397).

3) A "bill of attainder" is a legislative act which provides punishment for an individual, without benefit of trial, for an alleged crime. An "ex post facto law" is one which, after a particular act is committed, declares that act to be a crime and provides punishment for it; or, it declares the act to be a more serious crime than it had been when it was committed.

4. No Capitation, or other direct, Tax shall be laid, unless in Proportion to the Census or Enumeration herein before directed to be taken.

5. No Tax or Duty shall be laid on Articles exported from any State.

6. No Preference shall be given by any Regulation of Commerce or Revenue to the Ports of one State over those of another: nor shall Vessels bound to, or from, one State, be obliged to enter, clear, or pay Duties in another.

7. No Money shall be drawn from the Treasury, but in Consequence of Appropriations made by Law; and a regular Statement and Account of the Receipts and Expenditures of all public Money shall be published from time to time.

8. No Title of Nobility shall be granted by the United States: And no Person holding any Office of Profit or Trust under them, shall, without the Consent of the Congress, accept of any present, Emolument, Office, or Title, of any kind whatever, from any King, Prince, or foreign State.

4) This means that taxes must not fall more heavily on one group of people than on another. But decisions of the Supreme Court and Amendment XVI allow Congress to tax according to ability to pay. Thus in practice some people pay very high taxes; others none at all.

7) This is why the executive must prepare the annual budget in advance and "go to Congress" each year to ask for the money (see p. 170).

Section 10

1. No State shall enter into any Treaty, Alliance, or Confederation; grant Letters of Marque and Reprisal; coin Money; emit Bills of Credit; make any Thing but gold and silver Coin a Tender in Payment of Debts; pass any Bill of Attainder, ex post facto Law, or Law impairing the Obligations of Contracts, or grant any Title of Nobility.

2. No State shall, without the Consent of the Congress, lay any Imposts or Duties on Imports or Ex-

*Sec. 10, Cl. 1-3. These are the clauses which limit the states to powers **subordinate** to those of the United States. Powers denied to the states are those which always belong to a **nation**. Thus the Constitution sets up a **nation over the states**, not a league of nations, as the Articles of Confederation did.*

55

ports, except what may be absolutely necessary for executing its inspection Laws: and the net Produce of all Duties and Imposts, laid by any State on Imports or Exports, shall be for the Use of the Treasury of the United States; and all such Laws shall be subject to the Revision and Controul of the Congress.

3. No State shall, without the Consent of Congress, lay any Duty of Tonnage, keep Troops, or Ships of War in time of Peace, enter into any Agreement or Compact with another State, or with a foreign Power, or engage in War, unless actually invaded, or in such imminent Danger as will not admit of delay.

ARTICLE II

Section 1

1. The executive Power shall be vested in a President of the United States of America. He shall hold his Office during the Term of four Years, and, together with the Vice President, chosen for the same Term, be elected, as follows:

2. Each State shall appoint, in such Manner as the Legislature thereof may direct, a Number of Electors, equal to the whole Number of Senators and Representatives to which the State may be entitled in the Congress: but no Senator or Representative, or Person holding an Office of Trust or Profit under the United States, shall be appointed an Elector.

3. [*The Electors shall meet in their respective States, and vote by Ballot for two Persons, of whom one at least shall not be an Inhabitant of the same State with themselves. And they shall make a List of all the Persons voted for, and of the Number of Votes for each; which List they shall sign and certify, and transmit sealed to the Seat of the Government of the United States, directed to the President of the Senate. The President of the Senate shall, in the Presence of the Senate and House of Representatives, open all the Certificates, and the Votes shall then be counted. The Person having the greatest Number of Votes shall be the President, if such Number be a Majority of the whole Number of Electors appointed; and if there be more than one who have such Majority, and have an equal Number of Votes, then the House of Representatives shall immediately chuse by Ballot one of them for President; and if no Person have a Majority, then from the five highest on the List the said House shall in like Manner chuse the President. But in chusing the President, the Votes shall be taken by States, the Representation from each State having one Vote; A quorum for this Purpose shall consist of a Member or Members from two thirds of the States, and a Majority of all the States shall be necessary to a Choice. In every Case, after the Choice of the President, the Person having the greatest Number of Votes of the*

Sec. 1. President and Vice-President.

2) Under state laws the voter thus votes for "electors"; but the electors' names often do not appear on the ballot and the voter merely marks the presidential and vice-presidential candidates of his choice. In this way he votes for electors pledged in most cases to vote for his candidate for President (see pp. 76–77).

3) See Amendment XII, pp. 63–64.

56

Electors shall be the Vice President. But if there should remain two or more who have equal Votes, the Senate shall chuse from them by Ballot the Vice President.]

4. The Congress may determine the Time of chusing the Electors, and the Day on which they shall give their Votes; which Day shall be the same throughout the United States.

5. No Person except a natural born Citizen, [or a Citizen of the United States, at the time of the Adoption of this Constitution,] shall be eligible to the Office of President; neither shall any Person be eligible to that Office who shall not have attained to the Age of thirty five Years, and been fourteen Years a Resident within the United States.

6. In case of the Removal of the President from Office, or of his Death, Resignation, or Inability to discharge the Powers and Duties of the said Office, the same shall devolve on the Vice President, and the Congress may by Law provide for the Case of Removal, Death, Resignation or Inability, both of the President and Vice President, declaring what Officer shall then act as President, and such Officer shall act accordingly, until the Disability be removed, or a President shall be elected.

7. The President shall, at stated Times, receive for his Services, a Compensation, which shall neither be encreased nor diminished during the Period for which he shall have been elected, and he shall not receive within that Period any other Emolument from the United States, or any of them.

8. Before he enter on the Execution of his Office, he shall take the following Oath or Affirmation:—"I do solemnly swear (or affirm) that I will faithfully execute the Office of President of the United States, and will to the best of my Ability, preserve, protect and defend the Constitution of the United States."

Section 2

1. The President shall be Commander in Chief of the Army and Navy of the United States, and of the Militia of the several States, when called into the actual Service of the United States; he may require the Opinion, in writing, of the principal Officer in each of the executive Departments, upon any Subject relating to the Duties of their respective Offices, and he shall have Power to grant Reprieves and Pardons for Offences against the United States, except in Cases of Impeachment.

4) See Sec. 4, Cl. 1.

5) See Amendment XXII, p. 67.

6) There is no established method of determining the "Inability" of the President to discharge his duties, though many proposals have been made. Under law the succession to the Presidency, if both President and Vice-President die, is in this order: Speaker of the House, President pro tem of the Senate Secretary of State, and then other members of the cabinet in the order of the creations of their departments. No Vice-President, however, has ever died in office after succeeding to the Presidency. And no President has ever resigned or been judged unable to carry on his duties.

7) Present salary $100,000, plus $50,000 living expenses and $40,000 for official travel and entertainment.

1) See Art. I, Sec. 8, Cl. 15, and p. 165. "The principal officer in each of the executive departments" —this phrase is one of the constitutional bases for the cabinet. All executive departments have been created by acts of Congress. This clause has required the President to deal with many matters not specifically stated but necessary in the modern world (see pp. 166–167). Group pardons are called **amnesty.**

2. He shall have Power, by and with the Advice and Consent of the Senate, to make Treaties, provided two thirds of the Senators present concur; and he shall nominate, and by and with the Advice and Consent of the Senate, shall appoint Ambassadors, other public Ministers and Consuls, Judges of the supreme Court, and all other Officers of the United States, whose Appointments are not herein otherwise provided for, and which shall be established by Law: but the Congress may by Law vest the Appointment of such inferior Officers, as they think proper, in the President alone, in the Courts of Law, or in the Heads of Departments.

3. The President shall have Power to fill up all Vacancies that may happen during the Recess of the Senate, by granting Commissions which shall expire at the End of their next Session.

2) The reference to "Heads of Departments," again, indirectly authorizes the establishment of the cabinet and the executive departments to be made. Congress acts to give appointing power for most officials to agency heads. The President still appoints all top-level officials and U.S. attorneys and postmasters.

Section 3

He shall from time to time give to the Congress Information of the State of the Union, and recommend to their Consideration such Measures as he shall judge necessary and expedient; he may, on extraordinary Occasions, convene both Houses, or either of them, and in Case of Disagreement between them, with Respect to the Time of Adjournment, he may adjourn them to such Time as he shall think proper; he shall receive Ambassadors and other public Ministers; he shall take Care that the Laws be faithfully executed, and shall Commission all the Officers of the United States.

Sec. 3. The President's power to appoint Ambassadors, Ministers, and Consuls, and his power to "receive Ambassadors and other public Ministers" from foreign nations give the President control over foreign relations, though the Congress alone may appropriate money needed for foreign relations and the Senate must approve treaties.

Section 4

The President, Vice President and all Civil Officers of the United States, shall be removed from Office on Impeachment for, and Conviction of, Treason, Bribery, or other high Crimes and Misdemeanors.

ARTICLE III

Section 1

The judicial Power of the United States, shall be vested in one supreme Court, and in such inferior Courts as the Congress may from time to time ordain and establish. The Judges, both of the supreme and inferior Courts, shall hold their Offices during good Behaviour, and shall, at stated Times, receive for their Services, a Compensation, which shall not be diminished during their Continuance in Office.

See Art. I, Secs. 6-7.
For discussion of the federal judiciary as established by Congress see Chapter 9.
Federal judges may retire at seventy under present law but are not required to do so. For their compensation, see p. 227.

Section 2

1. The Judicial Power shall extend to all Cases, in Law and Equity, arising under this Constitution, the

Laws of the United States, and Treaties made, or which shall be made, under their Authority;—to all Cases affecting Ambassadors, other public Ministers and Consuls;—to all Cases of admiralty and maritime Jurisdiction;—to Controversies to which the United States shall be a Party;—to Controversies between two or more States;—between a State and Citizens of another State;—between Citizens of different States;—between Citizens of the same State claiming Lands under Grants of different States, and between a State, or the Citizens thereof, and foreign States, Citizens or Subjects.

2. In all Cases affecting Ambassadors, other public Ministers and Consuls, and those in which a State shall be Party, the supreme Court shall have original Jurisdiction. In all the other Cases before mentioned, the supreme Court shall have appellate Jurisdiction, both as to Law and Fact, with such Exceptions, and under such Regulations as the Congress shall make.

3. The Trial of all Crimes, except in Cases of Impeachment, shall be by Jury; and such Trial shall be held in the State where the said Crimes shall have been committed; but when not committed within any State, the Trial shall be at such Place or Places as the Congress may by Law have directed.

Section 3

1. Treason against the United States, shall consist only in levying War against them, or in adhering to their Enemies, giving them Aid and Comfort. No Person shall be convicted of Treason unless on the Testimony of two Witnesses to the same overt Act, or on Confession in open Court.

2. The Congress shall have Power to declare the Punishment of Treason, but no Attainder of Treason shall work Corruption of Blood, or Forfeiture except during the Life of the Person attainted.

ARTICLE IV

Section 1

Full Faith and Credit shall be given in each State to the Public Acts, Records, and judicial Proceedings of every other State. And the Congress may by general Laws prescribe the Manner in which such Acts, Records and Proceedings shall be proved, and the Effect thereof.

Section 2

1. The Citizens of each State shall be entitled to all Privileges and Immunities of Citizens in the several States.

Cases of "admiralty and maritime Jurisdiction" means cases arising not only on the high seas but on inland navigable waters such as rivers, canals, and the Great Lakes.

2) The power of the Supreme Court to decide the constitutionality of a law, when a case is appealed to the Court, is not found in the Constitution. It rests on the decision of the Court in the case of Marbury vs. Madison (see pp. 103–105).

3) There is no jury in cases before the Supreme Court. This clause applies to the Federal District Courts established by Congress under Sec. 1 of this article.

1) For discussion of national security, see pp. 362–363.

2) This means that the descendant of a person convicted of treason may not be punished for his ancestor's acts. Before the American Revolution such punishment was occasionally ordered under English law.

Secs. 1-2. These provisions guarantee the equality of the states.

2. A Person charged in any State with Treason, Felony, or other Crime, who shall flee from Justice, and be found in another State, shall on Demand of the executive Authority of the State from which he fled, be delivered up, to be removed to the State having Jurisdiction of the Crime.

*This procedure is known as **extradition** (see p. 285).*

3. [No Person held to Service or Labour in one State, under the Laws thereof, escaping into another, shall, in Consequence of any Law or Regulation therein, be discharged from such Service or Labour, but shall be delivered up on Claim of the Party to whom such Service or Labour may be due.]

3) See Amendment XIII, p. 64.

Section 3

1. New States may be admitted by the Congress into this Union; but no new State shall be formed or erected within the Jurisdiction of any other State; nor any State be formed by the Junction of two or more States, or Parts of States, without the Consent of the Legislatures of the States concerned as well as of the Congress.

1) See pp. 119 and 341 (Hawaii and Alaska).

2. The Congress shall have Power to dispose of and make all needful Rules and Regulations respecting the Territory or other Property belonging to the United States; and nothing in this Constitution shall be so construed as to Prejudice any Claims of the United States, or of any particular State.

2) This clause is the basis of American territorial governments (pp. 344–348), as well as federal control over public lands, forests, parks, etc. TVA was established under it (see p. 209–210). Also in the Tidelands controversy, Congress acted under this power to give lands to the states (see p. 582).

Section 4

The United States shall guarantee to every State in this Union a Republican Form of Government, and shall protect each of them against Invasion; and on Application of the Legislature or of the Executive (when the Legislature cannot be convened) against domestic Violence.

Sec. 4. For discussion of the states as "republics" see Chap. 11, pp. 270–271.

ARTICLE V

The Congress, whenever two thirds of both Houses shall deem it necessary, shall propose Amendments to this Constitution, or, on the Application of the Legislatures of two thirds of the several States, shall call a Convention for proposing Amendments, which, in either Case, shall be valid to all Intents and Purposes, as Part of this Constitution, when ratified by the Legislatures of three fourths of the several States, or by Conventions in three fourths thereof, as the one or the other Mode of Ratification may be proposed by the Congress; Provided [that no Amendment which may be made prior to the Year One thousand eight hundred and eight shall in any Manner affect the first and fourth Clauses in the Ninth Section of the first Article; and] that no State, without its Consent, shall be deprived of its equal Suffrage in the Senate.

No constitutional convention has been called since 1787. All amendments except Amendment XXI have been ratified by the state legislatures.

Prohibition (see Amendment XVIII) was repealed by state conventions.

ARTICLE VI

1. All Debts contracted and Engagements entered into, before the Adoption of this Constitution, shall be as valid against the United States under this Constitution, as under the Confederation.

2. This Constitution, and the Laws of the United States which shall be made in Pursuance thereof; and all Treaties made, or which shall be made, under the Authority of the United States, shall be the supreme Law of the Land; and the judges in every State shall be bound thereby, any Thing in the Constitution or Laws of any State to the Contrary notwithstanding.

2) The Supreme Court has held that "executive agreements" between the President and foreign powers have the force of law if made under law. In recent years there have been several attempts to amend the Constitution to eliminate "executive agreements" made without concurrence of the Senate or to declare them not to have the force of law.

3. The Senators and Representatives before mentioned, and the Members of the several State Legislatures, and all executive and judicial Officers, both of the United States and of the several States, shall be bound by Oath or Affirmation, to support this Constitution; but no religious Test shall ever be required as a Qualification to any Office or public Trust under the United States.

ARTICLE VII

The Ratification of the Conventions of nine States, shall be sufficient for the Establishment of this Constitution between the States so ratifying the Same. Done in Convention by the Unanimous Consent of the States present the Seventeenth Day of September in the Year of our Lord one thousand seven hundred and Eighty seven and of the Independance of the United States of America the Twelth. In witness whereof We have hereunto subscribed our Names,

Go Washington—Presidt
and deputy from
Virginia

New Hampshire	{ John Langdon Nicholas Gilman		Pennsylvania	{ B Franklin Thomas Mifflin Robt Morris Geo. Clymer Thos FitzSimons Jared Ingersoll James Wilson Gouv Morris	Virginia	{ John Blair— James Madison Jr.
Massachusetts	{ Nathaniel Gorham Rufus King				North Carolina	{ Wm Blount Richd Dobbs Spaight. Hu Williamson
Connecticut	{ Wm Saml Johnson Roger Sherman		Delaware	{ Geo: Read Gunning Bedford jun John Dickinson Richard Bassett Jaco: Broom	South Carolina	{ J. Rutledge Charles Cotesworth Pinckney Charles Pinckney Pierce Butler.
New York	{ Alexander Hamilton					
New Jersey	{ Wil: Livingston David Brearley. Wm Paterson. Jona: Dayton		Maryland	{ James McHenry Dan of St Thos Jenifer Danl Carroll	Georgia	{ William Few Abr Baldwin

AMENDMENTS

Amendment I (1791)

Congress shall make no law respecting an establishment of religion, or prohibiting the free exercise thereof; or abridging the freedom of speech, or of the press; or the right of the people peaceably to assemble, and to petition the Government for a redress of grievances.

For discussion of Amendment I see pp. 385–387. None of these prohibitions is absolute. You cannot freely shout "Fire!" in a crowded theater. Licenses may be required to bear arms, and incompetent persons (insane, convicts, etc.) are denied licenses.

Amendment II (1791)

A well regulated Militia, being necessary to the security of a free State, the right of the people to keep and bear Arms, shall not be infringed.

Amendment III (1791)

No Soldier shall, in time of peace be quartered in any house, without the consent of the Owner, nor in time of war, but in a manner to be prescribed by law.

Amendment IV (1791)

The right of the people to be secure in their persons, houses, papers, and effects, against unreasonable searches and seizures, shall not be violated, and no Warrants shall issue, but upon probable cause, supported by Oath or affirmation, and particularly describing the place to be searched, and the persons or things to be seized.

Amendments IV, V, VI, and VII are discussed in detail on pp. 387–396.

Amendment V (1791)

No person shall be held to answer for a capital, or otherwise infamous crime, unless on a presentment or indictment of a Grand Jury, except in cases arising in the land or naval forces, or in the Militia, when in actual service in time of War or public danger; nor shall any person be subject for the same offence to be twice put in jeopardy of life or limb; nor shall be compelled in any criminal case to be a witness against himself, nor be deprived of life, liberty, or property, without due process of law; nor shall private property be taken for public use, without just compensation.

Applies specifically to cases arising in federal Courts. All state constitutions give citizens similar but not identical protections. See also Amendment XIV. See Chapter 16 for detailed discussion of this extremely important protection.

*This power is known as **eminent domain** (see pp. 36 and 395).*

Amendment VI (1791)

In all criminal prosecutions, the accused shall enjoy the right to a speedy and public trial, by an impartial jury of the State and district wherein the crime shall have been committed, which district shall have been previously ascertained by law, and to be informed of the nature and cause of the accusation; to be con-

*Trials are often not "speedy." This is because court calendars are very crowded, or because the defense wishes time to prepare its case. "Compulsory process for obtaining witnesses" means **subpoena** (see pp. 250 and 396).*

fronted with the witnesses against him; to have compulsory process for obtaining witnesses in his favor, and to have the Assistance of Counsel for his defence.

Amendment VII (1791)

In Suits at common law, where the value in controversy shall exceed twenty dollars, the right of trial by jury shall be preserved, and no fact tried by a jury, shall be otherwise reexamined in any Court of the United States, than according to the rules of the common law.

See pp. 223–224 for discussion of unwritten or "common" law. See also p. 398 for meaning of this amendment as a safeguard to the citizen.

Amendment VIII (1791)

Excessive bail shall not be required, nor excessive fines imposed, nor cruel and unusual punishments inflicted.

Amendment IX (1791)

The enumeration in the Constitution, of certain rights, shall not be construed to deny or disparage others retained by the people.

Amendment X (1791)

The powers not delegated to the United States by the Constitution, nor prohibited by it to the States, are reserved to the States respectively, or to the people.

Amendments IX and X are the so-called "States' Rights" Amendments. See p. 99. They limit the powers of the national government and have often been appealed to when certain states have objected to federal laws, especially in such matters as civil rights.
Amendment X. **Reserved powers** includes, for example, the power to charter business corporations (see p. 537) and to regulate labor (see pp. 559–561).

Amendment XI (1798)

The Judicial power of the United States shall not be construed to extend to any suit in law or equity, commenced or prosecuted against one of the United States by Citizens of another State, or by Citizens or Subjects of any Foreign State.

Amendment XII (1804)

The Electors shall meet in their respective states, and vote by ballot for President and Vice-President, one of whom, at least, shall not be an inhabitant of the same state with themselves; they shall name in their ballots the person voted for as President, and in distinct ballots the person voted for as Vice-President, and they shall make distinct lists of all persons voted for as President, and of all persons voted for as Vice-President, and of the number of votes for each, which lists they shall sign and certify, and transmit sealed to the seat of the government of the United States, directed to the President of the Senate;—The President of the Senate shall, in the presence of the Senate and House of Representatives, open all the certificates and the votes shall then be counted;—The person having the greatest number of votes for President, shall be the President, if such number be a majority of the whole number of Electors appointed; and if no per-

See Art. II, Sec. 2. This amendment replaces Sec. 3 of Art. II. Since its adoption the election of a President has had to be made by Congress only once, in 1824. See also Amendment XX, Sec. 3.

son have such majority, then from the persons having the highest numbers not exceeding three on the list of those voted for as President, the House of Representatives shall choose immediately, by ballot, the President. But in choosing the President, the votes shall be taken by states, the representation from each state having one vote; a quorum for this purpose shall consist of a member or members from two-thirds of the states, and a majority of all the states shall be necessary to a choice. And if the House of Representatives shall not choose a President whenever the right of choice shall devolve upon them, [before the fourth day of March next following,] then the Vice-President shall act as President, as in the case of the death or other constitutional disability of the President.—The person having the greatest number of votes as Vice-President, shall be the Vice-President, if such number be a majority of the whole number of Electors appointed, and if no person have a majority, then from the two highest numbers on the list, the Senate shall choose the Vice-President; a quorum for the purpose shall consist of two-thirds of the whole number of Senators, and a majority of the whole number shall be necessary to a choice. But no person constitutionally ineligible to the office of President shall be eligible to that of Vice-President of the United States.

"Before the fourth day of March . . ." see Amendment XX, Sec. 1.

Amendment XIII (1865)

1. Neither slavery nor involuntary servitude, except as a punishment for crime whereof the party shall have been duly convicted, shall exist within the United States, or any place subject to their jurisdiction.

2. Congress shall have power to enforce this article by appropriate legislation.

Amendment XIV (1868)

1. All persons born or naturalized in the United States, and subject to the jurisdiction thereof, are citizens of the United States and of the State wherein they reside. No State shall make or enforce any law which shall abridge the privileges or immunities of citizens of the United States; nor shall any State deprive any person of life, liberty, or property, without due process of law, nor deny to any person within its jurisdiction the equal protection of the laws.

2. Representatives shall be apportioned among the several States according to their respective numbers, counting the whole number of persons in each State, excluding Indians not taxed. But when the right to vote at any election for the choice of electors for President and Vice President of the United States, Representatives in Congress, the Executive and Judicial officers of a State, or the members of the Legislature therof, is denied to any of the male inhabitants

See pp. 363–368 for limitations on the citizens here named.

1) This clause has been interpreted by the Supreme Court to make the first eight amendments binding against state governments in most cases, but not all. For example, states are not required to use the grand jury system (see p. 229). In Brown vs Topeka (1954) the Supreme Court held that segregation by color in public schools denies citizens "equal protection of the laws." In other cases, segregation in other public places has been declared unconstitutional for the same reason.

2) "But when the right to vote . . ." This clause has never been strictly enforced (see pp. 399–400).

of such State, being twenty-one years of age, and citizens of the United States, or in any way abridged, except for participation in rebellion, or other crime, the basis of representation therein shall be reduced in the proportion which the number of such male citizens shall bear to the whole number of male citizens twenty-one years of age in such State.

3. No person shall be a Senator or Representative in Congress, or elector of President and Vice President, or hold any office, civil or military, under the United States, or under any State, who, having previously taken an oath, as a member of Congress, or as an officer of the United States, or as a member of any State legislature, or as an executive or judicial officer of any State, to support the Constitution of the United States, shall have engaged in insurrection or rebellion against the same, or given aid or comfort to the enemies thereof. But Congress may by a vote of two-thirds of each House, remove such disability.

4. The validity of the public debt of the United States, authorized by law, including debts incurred for payment of pensions and bounties for services in suppressing insurrection or rebellion, shall not be questioned. But neither the United States nor any State shall assume or pay any debt or obligation incurred in aid of insurrection or rebellion against the United States, or any claim for the loss or emancipation of any slave; but all such debts, obligations and claims shall be held illegal and void.

5. The Congress shall have power to enforce, by appropriate legislation, the provisions of this article.

Amendment XV (1870)

1. The right of citizens of the United States to vote shall not be denied or abridged by the United States or by any State on account of race, color, or previous condition of servitude.

2. The Congress shall have power to enforce this article by appropriate legislation.

Amendment XVI (1913)

The Congress shall have power to lay and collect taxes on incomes, from whatever source derived, without apportionment among the several States, and without regard to any census or enumeration.

Amendment XVII (1913)

1. The Senate of the United States shall be composed of two Senators from each State, elected by the people thereof, for six years; and each Senator shall have one vote. The electors in each State shall have the qualifications requisite for electors of the most numerous branch of the State legislatures.

2. When vacancies happen in the representation of any State in the Senate, the executive authority of

Since the states retain the right to establish other voting qualificatons, many Negroes have been unable to vote or have been discouraged from voting in spite of this amendment (see pp. 399–400). But the Civil Rights Act of 1957 increased judicial power to protect the right to vote.

This made more democratic the method of electing Senators, since it put election in hands of the people rather than leaving it to the legislature of each state (see Art. I, Sec. 3, pp. 50–51).

such State shall issue writs of election to fill such vacancies: *Provided,* That the legislature of any State, may empower the executive thereof to make temporary appointments until the people fill the vacancies by election as the legislature may direct.

3. [*This amendment shall not be so construed as to affect the election or term of any Senator chosen before it becomes valid as part of the Constitution.*]

Amendment XVIII (1919)

1. [*After one year from the ratification of this article the manufacture, sale, or transportation of intoxicating liquors within, the importation thereof into, or the exportation thereof from the United States and all territory subject to the jurisdiction thereof for beverage purposes is hereby prohibited.*]

2. [*The Congress and the several States shall have concurrent power to enforce this article by appropriate legislation.*]

3. [*This article shall be inoperative unless it shall have been ratified as an amendment to the Constitution by the legislatures of the several States, as provided in the Constitution, within seven years from the date of the submission hereof to the States by the Congress.*]

This amendment was repealed by Amendment XXI.

Amendment XIX (1920)

1. The right of citizens of the United States to vote shall not be denied or abridged by the United States or by any State on account of sex.

2. Congress shall have power to enforce this article by appropriate legislation.

In recent elections women voters have sometimes outnumbered men.

Amendment XX (1933)

1. The terms of the President and Vice President shall end at noon on the 20th day of January, and the terms of Senators and Representatives at noon on the 3rd day of January, of the years in which such terms would have ended if this article had not been ratified, and the terms of their successors shall then begin.

2. The Congress shall assemble at least once in every year, and such meeting shall begin at noon on the 3rd day of January, unless they shall by law appoint a different day.

3. If, at the time fixed for the beginning of the term of the President, the President elect shall have died, the Vice President elect shall become President. If a President shall not have been chosen before the time fixed for the beginning of his term, or if the President elect shall have failed to qualify, then the Vice President elect shall act as President until a President shall have qualified; and the Congress may by law provide for the case wherein neither a President elect nor a Vice President elect shall have qualified,

2) This provision repealed Art. I, Sec. 4, Cl. 2.

declaring who shall then act as President, or the manner in which one who is to act shall be selected, and such person shall act accordingly until a President or Vice President shall have qualified.

4. The Congress may by law provide for the case of the death of any of the persons from whom the House of Representatives may choose a President whenever the right of choice shall have devolved upon them, and for the case of death of any of the persons from whom the Senate may choose a Vice President whenever the right of choice shall have devolved upon them.

5. [Sections 1 and 2 shall take effect on the 15th day of October following the ratification of this article.]

6. [This article shall be inoperative unless it shall have been ratified as an amendment to the Constitution by the legislatures of three-fourths of the several States within seven years from the date of its submission.]

Amendment XXI (1933)

1. The eighteenth article of amendment to the Constitution of the United States is hereby repealed.

2. The transportation or importation into any State, Territory, or possession of the United States for delivery or use therein of intoxicating liquors, in violation of the laws thereof, is hereby prohibited.

3. [This article shall be inoperative unless it shall have been ratified as an amendment to the Constitution by conventions in the several States, as provided in the Constitution, within seven years from the date of the submission hereof to the States by the Congress.]

Amendment XXII (1951)

1. No person shall be elected to the office of the President more than twice, and no person who has held the office of President, or acted as President, for more than two years of a term to which some other person was elected President shall be elected to the office of the President more than once. But this Article shall not apply to any person holding the office of President when this Article was proposed by the Congress, and shall not prevent any person who may be holding the office of President, or acting as President, during the term within which this Article becomes operative from holding the office of President or acting as President during the remainder of such term.

2. [This article shall be inoperative unless it shall have been ratified as an amendment to the Constitution by the legislatures of three-fourths of the several States within seven years from the date of its submission to the States by the Congress.]

1) Franklin D. Roosevelt was the only President elected more than twice, before this amendment took effect (1932, 1936, 1940, 1944). Harry S. Truman, President when the amendment was adopted, was exempted from its effect but did not seek another term.

CHAPTER 3

Backgrounds of American Democracy:
The Constitution

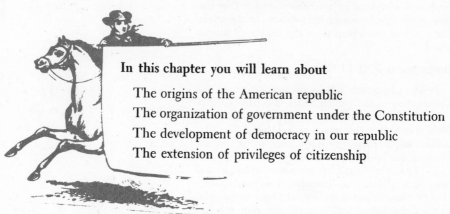

In this chapter you will learn about

The origins of the American republic

The organization of government under the Constitution

The development of democracy in our republic

The extension of privileges of citizenship

Can you imagine a time when the election of the President of the United States was page two news? Strange as it may seem, that is just where the news of the election of George Washington was placed in the April 13, 1789, issue of the *Pennsylvania Packet and Daily Advertiser*. Here is the news item:

Yesterday the Honorable Congress of the United States, having a quorum of both Houses, proceeded to business.

The Senate having chosen his Excellency John Langdon, Esquire, of New Hampshire, President, for the purpose of opening and counting the votes for President and Vice President of the United States, agreeably to the Constitution, the House of Representatives attended in the Senate chamber, when his Excellency opened and examined the ballots of the electors of the respective states.

The illustrious GEORGE WASHINGTON, Esquire, was then announced President of the United States of America, and his Excellency JOHN ADAMS, Esquire, Vice President.

It is true that part of the strangeness of the news item is due to the strange language. Newspapers and news reporting have changed greatly since the days of Washington. That is not the whole story, however. There has also been a great change in how much of a part the people of our country play—directly or indirectly—in making decisions in our political life.

WHAT IS AMERICAN DEMOCRACY?

Just how old is American democracy anyway? Didn't the Revolutionary War bring us democracy in the place of British tyranny? The answer to that question is not simple. Even asking such a question would show a great ignorance of history; we must draw on history to show how we gradually acquired what we now call American democracy.

Abraham Lincoln, in the Gettysburg Address, spoke of government of the people, by the people, and for the people. Yet over half the adults in the United States at that time were not allowed to take any part in "government by the people." In the early days of our republic an even smaller fraction of our people could vote. No, American democracy did not just happen as a result of the Revolution. It developed gradually, by fits and starts, by dissatisfaction, disagreement, and political working out of the disagreements through compromise.

Pure Democracy or a Republic?

Some Americans may be surprised at being reminded that in the early days of our country "democracy" was not a popular word. In some cases, it was even used as a term of insult. To the minds of many people, it suggested mobs and lawlessness. Consequently, when the delegates assembled in Philadelphia for the convention which was to result in a new constitution, they planned a government which would be a **republic.**

This idea of a republic is very ancient. Educated Americans in 1787 knew something about the idea of republicanism. The term suggested stable government under which personal liberties could be guaranteed by law. It suggested protection and safeguard against the fickleness and folly of the mob. We may distinguish the two terms in this way: a **democracy** is a political system in which the people themselves vote directly on what the laws shall be and directly choose those who shall administer the laws; a **republic** is a system in which the people vote for **representatives** who, in turn, make the laws and appoint most of the administrators.

Thus a republic is a form of government in which the laws are made by a legislative body chosen periodically by the people and administered by an executive chosen either by the people or by the legislative body. In 1787 the delegates at Philadelphia made plans for a new government in which "the people" (the minority who could vote) chose only the lower house, the House of Representatives. Senators, judges, and the President were elected or appointed by other officials—not by vote of the people. The President, for example, was to be chosen by the votes of persons called **electors.** These electors were to be "appointed" by the states in whatever manner the state legislature of each state might direct. In the beginning, this meant they were chosen by the state legislature itself or by the voters of the state. Once chosen, the electors met in their state capitals to vote. A few months later the votes of the "electoral college" were opened and counted in Congress.

These facts help to explain why the public did not find the election of George Washington a tremendously exciting affair. Had the public been allowed to choose a President, Washington might well have been the popular choice. What actually happened, however, was that a large portion of the people could not vote even for the state legislators. Secondly, the President was chosen by **electors** who in turn had been chosen by their states' lawmakers or by a minority of the people. It is true that in this way the people were rather indirectly represented. It is also true that within a few years, in most of the states, electors were chosen by popular vote. Nevertheless, this is the way, the unspectacular way, in which the idea of republicanism worked out in the earliest days of the United States.

Even in those days Americans differed among themselves on the extent to which a republic ought to be democratic. They disagreed on how far they should go in allowing the people to take part in the conduct of republican government. It has taken years to work out our present answer to this question of the people's participation in government.

A Democratic Republic

What we have developed in our country is a **democratic republic.** Our system is not a **true democracy** because all of us could not possibly vote on all the matters with which our government deals or on all the officials needed to carry out our laws. We have instead a republic where our officials are either elected by us or appointed by elected officials. Our laws are made by elected representatives. It is a **democratic** republic because all adult citizens may qualify as voters to elect their representatives. Thus the will of all the people (democracy) underlies our republican system. Today when we speak of the American democracy, what we really mean is our democratic republic. If you now understand the difference, you should feel free to use the popular term **democracy.**

To understand and appreciate how our democratic republic has developed, we must look at the past, particularly at the Constitution and the ideas of the men who made it.

REPUBLICANISM AND THE CONSTITUTION

The making of our Constitution was a dramatic and enlightening chapter in American history. The delegates to the Convention of 1787, appointed by their state legislatures, came together originally to revise the Articles of Confederation. Government under the Articles had proved both cumbersome and weak, but many delegates at first preferred to continue with a government that would really be a kind of league or treaty among the thirteen independent republics. They knew, however, that such a national government would have very little power.

Since lack of power in the national government was the chief difficulty to be met, the delegates soon found themselves considering new proposals. Though they could not agree at first on the plan of organization, most of the delegates would probably have agreed with James Madison's definition of a republic as "a government which derives all its powers directly or indirectly from the great body of the people, and is administered by persons holding their offices during pleasure, for a limited period, or during good behavior."

The Great Compromise

One of the principal issues the delegates faced was the important question dealing with the manner in which each state would be represented in the national government. They soon found themselves discussing new proposals, like the Virginia and New Jersey plans, which reflected the intense conflict of interests between the small and large states. Out of this disagreement and discussion came one of the first important compromises which were to play so vital and continuing a role in our democratic process. The Great Compromise, as it was later called by historians, provided in the Constitution, Article I (see pp. 50–51), that the members of the lower house of Congress, the House of Representatives, should be chosen directly by the voters of the states on the basis of population, and that each state was to have at least one Representative, regardless of population. Each Representative was to be elected for a two-year term (I, 2).[1] In the upper house, the Senate, each state would be represented equally, by two Senators. Senators were chosen by the legislatures of the states for six-year terms (I, 3). This meant that the Senators would represent the people in an indirect manner, since the members of the state legislatures were elected by the voters. The President was chosen indirectly, by a college of presidential electors (II, 1). Federal judges were further from the control of the people than were the other officials. They were to be appointed by the President (himself not elected by the people), with the approval of the Senate (another group not elected by the

[1] References to the Constitution throughout will be shown thus: II, 2, 4. This means Article II, Section 2, Clause 4.

voters of the states) (II, 2). Judges were appointed for life, depending on good behavior. A judge could be removed only if the House of Representatives brought charges against him and the Senate found him guilty as charged. Thus we find that under the republican principles of the Constitution the officials of the new government were to hold office "for a limited period or during good behavior."

The people would always be directly represented in the making of their laws, since no proposed measure could become a law without the majority approval of both houses of Congress. More important, only the House of Representatives could bring up new bills for taxing the people. This meant that the most direct representatives of the people would hold the purse strings. Such provisions also show how the principle of power "deriving from the people" secured both authority and responsibility in the new government.

The System of Checks and Balances

An important aim of the republican form of government is to prevent the growth of tyranny, that is, the concentration of too much power in the hands of one individual or group. The Constitution gave us very careful safeguards against this danger by dividing the powers of government and setting up the famous system of checks and balances. By this system, no one of the three branches—legislative (Congress, which makes our laws), executive (President and departments which enforce our laws), or judicial (courts which settle disputes under our laws)—was granted enough power either to run the government by itself or to threaten the powers of the other branches. (See chart, p. 73.)

ON THE PRESIDENT The result of this system, as we shall learn in detail in Chapter 7, is that the President 'of the United States, who is intended to be a powerful official, finds that powers given to other branches of government limit him in the carrying out of his powers. He is, for example, commander-in-chief of the armed forces, but Congress determines how large the forces shall be, sets up the rules for enlisting or drafting men, and votes the money to maintain these forces or any part of them. The President carries out the laws of the nation, but the laws are voted by the Congress. To carry them out, the President appoints a great number of officials—heads of departments, heads of bureaus, members of commissions, agency directors, and many others. These appointments must be approved by the Senate, a part of the lawmaking branch of government. The Senate must also give its approval or disapproval to men named by the President to be federal judges. The President is responsible for conducting our relations with other countries, but he may not commit us to treaties with other nations unless the Senate approves. Thus our chief executive is checked in a number of ways by one or both houses of the legislative branch of government.

Checks and Balances

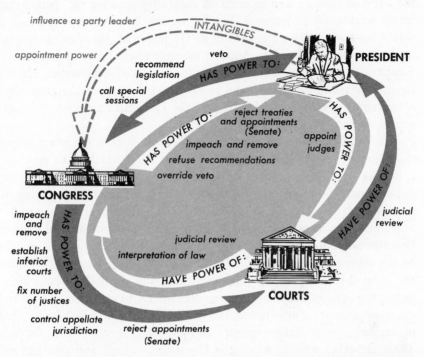

influence as party leader

appointment power

INTANGIBLES

recommend legislation

veto

HAS POWER TO:

PRESIDENT

call special sessions

HAS POWER TO:

reject treaties and appointments (Senate)

impeach and remove

refuse recommendations

override veto

appoint judges

HAS POWER TO:

CONGRESS

HAS POWER TO:

judicial review

impeach and remove

establish inferior courts

fix number of justices

control appellate jurisdiction

judicial review

interpretation of law

HAVE POWER OF:

HAVE POWER OF:

COURTS

reject appointments (Senate)

The powers of the national government are divided among three distinct branches, or departments: the legislative (Article I, section 1), the executive (Article II, section 1), and the judicial (Article III, section 1). These branches are not, however, completely independent of one another. For example, laws voted by Congress, the legislative branch, may be defeated by the veto of the President, who is not a lawmaker but is actually the chief of the executive department.

Note other examples of ways in which the powers of one department are subject to check by the powers of another branch of government. The "intangible" checks which the President can exercise will be discussed in Chapter 7.

ON THE LEGISLATURE   On the other hand, the President has ways of checking those who make the laws. He has the power to veto an act of Congress. In this way he may defeat a proposed law—unless two-thirds of both houses of Congress vote to pass the measure in spite of his disapproval. Thus the McCarran Immigration Law of 1952 was vetoed by President Truman, then re-passed over his veto. But in 1956 when President Eisenhower vetoed a bill to exempt natural gas producers from federal regulation, Congress could not muster enough votes to re-pass it.

The Congress is also dependent on the President for the way in which the laws are administered. It is even possible for a President who disapproves of a law so to administer it that the purpose of Congress is defeated. For example, President Truman repeatedly refused to use the Taft-Hartley labor law, of which he disapproved, in order to bring strikes to an end. This law gives the President power to declare that strikes in certain industries imperil the national security, and to order an eighty-day "cooling off" period during which work must be resumed. But to use the law, President Truman felt, would have implied his approval of it. He preferred, therefore, to use other methods to help end strikes. Another example might be an appropriation by Congress of more money for airplanes than the President wishes. He is not required to spend the money, and so can check the will of Congress. On the other hand, when a law is binding on the President's conduct, he must, of course, enforce it.

ON THE COURTS The courts act as a check on both the other branches, since they determine in cases brought before them whether the government is dealing with the people according to the law. Although the Constitution did not specify that one branch or body should interpret the meaning of its various parts, in a very few years after the government was started, the Supreme Court asserted its right to do so. This power of **judicial interpretation** or **review** has become a very important check by the judicial branch on the other two. The judges, in turn, are made by the Constitution dependent upon the President who appoints them and upon Congress which approves the appointments and appropriates money to pay their salaries and to operate the courts. Furthermore, the two houses of Congress have the power to impeach (bring charges against) and remove judges guilty of misconduct. There are other ways in which the Constitution itself, and practices which have developed under it, provide checks and balances against the misuse of power by any one branch of the government. These examples show how carefully the makers of the Constitution tried to protect the interests of everyone by not giving too much power to any one branch.

THE DEVELOPMENT OF DEMOCRACY UNDER
THE CONSTITUTION

In many ways, the whole history of the United States has been the history of the development and growth of democracy in social, economic, and cultural life, as well as in government. Some very important changes in our form of government have taken place since the Constitution was ratified. The first of these has to do with the rights of the people.

At the Philadelphia convention, several of the delegates argued that the Constitution should contain a statement of the rights of the people. Other delegates felt that a bill of rights was unnecessary, since the Constitution gave no power to the government by which the people could be deprived of their rights. The states, in most cases, already had bills of rights in their constitutions. This, some delegates felt, would make a national bill only a restatement of what was already in force. The Constitution was finally finished without a bill of rights.

Within a few months it became clear that those who favored a federal bill of rights were in the majority. When the Constitution was presented to the state conventions called to ratify it, this question was very vigorously argued. Several states agreed to ratify the Constitution only if it were amended to guarantee the rights of the people. President Washington, in his Inaugural Address, advised Congress to give careful attention to these proposals for amending the Constitution.

In the first session of Congress, in June, 1789, James Madison introduced a number of amendments. Congress passed twelve and submitted them to the states. The ten accepted by the states came to be, known as the Bill of Rights. The text of these amendments can be found on pp. 62–63, and some of them will be discussed later in this book. Amendment I is the key to the others.

AMENDMENT I.   Congress shall make no law respecting an establishment of religion, or prohibiting the free exercise thereof; or abridging the freedom of speech, or of the press; or the right of the people peaceably to assemble, and to petition the government for a redress of grievances.

Notice that the rights here guaranteed say nothing about citizens as distinct from "the people." *Every* American is protected by this amendment. Government must leave religion entirely alone. An American's faith and church cannot have anything to do with his fitness to take part in national affairs or to hold public office. The final clause in Article VI of the Constitution itself specifically declares that "no religious test shall ever be required as a qualification to any office or public trust under the United States." Americans are guaranteed the right to speak their minds freely and to publish their opinions, subject only to the laws against libel (written statements injuring one's reputation) and slander (oral statements injuring one's reputation). Government may not interfere with public meetings unless such meetings endanger the peace. These things, taken together, mean that the voices of all the people may be heard and must be reckoned with.

The Election of the President

Direct election of the President by the people was never seriously considered at the Philadelphia Convention. Hamilton eloquently expressed the fears of many delegates about the chaos which would result from "mob rule." The possibility of Congress's appointing a President was considered but also discarded. The delegates feared such a method would bring the office of the Presidency too much under legislative control. They finally decided that the President should be chosen by the votes of persons called **electors** (see p. 70 and Article II, p. 56, and Amendment XII, p. 63). Each elector cast

"SOMETHING TO
REMEMBER"

Carmack in
The Christian Science Monitor

two votes—one for President and one for Vice President, although he did not specify which vote was for which office. Also, electors were not pledged to vote for a party or a candidate, but used their own judgment.

In the election of 1796, the first in which political parties played a part, John Adams (a Federalist) received the highest number of votes and was therefore elected President. Jefferson (a Democratic-Republican), more popular than Adams's running mate Pinckney, received the next highest number of votes and became Vice-President. The awkwardness of having the President and the Vice-President of different parties led to agreement (not law) that each elector should be pledged to support both candidates of his party.

In 1800, the electors stuck to their party pledges. But since they did not label their votes for President or for Vice-President, there was a tie between Jefferson and Burr. This meant (by constitutional provision, Article II) that the vote had to be thrown into the House of Representatives for decision. Jefferson was chosen President.

Amendment XII to the Constitution, adopted in 1804, straightened out this kink in our election procedures by requiring that the electors vote for President and for Vice-President as distinct offices. By these means (party pledges and separate ballots), the choice of the President came a step closer to the people.

The provision of Article II that the choice of the electors is up to the states has never been repealed, and the great step of binding the electors to vote according to the will of the people had to be taken by the states themselves.

THE ELECTORAL SYSTEM TODAY   It is still possible for exceptions to occur, since not all states have bound electors by law. Nevertheless, nowadays the voter who marks a ballot or pulls the lever of a voting machine may normally be confident that the elector he chooses will vote for his candidate for President. The voter may scarcely notice he is not actually voting for the candidate he favors but for electors. When you vote for a party's candidates for President and Vice-President, it is only a technicality that your vote is not direct. The electoral system today is simply the means through which you express your choice.

There is still some possibility, under the working of our electoral system, that the candidate who wins may not have received the vote of the majority of the people who voted, even in a two-party contest. If a candidate wins in a big state like New York by a majority of only 1, he will get all 45 electoral votes of the state. His losing opponent may carry a smaller state like Michigan by a majority, say, of 500,000 but he will get only the 20 electoral votes of that state. In 1888 Cleveland had 5,540,309 votes to 5,439,853 for Harrison. But Harrison won by 233 to 168 electoral votes. Such facts call attention to the possibility for change in the future as we develop more democracy in our republic. On several occasions Congress has considered, but has not passed, proposals for changing our electoral college system.

In general, these proposals would provide that the number of electors be based directly on the popular vote in each state. Thus, the most populous states would have an even larger influence in the choosing of a President than they do now. The representatives in Congress of the smaller states quite naturally object and have enough votes to prevent the adoption of such amendments.

Changes which make the election of President and Vice-President more democratic have come about only gradually. Procedures in all states are not yet uniform. There have been cases in recent presidential elections where the candidate of a major party did not even get on the ballot of his own party in certain states. Because there are still weaknesses and irregularities in the system, many people are asking for a uniform national law covering presidential elections. However, in our time almost all citizens have a direct voice in the electing of the President and Vice-President. This fact is one of the most important advances in the United States toward making the republic more democratic.

SELECTING OUR PRESIDENTIAL CANDIDATES   Every fourth year now, over radio and television, the American people may hear and see the fascinating spectacle presented by our major political parties as they make their choice of candidates at the nominating conventions. In the early days of our republic, however, presidential candidates were selected quite differently. Political parties, as we have seen, came into existence very early in our history.

77

Their candidates for the Presidency and Vice-Presidency were selected by the party **caucus** (a closed meeting of party members). In other words, all members of Congress belonging to the same party held a closed meeting and made the selections. By the 1830's the state party leaders and the people were so dissatisfied with this method that they forced Congress to abandon it. A system of national party meetings in which all sections of the country were represented took the place of the caucus as a means of writing a platform and choosing candidates for the chief executive offices. In our time delegates from every Congressional District and from the District of Columbia, Virgin Islands, and Puerto Rico come together in highly publicized conventions. There they write a party platform and nominate candidates.

Again, there is no uniformity in the manner of choosing delegates to the conventions. In nineteen states, primary elections are held in which party members can vote to nominate the presidential candidates of their choice. They vote for delegates to the national convention who are pledged to support or are "favorable" to that candidate. In some states, like Minnesota and California, these delegate pledges are binding under state law, while in others, like Pennsylvania, the delegates are merely "advised" by the results of the primary. On the other hand, over half of the delegates at each national convention still are not chosen by the voters in their party but by the party leaders in the various states, so that they do not necessarily reflect the actual wishes of the people. As in the case of choosing presidential electors, there are many people today who are demanding a uniform national law under which party primaries would be held in each state with the results binding upon the delegates elected. But there can be no question that the national nominating conventions have helped greatly to make more democratic the process of choosing the President of the United States. We shall have more to say about this whole matter in Chapter 19 when we are studying the political parties.

Changes in Senate Elections and Traditions

The framers of our Constitution were indeed mindful of democracy when they provided that members of the House of Representatives should be elected *directly* by the people. They were not thinking of democracy, however, when they provided (I, 3) that two Senators were to be chosen from each state by the *legislatures* of the various states. This provision, as we have seen, was part of a compromise and reflects the intense interest of many of our Founding Fathers in maintaining the dignity, authority, and independence of the individual states. In fact, this provision for the Senate was one of the ways in which those framers who distrusted democracy intended to guard against too great a democratic tendency. It is true that some of the first critics of the Constitution, like James Monroe, opposed this plan for choosing Senators on the ground that it put lawmaking too far away from the control of the people. According to Monroe, the Senators would be more like diplomats than legislators. Such voices, however, were a distinct minority in 1789.

The Senate not only was removed from the direct control of the people but even chose to conduct its affairs in secret. There are no records of early Senate debates. But the public came to feel that it had a right to know what was going on among its lawmakers, and the growing clamor of the press eventually forced a change in the matter of secrecy. Before many years, the debates in the Senate drew so much public attention that the members began an uninterrupted tradition of oratory which has tended to set the standards of public speaking in America.

From the beginning, the Senate assumed an air of dignity and detachment quite unlike the more rough-and-tumble nature of the House of Representatives. Even today the Senate of the United States is sometimes spoken of as a kind of exclusive club. It is certainly true that the somewhat aristocratic origins of the Senate made it especially attractive to men of exceptional ability. Over the years some of our most eminent statesmen have made their careers as Senators. Men like Henry Clay, John C. Calhoun, William H. Seward, Daniel Webster, Jefferson Davis, Henry Cabot Lodge, Sr., Robert M. La Follette, Sr., William E. Borah, George Norris, Robert A. Taft, and Alben W. Barkley, to mention only a few, have won for themselves lasting recognition for their service in the Senate of the United States.

The appointment of Senators by members of the state legislatures remained as an undemocratic feature of the Senate until well into the twentieth century. Over the years, however, growing popular demand for a more democratic procedure forced a change. Amendment XVII, adopted in 1913, provided for the direct election of Senators (see p. 50 and pp. 65–66). This meant that candidates for the Senate would now have to go to the people to ask for their votes just as do congressional or presidential candidates. It made more democratic the method of electing the Senate. It did not, however, interfere with the rights of the states, because the states were left free as before to determine who could vote.

EXTENDING THE PRIVILEGES OF CITIZENSHIP

Thus, major changes in the method of choosing the President and Vice-President and of electing United States Senators were brought about by the consent of the governed. They illustrate ways in which our government remains experimental. As Amendment XVII suggests, the Constitution even as amended does not guarantee that our republic shall also be a democracy.

So much real power is left in the hands of the states that their actions to a great extent determine how democratic the nation is to be.

The Direct Primary

The states make some use of the **direct primary**, though only nineteen states have any form of presidential nominating primary, as we saw earlier. In the direct primary, party members vote for party candidates to run against the opposition party's candidates or for party officials or delegates to party conventions. This, too, represents an advance for democracy, since it gives the people a direct vote in the selection of a party's candidates, committee members, and delegates. A great many citizens, however, do not make full use of the primary elections. Often less than half the eligible voters actually go to the polls in primary elections. Thus they fail to take advantage of the chances they have to help select the leaders and representatives of political parties. Have you ever heard anyone complain that both candidates are bad and therefore it seems useless to vote? He is often the man who has never voted in a primary election.

The Initiative and Referendum

Just as our people as a whole can and do make the government of our republic more democratic through changes such as we have just seen, so also the people of the several states can and do make the republican government of the states more democratic. The people in some states have done so through the introduction of the **initiative** and **referendum.** These political devices give the people a more direct part in the affairs of government, though the people all too often fail to use the opportunity.

The **initiative** is a device enabling a specified percentage of voters to propose a bill by drawing up a petition. This bill will then become law if it is approved at a popular election or (in some states) if approved by the legislature. Suppose, for example, that you feel the lawmakers should enact a law requiring medical examinations for all people handling and serving food in public places, but the legislature has never acted on it. You and a group of friends could then draw up a petition. Getting enough signatures on the petition (most states require from 5 to 10 percent of the total number of eligible voters) can be a job of stirring up the community to realize how important their individual actions can be. With enough signatures, the petition will then go either before the legislature for consideration or directly before the people for a direct vote.

It might be, however, that what you want is to *prevent* passage of some law which you think undesirable. You can then use the *referendum,* that is, you can refer the law to the voters. If you get enough signatures to your petition, you can force the legislature to submit the law to the voters for

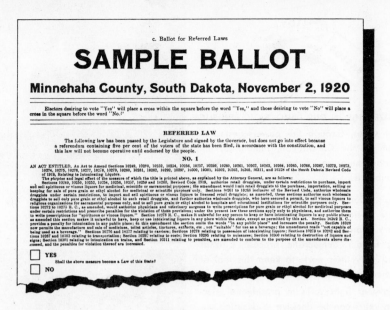

c. Ballot for Referred Laws

SAMPLE BALLOT

Minnehaha County, South Dakota, November 2, 1920

Electors desiring to vote "Yes" will place a cross within the square before the word "Yes," and those desiring to vote "No" will place a cross in the square before the word "No."

REFERRED LAW

The following law has been passed by the Legislature and signed by the Governor, but does not go into effect because a referendum containing five per cent of the voters of the state has been filed, in accordance with the constitution, and this law will not become operative until endorsed by the people.

NO. 1

AN ACT ENTITLED, An Act to Amend Sections 10249, 10250, 10252, 10254, 10256, 10257, 10259, 10260, 10261, 10262, 10263, 10264, 10265, 10266, 10267, 10272, 10273, 10274, 10275, 10276, 10277, 10278, 10279, 10280, 10281, 10282, 10292, 10293, 10300, 10301, 10302, 10303, 10305, 10311, and 10328 of the South Dakota Revised Code of 1919, Relating to Intoxicating Liquors.

The purpose and legal effect of the measure of which the title is printed above, as explained by the Attorney General, are as follows:

Sections 10249, 10250, 10252, 10254, 10256, 10257, 10259 and 10260, Revised Code 1919, authorize retail druggists, under certain restrictions to purchase, import and sell spirituous or vinous liquors for medicinal, scientific or sacramental purposes; the amendment would limit retail druggists to the purchase, importation, selling or keeping for sale of pure grain or ethyl alcohol for medicinal or scientific purposes only. Sections 10261 to 10266 inclusive of the Revised Code, authorize wholesale druggists under certain restrictions, to import and sell spirituous or vinous liquors to licensed retail druggists; as amended, three sections authorize such wholesale druggists to sell only pure grain or ethyl alcohol to such retail druggists, and further authorize wholesale druggists, who have secured a permit, to sell vinous liquors to religious organizations for sacramental purposes only, and to sell pure grain or ethyl alcohol to hospitals and educational institutions for scientific purposes only. Sections 10272 to 10273 R. C., as amended, would authorize physicians and veterinary surgeons to write prescriptions for pure grain or ethyl alcohol for medicinal purposes under certain restrictions and prescribe penalties for the violation of these provisions; under the present law these sections apply only to physicians, and authorize them to write prescriptions for "spirituous or vinous liquors." Section 10278 R. C., makes it unlawful for any person to keep or have intoxicating liquors in any public place; as amended this section makes it unlawful to have, keep or use intoxicating liquors in any place within the state, except as permitted by this act. Section 10302 R. C., provides a penalty for intoxication in any public place; in this amendment the section omits the words "in any public place" and increases the penalty. Section 10328 now permits the manufacture and sale of medicines, toilet articles, tinctures, extracts, etc., not "suitable" for use as a beverage; the amendment reads "not capable of being used as a beverage." Sections 10276 and 10277 relating to carriers; Sections 10278 relating to possession of intoxicating liquors; Sections 10279 to 10292 and Sections 10267 and 10303 relating to transportation; Section 10292 relating to costs; Section 10295 relating to nuisances; Section 10300 relating to destruction of liquors and signs; Section 10301 relating to intoxication on trains, and Section 10311 relating to penalties, are amended to conform to the purpose of the amendments above discussed, and the penalties for violation thereof are increased.

☐ YES

Shall the above measure become a Law of this State?

☐ NO

their acceptance or rejection. Sometimes a legislature itself refers a difficult question to the voters through a referendum.

For example, in New York State there was a hotly disputed issue over the building of a dam to be known as Panther Dam on the Black River. Professional conservation workers and the State Conservation Department wanted the dam built for flood control, and the power companies wanted it built to use its water power. Hunters and fishermen objected to the flooding of the area behind the dam, an area abounding in fish and game. The state legislature could not decide whether the public interest would be best served by building the dam or by not building it. Therefore, it referred the matter to the voters. When the referendum was held, a majority of the voters turned out to be sportsmen! The dam was not built.

Proposed amendments to state constitutions are also commonly referred to the voters in this manner. Unfortunately, many persons who vote in an election confine their voting to the choices of candidates for office. They neither read the referendum questions nor vote on them. In this way they deny themselves the democratic gains that have been made in their own states. When a citizen votes on a referendum question, he is taking a direct part in the lawmaking process.

The Recall

The **recall** is a method of removing officials from office. It is intended to make officeholders responsible to the voters more directly and continuously. It is another way in which "we the people" can take an active part in good government. Under this plan a certain number of voters may request, by petition, a special election to determine whether or not a certain official will be removed from office. Twelve states now provide that the recall may be

81

CITIZENSHIP IN OUR DEMOCRATIC REPUBLIC

Our states, through the powers vested in them by the Constitution, remain an important measure of how democratic our republic is.

Registration requirements may vary from state to state, but the vote in a state primary is an important means of participating in our democratic process. Citizens must play their parts to keep this tool of democracy from becoming rusty.

Heavy or light votes in presidential election years can be decisive in deciding our national policies, determining as they do who shall be our President and which party shall control Congress. It is the people who decide these things.

Two states have extended the voting privilege to 18-year-olds—Georgia and Kentucky—here shown voting.

used for removal of state officials. It is most commonly used, however, at the local level. In actual practice, few officeholders have been removed by use of the recall. Several cities have so removed mayors; city councilmen have been recalled in several other cities. On one occasion Pasadena recalled its entire city council. On the other hand, the recall election has frequently resulted in the victory of the official against whom the petition was aimed, as in the famous effort in Wisconsin to recall Senator Joseph McCarthy (1954). In either case, whether the removal does or does not take place, it probably operates to make holders of public office more keenly aware of their responsibilities to the voters. Thus the recall—like the initiative, referendum, and primary—extends the powers of the people at the state and local levels by democratic means. No one of them, however, has been used as widely as was expected by those who worked for these measures a half-century ago.

The Voting Privilege

To be a citizen in a democracy means that one shares in all of the privileges and responsibilities of that form of government. One of the most important privileges is the right to vote, since the "consent of the governed" lies at the very heart of the democratic process. If only *some* of the people are citizens, entitled to vote, a government will be something less than a democracy, even though some of its methods are democratic. Throughout its history the United States has continuously extended democracy by making it possible for more and more people to vote. First, there was a gradual elimination of property qualifications; then, freed slaves were made citizens and given the right to vote following the War Between the States; and finally, women were given the vote by constitutional amendment. This process has gone on throughout the whole history of the United States and is not entirely completed yet. For example, there is a growing movement today to permit 18-year-olds the right to vote; Georgia and Kentucky, as we mentioned on p. 36, have already extended the voting privilege to this group.

Nowadays, however, very few Americans are barred from the privilege of citizenship unless they have committed certain crimes or are unable to meet the tests of mental fitness and literacy which are usually administered objectively and without discrimination. Thus by the middle of the twentieth century, the American republic has become very nearly an American democracy as well.

One of the standing subjects for debate among Americans is the relation between democracy and economic status. It has been agreed that since the very poor have not always participated in the affairs of government, our democracy is not functioning at its best. On the other hand, this point is answered by asserting that a democratic government need go no further than

83

to provide by law the means of participation on an equal basis for everyone who can qualify for citizenship. Fortunately for the United States, this long-standing debate has become more and more a matter of theory rather than practice, since increasing numbers of Americans have begun to feel economic security as our country developed and prospered. The truth is that most citizens who do not take their proper place in the democratic process of government are indifferent, cynical, or just plain lazy. The United States today offers the widest opportunity to participate in public affairs ever offered by a great nation, and the American republic has come very close, insofar as laws and institutions make it possible, to realizing the ideal of democracy.

Remember that non-voting is actually a kind of voting. The non-voter not only excludes himself from making direct choices; he also indicates silent approval of the choices made by the voters. Non-voting weakens democratic government. But not to vote when you have the privilege is a quite different thing from not voting because you are forbidden to do so.

SUMMARY

There are important differences between a republic and a democracy. A democracy is a political system in which the people themselves vote directly on what the laws shall be and directly choose those who shall administer the laws; a republic is a system in which the people vote for representatives who, in turn, make the laws and appoint most of the administrators. The framers of our Constitution were chiefly interested in establishing a representative form of government with checks and balances to make sure that no one of the three branches could become dominant. They believed that through such precautions all forms of tyranny could be avoided. The framers favored a republican form of government; many were doubtful about democracy. This mistrust is reflected in certain governmental procedures established at the time.

Changes in governmental structure and practice have tended to make our republic more and more democratic over the years. The procedures for electing the President and Vice-President have been greatly changed; the Senate, formerly appointed by the state legislatures, is now elected directly by the people; and the growth of political parties, with their primary elections, has brought the average citizen into much closer relation with the conduct of government. At the state and local levels, the initiative, referendum, and recall are devices to provide greater popular control—more democracy. The privilege of voting has been extended, until now almost all adults who in other respects qualify for citizenship can vote. Perhaps before many years even 18-year-olds will be included (as they already are in two states).

Setting up laws and devices for popular participation does not guarantee that the people will use them, however. In our time almost every adult American can participate in the political process, but large numbers do not. Will you accept the challenge to make the most of your democratic opportunities?

KNOW WHAT YOU READ

1. What is the difference between a *democracy* and a *republic*?
2. How was the President selected in the early years of our Republic?
3. Why did the makers of the Constitution plan a *republic*?
4. What was the "Great Compromise"?
5. Explain how the Constitution provided that officeholders should hold their offices only "for a limited period or during good behavior." What is meant by "good behavior"?
6. What is the importance of the fact that the power to bring up new bills for taxing the people was given to the House of Representatives?
7. What is the purpose of our elaborate system of checks and balances?
8. Explain how the President is *checked* by officials in other branches of the government. How may he, in turn, check them?
9. How do the legislative and judicial branches of our national government check each other?
10. Why did the Constitution not contain a statement of the rights of the people? Why was such a statement (bill of rights) added to the Constitution?
11. Why may Amendment I be considered an important "cornerstone of democracy"?
12. How have the workings of the electoral college changed since the days of the "Founding Fathers"?
13. What changes have come about in the ways of *nominating* presidential and vice-presidential candidates?
14. In what ways might the Senate in its early days have been considered an *un*democratic body?
15. A people who understand that their government is an experiment in democracy will be willing to consent to changes in it. What change was brought about by Amendment XVII?
16. Summarize the extension of the privileges of citizenship since the days of the making of the Constitution.
17. ". . . The United States today offers the widest opportunity to participate in public affairs ever offered by a great nation. . . ." Why do so many people fail to take advantage of such opportunity?

WHAT DO YOU THINK?

1. Some people think that we can't expect to have government *by* the people in a country as big as ours, with problems as big as ours. What do you think?
2. Study the drawing Checks and Balances (p. 73), and discuss the "intangible" checks shown for the President on Congress. Can you think of others the President, Congress, or the Courts may have on any of the other branches?

PROBLEMS AND PROJECTS FOR YOU

1. Look up four different definitions of the word *democracy*. Write out and hand in the four, listing with each the proper references. What do they all have in common? In what ways do they differ? Which definition do you think most appropriately describes Amercan democracy?
2. Some of the delegates to the Constitutional Convention at Philadelphia were men who had read the history of Greece and of Rome. In what ways might this reading have influenced their ideas on *democracy*?
3. Write an essay on the meaning to you of the message the cartoonist is giving in the cartoon on p. 76.
4. Look up the popular vote of your state in the last presidential election. If the electoral votes of your state had been divided among the candidates in proportion to the popular vote each received, how many electoral votes would each candidate have received?
5. In Burns and Peltason, *Government of the People,* or in any other textbook which discusses the problem, look up the proposals that have been made for changing the electoral college system. Why have they failed to pass?
6. Interview ten adults in your community to find out their opinions on the electoral college. *Plan* your questions in advance.
7. President Truman appointed a Commission on the Rights of Americans. Look up the report of this commission. Report on it to the class as a study in the extension of democracy. (Report title: *To Secure These Rights*)
8. When Wendell Willkie failed to be nominated for the Presidency in 1944, one devoted follower wrote letters to editors urging that voters in November "write in" the name of Willkie on the ballot. What important fact did this person overlook?
9. One interested citizen, disappointed in both party conventions in 1956, wrote to an editor suggesting that conventions be dropped and candidates for the Presidency be selected by a meeting of members of Congress and governors of states. Write a "letter to the editor" defending the present system of conventions, or the system proposed in this paragraph, or any system you favor.

86

EXTEND YOUR VOCABULARY

extension of democracy
privileges of citizenship
republic
democracy
electors
electoral college

democratic republic
"the Great Compromise"
checks and balances
judicial interpretation or review
libel
slander

caucus
direct primary
bill of rights
initiative
referendum
recall

YOUR NOTEBOOK: THE GOVERNMENT OF ——

1. Can you find any examples of "checks and balances" in your local government? If so, write them in your notebook, showing checks clearly.
2. Does your state permit the use of initiative, referendum, recall, direct primary? If so, under what conditions? If referendum is used, list in your notebook some questions which have been on the ballot for the voters' "yes" or "no" vote.
3. Write in your notebook the names of all the people, Senators and Representatives, who represent you in Congress and in your state capitol.
4. Do political parties in your state also hold conventions? If so, what do they do?

READ MORE ABOUT IT

BURNS, JAMES M., and PELTASON, JACK W., *Government by the People*. Prentice-Hall, 1954. Chaps. 3–4.

DIXON, ROBERT G., JR., and PLISCHKE, ELMER, *American Government: Basic Documents and Materials*. Van Nostrand, 1950.
Brief discussion, illustrated with documents, of basic processes of government.

FENN, PERCY T., *The Development of the Constitution*. Appleton-Century-Crofts, 1948.
A standard text.

Formation of the Union of the American States. Government Printing Office, 1927.
A valuable source book of documents which includes among others the notes James Madison made at the Constitutional Convention.

IRISH, MARIAN D., and PROTHRO, JAMES W., *The Politics of American Democracy*. Prentice-Hall, 1959. Chaps. 3–4.

MASON, ALPHEUS T., *Free Government in the Making*. Oxford University Press, 1949.
A valuable book of source materials.

PADOVER, SAUL K., *The Living U.S. Constitution*. Praeger, 1953.
Useful study of the meaning of the Constitution, and very readable.

VAN DOREN, CARL, *The Great Rehearsal*. Viking, 1948.
Highly readable and accurate account of the founding of the nation.

CHAPTER *4*

Federalism

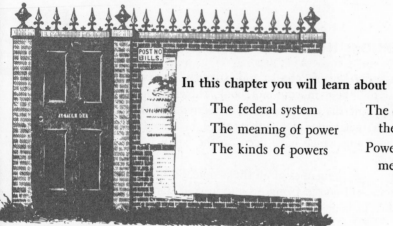

In this chapter you will learn about

The federal system

The meaning of power

The kinds of powers

The division of powers in
the federal government

Power and big govern-
ment

Imagine for a moment that a majority of the members of Congress believe that your community should be merged with another city nearby. Do you think your national government could *force* the local governments concerned into such a merger? Or suppose that your national government conducts a survey and finds the educational standards in one of our states to be somewhat below those in the other states. Do you think your national government, in the interest of the national welfare, could set up and administer a testing program in this state as a means of forcing the state to raise its educational standards?

Most national governments in our world today (even democratic governments) would have full authority to act in these situations. In England, for example, every bit of power the government has is concentrated in the hands of Parliament. Parliament could, at least in theory, wipe out all local governments overnight should it desire to do so. It may surprise some of you, therefore, to learn that the national government of the United States does *not* have the authority to act in either of the situations just described, even though such action might appear vital to the national welfare. In this respect, our national government is different from most national governments in the world today.

88

WHAT IS FEDERALISM?

The government of the United States, as distinct from the governments of the various states, is properly spoken of as the **federal** government. It is, of course, also a national government since its powers cover the entire nation. But there are important reasons why we retain the old word **federal** when we are precise.

A Confederation of States

As we saw in Chapter 3, the first government of the United States, under the Articles of Confederation, was really a league of sovereign states. Under this form the states retained their full powers as independent bodies. They sent representatives to a Continental Congress, but that body did not possess the necessary power to be a real national government. Such an organization is called a **confederation.** This system proved to be ineffective in so many ways that many of the leading men of that day undertook to revise it or to construct a new system which would make the whole country strong and win respect from the rest of the world. The Constitution of the United States was the result of their efforts. Under it the states *retained some* of their powers (such as education), but *surrendered others* (such as control of interstate commerce) to the new national government created by the Constitution. This meant that in the United States (1) there would still be state governments which would continue as before to deal with many matters pertaining only to their own people; (2) there would also be a new national government carrying out the powers surrendered to it by the states.

A Federal Government

Under the Constitution, the new national government would be **federal** because it would act on behalf of the associated states, with their consent and participation. It would be a **government** rather than a league or confederation, because it would have direct powers in many matters over both the states and the people. As we said earlier, a genuine government is one with power to make laws binding on the people and power to tax the people for the raising of money for public use. If Jonathan Smith was needed to fight the Indians in the 1780's, Congress could not force him to leave his comfortable home in New Jersey to fight savages in the far-away Northwest Territory. Likewise, Congress could not collect taxes from Jonathan. Congress could ask New Jersey to send soldiers or could ask New Jersey for money— and might or might not get either men or money. These powers were not granted to the Congress under the Articles; but both are given to the national legislature under the Constitution. Powers to act directly on the John Smiths today make ours a real government.

Federalism or a **federal government** should be contrasted, for clarity, with a **consolidated** or **unitary** government. By consolidated we mean that the sovereign states have come together to establish a government to which they surrendered all of their powers. Under such a plan of organization, there would be one central government at the top. There might or might not be local governments. Obviously this is not the kind of government we have.

The United States is governed by a national government which is **federal.** We may use this term because this government is carrying out powers given up or shared by the states. Other powers which affect us are carried out by the states, which are sovereign in these respects. John Smith, unlike his ever-so-great-grandfather Jonathan, now pays an income tax to the national government's collection agency, the Bureau of Internal Revenue. He may also be drafted for service in the armed forces of the national government. In some states he may also pay an income tax to his state government. Furthermore, he may discover, if he has joined the National Guard, that he may be called out for duty by the governor of his state. If he goes to work in a factory which makes packing cases, he may discover that in his industry hours and wages are subject to laws of the national government. Had he gone to work in a restaurant, he would have discovered that the state, through his local community, had a great deal to say about that particular business. Thus he would become acquainted with the distribution of powers between federal and state governments under the federal system.

Today most of us, like John Smith, are well aware of the influence of the powers of governments on our daily lives. Most of us, however, have given little thought to the nature and meaning of **power.**

THE MEANING OF POWER

The story used to be told by President Franklin Roosevelt of the experience he had shortly after his inauguration on March 4, 1933. The country was suffering from the worst phases of the great depression of the 1930's; many millions of people were out of work; many were starving; there was a bank panic. In an effort to bring about a drastic change, the people by a great majority elected Mr. Roosevelt. In his Inaugural Address he fired the imagination of the whole country with his cry, "This nation asks for action, and action now!" When the ceremonies were over, the President went immediately to his office at the White House, prepared to give the country the action it demanded. He rang for his secretary. There was no answer. She had gone to a party to celebrate. He rang for his assistants, one by one. All were out. He called the cabinet officers. None was available. And so it went, until he gave up and retired to his room to rest. The President of the United

States was completely frustrated. "There I was," he said, "the President of the United States, with a mandate for immediate and drastic action. They said I was the most powerful man in the world. But the fact was that I couldn't get anything done at all."

The Ability to Get Things Done

There is more than one valuable moral in that remarkable, true story. The meaning of the word **power** is contained in it. For power, as Mr. Roosevelt well knew, means nothing more nor less than the ability to get things done. Constitutions and laws, as he discovered, have no power at all in themselves. They are meaningful only when people act with reference to them. Titles, too, are meaningless unless *people* respond to them. Because the United States is a free nation, power for the most part depends upon coöperation, on *people* working together.

Since power, in itself, simply means the ability to get things done, we may define various kinds of power in terms of the kinds of things we wish to get done. Thus *governmental power means the ability to get the public business done*. The strength of a government, therefore, will depend upon the extent of its power and its ability to manage the public business.

Necessity for Organization

Another moral we may draw from President Roosevelt's· experience is that there can be no significant governmental power unless there is **organization**. When Mr. Roosevelt gave up the attempt to get anything done on that afternoon of his inauguration, he had actually tried to talk with only a few people. They were important, not in themselves, but because of their organizational positions. The Secretary of the Treasury, for example, is the responsible head of a great agency of the federal government having to do with the nation's finances. The Secretary of Defense, similarly, heads the organization of our military establishment. And so it goes throughout the whole roster of top-level officials.

None of these would be any more able to get things done than was Mr. Roosevelt, unless the organization which he headed was in working order. If he had been able to reach Secretary Woodin of the Treasury, President Roosevelt could have done no more than give an order under his limited constitutional powers. The Secretary himself could have done no more than alert other individuals within his organization to get the order into motion. If *his* secretary and assistants had also been unavailable, nothing could have been accomplished. Thus we may say that governmental power, the ability of the people to get things done for their common interest, is brought into being by appropriate organizations. The study of government in our free society is the study of the organizations, at the local, state, and national levels, which the people have established or authorized to bring their power into being.

Kinds of Power

We shall study these organizations in later chapters. First, however, we need to learn more about power. We must now try to see just what is meant by saying that some powers were **delegated** to the federal government, while others were **reserved.** We must examine, too, what is meant by the statement that some powers are **implied** as a result of those which are specified. In treating these three sorts of governmental power, we shall see that there is still another which we call **concurrent.** Each of these needs separate and careful attention.

Powers Delegated by the People

A constitution is simply a kind of contract or agreement entered into voluntarily by all parties concerned. A club in your school, for example, probably has a constitution drawn up by the persons who organized it. They had a right to enter into an agreement to form a club. They gave (delegated) certain powers to the club's officers. Those powers are probably stated, or **enumerated,** in the constitution of the organization.

In the making of the Constitution of the United States, there was also a question of powers for the new government. Because the states at that time were jealous of their independence, their delegates to the Constitutional Convention did not speak of "surrendering" powers to the new government, but rather of **delegating** powers. This means that they voluntarily authorized the new organization to do things for them. Thus we call the powers turned over by the states to the federal government **delegated** powers.

The effect of delegating powers to a new government was to create a **new sovereignty,** the federal government. **Sovereignty** means supreme political authority. Thus in the United States, under the Constitution, sovereignty was divided between the state governments and the federal government created by the states. In some things the states remained sovereign; in others, they became subordinate to the new sovereignty. What do we mean when we say that the "states" created the new government, that the states were sovereign?

Although these questions have been matters of controversy all through American history, there are some things we can say with assurance. For one thing, the Constitution was actually adopted by conventions in each of the states. The delegates to these conventions were elected by the people to represent them and vote "yes" or "no" on the question of whether to adopt the Constitution. This means that the Constitution was not an agreement among the state *governments,* but an agreement among the people of the states acting through special conventions set up to vote on the Constitution.

On the other hand, the state governments were established to handle the business proper to their states. To these state governments the people have delegated some of their powers. They established a national government to handle the business proper to the whole country. To this government, they have delegated others of their powers. Let us now see what their delegated powers are (see chart, p. 98).

Powers Delegated to the Federal Government

In general, the powers delegated by the people to the federal government (that is, the **enumerated** powers) are the powers to make and enforce laws, judge disputes which arise under the laws, provide for the defense of the country, and conduct relations with other countries. Though the power to make laws is the most important of these, the people have not delegated all of their lawmaking power to the national government. Article I, Section 8 of the Constitution contains a list of matters over which Congress has the authority to make laws sometimes known as **enumerated**; Section 9 contains a list of things which Congress may *not* do. (See pp. 53–55.)

Under the Constitution, the people delegated to the President powers not only to enforce the laws but also to do certain things on his own authority (II, 2, pp. 57–58). Finally, the people have delegated to the Supreme Court and to lower federal courts their power of judging, as specified in the Constitution (see III, 2, pp. 58–59).

Article V of the Constitution provides for the amending of the document as might from time to time be thought necessary. Through this article the people thus retained their right to change the manner in which their delegated powers are exercised, to add to these delegated powers, or to subtract from them.

Implied Powers

The powers which the Constitution specifically grants a branch of government are known as **express powers**. The right of Congress to coin money, for example, is an express power. From our earliest history, there has been an almost continuous dispute over whether an express power in the Constitution **implied** other powers. The basis for such implied powers was held to be in the so-called "elastic clause" of the Constitution, (I, 8, 18), where it is stated that "Congress shall have power to make all laws which shall be necessary and proper to carry into execution the foregoing powers and all other powers vested by this Constitution in the Government of the United States, or in any department or officer thereof."

The problem first arose in Washington's administration when Alexander Hamilton, the Secretary of the Treasury, sought to establish a national bank to aid him in restoring the credit of the United States. Hamilton maintained that the power to do this was implied in the Constitution because it gave

THE GENERAL WELFARE

The genius of the men who worked through that long, hot summer drafting the Constitution was that the document they produced has proved flexible enough to cover situations they never dreamed of. Congress, with its power to "lay and collect taxes, . . . to pay the debts and provide for the common defense and general welfare of the United States" has "stretched" the meaning of our "general welfare" to embrace a bewildering variety of government activity.

Building dams for flood prevention, irrigation, and power has been undertaken by the federal government under this clause.

The rich patchwork fertility of this farmland in the Columbia Valley resulted from federal conservation projects to irrigate formerly unproductive sagebrush prairie.

Relaxing in a national park, Americans are enjoying fruits of the government's power to promote the "general Welfare" under another clause of the Constitution—Article IV, Section 3, Clause 2.

Federal insurance of our banks seems a far cry from the work of the Founding Fathers; yet it also falls under that part of the Constitution called the "general welfare clause."

Fish and Wildlife conservation is a modern development of the interpretation of Article I, Section 8. Testing samples of water enables the government to improve fisheries for the "general welfare," thus increasing our natural resources.

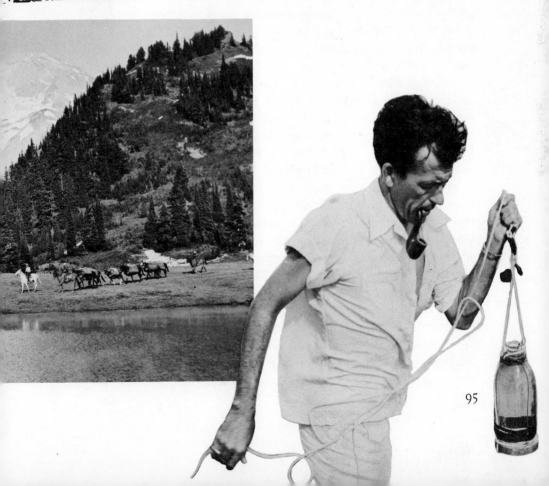

95

Congress authority over certain matters of finance, such as the power to borrow money on the credit of the United States. Thomas Jefferson, on the other hand, argued that Congress had no such power since it was not specifically set forth in the Constitution. The great political struggle which followed was won by Hamilton and his followers. The establishment of a national bank (Bank of the United States) in 1791 on the basis of power implied in the Constitution began a long history of increases in the powers of Congress by this principle that certain **express powers implied others.**

COMMERCE CLAUSE   Through the years the principle that certain delegated powers has been upheld by the Supreme Court and now is firmly established.[1] The so-called "commerce clause" provides us with an interesting example. Article I, Section 8, says that Congress shall have the power "to regulate commerce with foreign nations and among the several states." Obviously a Constitution adopted in 1789 could not have covered such matters as radio and television, yet today both are regulated by Congress through the Communications Act and the Federal Communications Commission (see p. 205). The power to deal with them is implied in the commerce clause because the air waves cross state lines and carry commodities (words, music, and pictures) for sale among the various states.

Again, the Constitution says nothing about the federal government's having power to inspect meat or analyze drugs in a laboratory to determine if the meat or drugs are suitable for sale to the public. Since meat and drugs are transported across state lines for sale, however, the power to control their standards of quality and purity is implied in the commerce clause.

By **implication** (sustained by the Supreme Court), the federal government has power to regulate not only interstate commerce but also the conditions under which products for interstate commerce are produced. Nowhere in the Constitution, for example, is anything said about the federal government's controlling or regulating the conditions of labor in any way. Most wage workers, however, are employed in industries which sell their products in more than one state. Because the products are transported across state lines and hence become interstate commerce, their production and distribution becomes subject to federal regulation. The Fair Labor Standards Act of 1938 (several times amended in later years) established 44 (later changed to 40) hours as the basic work week and set a minimum wage of 25 cents an hour (raised to $1.00 in later years). There are many hundreds of laws which depend, like the Fair Labor Standards Act, upon powers said to be implied by the commerce clause. There are also special commissions, such as the Interstate Commerce Commission, set up under this clause (see p. 199).

GENERAL WELFARE CLAUSE   Some of the most familiar legislation of our time comes from powers implied in the "general welfare clause." Article

[1] The decision in the case of *McCulloch vs. Maryland* (1819) established this principle.

I, Section 8, says that Congress shall have power "to lay and collect taxes, duties, imposts and excises, to pay the debts and provide for the common defense and general welfare of the United States." The interpretation of this clause has been debated almost from the beginning of our republic. Some have maintained that the clause was intended only to give Congress the power to lay and collect various forms of taxes. The purpose of the taxes would be to pay debts and to provide for our defense and welfare. Others, however, hold that this clause actually gives Congress *three different powers:* (1) to collect taxes; (2) to defend the country; (3) to provide for the general welfare. In other words, the latter interpretation means that the authority of Congress to provide for our defense and welfare is not limited by or dependent solely on its power to lay and collect taxes.

Over the years, the second interpretation has come to predominate. Under this implied power, Congress has enacted legislation to deal with matters as various as soil conservation, the building of national parks, providing unemployment compensation, insuring bank deposits, and building dams and power plants. As in the case of the commerce clause, the power to provide for the general welfare has been understood to imply powers covering countless activities not specifically mentioned in the Constitution at the time it was drafted, because the conditions requiring them did not then exist.

STRICT CONSTRUCTIONISTS AND LOOSE CONSTRUCTIONISTS At the outset of the United States in the 1790's, many leaders, like Jefferson and Madison, greatly feared that the principles of governing by implied powers would lead to tyranny. They took the position that the Constitution was to be interpreted, or construed, as literally as possible, in order to guard against excesses. They became known as "strict constructionists," a name since applied to a long line of American statesmen who have been conservative in their attitude toward the growth of power in the federal government. Those who favored the use of implied powers were known as "loose constructionists."

In an important sense, American political history has been the history of the shifting back and forth of control between holders of these two points of view. In the long-range view, we have favored the loose construction of the Constitution. In the twentieth century, the national power has grown far beyond anything dreamed by the Founding Fathers. Government, both federal and state, has become more and more centralized. This was caused not so much by a change in the principles of constitutional government as by the conditions faced by the country as it grew ever larger and more complex.

The fears of the strict constructionists have not been realized. Although the authority of the federal government to deal with more and more matters has continually expanded, at the same time the basic liberties of the people have been safeguarded. The Supreme Court, though it often seems to follow public opinion, has usually been jealous of individual liberty. Through the

Powers of Government

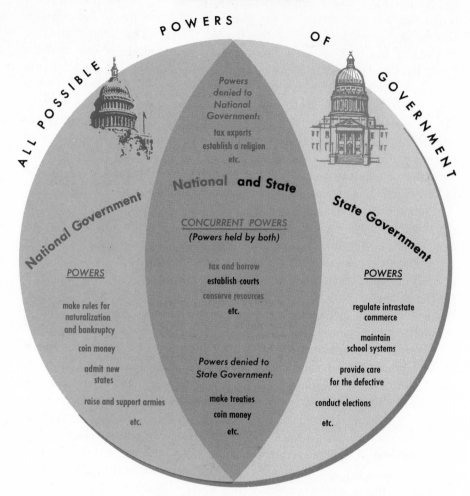

POWERS OF GOVERNMENT

ALL POSSIBLE

National Government

State Government

Powers denied to National Government:

tax exports
establish a religion
etc.

National **and State**

CONCURRENT POWERS
(Powers held by both)

tax and borrow
establish courts
conserve resources

etc.

Powers denied to State Government:

make treaties
coin money
etc.

POWERS

make rules for
naturalization
and bankruptcy

coin money

admit new
states

raise and support armies

etc.

POWERS

regulate intrastate
commerce

maintain
school systems

provide care
for the defective

conduct elections

etc.

The Constitution not only "enumerates" particular powers of the federal government, and implies others; it also expressly denies it certain powers (I,9). The Constitution also gives the states specific powers (I,10). The concurrent powers—held by both federal and state governments—are also "implied," since they are not expressly denied to either government.

years, it has declared unconstitutional certain apparently desirable measures which were, in the opinion of the Court, contrary to the spirit of the Constitution.

The principle of implied powers has become more necessary as the United States has grown and developed. It has been extended everywhere that national power is actually needed. Thus far it has not been abused, and the liberties of the people have not been curtailed.

Powers Reserved to the States and the People

The Constitution delegates certain powers **exclusively** to the national government. For example, the power to coin money is granted to Congress in Article I, Section 8, and forbidden the states in the same article, Section 10. The national government can and does exercise certain other powers which, though not expressly stated in the Constitution, are **implied** from the enumerated powers. The Constitution provides, however, that **all other political powers are reserved to the states or to the people.** (See Amendment X, p. 63.)

For example, the Constitution does not specify qualifications for voting; it says nothing about the qualifications and duties of our state and local officers; it does not attempt to regulate public institutions such as hospitals or colleges, nor does it determine automobile speed limits on our highways. These powers and many more are reserved to the states. Ultimately, of course, they are reserved to the *people*. We have already seen that in a democracy the supreme political authority (sovereignty) does not reside in any particular branch of government, but in the *people themselves*. In Chapter 3 we saw how the people of the various states can and do express their authority through their privilege of voting and also through such special political devices as the initiative, referendum, and recall.

Now we can better understand the two questions raised at the beginning of this chapter. Our national government could not abolish any unit of local government in your state, nor could it prescribe textbooks for the schools of your state. Under our federal system of government, these are powers reserved to the states. The reserved powers thus serve as important constitutional protections to our liberties and freedoms.

When a nation is founded, as is the United States, on the principle that its people are sovereign, safeguards will always be established to assure individual freedom and prevent tyranny. By limiting the powers given our national government, by reserving all other powers to the states and to the people, and by forbidding certain powers to both governments (see chart, p. 98), we have provided such safeguards. In Chapter 16 we shall learn more about the constitutional guarantees which protect our civil rights to speak, worship, read, publish, and assemble as we choose. In addition, however, as a sovereign people we have the right to work or not to work, to save money, to build a house, to cultivate a garden, to call a doctor, to go on a picnic, to choose a vacation. Many of us seldom give a thought to the fact that today there are ways of life and systems of government which would not permit us freely to exercise such rights. The important right to make choices in the common things of life is often taken for granted.

Concurrent Powers

Some powers delegated to the national government are also held by state and local governments. At many points these powers may overlap and the lines of division are often blurred. Food products may be inspected three times, for example: by federal officials, by state officials, and by city officials. Roads are built by the federal government, by the states, by counties, by townships, and, of course, by cities. Law enforcement often involves state police, city police, county police, and federal officials all working together in the same community. Their specific duties may, of course, be different, but they may nevertheless be working on the same case. Powers shared by two or more branches of government, like those of building roads or inspecting food, are called **concurrent powers** (see chart, p. 98).

Here is an example of concurrent power in action. The residents of a certain city may decide, through their local government, that a particular section of the city has become a slum and should be cleaned up. In order to tear down the old buildings and erect new ones, the following things may happen. The City Planning or Housing Commissioner may draw plans and specifications according to the city's building code and sanitation regulations. These plans, once they have been approved by the City Council, may then be submitted to the Director of Housing in the state government to secure his approval under state law. The state officials will determine whether the plan is in accord with the requirements for a grant of money from the state treasury to help pay the cost of the work. At the same time, the City Housing Commissioner may take his plans to the Federal Housing and Home Finance Agency to get federal approval and a federal loan. When the project is approved, there may be engineers and inspectors representing all three levels of government working together to bring it to completion. All three governments have powers in the field of housing—concurrent powers—which may need to be brought together in order to get this bit of public business done. For some other kinds of concurrent powers, see chart, p. 98.

Americans often complain of the "red tape" involved in governmental activity. Undoubtedly there would be a good deal of paper work, many conferences, and some delays in completing such a project as the cleaning up of the slum area in our example. Actually concurrent powers provide us with important safeguards against graft and corruption and against hasty and ill-considered planning and building. Each government tends to act as a check upon the others, while all are serving the interests of the people.

The Supremacy of Federal Law

In our federal system of government, where the powers of government are distributed between the national government and the states, conflicts in

100

Allocations of Powers of Government

Without the necessary powers, government can neither govern nor serve

These and other powers of government may belong to . . . . .

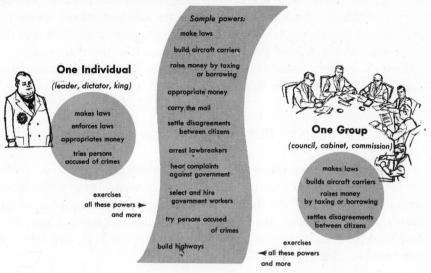

Sample powers:

make laws

build aircraft carriers

raise money by taxing
or borrowing

appropriate money

carry the mail

settle disagreements
between citizens

arrest lawbreakers

hear complaints
against government

select and hire
government workers

try persons accused
of crimes

build highways

One Individual

(leader, dictator, king)

makes laws
enforces laws
appropriates money
tries persons
accused of crimes

exercises
all these powers ➤
and more

One Group

(council, cabinet, commission)

makes laws
builds aircraft carriers
raises money
by taxing or borrowing
settles disagreements
between citizens

exercises
◄ all these powers
and more

or they may be divided among three separate groups . . . . .

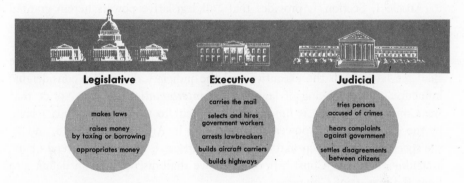

Legislative

makes laws
raises money
by taxing or borrowing
appropriates money

Executive

carries the mail
selects and hires
government workers
arrests lawbreakers
builds aircraft carriers
builds highways

Judicial

tries persons
accused of crimes
hears complaints
against government
settles disagreements
between citizens

Without the necessary powers, government can neither govern nor serve (see p. 91). Therefore in a large modern country, there must be great and extensive governmental powers. The sample powers listed above are only a few of the many necessary today.

Not all men are agreed on the question of who should have these powers. This chart suggests some of the ways in which men and nations have tried to answer the question. See pp. 102–105 for discussion of division of powers among the legislative, executive, and judicial branches of government in the United States.

authority are, at times, bound to occur. When a conflict occurs between a national law and a state or local law, the federal government must be and is supreme. The Constitution itself makes this clear in Article VI, Clause 2 (see p. 61).

For example, suppose a person from another city or state, while visiting in your town, is accused of committing a crime there. He could not be denied a trial simply because he is not a legal resident of your city or state. Such a denial would violate certain rights guaranteed by Amendment XIV. Again, no state today could decide to choose its congressional representatives through a state convention. Such an act would violate a federal statute which was enacted by Congress under its constitutional authority. While it is true that the powers of the federal government are limited by the Constitution, its authority is supreme within these limits, and no state or local laws can be enacted which conflict with federal law.

DIVISION OF POWERS IN THE FEDERAL GOVERNMENT

The powers of government in the United States are distributed between the federal government and the states. Those powers given to the federal government are divided by the Constitution among three branches of government—the legislative, the executive, and the judiciary. These three branches have been granted separate powers by Articles I, II, and III of the Constitution. (See pp. 50–59.)

Limitations of Powers

Article I, Section 1, provides that "all legislative powers herein granted shall be vested in a Congress of the United States, which shall consist of a Senate and a House of Representatives" (see p. 50). This means that the executive and the judiciary are not entitled to *make laws*, although, as we shall see later, both the executive and the judiciary do have a considerable influence on the making of law and the *interpretation* of law. Notice that the Congress, however, is *limited* in the extent to which it may enact laws, by the enumeration of powers which follows in Article I, Section 8, and by the specifically forbidden matters listed in Article I, Section 9. Several of the amendments to the Constitution, which we shall discuss later in detail, also limit the powers of Congress.

Article II vests "the executive power" in the President. The little word *the* is highly important, because it means that no other branch shares in the power of executing the laws and policies of the government. In parliamentary governments, like those of England and Canada, the same body both makes and executes the laws (see chart, p. 101). The United States Constitution separates these functions in order to make sure the power is not too highly concentrated in one body. If the powers of the President seem very great, it is because of the greatness of the country. Just what the executive power of the President means in practice we shall study in Chapter 7.

The third branch of government is established under Article III, which provides that "the judicial power of the United States shall be vested in one

Supreme Court and in such inferior Courts as the Congress may from time to time ordain and establish." The word *the* again means that there is no sharing of judicial power. The Courts, under the Constitution, were established as an independent branch of the government with definite jurisdiction over certain kinds of cases (III, 2).

The details of the work of the Courts will be examined in Chapter 9. However, one important aspect of their power, **judicial review,** directly concerns the distribution of powers which we have been discussing.

Judicial Review

Since the Constitution of the United States divides the powers of government among the three branches, it was inevitable that disputes would arise about which branch should have the last word on what the Constitution means. In our time, **judicial review,** the practice of having the courts decide whether a law is constitutional, is accepted by nearly everyone. In fact, many citizens know very little about the Supreme Court except that it does decide constitutional questions. (Turn to Article III, Section 2, pp. 58–59, for the constitutional provision covering the jurisdiction of federal courts.) Often in our history the Court has been called upon to determine whether a law is or is not "constitutional," and often our people and our leaders have awaited with some anxiety the decision of the Court.

We have not always had judicial review. The Constitution itself does not mention judicial review. When Washington, as first President, was in doubt whether proposed laws were in accord with the Constitution, he asked for the written opinions of his advisers, like Jefferson, the Secretary of State, and Hamilton, the Secretary of the Treasury.

MARBURY VS. MADISON In the case of *Marbury vs. Madison*, the Supreme Court established its power to decide whether a law passed by Congress is constitutional or unconstitutional. The importance of the Court's opinion, delivered by Chief Justice Marshall, is so great that most people have forgotten what the case itself was about. Actually it was a fairly simple matter. President John Adams appointed a man named Marbury to be a justice of the peace for Washington, D.C. His commission (certificate of appointment by the President), however, had not been delivered to him when Adams went out of office. James Madison, the new Secretary of State, refused to deliver the commission to Marbury because the new administration wished to make its own appointments. Marbury petitioned the Supreme Court to force Secretary Madison to give him his commission.

That was all there was to it. But Chief Justice Marshall saw in the case an opportunity to settle the tremendously significant question of the Court's power to determine whether or not laws made by Congress are in accord with the Constitution, and, if not, to declare them void.

103

"STILL THE CORNERSTONE"

Crawford in
The Newark News

This is the way Justice Marshall and his colleagues on the Supreme Court worked it out. They found that under both the law and the Constitution, Marbury was entitled to his commission. But did the Supreme Court have jurisdiction in such a case? They found that under the Judiciary Act passed by Congress in 1789 the Court might take action. A section of that law authorized the Supreme Court to issue *writs of mandamus* (court orders directing an official to perform an act). In this case, it would mean that such a writ, if issued by the Court, could direct Secretary of State Madison to deliver the commission to Marbury. The Constitution, however, gave no such power to the Supreme Court. The Court therefore noted that the law (Judiciary Act) and the Constitution were not in agreement. Chief Justice Marshall argued that the Constitution is the "supreme law of the land" and that all other laws must be subordinate to it. The Court then found that since the section of the act in question conflicted with the Constitution, it was not only unconstitutional but *void*. Marbury, we might add, never did get his commission.

This decision established the right of the federal courts, with final power resting in the Supreme Court, to review laws involved in cases brought before them. The Court might then decide whether such laws are constitutional

104

and declare them void if found to be unconstitutional. Actually, this very great power of the judicial branch does not often need to be used, since the Congress is careful to draw its laws in conformity with the Constitution and with earlier decisions of the Court. Only some eighty federal laws out of the many thousands passed have ever been declared unconstitutional.

The Courts cannot interfere in the making or administration of the laws. The power of judicial review can be exercised by the Courts only when cases are brought before them. It remains, however, a very great power indeed. Some people think that this power upsets the balance among the three supposedly equal branches, and the phrase **judicial supremacy** is sometimes used in characterizing the government of the United States. We must not forget, however, that the Court has no army or navy and no police force. The only force it has to make its decisions stick is the obedience by all of us to the rule of law, our voluntary acceptance of judicial action. If a Court became dictatorial through abuse of the power of judicial review, it would soon enough be checked by the powers of the other branches.

"Big Government" and the Distribution of Power

When the framers of the Constitution were struggling with the problem of distributing the powers of the people wisely between the states and the federal government, and among the branches of the federal government, they were dealing with a very small and very weak country. By no stretch of the imagination could they have foreseen a nation of over 180 million people, covering all the vast reaches between the Atlantic and the Pacific, and owning and consuming half the world's wealth. It would have been no great wonder and no fault of theirs if the government they planned and put into being had long since disappeared into history. What is remarkable is that it has in fact adjusted itself and survived through changes far more profound than those of the American Revolution itself. What was a tiny government, even by the standards of the eighteenth century, has become the largest free government in the world, with the original basic principles maintained and secured. The changes have come in the ways we apply the principles.

FINANCING THE GOVERNMENT The changes in size of the government can be illustrated by a look at the difference between the financing of the federal government in early days and at the present time. In 1805, federal tax collectors were simply unknown to the ordinary citizen. At the same time, Albert Gallatin, Secretary of the Treasury, was dealing with an annual budget of about fifteen million dollars, raised by import duties and the sale of public lands, and talking optimistically of paying off the entire national debt in a matter of five or six years. He offered to Congress in 1808 a plan to connect all sections of the country by roads and waterways, and showed that the total cost would be about twenty million dollars.

A hundred and fifty-odd years later, almost every adult American sees a "tax-gatherer of the United States" at least once a year and sometimes even more often. The Treasury employs tens of thousands of people to collect taxes and administer the public money. The budget of the United States government is well above seventy billion dollars, and the Secretary of the Treasury has to struggle with a national debt approaching 300 billion dollars. It costs more money to build two or three bombers for the Air Force than it cost to run the entire government for a year in Jefferson's time!

INCREASED DEMANDS ON GOVERNMENT Government has naturally changed with the expansion of the nation. At all levels, it now does an infinite number of things which were either unknown or thought not to be the business of government in the early years. The federal government in our time builds dams and power plants, provides financial security for old people, supports public education, gives direct benefits to farmers and businessmen, lends money to citizens for various purposes, and regulates competition in industry. It assumes a large share of responsibility for the economic prosperity of all our people, through such measures as those which provide old-age security and give assistance to the unemployed.

State governments, as far as their finances allow, carry on similar activities and undertake similar responsibilities within the areas they govern. Even local governments are involved in a host of activities of which early Americans never dreamed. "Big government," therefore, refers not only to the national government in Washington, with its numberless operations spread all over the country and the world, and with its two million or more employees; "big government" applies also to the governments of states, cities, and counties.

ORGANIZATION OF GOVERNMENT The contrast between Jefferson's time and the present also shows that we have learned a great deal about *organization*. In the period just after the Revolution, most Americans were skeptical of organizations, especially of governmental organizations. Government to them suggested interference with private life and the suppression of liberty. Years of experience under freedom gradually overcame much of this distrust. We have never, as a people, ceased to be on guard against encroachments by government upon our privacy and our liberty. We have learned that government can be the servant of the people without being its master.

Actually we have swung back and forth between great reliance upon government and fear of it. In the long run, however, our reliance has increased much more than our fear. This is because we have discovered much about the inner workings of organizations and how to keep them under control for purposes we approve. We have proved the truth of Madison's comment in the 10th *Federalist* paper, that large organizations involving large numbers of people and covering large territories are sometimes less dangerous to personal freedom than small, closely knit ones. In our times, for example, it has been the small, conspiratorial Communist and Fascist parties which have overthrown the liberties of the people in some countries, while the great political parties of the United States and Great Britain have served as guardians of liberty.

The dangers of big government and the centralization of power are avoided by public awareness and participation. It is, of course, possible for even a free government to extend its authority so far that individual liberty is threatened. But the American system provides a way to correct such tendencies. The people can remove the officers of government and elect new ones. Public officials who depend upon the good will and the votes of the people are not likely, in any case, to go much beyond the limits of what the people wish and expect of them. The penalty is defeat, and defeat for a man who makes his living in the public service is the one thing above all else to be avoided.

SUMMARY

Government in the United States is based on the principle of **divided sovereignty.** This system of government is called **federalism,** and our national government is called a **federal** government.

When the Constitution was ratified in 1788, it was *not* done by the state legislatures, but by conventions of delegates chosen by the *people* of the various states. Thus, our Founding Fathers recognized that political sovereignty rests ultimately in the *people* themselves.

The Constitution delegates certain specific powers to the national government, and lists certain things it cannot do. It also prohibits the states from doing certain other things. All other powers of government are reserved to the states or to the people. Many powers are exercised concurrently by federal, state, and local governments.

The powers of the federal government are distributed by the Constitution among the three divisions of our national government—the legislative, the executive, and the judiciary. All legislative powers are vested in Congress. The executive power—power to execute laws and policies of our government —is delegated exclusively to the President. All the judicial powers are vested in the Supreme Court and the other federal courts. The Supreme Court has in addition the important power of **judicial review.**

Through the years, the Supreme Court has tended to hold that additional powers are **implied** in the enumerated powers. The Constitution itself has

107

been amended 22 times to accommodate the growing needs of a rapidly developing nation. Finally, a free governmental system such as ours places the value of the individual above the value of the state, in contrast to totalitarianism, so that even "big government" will not cost us our liberties so long as we are vigilant in keeping the state the servant of the people.

KNOW WHAT YOU READ

1. Why do we speak of the government of the United States as a *federal* government?
2. In what ways is a true *government* different from a league or confederation?
3. How does a federation differ from a consolidated government?
4. Read Article I, Section 8 of the Constitution. List the powers given to Congress. Explain the importance of the word *herein* as used in I, 1.
5. Read the first sentence of Article II, Section 2. Explain the meaning of *executive power;* of *the* executive power.
6. In what ways is Congress limited in its power to make laws?
7. Why does the Constitution in Article III, Section 1, say *the* judicial power?
8. What is the meaning of *judicial review?*
9. Summarize the case of *Marbury vs. Madison.*
10. What is the meaning of this chapter's story about President Roosevelt's inauguration day?
11. Define: *delegated* power.
12. Why do we say the Constitution was an agreement among the *people* of the states?
13. Define *sovereignty.*
14. Explain the *meaning* of any two of the "things Congress may not do."
15. What is meant by *implied* powers? Give two examples.
17. Explain two meanings of the "welfare clause."
16. In what ways has the meaning of the "commerce clause" been enlarged to adjust to our country in the twentieth century?
18. Explain the difference between "strict construction" and "loose construction."
19. In what ways may the powers of state governments be limited?
20. What are *reserved* powers? Give an example.
21. Explain how reserved powers in our country differ from those of the person living in a totalitarian state.
22. What are *concurrent* powers?
23. What is *big government?* Do you live under one or several *big* governments? Explain.
24. What are the dangers of big government? How can they be avoided?

108

WHAT DO YOU THINK?

1. Political orators love to speak of "the sovereign people." Are we sovereign? Explain.
2. Would you agree that implied powers make it possible for Congress to do anything a majority wishes to do? Before answering, study the picture story, pp. 94–95.
3. Jefferson and others feared that use of implied powers could lead to tyranny. Implied powers have led to big, centralized government. Can the people really control the government?
4. Study the cartoon, p. 104. Why in the American system does the Constitution depend on individual freedom rather than individual freedom on the Constitution?
5. The drawing on p. 98 shows some of the possible powers of state and federal government: some exclusive to one or the other, some concurrent, and some denied. Discuss others not listed, bringing illustrations, if possible, from your newspaper or other reading.
6. Some people fear "big" government. Do you believe that bigness in government is a threat to democracy? Why?

PROBLEMS AND PROJECTS FOR YOU

1. Look up the powers of the Congress under the Articles of Confederation. Report to the class, pointing out important powers the Congress did have and important powers it did not have.
2. Examine the Constitution of your student-body organization. Does it provide for a separation of powers? A distribution of powers? Explain.
3. An American President once said, "John Marshall has made his decision. Now let him enforce it." Review the facts in this case and report to the class. Do you think President Jackson did the right thing?
4. Report to the class on the subject of powers delegated to your own state government. For this you will need a copy of your state's constitution.
5. Draw an original cartoon on the subject of big government.
6. Make a bulletin-board display of clippings illustrating the powers of Congress. On each article, picture, or news story, write (in ink or colored pencil) the appropriate power granted in Article I, Section 8.
7. In an American history book, read about the case of *McCulloch vs. Maryland* and report on it to the class. Explain its significance.
8. Write a report giving examples and case histories from modern history of the three different ways government may be exercised, as illustrated in the drawing on p. 101. Some examples may be from European history; others from local governments.

EXTEND YOUR VOCABULARY

federal government
confederation
federalism
consolidated (unitary)
  government
power
republic
delegated powers
reserved powers
express powers
implied powers

concurrent powers
enumerated powers
sovereignty
strict constructionist
loose constructionist
judicial review
Marbury vs. Madison
writ of *mandamus*
judicial supremacy
red tape

YOUR NOTEBOOK: THE GOVERNMENT OF ——

1. Who are the lawmakers in your community?
2. What local officials are responsible for carrying out the laws?
3. Does your community have a charter? If so, write up its history, and state the provisions it makes.

READ MORE ABOUT IT

BURNS, JAMES M., and PELTASON, JACK W., *Government by the People*. Prentice-Hall, 1954. Chaps. 4–5.

CORWIN, EDWARD S., *The Constitution and What It Means Today*. Princeton University Press, 1954.
    The text of the Constitution with notes that give its current interpretation by the Supreme Court, and showing relations with the states.

IRISH, MARIAN D., and PROTHRO, JAMES W., *The Politics of American Democracy*. Prentice-Hall, 1959. Chap. 5.

SWARTHOUT, JOHN M., and BARTLEY, ERNEST R., *Principles and Problems of American National Government*. Oxford University Press, 1955. Chap. 4.
    A reliable and readable text.

CHAPTER 5

The Legislative Branch

In this chapter you will learn about

The legislative ways of free government
The House of Representatives
The Senate

A great majority of all the people who have ever lived have been governed by laws not made by themselves or by their elected representatives. These people did not have rights with their own government. They were not able to remove officials from their governments or work openly and freely to change laws they did not like. Laws were for the people to obey but not for their rulers to obey. These people and nations were ruled by pharaohs, kings, emperors, "protectors," chiefs, "leaders," dictators—possessors of unlimited power.

In our free society, administrative officials give orders, but only so far as the laws give them the authority to do so. These laws may be changed by a vote of the people or their representatives. Furthermore, officials depend on the voters and their representatives to provide funds according to law. The laws approved by the majority also state how long officials will serve and on what conditions they can be removed from office. Finally, the representatives of the voters hold office for limited terms, and may be removed from office by being defeated in an election conducted according to law.

Since we do have government by laws rather than by men, the process of lawmaking lies at the heart of our whole common life. There is no better place to begin a careful description of the workings of American government than with a description of the process of lawmaking, that is, the legislative process.

THE LEGISLATIVE WAYS OF FREE GOVERNMENT

Stated in its simplest terms, a legislature is the branch of government which makes the laws. In a democracy such as the United States, a legislature is made up of representatives of the people who have been freely chosen by the people in open elections. The legislators thus act *for the people.* This method of lawmaking is the best protection a free people can have against dictatorship and oppression, against the tyranny we have previously described as "government by men."

Freedom means, above all else, freedom to differ among ourselves—not only to think and believe differently, but to express our differences without fear. As James Madison pointed out in the *Federalist,* differing opinions are the very stuff of freedom. If people do not agree on what should be done, how does anything get done at all? The answer is that a legislature manages somehow to settle differences well enough to get done what has to be done, without sacrificing anyone's freedom to differ and object. It does this through the important principle of compromise.

In addition to protecting our liberties and freedoms, however, we believe that the *legislative process provides us with the wisest course of action.* Suppose for the moment we imagine an individual who is equipped with knowledge of all the facts about a particular matter of common concern. Let us imagine also that his only desire is to serve the common good. Under such circumstances we might argue that his decision would be better and wiser than the decision of a legislature. There are, however, two things wrong with the idea. The first is that in a society as complex as ours, no individual can in practice know all the facts. Second, even if he could know all the facts and were concerned only with the public good, he would still have to decide on the basis of what *he* thinks the public good is, and that would be only one man's opinion. Certainly many people would disagree with him. Because equally wise, equally good, and equally just men differ as to what is wise, or good, or just, we need the legislative process. Laws enacted by a free legislature may often be less wise, less good, or less just than some citizens would like, or than you or I might think ideally desirable, but they will be the best *obtainable* by democratic means.

112

Privileges and Principles of the Legislative Process

The people who live in the world's democracies understand the privileges and agree to the principles involved in the legislative process. Nevertheless, conflicts do occur because all free men do not agree on the many measures and policies for which the legislature is responsible. Suppose you are the owner of a small business—say, a hardware store. You may want lower taxes, lower freight rates, and fair trade laws to prevent other dealers from cutting prices. You have your own ideas as to what is best for *your* particular business. Although other small businessmen—including other hardware men—may disagree with you on certain issues, many will share your views on the policies and laws which will best promote your business interests. You probably belong to a trade organization of hardware dealers which attempts to make your wishes felt in the city council, in the state legislature, and in the national Congress. As owners of small businesses, you are *all* anxious not to be squeezed out by larger businesses, and not to have prices you pay set too high by big corporations which supply you. If you employ some help in your store, you want to pay fair wages for their services. Thus you can find so much common ground with other businessmen that a law passed to help small business will certainly be of some use to you.

In the same way, you have something in common with even very large business. For example, both you, as a hardware dealer, and the president of a steel company hope for reasonable taxes on your profits. Together you are in competition with other groups and with other needs of the American people. If the United States Treasury has a surplus, you and other small businessmen may join with the managers of big business to demand that Congress reduce taxes. But other people argue that something should be paid on the national debt before taxes are reduced. The chances are that Congress will manage a compromise—it will reduce taxes just a bit, so that you will get a little of what you think you should have—but not all.

There are obvious disadvantages in living under *government by laws*— laws passed by a free legislature. Some people are always dissatisfied and most people never get all they think they deserve. But there are two overwhelming advantages. One is that you retain your freedom—freedom to do what the laws allow, to criticize, argue, and persuade others. The second is that laws enacted by free legislatures are never final. They are always subject to change when enough people have changed their minds, after argument or experience, to form a new majority. Thus it is always possible for a government of laws to be dynamic and creative. If it is "stand pat" and sluggish, the people have no one to blame but themselves.

A free legislature, then, is basic to our way of life. To understand how our own national legislature works is an important part of being a citizen.

The Constitution places all the legislative powers of the national government in the two houses of Congress (I, 1). This is not surprising. Most of the colonial legislatures were **bicameral** (composed of two houses), and the Founding Fathers were accustomed to this form of organization. As we saw in Chapter 3, the Great Compromise provided that each state should have two Senators and that House membership was to be based on the population of each state.

Today, both Senate and House elections are held on the same day in November of every even-numbered year. In some states, candidates are nominated in party primary elections (see Chaps. 3 and 18), while in others they are nominated by state conventions. In any case, except in southern states where there is only one effective party, candidates must campaign twice, once for the nomination and once for election.

Terms and Sessions of Congress

A new Congress is formed every two years, when new Representatives are elected. A **term** of Congress is two years, and each is numbered consecutively, beginning with the first Congress that met under the Constitution in 1789. The Eighty-Fifth Congress, for example, ran from 1957 to 1959.

The Constitution provides that "Congress shall assemble at least once a year." Amendment XX, enacted in 1933, specifies that the meetings should begin on January 3. This means that each term consists of at least two sessions. In recent times, Congressional sessions have lasted for seven or eight months. Although the Constitution does not set a definite date for adjournment, Congress customarily adjourns in mid or late summer.

In addition to the regular session of Congress, the President may call a **special session** if he thinks it necessary. Nowadays, special sessions are called only to act on emergency situations, such as, for example, the major war in Europe which broke out in 1939.

Privileges and Immunities of Congressmen

To protect the freedom of Congressmen to debate openly any and all issues, Article I, Section 6, provided that ". . . for any Speech or Debate in either House, they shall not be questioned in any other place." This means that no Congressman can be sued for anything he may say on the floor of Congress or in an official document such as the *Congressional Record.*

This privilege is an important one, if Congress is to operate efficiently. Since congressional speeches and debates today are so closely covered by television, radio, and the press, Congressmen could not be expected to speak out frankly if they were subject to civil suit. This is not to say, of course, that

THE CONGRESS OF THE UNITED STATES

(Numbers in parentheses refer to Constitution—Article, Section, and Clause; i.e., I, 2, 2, refers to Article I, Section 2, Clause 2)

	House of Representatives	Senate
Membership	435 Representatives,[1] elected by voters in Congressional districts (I, 2, 1, and acts of Congress)	100 Senators, elected by voters of states (Amendment XVII)
Qualifications [2]	25 years old, seven years a citizen, inhabitant of state from which elected (I, 2, 2) (customarily a resident of the electing district)	30 years old, nine years a citizen, inhabitant of state from which elected (I, 3, 3)
Term of Office	Two years (I, 2, 1)	Six years (I, 3, 1 and 2)
Sole Powers	Votes impeachments (I, 2, 5) (II, 4)	Tries all impeachments (I, 3, 6) (II, 4)
	Originates revenue bills (I, 7, 1)	Approves appointments made by the President (II, 2, 2)
		Approves treaties (II, 2, 2)
	Elects President of the United States in absence of electoral majority (Amendment XII, 1)	Elects Vice-President in absence of electoral majority (Amendment XII, 2)
Presiding Officer	Speaker of the House, elected by the House (I, 2, 5)	President of the Senate, the Vice-President of the United States (I, 3, 4)
		President pro tempore elected by the Senate (I, 3, 5)
Sessions	January 3 to adjournment; special sessions when called by the President (Amendment XX, 2; II, 3)	
Compensations	$22,500 plus allowances (travel, tax exemptions, offices and office help, stationery, telephone and telegraph, franking privilege,[3] free printing and distribution of speeches. Members of Congress also contribute to a pension system (I, 6, 1)	

[1] Temporarily increased to 437 when Alaska and Hawaii became states in 1959. After 1960, number will become 435 again.

[2] Article I, Section 5, 1: "Each House shall be the judge of the elections, returns, and qualifications of its own members."

[3] Right to free use of the mails for official business.

a Congressman cannot be censured by his own house. Under certain conditions he may even be expelled by his fellow Congressmen, and in the past some members have been expelled.

Both Representatives and Senators enjoy certain other less important privileges. For example, they cannot be arrested for speeding and other such offenses while traveling to or from a session of Congress. This immunity is to protect them from political opponents who might attempt to have them arrested on a "trumped-up" charge in order to prevent them from taking part in a congressional debate. Fortunately, Congressmen seldom find it necessary to exercise this latter privilege!

For compensations of Congressmen, see table.

Services Available to Congressmen

GOVERNMENT PRINTING OFFICE An agency of the Congress known as the Government Printing Office provides Congressmen with the printed records they need to conduct their business. It also prints the *Congressional Record*. The GPO, as it is known, is perhaps the largest printing house in the world. Under the authority of the Congress, it prints all government documents, journals, and records for all agencies of the federal government. The *Congressional Record*, containing the calendar of business and the debates of both houses, is published every day while Congress is in session, and the GPO often works around the clock to keep the Congress provided with printed copies of bills, hearings, committee reports, etc. Unless publications of the GPO are classified for restricted circulation because of their bearing on national security, they are available to any interested citizen at low cost. The shelves of a Congressman's office are literally filled with such documents all the time.

LIBRARY OF CONGRESS A Congressman's reading and research are immeasurably assisted by the Library of Congress, which is adjacent to the Capitol and is one of the finest libraries in the world. Its services are available to any government official, but its Legislative Reference Service is concerned chiefly with helping members of Congress—doing research, finding facts, figures, and publications, and otherwise serving Congressmen and their staffs. The Library of Congress is an agency of the Congress itself, but in a larger sense it is a national institution which serves any citizen who wishes to use it. Scholars, in particular, find its collection of manuscripts and books invaluable.

Copyright. Authors of books, magazines, pamphlets, and articles who wish to register their claims to published material, as they are entitled to do under the Constitution (I, 8, 8), are also served by the Library of Congress. The division known as the Register of Copyrights supplies forms to all claimants to literary property. When these forms are properly filled out and returned together with two copies of the published material and $4.00, they are permanently filed at the Library of Congress. Each such published piece of material is said to be copyrighted and is assigned a Library of Congress copyright number. Copyrights remain in force for twenty-eight years and may be renewed once for the same number of years.

THE HOUSE OF REPRESENTATIVES

The lower house of Congress—the House of Representatives—was intended by the framers of our Constitution to represent the people more directly than the Senate. Representatives have been directly elected by the voters in each state since the ratification of the Constitution in 1788. Representatives come up for election every two years.

There have been important changes in the methods of electing our Representatives. Before 1872, voting was **viva voce** (oral) and in public. In 1872 Congress decreed that voting be by secret ballot. Voting machines were later approved for use in place of printed ballots, and today several of our states use this method of recording votes. Before 1873, there was no set day for congressional elections, and the states held them at widely scattered times of year. In 1873, Congress set the Tuesday after the first Monday in November of even-numbered years as the date for congressional elections throughout the nation. If a vacancy occurs in the House between regular elections, most states require the governor to call a special election.

Powers Delegated Exclusively to the House

The Constitution delegates three powers or responsibilities exclusively to the House of Representatives: (1) it originates "all Bills for raising Revenue"; (2) it elects the President if there is no electoral majority; and (3) it impeaches federal officials. The table on p. 115 gives references to the Constitution for these powers. Note that **impeachment** does not mean that the House determines the guilt of those impeached. It means that, if the House feels there is sufficient evidence that a federal official has committed some high crime or misdemeanor, it may impeach (bring charges against) that official. If the official is impeached, as we shall see presently, he is brought to trial before the Senate.

Probably the most important exclusive power of the House is that of originating revenue bills. Since Representatives serve only for two-year terms, they may be more easily removed from office than Senators; they are, therefore, more responsive to the people. By placing control of all revenue bills in the hands of the House, the Constitution provides for the closest supervision possible—under representative government—of the public's money.

COMPTROLLER GENERAL Watch over all government expenditures (except secret funds for foreign relations) is kept by the General Accounting Office under the direction of the Comptroller General of the United States. The Comptroller General is responsible for checking all expenditures and auditing all books. He has power to disallow payment if he thinks public money is being spent contrary to law or that payments are too high. His signature is required on warrants issued to the various departments before money appropriated by Congress can be spent. The Comptroller General is appointed by the President, with the consent of the Senate, for a term of fifteen years, but he is not an officer of the executive branch and not subject to the orders of the President. His annual and special reports are made to Congress.

117

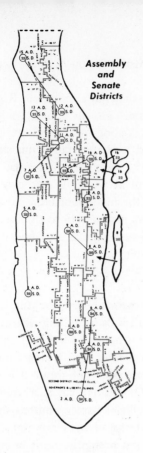

Assembly and Senate Districts

While Congressional districts are quite irregular in size and shape, as you can see, the legislative districts into which the states are divided for purposes of state government are frequently even more curious. In both cases, it is the political struggle over apportionment which affects the size of the districts (see p. 277).

Courtesy of League of Women Voters,
New York City

Qualifications and Compensations of Representatives

The table, p. 115, indicates the qualifications a Representative must have, as well as his compensation both in salary and in special allowances. Study the table carefully. Considering the responsibilities, duties, and expenses of a Congressman, his compensation is not high. He must keep up two houses—one in the state he represents and one in Washington. (He is allowed a tax exemption for this reason.) He must travel frequently to and from his home state to learn first-hand the problems of his constituents. A congressional career is indeed an expensive one, and the financial rewards are unquestionably less than those paid for equally (or even less) responsible positions in private business or the professions.

Apportionment of Seats

The Constitution provides (I, 2) that the number of Representatives for each state must be based on its population. Therefore, as our nation grew in population, membership in the House steadily increased. It was apparent that it would eventually become too unwieldy to carry on the public business. In 1929, the number of House members was fixed at 435, though Congress can change this number at any time if it should so desire. In 1958 and 1959, when Alaska and Hawaii became states, the number was increased to 437 for the 86th Congress only. After 1960 it becomes 435 again.

Every state, regardless of population, is entitled to at least one Representative. At present, Vermont, Wyoming, Delaware, Nevada, Hawaii, and Alaska have only one Representative. The question now is one of determining how the remaining 385 seats are apportioned (divided among the several states).

The Constitution provides (I, 2) for a census to be taken every ten years. After a decennial (ten-year) census has been completed, the Bureau of the Census, subject to approval by Congress, determines the number of Representatives each state is entitled to have. One state may gain new seats in Congress while another loses, as population increases or decreases in the various states. The determination of the number of Representatives a state may have is called **apportionment.** When the census indicates that a state must gain or lose seats in the House, a **reapportionment** is then necessary.

The District System

Before 1842 there was no set pattern for electing Representatives to Congress. In that year Congress declared that all states must be divided into districts—one for each Representative a state is entitled to have. For example, if a state is entitled to send five Representatives to Congress, the state must be divided into five districts. Later (in 1872) Congress specified that districts be contiguous (adjoining) and population of districts be as nearly equal as possible. The state legislatures were responsible for dividing their states into these Congressional Districts. This system, it was felt, would give political minorities a better chance to acquire representation in Congress, since the voters in each district could now select their own Representative (see Congressional District map, p. 118).

Today, if a census indicates that a state is entitled to additional seats in the House, the added Representatives may be elected-at-large (elected by all the voters of the state) until the legislature redistricts the state. If the census indicates that a state must lose seats, *all* Representatives must be elected-at-large until the redistricting is completed.

Problems in Redistricting

It is not always easy to divide a state into districts of approximately equal population. There have been cases in which one Representative has represented a district of 100,000 people, while another Representative—perhaps in an adjoining district—has represented nearly a million people. Such inequalities may occur when a state legislature does not keep up with population shifts within the state. Often, however, they are caused by political considerations. For example, political rivalry often exists between the rural and urban areas of a state. If the state legislature happens to be dominated by members from rural districts, they might wish to prevent the urban area from acquiring additional Representatives in the Congress. They could do this by simply refusing to redistrict the state, even though much of the population had shifted to the metropolitan center. In recent years, this situation has arisen in several states.

Unfair redistricting can result from still another kind of political maneuver. Suppose, for example, that a state is entitled to elect ten Representatives. The state legislature, under the influence of the majority party, might rearrange the ten district boundaries in such a way that most of the minority (opposition) party is lumped into, say, three districts. Although the minority party would undoubtedly win in those three districts, the majority party would be likely to win in the remaining seven districts. This kind of redistricting has become known as **gerrymandering.** The term was coined in 1812 when Governor Elbridge Gerry of Massachusetts was credited with originating (or at least permitting) this type of redistricting in his state. Similar problems exist at the level of state government (see pp. 276–278).

Organizing the House

The opening days of a new Congress are always busy (and frequently hectic) in the House of Representatives. The House must "begin anew" every two years, for all members of the House come to the end of their terms at the same time. The members-elect (representatives elected but not yet sworn in) inherit no parliamentary organization from the preceding Congress. On opening day of a new Congress, the House has no officers, no committees, no rules, and even no sworn members with which to begin conducting the public business. The majority party has the power to "organize" the House.

Before a new Congress opens, the majority party calls a **caucus** (a closed meeting of party members) to nominate its candidates for officers of the House. (The Republican party now calls it a **party conference.**) Though they will fail to be elected, the minority party also calls a caucus and nominates its candidates for House offices.

When the new Congress convenes for the first time, the **clerk** (of the preceding House) gets things under way by serving as temporary presiding officer and calling the roll. Next, the new presiding officer—the **Speaker** of the House—is formally elected by the House. Invariably, the House merely ratifies the choice already made by the majority party caucus. Even though the Speaker-elect probably has served in this capacity in past terms of Congress, he will be duly sworn in as the House Speaker for the new Congress. After this ceremony, he proceeds to administer the oath of office to the other members-elect. The House then elects the other officers—the clerk, sergeant-at-arms, a

120

Organization of the House of Representatives

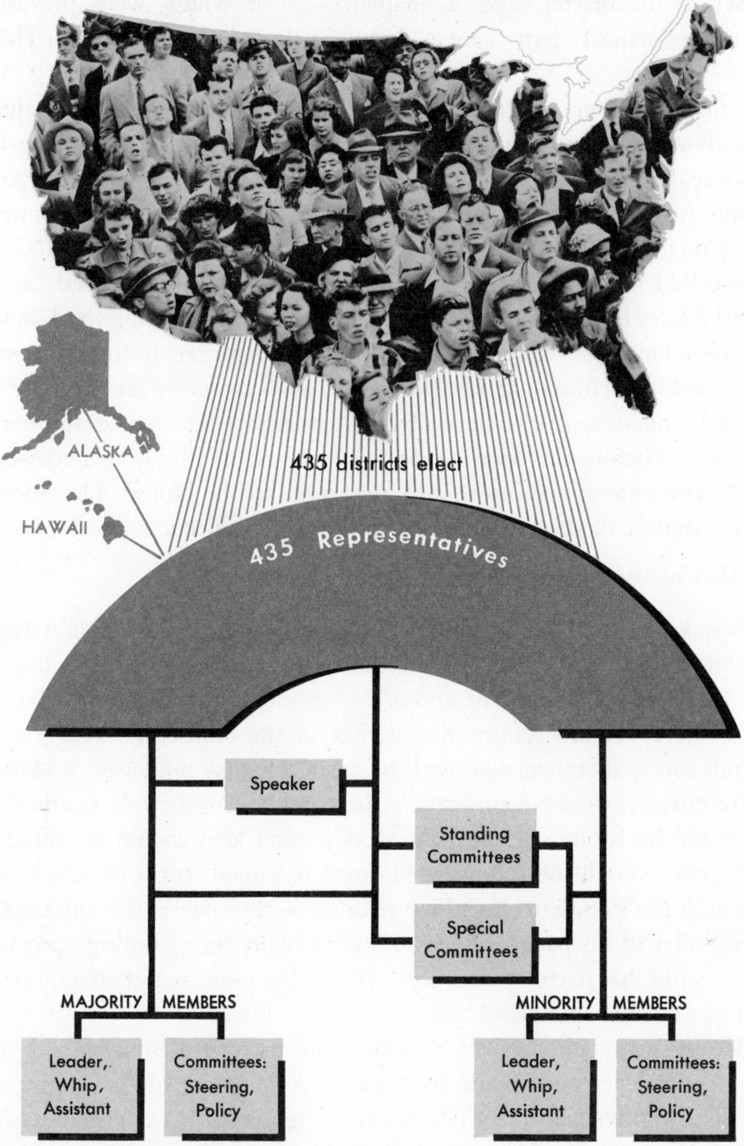

ALASKA

HAWAII

435 districts elect

435 Representatives

Speaker

Standing Committees

Special Committees

MAJORITY MEMBERS

Leader, Whip, Assistant

Committees: Steering, Policy

MINORITY MEMBERS

Leader, Whip, Assistant

Committees: Steering, Policy

The members-elect of the House choose their own officers. Most important of these is the *SPEAKER OF THE HOUSE,* who is the presiding officer and one of the chief figures of the whole national government. In the line of presidential succession, he follows the Vice-President.

Following the majority and minority leaders in importance are the *WHIPS* and their assistants, who keep the floor leaders informed on opinions of their party members and assist in influencing members to vote with the party leadership.

The House membership is set by statute at 435. This was temporarily increased to 437 to allow for one representative-at-large from each of the new states of Alaska and Hawaii. The number will revert to 435 for the 1960 Congressional elections, seats being reapportioned among the states after the 1960 census.

121

doorkeeper, a postmaster, and a chaplain—all of whom were previously selected by the majority party caucus. None of these latter officers is a House member.

After the House has elected its officers, a senior member of the majority party usually will move to adopt the rules of the preceding Congress. The rules of the House, based in part on the *Manual of Parliamentary Practice* prepared by Thomas Jefferson, have slowly changed and developed from the time of our first Congress. Although some members may propose new rules, the chances are that the rules of the preceding Congress will be adopted "as is."

After the rules have been adopted, the last stage in organizing the House— electing the committees—gets under way. The committee system is a most important aspect of House organization, as we shall presently see. Because the Speaker and a majority of the committee members are selected by the majority party caucus before the opening day of Congress, it is easy to understand why both parties are so anxious to win a majority in the House. The Speaker and the committee chairmen are the most powerful officers in the House.

The Speaker of the House

The Speaker of the House is one of the chief figures in the whole national government. Under the law of presidential succession, he is third in line for the Presidency; if both President and Vice-President should die in office, he would become President. As presiding officer of the House, he recognizes or gives permission to members who wish to speak. He may influence the fate of a bill by referring it to one committee rather than to another. As head of the majority party, he is one of those who decide what laws should be voted on and what policy should be followed. He may be called to the White House to confer with the President. For these reasons the Speaker is the outstanding legislative leader of his party. The same man usually serves during successive Congresses while his party is in power. When his party is out of power, he usually serves as minority leader.

The House always chooses the Speaker from its own membership though the Constitution does not require it to do so. As member of the House, the Speaker has the privilege of voting, but he is required to exercise this right only in case of a tie vote. He may also participate in House debates. When this occurs, he appoints a temporary officer to preside in his place.

The Committee System

Most people do not realize that as many as 5,000 bills may be introduced in a single session of Congress! Many of these bills are unimportant; many deal with minor issues important only to a small section of the country. Less than one-tenth of the bills introduced become law. It is obvious that the House, meeting as a body, would be unable to cope with the staggering number of bills it must face at each session of Congress. Committees are set up, therefore,

122

to weed out the less important bills and to evaluate the important ones that will eventually be put to the House for a vote.

Our first few Congresses studied legislative proposals by appointing a new committee to pass on each bill that came before them. At one point there were over 300 House committees. As the business of Congress continued to grow larger and more complex, permanent committees, known as **standing committees,** were appointed to study legislative proposals. Prior to 1946, there were so many standing committees that it was not unusual for a Representative to be assigned to three or four different committees. In 1946, the Legislative Reorganization Act fixed the number of standing committees at 19. (See table below, for committee names.) Representatives can today serve on only one standing committee by House rules.

HOUSE COMMITTEES

Agriculture	Interior and Insular Affairs
Appropriations	Interstate and Foreign Commerce
Armed Services	Judiciary
Banking and Currency	Merchant Marine and Fisheries
District of Columbia	Post Office and Civil Service
Education and Labor	Public Works
Government Operations	Rules
Foreign Affairs	Un-American Activities
House Administration	Veterans' Affairs
Ways and Means	

All the standing committees (except the powerful Rules Committee, with which we shall presently deal) tend to specialize in certain legislative areas. Bills dealing with farm problems, for example, are referred to the Committee on Agriculture. The Committees on Ways and Means and on Appropriations are major committees which deal with the financial responsibilities of the House. The Committee on Ways and Means must recommend the legislation which produces the tax money needed for federal expenditures. To a great extent, the Appropriations Committee decides *how* these large sums of money will be spent. Since no part of the government can operate without funds, these two committees are very powerful. Although the executive branch originally recommends expenditures and taxation, the congressional committees may cut the figures, increase them, eliminate them, or add others as they see fit. Bills recommended by these committees are sometimes amended on the floor of the House by the motion of an individual Representative, but usually the committees' recommendations become law. The leadership of the House and the majority party see to that.

In order for the committees to handle efficiently the tremendous amount of work they have to do, they often create subcommittees within their own membership to study specific proposals. Subcommittees may conduct their own investigations or hold their own public hearing, but they must report their findings to their main committee, not to the House.

Occasionally the House appoints special committees to deal with some unusual problem. Recently, for example, special House committees have been set up to deal with problems of defense. Unlike the regular standing committees, they are dissolved after they complete their particular study and make their report. In 1958, a temporary committee was set up to deal with outer space problems. It was called a Select Committee on Astronautics and Space Exploration.

SELECTING COMMITTEE MEMBERS Although Representatives are formally elected to the standing committees by House vote, they are actually nominated in advance by a caucus of each party. If one-third of the Representatives in the House are Democrats and two-thirds are Republicans, then one-third of the members on each committee will be Democrats and two-thirds Republicans. Thus, each committee is controlled by the majority party, but the minority party is usually well represented.

Committee chairmen are always members of the majority party and are chosen by the party chiefly on the basis of **seniority** (length of continuous service). As we shall see in Chapter 6, the chairmen are House officers of great importance.

THE RULES COMMITTEE The Rules Committee prepares the calendar of business for the House. When a bill is favorably recommended by a standing committee, it must then be submitted to the Rules Committee in order to get a place on the **agenda** (a list of items to be considered by the House). The committee places bills on a **calendar** (schedule of bills to be considered). Revenue and appropriations are placed on the **Union Calendar.** Such bills are "privileged" and may be introduced at any time. **Public bills,** dealing with matters of national concern (such as establishment of a Soil Bank), go on the **House Calendar.** They are taken up in the order in which they appear on the calendar, unless the Rules Committee passes a resolution declaring a bill privileged. **Private bills** deal with individuals and might concern a personal claim or granting a special status under the immigration and naturalization law. They go on the Calendar of the Whole House, usually called the **Private Calendar.** Such bills are introduced on the first and third Tuesday of each month.

The Rules Committee may also limit debate; it may determine what parts of the bill should be amended and how many amendments the bill may have. The Rules Committee can interrupt debate on the floor at any time in order to introduce a special rule to permit immediate consideration of a new bill, regardless of its place on the agenda. Although the minority party often sharply criticizes these practices, both parties use them when they are in the majority.

124

Majority and Minority Floor Leaders

The majority floor leader is strictly a party officer, chosen by the majority party caucus. He probably ranks next to the Speaker, however, in the power and influence he exerts over the business of the House. As floor leader, he guides his party's legislative program through the House. He plans debates, confers with the minority floor leader on the time that votes are to be taken, advises the Speaker who should be given the floor on particular issues and, in general, tries to keep the Speaker informed on the drift of majority opinion. With the steering committee (a committee to direct the policy of the party), he shares the responsibility of maintaining harmony within his party.

The floor leader of the minority party is also a party officer elected by a caucus of his party. His influence on the business of the House is, of course, much less than that of the majority leader, since his party commands fewer votes in the House. He is, in effect, the leader of the opposition in the House of Representatives.

Leaders of both houses also work closely with the President (see p. 180).

For functions of the party **whips** and assistants, see chart, p. 121.

THE SENATE

The Senate has sometimes been called a "snobbish men's club" and sometimes "the greatest parliamentary body in the world." It is probably neither.

A Senator, who is elected at large, comes up for election every six years. In a typical senatorial campaign, the candidate deals to a considerable extent with national affairs and with foreign policy. In choosing Senators, the people of a state have a valuable opportunity to make known their views on major issues before the country. Often a senatorial election provides a means for voters to show that they support a President or oppose him. Representatives more frequently hold their seats, or lose them, because of their stand on matters of special interest to their immediate communities.

The Senators know well enough that when they speak they command the headlines of the press and of the news broadcasts on radio and television. Their individual influence is such that what they say must be heeded.

Powers Delegated Exclusively to the Senate

The Constitution gives the Senate four exclusive powers: (1) it approves all treaties; (2) it approves appointments made by the President; (3) it tries impeachments; and (4) it elects the Vice-President if there is no electoral majority (see table, p. 115, for Constitution references).

NEXT!

Alexander in
Philadelphia Bulletin

The first two of these are important checks on the executive powers of the President. Senators make full use of their powers in the matter of presidential appointments of ambassadors, cabinet members, federal judges, and other important officials. It has long been a custom for the Senate as a whole to refuse to approve the appointment if one Senator objects to an appointment of a man from his state. For this reason, the President usually "clears" with the Senators any persons he wishes to appoint from their states, especially with a Senator of the same party as the President. This gives each individual Senator a certain amount of bargaining power with the executive branch. Sometimes dramatic rivalries develop between a President and a Senator, and their disagreement becomes a matter of wide public interest. Often, however, the Senators recommend to the President the names of people they would like to have appointed to federal posts. In this way, and through their approval power, the Senate as a body and Senators as individuals can exert considerable influence over the executive branch.

The power of the Senate to approve all treaties made by the President by two-thirds vote of the Senators present not only checks the President's power but also gives the Senate an important role in making foreign policy. We will learn more about this Senate function in Chapter 25.

In impeachment trials, the Senate serves as a jury. A vote of two-thirds of the Senators present is necessary for conviction. If the President is being tried, the Chief Justice of the Supreme Court presides.

Qualifications and Compensations of Senators

The table on p. 115 shows both qualifications and compensations of a Senator. As you can see, the Senator must be older than the Representative, and must have been a citizen for a longer time. His compensation and special privileges are the same as a Representative's (and his expenses are just as great); but he usually has better office space.

The campaign of a senatorial candidate is easier in some ways than that of a Representative; in some ways it is more difficult. He does not, on the one hand, have to pay quite so much attention to the wishes of a particular group. On the other hand, he has to please a great many more people and has to contend with a wider variety of opinions. For these reasons, senatorial candidates are most often outstanding party leaders or persons who have made a considerable reputation in state-wide civic affairs. In general, when a new Senator arrives in Washington, he is already a man of some stature and may even have a national reputation, while a new Representative may be younger and much less widely known.

Once elected, a Senator usually hopes to spend the rest of his active life in the Senate. He must, therefore, keep the wishes of the people in his state constantly in mind. Experience shows that it is much more common for a defeated Representative to return on another try, as opinion changes, than it is for a defeated Senator to regain his seat. Thus Senators campaign almost as much as Representatives do, day by day, month by month, and year by year.

Organizing the Senate

When a new term of Congress begins, the Senate faces only a few of the many problems which beset the House. Since normally only one-third of the 100 Senators are ever up for election at the same time, Congress always opens with a core of experienced Senators. Since the Senate is a continuing body, no complete reorganization is ever necessary (see chart, p. 129). New members-elect must, of course, be sworn in and then assigned to committees. The committee lists may have to be changed to accommodate any shift in Senate seats that results from the election. The number of Democrats on each committee, for example, would have to be increased if the Democrats gained new seats in the Senate.

The President of the Senate

By constitutional provision the Vice-President of the United States is the President of the Senate. He presides regardless of which party has a majority in the Senate.

The President of the Senate has few of the powers and little of the influence which the Speaker of the House enjoys. Since he is not really a member of the Senate, he may never take part in the debates and may vote only in the event of a tie vote. Often he is not even a member of the majority party that controls the Senate. He refers proposed bills to the appropriate committees and, as chairman of the Senate, presides over that body.

The President Pro Tempore

The President of the Senate is often unable to preside at Senate meetings because of his other responsibilities as Vice-President. When he is absent, the **President pro tempore** presides. (**Pro tempore** means "for the time being.") The President pro tempore is a senior member of the majority party and is elected by the Senate. Under law, he is fourth in the line of succession to the Presidency, following the Speaker of the House. For this reason, the senior leader of the majority party may prefer this office to that of majority leader. In any case, it is a position of great informal influence upon other Senators.

The Senate Committees

As in the House, the bulk of the Senate's work is done in committee. The Legislative Reorganization Act of 1946 reduced the number of standing committees in the Senate to 15. Most of them are smaller than the House committees, ranging in size from 13 to 21 members. By Senate rule, members can serve on no more than two committees. Again, as in the House, the majority party controls the committees, with the minority party well represented. Committee lists are drawn up by the party leaders and approved by their party caucuses prior to the opening of a new Congress. The Senate invariably approves these committee assignments without question.

The Committee on Rules and Administration is the Senate's counterpart to the House Rules Committee. The Senate Rules Committee is not nearly so powerful, however, because the Senate rules allow much more freedom of action to the individual Senators. The chart on p. 142 indicates the Senate standing committees.

The Committee on Government Operations serves as a kind of watchdog on the executive branch. Its subcommittee on investigations is empowered to investigate almost anything and to hold public hearings which may attract wide attention and give considerable influence to the committee. In recent years, the investigations conducted by Senate committees have become so important that they sometimes overshadow the work of committees in drafting legislation. We shall give special attention to congressional investigations in the next chapter.

Some committees are **joint committees,** consisting of members from each house appointed by their presiding officers. Most important of such permanent committees are the Joint Committee on Atomic Energy and the Joint Committee on the Economic Report. In 1958 the House rejected a Senate

Organization of the Senate

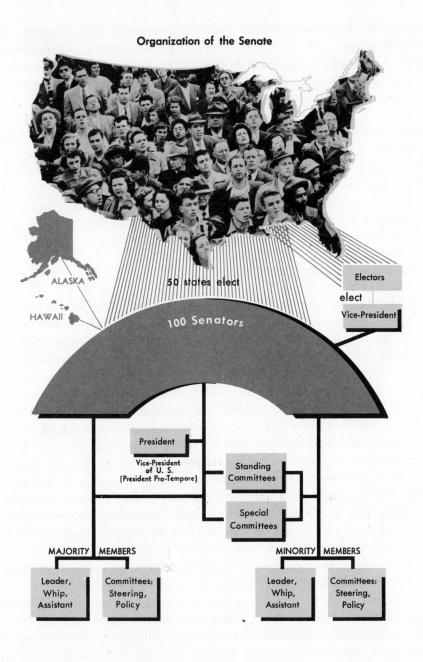

ALASKA

HAWAII

50 states elect

Electors

elect

Vice-President

100 Senators

President

Vice-President of U. S. (President Pro-Tempore)

Standing Committees

Special Committees

MAJORITY MEMBERS

Leader, Whip, Assistant

Committees: Steering, Policy

MINORITY MEMBERS

Leader, Whip, Assistant

Committees: Steering, Policy

The Vice-President of the United States is the presiding officer of the Senate. To preside in his absence, the Senate elects one of its members *PRESIDENT PRO TEMPORE*. This office frequently goes to the leading member of the majority party. As President of the Senate, he ranks behind the Speaker of the House in the line of succession to the Presidency. All other officers of the Senate are also chosen by its membership. Majority and minority floor leaders, whips, and assistant whips fulfill functions similar to those performed by members with the same titles in the House (see p. 121).

129

proposal for a joint Committee on Space and Aeronautics, declaring it would establish its own such committee. Senate and House agreed, however, on a bill for a space agency, the National Aeronautics and Space Administration.

In general, the committees of the Senate function in much the same way as those of the House. Nearly all legislation passes through their hands; they are served by staffs of specialists and lawyers. But legislation introduced without committee support is more likely to gain recognition, or even passage, in the Senate than in the House. The number of Senators is so small, by comparison, that each Senator soon comes to know every other Senator well. Many, regardless of party, become fast friends as they serve together through the years. Thus attention to the wishes of an individual Senator is common, and many a bill is passed by means of **logrolling**. This simply means that you agree to support my bill if I agree to support yours.

Majority and Minority Floor Leaders

Each party elects its own floor leader (see chart, p. 129). The party leader has great influence. If the division of the Senate is close, the majority leader must work very closely with the minority leader to get legislation enacted.

Unlike the House, the Senate allows unlimited debate, unless two-thirds of the Senators vote to close it. This privilege of unlimited debate has on occasion been abused. Sometimes a small minority—even one Senator—can hold up legislation by simply holding the floor and talking about anything, including matters which are not even remotely connected with the bill under discussion. Some Senators have read for hours to an empty chamber from a newspaper, a dictionary, or even a telephone directory to prevent passage of a bill or to secure a compromise amendment. This practice of "talking a bill to death" is known as a **filibuster**. It is possible for the Senate to invoke the **closure rule** (or **cloture rule**), which limits further debate on a particular bill if two-thirds of the Senators vote to close the debate. This is not often done, however, since the Senate is extremely proud of its tradition of free and open debate. Because of such unlimited debates, even in his own party the majority leader often has great difficulty in lining up his votes.

A Senator, as we have seen, can be a good deal more independent of his party than can a Representative. Democratic Senators from southern states and Republican Senators from certain northern states often serve for a great many years, regardless of changes in party fortunes. They become men of enormous power and influence in their own right. If they happen to disagree with party policy, they may well make a temporary alliance with members of the other party or pursue an independent course. The majority leader who, with the help of the party whip and other leaders, sees as many as 60 percent of the bills for which he is responsible enacted into law during a given session of Congress has done his job well.

Other Party Officers

The other party officers which exist in the House are also found in the Senate. The party caucus, as we have seen, elects party officers and committee members. The majority party steering committee works with the majority leader in setting up the Senate agenda and ushering the majority party program through the Senate. But neither the party caucus nor its steering committee has the power of its counterpart in the House. Influential Senators may even refuse to attend a caucus of their party. The party caucuses in the Senate are thus more like informal conferences, with little power to keep their members "in line" with their party leadership.

SUMMARY

The legislative ways of free government protect a democracy from the kind of dictatorship imposed by a government of men rather than laws. We enjoy such free government in the United States. Although it has some disadvantages—such as the fact that some people are always dissatisfied and most people do not get what they think they deserve—it has obvious advantages: it gives us freedom, and it is dynamic, that is, it changes to meet changing situations.

The Congress of the United States is the lawmaking body set up by the makers of the Constitution. Consisting of two houses, the Senate and the House of Representatives, it is a legislative body which carries out the will of the majority and safeguards our rights and freedom.

The House members, elected on the basis of state population, are closer to the people and are elected every two years. The House has three exclusive powers: (1) it originates all bills for raising revenue; (2) it chooses the President in case no candidate obtains a majority of electoral votes; and (3) it impeaches federal officials, including the President.

The Senate, consisting of two members from each state, has four exclusive powers: (1) it approves all treaties made by the President; (2) it approves or confirms presidential appointments; (3) it tries people impeached by the House; and (4) it chooses the Vice-President, if no candidate receives a majority of electoral votes.

Both houses of Congress operate through the committee system, with chairmen of the committees chosen on the basis of seniority. One important difference between the two houses is the matter of debate. The House limits debate sharply, while the Senate allows unlimited debate.

In our history, we have been fortunate in having elected many Congressmen who have shown real statesmanship by placing the good of the country above personal or local good.

131

KNOW WHAT YOU READ

1. What is meant by government of laws?
2. What is meant by government by men?
3. Was President Truman's action in the case of the steel strike (see Chap. 2) an illustration of "government by laws"? Explain.
4. In what ways do laws limit the power of administrative officials? In what other ways are their powers limited?
5. What are legislative powers? Where in the Constitution of the United States would you look to find the legislative powers of our national government?
6. Why is it that the laws made by our representatives in lawmaking bodies are so unsatisfactory to so many people? Why do most of us still prefer this way of making laws?
7. Why do we believe that lawmaking by elected legislatures "provides us with the wisest course of action"?
8. What is the difference between a term of Congress and a session of Congress?
9. What are the privileges and immunities of Congressmen? Why are they important?
10. What is the function of the Government Printing Office?
11. Explain what a copyright is.
12. What is meant by apportionment? Reapportionment?
13. The majority party has the power to organize the House. What does that mean?
14. Why is the Speaker of the House so important?
15. What is the work of the majority and minority leaders?
16. Which are the most important committees of the House? What is the work of each?
17. What is the work of standing committees?
18. In what ways is the Senate different from the House of Representatives?
19. Members of Congress cannot be expected to know everything about everything. How may they get help from specialists?
20. What powers does the Senate have which the House does not have? What are the exclusive powers of the House?
21. In what ways are campaigns for Senate membership different from campaigns for membership in the House?
22. Who are the officers of the Senate? How are they chosen?
23. Why is it possible for a small group in the Senate to "talk a bill to death"? What effect does the possibility of a *filibuster* have on the work of the majority leader?
24. Which are the most important committees of the Senate?
25. What part is played in federal appointments by the Senate and by individual Senators?

132

WHAT DO YOU THINK?

1. "The ways of freedom are at once political and slow." Discuss.
2. Study the cartoon, p. 126. What advantages and possible disadvantages do you see in the Senate procedure for presidential appointments?
3. Should the Senate presiding officer be elected from the majority party?
4. In recent years the order of Presidential succession was changed to place the Speaker of the House next in line after the Vice-President. Previously the Secretary of State had been next in line. Was this a good change?
5. Why is membership in the Senate usually considered more desirable than membership in the House?

PROBLEMS AND PROJECTS FOR YOU

7. Look up in any comprehensive history book President Jackson's action in the cases involving Georgia and the Cherokees. Report your opinion on whether this President did or did not violate the principle of "government of laws."
2. This chapter points out that the lawmakers may vote on taxes and military service for you. Make a list of the other ways in which the majority vote of lawmakers may affect *you* and the people of your community.
3. If Congress is in session, follow the news for one week, noting all references to congressional committees. Report your findings to the class.
4. Present to the class a carefully prepared point of view on the question, "Should unlimited debate be permitted in the Senate?"
5. "Laws enacted by a free legislature may often be less wise, less good, or less just than some citizens would like. . . ." Poll a dozen people to find their opinions on some controversial law recently enacted by Congress or by your state legislature. Then answer the question, "Was this law the wisest, best, and most just law possible under the circumstances?"
6. Study the two charts showing Organization of the House of Representatives (p. 121) and Organization of the Senate (p. 129). Discuss with your class the place and functions of the Whips.
7. Assign parts to members of the class; then enact opening day of a new term in the House.
8. Study the table (p. 115) and discuss differences (and likenesses) between privileges, qualifications, and powers of members of the two houses.
9. Make a map of the Congressional Districts of your state. For this activity, use the latest edition of *America Votes* by Richard Scammon (Macmillan), or your own state's handbook, manual, or blue book.
10. Report to the class on the origin and meaning of the word *gerrymander*.
11. Make a cartoon or poster on the subject of odd-shaped districts. You will find illustrations in various American history textbooks.

133

EXTEND YOUR VOCABULARY

legislative process	impeachment	agenda
bicameral	apportionment	calendar
term (of Congress)	reapportionment	party whips
sessions (of Congress)	gerrymander	president pro tempore
Congressional Record	caucus	logrolling
franking privilege	standing committee	filibuster
viva voce	seniority	cloture rule

YOUR NOTEBOOK: THE GOVERNMENT OF ——

1. How are the local laws (by-laws, ordinances) of your community made?
2. Attend a hearing in your own city, county, or other local government unit. Report to the class on how it was conducted and what topic was under consideration.
3. What committees in your state legislature correspond to the House's Committee on *Ways and Means* and the Committee on *Appropriations?*
4. On what committees do your representatives in your state legislature serve?

READ MORE ABOUT IT

Biographical Dictionary of the American Congress, 1774–1949. Government Printing Office, 1950.
  A source book of short biographies of Congressmen from 1774 to 1949.
BURNS, JAMES M., and PELTASON, JACK W., *Government by the People.* Prentice-Hall, 1954. Chap. 14.
Congressional Directory. Government Printing Office, published annually.
  A source book of value to the interested student.
GROSS, BERTRAM, *The Legislative Struggle.* McGraw-Hill, 1953.
  A study of conflicting interests.
IRISH, MARIAN D., and PROTHRO, JAMES W., *The Politics of American Democracy.* Prentice-Hall, 1959. Chap. 11.
RANNEY, AUSTIN, *The Governing of Men.* Holt, 1958. Chap. 17.
RIDDICK, FLOYD M., *The United States Congress: Organization and Procedures.* National Capitol Publishers, 1949.
  Comprehensive discussion of organization and procedures.
YOUNG, ROLAND A., *This Is Your Congress.* Knopf, 1943.
YOUNG, ROLAND A., *The American Congress.* Harper, 1958.
  Two interesting discussions of our Congress by the same author, the second more extensive than the first.

CHAPTER 6

Congress at Work

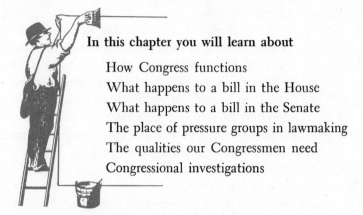

In this chapter you will learn about

How Congress functions
What happens to a bill in the House
What happens to a bill in the Senate
The place of pressure groups in lawmaking
The qualities our Congressmen need
Congressional investigations

The principal work of the Congress is lawmaking, and any Congressman in either house may introduce a legislative proposal. In many cases, however, the Congressman who introduces a new proposal is not the originator of that proposal. He may, for example, be petitioned by one of his constituents to propose a certain measure. An organized group of constituents, such as a labor union, a chamber of commerce, or a professional society, may petition him to initiate a particular piece of legislation. The right to petition is guaranteed to all citizens by Amendment I. The executive branch of the government and many independent agencies are also frequent sources of new legislative proposals. Again, a congressional committee might launch a research study on some particular problem that continues for a year or more. Out of that study could come a recommendation for important new legislation. Most of these sources have trained legal consultants on their staffs to draft measures for the consideration of Congress.

FORMS OF CONGRESSIONAL ACTION

When a proposal is drawn up for Congress to consider, it is known as a **bill.** As we have seen (p. 124), bills may be either **public** or **private.** Most bills today are public bills because the Legislative Reorganization Act of 1946 sharply curtailed the number of private bills that may be introduced. After any bill passes both houses of Congress and is signed by the President, it is called an **act** of Congress and becomes part of the law of the land.

Occasionally a measure that ordinarily would never be passed on its own merit becomes law because it is "tacked on" at the end of another bill which is certain to be passed. Such a measure is known as a **rider.** Since the President cannot veto a part of a bill, he sometimes signs an urgent bill in spite of a rider he does not like.

Another type of congressional action is the **congressional resolution.** Resolutions are formal statements expressing the will or the opinion of one house or both houses of Congress about a particular matter. They may be initiated in either house and are adopted by vote. **Simple resolutions** have to do with the conduct of business in one house and have no bearing on the other house. A resolution adopted by *both* houses but not intended to be law is known as a **concurrent resolution.** For example, a resolution fixing the date of congressional adjournment, when adopted by both houses, would be a concurrent resolution. Since concurrent resolutions are not laws, they do not require the signature of the President.

The most important type of congressional resolution is a **joint resolution.** Practically it is the same as a bill. When adopted by both houses of Congress and signed by the President, a joint resolution carries the authority of law. Joint resolutions are often used to amend or renew some existing law or to deal with a simple (though not necessarily unimportant) matter. Hawaii, for example, was annexed in 1898 by a joint resolution of Congress.

HOW A LAW COMES INTO BEING

In order to learn more about the actual workings of Congress, especially the lawmaking process, let us follow some of the events in the life of Mr. Jones, a new Representative. Jones represents a district which includes many dairy farmers. For several months the prices of milk, butter, and cheese have been steadily dropping while the prices of other commodities remain high. Thus the dairy farmers are losing income while their expenses do not go down.

In his election campaign, Jones promised that, if elected, he would take prompt action to help the dairy farmers. He was elected. He has just arrived in Washington to take his seat in the House of Representatives and do what he can to live up to his campaign pledges.

Representative Jones may be somewhat bewildered when he first arrives to take his place in the House, but he will soon enough be fitted into the organization described in Chapter 5. He is a member of the majority party and joins his party caucus at the outset. He is assigned to an office in the House Office Building and has a staff of two or three assistants and some office "help." His leaders will place him on a standing committee. As nearly as possible, his committee assignment will be in line with his interests and his known abilities. Quite possibly one of the veterans in his party will "take him in tow" and help him to learn his way in the organization of the House.

Since Jones comes from a farming district and has influential friends among farm leaders, his party leaders assign him to a place on the Committee on Agriculture. Mr. Jones soon finds that on this committee, as on all others, great importance is attached to what is called seniority (see p. 124). Below the chairman and the ranking minority member, Jones finds twenty-odd fellow Representatives ranked in order of their seniority in the party to which they belong. He finds himself at the bottom of the list on the majority side.

Jones observes that the committee members treat each other with great respect and courtesy. He finds that the "ranking minority member" is treated with as much deference as the chairman himself. This is because, with elections every two years, the chairmanship may change often, but the two senior members are likely to serve a long time regardless of which party is in power. It pays for committee members to be on good terms with both leaders, since the minority leader may very well be the chairman in two years.

When the committee meets, Jones sees in the room a number of people who are not members of Congress but have important standing with the committee. There is a counsel, who is legal adviser to the committee and who takes a leading part in its investigations of agricultural matters and in drafting and revising bills. There is a staff director, who directs the work of researchers, investigators, and specialists in economic and agricultural matters. There may also be special consultants to advise the committee on particular problems. In short, Jones is a somewhat inconspicuous member of a carefully organized group. As he becomes more experienced, he will see that the organization is indispensable to him. Literally hundreds of matters about which he knows either little or nothing at all will come before the committee. He must depend on the staff to provide him with enough information to form an intelligent opinion. There will be times when the work on the staff, the assistance of his own office co-workers, and his personal diligence will not be enough; he will be called upon to vote on questions he does not really understand. But Jones may get some satisfaction, and relieve his conscience a bit, by observing that there are always *some* Congressmen who *do* know. No Congressman can know about everything before Congress or even before his own committees. Hence Jones will find there is a division of labor, so that there are always some who are well enough informed to give leadership to others.

Setting the Stage for a New Bill

Most bills introduced by individual Congressmen are of minor importance; but let us assume, in order to learn more about legislation, that Jones, to carry out his campaign pledges, has in mind a bill of national importance. He wants to secure passage of a measure to enable the Secretary of Agriculture to maintain the price of milk at a level which farmers feel will yield them a fair profit. This is called **price support.** Jones thinks that the best way to do this is by a direct **subsidy.** This means that the government would pay the farmer the difference per pound between what he can get at the market and an agreed fair price. Jones sees that there are two ways to go about this task. He can draw up a bill himself, introduce it on the floor of the House, see it referred to his committee, and then do what he can in the committee to gain approval. Or he can discuss the whole matter first with his committee chairman.

The latter method is the more likely to succeed, although it may mean that he does not get recognition for his efforts, so that his constituents back home will not know what he has tried to do for them. If he is unsuccessful with his committee chairman, he can at least impress his constituents by introducing his bill on the floor of the House. His speech will be printed in the *Congressional Record* (see p. 116). A Daily Digest (started in 1947) gives a summary of each day's proceedings in both houses, as well as the program for each day and—at the end of each week—the program for the following week. Jones can have copies of his speech reprinted from the *Record* and sent free (by using his franking privilege) to as many farmer friends as he wishes.

Representative Jones, then, decides to try his luck first with the committee. His committee chairman will want to know whether the proposal is in line with party and administration policy. He will consult officials of the Department of Agriculture and, perhaps, members of the White House staff (see Chap. 7). If the bill is satisfactory to these people and to senior members of his party in Congress, the chairman will then need to think about the cost to the government and discover whether financial plans can be adjusted to it. He refers the bill to specialists working for the committee to make studies regarding finances, administrative methods, and its relation to the rest of the farm program. If the recommendations of the staff are favorable, Jones's proposal will then be drafted as a bill. Probably Jones himself will be consulted in the drafting procedure.

While all this is going on, if the majority party is enthusiastic about the bill, it is likely that an effort will be made to secure advance cooperation from the Senate. There may be informal conferences with the leaders of the Senate Committee on Agriculture, and Jones will probably have talks with Senators from dairy states. The bill will have its best chance of success if Jones can get a leading Senator to introduce the same bill in the Senate.

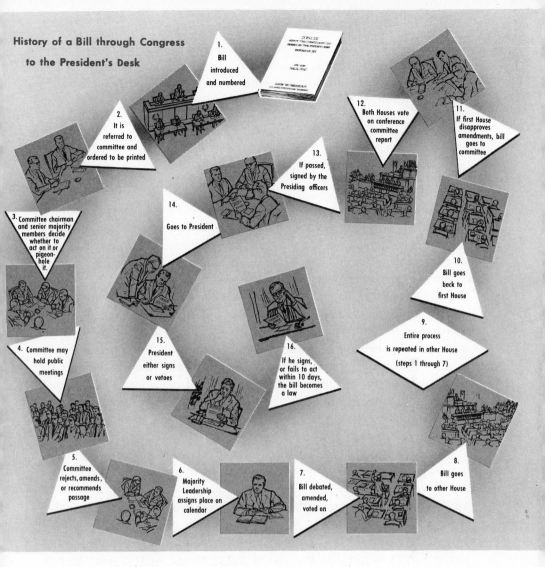

History of a Bill through Congress to the President's Desk

1. Bill introduced and numbered
2. It is referred to committee and ordered to be printed
3. Committee chairman and senior majority members decide whether to act on it or pigeonhole it.
4. Committee may hold public meetings
5. Committee rejects, amends, or recommends passage
6. Majority Leadership assigns place on calendar
7. Bill debated, amended, voted on
8. Bill goes to other House
9. Entire process is repeated in other House (steps 1 through 7)
10. Bill goes back to first House
11. If first House disapproves amendments, bill goes to committee
12. Both Houses vote on conference committee report
13. If passed, signed by the Presiding officers
14. Goes to President
15. President either signs or vetoes
16. If he signs, or fails to act within 10 days, the bill becomes a law

Introducing the Bill in the House

When the bill is finally ready, Jones is authorized by the committee to introduce it in the House. The first step is a simple one—he simply drops a copy of the bill, bearing his signature as sponsor, into a box near the presiding officer's desk. The clerk of the House assigns a number, say HR 126, to the bill, meaning it is the 126th bill to be introduced in the House of Representatives during this session. At this point, until recently, the bill received its "first reading" by title only. Nowadays, however, when a bill is introduced, its title appears in the *Congressional Record* for that day. The bill is then referred by the Speaker to the Committee on Agriculture. A copy of the bill is also sent to the printers, where it is printed for distribution to all Congressmen and any other interested parties.

139

After any bill has been referred to the appropriate committee, there are at least six different ways the committee may deal with it. (See chart, p. 139, for these.) We know that the Jones bill is not likely to be either killed or completely rewritten in committee since considerable party support was won for it before it was even introduced. There will nevertheless be many obstacles to overcome before the bill will ever become a law.

The Bill in Committee

The major standing committees in Congress will have scores (sometimes hundreds) of bills and problems with which to deal in any one session of Congress. The Agriculture Committee is no exception. To avoid tying down the entire committee for days or weeks, a temporary subcommittee of five members is appointed to study the Jones bill full time.

Any program like federal price support for milk would be highly controversial. To learn the opinions of all interested organizations and individuals on this measure, the subcommittee begins its work by holding public hearings on the bill. Speakers for and against the program are called to testify before the subcommittee. They are heard with courtesy and attention. Since what they say is reported in the press and on radio and television, it reaches not only the committee members but also their constituents. Members of the committee may hear opinions from people whose votes are very important to them, some favoring, others opposing the bill.

When the hearings are finally completed, the subcommittee has many conferences with representatives of the Department of Agriculture, since that department of the executive branch would have to administer the law if it passed. Criticisms and suggestions from that department must be seriously considered. This means that the bill gets a second working over by experts in the economics and politics of agriculture.

The Bureau of the Budget, also in the executive branch, must be consulted, since the program is going to cost a lot of money. The Treasury will demand to know where the money is coming from. Finally, the White House advisers to the President will be greatly interested, since Jones's bill will affect the whole country and will be politically important because it may stir up public controversy.

After weeks of study and consultation, a modified Jones Dairy Bill is reported by the subcommittee to the chairman of the Committee on Agriculture. The committee studies the modified bill and the report of the subcommittee. A majority of the committee members vote in favor of the bill, and it is then reported to the House with the recommendation that it be passed. The Rules Committee places it on the House Calendar (see p. 124), and it awaits its turn.

The Bill in the Committee of the Whole

When a bill of relatively minor importance comes before the House, it receives its "second reading" and is quickly passed or killed. An important measure like the Jones bill, however, requires lengthy consideration and debate. To speed up this process, the House adjourns and then, without even having the members leave their seats, promptly reconvenes as the **Committee of the Whole.** There are several advantages to this special parliamentary device. For one thing, only 100 members are required to be present for a **quorum** in the Committee of the Whole. (A **quorum** is the number necessary by law to be present for transacting business.) A House quorum requires 218 members to be present. Again, the House is not legally in session and the Speaker of the House steps down from his chair to let another member preside. Many House rules are suspended; there is no roll call and debate is freer, less formal. Many have said that Representatives appear at their best when debating in the Committee of the Whole.

Jones's dairy bill receives its second reading in the Committee of the Whole. This time it is read in its entirety. Each section is separately considered, approved or amended, and then voted upon. No member may speak more than once or longer than five minutes on any one amendment. Debate is thus rapid fire, to the point, and frequently very effective. Since votes are not published, voting is quicker and less restrained. After the entire bill has been debated and approved, the Committee of the Whole adjourns. Jones's bill is then sent out to be engrossed (reprinted) with all the changes included.

Action in the House

The report of the Committee of the Whole on Jones's bill is formally adopted by the House, and the bill receives its third reading, this time by title only. General House debate on the measure is now ready to begin. The overall time allowed for debate, divided fairly between both sides, has been determined in advance by the majority and minority floor leaders. Such a restriction on debate is always necessary because of the size of the House. A relatively small number of the 435 members will want to debate this (or any other) measure, but it is obvious that the privilege of unlimited debate, so cherished by the Senate, cannot be exercised in the House. A rule passed in 1841 limits House debates to one hour for each member. Unanimous consent is necessary to extend this limit. Moreover, any member has the privilege at any time to "move the previous question" (propose that a vote be taken). If this is done before any debate has taken place, each side is allowed twenty minutes for debate. If debate has already begun when a member "moves the previous question," no further debate is permitted.

When House debate on Jones's bill is over, it is ready to be put to a final vote. There are four possible methods of voting in the House: (1) by **voice**

Standing Committees of the Senate of the United States
(Each bill introduced into the Senate is referred to a committee.)

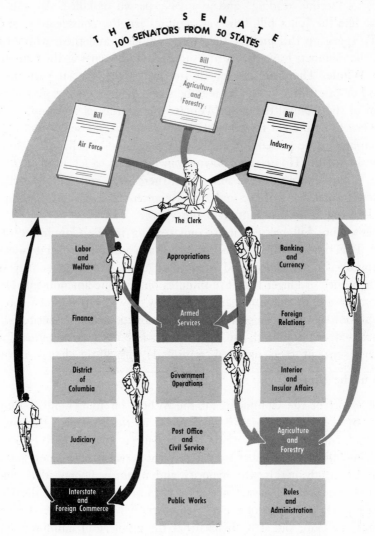

After being introduced in the Senate, a bill is numbered by the clerk. Then a messenger takes it to the appropriate committee, which appoints a subcommittee to study it. This subcommittee holds hearings to get opinions from many different sources; it requests suggestions from informed government officials. After many weeks of intensive study, it reports back to the committee. No Senator serves on more than two committees (see p. 128). This is an important limitation because most of Senate work is done in committees, and no Senator could keep well enough informed (considering all his other obligations) to participate intelligently in more than two.

The House committee system functions similarly though it has some differences (see pp. 122–124).

(those favoring the bill say "aye," those opposed, "no," and the speaker decides which prevails); (2) by a **standing vote,** used if a member questions the accuracy of the voice vote (in turn, members who favor and members who oppose stand and are counted by the clerk); if there is still a question about the vote, then (3) by a **teller vote,** used if one-fifth of the quorum (44 Representatives) demand it (tellers appointed from each side count the members who favor the bill as they pass between them and announce the number; then the tellers count those opposed as they pass); (4) by a **roll-call vote,** used if one-fifth of the members present demand it (each member replies "yea" or "nay" when his name is called, and his vote is recorded by the clerk).

The Jones Dairy Bill finally hurdles the last obstacle in the House when a majority of the members present vote in its favor. The Speaker signs the bill, and it is ready to be delivered to the Senate.

When all these aspects of the lawmaking process are considered, it is obvious that Jones will be very lucky indeed if a measure anything like the one he promised his voters back home is ever actually passed. Described in this way—and we could add still more detail—the legislative process seems both laborious and frustrating. It is. But this is ultimately a very good thing indeed. Freedom requires much restraint. Important restraints are written into the Constitution through checks and balances. Other restraints are written into law. But the most effective of all restraints against hasty and unwise lawmaking is found in the process itself. If at times we and our Congressmen lose patience, we at least retain our liberty.

A Bill in the Senate

Although, in general, a bill goes through the same steps in the Senate as it does in the House, there are some important differences. After a Senator introduces the bill, it is assigned a number and the presiding officer sends it along to the proper standing committee. If and when that committee reports it favorably to the Senate, it will be placed on the Senate Calendar. Unlike the House, the Senate has only one calendar for all bills. Bills are usually taken up in the order in which they appear on the calendar, although the majority leader may change this order should he so desire. Appropriation bills receive some priority over other measures, but no bills are considered to be "privileged" as some are in the House. When the bill finally reaches the Senate floor, the Senate does not resolve itself into a Committee of the Whole except when it deals with treaties. The Senate, a much smaller body than the House, has found it more practical to carry on the bulk of its business without using this parliamentary device. Debates on measures other than treaties are thus held in regular Senate meetings with a majority (51) of the Senators present to constitute a quorum.

Last Steps in the Lawmaking Process

An important measure seldom gets through either house without having a number of changes made in it. Sometimes a bill will emerge with little except its number and title still intact! Many amendments added in one house will not be acceptable to the other.

No bill can be acted upon by the President until it is passed by both houses in *identical form*. To work out a version of the bill acceptable to both houses, a **conference committee** is appointed by the presiding officer in each house. Eventually the conference committee works out a form on which it can agree, though on some measures it may take many days or even weeks of hard work. When a compromise is reached, the conference committee sends the new version of the bill back to each house. If approved by both houses, it is **enrolled** (printed in final form and signed by the presiding officer of each house). It is then sent to the White House for presidential action.

If the President signs the bill, it becomes law immediately. If he vetoes it, the bill is killed unless it is passed again by a two-thirds majority in both houses. He may not wish either to sign or to veto it; in this event he can simply ignore it. The bill would then become law automatically after ten days. If Congress adjourns before the ten days are up, and the President refuses to sign it, the bill "dies" at the end of the ten-day period. This is known as a **pocket veto** (see p. 53).

PRESSURE GROUPS AND THE PROCESS OF LAWMAKING

Almost every organized group in the country is concerned at one time or another about laws or policies that Congress may consider. Labor unions, religious organizations, wheat farmers, petroleum producers, manufacturers of heavy equipment, veterans, teachers, lawyers, physicians—almost any group you can think of has special interests which it feels Congress should nurture and protect. These special-interest groups, or pressure groups, make their views known through **lobbyists** in Washington. Lobbyists get their name from their practice of talking to Congressmen and Senators in the lobbies just off the floor of the two houses. Their activities, however, range far beyond corridor conversations with Congressmen. These people devote great time and energy to persuading members of Congress to vote for or against particular measures. In the case of Congressman Jones's dairy bill, for example, lobbyists for consumer groups, labor unions, business associations, and taxpayer groups interested in government economy may all oppose the measure and try hard to persuade members to kill or pigeonhole it. On the other hand, lobbyists

"HAIL, HAIL,
THE GANG'S ALL HERE!"

Pletcher in
Sioux City Journal

who represent dairy farmers' associations, some labor groups, and some business groups favoring Jones's bill will lobby vigorously to get it passed. Thus a Congressman reckons not only with the politics of congressional procedure but also with public opinion throughout the whole country.

Approximately 400 national organizations employ full-time lobbyists in Washington. Others hire lobbyists for temporary periods while a particular measure is before Congress. Many of them are paid high salaries—$60,000 a year or more, though the average salary is likely to be much lower. They serve as professional agents to push whatever cause their client has in mind. Sometimes ex-Congressmen become lobbyists, taking advantage of their knowledge of Washington politics and of the personalities in Congress who make our national policies.

Before 1946, Congress made little attempt to control the activities of professional lobbyists in Washington. In 1946, however, the Federal Regulation of Lobbying Act, part of the Legislative Reorganization Act, provided that lobbyists must register with the clerk of each house so that they are known for what they represent. The act provided that they must file an account of their expenses so that both members of Congress and the public may know how much a particular interest group is spending to influence legislation. However, enforcement of this act has failed to reduce noticeably the intense activities of the lobbyists.

Some good bills may have been killed and some bad bills passed through the influence of lobbyists. However, it is also true that such worthy causes as aid to education, civil rights legislation, minimum wage laws have been backed by lobbyists of special-interest groups. The lobby has been called a "third house of Congress." If all lobbying were outlawed tomorrow, the many diverse interest groups in our increasingly complex society would need to devise some other way to express their views to Congress effectively.

WHAT MANNER OF MEN?

What kind of men are they who serve in the Congress of the United States? Consider the three men from your own state who serve you in the Congress. What do you really know about the Representative from your district in the House of Representatives? What do you know about the two men who represent your state in the Senate? What sort of previous experience have they had? What positions do they take on issues? If you carefully think out your answers, you will have a better idea of a typical member of Congress.

Unfortunately, perhaps, the Senate is often best known to the general public through the activities of its "characters." Some Senators "make a career" of investigations. Others play the "lone wolf." Such Senators are not likely to be typical. On the contrary, the typical Senator is a quiet man who makes public appearances and gets headlines because his opinions are genuinely important or he has seniority in the Senate. He has often been a governor of his state with a long career in practical politics behind him. He is likely to be a lawyer, probably a specialist in some branch of the law. Typically he is well educated. He works hard in committee, studying problems, working at legislation, negotiating with colleagues. He gives much time to meeting visitors. While he is on the lookout to serve the interests of his state, he is also greatly concerned with matters of policy which affect his party, the nation as a whole, and the world.

A Senator actually speaks very little on the floor of the Senate, but he spends much time talking with other Senators and with lobbyists or members of the executive branch in the Senate cloakrooms. He does a good deal of traveling and public speaking. He is likely to be a very important figure in his party. His manner will be marked by good will, by easy accessibility, and by deference to his colleagues of both parties. In fact, the Senate itself, with its spirit of sportsmanship and good manners and its sense of its real dignity among parliamentary bodies, may mean more to him than his political party. Genuine ability and good judgment are his two most important characteristics.

In certain ways a typical member of the House is quite similar to a Senator: he is accessible, affable, hard-working, and does not come much to public notice. He is likely to be a lawyer and to have some useful specialized knowledge. In other respects the House member is less like his senatorial colleagues. The House member is younger than a Senator, is less well known, even in his home state, has less influence (as an individual) on public opinion and on shaping party or national policy. After all, he is one of 435 while the Senator is one of only 100.

The House member represents a district within his state, not the whole state (unless he is a Congressman-at-large from a state having only one member of the House). Thus he may be more closely identified with a particular interest group than the typical Senator. He may represent, for example, a farm district or a heavily industrial district, and he will be likely to think of himself as a spokesman for such a district. While some House members, like Democrat Sam Rayburn of Texas or Republican Joe Martin of Massachusetts, are very proud to make a career in the House, quite often a House member has other political ambitions, such as a seat in the Senate, his state governorship, or a judgeship. In a way, House members tend to be "on the way up," while Senators have "arrived."

A Congressman's Day

Although lawmaking is the main business of a Congressman, he does have other duties and tasks—many others—to fill his days and sometimes his nights.

Just what does he do? How does he spend his time outside of sessions of Congress? What are the various ways in which he represents us?

A member of the House of Representatives has his office in the House Office Building, close to the Capitol; a Senator, in the Senate Office Building opposite. A Representative's staff, provided by law, includes an administrative assistant, personal secretary, and four to ten other persons who work as researchers, assistants, and stenographers. Senators are allowed somewhat larger staffs than Representatives since they represent a whole state and have a larger volume of correspondence and other business.

The heaviest continuing responsibility of the Congressman and his staff is handling the mail and the telephone. A Congressman's constituents rightly expect him to look after their interests with the national government, do errands for them in Washington, and keep them informed on matters in which they have a particular concern. In addition, of course, he must represent the views of *all* his constituents on legislative matters.

147

An ordinary day's mail for a Congressman may contain requests for government documents from citizens concerned about a particular matter, publicists, journalists, professors in the local college or university, political clubs, labor union offices, business offices, and so on. Organizations ask him to use his influence for or against this or that program. There may be letters from business concerns in his district asking him to get them an opinion, a ruling, or simply information from such agencies as the Federal Trade Commission or the Interstate Commerce Commission. There may be letters asking him to make public appearances and speeches, to appear on radio or television, to write articles, or to receive visitors from home. National organizations write hoping to get him to support or oppose certain bills. There may be letters asking for help in getting jobs in government, or recommendations to employers, or appointments to military academies. Letters from local political leaders may come in, dealing with party political problems, finances, and positions. And then, though our list cannot be complete, there may be letters from individual constituents discussing public questions and offering advice, or criticism, or, less often, praise.

What happens to all these letters? Some, like requests for information, are handled by his staff. A large portion of the letters are answered over the Congressman's own signature. Many of them demand his careful attention. Because he must always be thinking of reëlection, a Congressman must never risk offending individuals or groups by ignoring them. Some requests will require the Congressman to make personal calls on other government officials; others can be handled by his staff. Much of his business is transacted by telephone, both by himself and by his staff. However it is done, every request gets some sort of attention. Many Congressmen say that they are more influenced by thoughtful letters from their constituents than by anything else.

Other demands require even more of the Congressman's time than the mail. As a member of at least two committees,[1] he must attend from two to six or eight committee meetings each week. He must go to public hearings on pending legislation, carry out research assignments, and hold conferences with colleagues. In these duties, he is aided by the committee staff as well as his own, but there are certain duties only he can carry out. Among other things, he must read widely to keep up with developments on matters covered by his committees, as well as on other legislation going through Congress. He must read committee reports, transcripts (written reports) of hearings, proposed bills, and other documents. And he must devote some time simply to reading the newspapers and the weekly and monthly magazines of opinion.

Then there are the visitors! From a delegation of home-town school children to the county chairman of his party or the mayor of the principal city in his district, the parade of callers is endless. All of them expect to see their

[1] One *standing committee* and one *subcommittee*.

Congressman, and most of them do. The visits may seem unduly short to the caller, but to the Congressman it seems as though he can never have time enough to collect his wits (or call his wife)!

Calls by newsmen and lobbyists always have to be handled with care and require a good deal of time. An offense to a newsman is bad politics, while lobbyists often represent groups of such great numbers or wealth or power that their views must be heard courteously and at length.

Finally, the Congressman has heavy social obligations. Entertainment is no small part of politics and government. There are invitations to receptions at the embassies and legations of foreign countries. There are dinners and parties given by members of the government—Congress, the executive, and the judiciary. And, of course, a Congressman is obliged to do some entertaining himself. He cannot function as an effective representative unless he is well acquainted with people of influence in all branches of government. Social acquaintance may often be more valuable than close working relationships. Time simply will not permit a Congressman to take part in all the social activities to which he is invited. But it is common for a Congressman to be engaged every night and every afternoon in the week. If he can find time to spend with personal friends, he is fortunate.

Washington does not consume the whole life of a Senator or Representative. Committee assignments frequently take him here and there about the country. Speaking engagements out of town must be filled. Most important of all, he must go home to keep close to the citizens he represents and to whom he must appeal for reëlection. He is invited to appear at an endless number of events back home. Since he can attend only a few, they have to be well chosen. And while he is at home, he must be sure to make himself available to the press, to his friends, and to fellow politicians.

If it makes you tired just to read such an account as this of the life and duties of a Congressman, you can perhaps get some notion of the kind of character and stamina the holding of congressional office requires. Too few of us understand how much work we expect of our Congressman—in addition to making the laws. We fail to realize to what an extent the Congressman is expected to take care of odd jobs and errands in the hours when he might be profitably working at making the nation's laws.

Today, as in the past, there are in Congress many persons who are outstanding in their ability and in their services to their country. Under the democratic process, we as citizens should work to increase their number.

What Are the Qualities of Leadership?

Young people who have been polled on the qualities of good political leaders regularly place high on their lists the characteristic of *honesty*. We do not expect our Senators and Representatives to be of average honesty. We expect them to be *outstanding*.

THE WORK OF OUR CONGRESSMEN

Work on the floor of Congress is only a small part of the duties of a Congressman. Committee meetings take a lot of time, and they must be prepared for. The Library of Congress, where a Legislative Reference Service finds facts, checks figures, procures publications, is one essential research center.

Campaigning in their home states is a continuing duty of Congressmen. This requires actual political speeches at election time, or appearances at picnics, dinners, and other such local functions between elections.

Congressmen must be prepared to meet the press between legislative sessions, committee meetings, and other duties, since the newspapers play a vital role in keeping the public informed of the activities of their representatives.

And a never-ending duty is that of answering the letters that pour in from constituents—raising questions, requesting favors, demanding action, asking for appointments—all of which must be answered carefully and promptly.

Fortunately, one important exclusive power of the Congress has had to be exercised only once in our history. The House voted to impeach President Johnson and the Senate tried him, issuing these tickets to the public to attend the emotion-packed proceedings. Johnson was acquitted in a one vote decision.

151

Another characteristic of the good political leader, in Congress or in any other part of government, is *courage*. He will need courage, in the first place, to go into a campaign, since his opponents can be expected to criticize him, misunderstand him, and misquote him. They will attack his record and his platform, and perhaps even his family. A campaign may be a nerve-racking experience. It is not the only test of a Congressman's courage. Sometimes he must stand up for what he knows is right and best, even though pressure groups and his own constituents are urging him to vote otherwise. Such a stand, since it may cost him votes, calls for courage.

It almost goes without saying that a Congressman should be *intelligent*. This does not mean that our representatives in either house must be experts in every subject from atomic power to social security. They must know how to use the services of experts, however; they must have that intelligence which enables them to work effectively with other members of Congress.

This suggests another important requirement for a Congressman. He must *genuinely like people* and be naturally sympathetic toward them. Unselfish and very nearly tireless, he must be ambitious to serve others, as well as to advance himself, and he must have confidence in his own ability.

Since in politics, as elsewhere, good men differ as to what is good, and just men differ as to what is just, a successful Congressman must also be able to *appreciate the merit of views other than his own*. A rare quality this may be; but the legislator must possess it or be a certain failure. His fellow Congressmen, a cross section of the American people, represent many more points of view than there are members in Congress. Under these circumstances, a Congressman will seldom get his own way. He must acquire great skill in the technique of compromise. He must understand the necessity for it and learn to excel in it. As a first-rate legislator, he will realize that it is this great principle of compromise that "makes democracy work."

It does not follow that a legislator must be spineless, or that he must have no opinions of his own. The good legislator does not search for compromise at the outset but knows when he must surrender some of his ground in order to hold the rest. Legislating is an art which can be cultivated. Skill comes through experience. For this reason some men serve for a great many years despite the changing fortunes of their party.

Some years ago Henry Ashurst of Arizona, who had been in the Senate for thirty years, was defeated for re-nomination in his party primary. His words spoken in the Senate following his defeat are well worth remembering.

Mr. President, I shall not waste any time on such miserable twaddle as to say that I ought to have been elected. A man only moderately versed in statesmanship, and with only a small degree of sportsmanship, is bound to admit that in a free republic, in a government such as ours, it is the undoubted right of the people to change their servants, and to remove one and displace him with another at any time they choose, for a good reason, for a bad reason, or for no reason at all. If we are to remain a free people, it is the duty of public servants not grumpily and sourly to accept the verdict of the majority, but joyously to accept that verdict; and I joyously accept the verdict of my party. . . . I should be lacking in frankness, I should be disingenuous if I failed to say that they probably had a fairly good reason for displacing me. . . .

It is certainly not easy to be a good Congressman. The requirements are high and the burdens are heavy. Why then do so many capable men—and women—go into this kind of political life? High on the list of reasons would be the recognition the Congressman gets from his fellow citizens as a person of importance. Furthermore, it must seem worth while to the Congressman to put in such long hours in order to take an active part in the great events of his country and age. And there must be a deep satisfaction in working hard at what one believes in deeply. This is a satisfaction the plain citizen can share, as we shall suggest in Chapter 18, by doing the kind of political work which is open to all.

CONGRESSIONAL INVESTIGATIONS

The subcommittees appointed by the standing committees in both houses do a great deal of the work in the field of investigation. Most of the investigations carried on by congressional committees have to do with preparing legislation. They rest on the right of Congress to collect any and all information which will aid it in enacting laws. The routine investigations as to cattle-marketing conditions, safety measures in the mines, numbers of fish exported and imported, number of employees needed in a certain bureau of one of the executive departments, cost of a certain type of heavy bomber, and so forth— these are colorless. The color and the public notice come with investigations of a different sort: investigations into crime, subversive activities, and corruption in government.

The power of Congress to investigate whatever it pleases is often disputed by students of American constitutional government. More than one committee has had its right to investigate challenged by citizens called before it who refuse to testify. But in general, the power has stood the tests both of court action and of custom. Almost any investigation can be defended as having a bearing on some possible law. Thus investigations into corruption on the part of executive officials may be related to appropriations for the executive branch; investigations into crime of big cities may be related to laws on federal aid to education; investigations of "racketeering" in labor unions may relate to the amending of labor laws; while investigations of Communist or other subversive influences in public organizations may be related to laws governing the punishment of conspiracy against the government.

Procedure of Investigations

The procedure of a congressional investigation is relatively simple. Either house may pass a resolution authorizing an investigation. It may also be launched by a committee having continuing authority granted at the time it was set up, as in the case of the Senate's Permanent Investigating Subcommittee.

Once a decision is made by the chairman and a majority of his committee to make a particular investigation, the first work is done by staff members. In their preliminary investigation the committee counsel and staff director hunt for suitable witnesses, interview them, and take testimony which may provide further "leads." When a substantial number of reliable witnesses and a fair volume of evidence has been accumulated in this way, the staff makes a report to the committee. The next step normally is to call witnesses before the committee, where they are interviewed under oath by the committee members guided by staff people familiar with the testimony to be offered. Sometimes the witnesses are brought to hearing rooms in Washington; on other occasions the committee, or one or two of its members, may travel to other places to conduct the investigation. The investigations into crime conducted by the Kefauver Committee of the Senate in 1950–1951 moved from city to city across the country. The McClellan Committee's investigation into the activities of labor unions in 1958 brought people from all over to Washington. Investigations of the Senate's Permanent Investigating Subcommittee are often held at governmental installations in various parts of the country or in cities where there are important defense production plants. On the other hand, a great deal of the work of investigating committees is completed in Washington after investigators have worked in the field during the preliminary stages.

Some of the hearings are held in what are known as **executive sessions.** This means that the press and the public are excluded. The record of testimony taken in executive sessions may later be published if a majority of the committee votes to do so. Frequently executive sessions are held as a kind of dress rehearsal for public hearings.

DOCUMENTS OF THE PROCEEDINGS When an investigation is completed, two documents are normally published. One is a report to the house of Congress in whose name the investigation was conducted. The other is the record of the proceedings. In general, the report is relatively brief, but the record may run to several volumes.

All such documents are available to the public from the Government Printing Office or from the offices of members of Congress. The materials thus available (from the Superintendent of Documents) are of enormous value to students of government, publicists, and politicians, as well as to citizens enough interested to ask for them. An example is the long series of reports and records issued by the House Committee on Un-American Activities. Such public papers as "100 Things You Should Know about Communism" give detailed and accurate information regarding not only the activities of Communists but also the theory and practice of communism, which is very helpful to anyone wishing to understand the nature of the Communist threat to freedom. Similarly valuable information has been published by the House Committee on Foreign Affairs, showing how the world Communist movement has developed, and making available the basic teachings of world Communist leaders.

The Citizen and Congressional Investigations

In recent years there have been times when the investigations of Congress have seemed to overshadow their lawmaking. The two functions are related, as we have seen. Investigations, however, sometimes get widespread publicity through newspapers, radio, and television. For this reason, every citizen should understand the procedures of congressional investigations and the purposes for which they are conducted so that he may decide what his own position is with reference to them. Unfortunately, citizens have often been more confused than enlightened by what are intended to be searches for information.

Amendment I, as we have seen, protects all citizens in their right to freedom of speech. Amendment V protects the citizen's right to refuse to give testimony which might incriminate him. Amendment XIV secures the civil rights of citizens against state governments as well as the national government, so that these rights also protect citizens in investigations conducted by state legislatures. These constitutional provisions have their bearing on the relation between citizens and congressional investigations. On the other hand, if Congress cannot obtain needed information, it cannot enact wise laws. It is therefore the obligation of citizens to provide whatever information they can to authorized officials of government at every level. In general, it is very much to their interest to do so. Thus, it is a good rule of thumb for the citizen to give full and truthful testimony whenever he is called upon by congressional committees. Occasions may arise when a refusal to testify, or to answer certain questions, may be to the interest of the citizen and entirely in keeping with law and democratic procedure. Let us consider some examples.

A Congressman conducting an investigation can use his position to harm a political opponent, by asking questions having to do with the private opinions of a citizen. Under such circumstances, it is proper for the citizen to refuse to answer if he so chooses, since it may be an invasion of privacy.

On the other hand, if a citizen is asked by a congressional investigator whether he has done such and such a thing or belonged to such and such an organization, it is not a matter of opinion but of fact. The citizen has a duty to answer the questions, unless truthful answers would lay him open to prosecution for a criminal offense. In that case, the citizen is entitled to plead the privilege of Amendment V and refuse to answer.

An interesting example of the use of Amendment V arises in the case of gamblers. Gambling is not a crime under federal law. Under the laws of some states gambling is illegal, while under others it is permitted. Thus, if a congressional committee investigating crime asks a witness whether he is a gambler by profession, the witness is in a difficult position. A truthful answer would not incriminate him under federal law, but the same answer, made under oath, appearing in the public record of the hearing, might be used by a state prosecutor to bring him to trial under the laws of a state. In such cases, the Courts have held that the witness is entitled to plead Amendment V and refuse to answer. On the other hand, a witness who refuses to answer may be cited for **contempt** of Congress. An act of Congress in 1954 provided that in certain cases a witness may be given immunity from prosecution by a Court order secured on committee request by the Attorney General. If the citizen then refuses to testify, he may by a vote of Congress be charged in federal court with **contempt** (illegal refusal to co-operate or illegal conduct before Congress). If the Court decides that truthful answers would not have incriminated the citizen, he may be fined or imprisoned or both.

Among the most common cases of refusal to testify are those of alleged subversive activities. A Communist may plead Amendment V when asked whether he is or has been a member of the Communist Party, since a truthful answer might show him guilty of a crime under the law. Sometimes, however, a witness who may not be and may never have been a Communist has refused to testify, either because he does not wish to give the names of friends who might be called before the committee or because he wishes to defy the committee. Such a witness runs a risk of being cited for contempt.

In the long run, it is wise for the citizen to coöperate with his government rather than to defy it. Through the democratic process, the citizen can work to defeat at the next election any Congressman who seems to be abusing his privilege.

When a congressional committee is investigating possible or alleged crimes, however, citizens may sometimes be subjected to treatment which would not be tolerated in a court of law. At times members of congressional investigating committees seem to have forgotten that they are *investigators*, not *prosecutors*.

156

Congress itself has become increasingly aware of the dangers of abusing its powers of investigation. Both houses are concerned to have rules which will at once bring in the maximum of needed information to Congress and protect the rights and reputations of individual citizens. It seems clear that the solution to the problem of abuse lies in the improvement of rules rather than in the curtailing of the powers of Congress. Current practice has gone far in this direction. Witnesses are now allowed to be accompanied by counsel, to make statements and file briefs in their own defense. Before some committees, they may now call witnesses on their own behalf and even cross-examine hostile witnesses. While, as we have said, congressional committees are not courts of law, Congress is improving rules and procedures by imitating many of the practices of our courts.

SUMMARY

In this chapter you have seen how the theory of lawmaking in a free legislature is carried out in practice. You have learned, through the example of Representative Jones's dairy bill, how the process works in the Congress of the United States, how public opinion is brought to bear on lawmaking, and what we mean by politics in the legislative way of life. At the same time you have had a glimpse of the complexities involved in our national governmental procedures—the interrelationships of individual legislators, committees, houses of Congress, and various agencies of the executive branch. You have noticed that legislation is normally a slow and somewhat frustrating process, but you should begin to realize how important these procedures are, in spite of delays, since they result in laws most representative of the wishes of the people and protect us from hasty and ill-considered measures.

You have considered the qualifications of Senators and House members and studied in detail how a Congressman spends his time. Now that you know what a Congressman actually does, you are in a better position to select your representatives intelligently, and to understand how heavy a load they carry.

Finally, you have considered the purposes and procedures of congressional investigations and have seen how important a part they play in the legislative process and in bringing citizens close to the lawmaking of the nation. You have learned that if the power of investigation is sometimes abused, it is nevertheless vitally important that Congress have the facts in order to legislate wisely. As a citizen you will need to form your own views as to where personal privacy ends and public responsibility begins in your own life.

KNOW WHAT YOU READ

1. What are the different forms of congressional action?
2. What requirements did Representative Jones meet to be eligible for election to the House?
3. In what ways is a first-year Congressman equal to members with more years of service? In what ways is he not their equal?
4. Why is it that a law often differs from the bill that was introduced in a house of Congress?
5. Outline the steps by which Representative Jones's bill became a law.
6. What is the purpose of forming the House into a Committee of the Whole?
7. "There are six different ways the committee may deal with a bill." Study the drawing on page 139, and list these six ways.
8. What activities must a Congressman perform as a member of a standing committee?
9. In what ways may groups of citizens try to influence lawmakers?
10. What are the qualities we citizens should look for in our representatives in government?
11. Describe the daily mail of a member of Congress.
12. Summarize the demands made on the time of a member of Congress.
13. What are the rewards a Congressman may expect from his service in Congress?
14. Why are congressional investigations necessary? Why do most of them receive so little publicity?
15. What are the steps by which an investigation is made? How are its findings reported?
16. What rights does Mr. John Citizen have when he is questioned by an investigating committee? What responsibilities does he have?
17. Under what conditions might a citizen plead Amendment V and refuse to answer a question?

WHAT DO YOU THINK?

1. Review the qualities we citizens should look for in our representatives in government. What qualities have they the right to expect in us?
2. Mr. Johnson has just been elected to Congress and means to be a good Representative. Why must he learn to respect and accept the judgment of other members of the House? Does this mean that he must have no mind of his own? Explain.
3. Mr. Smith is a member of Congress who would like to make himself nationally known in a hurry. Why might he try to use an investigation for this purpose?

4. William A. Citizen is going to testify before a committee of Congress. He does not know whether to defy the committee, since he disapproves of its work, or to coöperate despite his disapproval. What would you advise him to do?
5. What do you think of this statement? "Everybody who comes here to the capitol wants us to subsidize his group and regulate every other group."
6. "The precedent-setting even-year Legislature, filmed for the first time by TV movie cameras, began with the House sitting at 10:40 A.M. The Senate followed suit shortly after noon." This was reported in a Topeka, Kansas, newspaper. What do you think of having sessions of lawmaking bodies filmed for TV? What bearing on this question do the privileges and immunities discussed in Chapter 5 have?
7. Should a member of Congress vote for what he thinks best for the country as a whole, or as he thinks his constituents want him to vote? Explain

PROBLEMS AND PROJECTS FOR YOU

1. Prepare and present an original dramatization in which citizens—represented by people in your class—appear at a hearing to speak for and against proposed legislation. You may select for a topic some current issue, or you may invent an issue (such as the proposal to run a toll road through the middle of your community, or the abandonment of several small high schools to make one large consolidated school).
2. Use the following quotations as the subject of a report to the class, a panel discussion, or a cartoon. You might even interview adults in your community to find out what they think about the subject.

> This tendency to substitute a democracy for a republic began with the gradual and progressive reduction of a representative to the grade of a mere delegate. . . . It is commonly assumed that the first duty of a Senator or a Representative in Congress is to his constituency. . . . This is fundamentally wrong. . . . A national legislator is chosen to serve his country, not any section of it. He is paid by the United States, not by his particular district. (*John C. Clark*)

> This country is a republic. A Senator is supposed to hear all the arguments and decide every case by exercising his own judgment. If we merely counted the letters, pro and con, that would amount to a referendum. It would not be government by representation. (*Alex Holmes*)

3. The cartoon on p. 145 indicates the multitude of pressing problems with which members of Congress must deal each session. Considering these facts carefully, what do you think ought to be the character of the men you send to Washington as your representatives?
4. (*debate*) Resolved: That since the people are intelligent enough to govern themselves, they do not need protection by censorship—hence free speech, a free press, and academic freedom are necessary.

EXTEND YOUR VOCABULARY

simple resolution	rider	standing vote
concurrent resolution	price support	teller vote
joint resolution	subsidy	roll-call vote
bill	Committee of the Whole	pocket veto
public bill	quorum	lobbyist
private bill	conference committee	executive sessions
act	voice vote	contempt

YOUR NOTEBOOK: THE GOVERNMENT OF ——

1. Write down the names of your Senators and Representative in Washington.
2. Keep a record of the activities of your Congressmen—their votes on bills before Congress, their speech-making, and other activities reported in your local paper.
3. Make a record of which committees your Congressmen serve on in Washington. What issues before these committees have a special local interest for the people in your community?
4. Write a biography of one of your Senators or your Representative, describing his activity before he entered politics and the road by which he reached Congress.

READ MORE ABOUT IT

BAILEY, STEPHEN, and SAMUEL, HOWARD, *Congress at Work*. Holt, 1953.
    Accurate and interesting.
BURNS, JAMES M., *Congress on Trial*. Harper, 1949.
    Thoughtful and still timely.
FINLETTER, THOMAS K., *Can Representative Government Do the Job?* Reynal and Hitchcock, 1945.
    Thoughtful and provocative.
GRIFFITH, ERNEST S., *Congress: Its Contemporary Role*. New York University Press, 1956.
    An evaluation of the functions of Congress.
KEFAUVER, ESTES, and LEVIN, JACK, *A Twentieth Century Congress*. Duell, Sloan and Pearce, 1947.
    Very readable and thoughtful.
WHITE, WILLIAM S., *The Citadel*. Harper, 1956.
    Justly famous study of the Senate.

CHAPTER 7

The Executive

In this chapter you will meet, or become better acquainted with

The roles of the President
The Executive Office of the President
The President's sources of information
The qualifications of the President
The Vice-President

The Presidency of the United States is said to be the "most powerful secular office in the world"; indeed, our form of government is sometimes described as "presidential government." There is some truth in both these statements. Tradition, circumstances, legislation, and the Constitution itself have built into the presidential office enormous governmental power, a power which reaches directly or indirectly into the lives of all Americans, and even of most of the other people of the world. Thus, every young American male knows what may be meant by a personal "greeting" from the President. Every parent is immediately interested in what the President may say and do about vaccination for polio. Every taxpayer is concerned about the President's policy for spending the public money. In other lands, heads of government must watch the President's every word to see if it holds some significance for their relations with the United States and with each other; and people remote from Washington and knowing no word of English are affected by the President's views on such matters as technical assistance to "underdeveloped areas." For such reasons as these, it is sensible to speak of the American system as "presidential government."

That phrase also means other things. The chief executive of the United States has so many differing responsibilities that his office is closely related

161

to all other branches and functions of government. In a sense he and his office are the nerve center of public life in America.

GROWTH OF THE EXECUTIVE BRANCH

It was not always so. At first under the Constitution the President had, of course, powers of the highest importance, but the conditions of life prevented the concentration of power with which we are so familiar today. There were no telephones or other means of rapid communication. It took weeks for an order from the President to reach any distance from the capital. Without quick and efficient communication and transportation, it was necessary to allow great freedom of action to federal officials in the field. Most of the area of the country was outside the borders of the thirteen states. Although such territories were legally controlled by the President, it was obviously impossible for him to know much about what went on in such vast and remote areas.

The national government itself was extremely simple. In Washington's time there were less than a thousand regular employees of the national government, and there were only about 700 officials on temporary appointment, such as postmasters. By the early 1960's there were more than a thousand people employed in the Office of the President alone. In 1792, Secretary of the Treasury Alexander Hamilton had an assistant, a handful of clerks, and about 660 regular employees, including all the tax collectors for the whole country. Actually Hamilton had charge of about half of all the people working for the United States. Washington began with a secretary and a few clerks. By 1960 there were more than 700 on the immediate staff of the President. The entire executive branch, over which the President presides, has grown from perhaps 2,000 to more than 2,250,000.

But this tremendous growth seems less dramatic when we realize that it has come, over a century and three quarters, as the country itself grew from a small outpost of the Western world with a population of about 4,000,000 in 1790, to world leadership and a population of more than 180,000,000 in the 1960's. Actually the Presidency has struggled constantly to keep pace with events.

THE ROLES OF THE PRESIDENT

The roles of the President are both ceremonial and executive. Both are important. When we speak of a *ceremonial role*, we mean the part played by the President as symbol of the nation and its people. He is the chief of

162

The Executive Branch of the Government of The United States and the Independent Agencies and Commissions

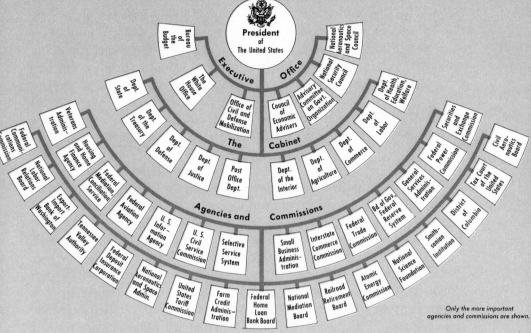

Only the more important agencies and commissions are shown.

Adapted from United States Government Organization Manual, 1959-60

The vastness and complexity of big government are suggested in this chart. Shown here are the executive branch and the independent agencies and commissions. To learn something about these—how they are staffed and how they serve the people of the United States, you will have to turn to other chapters, as suggested below.

Executive Office, Chap. 7
Dept. of State, Chap. 24
Dept. of the Treasury, Chaps. 20 and 21
Dept. of Defense, Chap. 27
Dept. of Justice, Chap. 10
Post Office Dept., Chap. 21
Dept. of Interior, Chap. 23
Dept. of Agriculture, Chap. 23
Dept. of Commerce, Chap. 21
Dept. of Labor, Chap. 22
Dept. of Health, Education, Welfare, Chap. 24
U.S. Civil Service Commission, Chap. 8
General Services Administration, Chap. 8
Veterans Administration, Chap. 8
Housing and Home Finance Agency, Chap. 24
Federal Mediation and Conciliation Service, Chap. 22
U.S. Information Agency, Chap. 8
Selective Service System, Chap. 27
Small Business Administration, Chap. 21
Interstate Commerce Commission, Chap. 8
Federal Trade Commission, Chap. 8
Bd. of Gov., Federal Reserve System, Chap. 21

Federal Power Commission, Chap. 8
Securities and Exchange Commission, Chap. 8
Federal Communications Commission, Chap. 8
National Labor Relations Board, Chap. 8
Export and Import Bank of Washington, Chap. 25
Tennessee Valley Authority, Chaps. 8 and 21
Federal Deposit Insurance Corporation, Chap. 21
United States Tariff Commission, Chap. 20
Farm Credit Administration, Chap. 23
Federal Home Loan Bank Board, Chap. 24
National Aeronautics and Space Administration, Chap. 27
National Mediation Board, Chap. 22
Railroad Retirement Board, Chap. 24
Atomic Energy Commission, Chap. 8
National Science Foundation, Chap. 8
Smithsonian Institution, Chap. 8
District of Columbia, Chap. 14
Tax Court of the United States, Chap. 9
Civil Aeronautics Board, Chap. 8
Federal Aviation Agency, Chap. 8

163

state under our form of government; that is, he is comparable to a king in a monarchy. The founders of the republic were keenly conscious of this role of the President, since in the eighteenth century nearly all governments were monarchies. The American experiment was to be republican, but in order to deal appropriately with foreign powers and to maintain the dignity of the new state, it was felt that the President should have a special place in government and in society. In fact, some Americans of those days would have preferred to make him a king, or at least to give him something like a royal title. At any rate, the idea of the President as chief of state quickly took hold.

The President as Chief of State

The President is always at the head of any list, whether at a state dinner for foreign diplomats and government leaders, at a parade or celebration, or simply at a private party among his friends. On state occasions, he is addressed as "His Excellency, the President of the United States"; otherwise, as "Mr. President." He is never publicly addressed by name.

He receives the credentials of ambassadors and ministers from foreign nations in formal audience. He can also refuse to accept credentials of a foreign representative; in such a case, the country from which the representative comes is not considered to be represented in this country. The President presents decorations and other awards. When he makes an appearance anywhere in the United States, all others present remain standing until he is seated or gives a sign to be seated. That goes for ladies too! American ministers and ambassadors to foreign countries represent the President and assume his ceremonial function at their overseas posts.

It is well to keep in mind that the great deference paid by Americans to the President is not directed to him as an individual. In fact, at any given time, about half of the people are likely to wish he were not in office at all. The deference is paid, rather, to his office as representative of the nation. In an important sense, he embodies our national pride. To help the President maintain the exalted station in which we place him, we provide a home for him—the White House—a salary of $100,000 a year, an expense budget of $50,000 a year, and many services and conveniences.

The President as Chief Executive

It is below the level of ceremony that the work of a republican government is done. When a state dinner is over and the visiting dignitaries have gone home in the late hours of the evening, a king can retire with his day's work done. Typically an American President retires to his study or his bed only to settle down with reports and memoranda, or even to confer with his assistants until the small hours of the following morning. This is because he is **chief executive** as well as chief of state.

Article II of the Constitution, which you should read carefully (see pp. 56–58), establishes the power and authority of the President. It says that the "executive power shall be vested" in him; that he shall have power to make treaties with other nations, "provided two thirds of the Senate present concur"; that he shall make all appointments not otherwise specified in the Constitution; and that he shall recommend to Congress measures to be enacted into law and shall "take Care that the Laws be faithfully executed." That last clause is buried among others, but it has become the most significant power of the President. What it means is that he is both the chief law enforcement officer of the land and the chief administrative officer. It establishes not only his power but also his responsibility to govern the country. Under this power the President may even grant reprieves or pardon convicted criminals.

In his capacity as chief executive, the President not only carries the laws of the land into effect but also issues **executive orders,** under his authorized powers, which have the force of law. For example, in wartime Congress may enact a law for the control of prices and wages in American industry, and the President by executive order may state specifically what these wages and prices shall be; or by executive order he may establish a temporary agency of the government to carry out the law. You should remember that though the executive orders of the President have the force of law, the President may issue them only when a law, or laws, passed by the Congress gives him the necessary authority.

In a different category are **executive agreements.** Article II limits the President's treaty-making power by providing that two-thirds of the Senate must approve. This allows a small one-third to thwart the President's plans for what he thinks is the good of the country; this has, therefore, been a much discussed provision. President Wilson saw the League of Nations rejected because of this very thing. However, sometimes executive agreements allow the President to get around this. These agreements do not require Senate approval; sometimes they are simply carrying out acts of Congress. In other cases, they are acts of the President. When President Franklin Roosevelt arranged to give England over-age destroyers in exchange for leases on strategic bases, it was done by executive agreement. Unless Congress disapproves the agreement, it has the force of law, and the judiciary has so ruled.

The Cabinet

Also in Article II, Section 2 (1 and 2), the Constitution says the President may "require the Opinion . . . . of the principal Officer in each of the executive Departments," and that power to make appointments "may be vested

in the President alone, . . . or in the Heads of Departments." These two references to "Departments" are the constitutional basis for establishment of the cabinet. There are ten departments today, shown in the chart on p. 163. The President appoints a head of each department (with approval of the Congress), and these men serve as his official cabinet (see pp. 179–180). Each department will be discussed in detail in later chapters.

The President as Commander-in-Chief

In Article II, the Constitution states that the President "shall be Commander-in-Chief of the Army and Navy . . . and of the Militia . . . when it is in the actual service of the United States." By making the President commander-in-chief of the armed forces, the Constitution made certain that the military in the United States would be under civilian control. To this important republican idea Americans have always been faithful. Military men elected to the Presidency have all resigned their commissions and entered office as civilians. The President as commander of the military is ultimately responsible for the entire defense program of the country in time of peace, and for the conduct of war when the United States may be engaged. As head of the military establishment, he appoints the Secretary of Defense, the subordinate Secretaries of the Army, Navy, and Air Force, and the military Chiefs of Staff, and heads of the National Security Council. We shall study the Department of Defense in detail in Chapter 27. In general, as commander of the military, the President must deal with certain matters of policy and administration not specifically stated in the Constitution, but certainly necessary in the modern world:

1. He determines the defense policy of the nation with Congress.
2. He recommends the defense budget to the Congress.
3. He appoints the responsible civilian and military officials in the Department of Defense.
4. He commissions the officers of all branches of the armed forces.
5. He administers all laws having to do with defense.
6. He directs the expenses of the defense budget.
7. He directs the stationing of all defensive forces.
8. He directs the strategy of war.
9. He appoints and removes the principal officers of the military command.
10. He presides over the National Security Council.

The largest share of the day-to-day work involved in such matters as these is, of course, delegated to hundreds, even thousands, of others. The point to remember is that the President alone is ultimately responsible for all of them. Washington as commander of the armed forces had a Department of War with about eighty employees and an army of some 5,000 men; a navy

166

was not even authorized until 1798, and then only on a pitifully small scale. President Eisenhower, in the mid-twentieth century, directed a Department of Defense (including Departments of the Army, Navy, and Air Force) with more than a million civilian employees and about three million soldiers, sailors, and airmen. The difference indicates the growth not only in power but also in responsibility of the Presidency. And this is in time of peace. In time of war, President Franklin Roosevelt commanded a military establishment with more than two million civilian employees and more than ten million service men and women. Whereas in the early years of the republic the military budget was counted in the hundreds of thousands, in our time it is figured in the tens of billions.

It is as commander-in-chief also that the President exercises, from time to time, extraordinary direct powers over the people. Congress can and does give the President power to take even extreme measures, such as declaring martial law, moving parts of the population from one place to another, as in relocating Japanese-Americans during World War II, or fixing prices and rationing goods and services. However, as we saw earlier, the President may not exercise such powers *without* acts of Congress. In time of war, regardless of which party controls Congress, great emergency powers are given to the President; but, unlike a dictator, he holds them at the pleasure of Congress, the elected representatives of the people. And he must account for his use of his great emergency powers to the whole people, who may reëlect him or defeat him at the polls.

The President as Budget-Maker

The notion of an executive budget (an annual detailed plan for spending the public money) was almost unheard of in the first years of the Presidency. Washington presided over a handful of departments, and such budget work as was done was managed by Hamilton as Secretary of the Treasury. Today the President is responsible for a budget of some seventy billion dollars (in peacetime). As chief budget officer, he must decide how much money to assign for defense, welfare, foreign aid, construction, education, operation of departments, and numberless other things. His budget in a real sense helps shape the course of American life, and affects the whole world.

Suppose you are working on the assembly line in a plant at South Bend, Indiana, which makes motors for bombers. It could mean a larger annual income to you if the President's budget increases the allotment of funds to the Air Force for the purchase of medium bombers. On the other hand, if the President decides to reduce the government's orders for these bombers, your company may not need so much of your labor and your income may go down.

If you are a public school teacher, the amount of money recommended in the President's budget for assistance to education may determine

167

THE ROLES OF OUR PRESIDENT

The duties of the Presidency have increased in number and become larger in scope every year—so that the roles the President must play tax the strength of the strongest man.

As a politician, the President is chief policy-maker. Theodore Roosevelt in this role persuaded the country to accept many reforms in which he believed.

The President must also be a budget-maker. Though he receives assistance from experts in all phases of the government, it is the President alone who must present the proposed budget to the Congress—as well as a State of the Union message, and an economic message. In the twentieth century, it has become the practice for Presidents to deliver such messages in person, and to address joint sessions of Congress on other occasions, as Coolidge is here doing.

President Franklin D. Roosevelt was acting as leader of the nation when he declared in this fireside chat over the radio in May, 1941, that a state of emergency existed, following the outbreak of World War II in Europe.

As Commander-in-Chief President Truman reviews troops at the airport in 1951, when General Eisenhower left for Europe to organize defenses against communism.

When he in turn became President, General Eisenhower, now a civilian, acted as chief executive in signing into law a Congressional resolution declaring an American Doctrine for the Middle East.

169

whether you continue to work in an old and outmoded building or have a chance to meet your pupils under pleasant and modern conditions in the new building your school district has been hoping to build.

A farmer in India may have heard about better wheat seeds from North Dakota. The amount of money assigned in the President's budget to foreign economic aid may decide whether the farmer will get a supply of such seeds.

PRESIDENTIAL MESSAGES   In his function as budget-maker, the President is assisted by the Bureau of the Budget in his own office, with more than 400 experts, and by substantial budget divisions in all departments of government. It is a duty of the President to present a budget message to the Congress each year, showing in detail how he proposes to spend the public money and requesting the Congress to approve and appropriate it.

The budget message is one of three messages transmitted by the President to the Congress at each of its regular sessions. The Constitution says that the President shall "from time to time give to the Congress Information of the State of the Union, and recommend to their Consideration such Measures as he shall judge necessary and expedient." In accordance with this provision, the President, in our time, sends (or reads in person) a message known as the State of the Union, in which he sets forth the general aims and programs of his administration; a budget message, as we have seen; and an economic message in which he gives an account of the state of economic life in the country and requests measures to maintain or improve it. In addition to these three set messages, the President also sends many special messages asking for particular measures or supplementary funds.

The President as Politician

The President is also the chief policy-maker of the country. In this role, he proposes to the Congress laws which in his judgment will be good for the country in both domestic and foreign affairs. He must take positions on the great questions of public concern which divide the people, and he must try constantly to persuade the Congress and the people to support his views. He is elected on the basis of a program outlined in his campaign, and, subject to changing circumstances, he must seek to have his program enacted. And he must accept responsibility for its success or failure. If he runs for reëlection, it must be on the basis of his record, so that, in addition to his other functions and roles, he must be above all a politician.

Politics, as has often been wisely said, is the "art of the possible." The politician must, therefore, concern himself with what is possible and, to the extent of his own convictions, do what he can to bring it about. He may stand or fall either on his judgment as to what is possible or on his skill in bringing it about. For this reason, it is a mistake to say that the office of the American Presidency requires a President to be "above politics."

At the beginning of government under the Constitution, many people felt that Washington was better qualified than any other citizen to serve as President because he was thought to be "above politics." Washington himself tried hard to live up to this image of himself. He had in his cabinet two men, Hamilton and Jefferson, who opposed each other on basic issues. He tried to bring them to agreement by appeals to patriotism; but, as another friend of Washington's, James Madison, wisely insisted, it is freedom itself which produces differences of opinion and partisanship. The two are inseparable. Washington learned this simple truth from sad experience. In our day, the President's political role is much more complicated. Our citizens should not only understand the necessity that the President be a politician but also applaud him for it.

In our country, public affairs are carried on and decisions made by persuasion. This, again, means that the President to be effective must be a politician. The politician, at any level of government, tries to judge what measures he can persuade a majority of the people to accept, what measures they will not accept, and what measures they might be persuaded to accept after longer experience and education. The President deals with measures and policies broader in scope and more complex than those with which other politicians are concerned. But that is the only difference—and politician the President must be or he cannot govern.

POLICY-MAKING What specifically does this role of the President as politician mean? It means, first of all, that he must be able to get himself elected (see pp. 465–470 for formal procedure). It means that because, once elected, he is a policy-maker, he must strive by persuasion to get his policies adopted. The means at his disposal are many. He is, for example, the head of a great political party (see Chap. 19), usually—though not always—the majority party. The party is more or less committed to the President's policies and program. It is represented in the Congress either by an actual majority of both houses or by very large minorities. In his relations with his party, the President can do much to bring about passage of the bills he wants and the appropriation of funds he needs for his program.

An American political party, as mentioned and as we shall see in Chap. 19, is not an organization of people all devoted to the same things and the same principles. The discipline of the party is loose at best, and it is part of the President's job to hold it as closely in line as he can. He must, of course, do his best to persuade his fellow party members by sheer argument, but when argument fails, he has other techniques available. (See chart, Checks and Balances, p. 73.)

APPOINTMENTS The President may appoint and remove a large number of federal officeholders. He can, if he wishes, approve appointments requested by members of Congress or refuse them, which is one important way in which he can influence legislation (see **patronage,** pp. 439–441). As chief administrator, the President can largely control the expenditure of public money, and he can make use of this power in such a way as to please or to displease a Representative or Senator. His prestige as President, however, may be more useful as a means of persuasion than any other, particularly if he is a popular President. A public appearance or a picture with the President may sometimes mean so much to a Congressman that he will "change his views" in order to get it. The fact is that the balance between a President and members of his party in Congress who may disagree with him is such that negotiation and compromise are always necessary and always in process. On the other hand, the President can usually count on the support of a big majority of the members of his own party.

SUPPORT OF THE OPPOSING PARTY   The President can also usually count on the backing of a significant fraction of the other party. This is because he is usually backed by a majority of the voters in order to be elected, and all politicians must respect the will of the majority. Thus, there will always be some members of the minority party who will support the President either out of conviction or because they wish to conform to majority opinion. On the other hand, the President can also count on a minority organized to oppose him. If it is small, he may choose largely to ignore it. But if it is very large, he must go a certain way to meet it and make every effort to get at least some support from it.

THE VETO AND CONGRESS   In some ways, the President's greatest power is his right—even duty—under the Constitution to veto legislation which he thinks is not in the public interest. If the President refuses to sign a bill passed by Congress, it cannot become law unless two-thirds of both houses pass the bill again. Often the division of party or of interest in one or both houses is so close that a bill cannot get the support of anywhere near two-thirds of the members. The President thus has the final say. The threat of a presidential veto always hovers over a congressional majority which differs from a President on important issues. Sometimes the mere threat of a veto causes Congress to modify the proposed legislation and work out an effective compromise. On the other hand, the President must also be very cautious in his use of the veto. For he must keep the good will of Congress, and he is dependent upon Congress for the appropriation of the money necessary to carry on his functions and program.

As we saw in previous chapters, much of any President's difficulty in controlling Congress arises from the fact that Representatives and Senators (the latter somewhat less so) are often elected on the basis of local or state issues and do not necessarily reflect the will of their constituents in matters of broad national policy. Party label and agreement to a national party platform are often less important to a Congressman than loyalty to his constituents and concern over issues at home. The President must grapple daily with these facts of political life.

THE EXECUTIVE BRANCH The President must also constantly play the role of politician within his own executive branch. The chief departments of the executive branch themselves represent various interests among the people. They reflect those constant differences of opinion which arise, as we saw in the opening chapters, among individuals and groups in our free society. Thus we have departments of labor, agriculture, and commerce which are required by law to serve as best they can the needs of laborers, farmers, and business-men. The departments are directed by secretaries who serve in the President's cabinet and advise him on matters coming under their jurisdiction. Because of their different interests and responsibilities, they often disagree—for exam-ple, over allocation of money. The President must find a way to bring about enough agreement to permit government to act. In doing this, the President is acting as a politician; he must work out compromises. And so it is with numberless relations the President must have with his co-workers in the executive branch.

In our time Congress has enacted broad and general laws which give to the President and the executive branch the right to make decisions and act in many areas. This means that administrators, under the authority of the President, make countless rules and regulations, having the force of law, which bear directly upon you and me as citizens.

**LONG-OVERDUE
PRUNING JOB**

Carmack in
The Christian Science Monitor

DECISION-MAKING Where matters of broad policy are involved, affecting many people or important interest groups, the President himself must weigh the relative strength of opposing forces, to consider how the matter under study fits his overall program, to judge public opinion, and to protect his personal relations with political leaders throughout the country.

This role of the President as politician is crucial to his office and important for us to understand and appreciate. The Dixon-Yates power contract controversy of 1954 is a good illustration. Briefly, this contract provided that the government, through the Atomic Energy Commission, should buy electric power over a period of twenty-five years from a private power company. That company would build a steam-generating plant to provide the electricity. The President favored this contract and rejected an alternative proposal, for Congress to provide money with which the Tennessee Valley Authority (another government agency) could build a new steam plant and supply the Atomic Energy Commission.

To make his decision, the President had to consider, among others, the following factors: (1) his own and his party's expressed policy of supporting private business enterprise wherever such support was consistent with the public interest; (2) the opposition to this policy from important members of his own party who lived in the Tennessee Valley area or in the Northwest and favored publicly owned power; (3) the effect of this disagreement within his own party, which was one short of a majority in the Senate; (4) the effect of his decision upon private businessmen who favored private utilities and had made large financial contributions to the President's party; (5) the effect of his decision upon voters in the border area who benefited greatly from the cheap power available from the publicly owned TVA—people whose future votes might be influenced by the President's attitude toward TVA; (6) the effect on voters in other parts of the country who hoped to get cheap public power in the future—for example, in the Northwest and in the mountain states; (7) the effect of his decision on the policy of the other party, which might choose to make the matter an issue in political campaigns or might itself be split on the question; (8) the immediate effect of his decision on the views of individual members of Congress and Senators whose votes would be needed on other measures important to the President's program.

Here are eight major aspects of one decision a President had to make, and each one suggests many others closely related. Actually the Dixon-Yates contract was finally cancelled, partly for reasons not included in this list, i.e., matters of legality and a decision by the city of Memphis to build a plant of its own. But we have enough here to see how highly political the Presidency is, and how skillful a politician a President must be to succeed as chief executive and as leader of the people.

The President as Leader of the Nation

Most important of all the many roles played by the President in our form of government is his role as leader of the nation. A free nation has many leaders: business leaders, farm leaders, labor leaders, educational leaders, leaders in science and the arts, and, of course, political leaders. Only the President under our elective system represents all of the people and so is responsible for leadership of the whole country.

The President must represent the people in relation to Congress and must recommend laws which he thinks will benefit all. In the executive branch, the President must represent the whole people in relation to his own cabinet and other administrative officials. The office of President has become not only so powerful but also so complex that it is almost literally impossible for any man to fill it well. However, the machinery of government developed to aid the President in his duties, while never entirely satisfactory, at least makes it possible for him to get his work done and makes his responsibilities bearable. At any rate, despite the awesome magnitude of the office, there seems never to be a lack of candidates!

The President is assisted in his mountain of work by various independent agencies and commissions, which we shall discuss further in Chapter 8. Here we shall see how his closest assistants work.

THE EXECUTIVE OFFICE OF THE PRESIDENT

Directly attached to the President, acting to coördinate his advice and carry out his immediate duties under the law, are six groups or divisions of officials known collectively as the Executive Office of the President. (For accounting purposes, the White House buildings and grounds staff are also included.) The Executive Office dates from 1939, and the various divisions are established by act of Congress.

The President has considerable power, under the law, to transfer agencies into or outside the Executive Office, as may seem to him desirable from time to time, depending on changing conditions. As you can see from the discussion of the roles of the President, a modern President needs a large and complex staff to carry out his immediate personal duties. All this is quite above and beyond his responsibility for each of the great departments established by law and represented in the President's cabinet.

The White House Office

The chart on p. 176 indicates the seven divisions in the Executive Office, with the staff and duties of each. In the White House Office are some of the

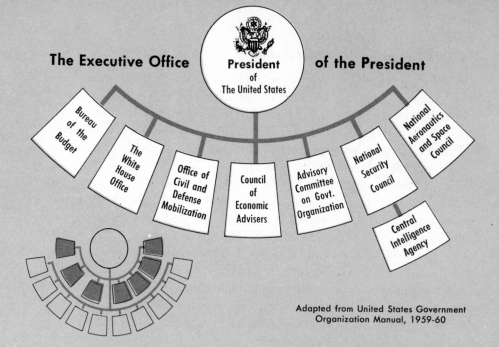

The Executive Office — President of the United States — of the President

Bureau of the Budget

The White House Office

Office of Civil and Defense Mobilization

Council of Economic Advisers

Advisory Committee on Govt. Organization

National Security Council

National Aeronautics and Space Council

Central Intelligence Agency

Adapted from United States Government
Organization Manual, 1959-60

THE WHITE HOUSE OFFICE

Staff: Assistant to the President; Deputy Assistant; military, naval, and air aids; administrative assistants for press relations, congressional liaison, cabinet liaison; President's physician; secretaries; stenographers and clerks.

Duties: Draft speeches and state papers; screen President's callers; arrange his schedule; brief him on political developments and press reactions; protect his health.

BUREAU OF THE BUDGET

Staff: Director (not Cabinet member, but attends meetings); assistants and experts in management and organization; statistics, accounting, finances, international affairs, legislative matters, labor and welfare; military matters, resources.

Duties: Assist in preparing budget and budget message; control administration of budget; coordinate work programs of agencies.

COUNCIL OF ECONOMIC ADVISERS

Staff: Three members, appointed by President with consent of Senate.

Duties: Analyze nation's economy; advise President on economic developments; study national investment, employment and standard of living; recommend action to help economy; forecast economic conditions.

NATIONAL SECURITY COUNCIL

Staff: President; Vice-President; Secretaries of State and Defense; Director of Office of Civil and Defense Mobilization and, if President wishes, Director of Budget or Secretary of Treasury; Advisers; Chiefs of Staff of Military Services; Director of CIA.

Duties: Help President to formulate policy, such as defensive treaties, military and economic support to free nations, relations with Soviet Union and satellites; conduct research; coördinate its work with departments outside Executive Office.

Under National Security Council is *CENTRAL INTELLIGENCE AGENCY*—top-secret agency; and *OPERATIONS COORDINATING BOARD* to coordinate work security.

CIVIL AND DEFENSE MOBILIZATION

Staff: Director and Deputy Director; assistants for Staff Coördination, Manpower, Plans and Readiness, Production, Stabilization, Telecommunications, Transportation and Labor; Counsel.

Duties: Advise President on defense and war production and on procurement of material for building armaments (such as copper, steel, oil, rubber); allocate these materials to suppliers; mobilize and relocate industry in emergency.

ADVISORY COMMITTEE ON GOVERNMENT ORGANIZATION

Staff: Three members appointed by President serving without compensation.

Duties: Advise President, his assistant, and Director of Budget of possible changes in executive branch in interest of economy or efficiency.

NATIONAL AERONAUTICS AND SPACE COUNCIL

Staff: The President (Chairman), Secretary of State, Secretary of Defense, Administrator National Aeronautics and Space Agency, Chairman Atomic Energy Commission, Director National Science Foundation, three private scientists.

Duties: Advise the President on all matters connected with the exploration of space.

most important—though little known—officials of the government, appointed by the President. President Franklin D. Roosevelt once appointed six administrative assistants among whose qualifications he rated first "a passion for anonymity." Behind that phrase lies an important situation with which the President was seeking to cope. Since the views of the President are of greatest importance, newsmen are forever trying to get "inside" information beyond what is available in the regular press conference. People working in the White House Office are natural targets for the attention of the press, but they cannot perform their duties properly if they become too well known. The executive head of the group—what President Eisenhower called a "chief of staff"—is well known, and the President's press and appointments secretaries are of necessity much in the public eye. Most others in his immediate "family" work quietly with as little public attention as possible. About the only aspect of his life the group is not responsible for—except the brief hours of family intimacy a President may snatch—is his physical security. That is in the charge of the Secret Service, an agency of the Treasury.

Bureau of the Budget

The **Bureau of the Budget** has a number of important functions, as the chart indicates. The experts who assist the Director are grouped according to specialties which correspond to the principal functions of the executive branch. There are, for instance, experts who specialize in analyzing the budget of the Army or of the Forest Service or of the National Health Institutes. Such experts are at work the year round studying the expenditure of the public money in the areas of their special knowledge.

A great deal of the budget preparation is done by the operating agencies, which make annual recommendations to the Budget Bureau. Within these agencies there must be officials who are expert, not only in such dramatic expenditures as the purchase of hydrogen bombs and the building of dams, but also in such petty details as estimating how many pencils, erasers, and paste pots a particular agency will need for a year's work.

In the Bureau itself every proposed figure must be checked and criticized in the interest of economy and efficiency and in terms of political expediency. In a sense, the most important work of the Bureau of the Budget is political. Negotiations between the operating agencies and the Bureau are carried on at every level, proceeding from minute detail at the lowest level to the very generalized figures at the top. The Director and the President obviously cannot concern themselves with small items in a budget of many billions, but the Bureau must have ready answers to any questions of detail the President, the Director, a presidential adviser, a member of Congress, or even an ordinary citizen might ask. Remember that all federal spending must also be approved by the General Accounting Office (p. 117).

The decisions made in the Budget Bureau have far-reaching effects. The President, of course is responsible for all decisions. Since he cannot make most of them himself, he must have the most competent and experienced staff that can be assembled. Budget examiners and analysts are normally trained in economics and public administration and have career status in the civil service (see pp. 195–197).

The Director and his immediate assistants are appointed by the President with the consent of the Senate; they reflect his political interests and program commitments. For their part, they must be experienced in management and policy-making. They must be at once flexible in their views and tough-minded, and they must have considerable imagination. It is their job to see the relation between the federal government in all its activities and the country in all its complexity. Upon their advice a President may succeed or flounder.

Council of Economic Advisers

The **Council of Economic Advisers** is a smaller organization within the Executive Office. As the chart shows, its function is to give the President every assistance possible to enable him to act to keep the economic state of the nation on an even keel.

National Security Council

The **National Security Council** advises the President on foreign policy as it relates to the security of the United States. It was established by law in 1947 when the Cold War showed that we needed a special agency to devote itself to the problems arising from a world of apparently endless strain and tension between democracy and communism. As the chart indicates, the members of the Council are top-level officials. The vital importance of its work is little known to the public because the greatest portion of its activity is necessarily secret.

CENTRAL INTELLIGENCE AGENCY   Under the National Security Council is the **Central Intelligence Agency.** The Director is adviser to the National Security Council, and the agency is a "top-secret" organization, whose activities are not known to the public. We do not even know how many employees it has; but we do know its functions and purposes. It receives and coördinates information to help the President understand plans, strength, political condition, and military condition of foreign powers, particularly those which may be unfriendly to the United States.

In short, the CIA operates what we may call an international spy system.

The CIA grew out of the experience of the government in World War II. It was discovered then that the usual intelligence services of the armed forces were both inadequate and in need of top-level coördination. Administratively the CIA functions as an operating agency of the National Security Council. It keeps the Council fully informed on all matters of interest to it.

OPERATIONS COÖRDINATING BOARD   Also under the National Security Council is the **Operations Coördinating Board.** As its name implies, it coördinates the functions of the other agencies relating to national security.

National Aeronautics and Space Council

Since 1958 the National Security Council has been supplemented in the Executive Office by the **National Aeronautics and Space Council.** This body, chaired by the President and composed of cabinet members and scientists from both government and private life, serves to advise the President on the latest developments in space science and help him to formulate national policy on all matters related to the exploration of space.

Two Other Divisions

The chart lists the organizations and functions of the other two divisions of the Executive Office: the **Office of Civil and Defense Mobilization** (see chart, p. 176, and Chap. 27) and the **Advisory Committee on Government Organization.** Their names describe the kind of work for which they are responsible.

THE PRESIDENT'S SOURCES OF INFORMATION

In order to manage his immense responsibilities wisely the President must, obviously, be well informed on all important matters of government. Thus the sources of information available to him are crucial to his office.

The Cabinet Members

Most of his information comes from the officials in the Executive Office. The President also gets information from the members of his cabinet. The cabinet meets at least once a week, with the President presiding, to consider general governmental policies. When the cabinet gathers in the cabinet room of the White House, each member finds before him a neat stack of papers providing him with concise background information about matters the President wishes to discuss. If the President is concerned about continued drought in the Southwest, the Secretary of Agriculture in particular will be asked for a report and recommendations. Other members of the cabinet will be briefed on the problem and may be invited by the President to express their views. And so with any other problem that has come to the President's attention on which he feels the need of advice from the entire executive branch. The President is not bound to accept the advice of the cabinet, but such advice is almost indispensable to him in the conduct of his office.

Each Secretary, as an adviser to the President and as a source of information, is responsible, at weekly cabinet meetings, for keeping the President informed on all important matters of his department. Often members of the cabinet bring to cabinet meetings deputies or assistants who have special knowledge of matters with which the cabinet will be concerned. In Washington's time, the President, as provided in the Constitution, asked for written opinions from the department heads. Washington soon found, however, that it was better to meet with the cabinet and conduct discussions around the table. This practice has been followed ever since. The President is at liberty to invite anyone he chooses to cabinet meetings. The Vice-President is frequently so invited, though he is not a department head and has no duties assigned by the Constitution except to preside over the Senate.

Members of Congress

The formal channels of information through the cabinet departments are by no means the only sources available to the President. He also receives much information from members of Congress. It is customary for the President to hold fairly regular meetings with the principal leaders of both houses. He must work closely with the Speaker of the House, the majority leader of the House, the majority leader of the Senate, and the chairmen of the principal committees of both houses. And he must not ignore the minority. Information received by the President from these officials is supplemented by innumerable personal calls from other members of Congress, who are free to offer their opinions to the President on any matters of interest to them, regardless of political party affiliation.

The Press

Another source of information of great value to the President is, oddly enough, his press conference. In modern times it has been customary for a President to meet the press formally at least once a month—some Presidents have met the press as often as twice a week. The stated purpose for these conferences is to give newspapers, radio, and television the opportunity to learn the President's views and plans so that the public may be kept informed. In the process, however, the President himself learns a great deal.

The newsmen present are experienced in national and world affairs and are normally exceedingly well informed as to what the public is thinking. The questions they ask indicate to the President the state of public opinion. This information, though it is indirectly presented, often plays a major part in helping the President to reach decisions. The presidential press conference probably serves as the principal channel of communication between the President, the only national official (except, of course, the Vice-President) who has been elected by a majority of all the people, and his constituents, the people themselves.

MR. PRESIDENT

It may have been true in the early years of the republic that certain men seemed "born to be President." Washington, John Adams, Jefferson, Madison, Monroe, and John Quincy Adams more or less fit such a description. In an era when broad education and worldly experience were available only to the few, it was natural that the President should be chosen from among a very small group of qualified people. The first six Presidents all came from social classes in which it was assumed that gentlemen had an obligation to serve the country rather than themselves. Each of these men, in fact, gave all of the best years of his life to public service, and all (with the exception of J. Q. Adams, who was too young) began that service with the Revolution or earlier. They had played leading parts in the war for independence and in the establishment of the new government. Their election to the Presidency was almost according to seniority, and each was well trained for it when his turn came.

Since the time of Jackson, the way to the Presidency has been entirely different. Jackson himself, though a military hero, had no aristocratic background and no inherited wealth. As President, he symbolized what has been called the "rise of the common man." After Jackson a new tradition of "log cabin" Presidents showed that a premium was placed on humble origin. In modern times, class distinctions have broken down. While the two Roosevelts, for example, came from very old and well-to-do families and received careful and "correct" education, President Truman came from a small town in Missouri and never went to college, and President Eisenhower was a farm boy who earned an education at West Point.

The Importance of Personal Popularity

The framers of the Constitution intended that the President should be chosen only by a small number of highly qualified men representing each of the states in the electoral college. The system as originally planned was republican and representative, but not actually democratic. The people had only an indirect role in selecting their President. Under such circumstances, personal popularity was not so important as experience and training in public service.

181

In modern times, personal popularity is very nearly as indispensable for election to the Presidency as character and intelligence. A winning smile, an open and sincere manner, pleasing appearance, a good speaking voice, and a certain sense of showmanship have become necessary to a presidential candidate in the day of mass communication when everyone can see and hear the candidate frequently.

The Vague Pattern for Advancement to the Presidency

The road to the Presidency is a long and tedious one. Usually the candidate must have very wide experience of public life, of government, and of handling men. Since the War Between the States, only two Presidents have not been politicians—Grant and Eisenhower. Usually a presidential candidate has served one of the great political parties for many years. He must know many people throughout the country, both in the ranks of his party and among the people at large. His record of performance must win the confidence not only of political leaders but also of the general public. A man who is merely likable cannot build such a record. He must also have faced many difficult situations which have tested both his intelligence and his character.

There is no set road of advancement to the Presidency, but many generations of experience do suggest a recurring pattern, which the illustration on p. 183 points up. Very few President's have come directly from the ranks of Congress without other important experience of public affairs. There are at least two good reasons for this. One is that the job of the legislator is separate from that of administrator, so that a Congressman does not acquire the best experience and training for the Presidency. Another is that Congressmen do not work so directly with political organizations as they do with one another in committees and in teamwork. When they appear regularly in the headlines and achieve widespread recognition, it is frequently because of their special interests or concerns. They become so identified in the public mind with particular causes or programs that they are very nearly disqualified for the more general functions of the Presidency.

On the other hand, many presidential candidates have been governors of their states. The reason is clear enough. The office of governor in many states is a kind of miniature Presidency. A governor must deal with nearly all of the fields of government with which a President deals, except foreign affairs and national defense. Governors, especially governors of very large and populous states, must take an overall view of the functions and policies of the government. They must make budgets, request legislation, deal politically with legislators and with administrators, conduct ceremonial functions, and represent all the people of their states, as the President represents all the people of the country. We shall discuss the work of the governor in Chapter 11.

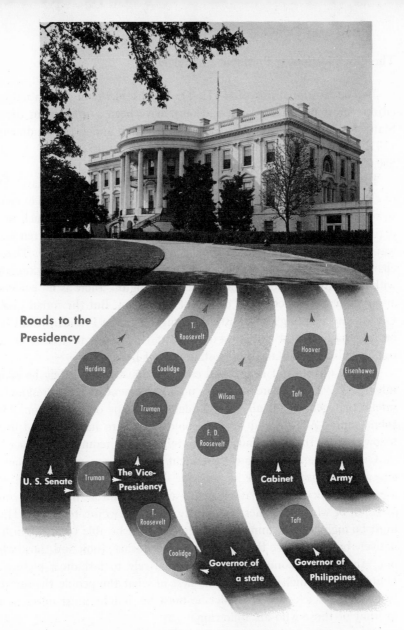

Roads to the
Presidency

Very few Presidents have come directly from the ranks of Congress, for the reasons given on p. 182. President Harding took that road, but he was nominated because he was not well known, and his party could not agree on one of two or three better qualified men. President Truman became President because of the death of Franklin Roosevelt. Truman often observed that his training as a legislator was insufficient for his tasks as President, and he found it necessary to devote a great deal of his time to study of the history and functions of the Presidency in order to meet his obligations as national leader and public administrator. As you can see, many of our Presidents have been governors. In that position their duties were somewhat similar to those of the President, as we shall see in Chap. 11. Of the ten successful candidates since 1900, five have been governors; of the ten defeated candidates, six had been governors. Ten of these eleven governors came from states with large cities and concentrated populations.

183

The Qualifications a President Should Have

By constitutional provision (II, 1), the President must be a natural-born citizen, must be 35 years old, and must have been a resident in the United States for fourteen years. His term is four years, and by Amendment XXII (1951), he can serve only two terms. His salary is $100,000 a year, plus $50,000 allowance for expenses, as we saw, pp. 57 and 164.

Beyond this, what are the qualifications a President must have? Strength of character and body would seem to be most essential. No one in civil life is so subject to constant pressure and heavy responsibility, or to such unceasing drains upon his sheer physical energy. Presidential candidates often find some way in which to demonstrate their good health to the public. That strong character and body must be matched by personal honesty and integrity goes without saying. In the long line since Washington, there is no evidence that any President was personally dishonest or corrupt. But the moral disasters of Grant's and Harding's administrations suggest that a President must not only be personally honest but must also insist that those to whom he entrusts responsibilities maintain similar standards of behavior.

To the qualities of health and character must immediately be added fine intelligence. To be sure, there is no requirement that a President be an intellectual genius. Of all the Presidents, perhaps only Jefferson, Madison, John Quincy Adams, and Wilson could be said to have towered over their fellows intellectually. Sound, active intelligence is required, however.

On the other hand, a great President must be a man of fine imagination and vision. This is because he must see so many aspects of life and so many aspects of policy all in relation one to another. And he must have some sort of vision of what he wishes his country, even the world, to be like. His ideals must be high but not unreachable, and he must be able to distinguish imaginatively between those things which answer to his vision and those which do not. Above all, he must be able imaginatively to fashion a picture of the United States which represents the best of what the people themselves wish to make of their country. Leader he must be, but he must never be too far in front of those who are following.

Thus, finally, we return to politics. For the qualities of intelligence, character, and imagination can be combined effectively only by a "political" turn of mind. This means that the President must know what his aims are and how close they are to the will of the majority into which he must have a clear insight. He must know how to move, now quickly and directly, now slowly and indirectly, to achieve his purposes. He must know when to be forthright and when to be reticent; whom to trust and how far; when to advance, when to retreat, and when to stand his ground. He must not fear compromise. Rather he must constantly seek workable and honorable compromises. He must know, too, with certainty when not to compromise, when to do so would lower the dignity or lessen the strength of the nation, or weaken the liberties of the people. The President sets the tone of the country and represents it to the world. In the long run, he can be no better than the people whom he governs. As citizens we do well to remember that fact, and to do whatever we can to help him.

THE VICE-PRESIDENT

Until recent years the Vice-President was the forgotten man of American government. A famous musical play of the 1930's, *Of Thee I Sing,* made the Vice-President (Alexander Throttlebottom) its chief comedian. As the play progressed, he kept appearing among groups of people looking for someone who had heard of him, or asking directions. This, of course, was a gross exaggeration. Yet it was an exaggeration of a fact—that Americans have traditionally paid too little attention to the Vice-President, to his office, and to his qualifications to be President.

Under the system of presidential elections, the Vice-President is chosen in the same manner as the President (pp. 76–77). His name, as candidate, together with that of the presidential candidate, constitutes what is called a party "ticket" in the elections. The only difference in procedure (see p. 76) is that, in case no candidate for Vice-President has a majority of the electoral votes, the Senate (not the House, as in the case of the President) chooses the Vice-President from the two candidates having the largest electoral vote. The legal qualifications for Vice-President are the same as for the President (see p. 184), since by the death or disability of the President the Vice-President automatically succeeds him. The Vice-President's salary is $35,000, plus a $10,000 allowance for expenses.

In the early days of the republic, before the party system came into being and before the electoral system was revised (see p. 77), the Vice-President was the man who polled the second largest vote for President. For this reason, such eminent founders of the nation as John Adams and Thomas Jefferson served as Vice-President. Since their time, the office of Vice-President has receded to the background of public interest, except at times when a President becomes seriously ill or dies. Political parties have treated the office lightly. How mistaken we have been is shown by the fact that already seven Vice-Presidents have succeeded to the Presidency through the death of the President. Fortunately, to offset this negligence, two of our stronger Presidents, Theodore Roosevelt and Harry S. Truman, were among the Vice-Presidents who succeeded to the Presidency. In recent years the public, as well as students of government, has become more aware of the problem. Our parties now more seriously try to select the best-qualified candidates for the office.

It has long been a tradition for the parties to select their vice-presidential candidates to "balance the ticket." Thus, if the presidential candidate is from one section of the country, his running mate is likely to be chosen largely because he is from another. If the party is split on certain matters, the candidate for President may represent one group and the candidate for Vice-President the other. Often a candidate for Vice-President is chosen simply because he is a respected member of the party who has long served in the Senate or in some party capacity. Very seldom have the parties seriously thought of the prospect that their candidate for Vice-President may become President. Yet the odds are about one in five that he will.

What does the Vice-President actually do? This is a question to which no general answer would be accurate. Under the Constitution his only duty is to preside over the Senate. But unlike the Speaker of the House, who is a member of the House, the Vice-President is not a member of the Senate, cannot serve on or appoint committees unless asked to do so by the Senate, and cannot vote except in cases of a tie. Thus he has no real influence in the Senate by virtue of his office. However, his personal standing in the party and his experience may in practice give him a considerable influence.

Another answer to our question as to the role of the Vice-President is that he plays as important a role in government as the President may wish him to. Henry A. Wallace, in the third administration of Franklin Roosevelt, was appointed by the President to be chairman of the Board of Economic Warfare, an important though temporary wartime agency. Richard Nixon, as Vice-President under Eisenhower, assumed many of the ceremonial functions of the President, presided over meetings of the cabinet and the National Security Council, and performed important political tasks during the various periods of the President's illness. In recent times, most Vice-Presidents have been asked by the President to attend meetings of the cabinet.

Under the Constitution the Vice-President may also succeed to the Presidency when the President suffers a disability and is unable to perform his duties. Just what this provision means in practice has never been legally determined, and in no case has a Vice-President succeeded to the Presidency for this reason. However, the illnesses of Presidents Wilson and Eisenhower have served to point up the importance of this clause and to focus public attention on the qualifications of the Vice-President. It may be necessary to amend the Constitution or to enact laws to clarify the matter and to prescribe the duties of the Vice-President under certain conditions. Above all, party leaders and the voters themselves should do what can be done without amendments or laws, namely, make sure that every vice-presidential candidate is the kind of man they would wish to see in the Presidency itself should death or disability overtake the President.

SUMMARY

The powers of the American President are vast and his office is vital to the welfare of our country and of the world. The President has many different functions and plays many different roles. To be sure, a number of administrative officials and offices serve him directly in the performance of his duties. The seven divisions of the White House Office assist him in many aspects of his work.

We have emphasized the importance of the *political* role of the President. Politics is the very life of free society, and the President must be the leading politician. He is first of all the people's politician. As the only national officer (except for the Vice-President) who is directly responsible to the whole people and elected by them, he is *your* agent in the government, charged with protecting *your* interests and seeing to it that you get a square deal. You have a direct and immediate interest in the qualifications of the President. As citizens you will do well to look carefully at all candidates to make sure that they have the character, health, intelligence, political good sense, imagination, and vision you would wish to find in the leader of the whole nation. And do not overlook the importance of the Vice-President; you as citizens ought to be equally concerned that he also be fully qualified to serve as President.

KNOW WHAT YOU READ

1. Why is our system sometimes called "presidential government"?
2. Contrast the executive department of George Washington's time with the executive department of today.
3. Why is so much deference shown to the President?
4. Describe the *ceremonial role* of the President.
5. Where in the Constitution do we find the statement of the powers of the President? Make a list of the powers stated in that Article.
6. What is an executive order? Executive agreement? Cabinet?
7. What are the things the President must do as commander-in-chief?
8. What extraordinary powers may be given the President as commander-in-chief?
9. Why is the President's budget responsibility so important?
10. What purpose does each of the President's three messages serve?
11. As chief policy-maker of the country, what things must the President do?
12. Why must the President be a politician?
13. What are the ways in which a President may try to win support for his policies?
14. What is the President's veto power? How important is this power?

15. Why does the President sometimes find it difficult to win the support of members of Congress?
16. What is the President's most important role? Why is this so?
17. Why should a President look upon himself as the *leader of the nation?*
19. Why might a President want assistants who "have a passion for anonymity"?
20. Members of the staff of the White House are important but little known. What work do they perform?
21. Explain how the federal budget is made.
22. What is the work of the Council of Economic Advisers?
23. Why is the National Security Council important to you?
24. For what reasons was the CIA established? What does it do?
25. What is the function of the Office of Civil and Defense Mobilization?
26. Explain the Advisory Committee on Government Organization.
27. List the many sources from which the President may get his information.
28. What legal qualifications must a person meet to become President of the United States? Where *in the Constitution* did you find the answer to this question?
29. How did the makers of the Constitution intend to have our Presidents selected? In what ways has the system changed?
30. Is it true that personal popularity is "very nearly indispensable" for election to the Presidency?
31. What kind of person should a candidate be to be worthy of, and equal to, the Presidency?
32. Why has the Vice-President been called the "forgotten man of American government"? What are the legal qualifications for the office?
33. How many Vice-Presidents have become President by the death of the chief executive?

WHAT DO YOU THINK?

1. Our President is our chief law-enforcement official. In recent years our country has seen a great growth in lawlessness. Does this suggest that our Presidents have not been on the job?
2. The powers to declare war (Article I, Section 8) belong to Congress. Can a President involve us in a war without a vote of Congress? Would you favor changing the Constitution to limit the power of either President or Congress? How?
3. In a public opinion poll a few years ago, it was discovered that most of the people polled did not want their children to go into politics when they grew up. Is such an attitude justified? Is it dangerous? Why?
4. Do you think it is ever possible for the President to please all of the people? Nearly all of the people? Why?

5. Discuss these quotations:

> The American presidency is the most exhausting job in the world. Soon after Theodore Roosevelt's retirement from the presidency, even he, with his abundant vitality, admitted that he had no idea that the office would take such a toll. He died at 61. . . . Toil and disappointment brought an end to Wilson at 68; frustration and despair drove Harding at 58 to death or suicide; even the cool Coolidge at 61 succumbed prematurely to cardiac exhaustion; and Franklin Roosevelt at 63 collapsed under the weight of inhuman responsibilities. Plagued with a hostile opposition, a slanderous press, a vicious radio, corrupt underlings, and a none-too-intelligent public, it is a wonder that the president survives as long as he does. He who would enjoy a ripe old age had better avoid residence at 1600 Pennsylvania Avenue, and he who would survive in that office should routinely go through a clinic every month after taking office.
> Victor L. Albjerg, "Qualities a President Needs," *Current History*, September, 1952.

> ". . . despite the awesome magnitude of the office, there seems never to be a lack of candidates." (textbook, p. 175.)

6. Study the cartoon, p. 173. Do you agree with the cartoonist? If not, why? If so, how do you think the job should be done?
7. It has been said that a man who would serve the public in a political office should have a thick skin. He should not be greatly disturbed by criticism; he should not be the kind of person who stays awake nights worrying. Is this statement justified? Is this an exaggeration?

PROBLEMS AND PROJECTS FOR YOU

1. Keep a five-day record of news items about the daily activities of the President.
2. Organize a committee and poll a number of adults in your community to find out what they think about "bigness" in government. Plan your questions and procedures carefully. Prepare an oral report to the class on your findings.
3. Draw an original cartoon to show the growth of the executive department.
4a. Poll adults in your school or community to find out what qualities they believe a presidential candidate should have. Report your findings.
  b. Run a similar poll among your fellow students concerning candidates for the top executive offices in your school and class. Compare the qualities of leadership suggested by both polls.
5. Report to the class on this question: Exactly how does a President "take care that the laws be faithfully executed"?

6. A President should be the kind of man who actually enjoys making decisions. From your study of American history draw up a list of outstanding difficult decisions American Presidents have had to make. Then,

   (a) Illustrate any of these decisions by a cartoon, or write an editorial for a newspaper of that period, attacking or defending the President's action.

   (b) Or write an editorial, or draw a cartoon, in which you favor one side of an issue now facing the President.

7. Go through your history book to find all the qualities of our Presidents mentioned therein. Make a list of these qualities. Tell the class which qualities were most frequently mentioned. To what extent were these the qualities of the candidates in the last presidential election?

8. While Congress is in session, follow the daily papers for one month, watching for examples of the use of the President's veto. Report your findings to the class, or post your clippings on the bulletin board.

9. Organize teams in your class to debate this question. Resolved: that a man who would be a good President must choose between being popular and doing what is best for his country. He cannot do both.

10. Make a collection of clippings or cartoons to show what a candidate will sometimes do to make himself popular.

11. Use this problem for a panel discussion or a debate: Suppose that a President is convinced that he would not have been elected if he had not received the support of labor, or of the farmers, or of some other very large group. Is he then justified in regarding himself as "Labor's President" or "The Farmer's President"?

12. Report to the class on any one of the following (as given in the year in which you are studying government): The State of the Union message, the budget message, the economic message. Point out to the class items in messages which affect the people of your community.

13. Organize a committee and undertake as a group project to ask ten to twelve adults to rate the men who have been President since World War I on their expressed aims, accomplishments, greatness. Compare their conclusions with those obtained from polling an equal number of students who have studied United States history.

    Report your findings to the class. How do you interpret the differences? How would you rate these men yourself? Read Chap. 5, A Yardstick for Presidents in *Paths to the Present* by Arthur M. Schlesinger, and compare with your class report. (Remember that the book was published in 1949, and therefore does not include later Presidents.)

14. Some families make budgets. Is it more necessary that families and individuals stay within their budgets than it is that the federal government stay within its budget? Is a government budget the same thing as a household account? Discuss the similarities and differences.

15. What is meant by "forecasting economic conditions"? Who makes forecasts? How is this done? Report to the class.

EXTEND YOUR VOCABULARY

presidential govern-
 ment
ceremonial role
executive order
executive agreement
executive departments

cabinet
budget message
State of the Union mes-
 sage
economic message
patronage

veto
politician
Executive Office
economic forecast-
 ing
commission

YOUR NOTEBOOK: THE GOVERNMENT OF ——

1. Does your local government have a budget? If so, who prepares it? Who has to approve the budget?
2. In your state, the group most like the White House Office is ——
3. How big was your last local budget? State budget?
4. What official(s) must carry out the executive power in your community?
5. What are the principal economic problems facing your community?

READ MORE ABOUT IT

BINKLEY, WILFRED, *The President and Congress.* Knopf, 1947.
 The relationship between two branches of our government.
BINKLEY, WILFRED, *The Man in the White House: His Powers and Duties.* Johns Hopkins Press, 1958.
 Careful and thorough.
BROWNLOW, LOUIS, *The President and the Presidency.* Public Administration Service, 1949.
 Discussion of adequacy of the office to meet the many demands on it.
BURNS, JAMES M., and PELTASON, JACK W., *Government by the People.* Prentice-Hall, 1954. Chap. 15.
CORWIN, EDWARD S., *The President: Office and Powers.* New York University Press, 1957.
 Standard reference book.
FENNO, RICHARD, JR., *The President's Cabinet.* Harvard, 1959.
 Unique and useful discussion of an important presidential aid.
HYMAN, SIDNEY, *The American President.* Harper, 1954.
 Readable and stimulating.
IRISH, MARIAN D., and PROTHRO, JAMES W., *The Politics of American Democracy.* Prentice-Hall, 1959. Chap. 12.
LASKI, H. J., *The American Presidency.* Harper, 1940.
 An English political scientist's thoughtful and interesting study of our executive.
ROSSITER, CLINTON, *The American Presidency.* Harcourt, Brace, 1956.
 The best popular study, highly readable, about the office of President.
WILLIAMS, IRVING G., *The Rise of the Vice-Presidency.* Public Affairs Press, 1956.
 Especially valuable because almost alone in its field.

191

CHAPTER 8

Independent Commissions and Administrative Agencies

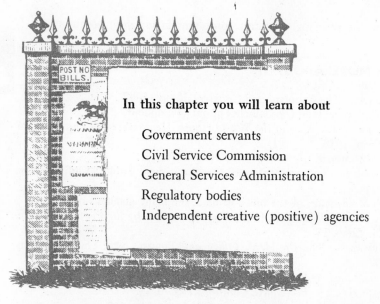

POST NO BILLS.

In this chapter you will learn about

Government servants
Civil Service Commission
General Services Administration
Regulatory bodies
Independent creative (positive) agencies

Some people are under the impression that "bureaucrats" (professional government servants) are somehow bad people who ought to be eliminated, that they are lazy and shiftless people who live like parasites on the money paid by the taxpayers, and that they are stupid and incompetent people who stand in the way of efficiency and progress. Such views of government servants frequently derive from the same ignorance which regards "politics" as a "dirty business." The truth is that just as we cannot have any free and democratic decisions or policies without politicians, so we cannot have government action to carry out our policies unless we have bureaucrats.

Who are the bureaucrats? If you stop to think about it, you may be surprised at the answers you are able to give yourself. Your mailman is a bureaucrat; so is an FBI agent. The clerk who helps your father with his income tax return, your neighbor who works with your state conservation officials on tree-planting projects, the weatherman at your local airport—all these are bureaucrats. So too are the engineers of the Tennessee Valley Authority, the stenographers in the American Embassy in Cairo, the men who stamp "U.S. Choice" on your beef, the physicists in the atomic energy plant at Oak Ridge, the chiefs of the great bureaus in Washington which deal with farmers, workers, businessmen, and housewives, and the policemen in the national capital. There are some two and one-half million government workers in 15,000 different occupations in the federal service—almost as many kinds of jobs as there are in private life. And most of these people do *not* work in Washington!

GOVERNMENT SERVANTS

The politician and the bureaucrat are the truly indispensable people in democratic government. American bureaucrats are not merely just as competent in their jobs, just as honorable, and just as necessary as are Americans in private employment; they are often more competent and more uniformly honest. In general, the standards of job competence met by civil servants are as high as or higher than the standards for comparable jobs in private life, though the rewards may often be less.

It is proper for citizens to debate the merits of any particular government program or criticize public officials, and to favor fewer or more government activities; it is not proper or sensible to attack government servants, or "bureaucrats," generally simply because you do not like the agency or office for which they work.

Political Appointees

There are two kinds of government workers: those in **classified** positions and those in **unclassified** positions. The power to decide which shall be which has been given to the President (by the Pendleton Act of 1883, see p. 196.) The positions on the classified list must be filled by people on the *Register*—civil service lists of those who have passed examinations and who meet requirements in other ways.

The overwhelming majority of those who work for the federal (and state) governments are professional career people in classified positions. Many very important positions, however, are filled by political appointments. This means that the President or the governor of a state or the mayor of a city appoints

INDEPENDENT AGENCIES

Conditions of modern life require regulation of certain aspects of our freedom in order to prevent others from irresponsibly interfering with them. Because of that, certain "regulatory" agencies have been set up—most of them having to do with economic aspects of our lives.

The oldest is the Interstate Commerce Commission. Any truck carrying goods of any sort between one state and another must get a license from the ICC. This kind of licensing protects the people against excessive charges and protects small companies against large in the matter of rates. Goods so carried must also be manufactured under conditions meeting other government regulations.

The Federal Power Commission does not install electricity—but it does protect the public by regulating rates of electric power if it is produced in another state and carried across the state border to you. When the electricity is used for telegraph, radio, and television transmissions, another agency, the Federal Communications Commission exercises regulation.

Airports have control towers maintained by Federal Aviation Agency. These towers control the traffic of incoming and outgoing planes; they also bring planes in by radar when poor weather conditions make visibility too poor for Visual Flight conditions.

to responsible offices people who are politically in sympathy with his program and loyal to him personally. Such people usually hold "policy-making" posts. That is, they carry out directives of the President, governor, or mayor. They will be helping their chief to make policy—advising him, interpreting his wishes, and carrying out the laws under their jurisdiction in such a way as to bring the most credit to the chief and his political party and program.

Such "patronage" appointments are very necessary. Because a President has been elected, he is a successful political leader, as we saw in Chapter 7; he is committed to a political program and needs political subordinates to help him with his task. If the President could not appoint cabinet members and deputies, agency heads, majority members of commissions, and other top officials, he might well find himself unable to do a good many things he promised to do if elected. Actually the people might be deprived of their control over the government. All top executive officials must be either directly responsible to the voters, as is a President, a governor, a mayor, or many another official elected on state or municipal ballots, or else responsible to an official who is so elected. At the level where policies are made in accord with the expressed will of the people, elected officials must have some independence in making appointments or removing personnel. This means, of course, that free government will not always be as efficient and professional as some people might wish, but it *will* remain free government, because it will be responsive to the will of the people.

Civil Service Workers

Below these top levels are our career civil servants in classified positions, who are actually limited in political action. The Hatch Act of 1938 forbids the vast majority of federal government workers to participate in partisan politics. The government worker is allowed the right to vote, but he cannot make speeches or work for a political party. This protects him from public criticism by people of the opposite party to his own, and protects the people from a government service overloaded with people who use their positions for partisan purposes.

CIVIL SERVICE COMMISSION

The Civil Service Commission (CSC) is in some ways the most important agency in the federal government. It is concerned with the personnel management of the whole government.

If you stop to look at the bulletin board at your post office, or perhaps the bulletin board in the corridor of your own school, you may see notices announcing examinations to be held at a certain time for stenographers or biologists, aeronautical mechanics or librarians—indeed, for almost any kind of occupation. These examinations are the opportunity for you and your fellow citizens to qualify for a job in the federal government. They are given by the U.S. Civil Service Commission.

Before 1820, when the federal government was very small, Presidents selected clerks, secretaries, and administrators on the basis of personal recommendations and merit. As government became more complex, the number of government workers increased to hundreds, then to thousands, and now it is up to millions. For a time, government jobs were controlled by the party in power. With each new administration, administrators and clerks were dismissed, and partisans of the new President were employed. As one Senator at the time of Andrew Jackson put it, "To the victor belong the spoils."

This "spoils system," as it was thereafter called, led to so many abuses that the people demanded reform. In 1883, Congress passed a Civil Service Law, the Pendleton Act, making merit rather than political affiliation the basis for appointment to certain government posts. This is known as the **merit system**. Since 1883, the standards and qualifications of civil servants have become steadily higher and the positions of government servants more secure. Pride of service and morale in the bureaus and other agencies have improved.

Selection of Government Workers

The civil service system makes government employment a career. It aims to recruit competent employees, pay them equally for equal work, and protect them from being arbitrarily fired. It is the duty of the Civil Service Commission to enforce the rules of the system. The Commission does not any longer actually conduct *all* examinations for admission to government service or hire the personnel who qualify. Much testing and hiring are done by the specialized agencies needing employees. But the Civil Service Commission sets the rules under which the employing agencies must operate, inspects their methods, and approves their examinations. The Commission itself still gives examinations for many types of government work and provides a list of persons qualified for employment known as a *Register*.

Make-Up of the Commission

The CSC consists of three members who serve six-year terms, but at the pleasure of the President so that the Commission has less independence than some other bodies. However, no more than two may be members of the same political party. The Commission is assisted by about 4,500 employees. More than 500 of these are investigators who check experience and background of applicants for jobs in the government. The law specifically forbids Congressmen to exert pressure on the Commission in order to get approval for their applicants, and makes it a crime for any citizen to try to influence a Commissioner or an employee of the Commission. However, it is difficult for the Commission to be non-partisan, because Presidents are careful to see that the Commission includes strong supporters of their administrations. Nevertheless, there has never been a serious scandal in the enormous business of the Civil Service Commission.

A Case History

The Civil Service Commission works to help both the government and citizens wishing federal employment. Take the case of a young man starting out on a government career, for example. Jim is a graduate of the state university and has served two years in the army. On his return he decides that he would like to work for Uncle Sam as a career. He goes to his local post office (or federal building in a larger city) and inquires whether any jobs are open for people with training in accounting, his college major. He finds that the Civil Service Commission is giving an examination the following month for people needed as statisticians. He gets an application blank, fills it out, and mails it. On the appointed day he takes the examination, along with a dozen other applicants. In a few weeks he is notified that he has made a high rating and will be placed on the register of people available for employment as statisticians. (See pp. 362–363 for "security" investigations.)

The Department of Commerce needs statisticians in its Bureau of the Census and has asked the CSC for the names of eligible candidates. Jim is recommended to the Bureau by the CSC, along with two others who qualified when he did. He is then called for an interview in Washington, or at a regional office of the Bureau. As it turns out, the employing officer finds that both Jim and another applicant have equally good records, characters, and personalities. The other man is not a service veteran. Jim gets the job because the law requires the government to give preference to veterans who are as well qualified as non-veterans. Incidentally, it does not matter what color Jim's skin is or what his religion is, for the CSC does not permit discrimination on such matters.

Jim receives notice of his employment and orders to report to work. He is given a classification number and paid a salary according to his classification. As the years go by, he may be promoted on his merits, his classification may be raised, and he will receive salary increases according to laws or regulations of his Bureau. He may be dropped if he is no longer needed, but he may not be fired unless he is guilty of misconduct. If he is dropped, he may be offered a lower-ranking post or cut from the payroll altogether. In any case, he will have preference for reëmployment if a job becomes available or if there is need for a man with the same qualifications elsewhere in the government. Thus the security of his career is protected. At the same time, the public is protected because the system has found a man qualified by training and experience to do the job—namely, Jim.

GENERAL SERVICES ADMINISTRATION

As head of the executive branch the President, of course, has final responsibility not only in matters of public policy but also for the efficiency of operations. One might say that he has a sort of giant household to maintain. To help the President keep his house in order, Congress established in 1949 a special department known as the General Services Administration.

The General Services Administrator, who is appointed by the President with the consent of the Senate, is a kind of housekeeper to the President. He oversees the purchase of supplies throughout the executive branch, maintains public buildings, and keeps permanent records. With the aid of a large number of employees, he takes care of the thousand and one details that must be attended to in so huge an enterprise as the executive branch of the United States government—from the purchase of pencils and typewriters, to the servicing of buildings, to the storage of old documents.

This agency establishes and publishes the rules for buying supplies which all department heads must follow, so that one agency does not pay one price for adding machines, for example, while another agency pays a different price. The General Services Administration includes the Federal Supply Service, Public Buildings Service, and National Archives and Record Service, among others. The Administrator reports directly to the President to keep him informed on all matters of housekeeping and carries out the housekeeping orders of the President as the law provides.

REGULATORY BODIES

Our people tend to believe that governments exist to protect life, liberty, property, and the pursuit of happiness. Experience has shown that some people, if left alone, will so operate their own automobiles that they are endangering the life and liberty of others. Likewise, some people will so operate their businesses or industries that they interfere with the liberty of others. This is why Congress has found it necessary to set up agencies to regulate certain parts of American economic life.

Like most other government bureaus, these agencies have arisen out of conditions following upon the scientific and industrial revolutions of the later nineteenth and twentieth centuries. The Federal Communications Commission, Tennessee Valley Authority, Atomic Energy Commission, Civil Aeronautics Board, Federal Aviation Agency, National Labor Relations Board, and Securities and Exchange Commission—names of such commissions and agencies taken almost at random—could have meant little in a previous age.

Congress has established these so that the President may organize them by executive order (see p. 165), but they report directly to Congress. Their function is executive since they administer laws and regulations. Since they also make rules, they function a little like a legislature. They also listen to appeals and make judicial decisions in the manner of the courts. Their decisions, however, are reviewable in the federal courts. The agencies are intended to be non-partisan. The commissioners and directors are usually given long terms in office, and the President is required to appoint an equal or nearly equal number of them from both major political parties. Their independence is also protected because the President does not have direct power to remove them from office, without consent of Congress, except for misconduct. Upon occasion, however, the President's influence may bring about resignations he desires.

It is almost impossible to make any other generalizations about the independent commissions and agencies. They were set up piecemeal, each to solve a different, special problem. Some, like the Interstate Commerce Commission, employ thousands, have large separate buildings, have a permanent function, and affect the livelihood of almost every citizen. Others, like the Rubber Producing Facilities Disposal Commission, have a personnel of a dozen or fewer people and serve a very limited and temporary purpose. Each agency is based upon the particular law by which it was set up and upon other laws pertaining to it alone. Commissions and agencies fall into two classifications. The first class of agency is the **regulatory**: bodies charged with setting and maintaining the conditions of life in America, especially business life.

Interstate Commerce Commission

The oldest of the regulatory bodies, and the model for most others, is the Interstate Commerce Commission (ICC). In the period of sudden and tremendous expansion following the War Between the States, farmers claimed that railroads charged excessively high rates, discriminated against some persons and localities, conspired to prevent competition, and, in general, cheated the public at every turn. They organized groups called Granges to demand public control of railroads. They were strong enough to get several states to pass Granger laws to regulate railroads. Challenged by the railroads, the Granger laws were overruled by the Supreme Court. Demands for regulation continued, however, and finally brought about establishment of the Interstate Commerce Commission under the Interstate Commerce Act of 1887.

Ineffective though regulation was at first—because the Courts ruled against the Commission time and time again—the act was very important. It set up the first regulatory commission—and it still affects our lives today

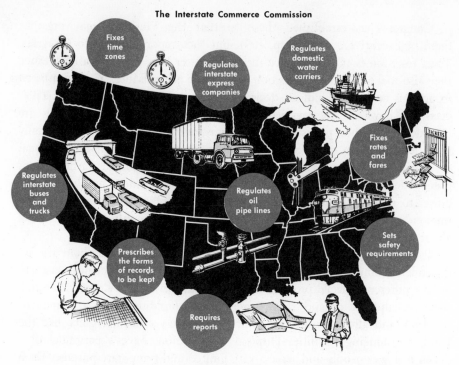

Originally there were five members, but today there are eleven, appointed by the President for six-year terms, only six from the same political party. They can be removed for proved misconduct. Many of the more than 2,500 employees are experts in economics and transportation, because the Commission deals with highly technical matters. In addition to the activities shown on the chart, the ICC investigates complaints of private citizens or companies about such things as train schedules and what services—such as diners—should be provided. It regulates bridges, ferries, and tunnels involved in interstate commerce.

through agencies which regulate television, air lines, labor relations, and many other areas.

Congress has no power to regulate commerce carried on exclusively *inside* (intra) any one of the states; but Article I, Section 8, gives it power to regulate commerce *among* (inter) the states. Thus, whenever a company engages in interstate commerce, or does any business that in some way *affects* interstate commerce (e.g., manufactures something sold in another state), it is subject to the authority of Congress. Under this power, Congress passed the Interstate Commerce Act.

The powers of the ICC were at first limited, both by the law and by decisions of the Court, to rather slight interference with railroad rates. However, in time the Congress greatly strengthened the Commission. Today the ICC reaches into your life in ways you may not suspect. For instance, if you find that a bus you use regularly to go to visit your grandmother in another state runs late and is so crowded that it seems unsafe, you (or a group of your fellow sufferers) have a way to register a complaint. You can write to the ICC. The Commission will also investigate your complaint about the absence of a diner on the overnight train you take to camp, and many other matters affecting your convenience and comfort. The drawing on p. 200 indicates some of the powers of the ICC today.

Let us take an example of the ICC in action. Suppose the Union Pacific Railroad finds its net income from carrying freight to points west of Chicago declining, though the amount of freight it handles remains about the same. The wages it must pay its workers are rising and the cost of fuel for its locomotives is also increasing. The company feels strongly that it is entitled to higher freight rates. Under these circumstances, the Union Pacific will apply to the ICC for a rate increase.

The ICC will then investigate. Experts from the Commission will examine the company's books, study wage rates, costs of material, and other pertinent matters, and report to the Commission. The Commission will hold a hearing at which representatives of the Union Pacific are given an opportunity to present their case for higher rates. At the same time, representatives of the companies shipping their goods over the Union Pacific will also present their case for keeping the rates down. The Commission must weigh all the evidence and all the claims and try to arrive at a decision that will be fair to all parties concerned. Whatever their decision may be, it will have the force of law.

If the Union Pacific disputes the rates thus set, it can appeal for a re-hearing to the Commission itself. If after such re-hearing the company still feels that it is being unfairly treated, it can appeal to the federal Courts. But it rarely does so, for the Commission's great experience and faithful protection of the public interest usually result in a rate which the Courts would uphold.

The ICC and Our Liberties You can see that the Interstate Commerce Commission seems to interfere directly in private business. Why do we permit such interference with our liberties without complaining? The Constitution (I, 8), as we have seen, gives Congress the power to regulate commerce among the states (see p. 53). When Congress, by authority of the Constitution, established the Interstate Commerce Commission, the idea was to protect the liberties of many by somewhat limiting the liberties of a few—namely, the railroads. Today the Commission regulates (limits the liberties of) railroads, bus and truck lines, express companies, pipe lines, water carriers, and others in the same way.

What has happened here is not that railroads have lost their economic liberty to make money. They have had this liberty restricted at the point where it interfered with the liberty of the shippers to ship their products at a rate which allowed them to make money, too.

The principle involved here is essential in a democracy. Liberty does not mean the right to do what you please *regardless* of others. It means, rather, the right to do what *you* please so long as it does not interfere with the rights of others to do as *they* please; the "others" are limited in the same way you are.

PRINCIPLES OF BUSINESS REGULATION Our whole system of business regulation is based on this principle. In other words, our laws and administrative agencies are intended to preserve the liberty of the individual by establishing fair rules applied equally to all. If there were no regulation, as Americans learned in the nineteenth century, one powerful company could squeeze smaller competitors out of business by operating for a time at prices other companies could not afford, or by giving special rates to a favored few. Thus the purpose of a regulatory body like the ICC is to establish uniform rates which are fair for all—providing greater equality of opportunity for any American going into business.

This is an entirely different notion from communism, under which the state controls and directs everything without regard to individual liberty. Having railroad and other transportation rates set by government is much like the decision many years ago forbidding pitchers to tamper with the cover of a baseball to make the ball do unpredictable things. The same principle of regulation protects railroads and trucking companies themselves. If the rates are the same for all, one company cannot drive another out of business by undercutting its prices.

Regulating Air Traffic

In the years immediately following World War I, when the airplane industry was in its infancy and young Charles A. Lindbergh was one of the few pilots carrying mail in small aircraft, there were only a few thousand miles of commercial airlines and almost no system of regulation and safety. Today the federal government, through the Civil Aeronautics Board and the Federal Aviation Agency, both independent bodies, controls and regulates more than 65,000 miles of carefully charted airways with hundreds of giant planes carrying millions of passengers and thousands of tons of freight and mail each year.

The Civil Aeronautics Board (CAB) is an agency of five men, appointed by the President with the consent of the Senate, who set the prices and fares on the airways, allocate routes to airlines, and investigate the causes of accidents in a continuing effort to improve air safety. The CAB coöperates closely with private airlines in all matters, and is charged by law with helping to

202

build our air transportation system. But CAB protects consumers as well, by setting fair rates and working for efficient routing and scheduling and safe flying.

The Federal Aviation Agency (FAA) replaced the old Civil Aeronautics Administration of the Commerce Department in 1959. FAA, whose Administrator is appointed by the President with the consent of the Senate, has great powers to make all traffic rules for domestic airways. It operates control towers, assists in designing and improving airfields, licenses pilots, inspects aircraft for commercial use, and manages all of the thousand details that are involved in regulating the operations of so complex an industry as air transportation. It coöperates closely with CAB, but has no responsibilities for policy on rates or route allocation. The Federal Aviation Agency also has full regulatory power over military aircraft when they are in flight on civil airways.

Federal Power Commission

If your electricity and gas are produced in another state, the rates you pay for them will be influenced by the Federal Power Commission (FPC). And if the river where you have been enjoying fishing is suddenly ruined for that purpose because a power company builds a plant on it, again you are being affected by the decisions of the FPC.

The FPC, established in 1920, is another important body which helps to regulate interstate commerce. It controls rates and conditions of transport of all electric power and natural gas which is sold across state lines. It must also pass on applications of private power companies wishing to develop new electric power resources on either navigable rivers or public lands. The FPC does not build dams or power plants but feels strongly the political pressure of those who do—private companies, which are often opposed by groups preferring to have the government build and own electric power installations like TVA (see pp. 209–210 and Chapter 21).

As we shall see in Chapter 11, much of the rate setting in public utilities (services used by everyone, such as electricity, gas, water, telephone, or telegraph) affecting the consumer is done by state regulating bodies. This is because much of our electricity and gas is produced from fuels in the state where they are used.

The Federal Power Commission is composed of five members, appointed by the President and approved by the Senate, serving terms of five years each. It is served by a staff of more than 600 experts and specialists, many of whom are accountants who do the technical work connected with setting power rates. Its procedures are much like those of the Interstate Commerce Commission.

HE CAN ADAPT IT
TO ANY NECESSITY

The late Hubert Harper in
Birmingham News

Federal Trade Commission

A different sort of regulation is carried on by the Federal Trade Commission (FTC). This Commission was established in 1914 to make rules of fair competition for businesses engaged in interstate commerce. It does not fix prices, but it does have the power to prevent companies from selling under cost in order to drive competitors out of business, as well as many powers over selling and advertising practices. Its usual procedure is to hear and act upon complaints brought by one company against another, or directly by consumers. It may also start investigations. Complaints are thoroughly investigated and heard by a trial examiner, who reports his findings to the Commission. The Commission, if it finds the complaint justified, has power to issue an order compelling the offending company to change its ways. These orders can be enforced in federal Courts, with heavy penalties attached for disobedience.

Here is a sample of the kind of national advertising that the FTC may force a business to discontinue.

> "The Deep-Freeze Home Freezer pays for itself in a surprisingly short time."
>
> "Cut food bills $200 a year."
>
> "Amazing, but true! You will cut your food bills 10 to 25 percent."

The Commission, of course, prohibited this advertising because the company could not prove that such savings could be made. Smear campaigns by one company against another, too close imitation of trademarks or slogans, and various kinds of bribery and corruption in order to sell goods or obtain contracts unfairly are also the concern of the FTC.

The Federal Trade Commission has five members appointed by the President, with advice and consent of the Senate, for seven-year terms. It is served by about 600 employees, of whom the largest number are trained investigators.

Federal Communications Commission

The Federal Communications Commission (FCC) was established in 1934 to regulate telephone, telegraph, radio, and television transmission across state lines. Such transmission for profit is considered interstate commerce, and falls under the commerce clause of the Constitution (see p. 53).

The FCC has seven members appointed by the President, with the approval of the Senate, who serve seven-year terms. Its employees number over 1,000, many of whom are skilled engineers. The FCC handles telephone and telegraph communications in the way the ICC handles transportation. It sets rates, or approves them, regulates the conditions of service, and in general protects the public interest by preventing telephone or telegraph companies which operate across state lines from discontinuing services unless the FCC approves. Nor can new lines be installed without FCC approval.

In the fields of radio and television, it does not set rates or prices, but it has the sole power to issue licenses to stations and authorize their use of frequencies or channels. When five corporations applied for the right to set up a high-frequency television station in the Boston area, the examiner representing the FCC decided which of the five would be given this privilege. The four losers then appealed unsuccessfully to the Commission, as is their right under the law.

By law the FCC must handle licensing to protect the public interest. Through this power, it helps to keep television programs reasonably varied. It also encourages cultural and educational programs.

The FCC assures non-partisanship or bi-partisanship in political or other highly controversial matters, by requiring that free time given to one political party must be matched by free time to the other. Stations will *not* sell time to *private* persons to make propaganda for a special cause. In Chapter 17, we will discuss the *sale* of time to a political party.

In many other countries, radio and television are operated as government enterprises. Thus, in England the British Broadcasting Company (BBC) divides radio and television time evenly between the parties during elections to the obvious advantage of the people. But the American tradition

205

favors private ownership in as many fields as possible. The solution to the American problems involved in the cost and assignment of time for political broadcasts will no doubt eventually be found within the system of *public regulation* of *private enterprise*.

The FCC has no power to censor actual broadcasts. However, since it does have power to revoke licenses (which have to be renewed every three years), it has made broadcasters develop their own codes of good behavior. These self-imposed broadcasting codes—against profanity, obscenity, partisanship (except in paid political broadcasts)—are good examples of the fact that freedom cannot be separated from responsibility. The broadcasters protect themselves against interference by the government and protect the interests of the public at the same time. Government, in the form of the Federal Communications Commission, is always in the background to see that the rules are enforced.

Securities and Exchange Commission

When the stock market crashed in 1929, the American public reacted strongly against irresponsible and misleading practices in the sale of stocks. During the "boom" of the 1920's, many Americans had bought stocks, either for invested savings or for speculation. Occasionally a company failed and many stockholders lost their money. In general, though, prices continued to go up and buying increased. Thus, when the prices of stocks on the New York Exchange began to fall rapidly in October, 1929, thousands of people were financially wiped out and millions more suffered to a greater or lesser extent. Many had bought their stock by borrowing money or by advancing only a part of the purchase price (buying on a **margin**). Unsound buying and dishonest selling were dramatized by the crash. Human suffering was great, and a number of people actually committed suicide. The need for government regulation to protect the public was obvious. The Securities and Exchange Act of 1933 was the response of Congress to a recommendation by President Franklin D. Roosevelt

The Securities and Exchange Commission (SEC), set up in 1934, has five members appointed by the President, with the consent of the Senate, for five-year terms. It now has more than 700 employees and authorizes all stock issues or other securities of companies which do business across state lines. It makes rules regarding the kinds of stock allowed to be sold and the places where they are sold (**stock exchanges**), and requires and publishes for public use all information about the companies selling securities (how much business they do, their assets, etc.).

In 1956, the Ford Motor Company sold stock to the public for the first time. The company was required to reveal certain facts about its operations. The people, for example, learned that Ford's 1954 sales were over four billion dollars, and that the corporation had assets of almost two and one-half billion dollars. This is just a part of the information that Ford was required to give before the Commission allowed the corporation to sell its stock. Incidentally, over 350,000 persons purchased these securities and thus became part owners of the Ford Motor Company.

Through the efforts of the SEC, stock and bond frauds have been reduced greatly, and public confidence in American stock traders and trading, which had fallen to a very low point in the early 1930's, has been revived. Much of the work of the SEC is technical, and it employs several hundred experts in accounting and finance. When a company wishes to sell stock to the public, the SEC holds hearings on request, makes its own investigations, and tries to make decisions which are fair to business and at the same time protect the public. As possible investors, you should know that the SEC could not and does not guarantee that companies which meet "truth in securities" requirements will be successful.

National Labor Relations Board

An agency which does not regulate business in quite the same way as the commissions we have discussed nevertheless serves very much to protect the public interest. This is the National Labor Relations Board (NRLB). The function of this vitally important agency of government is to regulate the relations between labor unions and industry.

If you were a factory worker, or an employer, you would know from your own experience what this kind of regulation means. You are free to join a labor union which represents you in bargaining with your employer about wages and working conditions, as we shall see in Chapter 22. If you are an employer, you must bargain with a union which has a majority of the workers in your factory and abide by the contract you negotiate with them. So must the union. The NLRB is the agency which enforces the rules covering all these matters.

The National Labor Relations Board was established in 1935 to carry out the provisions of the Wagner Act. This law stated that workers could join or form a union and bargain collectively—that is, through union representatives—for better pay and better working conditions. Employers were not allowed to discriminate against union members in hiring and firing, or to refuse to bargain with the union. The Wagner Act, based on the Interstate Commerce Clause (I, 8), referred to all industries which somehow crossed state lines.

While the NLRB under the Wagner Act protected the rights of unions, it did not force unions to fulfill their responsibilities and duties. Thus, in 1947, the Wagner Act was amended by the Taft-Hartley Act to protect also certain rights of employers as well as individual workers against unfair practices by unions. The law was further amended in 1959 to protect workers against corrupt leaders. (See Chap. 22.)

The NLRB now has five members appointed by the President, with the consent of the Senate, for five-year terms, who make all final decisions in labor disputes under its jurisdiction. Unlike other commissions, the Board has also a General Counsel who prepares cases and argues them before the Board. The Counsel of the NLRB has a great deal of power in matters of labor relations.

If a group of workers wish to be represented by a certain union at the bargaining table, they can ask the NLRB to conduct an election at the company; that is one of the two principal functions of the NLRB. NLRB staff men prepare the ballots, oversee the election, and report the returns. If a union wins a majority, the NLRB then orders the company to recognize the union and to bargain with it for a contract. We shall discuss labor contracts in Chapter 22.

The second function of the NLRB is to enforce rules against unfair practices either by unions or by employers. For example, employers are forbidden to: (1) interfere with attempts of workers to form unions; (2) refuse to bargain with union representatives; (3) support company unions; (4) punish an employee for activity as a union member; (5) use their influence to keep employees from becoming union members or taking part in union activities.

At the same time, unions are forbidden to: (1) refuse to bargain with employers; (2) charge excessive or discriminatory dues; (3) force an employer to hire more workers than he needs; (4) strike over the question of which of two unions should perform a job (**jurisdictional dispute**); (5) strike against an employer to force him not to do business with a different employer whose workers are on strike (**secondary boycott**); (6) strike against the federal government; (7) strike to force an employer to deal with a union which is not certified by the NLRB.

These and many other rules are enforced by the NLRB upon complaint from any aggrieved party by the usual means of hearing, investigation, perhaps an order to one of the parties to stop the practice complained of, and, if necessary, court action.

INDEPENDENT CREATIVE (POSITIVE) AGENCIES

The agencies we have just been discussing are all regulatory. There is a second class of agencies, called *positive* or *creative*, which carry on creative activity of the government on behalf of the people. While most of the creative services and activities (building dams, clearing harbors, erecting post offices) carried on by the federal government in the public interest are the responsibilities of the departments of the executive branch, several of the

208

most important, such as production of atomic energy, have been entrusted by Congress to certain special agencies. The chart on p. 212 shows the number and scope of such agencies. Four of them, which are of far-reaching significance, deserve special attention.

Tennessee Valley Authority

The Tennessee Valley Authority (TVA) may well be one of the most controversial agencies of a free government in the world. It is certainly one of the most spectacular.

If you had been a farmer in northern Alabama or a housewife in a small Tennessee town about thirty years ago, you would have had no telephone, no electric fixtures, and no running water. As a farmer, your crops would have been poor for lack of water and good fertilizers. As a housewife, you would have had none of the conveniences we call modern.

Today, as a farmer you have available electric power at rates you can afford, and the telephone connects you not only with your neighbors but also with any point in the country. As a housewife, you may have not only a telephone and running water but also a washing machine, an electric refrigerator, a freezer, and perhaps a television set. All these things have come to you through the Tennessee Valley Authority.

The act of Congress establishing TVA in 1933 was the climax of a great public debate raging since the end of World War I. During that war, the War Department had constructed a dam and chemical plants at Muscle Shoals, Alabama, for use in the war effort. After the war, advocates of government ownership of electric power wanted the federal government to use the property to provide power, flood control, and manufactured fertilizers to develop the Tennessee Valley. Those who favored private ownership of electric power argued that government should sell these properties to private companies.

TVA settled the issue. It is an independent agency which owns outright the old Muscle Shoals property. Under the 1933 act, it has developed electric power on a large scale and has carried on other extensive activities throughout the whole Tennessee Valley area, reaching into seven states (see p. 530).

TVA is an example of what is known as a **government corporation;** that is, it is organized like a business, but the stock is entirely owned by the government. As a corporation, it not only receives money by appropriation from Congress but also collects its own revenue from the sale of electric power and other products. It can carry on any activities allowed by its charter.

The constitutional basis of the law establishing TVA is Article IV, Section 3: "The Congress shall have power to dispose of and make all needful rules and regulations respecting the territory or other property belonging to the United States" (see p. 60).

The President appoints, with the consent of the Senate, a Board of Directors, three in number, who serve nine-year terms. The Board makes broad decisions on policy, appoints the general manager, and accepts responsibility for the entire operation. The Board reports annually to Congress. TVA has its own personnel system, including its own merit rating and civil service regulations outside the jurisdiction of the Civil Service Commission. TVA also has greater control over its finances than do other agencies. It may be sued in the courts of law, whereas other government agencies may not be sued unless they grant permission.

We shall consider other aspects of TVA in Chap. 21.

Atomic Energy Commission

The release of atomic energy was dramatized not only by the terrible destruction of Hiroshima and Nagasaki, which ended World War II, but also by the 60,000-mile cruise of the submarine *Nautilus* powered by a tiny lump of uranium. It brought the government of the United States into a new business, which can have far-reaching consequences, both for improving our way of living and for military purposes.

The use of atomic power—that is, the controlled splitting (fission) of the uranium atom—was developed as part of the war effort between 1941 and 1945. Research was under the military departments, and the first production was directed by highly secret organizations of civilian scientists and military personnel in specially built factories owned by the government. But in 1946, after the war was over, Congress passed the Atomic Energy Act to determine the future course of atomic research and production for both defense and peaceful uses.

MAKE-UP OF THE AEC   The Atomic Energy Commission (AEC) came into being under the 1946 law. It is a government-owned corporation, headed by a commission of five men appointed by the President, with the consent of the Senate, and serving five-year terms. The Commission is responsible for all atomic policy under the law, appoints the general manager and other high officials, and reports annually to Congress. It is aided by a nine-man Advisory Committee, whose members serve six-year terms. This body, consisting mainly of scientists, is also appointed by the President with the consent of the Senate. The Commission spends annual appropriations running into billions of dollars and employs about 6,000 people. This Commission works with a joint committee of the House and Senate (see p. 128).

RESPONSIBILITIES   The Atomic Energy Act made national defense the first responsibility of the AEC, but charged it also with "improving the public welfare, increasing the standard of living, strengthening free competition in private enterprise, and promoting world peace."

The AEC has six major divisions: Research, Production, Engineering, Military Application, Reactor Development, Biology, and Medicine. Their vast range indicates the tremendous possibilities in the use of atomic power, from making bombs and driving submarines to curing or controlling disease and breeding plants.

METHODS OF OPERATION To carry out its functions, the AEC owns several research centers, of which the largest is at Los Alamos, New Mexico. There most of the weapons development is carried on. This laboratory is run by the University of California for the federal government by contract. Many other universities are responsible for research programs by contract with the Commission. Actual production is carried on by private corporations under contract with AEC.

The AEC also owns factories and facilities, such as the huge installations at Oak Ridge, Tennessee, and Hanford, Washington, but contracts with private business for their operation. Under the law, the AEC owns all so-called fissionable material, such as uranium, used in producing atomic energy, and sets the price it will pay for such material. The Geiger counter which registers the presence of radiating minerals has become a familiar gadget. Though we may be envious, we are no longer surprised to read of a store clerk who has made a "strike" in the Adirondacks. The uranium "rush" has excited the imagination of many Americans in recent years because there is a guaranteed market for any ore the prospector may discover. In 1954 the law was modified to permit the AEC to sell some of its material to private industry for private manufacturing purposes, always subject to close watch by the AEC.

Atomic weapons are not the only concern of the AEC and private industry. They are deeply involved in research and production for peaceful purposes. Electric power plants, with boilers heated by atomic energy, are being built. It is possible that eventually such power will be cheaper than power produced by water or by steam plants burning coal or coke. Atomic-powered engines are moving from the experimental to the practical stage. Already atomic-powered ships have been launched. By-products of atomic manufacture have potentially great value for medical science. In your own lifetime, your electric power may come from an atomic power plant. You may travel in atomic-powered airplanes and ships. And you may well live to see such dread diseases as cancer overcome by controlled radiation.

Because atomic energy can be so destructive, it appears to be one field of enterprise in which government will have full control and the greatest part of ownership for a long time to come. However, as the law provides, private

211

The Executive Branch of the Government of The United States and the Independent Agencies and Commissions

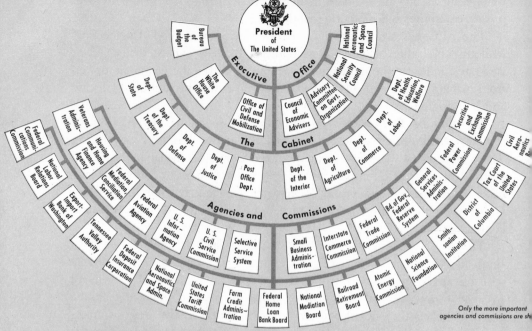

Only the more important agencies and commissions are shown

Adapted from United States Government Organization Manual, 195

NATIONAL SCIENCE FOUNDATION

Director, appointed by President with consent of Senate, with staff of about 300 employees. Is advised by **NATIONAL SCIENCE BOARD**, 24 members, representing scientific and educational field. Foundation makes contracts with private agencies, individuals, and universities. Promotes *basic research* (the kind of theoretical work which led to release of atomic energy) by awarding scholarships and fellowships to scientists to review scientific work of government and private interests, to exchange information with other countries, to keep roster of personnel available for its work.

SMITHSONIAN INSTITUTION

Sponsors scientific explorations and research and publishes scholarly papers. In CANAL ZONE BIOLOGICAL AREA in Central America (area set aside by Congress in 1940), the Institution carries on scientific investigation of plant and animal life. Its library, including works in Library of Congress, contains scientific publications from all over the world. With more than 900,000 volumes, this library is valuable research tool for scientists. (See also text, p. 214.)

See p. 163 for references to other agencies.

industry will benefit both from the eventual cheap power and from the opportunity to make atomic products commercially under AEC license. The AEC probably has more potential value for the public welfare than any other agency of government. In Chapter 25 we shall discuss the relations of atomic weapons testing to human health and international relations.

National Science Foundation

Not all the federal government's concern with science is as specialized as the AEC's. Recognizing that the advancement of science and technology are of the utmost importance in shaping the future of this country and the world, the government, by act of Congress in 1950, established the National Science

Foundation (NSF) as an independent agency to "promote the progress of science; advance the national health, prosperity, and welfare, and secure the national defense." (See chart, p. 212.) Its practical value to American citizens in such matters as technology, nutrition, and health is likely to prove great. You may some day be eligible for a scholarship for advanced study and research from the National Science Foundation. Your family—indeed, your whole generation—will certainly have better health and greater material comfort as a result of NSF research.

SPACE-AGE AGENCIES

Numerous agencies have been established by both the government and private organizations for such purposes as: (1) research into the development of rockets, missiles, and space vehicles; (2) evaluations of the means of defense against missile warfare; and (3) analyses of problems arising from space exploration. While there is some overlapping, one might break down the government agencies in terms of those concerned primarily with policy-making and coördination, and those under military or civilian control. The agencies established by private organizations concern themselves with various problems pertaining to the space age. (See also pp. 690–691.)

GOVERNMENT AGENCIES

Policy-Making and Coördination
NASC (*National Aeronautics and Space Council*). Under the chairmanship of the President, the NASC determines policy for all U.S. space programs.

MILITARY

ARDC (*Air Research and Development Command*). The ARDC coördinates and controls all of the Air Force's research and developmental programs.

ARPA (*Advanced Research Projects Agency*). The ARPA is in charge of all purely military space projects (the counterpart of the civilian NASA), and is also responsible for developing anti-missile missiles.

BMD (*Ballistic Missile Division*). A part of the ARDC, the BMD has developed such missiles as the Thor, Atlas, and Titan, and is also working on moon rockets and satellites.

ONR (*Office of Naval Research*). Controls research by the Navy in rocketry.

OSR (*Office of Scientific Research*). A section of the Air Force's ARDC, the OSR concerns itself with basic scientific research.

CIVILIAN

JPL (*Jet Propulsion Laboratory*). The JPL, managed by California Institute of Technology, is the NASA laboratory which developed the Explorer satellites and contributed its efforts and help to the Army in its moon probes. It was also the only U.S. agency to pick up signals from Russia's first moon rocket.

NASA (*National Aeronautics and Space Administration*). While the ARPA handles all military projects, the NASA controls all non-military space research.

ABMA (*Army Ballistic Missile Agency*). Headed by Dr. Wernher von Braun, the ABMA at Huntsville, Ala., has developed such missiles as the Redstone and Jupiter for the Army. Transferred to NASA in 1959.

PRIVATE ORGANIZATIONS

RAND (*Research and Development Corporation*). A private, non-profit organization, RAND concerns itself with analyzing and attempting to predict and solve future defense problems for U.S. agencies.

STL (*Space Technology Laboratories*). Another private organization, STL provides expert technical advice and assistance for governmental agencies when called upon.

Smithsonian Institution

Perhaps the most popular attraction for the tourist sightseeing in Washington is the Smithsonian Institution on the Mall. The world-famous museum is noted for its exhibitions of American natural science, ethnology, and history. The splendid collection of painting and sculpture at the National Gallery of Art and the oriental art at the Freer Gallery are also a part of the Smithsonian Institution. The National Zoological Park in Rock Creek Park completes the Smithsonian's exhibits in the District of Columbia. For other functions, see chart, p. 212.

Veterans' Administration

Another independent agency wholly different from these we have considered is the Veterans' Administration (VA). From the beginning of our government, people have wanted to reward and compensate our men and women who have served in the armed forces. After the Revolution the federal government offered free land to veterans who staked out homesteads. Over the years innumerable other benefits of all kinds have been gradually introduced.

The veterans, like other interest groups, have formed an effective lobby to persuade Congress to take action on their behalf. This lobby includes such important national organizations as the American Legion, the Veterans of Foreign Wars, and the Disabled American Veterans. However, some American veterans question the wisdom of special treatment for veterans other than disability benefits. After World War II a new organization, named the American Veterans Committee, was established with the slogan "Citizens first; Veterans second." It is against most special privileges for veterans. By the mid-twentieth century, veterans' assistance nevertheless constituted the largest cash outlay of the national government except for national defense itself.

MAKE-UP OF VA   The present-day Veterans' Administration was established by executive order in 1930 as an independent agency. However, the power of the President to appoint or remove the Administrator places the VA in a different category from most of the independent agencies we have been studying. The VA is independent of the departments of government but not of the chief executive.

The Administrator of Veterans' Affairs, as he is known, is assisted by more than 5,000 deputies and assistants and their staffs in the central office at Washington. Local and regional offices throughout the country, which do the largest part of the work, employ more than 160,000 persons.

214

FUNCTIONS The annual appropriations for the VA run into billions. The money is spent for many things. There is regular compensation for disability, and pensions for survivors of service people who died in service. Vocational rehabilitation for the disabled or partially disabled is another use. Education and training, such as the so-called G.I. Bill of Rights, which enabled service people of World War II and the Korean War to continue their education at public expense, uses much money. Then there is medical and surgical care at the many veterans' hospitals and mental institutions, allowances for unemployment, life insurance through a VA-operated life insurance company, and loans or subsidies for business, housing, or farming. The Veterans' Administration provides for our millions of veterans benefits and services affecting almost every aspect of human life. Nearly all these benefits and services are supplemented by veterans' agencies of the states which have similar functions.

A CASE HISTORY We can get some idea of how these benefits work by looking at the case of Joe, who served as a sergeant in the army during the Korean War. Joe was wounded in the leg and suffers from pain and a limp. Before he went into the service, Joe was a machinist, making a good income to support himself, his wife, and his two small children. But back home again things are tough for him. It is the VA that comes to his rescue.

His first step is to consult a counselor at his local VA office. He is given the necessary papers to admit him as an outpatient of the VA hopsital, where he receives weekly treatment for his leg. He files an application for educational benefits under the Korean G.I. Bill. Under this he goes to a refresher course for machinists for three months, meanwhile receiving an income from the VA to support himself and his family. When his training is completed, he goes to his *state* veterans' agency, where he is advised on job placement. In a few months, Joe is back at work as a civilian, more skilled than ever in his old trade. His family is insured against his death or permanent disability because he carries an insurance policy under the VA. If his leg should become worse so that he must give up work for a time, the VA will pay him an unemployment benefit to help tide him over.

Things go so well for Joe that he decides the time has come to buy his own home. Again the VA comes to his aid by lending him the money he needs to buy, on easy terms spread over many years. Under the state law, the taxes on his home will be reduced substantially below what non-veterans have to pay. There are still more benefits and services Joe might receive from the VA and from his state veterans' agency. These examples show to what extent Uncle Sam and the state governments look after the men and women who have served in our armed forces.

215

United States Information Agency

An important independent agency, established in the years since the Cold War began, is the United States Information Agency (USIA) which operates the famous overseas radio "Voice of America" (see p. 645). This agency was set up in 1953 after some years of experiment with agencies both inside and outside the State Department. Its purpose is to inform people everywhere about the ways of life in the United States and about American policies. Besides the radio stations which broadcast the Voice of America, USIA distributes books and periodicals to American libraries and information centers in dozens of foreign cities in some 80 countries. There are about 200 overseas missions operated by USIA. These are directly responsible to the chiefs of American diplomatic missions in the areas where they are situated (see pp. 632–635).

In recent years the USIA has given particular attention to cultural exchanges. The USIA is at work behind the scenes in connection with the scientific and cultural exhibits of the Soviet Union which you read about or, perhaps, have seen; and it is working to present American exhibits abroad, especially in the Soviet Union and other "Iron Curtain" countries.

The Director of USIA is appointed by the President with the consent of the Senate. He has a difficult political role to perform, since he must keep close liaison with other American operations overseas, especially the State and Defense Departments. And he must continually defend his policy of presenting America before Congress, some of whose members are almost certain to disagree with the Director as to what is "American."

SUMMARY

In this chapter you have seen that the typical "bureaucrats" do the work that you and I think of as indispensable—work by the government on behalf of all the people. You have read about independent agencies, belonging neither to Congress nor to the executive branch. One of these, the Civil Service Commission, sets the standards for government employment and safeguards the careers of government workers.

Other agencies which regulate various aspects of our business and commercial life are the Interstate Commerce Commission (transportation), the Federal Power Commission (public utilities), the Federal Trade Commission (business practices), the Federal Communications Commission (radio, television, telephone, and telegraph), the Securities and Exchange Commission (stocks and bonds and securities markets), and the National Labor Relations Board (labor-management relations). All these agencies serve the whole American people not by invading their private rights but by limiting these rights and privileges in such ways as to keep them safe and to provide fair rules of service and competition.

You have seen several of our great positive and creative agencies, which carry on enterprises either too expensive for private business or too closely bound up with our national security to be left in private hands. The Tennessee Valley Authority, a government corporation, controls a great river affecting seven states. It generates power at dams, conserves water, reclaims poor land, produces cheap chemical fertilizers, etc. The Atomic Energy Commission produces our atomic energy for both military and peaceful purposes and contracts with private business for the advancement of this wonderful new promise of material progress. A new agency, the National Science Foundation, gives national government backing to the fundamental scientific research needed to keep us in our position of world scientific leadership. The Veterans' Administration is a vast service agency to care for the millions of Americans who have served in the armed forces of the United States.

All these independent agencies, and many others we have not space to describe here, represent government activities of a special nature, outside the regular activities and services performed for us by the executive departments we shall study in later chapters. You may now have a better idea of how vast our government must be to serve our huge and growing nation.

KNOW WHAT YOU READ

1. What is a bureaucrat?
2. What is the difference between "classified" and "unclassified" positions in government?
3. Why was the Civil Service Commission established? What part does the Commission play in filling positions in the classified civil service?
4. Why are such agencies as the FCC, the AEC, and the NLRB called *independent*?
5. In what ways may such agencies be legislative, executive, judicial?
6. When and why did Congress establish the Interstate Commerce Commission? What powers does the Commission now have?
7. If you as a businessman believed that your section of the country should have lower freight rates, to what government agency would you express your opinion?
8. Two Providence, Rhode Island, firms applied for a channel 12 television station in that city. What government agency decided which firm should be allowed to set up the station?

9. Summarize the work of the Securities and Exchange Commission.
10. What is a *government corporation?*
11. State the provisions of the Atomic Energy Act of 1946.
12. What is the great importance of the research center at Los Alamos, New Mexico?
13. In what ways is atomic energy used for peaceful purposes?
14. What is *basic* research?

WHAT DO YOU THINK?

1. Just a few years ago an eastern railroad was investigated by several governmental agencies because a great number of railroad patrons complained that too many of the trains were late. To what agencies do you think the line's patrons complained?
2. In some countries radio and television are government monopolies. Would we get better programs under government ownership?
3. An honorably discharged veteran has 5 points added to his Civil Service examination score. Ten points are added to the scores of disabled veterans, as well as to the scores of wives of disabled veterans who cannot work. Why do you think this is done?
4. Why is such an agency as the General Services Administration necessary in the present-day executive branch? Discuss.
5. Why might the "new business" of atomic energy become "the most important in the history of man"?
6. Study the cartoon, p. 204. What do you think the artist is saying about independent agencies?
7. Should private industry also encourage basic research? Why?
8. Study the drawing on p. 200 of the Interstate Commerce Commission. Explain why the powers indicated fall under that Commission. Can you name some additional powers of the ICC?

PROBLEMS AND PROJECTS FOR YOU

1. The Federal Trade Commission has been called Uncle Sam's competition policeman. If you were a businessman engaged in interstate commerce, you might discover that you would be in trouble with this policeman if you engaged in any of the following practices:
   Selling below cost to destroy competition
   Advertising rebuilt merchandise as new products
   Misbranding your products
   For a more complete listing of forbidden practices, see Burns and Pelta-

son, *Government by the People*, chapter on Government as Regulator. Describe some of these to the class.

2. Read in *Only Yesterday* by Frederick Lewis Allen the chapter on the stock market crash. Report to the class. Be sure to point out why this experience led many people to believe that the market should be regulated.

3. Strictly speaking, the *civil service* means all government civilian employees except those in the high administrative positions. Look up in a dictionary of political terms the meaning of *merit system*. Use in a sentence each of these: civil service; merit system.

4. Five young ladies made these scores on a civil service test for the position of stenographer. Miss Green—92, Miss Smith—91, Miss Brown—89, Miss Jones (a veteran)—88, Miss White—69. At this time there is a stenographic vacancy in the Bureau of Motor Carriers. Which of the names do you think the Civil Service Commission will send to the Bureau? Why?

5. One way to operate the Tennessee Valley project would have been to have the flood control work done by the Army Engineers, irrigation by the Bureau of Reclamation, conservation by the Soil Conservation Service, and power by the Federal Power Commission.

    (a) What are the advantages of the form of organization which has been established for TVA?

    (b) Make an original chart to show the organization of TVA.

6. After studying the picture story on p. 194, make a list of additional agencies, listing the way they regulate economic aspects of our lives.

7. Report to the class on the Los Alamos research center.

8. Make a list of the agencies studied in this chapter. Place a check mark after the name of each agency which has some effect on your own life. Explain this effect. Double check those which do government business in your community.

9. What is the name of the agency which regulates public utilities in your state? Exactly what are its powers and duties? How are its members selected?

10. Many American scientists have expressed concern that our country's schools and colleges are graduating too few physicists, chemists, and other scientists. What is the National Science Foundation doing about this shortage? What recommendations would you like to make as to ways in which federal and state governments can do more to help increase the number of young men and young women going into science.

11. Read in Cushman, *Leading Constitutional Decisions*, the Supreme Court's decision on the regulation of interstate commerce. How might our history have been different if the Court had ruled in favor of state regulation?

12. Prepare a report on the work of the Federal Trade Commission, showing ways in which members of the general public are protected by this regulatory agency.

EXTEND YOUR VOCABULARY

bureaucrat	civil service	secondary boycott
bureaucracy	regulatory agency	creative (positive) agency
classified position	Interstate Commerce Act	government corporation
unclassified position	of 1887	board of directors
Register	Stock Exchange	fission
spoils system	Wagner Act	scholarship
Pendleton Act	Taft-Hartley Act	fellowship
merit system	jurisdictional dispute	G.I. Bill of Rights

YOUR NOTEBOOK: THE GOVERNMENT OF ——

1. Which government jobs (local, state, federal) in your community are filled through the merit system? List them, federal civil service jobs in one column, state or county civil service in another.
2. Name the agency, department, or commission in your state which (a) supervises state parks; (b) regulates intrastate commerce.

READ MORE ABOUT IT

APPLEBY, PAUL, *Big Democracy*. Knopf, 1945.
Interesting discussion of politics and merit in federal bureaucracy.
BLAU, PETER M., *Bureaucracy in Modern Society*. Random House, 1957.
A well-balanced evaluation.
BURNS, JAMES M., and PELTASON, JACK W., *Government by the People*. Prentice-Hall, 1954. Chaps. 17, 22–24.
CUSHMAN, ROBERT E., *The Independent Regulatory Commissions*. Oxford University Press, 1941.
Growth of a recent "arm" of the national government to help the President in administering government.
DIXON, ROBERT G., and PLISCHKE, ELMER, *American Government: Basic Documents and Materials*. Van Nostrand, 1950.
A valuable source book.
IRISH, MARIAN D., and PROTHRO, JAMES W., *The Politics of American Democracy*. Prentice-Hall, 1959. Chap. 13.
SWARTHOUT, JOHN M., and BARTLEY, ERNEST R., *Principles and Problems of American National Government*, Oxford University Press, 1955. Chaps. 16, 17, 22–26.
WHITE, LEONARD D., *The Federalists*. Macmillan, 1948.
——, *The Jacksonians*. Macmillan, 1954.
——, *The Jeffersonians*. Macmillan, 1951.
——, *The Republican Era*. Macmillan, 1957.
These four books form history of the growth of administration in our national government.

CHAPTER 9

The Judiciary

In this chapter you will learn about

The judicial process
Written, unwritten, and constitutional law
Independence and impartiality of judges
Government of laws and individual rights
The jury system
Federal Courts
State and local courts

It is remarkable how little the ordinary citizen knows about judges and courts of law. At the same time, Americans feel deeply the importance of judges and courts, and look upon them with something like reverence. In 1937 President Franklin Roosevelt became so exasperated with the Supreme Court of the United States, because it had declared unconstitutional a number of laws he favored, that he proposed to increase the size of the Court—to "pack" it with judges favorable to his point of view. Despite the popularity of President Roosevelt, this proposal met with an emotional reaction so strong that it was soundly defeated by a Congress overwhelmingly of the President's own political party. The people and their Congress seemed to rise up and say, "Hands off the Court!"

The independence of the judiciary and its separation from the legislative and executive branches of government began long before the American Revolution. In fact, each of the thirteen original colonies of the United States had independent courts and judges. When the national government was founded, no one even thought of national courts without the same independence.

The Courts are "government" in quite a different way from the executive and legislative branches. It is the job of the Courts to see that the rules are applied equally to government and to the citizens. Judges are called judges because they judge; that is, they are part of the government because their decisions have the force of law.

THE JUDICIARY AND THE LAW

Broadly speaking, the judiciary branch carries out its functions of judging in two different ways. First, it determines the guilt or innocence of persons accused by government of violating ordinances or breaking laws; that is, the courts make decisions regarding violations and crimes. Petty violations, such as illegal parking, are known as **offenses** and carry only light penalties—small fines, suspension of license, some hours or days in jail for repeated violations. There are two kinds of criminal lawbreaking: misdemeanors and felonies. **Misdemeanors** are petty thefts (**larceny**), disorderly conduct, or speeding. They are punished by small fines or brief jail sentences. **Felonies** are more serious crimes such as robbery (**grand larceny**), arson, and homicide in the first, second, and third degree. The punishments for these are heavier—long prison sentences or even death.

The second judiciary function is to judge disputes between citizens, groups of citizens, or citizens and their government. These cases are called **civil.** Civil actions in court include claims for wrongful injury to person or property, or for restitution of money or property lost by reason of fraud, or for harm caused by failure to perform a contract (see p. 246). If a person claims he has been damaged (he is the **plaintiff**), the court will either agree, and require **defendant** (the person accused of doing the damage) to pay a certain sum, or decide in defendant's favor, requiring plaintiff to pay court costs. In cases where a person *anticipates* damage—to his property, for example—by somebody else's intended action, he may ask the court to **forbid** the action. If plaintiff wins such a suit the court will issue an **injunction** (an order forbidding the action). The ancient term *equity* is sometimes applied to the latter type of case.

Thus, the two main branches of law are the **criminal law** and the **civil law.** Penalties for crimes are written down in statutes enacted by legislatures and known as the **penal** or **criminal code.** The civil law, too, may be statutory, but often is not written down at all. It is found, rather, in the decisions of judges in thousands and thousands of cases over several hundred years. Thus American law is of two sorts—**written** and **unwritten.**

Unwritten (Common) Law

These basic distinctions in the Anglo-American system of justice can best be illustrated by an all too common episode in our lives today—an automobile accident. Let us suppose that automobiles are so new that there are no laws about them on the books at all. Not too many years ago this was true. Now let us suppose that you are driving along at sixty miles an hour and run into a horse and wagon, causing, of course, very serious damage. Mr. Ichabod, the owner of the horse and wagon, decides to sue you.

Mr. Ichabod, like most citizens, will probably not know which court he should go to. He does know that he needs a lawyer and the lawyer knows what to do. He goes to the court which has the proper **jurisdiction**—that is, has authority under law to determine the question of your liability for the accident (whether you are responsible and how much damages you should pay), and the power to enforce its judgment. He serves you with a **summons** (see p. 247) to appear in that court on a certain day to show cause why you should not pay damages to Mr. Ichabod. This proceeding is a **trial**; Mr. Ichabod is the **plaintiff**; and you are the **defendant**. At the trial Mr. Ichabod's lawyer calls all the witnesses he has in order to prove Mr. Ichabod was damaged, and your lawyer (you will need a lawyer to defend you) puts in all his evidence as to what you claim to have happened. (We shall consider the citizen's privileges in civil suits in detail in Chapter 10.) Then your lawyer argues that the case should be dismissed because there is no law regulating the speed of automobiles.

To this the judge might reply as follows: "You are right. There is no **written**—that is, **statutory**—law governing automobiles. But there is an established principle of **common** or **unwritten** law that every person is bound to use his own property so as not to injure another.

"This principle has never been written down, nor has it been proclaimed by any king, parliament, Congress, state legislature, county board, or village council. It has, rather, been established and applied in thousands of cases by hundreds of judges over many generations. True, no judge before me ever had an automobile accident case. Many judges, on the other hand, have decided cases that are similar in principle. No one can write out in advance what is right and wrong in specific circumstances, but past decisions will help me determine the law in these specific circumstances. Ours is a flexible and dynamic system. I will find what has been ruled in past cases (unwritten law) and tell the jury how to apply the rulings (unwritten laws) to the facts as they find the facts to be." In consulting prior decisions as precedent for his determination, the judge is following a common law rule—*stare decisis*—to stand by decided matters.

Then, having looked up earlier rulings, the judge would charge the jury something like this: "Ladies and gentlemen of the jury, if you find the facts to be as claimed by Mr. Ichabod, and that no prudent person would at that time and place operate a car at that speed, and if you find that such speed was the real cause of the accident, and if you find that Ichabod was not at fault, then as a matter of law, you must bring in a verdict for Ichabod requiring that he be paid the amount of his damage." Of course the judge would also charge the jury to bring in an opposite verdict if they found *your* story to be true. The court—that is, the judge—decides the law; the jury decides the facts. If you are not satisfied with the law laid down by the judge, you may appeal to a higher court. If you are not satisfied with the facts found by the jury, you may secure a new trial, if the judge agrees with you.

Written (Statute) Law

Now let us suppose that the legislature of your state passes a law requiring drivers to operate cars at a reasonable rate of speed. We now have a written law, a **statute**. But actually this statute only declares the common-law principle stated above. Seventy might be a reasonable speed on a thruway; seven miles an hour might be unreasonable on a playground. In either case, judge and jury will determine what is reasonable, as before.

If the legislature passes a law before your accident making it a crime to exceed fifty miles an hour, then you are in trouble, because the state (a government) as well as Ichabod is involved. The state takes **criminal** action against you; Ichabod takes **civil** action. Mr. District Attorney, the state's enforcement official, brings you into court. His duties are discussed in Chapter 10. The point here is that as far as the courts are concerned, and even though our judges are considered a part of the government, the government through its enforcement officers comes into court on the same terms as you or I. The state is subject to the same rules of evidence and procedure as anyone else. If anything, at least in criminal cases, the rules work against the state because *it is presumed that the accused is innocent until proved guilty.*

There is another serious consequence of the legislation setting a speed limit. Since it corrects or remedies the unwritten law, it replaces it. Before it was passed, your lawyer could make a pretty good argument that sixty miles an hour was not always unreasonable. The judge had to tell the jury about various tests to be used, and the jury could use its own judgment. No longer, though. The legislature has written and proclaimed that speeds in excess of fifty miles an hour are unlawful.

Constitutional Law

So far we have considered the way in which the judiciary, through the judicial process, works in matters of civil and criminal law. The judiciary works in the same way in matters affecting the Constitution, which is, as we

224

have seen, the **supreme written law** of the land. The laws of the Constitution do not apply themselves; they must be applied by living judges. Constitutional law, like criminal and civil law, is subject to change. For example, there was nothing in the Constitution either permitting or forbidding Congress to pass an income tax law or to prohibit the sale of liquor. The courts, by interpreting the written words according to rulings of many judges in many cases over many years and applying their interpretation to the facts at hand, found that Congress had no power to do either. This became the unwritten law. Whereupon the people amended the Constitution and replaced the unwritten law with written law, making possible an income tax (Amendment XVI), and prohibiting the sale of liquor (Amendment XVIII).

When the judges find a change in the facts, they may reverse a law dramatically. This happened in the matter of segregation of white and Negro children in the public schools. In 1896 the Supreme Court declared, in a railway car case, that segregation was constitutional and satisfied the meaning of Amendment XIV, so long as the separate facilities offered were "equal." Upon the facts presented in 1954, the Court found that schools could not be both separate and equal. In a second decision, in 1955, the Court ordered that schools be desegregated "with all deliberate speed."

Uncertainty of the Law

Each of these examples points to a common criticism of our judicial system—the uncertainty of the law. People simply cannot be sure of the consequences of some of their acts. That is why we have lawyers. Actually only a fraction of a lawyer's work is in civil or criminal cases. Most lawyers rarely enter a courtroom. Much of their work consists of trying to tell in advance what certain important transactions and events in our daily lives will mean legally. Lawyers confess that theirs is an uncertain forecast.

This weakness points up the greatest virtue of our judicial process—its unending capacity to change. If people would stop inventing things like automobiles and stop trying to improve taxation, to control anti-social habits like immoderate drinking, to provide public education, or to abolish institutions like slavery, then we could have certainty in our law. If we all thought alike and acted alike, we could have certainty, but no freedom. Our judiciary and our legal system were set up to serve a dynamic people. To serve they must themselves be dynamic.

IMPARTIALITY OF THE JUDICIARY

If you were a British traveler observing American courts in action, you would probably conclude that in both civil and criminal cases our courts

WITH THE HARE GOING IN CIRCLES
One view of the Supreme Court contest.
Russell in *The Los Angeles Times*

are very much like those of England, and that they resemble the courts of Canada or Australia. Actually our American judicial systems are more like their English models than are our legislative and executive branches of government. This is so because our colonial ancestors believed strongly in principles which have been handed down to us with little change. The difference, indeed, between our courts today and English courts is no more profound than the fact that English judges wear wigs, while American judges wear whatever hair they have.

What are some of these inherited judicial principles? Many of them operate in the examples just given. One is that the courts of justice must be impartial. They must be free to be fair. This means that Judge Jones or Judge Smith or any other judge must be free to administer justice as he sees it without fear that he will be removed from his office by an executive official, or have his pay cut by the legislature because his decision is an unpopular one. He should be beyond the reach or influence of President or Congress, if he is a federal judge, or of governor or legislature, if he is a state judge.

Guaranteeing the Independence of the Judiciary

In order to be impartial, judges must be independent. They must not feel obliged to decide cases according to the wishes of others, but only according to their own best understanding of the law. A good example of judicial independence is the decision of the Supreme Court in 1952 ruling that President Truman's seizure of the steel companies (see Chap. 2, p. 30) was invalid. All but one of the nine judges had been a Democrat before he went on the bench. All nine had been appointed by Democratic Presidents. The seizure of the steel companies was considered vitally important by a Democratic President and a Democratic administration. If the judges of the Supreme Court were not in fact independent, they would certainly have found it possible to declare the seizure constitutional. Yet, by a vote of 6 to 3 they acted contrary to the will of the President and the administration.

In American government we have several ways of trying to guarantee the independence of the judiciary. The first of these is the long term for judges. Federal judges are appointed to serve during good behavior. This usually means that a judge may hold office for life, unless he wishes to resign or to retire at the age of seventy. In a few of the states, judges are appointed by the governor, or elected by the legislature, for long terms—sometimes during good behavior.

The second guarantee is in the Constitution of the United States and in some of the state constitutions: provision that a judge's salary may not be reduced during his term of office. This is another way of keeping the judiciary independent.

The third guarantee is the difficulty of removing a judge from office. Federal judges may be removed only by impeachment. This is a long and involved process; very few judges have been so removed. In the different states judges may be removed in different ways: by impeachment (p. 117), by vote of the legislature, by popular recall (pp. 81–82), and by action of the higher courts. Impeachment is the most common of these; but it has been used with respect to federal judges only nine times, and resulted in only four removals, since it requires that a judge be proved guilty of criminal conduct. Popular recall of judges is not generally favored by those students of government who are interested in assuring judicial independence. It is found in only a few states.

A final proposal to insure political and financial independence for judges is to pay them a good salary. Such a salary should make it easier for a judge to resist bribes or other outside influences, or to support his family without having to practice law on the side. Federal judges are paid from $21,500 to $35,000. The Chief Justice of the United States is paid $35,500. State judges' incomes range from fees collected by justices of the peace up to $35,500 paid to judges of the New York Court of Appeals and $38,000 paid to the chief judge of that court.

THE JURY SYSTEM

So far we have been discussing the judicial process in terms of the judges and of the individual. Several times we have spoken of juries. Juries, though they consist of ordinary citizens, are a vital part of the judiciary branch of government. In fact, they bring the plain citizen directly into government, just as much as does a town meeting, a referendum, or an election. How does the jury system fit into the total judicial process?

The American system of juries of common citizens was inherited in almost its present form from the English. The rights to investigation by a **grand jury** (if you are accused of a crime under the federal law or under the laws of many states) and to a trial before a **petit jury** are fundamental protections of the liberties of free men. They are rights won only by bitter struggle over many centuries. The jury system rests squarely on the assumption that ordinary people are capable of governing themselves, when given the opportunity, and that they are the only proper judges of the behavior of each other.

The Grand Jury

A grand jury is attached to the lower federal courts and to some state and county courts. Jurors are chosen by court clerks from panels of citizens residing in the judicial district. Such lists or panels are often compiled by a designated local officer from lists of registered voters in the district, or from tax rolls. Evidence of at least high school education and of responsible character is normally expected. Citizens may volunteer, but if not enough of them do, the clerk has the power to compel any citizen to serve by issuing to him a formal call to jury duty. A citizen who refuses such a call may be prosecuted for contempt of court.

The size of grand juries varies, but sixteen or eighteen members is an average number. It is customary for any one grand jury to serve during the term of a court. The year's work of a court is divided into two or more periods each of several months, called **terms** of a court. The grand jury has power to investigate anything it may suspect in the way of wrongdoing. In its regular relations with law enforcement officers, however, the normal practice is for the prosecutor to present his evidence to the jury, which then calls witnesses, questions officials, and otherwise accumulates enough information to satisfy itself that a crime has or has not been committed as charged. If the grand jury finds reason to believe that the accused has committed the crime, it sends to the court a statement to that effect known as an **indictment.** If not, the case is dropped.

All serious crimes under federal law and under the laws of many states must be presented to a grand jury, and the accused indicted, before there can be a trial. The accused, therefore, is protected from the very beginning of his troubles, since a jury of his equals must be persuaded of the probability that he committed a crime before he has to defend himself at all.

Amendment V covers all cases arising under federal laws except "cases arising in the land or naval forces, or in the Militia, when in actual service in time of War or public danger." The latter cases are tried in military courts. Thus indictment by a grand jury is a part of the due process of law guaranteed to civilian Americans by the government of the United States.

An Information

The Supreme Court has ruled that in cases arising under state laws a grand jury proceeding is not a necessary part of "due process." In 23 states a substitute proceeding known as an **information** is used. This means that a state prosecuting attorney may go to court and offer to a judge his evidence (information) that a crime has been committed. The judge may then authorize the trial of the accused without the action of a grand jury. The other states, however, still require an indictment by a grand jury, either under their constitutions or under statute laws.

The Petit Jury

The petit jury usually consists of twelve citizens. It serves for one trial only. In the presence of both the prosecutor and attorneys for the defense, the clerk of the court calls off the names of persons on his list of citizens available for jury duty. These citizens appear in person and are questioned by both the prosecutor and the defense attorney to make sure that they will be impartial if they serve at the trial. In some cases, many citizens are considered before the jury is selected. In a trial, the jury, which selects its own **foreman** (chairman), determines the facts of a case and decides, according to what the judge says the law is, whether the accused is guilty or innocent. Citizens can be made to serve on a petit jury by a court order or subpoena (see p. 249). The purpose is to guarantee that every accused person shall have a fair trial on the presumption of his innocence, and that no judge shall be able to order punishment for him unless an impartial group of his equals in the community is convinced that he is guilty as charged.

A petit jury is also a matter of right in the trial of many civil cases, if requested by either party to the action, and in such cases its function is also to determine the facts from the evidence, subject to instruction from the judge as to the law applicable to the case.

Importance of the Jury System

Neither the grand jury nor the petit jury is always perfect, but the instances of corruption and prejudice in juries are rare. What is more important is that the system normally works, and works well. Its failures are the failures of the people themselves to be worthy of their freedom and their responsibilities. Not many free men would prefer to transfer the powers and responsibilities of juries to officials or to judges beyond the reach of the people. Herein lies, perhaps, the most vital of all differences between freedom and tyranny.

THE FEDERAL COURT SYSTEM

Certain federal Courts, as we have already seen, are established by Article III of the Constitution (and are therefore sometimes called **constitutional** Courts). Others have been established by a long series of laws passed by the Congress. The system is headed by a Supreme Court. Below it are the Courts of Appeals and the District Courts. Certain other special Courts have been created by Congress to deal with particular kinds of cases. These are the **Territorial Courts** (see Chap. 14), the **Court of Claims**, the **Court of Customs and Patent Appeals**, the **Customs Court**, and the **Court of Military Appeals**. These Courts constitute the judicial branch of the *federal* government. (The **Tax Court** is an independent agency.) Under their **jurisdiction** fall all cases arising under the laws of the United States, as distinct from the laws of the states. However, even laws of the states may come under the jurisdiction of the Supreme Court when their constitutionality is in question, since state laws must not be in conflict with the federal Constitution.

As we shall see, some Courts have **appellate** jurisdiction, others have **original** jurisdiction (see chart, p. 234). Certain kinds of cases fall under **exclusive** jurisdiction of the federal Courts; other cases come under **concurrent** jurisdiction of federal and state courts.

The Supreme Court

The Supreme Court of the United States is unique among governmental bodies in the world. It is unique because of its power to determine whether laws of Congress or of the states are in accord with the Constitution and to declare void laws which it finds unconstitutional. This great power is not specifically granted to the Supreme Court by the Constitution itself. However, even very early debates in the Congress show that people looked to the Court to decide controversies as to the meaning of the Constitution. As we saw in Chapter 4, the matter was tested and decided by the case of *Marbury vs.*

230

Madison in 1803. Congressmen and Presidents since that time have questioned this power of the Supreme Court, but today the great majority of our people accept **judicial review** as an established principle of government in America. The people may amend the Constitution to alter a decision of the Court, and Congress sometimes writes new laws to avoid constitutional objections the Court has made. Thus, "supreme" as the Court is, it is not supreme over the people.

The Supreme Court is not simply a body of men who devote their time to passing judgment on the constitutionality of laws. Actually decisions on constitutional questions are only a small fraction of the Court's work. Its chief function is to act as a final court of appeal on any of the thousands of cases which arise under the laws of the United States.

SUPREME COURT JUSTICES Let us see just how the Court is composed. In our time, there are nine justices, each of whom has an equal vote with all others on every question before the Court. Judges are appointed by the President with the consent of the Senate, and serve during good behavior, unless they wish to retire at seventy or to resign. There is no restriction regarding their appointment. That is, they do not have to represent the political parties or geographical areas of the country. They must be citizens, of course, but all other qualifications are matters of custom and tradition. In practice, a President usually appoints to the Supreme Court men who have had substantial experience in the law. Most justices have held judgeships in lower courts or in state courts. There are, of course, exceptions, such as the occasional appointment of a man who has simply been of great service to the President or to his party, or of a distinguished professor of law.

It is probably true that Presidents hope to fill vacancies with men who will interpret the Constitution as the President would like it to be interpreted. Presidents have often been fooled in this respect. The fact that a justice of the Supreme Court serves for life, and is removable only by impeachment for a crime, gives him a sense of independence that he may not previously have felt during his public life. Thus views which he held as a member of a political party may change when he no longer feels the pressure of party loyalty. This is another illustration of the independence of the judiciary. There have been some cases in our history when the Supreme Court has seemed to "follow the election returns," and others when it seemed to be acting in defiance of the President. In general, however, we may say that the record of the Court in our history shows that the justices have decided each case according to their best understanding of the law.

The President appoints a Chief Justice, whose duties are to preside over the meetings and proceedings of the Court. His vote, however, carries no more weight than the votes of his colleagues. Cases are decided by a majority vote. If the Chief Justice has voted with the majority, he assigns the writing of the official opinion of the Court either to himself or to one of those who voted with him. If he is in the minority, the senior member of the majority (in point of service on the Court) assigns the writing of the Court's opinion to himself or to one of his colleagues. Any justice may write and read in Court a dissenting opinion, setting forth his reasons for disagreeing with the majority, or a concurring opinion, giving his own particular reasons for agreeing with a decision. The tradition of dissent has been very important, since it often happens that a dissenting opinion will at a later time become a determining influence on the majority. Justices Oliver Wendell Holmes, Jr., and Louis D. Brandeis became famous for their dissents, but after their time on the Court, the positions they had maintained in dissent became in many cases the majority opinion of the Court.

ROUTINE OF THE COURT The Supreme Court usually divides its work into two terms, from October to Christmas and from January to June. On the stroke of noon, the black-robed justices take their places on the bench in the handsome, dignified Supreme Court Building. The Chief Justice sits in the center, the others sit according to seniority. Attorneys who are presenting their cases sit at tables in front of the bench, the Department of Justice attorneys at the right. Then the arguments for each side start, each counsel being limited to one hour. The justices are free to interrupt at any time to ask for more information. They even discuss particular points among themselves in an informal way.

After about two weeks of such sessions, the justices retire to their chambers to study case records, meditate, discuss, vote, and write opinions. Then they will hear cases for another two weeks, and so on.

APPELLATE JURISDICTION Since there are literally thousands of cases under appeal in the federal Courts all the time, it would be physically impossible for the Supreme Court judges to hear them all. Fortunately they are not required to do so. In fact, as we have seen, the Court has full power to decide whether or not it will hear an appeal. There are certain cases which are actually tried before the Court, but most of its business is appeals. It has the power to hear or not to hear an appeal, which is a very great power indeed. If the Court refuses to hear a case, that is the end of it; the case is left finally as the lower court decided it. In practice, the Court normally grants the right of appeal in cases where one court has voted "yes," and the case was appealed to the next higher court which voted "no." Sometimes, if federal law is involved, it allows appeal in cases brought in from the highest courts in the states, and it hears appeals in most cases involving questions of constitutionality. Among all other cases, it refuses far more than it accepts.

ORIGINAL JURISDICTION Under Article III of the Constitution, the Supreme Court has **original** jurisdiction of all cases involving "Ambassadors,

232

other public Ministers and Consuls, and those in which a State shall be a party," if they arise under federal law. An action brought against an Ambassador under the laws of a state, for example, would not be the business of the Supreme Court. Cases in which a "State shall be a party" means cases in which the dispute is between a state and the United States or between two states involving federal law. The number of such cases is quite small, though sometimes they may be very important. For example, arguments before the Supreme Court may decide which state controls a certain piece of land, or whether certain mineral resources are on areas belonging to the state or to the United States.

The Supreme Court may also, if petitioned to do so by someone dissatisfied with a lower court decision, demand that the lower court send up all records of the case. This is called a **writ of certiorari.**

United States Courts of Appeals

The Supreme Court stands at the top of a pyramid of courts (see chart, p. 234). Below it are eleven United States Courts of Appeals, formerly called Circuit Courts. The United States is divided into ten judicial "circuits" plus one for the District of Columbia. The word comes down from a time when individual justices of the Supreme Court heard the appeals in various districts by "riding circuit" on horseback.

Each state, and each territory, is assigned to one of ten circuits, except for the District of Columbia, which is a circuit by itself. A justice of the Supreme Court is assigned to each circuit by the Chief Justice of the United States. In practice, these justices act only in an advisory capacity.

Cases in these courts usually are heard ordinarily by a "bench" of three judges. Each circuit has three to nine judges permanently attached to the circuit in which they hear cases. There are about seventy judges of the Courts of Appeals.

The function of a Court of Appeals, as its name suggests, is **appellate—** that is, simply to hear cases which have been decided in the lower courts and then appealed. Although the Court of Appeals may seem to be only a sort of way-station between the trial court and the Supreme Court, the Appeals Court's work is not really wasted, for two reasons. One is that the prestige of the Court is so great that very often the parties in a case take it for granted that the Supreme Court would uphold the Court of Appeals; therefore, they accept the decision and do not appeal further. The other reason is that the Supreme Court, in practice, very often refuses to hear appeals from the decisions of the Court of Appeals, because it is satisfied with the decisions as they stand. Thus the Court of Appeals performs a vital function in the federal court system and greatly lightens the load of the Supreme Court.

State and Federal Court Systems

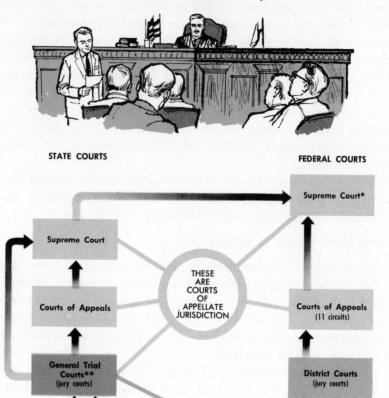

STATE COURTS   FEDERAL COURTS

Supreme Court*

Supreme Court

Courts of Appeals

THESE ARE COURTS OF APPELLATE JURISDICTION

Courts of Appeals (11 circuits)

General Trial Courts** (jury courts)

District Courts (jury courts)

Justice of Peace Courts

THESE ARE COURTS OF ORIGINAL JURISDICTION

Municipal Courts*** (misdemeanors and minor civil cases)

*Supreme Court has original jurisdiction in certain cases.
**County, Circuit, District and Superior courts.
***Or Police, Magistrates, and District courts.

The state system shown above is not the actual arrangement of courts for a specific state. The chart cannot show all the variations in state courts (for a specific illustration, see chart on p. 239, the Courts of Pennsylvania). All states do have, however, at least three levels of courts, as the chart does show. For special courts of the states, see pp. 238–246.

In addition to the federal courts shown here, there is a Court of Claims, a Court of Customs and Patent Appeals, and a Court of Customs (see p. 236). There is a Tax Court, an independent agency. The Court of Military Appeals operates as a part of the Department of Defense.

Federal District Courts

Below the Courts of Appeals are the Federal District Courts. There are 84 District Courts in the federal system, distributed among the states according to the volume of cases. The District of Columbia is a judicial district in itself. In each district there are from one to eighteen justices, depending on the volume of business carried on in a district. The Federal District judges, like those of the Supreme Court and the Courts of Appeals, are appointed to serve during good behavior and can be removed only by impeachment. It is the dream of many a practicing lawyer or state judge to be appointed to the Federal District Court, since the judges on this bench are among the most highly respected of our citizens and, as judges, deal with some of the most interesting legal matters.

JURISDICTION The Federal District Courts are the trial courts for all cases arising under the laws of the United States except for those over which the Supreme Court has original jurisdiction (Article III) and those tried in the special Courts. United States attorneys, in each District Court, are the prosecuting attorneys who represent the government in federal cases. Each Court has also a United States marshal, who makes arrests and carries out the orders of the Court. These officials are appointed by the President with the approval of the Senate (see Chap. 10). In each district, the Court also appoints a clerk, who keeps the official record of the proceedings, and United States commissioners, who conduct preliminary hearings after a person has been arrested for a federal offense.

The Federal District Courts are the only federal courts which use grand juries and trial (petit) juries. These courts handle the great bulk of the trials for alleged violations of federal laws. They bring the justice of the laws of the United States directly to the people. Suppose you are accused of passing counterfeit money. You will be arrested by an agent of the Treasury Department and brought before a United States Commissioner to plead innocent or guilty. Your case will then be brought before a federal grand jury, which investigates the charges against you, hears the testimony of the government's witnesses, and decides whether the government's case is strong enough to bring you to trial. If so, the grand jury will send to the Federal District Court in your area an indictment and, when your turn comes, you will be tried before a petit jury and a federal judge in the same Court. Cases involving lawsuits brought by the United States, cases having to do with offenses against the laws of the United States, cases involving the loss of civil rights, civil cases between a citizen of one state and a citizen of another state—these and many others are first heard in the District Courts. These Courts have the first responsibility for upholding the dignity and majesty of the law of the United States.

ADMINISTRATIVE OFFICE The business of the federal courts—supplies, records, calendars, buildings, payrolls, etc.—is managed by a Director of Administration, appointed by the Supreme Court, and a staff of assistants.

Special Courts

The judicial branch of the government contains also certain special Courts which have been established by Congress to handle specialized cases. The **Court of Claims** deals with claims for damages against the United States government (that is, any agency of the government)—for example, damage caused to your farm by the Air Force when they were building an airstrip, or damage to your store when the Post Office Department was blasting out cellar space for the new post office.

The **Court of Customs and Patent Appeals** deals with disputes regarding patents and trademarks [1] and hears appeals from a third special Court, the **Court of Customs.** To this latter court are taken cases arising when someone disputes a decision made by the collectors of custom duties on goods imported into the country. The **U.S. Court of Military Appeals,** established in 1950 as a permanent court, hears appeals from the courts of the military services. It is a civilian court located for administrative purposes in the Department of Defense. Finally, there is a **Tax Court** of the United States. This Court, which hears disputes regarding income and other tax assessments (see Chap. 20), is an independent agency and thus technically not a part of the judicial branch. But in other respects it is similar to the special courts of the judiciary branch.

STATE AND LOCAL COURTS

The study of the state courts is more complicated than the study of the federal courts because there are no two state systems that are quite the same. It is impossible to examine them all here, in detail. If you wish to find specific information about the courts of your own state, you should consult the manual, guide, or handbook of your own state's government. (See chart, p. 239, for the court system of Pennsylvania.)

If you were to study and compare all American court systems, you would find that they do not differ greatly on fundamental principles or in the way they do their judicial business. They *do* differ in names of the courts, in methods of selecting and removing judges, in jurisdiction of courts, and in many other

---

[1] Patents and trademarks, provided for in the same clause of the Constitution as copyrights, are handled by the Patent Office. (See Chap. 21, pp. 513–514). A **patent** is a government grant to an inventor of exclusive use of his invention for seventeen years. A **trademark** is an exclusive name or symbol by which a manufacturer or merchant distinguishes his product from all others.

ways. The rather common pattern of state systems is shown in the chart, p. 234. They all have a high court, usually called the supreme court, and several levels of inferior courts. Civil and criminal cases are tried in the inferior courts. Persons may appeal cases to higher courts and to the supreme court. Procedures in civil and criminal cases in one state are very much like those in another. Basically the state courts are more alike than different.

The common law (the **unwritten law** that we studied earlier in this chapter) is the basis of the legal systems of 49 of the states. The state courts have jurisdiction over all cases arising at common law as well as all cases under the laws of the states as enacted by their legislatures. Louisiana is the one exception to this system. Louisiana was a part of the French empire before it was purchased by the United States in 1803. As a part of Napoleon's empire, the territory was governed by a system of laws known as the Code Napoléon, a re-writing of the old laws of France. These were different from the legal systems of England and the United States. It was a part of the Louisiana Purchase agreement that the Code Napoléon should remain in force in Louisiana as long as it was not in conflict with the Constitution and laws of the United States. In practice, the Louisiana system has become more and more like that of her sister states.

Selection of State Judges

One outstanding difference between the federal system and most of the state systems is in the way judges are selected. In some states, judges are appointed by the governor; in some, they are elected by the legislature. But in most of the states, judges are chosen by popular election. In these states, terms of judges of the higher courts are usually longer than terms of judges of the lower courts.

The question of whether judges should be elected or appointed is one on which there is considerable disagreement. Good judges and poor judges have been selected by both methods. It is important for us to realize that people, not systems, determine whether we get good or poor officials. In general, the standards of the state courts are high, and most judges, whether elected or appointed to the bench, do it credit. A state's bar association, the professional organization of lawyers, often takes an active part in recommending candidates for judgeships. Such non-partisan recommendations may have great influence on the political parties, the voters, or appointing officers.

The American Bar Association has shown its interest in working out better methods of selecting judges by giving its approval to a plan using the best features of both the elective and the appointive systems. Under this plan, state judges would be appointed by the governor, who would make his choice from a list presented by a commission or board of lawyers and laymen. At the end of a certain period, these appointees would have to stand for election, as would all judges at the end of their terms. In this election the voters would vote on the question of whether each judge should stay in his office. If the voters do not reëlect a judge, then a new appointment must be made, and referred to the voters at the next election. Two states, California and Missouri, have tried systems similar to this proposal.

The State Supreme Court

At the head of each state's court system is a highest state court, which hears appeals, interprets the state constitution, and, in general, is somewhat like the Supreme Court of the United States. In some states the highest court will give **advisory opinions** to the governor or the legislature as to whether a proposed measure conforms to the state's constitution. This court may be known as a Court of Appeals, or Supreme Judicial Court. In most states, it is known as the Supreme Court.

Courts of Appeals

A number of states maintain courts of appeal between their general trial courts and the supreme courts, as the chart, p. 234, shows.[2]

In general, state appeals courts operate much like United States Courts of Appeals. The judges often sit in teams of three or more. There are no juries since the proceedings are not a trial—they are a review of a trial. In some cases, the decision of an appeals court is final; in others, a final appeal may be taken to the highest court in the state.

General Trial Courts

The "big" cases which reach the headlines of the newspapers—murder, million-dollar lawsuits, armed robbery—are tried in the general trial courts. These courts may hear civil cases involving any amount of money and trials for felonies. In most states they will render **declaratory judgments.** This means that disputes between citizens or organizations may be settled without a damage action. The two parties go to court and ask what their rights are in a dispute—whether, for example, Business A has a right to buy a piece of land and build a warehouse on it when Business B claims that it has an option to buy the land. The court studies the problem and issues a judgment declaring what the rights of each party are. This judgment is binding on both parties and settles the dispute.

The judges of these courts are usually elected from a county or a district. The courts themselves are known as county courts, district courts, circuit courts, or courts of common pleas, depending on the laws or customs of the

[2] In New York State, the Supreme Court is a trial court; the Appellate Division of the Supreme Court is the normal appeals court; and the Court of Appeals is the highest court in the state.

238

The Courts of Pennsylvania

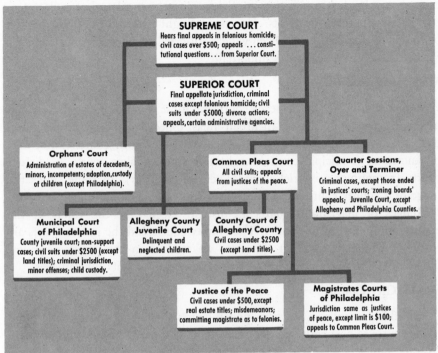

SUPREME COURT
Hears final appeals in felonious homicide; civil cases over $500; appeals ... constitutional questions ... from Superior Court.

SUPERIOR COURT
Final appellate jurisdiction, criminal cases except felonious homicide; civil suits under $5000; divorce actions; appeals, certain administrative agencies.

Orphans' Court
Administration of estates of decedents, minors, incompetents; adoption, custody of children (except Philadelphia).

Common Pleas Court
All civil suits; appeals from justices of the peace.

Quarter Sessions, Oyer and Terminer
Criminal cases, except those ended in justices' courts; zoning boards' appeals; Juvenile Court, except Allegheny and Philadelphia Counties.

Municipal Court of Philadelphia
County juvenile court; non-support cases; civil suits under $2500 (except land titles); criminal jurisdiction, minor offenses; child custody.

Allegheny County Juvenile Court
Delinquent and neglected children.

County Court of Allegheny County
Civil cases under $2500 (except land titles).

Justice of the Peace
Civil cases under $500, except real estate titles; misdemeanors; committing magistrate as to felonies.

Magistrates Courts of Philadelphia
Jurisdiction same as justices of peace, except limit is $100; appeals to Common Pleas Court.

Court systems differ from state to state. Here you see the names and jurisdiction of the courts of one of our largest states. From the chart you can find out where various kinds of cases (see pp. 238–241) are tried. When you study fundamental principles and ways of doing judicial business, you will find that the state systems are more alike than they are different.

individual states. In some states, these courts may hear appeals from lower courts, and they sometimes share authority with justice courts over minor cases. It is these general trial courts which regularly make use of both grand juries to indict or accuse and petit (trial) juries to try accused persons.

Justice-of-the-Peace Courts

If a policeman overtakes you on a country road and stops you for speeding, you will probably meet an important town or township official—the justice of the peace. You will probably be some few dollars poorer when you leave this official than when you met him! The "J.P.," as he is often familiarly known, does not merely fine people for speeding. People arrested for petty crimes may be brought before him to plead "guilty" or "not guilty"; disputes between neighbors involving small sums of money, trespassing, etc., may be settled by the justice of the peace.

In most states, justices of the peace are elected by the voters of some subdivision of a county. In a few states they are appointed by the governor.

Justices of the peace are not required to have legal training or formal education of any kind. Most justices of the peace get no salary but collect fees charged as a part of the "costs" for cases brought before them. This method of compensating justices has been widely criticized as making it more difficult for the justice to decide cases impartially.

Magistrates Courts

In general, justice-of-the-peace courts are most common in rural areas and in small towns and villages. In urban areas, especially in large cities, minor civil cases and misdemeanor cases are heard before county courts. These may be known as municipal courts, magistrates courts, police courts, or district courts (sometimes a district includes several counties). In some states the judge of a county court may hear appeals from the justice-of-the-peace court.

Judges of magistrates courts are usually elected by the voters of the county, municipality, or district. The county courts and the justice courts are the ones which try most of the cases we read of in the paper—vagrancy, drunkenness, disorderly conduct, petty larceny, minor suits for damages.

Special City Courts

In addition, most cities have police courts to handle minor crimes, and traffic courts to deal with offenses like speeding or going through "Stop" signs. In some larger cities, there are even more specialized courts such as juvenile (children's) courts or domestic relations courts and small claims courts (see Chap. 10).

Surrogate Courts

In some states there are special courts at the county level for the **probate** of wills (proof of legality before estates can be settled), appointment of executors and trustees, and other matters connected with estates of deceased persons. The judges of such courts are known as **surrogates.** In other states these matters are handled in the regular courts.

SUMMARY

In this chapter we have discussed the judiciary and its place in the American government. We have examined criminal and civil law and have seen how the unwritten or common law developed before written or statute law. The judiciary also works in matters of constitutional law, the supreme law of the land.

In order to insure that our judiciary be both impartial and independent, we have provided long terms—sometimes life terms—for our judges; we have guaranteed that their salary will not be reduced during their terms of office; and we have made it difficult to remove a judge from office. We also see to it that judges' salaries are good, so that they will not be subject to influence by bribery.

We have examined the federal and state system of courts, and certain special courts, and have seen which courts have original jurisdiction and which appellate. We have seen the kinds of cases each court is concerned with. We have also discussed briefly certain municipal courts dealing with special kinds of cases.

All of this system of law and courts is set up with one purpose first and foremost—to protect the rights of the individual. The courts, though a branch of government, treat both citizen and government equally, so that unreasonable action by government officials can be avoided, and citizens can meet each other on equal ground.

KNOW WHAT YOU READ

1. In what two ways does the judiciary branch carry out its judicial function?
2. How are civil cases different from criminal cases.
3. What are three classes of violation of criminal law? Give an example of each.
4. What is the meaning of common law? How is it different from statute law?
5. Why is it important to you as a citizen that our courts be independent?
6. In what ways does the federal government try to protect the independence of the judiciary?
7. How do the states protect the independence of the judiciary?
8. What is the meaning of "government of laws, not of men"?
9. Describe the jury system. Why is it important?
10. List the regular courts of the United States.
11. Why is the United States Supreme Court *unique* among governmental bodies?
12. How is the official opinion of the Supreme Court made known?
13. When and where does the Supreme Court meet?
14. In what kinds of cases does the Supreme Court have *original* jurisdiction?
15. The Supreme Court hears only a fraction of the total number of cases appealed. Why is this so?
16. What is the work of the U.S. Courts of Appeals?
17. Which federal courts are the trial courts for most cases arising under the laws of the United States?
18. List the special courts of the United States. State briefly the kind of cases heard in each.

19. What method of selecting judges has been proposed by a professional organization of lawyers?
20. What is the work of justices of the peace? How are these officials selected? How are they paid?
21. Summarize the ways in which state court systems are like the federal system and ways in which the state systems are different from the federal system.
22. Give one example of the kind of case each of the following state courts hears: Supreme Court, Court of Appeals, General Trial Court?

WHAT DO YOU THINK?

1. What are the most important characteristics that a man or woman should have to be a good judge?
2. We elect lawmakers, governors, and the President. Why is there disagreement over the question of electing or appointing judges? Which method do you favor? Why?
3. Would you favor the judge-selection plan approved in 1937 by the American Bar Association? This plan is described briefly in this chapter.
4. Should a President appoint to the Supreme Court only persons whose views agree with his own?
5. Are cases appealed in state courts ordinarily based on questions of constitutionality?

PROBLEMS AND PROJECTS FOR YOU

1. Try to find out by asking a lawyer, or by looking it up with the help of your school librarian, exactly how a case is *appealed* in your state. Explain this procedure to the class.
2. Post on the bulletin board clippings about the work of the regular and special courts of the United States. (This could be done by an individual or by members of a committee.)
3. Write a biographical sketch about one of the Justices of either the United States Supreme Court or of the highest court of your own state. Be sure to include a summary of the judge's experience in the law.
4. On a given day a local newspaper reported the following cases heard in a court of the city in which the paper is published.
   (a) Four youths were found guilty of disturbing the peace.
   (b) Two juveniles were held on charge of larceny. They stole from a used auto parts yard.
   (c) A man was fined after being arrested for teaching himself to drive. Before what court, or courts, would these cases have been heard in your community or county?

5. Report to the class on the attempt of President Roosevelt in 1937 to change the make-up of the Supreme Court. In this report give your answer to these questions:
   (a) Was this an attack on the independence of the judiciary?
   (b) What factors other than a Justice's knowledge of the law will influence his decision on a case brought before the Court?
6. "Those who insist that the law is only a reflection of the biases of the judges are as extreme as those who insist that these biases have no effect on the law." What do you think of this statement?
7. You may get a better understanding of the common law if you will look up the meaning of the rule of *stare decisis*. Explain this rule to the class.
8. In this chapter you read that lawmaking bodies have sometimes been known to enact laws contrary to the constitutional liberties of the people. What liberties might be involved in each of these:

   (a) a state law requiring that Indian children in the state be educated in separate schools?
   (b) a state law requiring employers to pay a minimum wage to women workers?
   (c) a city ordinance forbidding the distribution of handbills on the streets?
   (d) a state law requiring employers to hire, pay, and promote workers without racial, religious, or national-origins discrimination?

   Any or all of these might be discussed in a panel. Be sure that you do not overlook the possible existence of conflicting liberties on both sides of each question.
9. Finley Peter Dunne had Mr. Dooley say, . . . "th' Supreme Coort follows th' illection returns." Can you find evidence from our history to support or contradict this point of view?
10. "The doctrine and practice of judicial review has a *prima facie* reasonableness, especially in a common law country, used to judge-made law." What does this statement mean? Do you agree?

EXTEND YOUR VOCABULARY

offenses	criminal law	petit jury
misdemeanors	written (statute) law	indictment
felonies	unwritten law	information
civil case	summons	appellate jurisdiction
equity	*stare decisis*	original jurisdiction
plaintiff	surrogate	concurrent jurisdiction
defendant	probate	advisory opinions
injunction	grand jury	declaratory judgments

YOUR NOTEBOOK: THE GOVERNMENT OF ——

1. Draw a diagram showing the system of regular courts in your state. Name these courts correctly.
2. Write in your notebook the name of the judge of the court nearest your home. Indicate whether he is elected or appointed. Watch for newspaper items about this judge. From your study of these items, you will be able to learn important facts about this judge and his work. Write these in your notebook.
3. Who are the judges of the highest court of your state? Write in your notebook the names of these judges and brief facts about them and their work which you have gathered from the newspapers or from friends in the legal profession.

READ MORE ABOUT IT

Burns, James M., and Peltason, Jack W., *Government by the People*. Prentice-Hall, 1954. Chap. 16.

Commager, Henry Steele, *The American Mind*. Yale University Press, 1950. Useful chapters on law and significant individuals in law in America.

Irish, Marian D., and Prothro, James W., *The Politics of American Democracy*. Prentice-Hall, 1959. Chap. 14.

Jackson, Robert H., *The Supreme Court in the American System of Government*. Harvard, 1958.

Peltason, Jack W., *Federal Courts in the Political Process*. Doubleday, 1955.

Rodell, Fred, *Nine Men*. Random House, 1955. A lively book about the Supreme Court.

Westin, Alan, *The Anatomy of a Constitutional Law Case*. Macmillan, 1958. Analysis of steel seizure case, Youngstown Sheet and Tube Co. v. Sawyer. Readable and thoughtful.

CHAPTER 10

The Citizen and Law Enforcement

In this chapter you will learn about

Law enforcement
State agencies of law enforcement
The Department of Justice
Other agencies of federal law enforcement
Prisons
Standards of public morality

Through their elected legislators, the people make the laws. Through the judges, who are also publicly selected, the people provide for the interpretation of the laws. It is not surprising, therefore, that our citizens, for the most part, obey the laws which they themselves approve and understand.

Of course, there are many exceptions. We need only look at the morning newspaper. Still, generally speaking, people obey laws which they understand. For example, we read about lots of traffic violations and accidents because of violations. Actually, however, when you think of the millions of miles that are covered by individual automobiles every day, the speed and power of our automobiles, and the great differences among individuals, it is amazing that we do as well as we do.

We are, generally, a law-abiding people—and not because of fear of the policeman on the corner. On the contrary, we have demonstrated in our own history that no matter how much effort is put into law enforcement in terms of policemen, prosecutors, and detectives, and even jail sentences, the laws that people do not believe in cannot be enforced. The best example, of course, is Amendment XVIII to the Constitution, which formerly prohibited the sale of intoxicating beverages.

Nevertheless, there are inevitably cases of lawbreaking in a society as complex as ours. To handle these, we need more than just a system of courts where justice can be handed out. We need machinery to institute proceedings in court. The courts act only upon disputes brought before them. The process of bringing the matters into court is what we call law enforcement.

HOW LAWS ARE ENFORCED

There are many ways to enforce laws. In one sense, an ordinary civil action (see Chap. 9) between private individuals is law enforcement. If your government or your landlord breaks a contract with you, you can go to court about it and be awarded a sum of money (compensation) to make up for the damage you have suffered. This is supposed to deter people from breaking contracts, and thus enforces the law that a person must pay damages if he does not live up to his contract. Or if two people are involved in an automobile accident, one can take the other to court and try to prove that the accident was caused because the other one was driving carelessly. If he proves it, the court can make the careless driver pay damages.

Civil Actions

All Americans have the privilege of having their disputes settled in the courts. You may have heard someone say, "If you do that (or don't), I'll sue you." That means that if you feel you have been seriously abused or cheated by someone with whom you are dealing, you can take him to court. In business transactions, even in neighborhood disputes, if you believe that a contract to which you are a party has been broken or your rights have been infringed, you may get a lawyer and start a legal action to have your grievance heard by an impartial judge (and jury, in serious matters). The judge (and jury) can decide how to correct the situation: by forcing people to carry out a contract or by assessing them damages for breaking it.

This is the way civil cases work. You consult a lawyer for advice. He studies your account of the matter and gives you his opinion as to whether you are likely to win a lawsuit. If, between you, you decide to sue, your lawyer has a paper known as a **summons and complaint** made out and served on (delivered to) the person (or organization) against whom you are making your complaint. When he receives the summons, he will also get a lawyer. Often civil disputes are actually settled by negotiations between the two lawyers. If not, your lawyer requests a place on the calendar of your local county court or state court district. In some states the amount of money involved decides which court will be used. Thus disputes involving only a few dollars may be settled in small claims courts, while larger amounts mean that a case goes directly to a county or district court.

At the trial the two lawyers argue before the judge (and jury, if a jury trial is appropriate), call witnesses, and submit all the evidence they can. Then the court announces a decision. It may, for example, decide that your opponent must pay you money for damages you have suffered, including normally the costs of the trial itself (costs of keeping the minutes, paying the clerk, the expenses of witnesses, and even renting the courtroom). It may find that your evidence is insufficient and dismiss the case. If that happens, you are obliged to pay the court costs.

More dramatic examples of the use of civil actions as a weapon of law enforcement are those laws which provide that individual citizens, where injured by particular kinds of unlawful conduct, can recover both the amount of their damages and also a penalty. A well-known example of this was price control during World War II. Anyone accused of charging more than the highest (ceiling) price set by law could be made to pay not just the amount he had overcharged but three times the amount, and the attorney's fee of his opponent as well. As we shall see (pp. 259–261), antitrust laws also provide that any person who is injured by an unlawful combination of business or monopoly can recover from his competitor three times the amount of his actual damages plus his attorney's fees.

Criminal Prosecutions

By far the most common and most important method of law enforcement is a criminal prosecution by the government—most often *state* government. When a law has been violated and the legislature has provided a penalty for that violation, then it is up to the prosecuting officials of the government to bring the violator before the court. In performing the duties of his office, the *prosecutor* acts as part of the executive branch of the government. The legislator makes the laws; the prosecutor determines what action should be taken, and he then asks the court to interpret the law and impose the penalty. The prosecutor comes before the court like any other party, excepting, as we shall see, the accused. Criminal proceeding has all kinds of constitutional protections for the accused that are not provided to other parties.

Safeguards of the Citizen

Fortunately, most of us will never have any occasion to become familiar with the intricacies of criminal procedure in day-to-day criminal law enforcement. On the other hand, the safeguards which the Constitution gives individuals charged with a crime are among the most important traditions of free

FOR OUR CHILDREN AND
OUR CHILDREN'S CHILDREN

With permission of
Vaughn Shoemaker

people. For this reason alone, it is worth reviewing some of the safeguards.

We are proud of our American Bill of Rights, the first ten amendments, which we shall consider in Chapter 16. We rightly emphasize as the best part of our Bill of Rights the freedoms of worship, speech, press, assembly, and petition. We too often forget that most of the first ten amendments were devoted to protecting the individual citizen from the abuses of criminal prosecution. Our constitutional safeguards against abuses and tyrannical law enforcement, though they came almost entirely from England, are an essential part of the American notion of freedom.

SEARCH WARRANT Let us take the case of Mr. Z, a professional thief. There is a holdup at a supermarket on the edge of the city. As soon as the robber has left, with $1,000 in cash, the police are called. A city police department has several divisions—traffic, burglary, homicide, etc. In this case, the police department orders a "squad car" cruising a few blocks away to go to the scene of the holdup and keep the witnesses together until a detective who specializes in such cases arrives. The police question witnesses on the scene and immediately think they recognize Z as the criminal from his description. They would have a better chance to catch him if they could go straight to his house and search it. But Z is protected from such a search until the police secure a **search warrant** from a judge. This means that a judge must first be persuaded that such a search is likely to help solve the case.

ARRAIGNMENT AND INDICTMENT Let us now suppose that Z is caught. He is arrested and taken to police headquarters, and held under suspicion until a witness identifies him. Then he is charged with armed robbery (a **felony**). If he were not brought before the judge, his lawyer could get a court order called a writ of **habeas corpus** requiring that he be formally charged and bail fixed or denied. (If you are held under arrest by the police, your friends or lawyer may also go to a judge and get a writ of *habeas corpus*, requiring the police to bring you before the judge to determine whether you are entitled to bail. *Habeas corpus* is included in both the federal and state bills of rights.)

Z's lawyer advises him to plead "not guilty." He is **arraigned** (or called) before a judge, and denies the charge.

BAIL Z is entitled to go free on **bail** from the time he is arrested until he is convicted and sentenced. That is, he posts a sum of money, set by the judge, as a guarantee that he will appear when requested during the proceedings involved in his case. (If you are accused of a very serious crime, bail may be set at a figure so high that you cannot meet it and will have to stay in jail. However, there are private finance organizations available in many cases to lend you the money. The Constitution (Amendment VIII) forbids "excessive bail," but it is left to the court to determine what "excessive" bail means in any specific case.)

Next the district attorney, an elected official who is the state's law enforcement officer in a local area (county or judicial district), prepares the case against Z and presents it either to a grand jury or (in a state allowing use of information) directly to the judge. The grand jury calls witnesses and then deliberates in secret. It decides that Z may be guilty and sends its decision to the court. This decision is known as an **indictment** and means that Z will be tried for the crime of which he is accused.

TRAIL BY JURY Now Z and his lawyer prepare for the trial, as does the district attorney. The petit jury is chosen from a panel of citizens in the area (see Chap. 9, p. 229). Z's lawyer makes sure by questioning that no juror is prejudiced against Z. At the trial Z need not testify at all. The state must prove that he is guilty. The prosecution (the district attorney and his staff acting for the state) calls witnesses against Z, and the district attorney sums up the state's case for the judge and jury. Z's lawyer, the defense counsel, calls witnesses to prove Z's innocence. If anyone needed for such testimony refuses to appear, Z can have him subpoenaed. A **subpoena** is a court order requiring appearance and testimony.

When all witnesses have been heard and **cross-examined** by the district attorney and defense counsel, defense counsel makes his plea to the judge and jury. The judge then instructs the jury as to the law, and the jury retires to a room reserved for it to study and decide on the facts. In this case, the jury finds that the facts prove Z guilty under the law. The judge then sentences him to twenty years in prison.

APPEAL Defense counsel appeals the case to the state's court of appeals (see Chap. 9). Z remains free on bail. The appeals court of three judges hears the district attorney and defense counsel argue the case. It upholds the trial court's decision, and Z finally goes to prison.

PROTECTION FOR ALL Through all the weeks and months of this proceeding, even though he is a known criminal, Z has been protected at every point. At the trial he was given every opportunity to defend himself. The government had to prove that he was guilty; he did not have to prove himself innocent.

Z's case illustrates the safeguards you would have if you should ever be arrested.

You are entitled to the services of a lawyer to defend you. If you cannot afford to pay a lawyer's fee, the court in some states will appoint a lawyer to defend you at public expense ("public defender"). In other states the court appoints a lawyer who serves without fee as a part of his professional obligation. At your trial, the court must assume that you are innocent until the government proves you guilty, if it can. You are entitled to know in detail what the charges against you are, to confront witnesses who testify against you and to cross-examine them, to bring in any witnesses you may wish to testify on your behalf. If someone does not wish to testify at your trial, the court can, as we have seen, make him appear to answer questions by issuing a document known as a subpoena. If he does not appear when subpoenaed, such a witness will himself be prosecuted for contempt of court.

As for yourself, though you must appear at court, you are not required to testify at all unless you wish to do so. If you do testify, you may not be forced to answer any questions whose answers might incriminate you (Amendment V); that is, you cannot be made to testify against yourself. Fair and long-tested rules protect you from being convicted for reasons not directly related to the crime of which you are accused. For example, a previous bad reputation is not evidence in a trial for a specific crime. It is up to the judge to see that such evidence is not considered by the jury. He instructs the jury as to exactly what the law is as it applies to your case, and charges the jury to confine itself to finding the facts only so far as they relate to the law and to your case. If you are convicted, you may appeal, as we have seen.

250

Our legal system carefully protects criminals in order to protect us all, especially the innocent. Because we have these safeguards, we cannot be arbitrarily imprisoned at the whim of officials. Our freedom rests on a system which protects everyone. If *anyone* may be ill treated by the law or have his freedom arbitrarily abused, *you* could be the *anyone*.

STATE AGENCIES OF LAW ENFORCEMENT

The criminal laws of the states, which cover most of the common crimes, are enforced by state departments of justice under state **attorneys general** and by **district attorneys** who prosecute cases in the county or district courts. Many states maintain a state police force to detect crimes against state law and enforce many state regulations (such as speed limits), and each county and city, and many villages or town, maintains a police force for the detection and arrest of criminals as well as for routine policing duties, such as patrolling the streets and roads, guarding buildings, and regulating traffic.

The Attorney General and the Solicitor General

The state attorney general, usually elected like the governor on a state-wide basis, is the chief law officer of the state. He prosecutes, or directs others to prosecute, cases at the highest levels of the state courts, advises district attorneys, and serves as legal adviser to the governor and other state officials. Under the broad constitutional powers entrusted to most attorneys general, he may interfere when necessary in local matters, either to support local law officers or, under special circumstances, to oust them and take command of a troubled situation—like a major riot that has got out of control. In such cases, the governor has power to call out the militia (National Guard). On pp. 285–286, we shall see what other duties he has.

Commonly the state attorney general is assisted by a state **solicitor general**, who handles cases for the state before its highest courts and serves for the attorney general in advising local prosecutors. The solicitor general also normally handles important civil cases to which the state may be a party, like suits for damages against state agencies, or questions of jurisdiction between the state and private individuals or agencies.

The District Attorney

In state systems of justice, the chief burden of criminal law enforcement falls on the **district attorney**. There is, in each state, a district attorney for each judicial district (district where a justice of the state trial court holds his

The prosecuting attorney has turned to call the jury's attention to an important point in the testimony of the witness he has been questioning. This might be the trial of Mr. Z (pp. 249–250). The jury and judge must presume that Mr. Z is innocent. The PROSECUTOR must prove that Mr. Z is guilty. *He does not have to prove his innocence.*

court). He is elected by the people, for either a two- or a four-year term. The elections are often seriously contested because of the important place the district attorney has in the community. Lawyers with political ambition are often interested in the office as a place in which to make an outstanding record that may lead to political advancement or to a seat on the supreme court of the state.

The duties of the district attorney are to enforce all state laws within his district and to prosecute (usually with the assistance of one or more assistant district attorneys) all felonies. He directs the investigation of charges, tries to secure indictments by presenting evidence to the grand jury, or in some states supports an information before a judge with such evidence. When indictments or informations are secured, he tries cases before the courts.

Prosecution for Minor Offenses

The prosecution of minor criminal offenses (misdemeanors) is normally handled in city or county courts by an assistant district attorney or an attorney for the municipality. In such cases, the evidence is presented to the judge by policemen or by witnesses called by the police and argued by the assistant D.A. or other attorney assigned by law or custom to prosecute. Frequently—indeed, most commonly—there is no jury, but the accused may always ask for a jury trial. The request may be granted or refused by the trial judge. If refused, the refusal itself may be grounds for the defendant to appeal to a higher court. Most misdemeanors, however, are handled as a matter of routine; that is, the evidence provided by the police is so clear that the accused admits his guilt and is immediately sentenced.

Many offenses brought before city, county, and justice-of-the-peace courts (see p. 241) are not crimes. It is not, for example, a crime to break the speed laws in most areas. An offender is simply brought before a judge or justice of the peace, asked whether he is guilty, and either dismissed or punished by a fine. Violations of parking and other traffic regulations are frequently handled without any court procedure at all. These are the familiar cases in which the citizen is handed a "ticket" for, say, illegal parking by the police officer. He signs the ticket, thereby pleading guilty to the charge, and mails it with his fine to the courthouse or traffic violations bureau. We must not take this sort of law enforcement lightly. Traffic and speed regulations are important protections of our safety and our freedom.

Juvenile Courts

The people are served in many states and cities by special courts devoted to particular needs and problems. There is, for example, in many cities, a children's court, or juvenile court, intended to restrain juvenile delinquency and to protect youthful offenders from developing criminal records. Usually it deals with offenses committed by persons under sixteen. It has power to sentence offenders to reform schools or place them on **probation** (that is, allow them to go free under supervision for a specified length of time on promise of good behavior). Or it can give them **suspended sentences** (release them without punishment, holding the sentence back to be applied if there should be another offense). Very frequently it functions as a place where children simply "learn a lesson" they did not learn at home. Such courts are often today assisted by staffs of professional experts in psychiatry, child guidance, probation, and family welfare.

253

Frequently the procedures in juvenile courts are less formal than those for adult offenders. The judge may call the child and his parents to the bench and talk over the child's behavior in detail, impressing him with the seriousness of what he has done and the meaning and purpose of the law. A stern lecture by the judge in his judicial robes in the solemn surroundings of a courtroom sometimes impresses young people with the need for decent behavior. There is no freedom either in lawless behavior or in prisons.

Domestic Relations Courts

Some states have special courts to deal with domestic relations. The chief problem coming before such courts is divorce or separate maintenance. The laws of marriage are fairly uniform among the states. A marriage is a legal contract; violation of its provisions constitutes an offense both against the state and against the other party in the contract. The states differ widely in their laws respecting divorce. Wherever domestic relations courts are found, however, their function is the same, namely, to prevent if possible the disruption of families and to help couples to solve their problems.

In domestic relations courts, the judge has power to delay a decision while he attempts to reconcile the husband and wife. He calls to their attention the unhappy consequences which sometimes come with broken homes, explains the complicated process of property division, and tries to impress upon both husband and wife their responsibilities under the marriage contract. In other words, domestic relations courts are intended to prevent divorce if possible and grant it only as a last resort. These courts play an important part in life in the United States today. Many more of them are needed.

THE DEPARTMENT OF JUSTICE

The laws of the United States are the Constitution itself and those statutes enacted by Congress which are at any given time in force. The responsibility for federal law enforcement is given by the Constitution to the President. Through the President's powers, the whole executive branch becomes a kind of vast agency of law enforcement.

Most laws, however, are of a positive sort. That is, the executive branch is authorized by Congress to do something for the people—build roads, coin money, maintain the army. These functions of the President and the executive branch were considered in Chapters 7 and 8. Here we are concerned with federal laws providing a penalty for misconduct defined in the laws, and with legal aid to the executive branch. The first Congress in 1789 established the office of Attorney General of the United States to act on behalf of the President in discharging this part of his responsibilities for law enforcement.

In 1870 the Congress established a department for the Attorney General and his staff, the Department of Justice. Based in its majestic stone building in Washington, this Department (with some 30,000 employees) is today one of the most important parts of the executive branch. It has many divisions and bureaus, as the chart, p. 258, shows, all under the direction and leadership of the Attorney General. Between these agencies and the Attorney General are eleven top-level policy-making and administrative officials: the Deputy Attorney General, the Solicitor General, and nine Assistant Attorneys General.

The Attorney General

The Attorney General is the chief law officer of the federal government. The chart, p. 258, indicates how he is appointed and what his duties are. Because almost everything the government does is in some way or other related to questions of law, the Attorney General is a central figure in the government and often one of the President's closest advisers. This means that the Attorney General must be carefully selected. He must, of course, be a lawyer. In particular, he must be a lawyer who is thoroughly acquainted with federal law and the federal Courts.

Legal opinions are often anything but cut and dried statements of fact about the law. Typically they are matters of judgment in which at least some other lawyers—and judges!—may be expected to differ. There are so many laws on the statute books—not always consistent among themselves—that frequently the Attorney General has a great deal of leeway in forming an opinion. His job is not only to protect the government, by good legal advice, from acting contrary to law but also to find ways and means within the law by which government can carry out its programs. He must expect that some of his opinions will be tested in the courts by individuals or groups who disagree with his judgment, or who may feel themselves aggrieved by the program of the administration. Thus the Attorney General must exercise careful judgment to make sure that the government will have a good case if its measures are tested in the courts. Since he is responsible for representing the United States in all cases before the courts to which the United States is a party, his judgments and decisions have the greatest importance for the government as well as for his own standing as a lawyer and a statesman.

As legal adviser to the executive branch, the Attorney General is in constant close relations with Congress. He is frequently asked to testify in support of bills the administration is asking Congress to pass. Senator A may want to know whether a bill to fix the price of milk in a certain region is constitutional. "Mr. Attorney General, can you show that this bill is within the letter as well as the spirit of the Commerce Clause, Article I, Section 8?"

A Representative may have a different kind of question. "Mr. Attorney General, in what way will this bill affect other statutes on marketing? In other words, sir, what happens to the price of milk in my home state, which is covered by the law we passed last year?"

The Attorney General must be skillful in answering such questions convincingly because it is his job to persuade Congress that if the bill is enacted into law it cannot be successfully challenged in the courts by citizens who may not like it. Thus, the Attorney General's personal relations with Congressmen may be crucial to the success of the administration. This is why he must be a good politician.

Other Officers and Divisions of the Department

The chart, p. 258, shows the complete organization of the Department of Justice, as well as the important duties of each division. You should study it carefully. Immediately under the Attorney General is the Deputy Attorney General, who shares the responsibilities of his office and acts for the Attorney General when he is absent or ill. He directs the United States attorneys and United States marshals.

Let us see how the United States attorneys proceed. If counterfeit money is found in circulation in his district, for example, the United States attorney tries to find its source and arrests anyone found passing it or printing it. In this he will coöperate with the Secret Service of the Treasury Department (p. 521). He presents his evidence to the federal grand jury and, if he secures an indictment, prosecutes the case in the federal District Court.

The Solicitor General of the United States has important duties in the Department of Justice. To discharge them, he must be an expert in constitutional law and in the statute law of the United States. In particular, he represents the United States in cases before the Supreme Court, and he must be able to present skillfully the government's position before the Court.

The criminal laws of the United States, except those involving taxes and sedition, are enforced by the Criminal Division under direction of an Assistant Attorney General. There are more than 120 federal criminal laws with which the Criminal Division is concerned. They include laws against counterfeiting and forgery, bribery, customs violations, extortion, larceny and theft, impersonation (for example, impersonation of a military officer), kidnaping, violations of the narcotics laws, passport fraud, racketeering, frauds in stocks and bonds, violations of fair labor standards and labor-management laws, crimes on the high seas or on government property, violations of laws regulating the use of firearms and the mails and of the atomic energy laws.

The Civil Division supervises such civil suits as admiralty and shipping cases, certain Court of Claims cases, fraud cases on the government, patent cases, veterans' affairs cases under certain Acts, customs cases and general civil suits by and against the United States.

256

The Internal Security Division prosecutes those accused of treason or sedition. The Civil Rights Division is directly responsible for enforcing the Bill of Rights, especially voting rights. (See Chap. 16.) Many civil liberties cases arise in the state courts. The Department of Justice intervenes when such cases are appealed to the federal Courts on constitutional grounds or when states fail to protect the rights guaranteed to citizens in the Constitution. An example of the sort or case in which the Civil Rights Division defends the rights of the individual would be one in which a citizen was denied the right to vote in a national election.

Federal Bureau of Investigation

FBI NABS KIDNAP SUSPECT

This headline highlights the activities of one of the most famous agencies in the United States government. The name FBI means to many such spectacular work as detecting kidnapers or dramatic closing in on agents of foreign powers. On these activities plays, movies, and novels have been based. The FBI's long-time chief, J. Edgar Hoover, has impressed the nation as one of our most efficient public servants.

Behind the dramatic cases that burst into headlines, however, are the patient and painstaking activities of more than 13,000 people, doing routine work. The FBI is the chief investigating agency of the federal government. Through its network of offices and agencies all over the country, it investigates all alleged violations of federal laws except those specifically assigned to other federal agencies for enforcement. Tax frauds, counterfeiting, and customs violations, for example, are investigated by the Treasury Department (Chap. 21).

The FBI undertakes many additional assignments from the Attorney General or the President, including **security** and **loyalty investigations** of federal employees (see Chap. 15, Citizenship). It coöperates closely with other federal agencies, such as Military and Naval Intelligence, and with the Civil Service Commission, on any investigations they may be carrying out. A sober look at the duties of the FBI shows that its more newsworthy activities, like hunting for spies, are a very small part of its enormous routine load.

Immigration and Naturalization Service

Before 1940 the administration of our immigration and naturalization laws (Chap. 15) was in the hands of the Department of Labor, because by far the largest proportion of immigrants came to work as wage laborers. In recent years, the flow of immigration has slowed down. Most of the recent immigrants have been refugees from dictatorships in their own countries.

Department of Justice

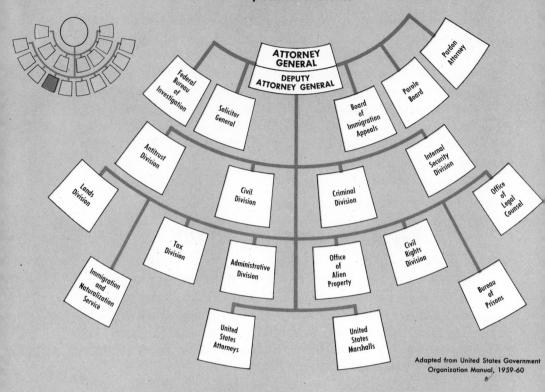

ATTORNEY GENERAL
DEPUTY ATTORNEY GENERAL

Federal Bureau of Investigation
Solicitor General
Board of Immigration Appeals
Parole Board
Pardon Attorney
Antitrust Division
Lands Division
Civil Division
Criminal Division
Internal Security Division
Office of Legal Counsel
Tax Division
Administrative Division
Office of Alien Property
Civil Rights Division
Immigration and Naturalization Service
Bureau of Prisons
United States Attorneys
United States Marshalls

Adapted from United States Government
Organization Manual, 1959-60

Attorney General; Deputy Attorney General, Solicitor General, 9 Assistant Attorneys General.

ATTORNEY GENERAL (1789). Chief law officer of the federal government; investigates, prosecutes in federal courts, acts as counsel for U.S. Appointed by President with consent of Senate.

U.S. ATTORNEYS. Initiate prosecution of violators of federal laws, present evidence to grand juries, argue the government's case. Represent the federal government legally in their districts.

SOLICITOR GENERAL. Acts for Attorney General in arguing cases before the Supreme Court. May represent the federal government in any court of the United States. Must authorize appeals made by the United States.

CRIMINAL DIVISION. Assistant Attorney General. Prosecutes federal offenders on evidence provided by any agency of government which is responsible for enforcement of laws, except those involving taxes. At the request of any of these agencies, the Federal Bureau of Investigation may investigate and give its evidence to the Criminal Division. Federal criminal laws include those against counterfeiting and forgery, bribery, customs violations, illegal use of firearms, extortion, larceny and theft, impersonation, kid-

naping, violation of liquor or narcotics laws, passport frauds, crimes on the high seas or on government property, violation of labor laws, violation of atomic energy laws.

CIVIL DIVISION. Assistant Attorney General. Supervise civil suits and claims involving the U.S., its officers and employees in cases of civil fraud, customs, veterans' affairs, patent, etc.

INTERNAL SECURITY DIVISION. Assistant Attorney General. Enforces laws against subversion.

IMMIGRATION AND NATURALIZATION SERVICE (1891). Commissioner. Administers the immigration and naturalization laws. Polices our borders to prevent illegal entry, deports aliens whose departure has been ordered as punishment for violation of the laws. Admits those aliens permitted under quota laws. Supervises procedures under which aliens become citizens. See pp. 367–368.

CIVIL RIGHTS DIVISION. Assistant Attorney General. Investigates complaints about matters affecting civil rights. Initiates appropriate actions. Coördinates all civil rights matters, state or federal. Does research on civil rights and makes recommendations to Attorney General about proposed policies and legislation.

Because of possible political ties, it seemed more appropriate for the Department of Justice to take over the handling of immigration and naturalization (that is, procedures under which immigrants become citizens). The work is carried on through the Immigration and Naturalization Service, numbering about 7,000 employees. It is headed by the Commissioner of Immigration and Naturalization, who is appointed by the President with the consent of the Senate.

The Immigration and Naturalization Service has offices in all larger communities and at all border points and representatives at consulates in certain foreign countries. If you have crossed the border from Mexico or Canada, you will remember the Immigration man who asked you politely where you were born, while the Customs man inspected your luggage. The Service is responsible for policing the borders to prevent illegal entry (coming into a country without authorization). It must consistently try to detect agents of foreign powers trying to enter the United States illegally and stop such persons at the borders.

See chart and caption, p. 258, for duties of the Service. Although the police work is dramatic, in practice it is really less important than the contribution the Service makes in training and assisting friendly immigrants who seek United States citizenship.

Antitrust Division

The Antitrust Division of the Department of Justice, under an Assistant Attorney General, influences greatly the economic life of the country. Specifically, it enforces the federal laws against monopoly, trusts, and other practices "in restraint of trade." It helps to maintain competition in private business enterprise, working closely with regulatory agencies like the Federal Trade Commission (p. 204). It protects the liberties of business, commerce, and consumers, by fair enforcement of the rules (see Chap. 21).

THE ANTITRUST LAWS   The principal federal laws now enforced by the Antitrust Division are the Sherman Act (1890), the Clayton Act (1914), and the Robinson-Patman Act (1936). The Sherman Act makes it a crime (misdemeanor) to "monopolize, or attempt to monopolize, or combine or conspire with any person or persons to monopolize any part of the trade or commerce among the several states, or with foreign nations." It was enacted at a time when the oil, steel, railroad, tobacco, and other industries were being pyramided into giants so big that small business was squeezed out or unable to get started. Under the law, a number of famous cases were tried, and the government succeeded to some extent in breaking up such huge corporations as the Standard Oil Company and the American Tobacco Company.

259

The Sherman Act sets the basic policy for business competition by making it illegal for one corporation or business organization to monopolize the business in which it engages. The Clayton Act, passed in 1914, enforced the principles of the Sherman Act. The new law made it an offense for one company to control another by means of "interlocking directorates" (the same individuals serving as directors of "competing" companies), to require dealers to sell its products only, and to charge different prices for the same product to different purchasers. The Robinson-Patman Act further tightened these laws and further defined unfair price competition to include secret agreements between companies.

EXCEPTIONS TO ANTITRUST SUPERVISION Congress has made a number of exceptions to the laws. Notable among these are the public utilities. Providing electric power or telephone service to a community is a kind of "natural monopoly" where competition among several suppliers would obviously not be in the public interest. Congress therefore exempted the utilities by law from many of the provisions of the antitrust laws. They are regulated through the Federal Power Commission and the Federal Communications Commission, and also by certain state laws (see pp. 199–206). Another important exception to antitrust regulation is the labor unions, as we shall see in Chapter 22. The courts and the Congress have decided that "labor is not a commodity of commerce"; therefore, Congress does not have the same power to regulate unions under the Commerce Clause of Article I, Section 8, that it has to regulate business. However, as we saw in Chapter 8 and shall learn more fully in Chapter 22, Congress does have power to make rules for labor-management relations and to regulate conditions of labor.

ANTITRUST SUITS AND TRIALS In spite of numerous exceptions, the laws do apply to much of American business. The Antitrust Division represents the government in important prosecutions or civil suits for damages under the laws. Some offenders have been fined or jailed as criminal punishment. More commonly the government has been content to bring civil suits as a result of which the offender pays for damages. The Antitrust Division asks for an injunction from the federal Courts to restrain offenders from continuing practices that violate the laws. Thus, in 1957 the Antitrust Division won a case in the federal Courts against the Du Pont Corporation because it owned a very large portion of the stock of the General Motors Corporation. The Court ordered the Du Pont Corporation to sell its General Motors stock. Sometimes small businesses have brought suit for damages against large companies, for violation of the antitrust laws. In such cases a judge may award triple damages if the complaint is found to be valid.

The Antitrust Division acts as a kind of policeman enforcing the laws regulating business. The antitrust laws have succeeded to a considerable extent in holding back the formation of trusts and monopolies. If business has become big, it has most often been through the successful sale of its product and well-warranted expansion of its plant and operations.

Tax Division

The Tax Division of the Department of Justice, under an Assistant Attorney General, frequently makes the headlines of our newspapers because it is involved in notorious cases. Gangsters, hoodlums, and illegal gamblers about whose activities local police departments have not been able to gather enough evidence, have often been caught when Internal Revenue investigators (see p. 495) prove that they have failed to report all of their income or have otherwise avoided tax obligations. In such a case, the evidence is turned over to the Tax Division of the Justice Department, and the man is prosecuted for violation of federal tax laws. The most notorious of all American mobsters, Al Capone, was finally caught and imprisoned by this means.

Such cases are so dramatic that the bulk of the important work done by the Tax Division is overlooked. It also acts for the government in all lawsuits based on federal tax laws, except those argued before the Tax Court (see p. 236). This means that the attorneys of the Tax Division work with United States attorneys in cases before the District Courts and Courts of Appeals to collect taxes from delinquent taxpayers. Or they defend the government when it is sued by taxpayers claiming refunds denied by the government. The volume of such business is enormous. Court dockets are crowded to overflowing, and cases often go on for many years. Through the Internal Revenue Service and the Tax Division, however, Uncle Sam has a way of getting his due sooner or later. Conversely, citizens are guaranteed fair treatment when they have grievances against the government, since in the federal Courts citizens have the same standing as government prosecutors.

OTHER FEDERAL LAW ENFORCEMENT AGENCIES

There are several other important but specialized federal law enforcement and investigating agencies shown on the chart, p. 262. You can get an idea from this chart how complex our law enforcement system is. Eight of the departments play a part in it, and so do numerous independent commissions and administrative agencies.

The record of all these agencies is a good one. Nevertheless, new techniques of detection and investigation must constantly be developed so that the law can outwit the criminal. And more trained men are needed in every agency. Some agencies, those whose work comes more frequently to public attention, have little difficulty in persuading Congress to appropriate sufficient

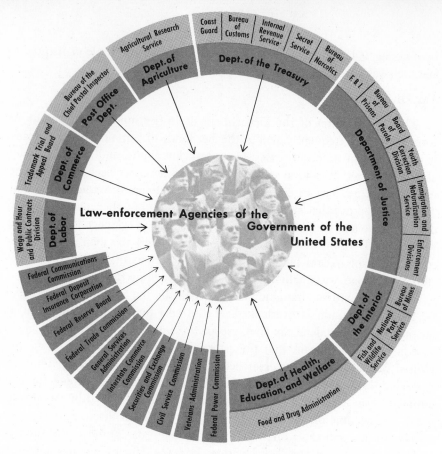

Law-enforcement Agencies of the Government of the United States

We are apt to think of federal law enforcement as something spectacular—such as Secret Service men guarding the President, or the FBI hunting down public enemies. Most law enforcement is less exciting. Nevertheless, your government is quietly at work when:

the Veterans Administration analyzes handwriting to detect an impostor; or the Agricultural Research Service enforces the meat inspection laws; or representatives of the Bureau of Mines make investigations.

These, as you can see from the chart, are only a few of the many law-enforcement activities of your government. And there are more not even shown on the chart. In one sense, all administrative and executive agencies are engaged in law enforcement as they perform their regular duties. For example, the Civil Service Commission administers examinations, and the Department of Labor draws up apprenticeship standards.

funds for their work. It has always been difficult to obtain enough money for the routine, humdrum kind of labors on which all good law enforcement ultimately depends.

Prisons

Over the generations almost all trace of "cruel and unusual punishments" has disappeared throughout the United States. Amendment VIII to the Constitution, an important part of the Bill of Rights, prohibits the federal government from inflicting such punishments, but the states were slower to act.

For example, the practice in some states of chaining prisoners together and sending them out to do hard labor on roads has only begun to disappear in recent years. On the whole, the record is good, and American penal actions tend pretty well to "fit the crime."

Prison reform has been much slower. In fact even today some state prison systems are poor, and many local jails are disgracefully inadequate. The reason is usually lack of money. Legislatures tend to be as economical with the taxpayers' money as possible. Prisons "don't show," so it is rather easy to neglect them when appropriations are under debate. Citizen lack of interest is probably the most important reason for the lag in prison reform. People do not like to think about prisons (for long sentences) and jails (for short sentences). This negligence is harmful to the community and to the nation. Many studies have shown that the worse the conditions of prison life, the more likely a prisoner is to revert to his criminal ways when his sentence has been served. It is only good sense to invest public money wisely in improving, and enlarging, our backward and overcrowded prisons, since all the evidence indicates that the investment would significantly lower the crime rate. One of the most useful answers to the common citizen question "What can I do?" is to say that you can take an active interest in our penal institutions.

FEDERAL SYSTEM   The six federal penitentiaries—at Alcatraz, California; Atlanta, Georgia; Leavenworth, Kansas; Lewisburg, Pennsylvania; McNeil Island, Washington; and Terre Haute, Indiana—are administered by the Bureau of Prisons in the Department of Justice. This Bureau, staffed by career experts in prison administration, also has charge of federal reformatories (four—one of which is for women), juvenile institutions (four), correctional institutions (seven), and detention camps (four). In general, the federal prison system is more modern and better administered than many state systems. Prisoners are sorted out according to the seriousness of their crimes against federal law and are assigned to specialized prisons or prison divisions. They are required to work at occupations suited to their abilities, for the most part, and are given extensive vocational and rehabilitation training. The system results in the production of many useful articles in prison industries, and a record of good behavior for ex-convicts after sentences are completed. Of course, some habitual criminals do not change their ways after federal prison experience, but there are relatively few of them. The occasional serious disturbances inside the prisons usually occur among men serving sentences of many years for the most serious crimes. In general, federal prisoners are well behaved and good discipline is maintained, and prisoners are given increasing responsibility as their conduct warrants.

The President of the United States has constitutional authority to pardon offenders against the laws of the United States. Such pardons are uncommon, but are occasionally granted to individuals whose record is good except for one offense, and who have served at least a portion of their terms. **Parole** (release under oath to obey the laws) is granted in most cases except those involving very long sentences. The Board of Parole in the Department of Justice makes continuing studies of the records of prisoners as referred to them by prison wardens and administrators, grants hearings to attorneys representing prisoners, and grants parole on its best judgment. In some cases the law provides that parole must be granted after a certain portion of a sentence has been served, providing the prisoner's record is good. Youthful offenders (under 22) are given special treatment by the Board of Parole, and all parolees are supervised by probation officers of the Department of Justice.

STATE AND LOCAL SYSTEMS   At the state level, there are three classes of prisons and jails: state, county, and city. State prisons are usually administered by an official under the state Attorney General and by wardens for each separate prison. Commonly only felons are sentenced to state prisons, though some state prisons handle the overflow from inadequate local prisons and jails. The more common types of crimes are punished by sentence to the county jail, while city jails are used principally for detention of persons charged with offenses or for sentences of a few days, such as may be handed out for such minor crimes as vagrancy or disorderly conduct.

There is no uniform standard, either of management or of equipment, among state and local jails and prisons. Conditions in institutions for "reform" of youthful offenders, for mental defectives, and for women delinquents also need to be improved, especially at the levels of the states, counties, and cities. Some states and the more progressive cities have remarkable records of penal and prison reform, and have built institutions and carry on programs among the inmates of which all citizens may be proud. The moral of the prison tale, as in so many other aspects of American government, is that the citizens who let things go are always poorest served by their government; those who are willing to take responsibility and work hard at their problems are rewarded by institutions in which they can take pride and which serve them well. As an adult citizen you have not only the right but also the duty to inspect the prisons in your state. If you are not satisfied with what you find, you should talk to your state representative about it, and if necessary organize your friends and neighbors to protest. If you do, you will be heard, and if you have enough facts, sooner or later the legislature will take action.

STANDARDS OF PUBLIC MORALITY

In some states the State Board of Education is responsible under law for such things as deciding whether motion pictures may be shown, licensing professional people like physicians and dentists, and other functions having to do with public enlightenment, health, and morals. This work is a kind of law enforcement. For this reason, a Board of Education has a very difficult and sensitive position in the social structure.

Censorship

An example would be its powers of **censorship.** Freedom does not mean unlimited power to do what one wants to do. You may not publish anything you wish, show any kind of film you choose to make, or otherwise exercise the freedoms of speech and publishing without restriction. A Board of Education given the responsibility of licensing motion pictures is under constant pressure to censor. A film may strike one religious group in the state as offensive to good taste, while others wish it approved because they fear any decisions allowing religious influence on the government. In at least one state, certain questions have been removed from state public school examinations because they seem offensive to a religious group. When to censor and when not to censor, when to license and when to refuse, are matters calling for exercise of the most careful judgment and strong character. Certain outstanding cases, of course, are tested in the Supreme Court of the United States, and when this happens, often the power of the state, through its Board of Education or other agency, is found to be limited by the Constitution.

SUMMARY

Although our federal and state constitutions separate the powers of the judiciary and the executive branches, there is a very close relationship between the courts and executive law enforcement. The task of the executive is to bring cases of violation of law into the courts for trial and decision. This function is known as **prosecution.** Government lawyers also argue civil cases before the courts, pleading the government's side in a controversy.

In this chapter, you have seen how civil actions are used to enforce the law and prosecutions for crime are conducted. You have learned about the safeguards our laws provide for persons accused of crimes and seen what it means to say that the burden of proof rests on government. In particular, you have studied the agencies of law enforcement at the state and local level, where citizens most commonly meet with law enforcement officers and agencies, and you have seen how the Department of Justice is organized to enforce the laws of the federal government.

You should now understand the duties and responsibilities of law officers, from the local policeman on the beat to the District Attorney, and from an

FBI agent to the Attorney General of the United States. And you should understand the relation of yourself, as citizen, to the law and its enforcement. You have also examined our prison system, local, state, and national, and have seen how government works to maintain standards of public morality. Police law enforcement, at all levels of government, can protect us to some extent against criminals and against indecent, unfair, or dishonest conduct, but police work usually comes only *after* wrong has been done. It is the people who decide *whether* wrong will be done.

KNOW WHAT YOU READ

1. Review the difference between civil and criminal cases. Explain how civil cases also may be law-enforcement cases.
2. John Doe believes that he ought to sue Richard Roe. What are the steps by which he goes about this? What does Richard do? What does the court do?
3. Explain how a criminal prosecution brings in all three branches (legislative, executive, judicial) of government.
4. What is the purpose of most of the first ten amendments? Locate each in the Constitution. What is the significance of the cartoon, p. 248?
5. Outline the steps by which a criminal may be brought to trial and tried.
6. Why are American laws and American courts so careful to protect the rights of persons accused of crimes? Give two examples.
7. Summarize the work of the state attorney general.
8. Lawyer Schmidt wishes to rise in politics. He would like to become a district attorney. How may one obtain this office? Why is this an important office to a man who has political ambitions?
9. What are the duties of a district attorney?
10. How are persons accused of misdemeanors prosecuted?
11. What cases brought before our courts are not *crimes*?
12. In what ways is the work of a juvenile court different from that of a regular trial court?
13. What is the chief purpose of the Court of Domestic Relations?
14. Why must the Attorney General of the Department of Justice be a good politician?
15. What are his duties?
16. List any ten of the 120 federal criminal laws.
17. What agency of government is responsible for the enforcement of the Bill of Rights?
18. What is the work of the Civil Division?
19. What are the responsibilities of the FBI? Why is this the best known of all our law enforcement agencies?
20. What are the chief tasks of the Immigration and Naturalization Service?

21. In what ways does the Antitrust Division of the Department of Justice "police" business?
22. What are the responsibilities of the Tax Division?
23. What law-enforcement work is carried on with each of the following, shown in the drawing, p. 262: (a) Secret Service; (b) Bureau of Narcotics; (c) Postal Inspection Service.
24. Why have so many states been slow in reforming their prisons?
25. In many ways the federal prison system is considered modern. What does this mean?

WHAT DO YOU THINK?

1. How are adults responsible for juvenile delinquency? In what ways are young people responsible for their own delinquency?

> "A bill holding parents legally responsible—up to $250—for acts of vandalism by their children has been passed by the State Assembly.
>
> This strikes us as a basic ingredient of any plan to curb delinquency. Until parents can be made more responsible—legally, financially, morally—the war on youthful crime will lag.
>
> We hope this bill gets final approval, but we would suggest one deletion. Why limit financial responsibility to $250? Why limit it at all?"
>
> Editorial, New York *World Telegram*, February, 1956

2. The bill discussed in the above editorial was passed and sent to the governor. If you had been the governor, would you have signed the bill or vetoed it?
3. In 1956 the Legislative Research Council of Massachusetts reported that its investigations showed that the worst drivers in that state were teenagers. This report indicated an average of 89.1 accidents for every one-thousand teen-age operators. The second worst record was held by the age group 20 to 24 with 50.9 bodily injury accidents per one-thousand drivers. Would you justify making young people pay higher rates for automobile insurance?

PROBLEMS AND PROJECTS FOR YOU

1. Within the last 24 hours, how many opportunities have you had to break laws? Why didn't you do so? This might make a good discussion question or a topic for a paper. A suggested but not required title for the paper might be "Living Within the Law."

2. Your textbook says that the laws that people do not believe in cannot be enforced. Do you agree? Is this true of student obedience to the rules and regulations of your own school? Do you find any difference in the case of those rules and regulations which have been made by elected student leaders? This whole area might be good for a panel discussion.

3. In 1905 Pennsylvania established a State Constabulary which was the first real state police system. Thirty-six states now have such forces. If you live in one of the 36, report to the class on the history, organization, and achievement of your state police.

4. For your bulletin board, collect items about the work of the attorney general of your state. If you are doing this assignment in an election year, collect items listing the reasons each candidate claims *he* is the one who should be elected.

5. Report to the class on how misdemeanors are prosecuted in your state.

6. Interview an attorney or a judge to find out how juvenile cases are handled in your state.

7. In a speech in San Diego a few years ago, J. Edgar Hoover said in reference to the cities' difficulty in recruiting police:

   "Entrance standards should never be lowered. Salaries should be increased. It is better to keep a high-class force by raising their pay instead of lowering their standards. Law enforcement is a profession. Police . . . are underpaid at a serious cost to communities."

   Report to the class on the methods by which local or state police are recruited, promoted, and paid.

   > The sheriffs (in South Dakota) are now paid on a fee system—a carry over from the old days when that was the common method. But in respect to virtually all other offices, the system has been discarded. It should be abandoned in respect to the office of sheriff. The legislature should amend the law to provide a direct salary system in conformity with modern practices and common sense. *Sioux Falls Argus Leader*

8. Report to the class on how sheriffs are paid in your state.

9. A few years ago, a citizen was arrested in Boston for refusing to help a uniformed policeman in making an arrest. Does the law of your state require you to give assistance to the police if they ask for it?

EXTEND YOUR VOCABULARY

civil action	search warrant	appeal
summons	arraignment	attorney general
complaint	indictment	district attorney
damages	cross-examine	prosecutor
bail	habeas corpus	subpoena

probation   naturalization   interlocking directorates
suspended sentence   monopoly   pardon
immigration   antitrust   parole
                                                 censorship

YOUR NOTEBOOK: THE GOVERNMENT OF ——

1. What kind of specialized courts does your community have? Make a record of the names in your notebook, and give an example of the kinds of cases each court has had before it during the past month.
2. Here are a few of the items on the night blotter of the police of a Massachusetts town for an October night:

   8:30—Fire alarm: rubbish fire in truck.

   8:45—Policeman reports horses and lanterns blown over near construction.

   9:00—Mr. S reports that his dog is lost.

   9:55—Mr. C telephones to report that someone has broken his aerial off his automobile.

  10:10—Mr. T calls in to report that someone has taken a pumpkin from his front yard.

  10:20—Officer D reports that he has locked the side door of a used car agency.

  10:45—Automobile accident, property damage only. A car struck a tree and stone wall. No damage to tree or wall.

  12:30—Mr. L calls that someone has taken two hubcaps from his car.

  12:57—Mrs. T telephones to ask the police to have her daughter call her. (Mrs. T has been trying to call the daughter and has gotten a busy signal.)

   1:23—Recovered stolen car.

Interview your local law-enforcement officers for a similar report on the everyday work of the police. Write a report similar to above in your notebook.

READ MORE ABOUT IT

IRISH, MARIAN D., and PROTHRO, JAMES W., *The Politics of American Democracy.* Prentice-Hall, 1959. Chap. 14.

RANNEY, AUSTIN, *The Governing of Men.* Holt, 1958. Chap. 20.

SWARTHOUT, JOHN M., and BARTLEY, ERNEST R., *Principles and Problems of American National Government.* Oxford University Press, 1955. Chap. 25.

CHAPTER 11

State Governments

In this chapter you will learn about

The scope and power of state governments
State legislatures
The governor
The executive branch of the state
Governmental programs of the states

The state governments in our country are older than the federal, but they have been based on certain constitutional provisions since 1789. Amendment X (p. 63), as we have seen, states that powers not delegated to the United States or prohibited to the states are "reserved to the States respectively, or to the people." Article IV, Section 4, says that "The United States shall guarantee to every state in this Union a Republican Form of Government" (p. 60). Thus each of our states is a **republic,** that is, a form of government in which the public business is carried on by representatives of the people, elected by the people for relatively short periods, and subject to being replaced by the people, either in elections or by recall or by impeachment for misconduct.

Each of these 50 republics exercises the powers **reserved** by the Constitution to the states and delegated to the states by the people in written constitutions. You, the citizen, are therefore a full-fledged member of *two* republics—your state and the United States. You are, indeed, a citizen member of certain other governments, too—your town, county, and city and, perhaps, even certain "special districts," as we shall see in Chapter 12. These local governments have no independent authority of their own. They are created by the state governments and are dependent on the state governments. They are not independent republics like your state and the United States.

As one of the 50 republics which make up the United States, what can your state do? What power does it have? Here are some answers. The law requiring you to go to school is a state law; the curriculum of studies you have gone through ever since you started in the first grade is partly or wholly prescribed by the education department of your state government; and the buildings housing your public schools were built either with money from the state treasury or with money raised by your local government under state authority, or both. The main roads connecting cities in your state are state roads; the serum with which you were vaccinated against polio was distributed under rules laid down by your state health department; the barber who cuts your hair has a license issued by the state, which means that he has met standards of skill and sanitation set up by your state; the monthly rate you pay for your telephone service is fixed by an agency of your state government. The trout you caught in a country stream were probably placed in that stream by your state wildlife officials; your doctor complied with state requirements of medical training in order to get a license issued by the state; the weight of trucks allowed to use your highways is determined by state officials; the punishment for armed robbery in your town is fixed by state law. These are almost random examples of the things your state government does and is empowered to do by your state constitution.

STATE CONSTITUTIONS

There are many differences among the 50 state constitutions. We shall consider here some of the elements these constitutions have in common, and some of the more important differences, but you should obtain a copy of the constitution of your state in order to be sure just what its provisions are.

Preamble

All state constitutions resemble the federal Constitution. Each has a preamble setting forth the purposes of the state government. Emphasis is on securing freedom to the citizens. The preamble to the constitution of New York State is brief and to the point: "We, the People of the State of New York, grateful to Almighty God for our Freedom, in order to secure its blessing, do establish this Constitution." Other preambles include references to security and public welfare, as does the national Preamble. In every case, however, there is strong emphasis on securing freedom; and in every case it is "We the People" who speak—for themselves.

Bill of Rights

The people of each state took measures to protect their individual liberties, even before the federal Constitution was written, by writing bills

ARTICLE I

DECLARATION OF RIGHTS

That the great and essential principles of liberty and free government may be recognized and established,

WE DECLARE

Sec. 1. [Equality of rights] That all men when they form a social·compact, . . .

Sec. 2. [Popular sovereignty] That all political power is inherent in the . . .

Sec. 3. [Freedom of religion] The exercise and enjoyment of religious . . .

Sec. 4. [No religious preference] No preference shall be given by law to . . .

Sec. 5. Every citizen may freely speak, write and publish his sentiments on . . .

Sec. 6. [Freedom of speech and press] No law shall ever be passed to curtail . . .

Sec. 7. [Prosecutions for libel] In all prosecutions or indictments for libels, . . .

Sec. 8. [Searches and seizures] The people shall be secure in their persons, . . .

Sec. 9. [Conduct of trials] In all criminal prosecutions, the accused . . .

Sec. 10. [Personal liberty] No person shall be arrested, detained or punished, . . .

Sec. 11. [Eminent domain] The property of no person shall be taken for . . .

Sec 12. [Judicial remedies] All courts shall be open, and every person, . . .

Sec. 13. [Bail] Excessive bail shall not be required, nor excessive fines im- . . .

Sec. 14. [Habeas corpus] All prisoners shall, before conviction, be bailable by . . .

Sec. 15. [Bills of attainder] No person shall be attainted of treason or felony, . . .

Sec. 16. [Right of assembly] The citizens have a right, in a peaceable man- . . .

Sec. 17. [Right to bear arms] Every citizen has a right to bear arms in . . .

Sec 18. [Military power subordinate] The military shall, in all cases, and . . .

Sec. 19. [Quartering of soldiers] No soldier shall, in time of peace, be . . .

Sec. 20. [Titles of nobility] No hereditary emoluments, privileges or . . .

Sec. 21. [Trial by jury] The right of trial by jury shall remain inviolate. . . .

---

of rights into their state constitutions (see pp. 62–63). These bills include guarantees of free speech, free press, freedom of assembly, freedom of religious worship, trial by jury, the writ of **habeas corpus,** the privilege against self-incrimination. The difference between the federal Bill of Rights and those of the states is that the latter are even more detailed and "spelled out." The bill of rights in a state constitution shown above is a fair illustration.

Separation of Powers

A third feature that state constitutions have in common is the provision they make for the organization of the state governments. Each provides, like the national Constitution, for an executive branch, a legislative branch, and a judiciary. The state judiciary systems are discussed in Chapter 9. Thus the republican structure of each state is typical of all. There are, however, many differences in the details of structure of state governments. For example, one of the states, Nebraska, has only one legislative chamber, but each, including

Nebraska, provides for a separation of powers like that in the federal government (see pp. 102–103) through three independent branches.

Provisions for Amending

Finally, all of the state constitutions provide means whereby the citizens can amend them from time to time, or even re-write them completely. And the citizens do use their powers of amendment—in some states very often indeed. While Missouri has amended her constitution only four times and Illinois only eight times, California has enacted 372 amendments and Louisiana 326. Between these extremes, most of the other states have amended their constitutions between 20 and 100 times. Massachusetts adopted her constitution in 1780 and has never re-written it completely; most states, however, have drawn up new constitutions, in constitutional conventions, at least once. The length of these state constitutions varies greatly—from Vermont's, which has less than 6,000 words, to Louisiana's, which has more than 200,000. In general, greater length means more amendments.

You may well ask why the states generally have amended their constitutions so many times. The answer is that the citizens of the states have tended to keep their government close to themselves, using the amending power to make their own decisions on matters of great and continuing importance. Some students of government feel that the amending power is used too often in some cases. Many amendments to state constitutions grow out of the unwillingness of legislators to take full responsibility for making certain controversial decisions. Decisions on such matters can be passed along to the citizens to vote on at election time as proposed constitutional amendments, as we saw on p. 81, when the question of building a new dam arose in New York.

In most states a constitutional amendment goes on the ballot for the voters to decide if two-thirds or three-fifths of the state legislature approve. In a few cases the legislature must act favorably in two successive sessions before the proposed amendment can go to the voters. Thirteen of the state constitutions have provisions enabling the citizens to initiate a referendum on an amendment (see pp. 80–81). In most states, amendments are adopted by a simple majority of the voters at the election, but Minnesota requires a three-fifths majority and New Hampshire ratifies amendments by a two-thirds vote of those voting in annual town meetings.

Forty-three states have some provision for calling a constitutional convention. The usual procedure is similar to the amending procedure. If a majority of the legislature approves of the proposal, it goes to the people for referendum at election time. A majority vote for the proposal means that the state will have a convention to reconsider its constitution, usually the year following. In some cases a convention is held two years following the referendum so that delegates to the convention may be elected in the regular fall election of the year following the referendum. You should examine the constitution of your state to see what kinds of matters have been added to it by amendment, how amendments may be made, and whether there is a provision for calling constitutional conventions. Many state constitutions, as we have seen, are so long that they are unwieldy. Check your state constitution for length and age.

STATE LEGISLATURES

The following paragraph from a popular magazine suggests something of what lawmaking is like in the 50 republics which are the states of the United States:

> The Legislature [Illinois] no longer possesses the powers it abused when Abraham Lincoln was a member—to grant divorces and give away state land to railroad promoters. But there still is very little it cannot do. The problems it dealt with in 1953 ran from accounting to zoning and included alcoholic beverages, atomic energy, auctioneers, brucellosis in cattle, burglary, cats (stray), detectives, fireworks, garbage, hypodermic needles, jailbreaks, Lake Michigan, mosquitoes, plumbing, rape, slaughtering, and the Walcott-Marciano fight.
>
> The Legislature appropriates one and a half billion of the taxpayers' dollars to build highways, run prisons and welfare institutions, and perform other important functions. It killed a bill to protect the mourning dove. It considered measures to reform by constitutional amendment the entire court system of Illinois and to permit sport fishermen to use fifty hooks on a trot line. It appropriated $15,000 to air-condition the Governor's Mansion, but decided not to require the reading of five verses of the Old Testament in public schools daily. It revised the divorce law and congratulated the American Bowling Congress "for fifty years of dynamic service to the bowling public." [1]

By far the largest proportion of all the laws that affect you as an individual citizen are state laws; and there are thousands and thousands of them. It has always been so. When the original thirteen states gained their independence and formed the United States, each retained most of the governmental power for itself under the Articles of Confederation. Later, when the Constitution was adopted to build a strong national government, there was little thought that such a government would often deal directly with the citizens. The state governments were created directly by the citizens and were expected

---

[1] Copyright © 1953 by Curtis Publishing Company. Reprinted by permission of Harold Ober Associates Incorporated.

to do everything a government should do within the borders of the states. Over the years, of course, the national government has taken on many important responsibilities of lawmaking for the whole nation; but the states have not only retained the powers they always had, but also developed new ones as they have grown in size and needs. Thus the state legislatures are still at the center of the lawmaking process.

In important respects the state legislatures are like the Congress of the United States. All but one have two houses. Nebraska has adopted quite successfully a unicameral (one chamber) legislative body; but in each of the

Here you can see the makeup of a state legislature. State senates usually have from 30 to 50 members; but Delaware and Nevada have only 17, and Minnesota has 67. The lower houses (House of Representatives, or Assembly, or House of Delegates) vary from 35 (Delaware) to 399 (New Hampshire), but the membership is usually between 100 and 200. Nebraska has only one house, a Senate of 43 members. All but four states have two-year terms for members of the lower house; in Alabama, Louisiana, Maryland, and Mississippi the term is four years.

North Carolina General Assembly

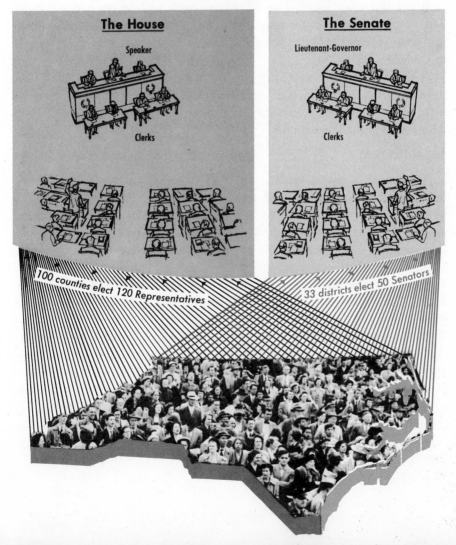

other states there is an upper chamber, called the Senate, and a lower chamber usually known as the House of Representatives (see chart, p. 275). In Nevada, New Jersey, New York, and Wisconsin the lower house is called the Assembly, while in Virginia it has always been known as the House of Delegates. Nebraska's one house is called the Senate. For number of members and length of terms, see table, pp. 282–283.

State Senate and Lower House

The electoral base of the state senates varies. In some states one senator is elected from each county. In others the state is divided into senatorial districts according to some formula of population. In every case, however, the state senate is substantially smaller than the lower house. See chart, p. 275, for the organization of the state government of North Carolina. The state houses of representatives are normally based on population, one representative to so many thousands of people.

Both the national and state lower houses are based on election districts (but not the *same* districts) in accordance with population, and the members are elected for two-year terms. The state senates, however, have no such firm basis as does the Senate which represents each of the fifty states equally in Congress.

The state senates play a very important part in state government. They serve as checks on the lower, more popular houses, and represent larger areas with ranges of interest which may be broader than they are in the districts represented in the lower houses.

Apportionment

In general, however, we may say that state legislatures apportion their seats according to some kind of population formula. This relation between legislators and population is known as apportionment (see pp. 118–119), and presents a serious continuing problem of state government. On pp. 119–120, we discussed the difficulties of solving this problem for federal Congressional districts. The problem is somewhat different in different states, and the states have devised a variety of ways of solving it. You should ask your own representative how the seats in your state legislature are apportioned and how and when changes in apportionment are made.

There are some common elements in the apportionment problem. As the population of the United States as a whole grows, population grows unevenly in various states and in particular areas of the states. For example, rural areas tend to lose rather than gain population. At the same time, many cities are losing population to suburbs. Thus election districts laid out according to population some time ago often bear little relation to the distribution of population now. In theory legislative seats should be reappor-

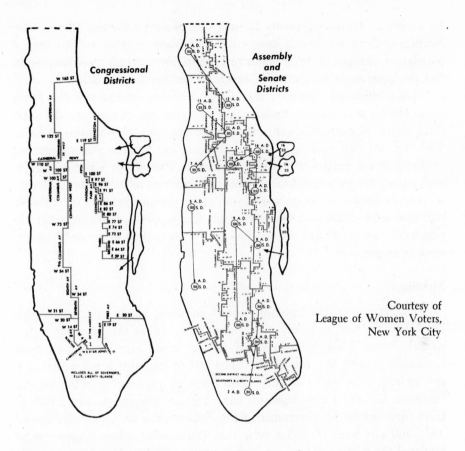

Congressional Districts

Assembly and Senate Districts

tioned as populations grow or shift. In practice this often does not happen, or happens very slowly. The reason is usually to be found in the interest of political parties in protecting their control over legislatures. In early days the states were, of course, predominantly rural. Legislative districts gave the larger share of seats to rural representatives. But as cities grew into large concentrations of population, the representatives from rural areas, who had a majority in the legislature, were reluctant to reapportion the seats accordingly. Such reapportionment could mean losing their own seats as well as turning the majority from the country to the cities. Of course some changes were made, but even today the rural areas of the states are much more heavily represented in the state legislature than are the cities. It is not uncommon, for example, to find a legislator whose district contains 10,000 people seated in the chamber next to a man from a city whose district has 150,000 people.

In most states the power to reapportion is vested in the legislature itself. If a political party holds a majority in the legislature, and these legislators come mainly from rural areas, you can see why the majority is unlikely to look

277

favorably on reapportionment. In such states as California, Illinois, and Michigan, there are boards especially established to plan redistricting as population changes. In these states reapportionment occurs more frequently, and the legislatures are chosen in better proportion to population.

This problem of apportionment shows a serious weakness in our democratic system and suggests something which you, the citizen, can do something about. In many states citizen organizations have taken up this problem. They are not only making useful suggestions, but are also putting pressure on the political parties to make the necessary changes. It was the work of such citizen groups which brought about the reforms in states like California. As you become an active citizen in your state, you may wish to see for yourself how well democracy works through the proper representation of the people in your legislature. If you find your state system outmoded, you can work to improve it.

Meetings

In sixteen states the legislature meets annually, but in other states legislative sessions are held only every other year, unless the governor calls a special session. Though sessions may last up to six months, they are more commonly limited to a few weeks. Thus a state legislator is not expected to give so large a portion of his time to his duties as is a member of the national Congress. Usually a state legislator has a regular occupation, from which he takes time out for his government work. Salary scales are established accordingly, and vary from $15,000 in New York (biennially), where sessions are annual and the volume of business is very great, to $200 in New Hampshire. In general, salaries run from $1,000 to $5,000 biennially. (See table, pp. 282–283.)

Organization

State legislatures are organized much like the Congress. Each house has a number of standing committees charged with considering legislation in specialized fields. The names of committees vary, but all legislatures have committees on finance, taxation, education, welfare, labor, business, agriculture, health, etc. In addition there are usually a number of temporary committees dealing with specialized matters as they arise.

In the 39 states which elect a lieutenant governor, that officer presides over the senate; in the other 11 states the senate elects its own presiding officer. The lower houses elect a speaker from their membership. The speaker, like the Speaker of the House of Representatives, is actually chosen in the caucus of the majority party, which also chooses a majority leader and sometimes one or more assistants, and assigns its members to committees. The minority, for its part, chooses a minority leader and designates committee

278

assignments for its minority memberships. The speaker, the majority and minority leaders, and the committee chairmen usually achieve their important positions through seniority (see p. 124).

In many states an even greater share of legislative work is done by committees and directed by committee chairmen than is the case in Congress. It often happens in states where one party has a substantial majority in the legislature, and the governor is of the same party, that legislation is almost entirely decided upon in meetings of the governor with the legislative leaders. In such circumstances, the rank-and-file legislator has little to do but appear at sessions of his house and vote. To some extent, this condition displays a weakness in the democratic process. But the fault, if any, lies ultimately with citizens who are too indifferent to become active in opposition.

The Scenes of Action

When a state legislature is in session, the state capitol is somewhat like Washington on a small scale. The corridors of the legislature are crowded with people seeking favors and influence. Committee hearings are held. Legislators are "buttonholed" by lobbyists pressing for enactment of laws in their interests or seeking votes against other proposed measures. Legislators receive petitions, letters, wires, and telephone calls from organizations and from individuals. They negotiate with one another in the hope of securing laws favorable to the districts they represent. Logrolling is common—you vote for my bill and I'll vote for yours.

At the heart of the legislative process, again, is compromise. Many legitimate interests come into conflict. Teachers looking for higher salaries run head-on into groups seeking to cut state expenses and taxes. People who believe in conserving our natural resources vie with power companies wanting to use the resources. Labor unions and consumer groups seeking higher minimum wage laws or lower milk prices compete with farmers needing lower-priced hired hands and higher prices for their produce. State regulation and state policy are vital to all such people and organizations. Often the central issue is between cities seeking greater financial aid from the state, or more state services, and rural areas wishing to hold costs down but eager to have roads to service the farms and money for consolidated schools. In states like Massachusetts, Illinois, Pennsylvania, or New York, this conflict of interest between city and country frequently gives the chief color and meaning to sessions of the legislature.

To compromise such differences successfully is not easy. No group is ever satisfied with the result. The process of democratic legislation remains always open to new solutions, however; and the citizens have always another chance. The state legislator, for his part, like the Congressman, seldom holds his seat so safely that he can ignore the majority opinion in his district. He must

PLENTY OF WOOD TO CUT

Messner in
Rochester Times-Union.

go back, usually every two or four years, to ask for reëlection. The voters will hold him to his record. Thus the best state legislator, like the best Congressman, is the one who advances the interests of his constituents as far as possible, compromising when he must. He must continually educate the voters to understand that their claims must always be weighed against others, and that their best interest in the long run is the good of the whole state. The legislator, in state government or in Congress, who can "raise the sights" of the voters he represents, persuade them to check and modify self-interest by recognizing larger interests and broader values, is most likely to succeed in his job and secure continuing reëlection.

A State Legislator

A good example is that of a doctor who has been a state representative from a small town in one of our eastern states for many years. Most of the people he represents are dairy farmers or people whose business is to sell supplies and services to dairy farmers. The doctor himself grew up among these people and understands their problems and point of view very well. But experience soon taught him that a state government cannot be run just to satisfy dairy farmers—there are too many other kinds of people in the state, and too many points of view just as worthy. So he set out, in his first term in the legislature, to do two things: (1) learn to understand and appreciate the needs of people in the cities and larger towns of the state and to help them when he thought their requests were justified, and (2) persuade his neighbors who had sent him to the legislature that each group or area is best served in the long run by what is best for the whole state.

The doctor-legislator did not always succeed, of course. But he played an important part in getting through a law 'governing milk distribution which gave less to his own constituents than they thought they should have and higher prices to city consumers than they wished to pay—and he "sold" his farmer friends on it. He supported a bill to give certain cities a larger share of tax money for schools, a bill his friends at home were against; but he persuaded a number of legislators from the cities to go along with his bill for consolidation of rural schools so that the new large central school in his district also received a greater share of tax money. He also persuaded those same city legislators to support his bill to supply young evergreens without charge to farmers who would reforest worn-out land and thus conserve it for future generations. The doctor, as we said, sometimes fails, but over the years he has been more and more valuable to his constituents and is not likely to lose his seat for a good many years to come.

STATE GOVERNORS

The executive branch in each of the 50 states is headed by the governor. The office of governor was inherited by the newly independent states from their previous colonial status. Under British rule each of the American colonies had a chief executive appointed by the king—a governor—and a legislature elected by those colonists who were entitled to vote. With the coming of independence, the legislatures were given far greater authority under the new constitutions, but less change was generally made in the office of governor as it was adapted to republican government. State governors have always been important leaders of the country—though in some states their powers are greater than in others. In our time their importance has for many reasons continued to grow. In a recent public opinion poll, it was discovered that more than 80 percent of the people of a state could name their governor, though only about 65 percent could name the Vice-President of the United States. What would your answers be to such a poll?

State governors are rather like small-scale Presidents, though in some of the very populous states the scale is not so small. They are elected on a state-wide basis, as the President is elected on a nation-wide basis. Thus they represent all the people of the state, while state legislators are chosen to represent certain districts. Though the constitutions and laws of the states differ in the amount of power they give to their governors, the governors are nevertheless the natural leaders of their states simply because they are

STATE GOVERNORS, LEGISLATURES, AND CONSTITUTIONS

State	Term of Governor (Years)	Governor's Salary (Annual)	Senate Members	Senate Term (Years)	Lower House Members	Lower House Term (Years)	Pay of Legislator	Constitution Date	Constitution No. of Amendments
Alabama	4	$12,000 (r)	35	4	106	4	$ 10 per day	1901	140
Alaska	4	25,000 (r)	20	4	40	2	6,000 biennially	1958	—
Arizona	2	18,500	28	2	80	2	8 per day	1912	40
Arkansas	2	10,000 (r)	35	4	100	2	1,200 biennially	1874	46
California	4	40,000 (r)	40	4	80	2	12,000 biennially	1879	321
Colorado	4	20,000	35	4	65	2	3,600 biennially	1876	58
Connecticut	4	15,000 (r)	36	2	280	2	600 biennially	1818	49
Delaware	4	17,500	17	4	35	2	2,000 biennially	1831	69
Florida	4	22,500 (r)	38	4	95	2	2,400 biennially	1886	105
Georgia	4	12,000 (r)	54	2	205	2	10 per day	1945	26
Hawaii	4	18,000 (r)	25	4	51	2	4,000 biennially	1959	—
Idaho	4	12,500 (r)	44	2	59	2	10 per day	1890	55
Illinois	4	25,000 (r)	58	4	177	2	12,000 biennially	1870	13
Indiana	4	15,000 (r)	50	4	100	2	3,600 biennially	1851	18
Iowa	2	12,500 (r)	50	4	108	2	30 per day	1857	19
Kansas	2	15,000 (r)	40	4	125	2	5 per day	1859	42
Kentucky	4	15,000 (r)	38	4	100	2	25 per day	1891	18
Louisiana	4	18,000 (r)	39	4	101	4	50 per day	1921	356
Maine	4	10,000 (r)	33	2	151	2	1,400 biennially	1820	84
Maryland	4	15,000 (r)	29	4	123	4	3,600 biennially	1867	86
Massachusetts	2	20,000	40	2	240	2	10,400 biennially	1780	81
Michigan	2	22,500 (r)	34	2	110	2	8,000 biennially	1908	63
Minnesota	2	19,000 (r)	67	4	131	2	4,800 biennially	1858	83
Mississippi	4	15,000 (r)	49	4	140	4	3,000 biennially	1890	35

State									
Missouri	4	25,000 (r)	34	4	157	2	3,000 biennially	1945	6
Montana	4	12,500 (r)	56	4	94	2	20 per day	1889	28
Nebraska	2	11,000 (r)	→ Unicameral Legislature, 2 yrs.				1,744 biennially	1875	72
Nevada	4	18,000 (r)	17	4	47	2	15 per day	1864	47
New Hampshire	2	15,500	24	2	400	2	200 biennially	1784	34
New Jersey	4	30,000 (r)	21	4	60	2	10,000 biennially	1947	2
New Mexico	2	17,500 (r)	32	2	66	2	20 per day	1911	40
New York	4	50,000 (r)	58	2	150	2	15,000 biennially	1894	127
North Carolina	4	15,000 (r)	50	2	120	2	15 per day	1868	(a)
North Dakota	2	10,000 (r)	49	4	113	2	5 biennially	1889	65
Ohio	2	25,000 (r)	34	2	139	2	10,000 biennially	1851	67
Oklahoma	4	15,000 (r)	44	4	121	2	15 per day	1907	39
Oregon	4	17,500 (m)	30	4	60	2	1,200 biennially	1859	97
Pennsylvania	4	25,000 (r)	50	4	210	2	6,000 biennially	1873	58
Rhode Island	2	15,000	44	2	100	2	5 per day	1843	33
South Carolina	4	15,000 (r)	46	4	124	2	2,000 biennially	1895	223
South Dakota	2	13,000 (r)	35	2	75	2	1,800 biennially	1889	60
Tennessee	4	12,000 (r)	33	2	99	2	10 per day	1870	8
Texas	2	25,000 (r)	31	4	150	2	25 per day	1876	133
Utah	4	12,000 (r)	25	4	64	2	1,000 biennially	1896	29
Vermont	2	12,500	30	2	246	2	1,750 biennially	1793	43
Virginia	4	20,000 (r)	40	4	100	2	1,080 biennially	1902	90
Washington	4	15,000 (r)	46	4	99	2	2,400 biennially	1889	32
West Virginia	4	17,500 (r)	32	4	100	2	3,000 biennially	1872	29
Wisconsin	2	20,000 (r)	33	4	100	2	7,200 biennially	1848	61
Wyoming	4	15,000 (r)	27	4	56	2	12 per day	1890	22

(a) not available
(r) salary plus residence or residence fund
(m) maintenance or other expenses

elected state-wide. A state governor is like the President, again, in many of his functions. He is chief executive of his state, chief ceremonial leader, and, often though not always, leader of his political party. He also has power to pardon or reprieve, stay executions, and commute sentences. Of course, he has no responsibility for the conduct of foreign relations, since the Constitution vests all power over foreign relations in the national government. As the chart on p. 183 shows, state governorship is the most common breeding ground for Presidents.

Terms of Office and Compensation

In 31 states the term of the governor is four years; in nineteen it is two. In sixteen states a governor cannot succeed himself at the next election, in seven states he is limited to two terms, while 27 states have no such restrictions. There are other important differences among the states in the powers allowed to governors, but in general the governor is the most powerful individual official in his state and is the chief representative of the republic over which he presides. Examine the constitution of your state to see how long your governor may serve and what limits are placed on his powers.

Governors' salaries vary from $10,000 a year in North Dakota to $50,000 a year in New York (see table, pp. 282–283).

Limitations on Powers of Governors

Although all state governors are chief executives of their states, there are many differences of power and duty among the various state governors. We can put the matter rather simply: the President is the only executive officer elected by all the people of the United States and is charged by the Constitution with responsibility for carrying out all the laws of the United States (see p. 165). By contrast, in all the states, other administrative officials besides the governor are also elected by all the voters and are charged with certain executive responsibilities either wholly or partly independent of the governor.

The 39 states which have a lieutenant governor elect him at the same time and for the same term as the governor. The lieutenant governor is in some respects like the Vice-President. He usually has no administrative duties, but presides over the upper house of the legislature. He succeeds to the governorship when the governor dies or is unable to carry on his duties.

Typically the states elect their attorney general (all but seven), secretary of state (all but nine), and often such other officials as auditor (comptroller), treasurer, and superintendent of public instruction. In some states, still other executive officials are elected on a state-wide basis. We shall consider the duties of these lesser officials later; the point here is simply that because of their constitutional responsibilities, they limit the powers of the governor. The governor is chief executive in the sense that he is most important, but in every state there are at least some aspects of the executive branch placed in the hands of others.

Roles of the Governor

In spite of the limitations on the governor's power, he is a very potent agent of the people. What powers does the governor have, and what does he in fact do? Satisfactory answers to these questions require whole books— even a whole book for each state. The chart on p. 286 indicates how extensive his powers and work are. A governor, for example, administers those laws entrusted to him either by his state constitution or by the laws of his legislature—not *all* laws, but still very many laws. In addition, in every state except North Carolina he has the power to veto legislation. In four states— Alabama, Massachusetts, New Jersey, and Virginia—the governor even has the power of executive amendment; that is, he may send back a bill passed by the legislature with an amendment suggested by himself on which the legislature must proceed to vote. The special sessions he calls in some states consider only matters specifically recommended by the governor. He has the power of **reprieve** (to postpone an execution), **pardon** (in most states), and **extradition** of persons wanted in other states (see p. 60).

The governor's informal power as a party leader adds to his strength as chief executive. Like the President, he can use his power of appointment to influence the legislature in his favor. Thus, suppose a measure is pending in the legislature which he is anxious to see passed but which some members of his party oppose. He can call them to his office and offer to make certain appointments these members are anxious to obtain in exchange for their support of his measure. As political leader, he has the chief voice in naming candidates for elective office on the state-wide ticket, sometimes even the power to choose candidates for the United States Senate. All politicians must

Even the governor's role as chief ceremonial officer of his state adds to his power. You may not, at first sight, think that such duties as laying a cornerstone for a new building, cutting the ribbon to open a new bridge, greeting distinguished visitors, and attending banquets would mean much in terms of getting things done. Remember, however, that in every community in the state, politicians of the governor's party are constantly searching for ways to impress the people and gain publicity. From that standpoint, an appearance by the governor at the kinds of ceremonies mentioned can be very important. To be seen publicly with the governor is helpful to the politician, and the governor can select the appearances of this sort he makes in order to be most useful to himself.

Finally, the governor has an opportunity to exercise great influence on public opinion through the newspapers and on radio and television. What he does, where he goes, who is with him, his opinions on all sorts of matters are news. Newsmaking is often opinion-making, and favorable public opinion tends to increase the governor's power over and above the authority given to him by the laws. This means that the kind of person a governor is makes a great difference both to himself as governor and to the people he governs. A successful governor must have the characteristics of leadership. Knowing when to advance new ideas and how to advance them is almost as important as having them, for the very best ideas about government are useless unless the people can be persuaded that they are wise.

To lead, the governor must make a favorable and friendly impression on newsmen, politicians, and citizens generally. To be likable is not enough,

A governor's life, as you can see, is a busy one; many of his duties are like those of the President. As commander of the National Guard, he may call out the militia and declare martial law, placing the militia temporarily over local governments in such cases as severe floods which upset civil life. Although the governor prepares the budget, the legislature authorizes expenditures and levies taxes. Three of the governor's duties give him special strength: those of party leader, of appointing and removing officials, and as ceremonial officer (see text, pp. 285–286).

Commander of National Guard

attend ceremonial functions

Work of a Governor

act as party leader

appoint and remove office holders

prepare budget

approve or veto legislation

call special sessions of legislatures

recommend legislation to state legislatures

supervise administration organization of state

use "mercy" powers pardon, stay executions, commute sentences however; the governor must also be firm. Again, it is fair to say that the qualities that make a good governor are similar to those that make a good President—attractive personality, vigor as a leader, willingness to listen, appreciation of people's needs and hopes, and willingness to compromise, but compromise only when it will produce the best obtainable results for the people of his state.

THE EXECUTIVE BRANCH OF THE STATE

The executive branch of state government carries on activities, under state laws, that range from aeronautics to welfare, from agriculture to water supply, from banking to workmen's compensation, and from civil defense to veterans' assistance. Some states carry on more extensive activities than others, depending upon size and population; but in all states, government in the twentieth century has become large and complex. In order to familiarize yourself with the extent of your state's executive (as well as legislative and judicial) agencies and functions, you should write to the clerk of your state's legislature or to the secretary of your state and ask for a copy of the manual of your state's government.

Secretaries of State

We have already mentioned two of the most important state administrative officials, the secretary of state and the attorney general. The secretary of state in a state government must in no way be confused with the Secretary of State of the United States. He is not usually a policy-making officer and, of course, he does not have anything to do with foreign affairs. The secretary of state is in many ways like the secretary of any organization. He keeps certain records and affixes his signature or seal to official documents such as proclamations, laws, and letters of appointment to office. In some states he is also the chief licensing officer. He issues charters of incorporation to businesses and to local governments and certifies licenses—many of which may actually be issued under authority of other departments—for barbers, restaurant operators, doctors, engineers, etc. He does not, however, decide who shall have a license or a charter of incorporation; such decisions are made by the appropriate agencies. He acts as a secretary, certifying that the laws and regulations have been complied with by the applicants. In many states, the duties of secretary of state are not heavy and the party nomination or the appointment sometimes goes to a prominent party leader as a reward for party work. In Alaska, however, the secretary of state is elected and succeeds to the governorship if the governor is incapacitated or dies.

An Interstate Administrative Agency   Upper Colorado River Commission

WYOMING

Pinedale

Rock Springs

Salt Lake City

FLAMING GORGE DAM

Vernal

Craig

Yampa R.

Hot Sulphur Springs

ADAMS TUNNEL

STRAWBERRY TUNNEL

White R.

Denver

SPRING CITY TUNNEL

Price

Grand Junction

Glenwood Springs

MOFFAT TUNNEL

EPHRAIM TUNNEL

Green River

COLORADO

BUSK-IVANHOE TUNNEL

TWIN LAKES TUNNEL

Dirty

Devil R.

UTAH

Green River

Gunnison R.

Dolores R.

Gunnison

Loa

Moab

CURECANTI DAM

Monticello

GLEN CANYON DAM

San Juan R.

Durango

ARIZONA

Shiprock

NAVAHO DAM

Chinle Cr. L.

NEW MEXICO

Chaco R.

Legend
- Oil
- Gas
- Coal
- Minerals
- Metals
- Uranium
- Irrigated land

0   Miles   100

This interstate administrative agency, representing four states and the federal government, is based on the Upper Colorado River Basin Compact. The Commission administers water resources developed by the Colorado River Storage Project. The storage dams and irrigation projects are being constructed by private companies under Bureau of Reclamation contracts. The federal government is paying the bill but expects to be repaid by the people who use the water and power of the project. The project will provide power for development of the resources of the area. Both agriculture and industry expect to benefit from the project.

Attorneys General

On p. 251 we saw what duties the attorney general has in state law enforcement systems. In most states the division he heads performs a number of services for other branches of state government; for example, experts in the attorney general's office may draft bills for members of the legislature. This does not mean that such experts make the actual suggestions for legislation, but rather that they make sure bills are in proper legal form.

Auditors and Treasurers

Other important state officials found in all our state governments, though sometimes with different titles, are the auditor and the treasurer. The auditor (comptroller) is elected in 42 states. In the others, he is appointed by the governor. His job is to keep track of all state expenditures to make sure that the public money is spent according to law, and that the books are accurately and honestly kept. He must approve all money spent from the state treasury.

The treasurer is also elected in 42 states. As his title suggests, he is the custodian of the state's money. He receives the state's income from taxes, borrowing, and other sources, and pays it out on the authority of the auditor.

GOVERNMENTAL PROGRAMS OF THE STATES

State governments provide services to the people in a great many ways. In later chapters you will learn how the more important of these services are administered and will see the relation between what the states do for the farmer (p. 576), the laborer (p. 559–561), the businessman (pp. 536–538), and the consumer (p. 598); for the people's health, education, and welfare (p. 596); and for preservation and improvement of their natural resources (p. 576). Most of these activities at the state level are administered by the executive branch under the general supervision of the governor. The table lists these functions of state governments.

PROGRAM ACTIVITIES OF THE STATE GOVERNMENTS

(usually carried on by the executive branch under the general supervision of the governor)

ADVERTISING—attracting tourists and business concerns to the state
AERONAUTICS—licensing pilots and planes and regulating air traffic within a state's borders

AGRICULTURE—providing benefits to farmers such as pest control, information on soils, crops, and seeds, assistance in marketing produce, and working in cooperation with the U.S. Department of Agriculture

BANKING—chartering state banks and regulating banking within the state

CIVIL DEFENSE—coördinating civil defense activities of the towns, cities, and counties; promoting understanding of civil defense needs among the citizens; channeling information, advice, and supplies to local units from the national Office of Civil and Defense.Mobilization.

COMMERCE—chartering corporations, issuing licenses, aiding business development, regulating sales procedures and (sometimes) prices within the state

CORRECTIONS—operating the state prison system, maintaining institutions such as prisons, reformatories, and industrial schools, and administering a parole and probation system

EDUCATION—directing and financing the public school system in cooperation with local boards of education, also state universities, professional schools, and technical institutes; channeling information and money to local boards from the federal government

CONSERVATION—caring for natural resources such as fish, game, and other wildlife; coöperating with state and federal agencies for the improvement of land

FOOD AND DRUGS—inspecting foods and drugs and regulating their sale and use

FORESTRY—maintaining and improving state forests, and assisting private citizens to reforest their lands

HARBORS AND DOCKS—maintaining and improving conditions for commercial shipping, usually in collaboration with federal government agencies and, in the larger cities, also municipal bureaus.

HEALTH—maintaining a state public health service, coördinating and administering state-wide health programs, such as vaccinating; distributing scarce medicines; maintaining state hospitals and institutions for the mentally ill, chronic sufferers, and disabled persons; maintaining clinics or assisting local governments to maintain them

HIGHWAYS—building and maintaining the state roads, channeling funds and advice to local units from the national Bureau of Roads

INSURANCE—regulating the sale of insurance policies within the state, requiring companies to meet standards of financial integrity established by state law

LABOR—operating a mediation service to help settle labor disputes, administering programs of unemployment insurance and job placement in coöperation with the federal government, setting standards for various laboring occupations and issuing working papers

290

LIQUOR CONTROL—regulating the manufacture and sale of alcoholic beverages within the state, licensing wholesale and retail dealers, taverns, and restaurants, and in some states managing a state-owned liquor business

MOTOR VEHICLES—administering regulations for the ownership and operation of motor vehicles, issuing registration certificates and drivers' licenses

MINES—administering rules and regulations covering mining methods, health, and safety

PARKS—operating and maintaining the state's public parks system

POLICE—patrolling the state highways, controlling traffic, assisting local police in all aspects of law enforcement

VETERANS' PROGRAMS—assisting veterans in matters of health, education, employment, and home ownership to supplement the assistance given to veterans by the national Veterans' Administration

In addition to these many activities, the states often coöperate with adjoining states in projects to their mutual advantage. There are interstate bridges, tunnels, and harbor controls. The map on p. 288 shows how five states have formed an Upper Colorado River Commission which provides wide benefits to all.

SUMMARY

In this chapter you have seen how our 50 state governments are organized under republican constitutions guaranteed by the federal Constitution. Thus you are a citizen of two republics—the United States and your own state. State constitutions resemble the national Constitution in important ways: each contains a preamble and a bill of rights. Each provides for three separate branches of government—executive, legislative, and judicial; and each makes some provision for amendments.

Nearly all of the laws which affect you, the citizen, directly, are state laws passed by your state legislature. In this chapter you have examined the state legislatures. You have seen what their powers are in some detail; you have examined their structure and seen in what ways they resemble the Congress of the United States. You have also learned something about the serious problems Americans are now facing in trying to have legislatures which fairly represent the people of the states by fair apportioning of the seats. And you have seen again how important a part is played by compromise in the democratic political process. Meeting the other fellow halfway, because he is just as honorable as you are and his claims are just as reasonable—this is the essence of democracy.

291

You have studied the role and functions of the state governor—as chief ceremonial officer, as chief executive, as commander-in-chief of militia, and as political party leader. State constitutions and state laws limit the powers of most governors by assigning important executive functions to other elected officials: the attorney general, the secretary of state, the auditor (comptroller). Finally, you have been introduced to the large number of programs and services maintained by the states for the people of the states. The more important services are discussed in later chapters.

KNOW WHAT YOU READ

1. Name some powers every state government has.
2. Describe the features all state constitutions have in common. Then name certain differences among the various state constitutions.
3. Why are some state constitutions so long? Is this inevitable, or is there some constitutional way to avoid it?
4. Compare state legislatures to the U. S. Congress.
5. Compare apportionment for congressional representation (discussed in Chap. 5) with apportionment in the states for state legislatures. What are some of the problems of each kind of apportionment?
6. Why do many state legislators have regular occupations outside of their activity in politics? Study the table on pp. 282–283 and decide whether your own state legislators make lawmaking their career, or have other jobs.
7. In what ways are a governor's duties like those of the President? What duties of the President does the governor *not* have?
8. Describe some of the roles of a governor. Is some of his influence intangible? If so, describe.
9. What kind of man must a governor be, to be successful? Is the governorship a stepping stone to other things or not? Why?
10. Name several state officials below the rank of governor who are in the executive branch of the state. What are their duties?
11. List ten of the many services and activities carried on by the states. (See pp. 289–291.)
12. What are some of the advantages of interstate coöperation on projects affecting a wide region? The map of the Upper Colorado River Commission (p. 288) will suggest some of them.

WHAT DO YOU THINK?

1. Do you think your state congressional district gives you fair representation in your state legislature? Why or why not?

2. See chapter on State Government in *American Government: Basic Documents and Materials* by Dixon and Plischke for maps of state senatorial and assembly districts. Make a map showing the districts of your state.
3. On pp. 289–291 are listed some of the powers of your state government. Find out additional ones. Do you think these powers give your state more or less control over your personal life than the powers of the federal government? Give details in your answer.
4. Do you think the people of your state have used the amending power too often? Or have they been wise in thus keeping their government close to themselves by making their own decisions?
5. What are some of the problems of reapportionment? How do you think the inequality between rural and city representation can be corrected?
6. Resolved: That state legislators should be paid high enough salaries to enable them to devote all their time to legislative matters instead of having to earn a living at another occupation. Use the cartoon, p. 280, in your argument.
7. Study the drawing on p. 286 showing the Work of a Governor. What do you think are the two most important duties listed? Give illustrations of your own governor's performance of each of these duties.

PROBLEMS AND PROJECTS FOR YOU

1. If your state legislature is in session, watch for news of hearings. Assemble a bulletin-board display of news items about the hearings.
2. Ordinarily newspapers in the region of the capital city list the hearings to be held by committees of the state legislature. Here is a partial list of hearings for one day:

Committee on Highways and Motor Vehicles
   - bills to change the name of a bridge
   - bill authorizing the state department of public works to construct an overpass

Committee on Legal Affairs
   - bill for licensing dog racing at county fairs
   - bill relative to disposition of legacies of persons in countries under Communist control
   - bill to provide for the resting of certain race horses

Committee on Pensions
   - bill to reclassify certain employees of publicly-owned gas and electric plants under the state retirement system

As a group activity, plan and present a mock hearing. Use actual bills under consideration in your state, or invent original proposals suggested by the above items or by your study of the courses you are now taking.

3. A newspaper reporter in Worcester, Massachusetts, studied the demands people in his area made on their representatives in the state legislature. He found that voters have asked their representatives to do many things besides making laws. Here is a partial list of constituents' requests:

exchange boxtops for a prize	get back revoked drivers' licenses
arrange for a constituent to take a civil-service examination	obtain airplane reservations
	get tickets for plays
identify historical landmarks to help constituent win a contest	find out how a pine tree may be bought from the state

Why do representatives hesitate to refuse such requests?
Interview a lawmaker who represents you to find out if his constituents make similar requests. Report your findings to the class.

4. Study the nature and purpose of districting for your state legislature. Report to the class on the variations in size, population, make-up (rural or urban), and natural boundaries of the districts. In your report recommend changes, if you think them desirable, giving your reasons.

5. Make a study of some of the services provided by your state. How are they paid for? Do they overlap similar services from the federal government? Should such overlapping be avoided? How?

6. Find out what committee in the state legislature your own representative serves on. What issues has that committee considered in the current term? Report on the part your representative played on the committee, and what recommendations the committee made on two issues.

7. Make a report on the organization of the government and the constitution of either Alaska or Hawaii, our two newest states.

> Lobbyists flocked into the State House Tuesday for opening day of the 1956 budget session of the Kansas legislature. A total of twenty-eight legislative agents and seven legislative counsels signed the official book in the office of the Secretary of State, Paul Shanahan.
>
> *Topeka Daily Capital*, January 11, 1956

8. The news story then lists the names of the lobbyists and their employers. The latter list includes: Kansas Power and Light Company, Farmers and Bankers Life Insurance Company, Southwestern Bell Telephone Company, Kansas State Chamber of Commerce, Kansas Savings and Loan League, Kansas Electric Coöperatives Incorporated, United Brewers Foundation, Kansas Motor Car Dealers Association, Kansas Medical Society, Kansas State Federation of Labor, Kansas Teachers Association, Western Union Telegraph Company, Committee of Kansas Farm Organizations, Kansas United Dry Forces, Brotherhood of Railway Trainmen, Kansas Industrial Union Council, Motor Carriers Association, League of Women Voters of Kansas, Kansas Independent Oil and Gas Association.

What kind or kinds of legislation do you think each of these organizations would favor? Oppose?
What constitutional rights are lobbyists putting into practice?

EXTEND YOUR VOCABULARY

republic	bicameral	reprieve
reserved powers	Assembly	stay of execution
preamble	House of Delegates	commute sentence
bill of rights	election districts	(state) secretary of state
amendment provisions	apportionment	state auditor
unicameral	pardon	state treasurer
		interstate activities

YOUR NOTEBOOK: THE GOVERNMENT OF ——

1. What is the name by which your state legislature is known? If it has two houses, what is each called?
2. Write down the names of the several representative (Congressional, upper house of state legislature, lower house of state legislature) districts in which you live.
3. How long are the terms of lawmakers in your state government?
4. What questions (if any) have been referred to the voters of your locality through the referendum in the last four years?
5. Write in your notebook the name of your governor; your lieutenant governor.

READ MORE ABOUT IT

AMERICAN ASSEMBLY, *The Forty-Eight States: Their Tasks as Policy Makers.* Columbia University Press, 1955.

BABCOCK, ROBERT S., *State and Local Government and Politics.* Random House, 1957. Chaps. 1–5, 9–20.

Book of the States. The Council of State Governments, published biennially. Valuable information on many phases of state government, including details on interstate relations, state constitutions, make-up of every state government, etc.

DEUTSCH, ALBERT, *The Shame of the States.* Harcourt, Brace, 1949. Readable and debatable.

GRAVES, W. BROOKE, *American State Government.* Heath, 1953. Chaps. 1–3, 6–8.

MACDONALD, AUSTIN F., *American State Government and Administration,* Crowell, 1955. Chaps. 5, 8, 10, 16, 17.

CHAPTER *12*

Local Government:
The Counties, Towns, Townships, and Villages

In this chapter you will learn about

Citizens and local government
How local governments are formed
County governments and their problems
Towns, townships, and villages
Special districts

Most people, when they think of government, think of what Congress did yesterday, or of what the President said, or of the governor's television appearance. There is another kind of government, however, which is actually much closer to your daily life. When the trashman empties the baskets or cans in front of your house, when a crew of workmen paves the holes in the street, when the policeman stops your car at an intersection, or when a social worker visits the family next door, you see government in action. It is local government, of course. It is taken so much for granted that it hardly seems like "the government."

THE NATURE OF LOCAL GOVERNMENT

If all local governments were suddenly wiped out, there would be no public schools, no parks or playgrounds, no public libraries or museums, no policeman on the beat, no deputy sheriff patrolling the highways, no firemen to save your house, no paved streets or sanitation or traffic control, no municipal water supply, and, perhaps, no hospital or community service center. In short, without local government, people could not live together in communities. They would be isolated from each other.

The Units of Local Government

Local government is all government that functions below the state level. Each state creates by law and supervises the units of local government within its borders. The chart on p. 298 shows state-local relationships in detail.

The political unit immediately below the state is the **county** (borough in Alaska). Every state, except Louisiana (which has parishes) and Connecticut (which abolished counties in 1959), is subdivided. There are more than 3,000 such subdivisions or counties in the United States, varying greatly in size and population: from 25 square miles to more than 2,000 square miles, and from a few hundred to more than four million inhabitants.

Another unit of local government (within the counties) is the **municipality**. A municipality can be a **city**, a **township**, a **town**, a **village**, or a **borough**. Municipalities, like counties, are created under state law. Also like counties, they vary so much in size and population that a community which might in one state be called a town or village would in another be regarded as a city.

The Citizen and Local Government

Unfortunately even otherwise well-informed citizens frequently do not understand or have little interest in the government closest to their daily lives. In years when only local officials are running for election, often as few as one-third or one-fourth of the eligible voters bother to go to the polls. Very few citizens know the names or public records of their city councilmen or of the members of their county board of commissioners. Yet, unspectacular as it may be, it is through local government that free men first show that they are responsible and can coöperate effectively.

How Local Governments Are Formed

Local governments arise out of the needs of people as communities develop. If you live on a farm several miles from any neighbor, your home is likely to be very nearly self-sufficient. You will pay taxes to your county and state governments to support the public school and to maintain the roads. You will supply most of the other goods of life for yourself—or do without

State and Local Powers

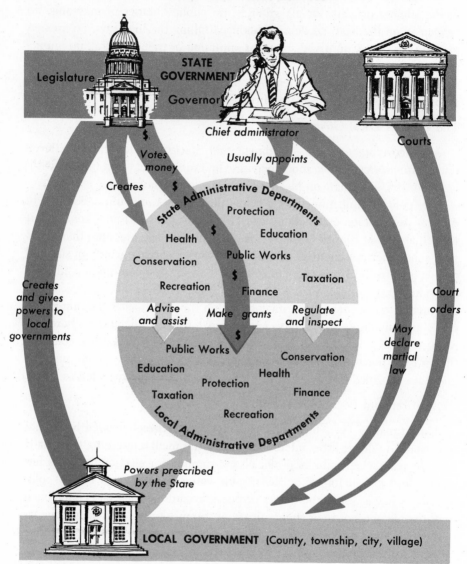

STATE GOVERNMENT

Legislature

Governor

Chief administrator

Courts

$ Votes money

Usually appoints

Creates

State Administrative Departments

Protection

Health

Education

Conservation

Public Works

Recreation

Taxation

Finance

Advise and assist

Make grants

Regulate and inspect

Creates and gives powers to local governments

Court orders

May declare martial law

Local Administrative Departments

Public Works

Education

Conservation

Protection

Health

Taxation

Finance

Recreation

Powers prescribed by the State

LOCAL GOVERNMENT (County, township, city, village)

Local governments are all created by the power of the state government and are subordinate and responsible to it. Here you can see how power, and the services that go with it, flows down from the state to the local level, and how local functions supplement state functions.

them. But if other farmers come into your area, a cross-road is built, a general store is established. As the population continues to increase, you will begin to consider the advantages of local government. You may consult with your neighbors about the need for such things as fire protection, police protection, a local school, a central water supply.

INCORPORATING When you and your neighbors agree on these needs, you may jointly sign a petition to your state legislature asking to be **incorporated** as a village or town. Your state has laws allowing communities of a certain size and having such needs to "go into business" for themselves as units of local government. Once your town has been incorporated by act of your state legislature, you may proceed to elect public officers, establish your police and fire departments, set up a water supply system, and other services.

FINANCING You will need money for all these things, of course. Your state will allow your town as an incorporated unit of local government either to collect taxes from the residents or to receive a share of the taxes you pay to the county. At the same time, the state will pay back to your town treasurer, either directly or through the county treasurer, a substantial share of the money you have paid the state in taxes. From these financial resources, you may be able to build and maintain paved streets and a school, as well as pay the salaries of the people you need to carry on the work of the town. The federal government will set up a post office for your town and you may be eligible for some kinds of federal assistance, such as help in building your school, training for your policemen, money for children's lunches, money to help build a community hospital, and other such things.

BECOMING A CITY You may live in a large town in which various kinds of private businesses and services employ many people. You may need several schools, and fire protection may require fire stations in various sections. The police department must keep expanding; public buildings are in demand, and you and your fellow citizens will find it desirable to regulate for the public interest a good many activities. In that case, you may wish to give your town the status of a city. As a city, you and your neighbors will have much more control over your affairs directly and much greater authority to do things for the community. To become a city you petition your state legislature for a **charter,** that is, a city constitution approved by the state.

Both incorporation papers and city charters are secured from state legislation by the petitions of residents. The number of signatures on these petitions is specified by the laws of various states, which also require the residents to make geographical surveys to define the boundaries of proposed towns, villages, or cities.

When you go to the county clerk's office to get a fishing license, or pay your annual tax on your home to the county treasurer, or "step on it" as you drive out of the city into the country and get arrested by the deputy sheriff for speeding, you, the citizen, are in direct relation with your county government. It is one of the oldest units of government in the English-speaking world.

The political subdivision known as the county was inherited from England and formed the basis of much local government in America during colonial days. Many of our early leaders began their public careers by county service. When Tammany Hall, the nation's oldest political organization, was founded in New York City in the 1790's, it tried to control the county courthouse, as county governments are often called. Only in relatively recent times have political parties developed a greater interest in cities. As we shall see in Chapter 18, the county is still typically the essential unit of party organization. It continues to be a training ground for political leaders. Furthermore, the county is responsible for numerous important governmental functions, such as maintaining law and order, constructing and maintaining roads, keeping official records, maintaining public school systems, and many others. There are over 3,000 counties in the United States and their powers vary from state to state and sometimes within a state. County government in many rural states continues to be the important local government, and the county seat is a sort of capital city for the area served by the county. In states with large concentrations of population, the county may be a less useful unit. Connecticut, as we have indicated, decided in 1959 to abolish counties and reassigned their powers to the state, towns, or cities.

Unlike some other governmental structures, county government has not changed much. In England, counties were administered by justices of the peace. Justices of the peace now administer counties in Kentucky, Tennessee, and Arkansas. The office of the sheriff, which is one of the oldest known of English offices, is found in every state of the Union. The courts continue to be quite like those of the English counties.

The County Board

Typically a county government is centered in a board with legislative and administrative powers. This board is known variously as the board of commissioners, the board of supervisors, the board of revenue, the board of freeholders, the county court, the fiscal court, or the levy court. For simplicity, we shall use the best-known term, **county board**. Sometimes board members are appointed, but usually they are elected by the voters. In the states of the South and West, as well as in some others, board members are elected at large. In some states, board members are known as "supervisors" and often are elected by the townships (see p. 308) and by city wards. Under this system boards may be quite large, numbering as many as eighty members. The supervisors look after the interests of their own township but work as a body on matters concerning the whole county.

The county board elects its own chairman, but he is not a true chief executive. The administrative and executive powers belong to the board and are carried out by employees of the board. The administrative powers may include any or all of the following: managing county institutions—the courthouse and county jail, the almshouse (poorhouse), and the home for the aged; making contracts in the name of the county for all sorts of services and construction, such as water supply, roads, buildings; fixing the compensation of county employees; and supervising the conduct of elections. The board is also a "legislative" body in that it votes county appropriations and county taxes, and borrows money on the promise of the county to pay. Sometimes a county board has power to zone rural and suburban areas, or to regulate amusement places in the county. Board powers vary greatly from state to state, but all board powers in all states are those granted by the state to the county government.

Officials of the County

Other officials found in a typical county system include the sheriff, county clerk, county assessor, county treasurer, coroner, recorder of deeds, and county school superintendent. These officials are usually chosen by the voters (see chart, p. 302).

The sheriff is the chief police officer of the county. He is also keeper of the jail and an officer of the county courts. As a police officer, his work is chiefly in rural areas. If the sheriff and his deputies need assistance, he may summon the "power of the county" (**posse comitatus**) to his aid. Able-bodied men summoned to serve on a posse must assist the sheriff. The TV or movie "western" keeps us familiar with the posse and the sheriff—though most real sheriffs have rather less glamorous lives than do those we see on the screen!

The county clerk keeps the records of the county board and of the county as a whole—births, deaths, marriages, as well as records of county business. He may also receive nomination papers of candidates for county office, issue hunting and fishing licenses and marriage licenses, and prepare the agenda for meetings of the county board.

In those states where the county is the unit for the property tax (see Chap. 20), the county assessor is responsible for determining property valuations for taxes. In other states, the county assessor may advise or assist township or district assessors.

Organization of a County in Wisconsin

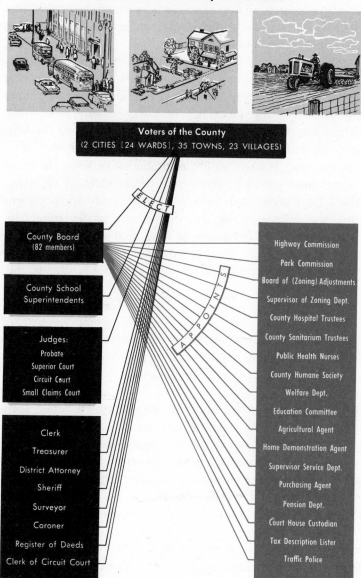

Voters of the County
(2 CITIES [24 WARDS], 35 TOWNS, 23 VILLAGES)

ELECT

APPOINTS

County Board
(82 members)

County School
Superintendents

Judges:
Probate
Superior Court
Circuit Court
Small Claims Court

Clerk

Treasurer

District Attorney

Sheriff

Surveyor

Coroner

Register of Deeds

Clerk of Circuit Court

Highway Commission

Park Commission

Board of (Zoning) Adjustments

Supervisor of Zoning Dept.

County Hospital Trustees

County Sanitarium Trustees

Public Health Nurses

County Humane Society

Welfare Dept.

Education Committee

Agricultural Agent

Home Demonstration Agent

Supervisor Service Dept.

Purchasing Agent

Pension Dept.

Court House Custodian

Tax Description Lister

Traffic Police

Counties differ somewhat in organization, but this one is fairly typical. See the text for the various duties of the elected officials shown here, as well as others, and for the executive and legislative powers the Board has over the bodies it appoints.

The county treasurer receives, holds, and disburses money raised by taxes, received from the state government for specified purposes, or received from the sale of county services and water supply.

In most of the states there is an official called the coroner whose duty it is to hold inquests to determine the cause of deaths occurring under violent or suspicious circumstances. The coroner is frequently a physician, although most states do not make this a requirement.

The recorder, or register of deeds, is responsible for keeping records of deeds (certificates of property ownership), mortgages, and leases. In the past, these records were always written out in longhand. This is still done today in most counties, but in some counties microfilming is permitted.

Thirty-eight states have county superintendents of schools. The superintendent is the chief administrative and supervisory official of a school system, sometimes elected and sometimes appointed by the county board.

An important appointed official in most counties is the county highway superintendent. He supervises the construction and maintenance of county roads and bridges.

County Agent

In the strictest sense, the County Agricultural Agent is not a county officer. He serves federal, state, and county governments, as well as private farm organizations. His work is to improve the earning power of the farmers of his county; his program is financed by funds from the federal government, his state government, his county, and the local farm organizations. A county agent is supervised by the United States Department of Agriculture, the state agricultural college, and the county board. In turn he may draw on each of these for aid in his own work, which may include such activities as sponsoring 4-H clubs, administering soil conservation programs, conducting farm demonstrations, and organizing coöperative marketing associations (see Chap. 23).

Problems of the County

County governments consist largely of independent agencies, functioning without centralization and without an executive head. It is difficult to fix responsibility for poor administration of county government. In general, county government needs reform. In particular, residents of the county's cities are likely to be critical of county governments, since they feel that they are paying, through their taxes, for the services the county performs for rural communities. Thus city residents whose tax money has been used to build a swimming pool in a city park may object when the county board decides to build a swimming pool in a county park. In such instances, city residents are actually taxed twice, once by the city and once by the county. The county governments—in the city dweller's opinion—represent the smaller communities and not the cities. Their functions, except for the judicial, are duplicates of those the city performs for its residents. Consequently, some cities have sought and achieved independence of their counties.

County-Manager Plan

One attempt to bring greater efficiency into the county is the county-manager plan. In some respects, this is like the better-known city-manager plan, which we will discuss in the next chapter. The elected body, the county board, appoints a professional executive to run the affairs of the county. The duties of the county manager are to prepare and present to the board the annual budget, to appoint the operating personnel of the county services, and to superintend the various departments.

The county-manager plan has been tried chiefly in counties of large population where people have many common problems, whether they live in or outside the city. It has worked out quite well in terms of service to the public, economy, and efficiency. It has not, however, spread rapidly. Tradition, lack of citizen interest in county government, and the opposition of officeholders combine to prevent the average county from trying this plan.

The county-manager plan is open to the criticism that it tends to remove public matters from the scrutiny of the citizens and from effective public debate. A few counties, like Nassau, New York, have tried to avoid this objection by electing a county executive who functions much like a mayor in a city.

Experience is still too limited for us to be certain as to the best way to reform county governments. There is, however, almost general agreement that the services of county government could be more efficient and responsible. It is also agreed that financing of county government could be reformed to spread the costs more equitably among taxpayers. For example, in counties where one large city is spreading out to cover practically the whole county, what we call a **metropolitan area**, it may be possible to work out a system of single government for one whole area. Such a system would have one administration, one legislature, and one taxing system to provide services for all. Either city government or county government would disappear, or both would disappear in favor of a wholly new form of local government. On the other hand, in areas where cities and counties retain their basic differences, a single government may not be practical. It may be necessary to work out means by which the city and county governments can cooperate much more closely than they now do to the benefit of all. This is a job which challenges the imagination of new generations and offers endless opportunity for free citizens to display their ability to coöperate in their own interest.

TOWNS

The best examples of government by direct democracy in our country today are to be found in the New England towns. From the time of the settlements at Plymouth and Massachusetts Bay, it has been the custom in New England to handle local matters in "town meeting."

Town Meeting

What this means is that all the legally qualified voters of a town are entitled to meet, one or more times a year, and act as the legislative authority for their local government. The town meeting elects a moderator (presiding officer) and proceeds to business. The voters hear the reports of their town officers, appropriate money to provide the local services for the coming year, vote the taxes to pay for these services, authorize the borrowing of money for costs that cannot be met by the taxes voted, and enact the by-laws (local laws) of the town. Town officers are also elected at town meetings, usually before the business session begins.

While the town meeting gives the individual citizen a chance to participate directly in the lawmaking process, it is not as important an institution as it was in earlier days. It functions most satisfactorily in smaller communities; in larger towns the "meeting" may become too large. Many of the larger towns have adopted a **representative** meeting, which is attended by citizens who have been elected to represent their neighbors.

Town Officers

The principal administrative officers of a town are the board of selectmen, or town council. They are elected by the voters, usually for one year. They carry on the work of the town between town meetings. If a street needs fixing, they arrange to have it done. If the roads are clogged by snow, they order out the snow plow. If you live in a community of this type, you should examine your annual town report to find out just what the selectmen do. In some of the larger towns, the selectmen appoint a town manager, if voters have voted for a town-manager plan and if the state permits. The town manager carries on the work usually done by selectmen.

Citizens of a town also elect a clerk, a treasurer, an assessor, constables, and a school board or committee, whose duties are much like those of county officers. Larger towns may also elect a library committee, a parks commission, a board of health, a planning board, a water commission, and trustees of various charitable or educational funds. Many minor officials, such as the town counsel, tree warden, plumbing inspectors, wiring inspectors, and others, are usually appointed by the selectmen.

305

"ANOTHER SUMMIT"

Lee Roche in
Buffalo Courier-Express

LOCAL GOVERNMENT AND THE CITIZEN

To bring the benefits of the world of books to rural regions, Montpelier sends out a Bookmobile through which readers can browse.

Of continuing concern to towns, villages, and cities is the higher and higher cost of education—one of the indispensable services of government.

Children of a community can enjoy a swimming place, courtesy of one of the local units of government which maintains the lake.

306

A county in California builds a road from one town to another—on this particular project even diverting a creek so that it will run under the highway in the course of the work.

Special districts give people of a region special services. Here farmers of a conservation district meet with soil conservation experts to make plans for improving the productivity of land in their area.

To provide for careful advance study of local finances, some towns now provide for a committee on finance (or budget, or warrant, committee), which puts together the estimates of the various committees as to their financial needs and submits a proposed budget to the voters at town meeting. The voters usually accept the recommendations of this committee. But in the town meeting, individual citizens have their chance to argue about how public money shall be spent. The citizens themselves make the decisions directly.

TOWNSHIP GOVERNMENT

In sixteen states, the counties are divided into townships, somewhat like the towns of New England. In eight of the sixteen, the state provides that township meetings, modeled after New England town meetings, shall be held. All voters of the township may attend. There they vote appropriations for conducting the affairs of the township, as well as the taxes to pay the required costs. Township meetings are not, as a rule, so well attended as town meetings. It sometimes happens that the only persons present are the township officers.

Township Boards

In states which have township government, whether they do or do not have township meetings, the general governing authority is the township board. The name of this board varies from state to state. It may be known as a board of supervisors, board of trustees, township committee, advisory board, or board of auditors. Usually the board is elected; it may in some states, however, be made up of such elected officials as a clerk, a treasurer, and a justice of the peace.

In several township-government states, the township board votes appropriations and levies taxes. In general, the board of a township has charge of all affairs not given by state law to any other officials.

Township Officers

In some of the states, one member of the board (in some cases elected, in others chosen by the board) is the head official of the township, being known as the supervisor, trustee, or chairman. He has much greater powers than do the other board members. He may, as in Indiana, have powers much like those of a city mayor. In New York State, the chief official of a township is the township's elected member of the county board of supervisors, who thus participates in two levels of government.

Other township officers may include clerk, treasurer, assessor, collector of taxes, constables, and justices of the peace (see Chap. 9 for discussion of the latter). These officials are appointed or elected, depending on the laws of the state. If you live in a township, you should find out the facts about your own local government.

THE VILLAGE

Finally, we have village government. Villages are miniature cities, though sometimes their population may reach many thousands. This means that their governments are similar to those of cities and perform as many of the same functions as their financial resources will permit.

Villages are normally governed by an elected board of trustees (sometimes called selectmen) and an elected mayor, sometimes called president, or warden, or burgess. The mayor does not have the heavy responsibilities of a city mayor, but he does preside over board meetings, and he enforces the village ordinances. These ordinances are made by the board, and they usually concern building and maintaining roads, sewers, street lights, and schools, as well as snow removal, sanitation, etc. Villages sometimes support and administer their own fire departments and police departments. Of course, to do this, a village must have power to tax in order to raise the necessary money.

Occasionally, small villages belong to special districts, as we shall see presently, or are merely part of a county or township system.

SPECIAL DISTRICTS

As we have seen, there are a great many different kinds of units of government in the United States below the state level. Even those roughly in the same category, such as county governments or city governments, vary greatly in structure and function. Often these functions overlap, so that one would think that every possible local need was taken care of somehow, if not by the town or city government, then by the county. But the needs of modern people with a high standard of living are so vast and complex that in many areas counties and townships are divided into special districts for special administrative purposes.

Purposes of Special Districts

Of the more than 150,000 local government units in the United States, most are organized for one special purpose only. More than 100,000 of them are districts established for supporting and administering schools (see Chap. 24). Others are organized for soil conservation, parks, sewage disposal, lighting, fire protection, cemeteries, parkways, mosquito control, irrigation, bridges, agricultural development, police protection, recreation, libraries and flood control. This list is not complete but gives some idea of the variety of reasons for which a special district may be organized.

Special districts are set up to meet special needs of an area, needs which the existing local governments are unable to meet by themselves. For example, Massachusetts set up in 1889 a Metropolitan Sewage District of Boston. This step was taken because the city of Boston found itself unable to do anything about the sewage which upstream suburban communities were dumping into the Charles River. The new district proved so satisfactory that the state later organized a Metropolitan Park Commission and a Metropolitan Water Board. Then the three were combined into the Metropolitan District Commission, which has complete charge of water, sewage, park, and highway systems in the metropolitan area of Boston.

Reasons for Special Districts

Special districts normally come into existence for one of two reasons. The first is that the creation of a special district, since it may include townships, villages, cities, towns, and counties, makes it possible for the people of a **region** to obtain a service which the various local governments of the region could not provide as well.

The other reason for setting up special districts is that states usually place limits on the taxes or debts of local governments. This means that, when the people of a local-government area wish to borrow money for some such purpose as bridges, roads, a sewer system, or other item of great expense, they may find that under state law they have already borrowed all the money allowed. With the state's permission, they may set up a special district to borrow the money and provide and pay for the new service.

Special districts are usually administered by boards of commissioners. These commissioners may be chosen by the voters of the district or they may be appointed by the state, by a judge, by a county board, or by a mayor. In some cases, a county board acts as commissioners for a special district.

SUMMARY

In this chapter you have been introduced to the local forms of government which are so close to our everyday life that we often do not think of them as governments at all. You have learned how these governments are formed at the desire of the people and by the authority of the state. You

310

studied the general forms of the more than 3,000 county governments into which our states are divided. You then examined our smallest political units—towns, townships, and villages. Finally you learned something about what are called "special districts," units of government which serve only one specified purpose, like school districts.

KNOW WHAT YOU READ

1. List the various units of local government.
2. What is a municipality?
3. How is a petition of incorporation made?
4. What are the responsibilities of county government?
5. How are county boards chosen? What are their usual powers?
6. Name the other principal officers of a county and their powers?
7. What is unusual about the work of the county agricultural agent?
8. What is the work of a county manager? How is he selected?
9. What are the principal arguments for and against the county-manager plan?
10. Explain how the citizens act as a legislature in a New England town meeting.
11. Name the principal officers of a *town*. Of a *township*. How are they governed?
12. In what ways are *towns* different from *townships*?
13. What is a *village*? Name the officials of a village.
14. What is a special district? Why are they organized? How are they governed?

WHAT DO YOU THINK?

1. "If we are alert, well-informed, and active citizens, we may get good local government. If we are indifferent, we are more likely to get low quality local government." Do you agree? Defend your answer.
2. "In the years between 1950 and 1955 . . . the number of U.S. children under the age of 14 increased by 20 per cent, while the number of persons over the age of 65 increased by approximately 15 per cent. During this same period, however, the number of persons of working age—in the 16 to 64 age bracket—increased by only 3.8 per cent."

   How will these population trends affect the problems of local government services and costs?

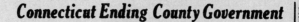

Connecticut Ending County Government

By RICHARD H. PARKE
Special to The New York Times

HARTFORD, May 7—Connecticut's historic form of county government was ordered abolished tonight by the General Assembly.

A bill transferring the already restricted powers of the eight counties to the state, effective Oct. 1, 1960, was passed by the House by a vote of 144 to 129. The Senate had approved the measure by an overwhelming voice vote.

The passage of the bill represented a victory for Gov. Abraham A. Ribicoff, a Democrat. He had urged the step as a part of his governmental reorganization program.

Under the legislation the three county commissioners in each county will lose their posts, the county buildings will be turned over to the State Public Works Department and the administration of the jails will be placed under a new State Department of Correction.

When county government was established in 1666 the units maintained their own courts, jails and child care institutions. The counties lost court jurisdiction in 1855. They retained the management of children's homes until four years ago.

In recent years the counties' only major function has been the operation of the county jails. Each county has its own sheriff and his deputies, who manage the jails and serve court orders. They will now lose these powers. Today's vote followed a four and a half hour debate.

Courtesy of *The New York Times*

3. From facts given in this news story, why do you think Connecticut took this step? Do you think it was wise? Explain your position.
4. Are town meetings an effective way to run a local government? What do you think prevents this form of direct democracy from being more widely adopted today?
5. Do you think there is a sound reason for special districts? If your community is included in such a district, what benefits do you get from it?

PROBLEMS AND PROJECTS FOR YOU

1. Below is a list of the responsibilities of a county board chairman in a Wisconsin county. What official or officials in your local government have these duties?
   (a) He must sign all ordinances passed by the board, all orders drawn on the county treasurer, all vouchers and checks issued against the county treasurer, and all bonds authorized by the county board.
   (b) He may examine and settle accounts or claims against the county.
   (c) He may administer oaths to persons who must be sworn concerning board matters.

312

(d) He, with four members selected by the board, appoints all board committees.

(e) He is chairman of the audit committee.

(f) He is an ex-officio member of the County Agricultural Committee.

2. Resolved: That our county (township) should adopt the manager system. Choose two teams to debate on this subject.

3. From a local newspaper, assemble a bulletin-board display of clippings which illustrate the functions of county government and the duties of county officials.

4. In some New England towns, high school students hold their own "town meeting" before the regular town meeting is held. They debate and vote on the proposals which their parents will act on. Then the young people attend the town meeting to compare their decisions with those of the adult citizens.

   Plan and conduct a model town meeting. If you have an opportunity to do so, attend a town meeting. Report to the class on the extent to which you think the meeting illustrated democracy in action.

5. Invite one or more of the following to visit your class, describe his or her work, and answer questions asked by your classmates (it is a good idea to have some questions prepared in advance): Assessor, clerk (city, township, county), district nurse, county agent, county commissioner, chief of police, fire chief, or any other whose work might be of interest to the class.

6. Investigate the county organization in your own state and discuss its duties, functions, and effectiveness. Study the picture story, pp. 306–307.

7. Study the history of your community and report on how the present form of local government was formed.

8. Read and write a report on "The Councilman as a Political Broker," by Arthur W. Bromage. You will find this in a book, *On the City Council*, or in Morlan's *Capitol, Courthouse, and City Hall*.

9. To find out more about direct legislation, read "The Initiative and Referendum in Action" in *Capitol, Courthouse and City Hall*. Read and report.

EXTEND YOUR VOCABULARY

municipality	county	metropolitan
city	*posse comitatus*	moderator
township	county-manager plan	town meeting
town	sheriff	constables
village	coroner	board of trustees, selectmen
borough	county assessor	special districts
charter	register of deeds	

YOUR NOTEBOOK: THE GOVERNMENT OF ——

1. In what ways does your local government depend on your state government? Investigate the charter given by the state government to your community, and record details of it.
2. How has your community benefited from some services provided by the state? Does your local government contribute anything toward that service—in taxes or personnel or in any other way? Write a report in your notebook.
3. Investigate several businesses in your community, and find out what kind of license or charter they had to obtain from the state before starting in business. Write all details in your notebook.

READ MORE ABOUT IT

BABCOCK, ROBERT S., *State and Local Government and Politics*, Random House, 1957. Chaps. 6–7, 16–18.

BROMAGE, ARTHUR W., *On the City Council*. Wahr, 1950.

GRAVES, W. BROOKE, *American State Government*. Heath, 1953. Chaps. 21–23.

LANCASTER, LANE, *Government in Rural America*. Van Nostrand, 1952.

MACDONALD, AUSTIN F., *American State Government and Administration*. Crowell, 1955. Chaps. 13–15.

MARTIN, ROSCOE C., *Grass Roots*, Alabama, 1957.
    Very lively and full of useful information.

MORLAN, ROBERT L., ed., *Capitol, Courthouse, and City Hall*. Houghton Mifflin, 1954.

RANNEY, AUSTIN, *The Governing of Men*. Holt, 1958. Chap. 21.

SCAMMON, RICHARD M., *America Votes*. Macmillan, 1956.
    Useful information on American election statistics, by states.

SNIDER, CLYDE F., *Local Government in Rural America*. Appleton-Century-Crofts, 1957.

CHAPTER *13*

Local Government:
The Cities
and Their Problems

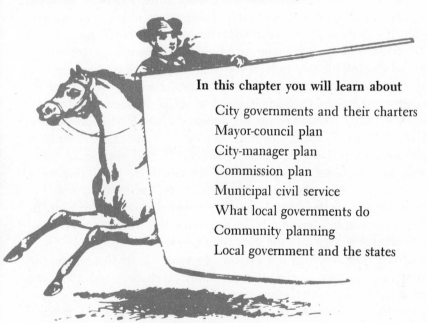

In this chapter you will learn about

City governments and their charters
Mayor-council plan
City-manager plan
Commission plan
Municipal civil service
What local governments do
Community planning
Local government and the states

Whenever the people of one community organize themselves for self-government under the laws of their state, a municipality is created. If the community is large enough and meets other requirements of state law, it is usually a city. In 1790, there were only six communities large enough to be called cities, and Philadelphia, the largest of these, had only 40,000 people. Only 3.3 percent of the entire population at that time lived in cities; the rest lived in smaller towns or villages or on isolated farms. The great shift in population brought about by the industrial revolution changed America from a rural to an urban civilization. Today, more than half of the people live in 1,200 cities, each of which has a population of 8,000 or more.

CITY GOVERNMENTS

Because cities depend for their existence on the laws of their states, they vary greatly from state to state. In Nebraska, for example, a community of more than 1,000 people may become a city; in Ohio it takes 5,000; and New York and Pennsylvania demand that every city have at least 10,000 inhabitants. Since cities can grow or decline once they are established, there is even greater variety among American cities. About eight million people live in the city of New York, more than twice the population of the entire United States in 1790. For these reasons, it is easy to see that there is really no such thing as a typical American city.

Generally, the provisions of a city's charter—stating the self-governing rights of the city as well as the obligations it owes to the state—are the same for every city in that state. But since every community is different in area and population, it is not easy for one city to operate under exactly the same charter as a totally different city does. Some state legislatures, therefore, grant certain cities **special charters,** drafted to meet the needs of these cities. Thus the city of New York has a structure unlike that of any other city because of its enormous population and the complexity of its public business.

Other states have a **classified charter system,** by which cities are divided into classes or types according to area, population, and location, such as cities providing water power or mining communities. Still other states allow **home rule** to their cities. This means that the people of a city vote on a charter prepared (within the limits, of course, of the constitution and laws of their own state) by the city council or by a group chosen to write it. In some states, home rule is granted by an act of the legislature; in others, the home-rule grant is written into the state constitution.

The newest charter system is the **optional system.** Under this system, the state legislatures prepare several different kinds of charters and allow the residents of a city to choose the one they like best.

The charter of a city specifies the type of government that city is to have. There are three principal types of city government: mayor-council, city-manager, commission.

THE MAYOR-COUNCIL FORM

The oldest and most common type of city government is known as the **mayor-council** form. Under this form, adapted from the English usage in colonial days, cities are governed and served by an elected **mayor,** who is chief executive, and a **council** of elected representatives, who make the city's laws, called **city ordinances.**

316

Most of our largest cities have this form of government, but Washington, D.C. (see Chap. 14), Kansas City, and Cincinnati are among the important exceptions.

In this form, the mayor is the executive, and the council is the legislature. At one time, most of these local legislatures were **bicameral**, having an upper house, or board of aldermen, and a lower house, or common council. Now only a few cities, found chiefly in New England, have two-house legislatures. In the remaining cities, members of the local legislative branch are known either as councilmen or as aldermen. We shall use the terms **council** and **councilmen** in the following paragraphs. The chart, p. 319, gives details about this form of government.

The Council

As a lawmaking branch, the council has several different functions. As you can see, it has lawmaking, financial, and regulatory powers. Regulatory powers involve such matters as licensing and inspecting restaurants, setting water rates, making rules for the operation of trucks on city streets (which streets they may use and what weights will be allowed), zoning (restricting) sections of the city for business or for residential building, and many others. The **franchises** they grant are legal authorizations to perform public services, as, for example, to bus companies. To learn what powers the council of your own city has, you may have to study its charter. You can find out a lot about the council's power by regularly reading a local newspaper.

Recently the citizens of a large eastern city were greatly interested in a public housing development proposed by their City Planning Commission (see p. 332). Many citizens went regularly to meetings of the council and expressed their opinions when the presiding officer declared the meetings open; others tried to influence their councilmen in private conversations; nearly everyone followed the matter closely in the paper. A large sum of money was available to build low-cost housing and eliminate a slum area. The trouble was that the citizens and their council could not agree on a location for the project. Some objection was found by some group or other to every suggestion. Finally the council, realizing that the debate could not go on forever, reached a firm decision. The next day the newspapers had great fun at the expense of the council by pointing out that they had chosen a site on which work had already been commenced to build a private bowling alley! But the council had the last laugh. The charter of the city gave the council power to condemn property (take it over for public use). The council ordered the bowling alley property condemned and paid the owner a fair sum for his land and investment. At last work began on the housing project.

ORDINANCES, ORDERS, AND RESOLUTIONS If you read about the work of your own city council, or of the council of any city, you may notice that the council's acts are in the form of ordinances, orders, or resolutions. Local laws are **ordinances.** By ordinance, the council controls a great variety of activities. For instance, the council may regulate the sale of ice cream by street vendors (loudness of their bells, streets to be used, etc.), zone a section of the city for one-family houses, change the building code, or forbid the playing of baseball on Sunday.

A command of the council is in the form of an **order.** For example, the council may vote an order for the sale of city property. The condemning of the bowling alley was an order. A **resolution** is voted when the council wishes to express an opinion, state a principle, or declare a purpose. In your reading, you may notice some statement such as this: "Resolved: that the 24th day of October be observed as United Nations Day," or "Resolved: that a park commission of five members be set up to study undeveloped land in the city which might be taken for use by the recreation department."

Council Meetings

The business of a city council is carried on in a public building readily accessible to the citizens. Citizens may attend the meetings in groups or as individuals. The usual practice is for the presiding officer, at some time during a legislative meeting, to allow any citizen to address the body on the floor. Thus the citizen participates, if he wishes, directly in legislative deliberation.

As a legislative body, the council often holds public hearings (posting notices and informing the press) before deciding what action to take on a proposal. For example, at a recent meeting of a city council, citizens appeared to speak for or against such matters as these: a petition for storing gasoline in underground tanks at a specified location, a petition for locating poles and wires (electric company and telephone company) on a new street, an order for the construction of a sewer, an order for taking a certain piece of land for city use.

A large city council may also be divided into "standing" committees, which work in much the same way as do the committees of Congress or your state legislature. The standing committees of one city council are as follows: finance, public works, claims and rules, franchises and licenses, public buildings, education, and legislation. Legislative matters are referred to the appropriate committees, which, in turn, make studies, hold hearings, and report their recommendations for council action.

The Council and the Citizen

Everything a city council does is subject to the scrutiny of the voters. Because they are small in number and close to the people, councilmen must be highly responsive to public pressures. If you own a large house and wish

MAYOR. Elected, 2- or 4-year term.

Ceremonial duties: Dedicates buildings, receives visitors, etc.

Executive duties: Carries out ordinances, recommends legislation, prepares budget, appoints department heads, etc. (See p. 321.)

COUNCIL. Elected, 2- to 4-year term; 3 to 50 members.

Legislative duties: Determines city taxes; borrows money; fixes city employee wages; regulates licenses and zoning laws; grants franchises; approves appointments; awards contracts. (See pp. 317–320.)

Shared responsibility: In strong-mayor government, council approves mayor's decisions and appointments. In weak-mayor government, mayor carries out decisions of council. City charter and traditions determine which form will be used, although sometimes the personality of the mayor is also a factor.

(See pp. 321–322 for advantages and disadvantages of Mayor-Council government.)

CITY MANAGER. Appointed by and responsible to council.

Executive duties: Appoints department heads, recommends way city's facilities and services shall be maintained and approved; oversees operations of city government; makes annual report to council. (See p. 323.)

COUNCIL. Elected.

Duties: Appoints city manager; passes ordinances and budget.

DEPARTMENT HEADS. Appointed by manager for experience, training, and skill in specific duties of department, i.e., engineers, technicians, etc.

TREASURER, CLERKS, AND AUDITOR. Elected.

(See pp. 323–324 for advantages and disadvantages of City-Manager government.)

COMMISSION. Elected; 3 to 7 members.

Executive duties: Each member a responsible head of a department: Health, Safety, Finances, etc. (See p. 324.)

Legislative duties: As a whole, passes ordinances, and makes budget. Mayor is merely ceremonial.

(See pp. 324–325 for advantages and disadvantages of Commission government.)

STRONG MAYOR GOVERNMENT

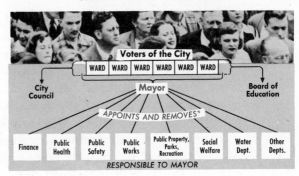

WEAK MAYOR GOVERNMENT
(Divided Authority)

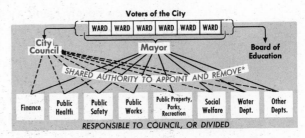

CITY MANAGER GOVERNMENT

COMMISSION GOVERNMENT

*Appointments and removals may be limited by a city's merit system

319

to convert it into a double house so that you can make some money from rent, all your neighbors may be directly interested. You go to the council and ask that the zoning ordinance be changed so that double houses are permitted on your street. Perhaps your own councilman will agree to introduce an ordinance calling for the change, but other councilmen may feel differently about it, and so may some of your neighbors. In any case, the whole matter will be publicly debated and everyone will know how the councilmen vote.

If the council is considering a measure to appropriate money for supervised recreation in the city park near where you live, you and your neighbors may wish to appear at the council meeting and argue in favor of the plan. Residents in other sections may oppose it.

In these and countless other kinds of cases, a city's problems are frequently argued by the citizens in open meeting before the council, and the council's action is taken openly before the interested citizens. Of course, in larger cities there are administrative departments and commissions, having authority over most of the public business. You, the citizen, may go to the administrative agency, such as the zoning board or the recreation commission, with your proposals or complaints. But the council usually has final authority and always has the power of the public purse. Thus you, as a citizen, have a deep concern in the kind of people you nominate and elect to serve on your city council. Too many citizens pay little attention to the choice and election of the city council. If you are one of those who neglects your responsibilities as a democratic citizen in the selection of your city's legislators, you have no one to blame but yourself if your city's business is not handled the way you would like it to be.

Electing Councilmen

Councilmen may represent fixed districts (sometimes called **wards**) or they may be elected at large, that is, to represent all the citizens. Candidates for the council are ordinarily selected by primary election, by petition, or by caucus. Election may be on a party basis, or a city may have a non-partisan election.

In a few American cities the council members are elected by the method known as PR (**proportional representation**). Under the PR system most commonly used (the Hare system), the voter votes for as many candidates as there are positions to be filled. If, for example, your city is choosing a city council of five members, you mark on your ballot your first choice, your second choice, and so on through your fifth choice. This method of voting is intended to give minority groups and independent voters some representation in government, since less popular candidates are not automatically eliminated as they are in the more common system of voting for one of two candidates for each position.

320

The Mayor

The mayor is a miniature governor, just as the governor is a miniature President. The candidate for mayor is nominated either by a political party or on a petition of citizens. He runs for election, like a candidate for governor or President. In most cities, the mayor is elected for a two- or a four-year term. In some cities, he may not succeed himself. Usually, he serves for one or two terms. Sometimes, however, if he is exceptionally popular, he may serve his city for twenty years or longer, as did former Mayor Daniel W. Hoan of Milwaukee, Wisconsin, or Mayor Jasper McLevy of Bridgeport, Connecticut.

Mayor-council government requires ceremonial and executive duties of the mayor. In a small city of only a few thousand inhabitants, there may be few ceremonial functions to attend to. The mayor may finish his work in an hour or so a day and spend the rest of the time on his private business. The mayor of a small community may earn only a few hundred dollars a year. In such communities, the office of mayor is often an honor given a leading citizen rather than a political job.

In a large city, the ceremonial duties alone may place so heavy a burden upon the mayor's time that he simply cannot perform them at all. Since this is the case in New York, for example, a special office was established, that of official "greeter," or chairman of a civic reception committee. In several other large cities, civic committees, other designated officials, or other members of the mayor's family take over some of the ceremonial tasks.

The more important duties of a mayor, of course, are those of chief executive. The chart indicates some of these. Like a President or a governor, his responsibilities are great. In a large city, the mayor must spend many hours every day going over papers, attending to correspondence, conferring with officials, and meeting citizens and groups. The bigger the city, the heavier his responsibility, the larger the sums of money he controls, and the greater his power. In the huge and complex city of New York, the mayor controls the second largest budget in the country—second, that is, only to the federal government budget itself—and directs administrative agencies more complex and varied than does any other public official except the President.

Under any system, of course, the people may choose a "weak" or a "strong" leader. But we should understand that some city charters give great power to the mayor, while others reserve most of the power to the council (see chart, p. 319).

Advantages and Disadvantages of Mayor-Council Government

The mayor-council form or system of city government has been both good and bad. Some of the worst corruption and scandal in our history have arisen under this form, but some of the best work in local government has also been done under it. At its best, the system keeps people close to their government and keeps the government responsive. The mayor gives leadership at once effective and responsible.

The chief disadvantage of the system is that it may enable a political party machine (see Chap. 19) to gain and keep control of a city's government. In the mayor-council form, a corrupt political organization can get weak men elected and, by controlling or bossing them, manage to pad contracts or accounts. That means that the organization can make costs on a contract higher than the contractor asks and get back from him the extra money for the organization. In this way, the leaders of the organization can put public funds into their private pockets. The organization can stay in power by doing endless favors for influential citizens who are more concerned with money and power than with decent government. They can control votes by patron-age—seeing to it that jobs are passed out to the party faithful. Thus cities like New York, Boston, Chicago, Philadelphia, Kansas City, and San Francisco, to name only a few, have suffered long periods of shabby and dishonest government under the mayor-council system. These same cities have also had remarkable periods of reform in which the city government has been over-hauled and made to serve the people honestly and well.

Under any form of local government, the quality of government depends on the quality of local politics and the sense of responsibility for it. Several efforts have been made, however, to develop forms of city government which will reduce the likelihood of political corruption.

THE CITY-MANAGER PLAN

After many years of experimenting with municipal reforms, experts devel-oped a different system of local government which, they believed, would improve the quality of local governments; they removed some of the tempta-tions to fraud and graft and inefficiency by placing most of the city's business in the hands of professional public servants. This form, developed during the first quarter of this century, is known as the **city-manager plan.**

While the mayor-council form is like the American national and state systems on a smaller scale, the city-manager plan is more like the administra-tion of a business corporation or a special agency. This plan assumes that since most of the functions of city government are services which require skilled executives, engineers, and technicians, they are not proper subjects for political action. City government, for example, is not so much a matter of deciding whether the streets should be kept clean, as of working out the details of cleaning them. Thus the plan turns over to a professional manager the practical administration of the city.

322

The Job of City Manager

Several hundred cities, scattered throughout most of the states, especially in the South, along the Pacific Coast, and in the Middle West, have adopted the city-manager plan.

The position of city manager has become a specialized career—a profession. Several universities now have graduate programs for the training of city managers, as well as town and county managers. Practicing managers are often chosen on a professional rather than on a political basis. A manager may, in the course of his career, move from city to city, usually from small to larger cities, until he reaches the city in which he can do his most effective work and serve the community best.

Advantages and Disadvantages of the City-Manager Plan

The merits of the city-manager plan are under constant debate. In nearly all of our cities there are pro-city-manager and anti-city-manager groups, no matter what kind of charter a city may have. Those who argue in favor of the plan say that it is efficient and economical, because it allows experts to handle those aspects of municipal government which are technical, and keeps political organizations from exercising undue influence upon the ways in which the city's money is to be spent.

On the other hand, opponents of the plan argue that the trouble with the system is precisely that it does remove so much of city government from politics. As they see it, the manager, since he is not an elected official, does not have to account to the people for his management of their affairs. Because he is an expert and a professional, he may unduly influence councilmen less well informed than he and dictate the policy of the city without having to report directly to the people or their representatives. Thus, much of the government of the city is carried on outside the political process and outside the realm of public debate. This discourages citizen participation in public affairs, the critics of the city-manager plan believe, and does a disservice to democracy.

Whatever view a citizen may have, for or against the city-manager plan—and the issue is both difficult and important—the final decision rests with him. The community may adopt a city-manager charter or throw it out, as the majority sees fit.

In general, cities which have adopted the city-manager plan have been successful with it. Examples are Cincinnati, Ohio; Norfolk, Virginia; Schenectady, New York; Hartford, Connecticut. A few have given it up after a trial, such as Cleveland and Houston. Like all plans studied here, it does not guarantee good government. By way of example, we may note the case of one large midwestern city which adopted this plan in 1926. The first election under the plan resulted in the choice of a partisan council which appointed a local politician as manager. For the next fourteen years, this city was administered by a government no better than that which preceded the change to the city-manager plan. Payrolls were padded (larger sums appropriated for salaries than were paid to workers), taxes were high, graft and corruption prevailed. The voters finally revolted, electing a reform council which chose an experienced, professional manager. Since then this city has been as well governed as any in the country.

Note that the choice of a particular *form* of government did not provide good administration for the city. This result was not achieved until good councilmen were elected because a majority of plain citizens proved in political action that they really cared about good government.

THE COMMISSION PLAN

There is still another form of city government, the **commission plan.** This plan was developed in Galveston, Texas. In 1900, that city was almost completely destroyed by a tidal wave from the Gulf of Mexico. The city was already heavily in debt before the disaster struck, and the city government was known to be corrupt and inefficient. Texas decided to take drastic steps to meet the new emergency.

The state legislature appointed five businessmen to take on the task of reconstruction and to run the city's government. The city commissioners, as they were called, were so efficient that soon Galveston enjoyed better government than it had ever had before. In spite of the heavy cost of rebuilding after the flood, the city's finances were far sounder than they had ever been. The citizens of Galveston then requested the Texas legislature to make the commission plan, as they called it, permanent. Other cities followed suit. Now about 300 medium- and large-sized cities, such as Birmingham, Alabama, New Orleans, Louisiana, and Nashville, Tennessee, are governed by the commission plan.

The chart, p. 319, shows how this type of city government functions. This plan combines the executive and legislative functions of government in one body, the city commission.

The Merits and Weaknesses of the Commission Plan

Commissioners elected by the voters may not always be qualified for positions they are to hold. Any citizen, for example, may be a candidate for the position of commissioner of public works. He may be elected because of his popularity, even though he is not properly qualified to handle the job, and the city services may then suffer. This is a particularly serious weakness in a large city, where a large number of functions must be divided among the various elected administrators, many of whom are inexperienced as administrators. Commission government seems to work best in medium-sized cities, such as Galveston and Nashville.

Commission government has one great advantage: voters may find it less complicated and easier to understand than the mayor-council and city-manager plans. In a number of cities, it has worked well, providing services with a minimum of political pressures. It uses the short ballot, which, as we shall see in Chapter 16, p. 385, makes the voter's task easier; this is also an advantage. On the other hand, it is harder to place responsibility under this plan than under the others; commissioners may be able to "pass the buck" on difficult or unpopular decisions. This plan also violates what many students of government believe to be a sound principle: that administrative officials should be *appointed* on the basis of their qualifications for administrative posts. In general, this plan has not proved as popular among the voters as has the manager plan.

CIVIL SERVICE

Although there are considerable differences among the three plans of city government, one device for improving efficiency in all municipal governments is very widely used. This is the civil service or merit system for city employees.

In general, such systems operate in much the same way as federal or state civil service systems. Thus city employment may become a career. Examinations are given to applicants for various types of positions. Successful candidates are interviewed, and the employing officer must appoint one of the two or three best qualified. Once in service, the employee has some protection in his career, against both arbitrary dismissal and arbitrary refusal to promote him. Normally cities have a civil service board or commission which administers examinations and supervises the system.

Civil service practices have done much, especially in the twentieth century, to improve public service in local government, both by reducing the number of city positions open for appointment by political bosses as patronage, and by providing government with better-qualified personnel.

THE SERVICES PERFORMED BY LOCAL GOVERNMENTS

The forms of local governments which we have been discussing do not tell us the many things they actually do for us. In general, their functions fall under six headings, but it would be difficult to list *all* of the services per-

CONDUCT: POLYTHEISM

GANGSTERS

RACKETEERS

GRAFTERS

LA GUARDIA
ADMINISTRATION

CITY SERVICES

Whatever the form of city government, certain services which benefit us all are performed by the government. In big cities, the traffic policeman is indispensable at busy corners. The street cleaner is essential to our physical health. In this cartoon, he is also removing from the city political undesirables.

Keeping the streets paved and in good repair is an important duty of the city. And fire-fighting, night and day, helps to save lives and prevent property damage. School buses to take students to and from distant schools are also a responsibility of city government.

THE CAMPAIGN
FOR A CLEANER CITY
IS WELL UNDER WAY
Marcus in
The New York Times

327

formed by all of our local government units. The chart, p. 330, indicates how two local communities pay for the services.

Roads and Water Supply

It has long been a basic principle among free men to ask government to do for them only those things they cannot do for themselves, or cannot do as well themselves. This principle is well illustrated in the services of local government. The building and maintaining of roads, one of the oldest functions of local governments, shows how governments now perform services which individuals tried to manage in pioneer days. Government now builds and keeps up the roads because government can do it better than can individual citizens, even when individuals try hard to coöperate with one another. In the old days, farmers cut and "improved" their own roads to the village, each man taking responsibility for roads on his own land, but often on the basis of "you help me, I'll help you." Now, through payments into a common treasury, the citizens provide the money for the machines and the hired employees who do the required work, under the control of the citizens' chosen local officials. In most of our local units today, more money is spent for roads than for any other item in the budget except education.

Another old and important local service is the supplying of water to homes, stores, and places of public business. In some places in our country, privately owned businesses sell water to the residents of the community. It is more common for government to supply water to the citizen, who pays "water rent," or a "water tax," or some other charge for this service. In some communities, this charge is a flat amount; in others it may be determined by the number of outlets the property owner uses or by a water meter's measure of the amount of the precious liquid used. With the income derived from these charges, the local unit then pays for the reservoirs and pipe lines, and the work of engineers, laborers, and others who bring the water to its homes, barns, factories, public buildings, stores, and other users of water.

Public Health and Welfare Services

In recent years public health services have taken a place among the most important services of local government. Local units now provide (when they can afford it) hospitals, sanitariums, medical centers, and clinics for treatment of people who cannot afford private medical service. Counties, cities, and other local units take care of the health of children in their schools, by vaccinating against disease, checking teeth and eyes, giving X-rays for tuberculosis detection, and performing other services. Psychiatric service, which has long been neglected, is now provided by some local governments.

Also growing in importance among the functions of local governments are those classified as welfare services. Many local governments now provide care

328

for the aged and infirm, give public assistance to the needy and the unemployed, offer rehabilitation and vocational training for the handicapped, and maintain institutions for the care and training of the mentally deficient or retarded and for delinquents. The federal and state governments have, in recent years, taken a more active part in public welfare activities, particularly in the granting of funds for services. These will be discussed later, in Chapter 25.

Police and Fire Departments

Among the most familiar and important services of local government are the police and fire departments. In Chapter 10 we studied the various police agencies of local government—the county sheriff and his deputies, the city policemen, and the town or village constable and his staff. Here it is enough to say that the maintenance of law and order, the regulation of traffic, the safeguarding of lives and property are all basically functions of local government. Policing is an expensive item in municipal budgets. One of the chief problems facing modern American local governments is the lack of adequate funds to pay policemen the salaries they should have and to employ enough of them. The increase of population and the crowding of people in residential areas seem to bring an increase in crime and in delinquency. While police work is not the solution to this problem, it is vitally necessary so long as the problem continues to plague us.

Fire protection has always been the responsibility of local government. In early times firefighting was managed on a volunteer basis everywhere. Even today most towns and villages depend upon volunteer firefighters. However, modern firefighting equipment is costly and must be paid for from tax income. The day of the citizen bucket brigade is gone. In larger communities, and in all cities, the fire department is a major item of the budget and a major public service. Fire departments today face the same problem as do the police—lack of funds to pay good salaries and maintain sufficient force. Improvements in firefighting equipment put an additional strain on the public treasury, since machines are expensive and tend to go out of date in a few years.

Both police and fire departments are usually based on a merit system of employment and promotion. The police chief and fire chief are leading city officials who must be highly competent in their fields. In some of the largest cities, like New York, Chicago, or Los Angeles, it may be more important that police and fire commissioners (as they are often called) be experienced administrators than actually policemen or firemen. This is only because the departments under them are well staffed with high-ranking experts. In most cities the chief or commissioner will need to have great experience in his field of public protection. Below the top level, policemen and firemen are career

Where cities of over 25,000 get their tax dollars

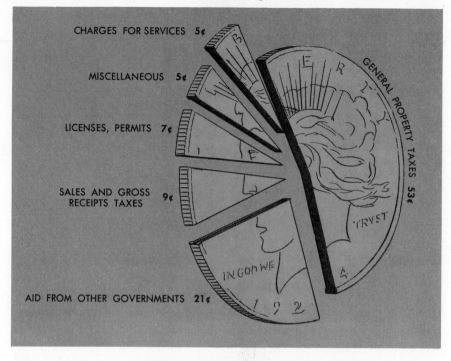

CHARGES FOR SERVICES 5¢

MISCELLANEOUS 5¢

LICENSES, PERMITS 7¢

SALES AND GROSS RECEIPTS TAXES 9¢

AID FROM OTHER GOVERNMENTS 21¢

GENERAL PROPERTY TAXES 53¢

What the tax dollar buys

in a city of over 25,000   in a small college town

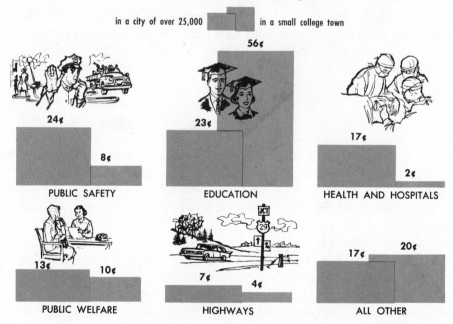

56¢

24¢   8¢

23¢

17¢   2¢

PUBLIC SAFETY   EDUCATION   HEALTH AND HOSPITALS

13¢   10¢

7¢   4¢

17¢   20¢

PUBLIC WELFARE   HIGHWAYS   ALL OTHER

Here are the chief sources of a city's income and the chief channels of outgo. "All Other" outgo means the cost of administration, including such supplies as typewriters, pencils, adding machines, and paper towels; cost of the legislative chamber, including salaries of councilmen; civic entertainment; insurance premiums; and workmen's compensation.

officials who earned their jobs in competitive examinations and interviews, and who achieve promotion and salary advances through merit.

Housing and Slum Clearance

In the period since World War II, when population has been increasing rapidly, local governments have taken on important responsibilities in housing and slum clearance. This work is usually locally administered but is also supported by funds from both the state and the national governments (see Chap. 24). In many areas, public housing projects have changed the faces of communities almost beyond recognition, removing ancient eyesores and providing low-cost modern dwellings of which the people may be proud. Housing is a matter of continuing controversy. Many people feel that dwellings ought to be built and sold or rented only by private business—that for government to go into the housing business is "socialism." Others feel that good housing is a community responsibility, since slums not only run down the community, but also run down the people who live in the slums. Therefore, good housing is important to the community as a whole to improve its conditions of life.

Education

Education has always been a function of local government, in some ways its most important function. The public schools—buildings, facilities, and teachers—are provided from the tax money paid into local and state treasuries by the citizens of the community, supplemented by money returned to school districts from the state treasuries. The school system itself is based on the will of the people, who elect their school boards. The public schools are by far the largest business of local governments. They are so important, in fact, that we shall consider them separately in Chapter 24, where we shall deal with the whole structure of public education in a free society.

Public Libraries and Museums

While culture—literature, music, and the arts—is in the United States very largely a private matter, it is fostered and supported to a considerable extent by local governments. Your town or your district in the city will almost certainly have a public library. You probably use it yourself and appreciate a service that enables you to get books you want to read and take them home for a reasonable length of time. You may well have discovered how helpful a public librarian can be in getting just the book or article you need in pursuing your hobby (or doing your homework project!). Andrew Carnegie, the great steel manufacturer, gave library buildings to several thousand communities on condition that local governments would keep them up and build

331

collections of books. This philanthropy stimulated our fine public library system. Today our public libraries are a very large business indeed.

It is a similar story with art museums, though American cities and towns have never been so willing to spend money for art or music as for books. Nevertheless, most medium-sized and large cities have good museums and art galleries operated in whole or in part at public expense. Many communities own their own concert halls and public auditoriums. Frequently libraries, museums, and art galleries are supervised by the local board of education, though in some cases special agencies have been established to run them. It may strike you that "politics" and your local museum are a pretty far cry from each other. But the latter is no less a part of government; and if you become actively interested in your museum or library, you may find out to your surprise that "politics" is at work there too.

COMMUNITY PLANNING

It takes too long to get to work, too long to shop, too long to get to the park, too long to get out of town, too long to get into town, too long to get to school, to the train, to the airport. It costs too much in terms of wasted time, rubber, gasoline, and nerves to transfer goods, to make deliveries, to make business calls. It costs too much in terms of the city's most important task—the growing of normal, healthy children. There isn't enough air, enough sun, enough open space in our big cities. There isn't enough privacy, and what there is costs too much. There's too much noise. There is too much bustle and agitation, too little peace, dignity, and human warmth.

This was written about one American city, a twentieth-century industrial city which was a small New York village when the Erie Canal came to its doors to stimulate its growth. Other communities have also learned what happens when growth takes place without plan. In the years since World War II, many of the small communities within daily driving distance of our cities have been suddenly confronted with results of a lack of planning; hundreds of thousands of city people have moved out of the cities to the smaller places, bringing some of the very conditions, mentioned in the quotation, which they moved to get away from. In fact "Suburbia" is becoming more and more the typical residence of mid-twentieth-century Americans.

Today in over three-fourths of our cities of more than 25,000 people, the citizens have established some kind of planning agency, frequently called the planning board or commission, and have passed legislation called zoning laws. These ordinances usually divide the community into zones, some for

Pittsburgh's "Golden Triangle"

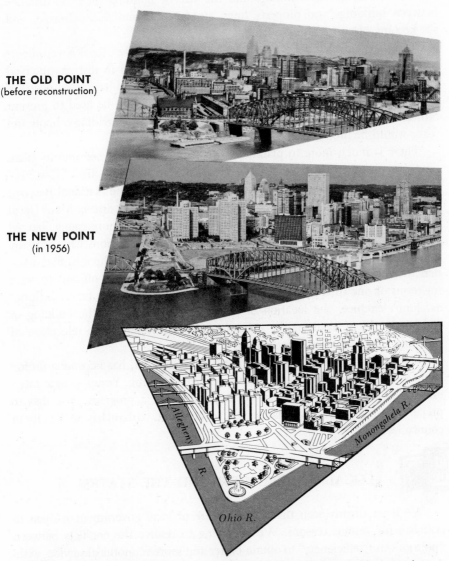

THE OLD POINT
(before reconstruction)

THE NEW POINT
(in 1956)

The "Pittsburgh Renaissance" is an outstanding example of what planning can do—planning along with leadership, money, and favorable community attitudes. Shown here is the city's business district, where the Allegheny and Monongahela rivers come together to form the Ohio. Here was a blighted area in which no new structure had been built in 25 years. Here too the city had a traffic problem, a flood problem, and a smoke problem.

Federally-built dams have brought the rivers under control. City and county ordinances now regulate smoke density. Fifty-nine acres of blighted area have been cleared as workers demolished old buildings in the "Golden Triangle" region. Thirty-six of these acres have been reserved for a new park, new bridges, and a traffic interchange. Handsome skyscrapers have been erected on the rest of the cleared area. The drawing at the bottom shows how this fine city planning has earned for the section the name Golden Triangle.

333

industry, some for residence, some for stores and offices. Zoning laws may also regulate the height of buildings and the size of building lots, the distance between buildings and property lines, storage of flammable materials, and the keeping of animals or poultry.

Rural areas may also be zoned. In several of the states, local governments may by zoning prevent the cultivation of lands situated in districts reserved for recreation and forestry. The state of Wisconsin alone has zoned over five million acres for forestry and recreation. Zoning may also be used to prevent farmers from settling in remote areas where the costs of providing schools and roads would be prohibitive.

There is much more to planning than zoning. Actually community planning may involve anything from a great athletic stadium like Milwaukee County Stadium, the home of the Milwaukee Braves in the National Baseball League, to county-wide sewage disposal plants and facilities. Many local governments now have their own planning councils or commissions charged with drafting plans for the future. Some planning commissions have as many as 55 members, but most of them are small, consisting of three to five members. Members are usually appointed by the local executive officials to serve for terms of one to seven years. Their work includes planning for such things as slum clearance, the location of public housing projects, the building of civic and athletic centers, the extension of road systems, the relocation of railroads, and a host of other things.

The field of planning, like that of city management, has become a profession for which universities now offer specialized training. Young people interested in this kind of public service may undertake a program of studies to prepare them for careers as planners in government, particularly at the city or county level.

LOCAL GOVERNMENT AND THE STATES

We have already seen that the structure of local government is open to criticism for various reasons. We are trying to resolve the conflicts between "politics" and "efficiency," to obtain better and more economical services without surrendering our political control over government. Regardless of how these problems are solved, we shall continue to face another still more baffling one: the problem of costs. As cities grow and people require ever more and better services, the cost of their government continually rises. Their financial resources, however, may not grow at the same rate. This problem makes the relationship between city and county government difficult, especially in counties where a very large city has grown up. It complicates even more the relation between local government and the states. In many states we now have cities whose government is larger and even more costly than the government of the state. New York, Pennsylvania, Illinois, Massachusetts, Ohio, and California are well-known examples, but many other states are fast approaching a similar condition. Ways must be found to spread the cost of government in cities and large metropolitan areas more evenly among the people of the state, in proportion to what they receive.

This problem is dramatized in New York State. For generations there has been constant friction between "upstate" and "downstate"—meaning actually between New York City and the rest of the state. Once this friction was mainly social. It meant simply the age-old difference between country people and city people lampooned in the wisecracks about "hicks" and "city slickers." In our time the friction has become immediate and compelling.

New York City, like cities everywhere in the country, depends upon the state government for its charter and its authority. Thus it can tax its people only to the extent permitted by the state legislature, and it is entitled to only such money from the state treasury as the legislature agrees to give it. As its costs increase, the city asks for both more taxing power and more assistance from the state. But the legislature represents all of the assembly districts in the state equally; it includes a large number of assemblymen from small cities, towns, and rural areas. These legislators, and the constituencies they serve, are not anxious to spend any more state money for New York City than they have to. After all, they need more money for their own school districts, for parks, roads, and many other things, and are concerned with dividing the state's income so that they will get a fair share.

The question then arises as to what a "fair share" is—and the argument is on. There is no end to it, because there is not enough money to satisfy everyone, and no one will agree that someone else needs it more than he does. On the other hand, the people of New York City, who must pay their full share of state taxes, naturally resist as strongly as they can the steady increase in their local taxes. They argue that their needs are more pressing than those of "upstate." Nor does the problem end here. The fact is that New York City is not the only large city in the state with a big and costly government. There are also Buffalo, with nearly a million people, Rochester, with half a million, and Syracuse, with a metropolitan area of nearly half a million. Other cities, like Utica, Albany, Schenectady, Binghamton, and Elmira, also make strong and legitimate demands for greater state assistance.

The basic problem illustrated by the case of New York State is how to adjust the structure and financing of local governments to deal with conditions which could not have been foreseen at the time they were established. No one can be sure how this problem will eventually be solved. Certain things, however, are clear. A better system of taxation and finance will have to be devised. Governmental responsibilities will have to be placed more effectively where they are needed in relation to population. There will have to be more centralization of services. At the same time, the relation of the citizen to local government must be kept direct and immediate. We must not lose the idea of "grass roots" politics and "grass roots" government.

This is a challenge, not only to students and experts in the field of government and administration, but to the citizens themselves. Lest the whole system of local government collapse of its own weight, coming generations may need to revise the form of it. If they are true to our democratic traditions of freedom and individual responsibility, they will meet the challenge wisely, cautiously, yet imaginatively, and the United States will enter a new and better era.

SUMMARY

In this chapter you have made a study of our cities, where a great and growing majority of Americans live. You have examined the three chief plans used to govern cities—mayor-council, city-manager, and commission—and learned about the strengths and weaknesses of each. The dangers of city government are inefficiency and corruption. No system is foolproof. Many cities are working to protect the public and city employees by a system of career civil service. You have explored the substance of city and other local governments—what they actually do for the people—and you have seen the growing need for broader and more farsighted community planning. Finally, you have considered some of the perennial as well as new problems involved in the relations of the local governments to the states.

KNOW WHAT YOU READ

1. What is a charter? How is it obtained? What are the different kinds of charters?
2. What is an ordinance? Give some examples of ordinances. (See also page 36 of Chap. 2.)
3. How does an *order* differ from a *resolution?*
4. How are councilmen chosen?
5. What are some of the steps taken by a council in its work of legislating for a city?

6. What are the powers and responsibilities of a mayor?
7. Why is the mayor-council plan so often criticized? Under what conditions does the mayor-council plan result in good government?
8. How does the "strong" mayor plan differ from the "weak" mayor plan? (See drawing, p. 319.)
9. Why have some cities tried the city-manager plan? Under this plan, what is the work of the council? Of the manager?
10. Like all the plans studied in this chapter, the city-manager plan does not guarantee good government. Why is this so? What are the arguments for and against this plan?
11. How did the commission plan come into existence? How does it operate? What are its advantages and disadvantages?
12. How have civil service practices improved local government?
13. What are the principal services performed by local governments?
14. Explain the relationship between services of government and local taxes.
15. What happens to communities which grow without planning?
16. What are zoning laws? Planning commissions?
17. In what ways may the activities of private citizens be regulated by zoning rules? By other aspects of community planning?
18. What is the reason why so many large cities are having financial difficulties?
19. What is the relationship of local government to state government?

WHAT DO YOU THINK?

Reform government operates best when it is solidly supported by a civic organization. The one which supported the city-manager plan in our city when it was first adopted has now completely evaporated. Several months ago, the organization held a meeting but no one would agree to act as its president. Two meetings have been called since then, but could do nothing since there was no quorum.

1. What do you think finally happened to city-manager government in the city discussed in the above quotation?
2. Local governments, in general, now offer the services described in this chapter. Some also provide concerts, zoos, swimming instruction, airports, playgrounds, skating rinks, libraries, and others which are sometimes classified as "desirable but not necessary." The number of services seems to be on the increase. Under what conditions would you vote against local government offering a new service?
3. Voters of an eastern city recently voted out their seven city councilors because, under their administration, the tax rate went from $30 to $60.60 per thousand in ten years.

In that same period the city built six schools (76 classrooms), built a $250,000 power plant, bought 26 new refuse trucks, laid 13.8 miles of waterways, 11.4 miles of sanitary sewers, 7 miles of storm sewers, built 6 miles of new roadways, reconstructed 5.3 miles more, plus 36.9 miles of asphalt resurfacing and 12 miles of seal coater.

Do you think the voters wanted these services? Why did they defeat the administration that provided them?

4. Halloween parties are a comparatively new local government service. In a recent year one city reported that on October 31, 260 parties were held, attended by over 12,000 school children. These parties were made possible through the work of over 1,800 parents who served as coördinators, committee chairman, and program-committee members. Coöperating organizations were the Chamber of Commerce, the school, police, health, fire, and library departments, the PTA's, and the American Legion. Costs were met from token tickets, fees, donations from public-spirited citizens, and from a special fund in the budget of one of the city departments. Which city department do you think provided the money and the leadership for these parties? Is this a good idea for the celebration of Halloween? Does your local government make any special provision for this kind of recreational service? Should it?

PROBLEMS AND PROJECTS FOR YOU

A complaint frequently heard about local government is that there are altogether too many separate jurisdictions and too many local officers who have powers to impose taxes for this, that, or the other purpose. In addition to the county, city, and township jurisdiction, the taxpayer is likely to find himself living within many other minor jurisdictions and subject to their taxes. These are school districts, park districts, drainage districts, forestation districts, road districts, mosquito abatement districts, sanitation districts, etc. Each district has its own set of officials and its own precious tax rate. . . .

1. In how many special districts do you live? What services do they perform? What does it cost to maintain them? This information might make a good subject for a cartoon, poster, or diagram.
2. From time to time citizens appeal to their local governments to have zoning exceptions made for their own benefit. In your own local government, what officials hear these appeals? Do they usually decide in favor of the citizen seeking an exception?

> A new 1,000 gallon pumping engine has been delivered to the Fire Department. The $16,000 vehicle was formally accepted at City Hall Wednesday by Mayor Swanson. It will replace an engine purchased in 1929 and will be attached to Station 7.

3. What role of the mayor is illustrated above? Who takes this part in your local government?

In the case of the purchase of this fire engine, what other activities did the mayor perform? What had to be done by the local legislative branch? What officials would be responsible for the purchase of fire-fighting equipment for your protection?

> What is city planning? In its simplest terms, it is the business of looking ahead—of studying the city with the aid of modern science and of working to improve the city and protect its good features. City planning deals chiefly with the arrangement of things in an urban community. The streets, parks, schools, stores, factories, and houses all need to be fitted together in a common-sense way, and this is what city planning tries to do. Each of these has many effects—economic, social, and even psychological, on the people living in the city. Therefore, city planning touches on many other subjects, including geography, engineering, architecture, sociology, law, and finance. The objective of city planning is efficient progress toward the best sort of urban community we can build.
>
> The City Plan Commission of Providence, R.I.

4. Who is responsible for planning in your locality? In what ways does the above definition describe the work of your own planners?
5. Report on proportional representation, what it is and how it operates.
6. Attend a public hearing. Find out in advance all you can about the subject of the hearing. At the hearing, note particularly who are present. Report to the class on what you saw and heard.
7. From your local newspaper, assemble materials for a bulletin-board display which will illustrate the work of the mayor and the council.
8. Look up zoning in other localities. Report to the class on the variety of regulations you have studied.
9. Plan and conduct a model "public hearing" on some question of local importance. For this some students of your class will act as government officials; others will be interested citizens. What good use might be made of the arguments presented at this "hearing"?
10. The profession of city manager offers both opportunities for the public service and for good income. One successful manager has held positions as follows:

Location	Salary
Cincinnati, Ohio (assistant)	$ 4,200
Portsmouth, Ohio	8,000
Binghamton, N.Y.	9,000
Schenectady, N.Y.	10,800
Norfolk, Va.	20,000
San Antonio, Texas	27,500 plus expenses

Obtain university catalogs from your school library or guidance office and find out what studies should be pursued by a person who wishes to prepare for this profession. Report your findings.
11. Make a list of all the local government services you observe from the time you leave home in the morning until the time you return to your home. You should list more than are shown in the picture story, pp. 326–327.

EXTEND YOUR VOCABULARY

special charter	resolution
classified charter system	franchise
optional system	proportional representation
home rule	city-manager plan
mayor-council government	commission plan
city ordinance	planning board
order	

YOUR NOTEBOOK: THE GOVERNMENT OF ——

1. Does your community have a planning agency? If so, who are its members?
2. Do you have a zoning ordinance? Who is responsible for making it work? Who hears appeals from persons wishing exceptions made in their favor?
3. Make in your notebook an original diagram showing the relationship of the voters to your legislative and executive officials.
4. What is your local lawmaking body called? Name your representative in that body.
5. How long are the terms of your local lawmakers? Where do they meet? When? Do they hold public hearings? When?

READ MORE ABOUT IT

ALLEN, ROBERT S., *Our Fair City*. Vanguard Press, 1947.
Readable and provocative.

BABCOCK, ROBERT S., *State and Local Government and Politics*. Random House, 1957. Chaps. 8, 10, 18.

EDITORS OF FORTUNE, *The Exploding Metropolis*. Doubleday, 1958.
Exciting and reliable.

GRIFFITH, ERNEST S., *History of American City Government*. Oxford University Press, 1938.
Useful for earlier periods.

MACDONALD, AUSTIN F., *American State Government and Administration*. Crowell, 1955. Chaps. 13, 30.

STEFFENS, LINCOLN, *The Shame of the Cities*. Sagamore Press, Inc., 1957.
First printed in book form in 1904 from a series of articles from *McClure's Magazine*. Classic study of big city political corruption.

WOODBURY, CULEMAN, ed., *The Future of Cities and Urban Redevelopment*. University of Chicago Press, 1953.
Valuable discussions of current problems.

CHAPTER 14

Puerto Rico, the Territories, and Washington

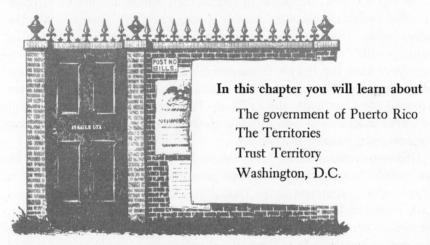

In this chapter you will learn about

The government of Puerto Rico
The Territories
Trust Territory
Washington, D.C.

Since the United States was born in a colonial rebellion, we have a special obligation to treat with fairness and full self-determination those people who have come under our control. Some people may have felt that we have not always conducted ourselves according to our ideals. Indeed, we were long accused, in the old world, of aggressive imperialism because of our war with Mexico in 1846 and, to a lesser extent, our war with Spain in 1898. But whatever you may think about American empire building in the nineteenth century, you may be justly proud of the American record in the twentieth. Two great territories have been granted their wish for statehood—Alaska and Hawaii—and Puerto Rico has exercised her free choice to become a "commonwealth," as you will see in this chapter. The Philippine Islands, according to a solemn agreement, were given outright independence in 1946 after almost fifty years of preparation. All our remaining possessions have a large measure

341

of self-government and, unlike the colonies of most other nations, none has ever complained of exploitation.

The United States still has a large overseas "empire" including many islands in the Pacific Ocean, the Virgin Islands, the Canal Zone, and the Commonwealth of Puerto Rico. All these territories are governed in accordance with Article IV of the Constitution: "The Congress shall have Power to dispose of and make all needful Rules and Regulations respecting the Territory or other Property belonging to the United States." The Congress, in addition, exercises under the Constitution exclusive jurisdiction over the national capital, Washington, D.C.

PUERTO RICO

On July 25, 1952, the island of Puerto Rico, which had been a territory like other overseas possessions, became a commonwealth in union with the United States. This is a new idea in American government. It is not to be confused with "commonwealth" as applied to countries like Canada or Australia within the British Commonwealth of Nations. They are wholly independent and sovereign nations joining together voluntarily for certain purposes. The Commonwealth of Puerto Rico, on the contrary, is a part of the United States, by its own will, though Congress has said that it may have complete independence if it wishes.

Under its commonwealth form, Puerto Rico is governed internally by its own elected government, as we shall presently see. In foreign affairs it is subject to the government of the United States, and its residents are citizens of the United States, subject to the laws of the United States, except tax laws, just like residents of the various states. Unlike the states, however, Puerto Rico does not participate in the national government, except to send a kind of ambassador known as the Resident Commissioner to represent it in Washington. The Commissioner is elected for a four-year term. He sits in the House of Representatives by the rules of the House and may sit with committees, but has no vote. Again, unlike the states, Puerto Rico is not subject to federal excise tax or the federal income tax. It has its own system of taxation.

The Legislature

The legislative power of Puerto Rico is vested by its constitution in a Legislative Assembly of two houses. The Senate has 27 members, two from each of eight senatorial election districts, and eleven elected by the whole population (at large). The House of Representatives has 51 members, one from each of forty districts and, again, eleven elected at large. The term for both houses is four years. A unique provision of the constitution is that the minority party can increase the number of its seats in either or both houses whenever the other political party controls more than two-thirds of the seats. Thus the minority party can never have less than one-third of the seats.

The powers of the Legislative Assembly are similar to those of state legislatures in many respects. It has great powers of raising money by taxation. Whereas a state cannot tax imports, the Puerto Rican Assembly places duties on goods imported into Puerto Rico, except those which come from the United States. It applies excise taxes to all goods including those from the United States. Puerto Rican revenue is supplemented by the return from the federal government of internal revenue taxes collected by the federal government on Puerto Rican goods sold on the mainland, especially rum.

There is only one limitation specified in the constitution of Puerto Rico and approved by the Congress of the United States on the legislative powers of the Puerto Rican Assembly: it may not enact laws contrary to the Constitution, laws, or treaties of the United States. Thus Puerto Rican laws, like those of the states, are subject to review for constitutionality in the federal Courts.

The Executive

The Governor of Puerto Rico, the chief executive, is popularly elected for a four-year term and has all the powers of a strong state governor. The Governor has a veto power over legislation, which may be overridden only by a two-thirds vote of both houses; he appoints the heads of government departments, with the consent of the Senate; he prepares the budget, recommends legislation, and carries out the laws enacted by the Assembly. There is no lieutenant governor; if the Governor dies or becomes incapacitated, he is succeeded by the senior executive official, the Secretary of State.

The Judiciary

Puerto Rico has its own judiciary system, ranging from justice-of-the-peace courts to a Supreme Court consisting of a Chief Justice and four associate justices. These judges of Puerto Rican courts try all cases of law arising under civil law or the laws of Puerto Rico. The commonwealth is also a federal judicial district, and the federal Court deals with cases arising under the laws of the United States.

The Commonwealth Plan

The decision of the Puerto Ricans not to press a claim for statehood, but instead to take on their semi-independent status, means that their very active political life is largely confined to internal rather than national or foreign issues. They have their own political parties quite distinct from those of the mainland and the other parts of the United States. But both our national Republican and Democratic parties maintain commonwealth committees

343

which send delegations to presidential nominating conventions. Puerto Ricans do not, of course, vote in national elections.

The commonwealth plan in Puerto Rico is, as we have said, a new idea in American government, and is thus far highly successful. The large measure of independence the plan gave them seemed to the Puerto Ricans the best expression of their political maturity. Since a great majority of Puerto Ricans are Spanish-speaking and have a common cultural inheritance different from the Anglo-Saxon tradition, Puerto Rico has a very small nationalist party which agitates for complete separation from the United States. But the overwhelming majority, under the leadership of Muñoz Marin, first native governor, prefers to retain the advantages of the moderate ties to the United States which exist under the new constitution of the commonwealth.

THE TERRITORIES

With the independence of the Philippines and the new states of Alaska and Hawaii, and Puerto Rico, America's overseas territories have been very greatly reduced. Nevertheless, we still have substantial possessions in both the Atlantic and Pacific oceans and the Canal Zone in Central America. In general, these territories fall into one of two classes, unincorporated and trusteeship. Unincorporated territories are governed chiefly by officials appointed in Washington and responsible to agencies of the federal government; trusteeships are territories belonging legally to the United Nations and governed by the United States on behalf of the United Nations.

The Canal Zone

The Canal Zone is a strip of land five miles wide on either side of the Panama Canal. It is governed directly by the President through a Governor appointed by the President and chosen from the Army Engineers. You will remember from your study of American history that the Canal Zone was purchased from Panama by President Theodore Roosevelt in 1903, in order to guarantee American control of the great new waterway. In view of the recurring wars and crises of the twentieth century, President Roosevelt's foresight has been fully proved. The strategic value of the zone is made very clear to us when we contrast its status with that of the Suez Canal, so often the source of crisis and uncertainty for the Europeans dependent upon it.

Laws for the Canal Zone come either through presidential orders authorized by Congress or directly by acts of Congress. The Canal Zone has its own system of courts to handle criminal offenses and civil actions. However, at any particular time a large number of residents are military personnel on active duty and subject to military courts.

See table, p. 345, for other territories.

INCORPORATED AND UNINCORPORATED ¹ TERRITORIES

	Size, Square Miles	Population (1950)	Citizenship	Executive	Legislative	Judiciary	Federal Agency Responsible	Special Value to U.S.
VIRGIN ISLANDS	133	26,665	Yes; granted by Congress in 1927	(Organic Act of 1954/Pub. Law 517) Governor appointed by President; limited veto powers	Unicameral: 11 Senators elected for 2 years	U.S. Attorney; also Judge of District Court of Islands	Dept. of Interior	Defense: protects entrance into Caribbean and Panama Canal Zone
				Unincorporated territory (Organic Act of 1950/Pub. Law 630)				
GUAM	206	59,498	Yes; granted by act of 1950; but no right to vote in U.S.	Governor appointed by President	Unicameral: 2-year term	Island courts in local matters	Dept. of Interior	Naval and air base; center for Strategic Air Command in Pacific
				Unincorporated territory				
SAMOA	76	18,937	Yes	Governor appointed by Secretary of Interior	Bicameral: 15 Senators; 18 members of House	One high court; also appellate, trial, and probate	Dept. of Interior	Defense: naval base
WAKE	3	349	No natives				U.S. Navy	Defense: naval base
MIDWAY	2	416	No natives on island				U.S. Navy	Defense: air base
BAKER	1	?	No natives				U.S. Navy	Defense: air base

¹ An *incorporated* territory (Virgin Islands) can carry on such fiscal functions as floating a loan; an *unincorporated* territory (Guam) cannot undertake any functions on its own.

A COMMONWEALTH AND SOME TERRITORIES

The Commonwealth of Puerto Rico functions much as do our federal and state governments, with a Congress, a Supreme Court, and an executive. Congress makes the laws (House of Representatives is here shown in session); the Supreme Court, housed in this modern building, interprets the laws; under the strong executive, Muñoz Marin, the laws are executed. The Commonwealth has forged ahead in many areas.

From Truk, our Trust Territory in the Pacific, copra is shipped to many markets all over the world. Copra oil is used for soap, margarine, and other products.

346

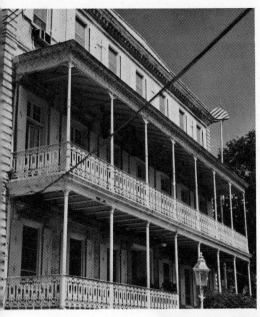

Our territories include many different kinds of civilizations.

Reminiscent of New Orleans is Government House in the Virgin Islands (shown at the left). Modern government offices, in the unincorporated territory of Samoa (below), are dominated by Rainmaker Mountain. But housing on the palm-fringed shores represents a very different culture.

TRUST TERRITORY

The Trust Territory of the Pacific, consisting of the Marshall, Marianas, and Caroline Islands in the South Pacific, was formerly held by Japan. These islands were conquered by the United States in World War II and were officially turned over to the American government in 1947 to be held in trust for the United Nations. They are governed by a High Commissioner, appointed by the President, who is in the Department of the Interior.

As a trusteeship power, the United States reports regularly to the Trusteeship Council of the United Nations. We assume obligations under the Council to help the peoples of these islands to improve their industry, agriculture, and commerce, to raise their educational standards, and to maintain health and sanitation.

WASHINGTON, D.C.

One of the early compromises in American politics was that between Thomas Jefferson and Alexander Hamilton on the matter of the location of the national capital. Hamilton, the first Secretary of the Treasury, proposed to Congress in 1791 that the new federal government assume the debts contracted by the states during the Revolution, and pay them off gradually as a part of the national debt. Many members of Congress were opposed to this idea, especially the members from Virginia. Virginia had already paid off its debt, and objected to being taxed to help pay off the debts of states like Massachusetts or New York. Northern Congressmen, however, supported Hamilton's proposal.

At the same time, the Congress was discussing the location of the future national capital. The Virginians were anxious to have it in Virginia or elsewhere in the South, so that it would not be too near the northern financial centers. Many northern Congressmen were anxious to have the national capital situated well to the north, in New York or Philadelphia (where it then was temporarily).

The Location

The votes of the two groups appeared to be nearly evenly divided on both issues. At this point, Secretary of State Jefferson and Secretary of the Treasury Hamilton made "a deal." Hamilton would receive the support of two or three Virginia Congressmen for his debt assumption bill, and Jefferson would receive the support of two or three New York Congressmen for a bill to put the capital in or near Virginia. And so it happened. The debts were assumed, and the national capital, named after President Washington, was situated between Maryland and Virginia on land ceded to the government by the two states. Whenever you are in Washington, stop for a moment to realize that your great modern-day capital is itself a product of the process of democratic compromise we are stressing throughout our study of American government.

The capital district, set up under Article I, Section 8, of the Constitution (see p. 54), is known as the District of Columbia and contains the city of Washington. The entire District (seventy square miles) is governed by Congress, but much of the area outside the limits of the city of Washington is more directly administered by executive agencies which occupy it. The whole of the District of Columbia is on the Maryland side of the Potomac, since Congress returned the land on the other side to Virginia in 1846. However, so many thousands of people who work in Washington live on the Virginia side of the river that communities like Alexandria and Arlington are in many ways parts of the metropolitan area of Washington. Many federal buildings, such as the Pentagon, are in Virginia on federally owned land.

The Government of the District

From its beginnings in 1800, the government of Washington has always been a serious problem. Various systems of government have been tried, including a long period in which Congress authorized the residents to govern themselves by electing a mayor and council. Under this system government was inefficient and a large debt was accumulated. Since 1878, the District of Columbia has been administered by a board of three commissioners estab-lished by Congress. Two of the commissioners must be residents of the District and are appointed by the President with the consent of the Senate to serve three-year terms. The third commissioner is an Army Engineer who is assigned by the President for an indefinite term. The commissioners, in turn, appoint the specialized officials of the city government.

THE LEGISLATURE In practice the legislature of the District consists of the House and Senate Committees on the District of Columbia. Officials of the city and private citizens appear before these bodies to ask for legislation and to debate policies of city government. The decisions of the committees must, of course, be written into bills and passed by Congress. The budget of the city comes from two sources: taxes on the residents (property taxes, licenses, etc., and sales taxes) and direct appropriations by Congress from the federal Treasury.

In early days Congress provided all or most of the money needed to maintain a national capital, since the sole purpose of the district was to accommodate the government. As Washington grew in population and economic activity, tax revenues produced an even greater share of the money needed to run the city. Today congressional appropriations form only a small share of the city budget, chiefly to make up deficits and assist welfare and education. Federal money, of course, supports the services in the District outside of the city.

THE JUDICIARY The District of Columbia is a federal judicial district, and the courts are operated directly by the judicial branch of the federal government.

Problems of Washington

The chief problems of Washington are financial difficulties and the fact that the citizens cannot vote. In modern times, the financial situation has improved as the city became a great metropolis. On the whole, the city has a fair measure of economy and efficiency.

On the other hand, the voting problem seems to be no nearer solution than formerly. Congress denies the residents of the District the right to vote in either local or national elections. Thus government workers as well as others who make their residence in the District are disfranchised.

We must understand that when Congress established the capital district, its purpose was not to develop the great modern city of today. It was meant only to accommodate the necessary public buildings of a national capital, and to provide places to live for government workers and foreign representatives. It was assumed that citizens who work for the government in Washington would have homes elsewhere where their rights as citizens could be exercised. But as the city grew, it inevitably accumulated a large permanent population not only of government workers but also of people engaged in nearly all the numerous occupations of a city.

350

Today all Congressmen make their legal residences in the states from which they come, and all other government employees who can afford it live outside the District and vote from their homes, for example, in Maryland or Virginia. There are nevertheless several hundred thousand citizens who make their legal residence in Washington and are not allowed to vote. They agitate continuously for the vote, using the old slogan "Taxation without representation is tyranny!" and bills to allow it are introduced in almost every session of Congress. But Congressmen, more concerned with national and their own local affairs, let the bills die in committee. Washingtonians continue without the basic privilege of citizens of a democracy.

A small step forward was taken in 1956 when Congress authorized political parties to hold presidential preference primaries. Since Washington could elect only half a dozen delegates to each of the national party conventions (out of twelve or thirteen hundred!), this privilege was not very significant. We are thus faced with the paradox that the citizens of the capital city of the world's most powerful democracy are governed without elected representation.

SUMMARY

In addition to the fifty states, the government of the United States controls many territories and the national capital—Washington, D.C. From the beginning, American statesmen envisioned an extension of the "empire of liberty" and made provision for it. Today wherever the American flag flies—in mid-Pacific, the South Pacific, the Caribbean, or Central America—Americans are protected by the Constitution, and most of them have some measure of self-government. In this chapter you have examined the new status of Puerto Rico as a commonwealth in union with the United States under a system drafted by the Puerto Ricans. You have seen how our unincorporated territories are related to the federal government, and learned about our trusteeships under the United Nations. Finally, you have studied the government of Washington, D.C., and discovered how it differs from all other American cities as it is directly governed by the national government.

KNOW WHAT YOU READ

1. Explain the unusual arrangements by which Puerto Rico is governed.
2. Into what two classes do our overseas possessions fall?

3. How is each of these governed: Guam, Wake, The Canal Zone, The Marshall Islands?
4. What is a trust territory?
5. Explain the compromise by which Congress agreed on the location of our nation's Capital.
6. Who governs Washington? The District of Columbia?
7. What form of government does Washington have? How are its officials selected?
8. What is the lawmaking body for this city?
9. If you were a resident of the District of Columbia, what voting rights could you expect to have when you reached the age of 21?
10. What new voting rights have been won by residents of the district?

WHAT DO YOU THINK?

1. Do you favor commonwealth status or statehood for U.S. territories?
2. Why are residents of the capital denied the vote? Study the cartoon on p. 350, and give arguments for and against the vote.

PROBLEMS AND PROJECTS FOR YOU

1. On an outline map, locate the possessions of the United States.
2. Report to the class on how Alaska and Hawaii won statehood.
3. Report to the class on that part of the report of the President's Commission on Civil Rights which had to do with the District of Columbia.
4. What advantages did Puerto Rico gain and lose by deciding to become a commonwealth instead of a state?

EXTEND YOUR VOCABULARY

territory	unincorporated territory	trusteeship
commonwealth		territorial courts

YOUR NOTEBOOK: THE GOVERNMENT OF ——

1. When did your state become a state? What was its status before that?
2. List the steps by which your state agitated for, applied for, and was finally granted statehood.

352

READ MORE ABOUT IT

BURNS, JAMES M., and PELTASON, JACK W., *Government by the People*. Prentice-Hall, 1954. Chap. 5.

DEPARTMENT OF STATE, *The United States and Non-self Governing Territories*. Government Printing Office, 1947.
Useful handbook.

SWARTHOUT, JOHN M., and BARTLEY, ERNEST R., *Principles and Problems of American National Government*. Oxford University Press, 1955. Chaps. 4-5.

THINK ABOUT

THE NATURE OF OUR GOVERNMENT

It is fitting and proper that the document used to introduce a unit entitled THE NATURE OF OUR GOVERNMENT should be the Constitution of the United States, especially the Preamble, which states the purpose of what has been called (by English statesman William Gladstone), "the most wonderful work ever struck off at one time by the brain and purpose of man." Certainly it is a work which has kept up with the times. The chapters in this unit have showed how and why it has done so. Reread the Preamble and refer to the Constitution and the notes beside it as you work on the following activities.

1. In what ways does the Constitution help us to "establish justice"? What do you think is meant by "justice"? In answering this question, mention not only the structure discussed in the various chapters, but also the basic philosophy underlying the structure. There have been ups and downs in our achievement of this goal. Give specific instances of them.

2. Has the history of our country demonstrated that we are able to "promote the general Welfare"? Make a table of our advances in that direction, mentioning specific provisions of the Constitution which have been interpreted as the basis for each, as well as specific instances in history to illustrate each.

3. List as many meanings of "welfare" as you think are justified by the Constitution.

4. Write an essay on the "blessings of Liberty" secured for us and "our Posterity" by the Constitution and the form of government we have developed in this country. Compare with other forms of government.

5. Show how and why our government is a "democratic republic." List ways in which our Constitution makes it a republic; ways in which it makes it a *democratic* republic.

FORM 262A .54-5M

Mr. STUART GERRY BROWN

of 822 MAR

Sir—You have been drawn to serve as a

to be held at the Court House in Syracuse, on the

at 9:45 o'clock A.M., whereat you are required to

Report to Supreme Court
JURORS ROOM No. ~~311~~ 317

YOU

AND YOUR

GOVERNMENT

Unit III

CHAPTER *15*

Citizenship

In this chapter you will learn about

How the idea of citizenship developed
Citizens and their rights
Who are citizens and who are not
Naturalization
Responsibilities of Citizenship
  1. under law   2. voluntary
Privileges of citizenship

The best-known but perhaps the least-understood idea in American political thought and life is the idea of **citizenship.** You probably think of citizenship as voting on election day, paying taxes on time, obeying the law, respecting property, and other related activities which everybody expects everybody else to do without much question. And you are partly right. These things are, of course, included in the idea of citizenship, and no one would deny their importance in the United States or in any other democratic society. You have only begun to define the term, however, for these activities do not convey the essential meaning with which we are concerned. The word **citizenship** refers to the status of a person in his social order. It must be distinguished from such words as **slave, alien,** or **subject.**

THE DEVELOPMENT OF CITIZENSHIP

In the fifth century B.C., Athens was the strongest of the city-states (or small nations) into which Greece was divided. In Athens, which was a republic, the idea of citizenship first arose. The people were divided into four classes: women, slaves, aliens, and citizens.

Strangely enough, *women* had no legal standing in one of the most highly developed cultures in history. They could not take part in public life. Except for religious festivals, they seldom left their houses. A Greek proverb of the day was: "Silence graces woman." **Slaves**—forced, unpaid laborers captured in war—though generally well treated and sometimes well educated, were treated as the property of their owners, and had no rights. **Aliens** were simply strangers who lived in Athens, mostly as merchants, bankers, artisans, and skilled craftsmen. They had no voice or vote in public affairs, although they were taxed and sometimes had to serve in the army.

Citizens were the important people in Athens. They voted, held office, took part in debate and public discussion, served in the military establishment, owned property, engaged in business or professions, and used the courts. The citizens were the **body politic**, that is, the **republic**. Citizenship was a mark of great distinction; a severe punishment for crime was taking away citizenship. The obligations of citizenship were also great. Citizens had the responsibility for good government in the city and for its destiny in both war and peace. That is, the idea of citizenship meant the condition of sharing public power, exercising it in the common interest, and receiving the privileges and protection of the state.

In Rome, too, when it was a republic, the citizen had privileges and responsibilities not enjoyed by aliens or slaves. We inherited our ideas of citizenship, however, directly from the English. Englishmen struggled with their kings for centuries to establish "the rights of free-born Englishmen." **Magna Carta** in 1215 and the common law in the following centuries gradually strengthened these rights against the power of the king. Under Magna Carta, for example, no freeman could be arrested, imprisoned, or deprived of his property unless he was immediately sent before a court of his equals for a trial. At that same time in France (and for almost six centuries after), the king could arrest anyone he wished and hold him in prison as long as he wished without trial. He did not even have to let the arrested man know the charges against him.

The Mayflower Compact

The English colonists in America naturally followed the English tradition. In 1620 the colonists in Plymouth signed the Mayflower Compact, saying: "[we] solemnly and mutually . . . covenant and combine ourselves together into a civil Body Politick for better Ordering and Preservation, and Furtherance of the Ends aforesaid; And by virtue hereof do enact, constitute, and frame, such just and equal Laws, Ordinances, Acts, Constitutions, and Offices, from time to time, as shall be thought most meet and convenient for the general Good of the Colony; unto which we promise all due Submission and Obedience. . . ."

The key word in this landmark in the literature of freedom is **covenant.**
We would say **contract** today. The point about making a contract is that the
parties who enter into it do so because they wish to do so. There is no such
thing as a contract made under compulsion. One who makes a contract is a
freeman, free to enter into the agreement. To appreciate the meaning of
citizenship, we must understand the importance of the action of the Plymouth
colonists. They formed a society in accordance with their own wishes and in
their own interest. They did this as free men entitled to manage their
affairs in any way they chose. They met together as equals, and assumed equal
responsibilities for their equal protection. In many ways the "Body Politick"
they formed was like a Greek city-state, and the Pilgrims themselves were
the citizens.

The Fundamental Orders of Connecticut

A few years later, still another group of Englishmen moved down the
Connecticut Valley from Massachusetts Bay and founded their own "plantation," at Hartford, Connecticut, on January 14, 1639. Their contract, known
as **The Fundamental Orders of Connecticut,** contains language very similar
to that of the Mayflower Compact: ". . . there should be an orderly and
decent Government established according to God, to order and dispose of
the affayres of the people. . . ." And "[we] doe therefore assotiate and
conioyne our selves to be as one Publike State or Commonwelth; . . .
and enter into Combination and Confederation together."

The signers of this document considered themselves free-born Englishmen
entitled to enter into an agreement for the management of their public
affairs. Though subjects of the king, they nonetheless took it for granted
that they had the right to establish a government according to their own wisdom and pleasure—and that it was the will of God that they should do so.
The establishment of government in Connecticut on this basis is a long step
toward the modern American idea of citizenship. Neither slaves, nor aliens,
nor subjects of a despot could think of acting in such a manner.

Changes in England

In the meantime, in England the status of free-born Englishmen was
rapidly changing. After much turmoil in the "Glorious Revolution" of
1688–1689, King William III and Queen Mary II came to the throne of
England. They became rulers on the invitation of Parliament and under
the terms set down by Parliament. Thus constitutional monarchy (see Chap.
2) was established. Parliament's terms were the rights stated in the "Bill of
Rights." These rights will be considered in Chapter 16; they are mentioned
here because the "Bill of Rights" was an expression of the belief in the
existence of a body of powers and privileges which were the rights of "free-
born Englishmen."

Developments in America

The colonists of New England—and of Virginia—appealing to traditional English rights and freedoms, considered themselves free to enter into contracts for the establishment of governments. Not all the people of the new world were citizens in our modern understanding of the word, however. Slaves and indentured servants in the colonies were denied some of the privileges of citizenship. The large group of freemen—chiefly dock workers, fishermen, sailors, tenant farmers, and farm laborers—enjoyed most of the traditional rights of Englishmen, but since they were not property owners, they were not allowed to vote.

At the time of the American Revolution, the right to vote was commonly restricted to persons who owned at least a specified amount of property, as we saw in Chapter 3. There was even a period in Massachusetts when every voter had to be a member of the established church. Thus, in one way or another, large numbers of individuals throughout the colonies were barred from the right to vote. The *methods* of government used by our colonial ancestors involved the *forms of democracy* to a considerable extent but excluded many inhabitants from participation in government. Few people were actually citizens and able to claim these rights for themselves.

Yet American colonials of the eighteenth century were in many ways nearer to the modern idea of democratic citizens than most people had ever been. The American Revolution is all the more remarkable a landmark in the history of freedom and citizenship because it was made by a relatively free people who wished to extend their freedom still further. The Declaration of Independence declared the equality of human beings and stated that they were entitled to equal rights and liberties. In an important sense, it was a declaration of war aims. Once the support of common men had been enlisted in the cause, it would become impossible to return entirely to the old ways. Reforms at home would be required to satisfy a people who had fought for and won independence. And new governments would be needed to replace those which had served the purpose of the people when they were English colonists.

The question of who should establish the new governments again raised the question of who was a citizen and what were the rights of citizens in a brand-new country. The Americans could no longer appeal to the "rights of free-born Englishmen"; they were no longer Englishmen! The Revolution required us to work out our own meanings of citizenship, rights, and duties.

New Constitutions

In Virginia the legislature had adopted a "Declaration of Rights" in 1776, less than a month before the Declaration of Independence was adopted. In the second paragraph it stated:

That all power is vested in, and consequently derived from, the people; that magistrates are their trustees and servants, and at all times amenable to them.

"The people" as used in this "Declaration of Rights" and in other documents of the period really meant only the part of the people with enough property to vote or hold office. For a long time, the idea prevailed that "those who own the country ought to govern it." But when the laws of Virginia and other states were revised, the amount of property necessary for voting was reduced. In 1780 the people of Massachusetts adopted a new constitution. Though it stated property requirements for voting and officeholding, its preamble shows clearly how the idea of the citizen was taking on broader meaning. Here is the second paragraph:

The body-politic is formed by a voluntary association of individuals; it is a social compact by which the whole people covenants with each citizen and each citizen with the whole people that all shall be governed by certain laws for the common good. It is the duty of the people, therefore, in framing a constitution of government, to provide for an equitable mode of making laws, as well as for an impartial interpretation and a faithful execution of them; that every man may, at all times, find his security in them.

In such a passage as this, the idea of citizenship is well on the way to its present meaning. The changes caused by the Revolution brought citizenship closer to this broader idea. The entrance of new states into the Union also brought more democracy. The first two new states to join the Union, Vermont and Kentucky, gave the vote to all free white males. Other new states did the same.

There was still much to be done before every resident of the United States could become a citizen. In particular, American Negroes and American women have had a long struggle to achieve the full rights of citizenship, as we shall see in Chapter 16.

CITIZENSHIP AND LOYALTY

Some people find it difficult to understand that allegiance to the United States, which is required of all citizens, may include the right to find fault with injustice or with wrongdoing in the United States. Loyalty, thus, means devotion to or allegiance to those principles and ideals for which our country stands. At any one time, almost 50 percent of our people may be dissatisfied with the results of an election. They voted for the candidate who lost;

they may work to defeat the winner in the next election. But this is in no way disloyalty to the United States.

Loyalty, as explained here, means respect, devotion, allegiance. It is *voluntary*. We give respect and devotion to our country because we wish to do so. This is not the same thing as the forced show of allegiance which the subjects of a dictator must display toward their leaders. These people must pretend that the dictator's government is never wrong, that nothing should be improved. That is a totalitarian definition of loyalty, not our kind. In such a society, he who dares to find fault with the deeds, policies, or personalities of the leaders is disloyal. When Juan Peron was dictator of Argentina, he put out of business newspapers which were critical of his government. A few years later the government of General Pinilla, in Colombia, suppressed an opposition newspaper which refused to publish an apology dictated by the government censor. Read your own newspapers to see how critical some of them can be toward the persons who hold office in federal, state, or local government in our country. They are critical, even hostile, but criticism and hostility do not equal treason, or disloyalty.

Problem of Loyalty in a Democracy

You can now see why the emergence of communism and fascism in the twentieth century has produced such great problems of loyalty for free nations, including the United States. People who accept the doctrines of communism or fascism are not loyal to the democratic processes of government and the ideals of individual liberty, even though they may claim to be. They are glad to make use of our liberties of speech, press, and assembly, but their purpose is to set up a government which would do away with precisely those liberties. Thus it is not because Communists and Fascists propose ideas which are unpopular or radical that they are considered subversive. Rather it is because they would establish by force if they could a system in which no ideas except theirs could be heard.

You may ask, What about the right of our citizens to make drastic changes and reforms? That right still exists, as strong as ever. In fact, it was written into our Constitution by the framers in 1787. Read Article V carefully. You will see that it provides the machinery for amending the Constitution in any way the people choose, except that it forbids us to take away the equal voice of the states in the Senate. By amendment we can adopt any policy, no matter how radically it might alter our accustomed way of life.

Loyalty and Ideas

Violence against the government has always been a crime. In 1940 the Congress passed a law (the Smith Act) which makes it a crime to "conspire to teach or advocate the overthrow of the government by force or violence." This law is aimed at people who wish to change our form of government by secret means, who could not openly persuade a majority to agree with them, and who are not willing to abide by the peaceful decisions of the democratic process. Under this law, a number of Communists have been tried, convicted, and sent to prison. They were convicted not because they wished to change our form of government or our policies, but because they refused to abide by the will of the majority and engaged in a conspiracy to overthrow the government or preached the overthrow of government by force.

People who believe in democracy are not afraid of *ideas*, no matter how radical. As Jefferson said in his First Inaugural Address, "If there be any among us who would wish to dissolve this union or to change its republican form, let them stand undisturbed as monuments of the safety with which error of opinion may be tolerated where reason is left free to combat it." President Jefferson, however, was thinking of people willing to stand up and be counted for their principles, not of those who work secretly either to overthrow the government or to inspire others to do so. The majority of Americans in our time have felt that measures like the Smith Act are necessary because of the conspiratorial nature of our Communist enemies. In recent decisions, the Supreme Court has reminded us that free speech is still the best answer to the opponents of freedom, and has warned us that too great stress on security is like too much of anything else—it can bring down on our heads the very troubles we are trying to avoid.

Security in the National Government

Some security measures are necessary, however. To protect us against subversion and betrayal by any who may be unwilling to accept the discipline of democratic citizenship, our government has a system for carefully screening its employees. Investigations are conducted by the F.B.I., the Civil Service Commission, or the intelligence services of the military departments to make sure that employees are loyal citizens. If they hold positions in which they would handle government secrets, they must be not only loyal but positively not "security risks." The latter term means a person who, though loyal, has some weakness of character or behavior which makes it uncertain that he can keep a secret—he may drink too much, for example. Such people are not allowed in "sensitive" positions in the government.

From time to time the security system has accused or even dismissed people on inaccurate evidence. Reliance on unidentified informers has been seriously criticized. To make the system as fair as possible, the government allows those who may be declared "security risks" to appeal. All decisions on these matters are subject to a final appeal to the Supreme Court. It speaks well for our government and for our devotion to freedom that only a tiny handful of loyalty or security risks have ever been found—a few thousand out of millions. The best protection a government can have is the devotion of its citizens—devotion freely given because the citizens are free.

CITIZENS OF THE UNITED STATES TODAY

Citizenship is an idea which can have meaning only in a land of freedom, or apply only to those who are free. It means the freedom to enter into agreements, to share in the power and authority of government, and to exercise the liberties established by laws. Citizens are those who are governed by their own consent. The children born in the United States are called citizens (see Amendment XIV, pp. 64–65, but until they reach the age of 21 (18 in Georgia and Kentucky), they are denied by state laws a number of the other privileges accorded to adult citizens, such as holding office and voting.

Citizenship means also the obligations and responsibilities to maintain public order, to enforce the laws, and to conduct public affairs generally. It is the responsibility of all citizens to see to it that the purposes for which our national government was established are carried out—a more perfect union, justice, domestic tranquillity, defense, the general welfare, the blessings of liberty. The *idea of citizenship,* with some of its roots in ancient Greece and others in English history, as we have seen, has rich and rather complex meanings. Citizenship in our republic has come, indeed, to be a most desirable possession. Millions of people in lands where they are oppressed would give much for the rich heritage of American citizenship which so many of us have acquired by no effort of our own.

From 1789 until 1868 the legal question of citizenship was left largely up to the states. The original text of the Constitution does not say who is to be a citizen. Amendment XIV, adopted in 1868, established constitutional definitions:

Sec. 1. All persons born or naturalized in the United States, and subject to the jurisdiction thereof, are citizens of the United States and of the State wherein they reside. No State shall make or enforce any law which shall abridge the privileges or immunities of citizens of the United States; nor shall any State deprive any person of life, liberty, or property, without due process of law; nor deny to any person within its jurisdiction the equal protection of the laws.

Thus citizenship comes either from **birth** or from **naturalization.** Article I, Section 8, Clause 4, of the Constitution had provided in the beginning that Congress should have power "to establish an uniform rule of naturalization." In its simplest terms, this means that Congress shall make the laws

363

RESPONSIBILITIES OF THE CITIZEN

Citizenship is a precious privilege, but it must be worked at to provide continuity and attain meaning. The responsibilities of citizenship are numerous and varied. Many of them are directly tied up with the rights we enjoy. To protect these rights, we must work assiduously in discharging our responsibilities. The League of Women Voters' representative is discharging both facets of this when she works at persuading people to register so that they can exercise their right and duty to vote.

The right of education, one of the cornerstones of American democracy, must be worked at if it is to be effective. Citizens must take an intelligent interest in what goes on in schools, to ensure adequate facilities and teachers so that the best possible education can be given to their children. Here the New York State Citizens Committee for Public Schools meets to plan ways to improve their school systems.

Good citizenship is also displayed by the Better Business Bureau which is vigilant in protecting citizens from fraudulent advertising or business practices.

364

Informed citizens also have duties beyond local interests. Audiences at UN meetings can be alerted to events and ideas if they not only attend meetings such as this, but take pains to keep themselves intelligently informed about them.

governing the process by which a person not born in the United States may become a citizen—or be refused citizenship. In the period before the War Between the States, Congress made laws affecting immigration and naturalization, while the states determined other questions of citizenship. Amendment XIV brought the definition of citizenship into the Constitution itself.

By Birth

What is meant by citizenship by birth? An American becomes a citizen through birth in the United States or in territories which are subject to the jurisdiction of the United States. To be a citizen by birth, not only must a child be born in this country or one of its territories, but the parents must be permanently subject to the jurisdiction of the United States. Thus a child born to French tourists would not be a citizen, nor would the child of the French Ambassador living in the United States. The child of an alien resident of the United States does become a citizen, even though the parents have not been, or may not be, naturalized. You may have read about the most decorated unit in the United States Army during World War II. It was made up entirely of Japanese-Americans, citizens whose parents under the law of that time were not allowed to become naturalized.

Children born of American parents living abroad are by law citizens under certain conditions. If both parents are American citizens and normally live in the United States, there is no question. If only one parent is an American, the child may be a citizen (if he chooses) if the American parent has lived in the United States for ten or more years, of which five are after the age of sixteen. In this case, however, the child himself must live in this country for at least five years between the ages of thirteen and twenty-one or his citizenship is forfeited. All these conditions do not apply if the child is born of parents who are living abroad as representatives of the United States government. This is because official members of the American government are considered to be living under our jurisdiction wherever they may be sent on an official assignment.

By Naturalization

A great majority of citizens attain their citizenship through birth. Congress may also confer citizenship upon the inhabitants of a territory. The rest of our citizens have had to win their citizenship through the process of naturalization. In the early days of our republic, some Americans thought that anyone who wished to become a citizen, who would swear to abide by the laws, and who would declare his willingness to bear arms in defense of the United States should be admitted to citizenship without other requirement. On the other hand, other early statesmen believed that it was such a privilege that people wanting it should serve a long apprenticeship before being admitted to citizenship. At one time people had to live in the United States for fourteen years before they could become citizens. Today's law, as we shall see, is a kind of compromise between the two views.

Until recently we as a nation thought that people of certain races should be barred from the opportunity to become naturalized. During World War II we found ourselves fighting a war in the Far East where China was our principal ally. At the same time we refused to naturalize—or admit—Chinese people. A great many Americans had long been dissatisfied with such a policy, and in 1943 Congress voted to permit the naturalization of Chinese. Since then the same privilege has been extended (1952) to Filipinos, Asian Indians, Koreans, and Japanese.

If you were an alien who had come to the United States under the immigration quota for your country (Congress fixes the number of immigrants from each country who may be admitted each year), you could obtain your citizenship in the following way. You would appear before the clerk in any court of law (above the level of justice-of-the-peace court) and declare your intention to become a citizen. A preliminary examination of your character and sincerity would be made. You would probably enroll in an evening course at your local high school to study American government, particularly the Constitution, since you are required by law to understand it before being admitted to citizenship. After you have lived at least five years in the United States—but not more than seven years—you again go to court. This time you must be accompanied by two American citizens who will swear to your loyalty to the United States and certify your character and residence here for the required number of years. You renounce allegiance to the country from which you came and take an oath to uphold the laws, not to engage in subversive activity, and to bear arms in defense of the United States if required. There follows a waiting period of ninety days during which your application is checked by the Immigration and Naturalization Service in the Department of Justice (see Chap. 10). If the investigation shows you to be worthy of citizenship, and if the judge is satisfied from questions and a written examination that you are literate, that you understand the fundamentals of the history and government of this country, and that you meet all the other requirements, the judge gives you the oath of allegiance and issues to you a certificate of citizenship.

In wartime, the process of becoming a naturalized citizen is considerably simplified and speeded up for aliens who serve in the American armed forces.

A naturalized citizen is entitled to the same privileges as a citizen by birth, with two major exceptions. He may not become President of the United States (Article II). He may, since he has taken an oath, be deported if he violates that oath. Thus if he commits certain crimes, or engages in efforts to overthrow the government, he may be deported. In this connection, you should note that the record of naturalized citizens, both in obedience to law and in loyalty to the United States, is as good as the record of native-born citizens.

By Derivation and by Marriage

Two other ways of gaining citizenship need to be mentioned. One is called **citizenship by derivation**. This applies to children who were born abroad of naturalized parents. Such children, if *under* eighteen years of age, become citizens when their parents' naturalization is completed. If they are *over* eighteen, they themselves must go through the naturalization process. The other case is that of marriage to an American citizen. Before 1922 the citizenship of the wife depended on that of the husband; a woman who married a citizen became a citizen. Now, under the terms of the Nationality Act of 1940, an alien man or woman who marries an American citizen must be naturalized in order to become a citizen, but only one to three years' residence is required. During recent years, this has been an important law to many American families, for young men serving overseas in the armed forces have found wives in foreign countries.

In summary, American citizens today are: (1) those who are born in the United States or its possessions to parents who are subject to the jurisdiction of the United States; (2) those who are born elsewhere but become naturalized according to law; (3) those who "derive" their citizenship from the naturalization of their parents; and (4) those who are quickly naturalized after marrying American citizens.

As we saw earlier when we were discussing the idea of citizenship, the legal status of being a citizen is no more than the *beginning* of citizenship. For the American who is already a citizen, and for the alien who is applying for citizenship, the chief meanings of the word are in the responsibilities and privileges which go with being an American citizen.

THE RESPONSIBILITIES OF CITIZENSHIP

For every right, there is a duty. The right to a jury trial is a right for which English-speaking peoples have struggled since the days of King John. But of what importance to any of us is a jury trial unless persons of ability and character serve on the jury? In 1954, more than 700 years after Magna Carta, the newspapers reported that a man who neither spoke nor understood English served four times as foreman of a jury in a Canadian court, where the trials were carried on in English. Or you may have read of a case in which an American jury reached a decision quickly—and contrary to the facts of the case—because the jury members did not wish to remain indoors on a

368

"YOUR VOTE MAKES
YOUR GOVERNMENT."

Fitzpatrick in
The St. Louis Post-Dispatch

pleasant Saturday afternoon. We must wonder what happened to justice and to the rights of persons involved in the trial.

We have said much in this chapter about the right to vote. Suppose that Mrs. Smith, whose right to vote is a very new right in our country (Amendment XIX), goes to the polls at the time of a local election. She looks at her ballot and discovers that all the candidates are third-raters. Her choice is between the poorly qualified candidates of Party A and the poorly qualified candidates of Party B. Mrs. Smith may well decide that her voting privilege was hardly worth the effort which so many people put forth over so many years to get.

Mrs. Smith's feeling would be understandable; but she would be mistaken. The trouble is not with voting but with the citizens in the two parties who have been lazy and irresponsible in not striving to get the best possible candidates on the party tickets. Mrs. Smith's experience may not be typical, but it is true that this sort of thing does happen and does cause some people to feel that "democracy is fine in theory but will not work in practice." This is misleading. Democracy does not work by itself; it is the citizens who must work. They must work at the responsibilities of citizenship.

These responsibilities may be divided into two classes: those which are *compulsory*, and those which a citizen undertakes *voluntarily*. In general, we can say that the compulsory responsibilities are those which are written down in the law, on local, state, and national levels. There are two kinds of com-

369

pulsory responsibilities: **restrictive** and **constructive.** First let us examine the responsibilities of the citizen in his home community.

Compulsory Responsibility to Obey Laws

Everyone knows that one of the chief responsibilities of a citizen is to obey the law. Often we think of this statement in a negative way; that is, the law means No. Actually, as you learned in Chapter 9, most crimes are **not** prohibited by law. The law prescribes the penalties and punishments **if** you **do** commit crimes, but you are "free" to commit them. We must not, of course, commit crimes—such as stealing, setting fire to buildings, or urging the overthrow of government—but we sometimes overlook the reasons why. We may not steal our neighbor's property or set fire to his buildings without punishment because we would thereby deprive him of his right to own property. The overthrow of government would take away from us the agency whose job it is to protect and maintain our rights. For similar reasons we must not trespass, we must not exceed the speed limit or "go through" traffic lights, and so on.

RESTRICTIVE LAWS At the local level, as we have seen, the laws which regulate our behavior—to the advantage of all of us—are usually called ordinances. The **restrictive** laws place limitations on some of the freedoms of individuals in order to protect other freedoms of the rest of us. These are the regulations worked out by local government for the greatest welfare of everyone living in the local community. There are hundreds of such ordinances. They are not the same in all localities, since not all have the same problems or try the same way of regulating acts even in similar situations. Here are a few examples which may suggest the variety and importance of ordinances.

If you own a house on an ordinary city or village street, an ordinance may make you responsible for keeping your sidewalk in repair. If you allow it to break up, someone may injure himself in a fall. Such an ordinance protects you and your family, as well as others, since you must also depend on your neighbors to keep their sidewalks in good condition if you are to pass in safety. It is also common to require that you remove ice and snow from the sidewalk adjoining your property.

In the fall when you rake up your leaves, it might be convenient simply to burn the pile where it is. But in most communities there is an ordinance which forbids this because of the danger of spreading fire to nearby houses, including your own. In fact, a great many ordinances are against fire hazards. Thus there is almost always a "building code" which requires certain specifications on the kind of house or other building you may wish to erect in order to insure protection against fire.

Just as it is a violation falsely to shout "Fire!" in a theater, so the citizen's freedom is limited by ordinance when he is on the public streets. He may not obstruct traffic by conducting a meeting in an unauthorized place. He may not "jaywalk" without risking arrest. He may not block off the sidewalk with a display of his merchandise.

Many important ordinances are intended to protect health. The citizen is forbidden to throw garbage into the street. If his home is quarantined because some member of his family is suffering from a contagious disease, he must obey the regulations and he may not send his healthy children to school, even though it would be very helpful to him if he could.

Ordinances also regulate such matters as these:

ball playing in the streets
storage and sale of gasoline
driving of animals in the streets in droves of more than twenty
use of bicycles
displays of fireworks
zoning regulations
shaking dust mops from windows in crowded areas
operating a loud-speaker system

CONSTRUCTIVE LAWS   Among the constructive laws to which the citizen is responsible are those which levy taxes upon him. It is not enough to say that the good citizen pays his taxes on time. He is penalized if he does not do so. He should, moreover, understand that by paying taxes, he is making a positive contribution of the utmost importance to himself and to his community. Many of the good things of life which you take for granted are supported entirely by tax money. When you walk on a sidewalk or ride along the highway or city street in a car, you are sharing the benefits provided by taxpayers' money. Your place of residence is provided many services, such as fire protection, snow removal, garbage collection, rubbish collection, and police protection. Some or all of these, depending on where you live, are supported by tax money.

Other constructive laws are those relating to public education. All citizens, whether or not they have children who use the public schools, are required to pay taxes for the support of schools. This is their positive contribution to the general welfare. The laws of all the states also require children to go to school. Out of regard for our differences, however, the citizen is not required to send his children to public school, or to one particular kind of public school—if his community is large enough to maintain different kinds. The parent may, if he prefers, send his children to a church-supported school, or to one of the independent private schools. He may send the child to a public high school which concentrates on college preparation, or to a trade school, or to an agricultural school. Within one school the pupil may choose one of several programs of study, commercial, vocational, or academic. In short, in the interest of all of us, the law requires that young people receive an education. Out of respect for our different backgrounds, interests, and abilities, the law does not require us all to receive the same kind of education.

Voluntary Responsibilities

The second class of responsibilities of citizenship, which are not binding in law are voluntary. Unless the great majority of our citizens accepted them, however, we would shortly lose much of our freedom.

Three things of outstanding importance in the success or failure of our experiment in free government are almost wholly dependent upon the voluntary action of our citizens. These are *religion, social progress,* and *political organization.*

RELIGIOUS FREEDOM The variety and freedom of religion in the United States is one of the chief qualities accounting for the uniqueness of the American experiment, as we saw in Chapter 1. Our modern system (a system found in few countries of our world today) of voluntary support and attendance did not develop until after the time of the American Revolution. Amendment I to the Constitution provides that "Congress shall make no law respecting an establishment of religion, or prohibiting the free exercise thereof. . . ." As interpreted over the years by the Supreme Court, this clause has come to mean that religious activity must be private and separate from government. Thus the burden of supporting our churches and church-related institutions is borne by the church-goers. The sanctuaries, parish halls, meeting houses, school and college buildings, furnishings and equipment, salaries and homes of clergymen, salaries of other employees—all these and other expenses are paid out of the contributions of those whose beliefs lead them to give.

In the early days of the United States, many prominent men believed that churches should be supported by government lest they become so weakened that they would lose their influence for good in the country. This view was shared by men like John Adams, George Washington, and Patrick Henry. Men like Thomas Jefferson and James Madison opposed it. The latter argued that religion would become stronger if no one were forced to go to church or to pay for the support of religion. This view prevailed. In the United States, the government does not require anyone to support any church or, indeed, to pay any attention to religion unless he wishes to. Yet religious institutions flourish in the United States today. Catholic and Protestant churches and Jewish synagogues and temples have a higher proportion of the people as active church supporters than have those in many countries where churches are still established and supported by law.

SOCIAL RESPONSIBILITIES. *Social progress* includes the improvement of health, housing, recreational facilities, and educational and charitable activities. It is true that government bears an increasing burden of the cost for social services. Yet it is still an important fact that voluntary action through civic organizations contributes greatly to the social well-being of the American people.

All of us know what it means when we hear, "Mr. and Mrs. Doe are *civic-minded* citizens." We know that the term *civic-minded* is used to describe persons who work to make their community, state, and nation better places, not just for themselves but for their fellow citizens as well. Too often we may not know of or appreciate the benefits that come to us from the efforts of such people. They are the ones who serve without pay—and usually without praise or thanks—as library trustees, members of the school committee, aldermen, park commissioners, and members of one thousand and one committees which deal with such vital matters as our community's school building program, our drinking water supply, or civil defense. They put in the long hours of work necessary for carrying on the programs of the youth-service organizations, the PTA, and many others. They call on us for the money needed to conduct our settlement houses, homes for crippled children, scout and campfire groups, hospitals, disaster relief, educational television, the fight against polio. These people, the civic-minded, work without compensation for the Red Cross, and for the churches. They campaign for better schools, for playgrounds, for hospitals, for the cleanup of unsanitary conditions or of corruption in government. They pick up the broken glass some other person left on the beach. They may not make page one of the newspapers, but there are millions of such citizens, and they are indispensable in a free society.

The civic-minded individual working alone can accomplish very little as compared with what he can do when he associates himself with others who share his interest in those things which make a better society. Much work can best be done through organizations. We Americans are sometimes known as a nation of "joiners." Some of our organizations exist for the pleasure of the members; others have more serious purposes. An American citizen is not required to join any of them. It is the fact that we join voluntarily that gives our organizations their vitality. No nation has had so many organizations, or so many which perform useful public services. The overwhelming majority of us belong to at least one active organization. We can select representative groups almost at random:

The Lions, Kiwanis, and Rotary clubs are formed by business and professional men who voluntarily give both time and money to many different causes, such as extra milk for underprivileged children, athletic facilities for

You and others have

of Freedom of Speech

...the right to say what you and they believe is true, right, and worth saying.

b

to Vote

...to take part in picking people who are to hold the elective positions in your government, and to have your vote counted honestly.

b

to Equality of Opportunity

...the right to a fair chance to make good in school, in employment, in civic life.

but

you must make the most of your abilities, make an honest effort to succeed on merit. (The world does not owe you a living.)

the right ...

you must try to find out what is true and think carefully about what is right and important.

and you must not do anything as an individual or member of a group to take away from others their right to say what they believe is true and right — even if they disagree with you.

you should do your best to find out which parties and which candidates are best for the general good; and then cast your vote.

and you must not deprive others of their right to vote and have their votes counted honestly. You should not support officials who deprive others of this right, by discrimination or by fraud.

and you must not through discrimination deprive others of their chance to make good.

"This company will not hire people who are different from ME — in religion, race, national origin, political belief."

boys and girls, and entertainment for people who cannot afford it. These service clubs also frequently are the leaders in planning broad community improvement.

A fraternal organization like the Shriners provides medical and orthopedic care for crippled children. Women's organizations like Zonta, or the Business and Professional Women's Clubs, raise money for scholarships to send deserving girls to college, and perform many other socially useful functions. The League of Women Voters, a non-partisan organization, works constantly for adult education, better citizenship, and the improvement of schools and other local services.

The American Legion encourages the acceptance of civic responsibility by awarding medals for good citizenship, and has contributed greatly to health and sportsmanship, as well as to reducing juvenile delinquency, by sponsoring amateur baseball for teen-age boys. Baseball fans can thank the Legion for starting in baseball many of our famous big league stars.

Two other quite different kinds of organization need to be mentioned here. Each of the professions has at least one association which brings its members together primarily for the purpose of setting and maintaining standards of excellence and encouraging the advancement of knowledge. The American Medical Association and the Society of Chemical Engineers, as examples, have a great influence on American life. Our knowledge of medicine and our scientific skills and accomplishments are continually improved by the efforts of such organizations. Another type of voluntary activity is the organization of groups to support the fight against major diseases.

Such a list as this could go on and on. The few examples given help to show how enormously America has benefited by the voluntary and cooperative work done by people like ourselves. The responsibilities to do such work are not included in any legal **definition** of citizenship, but the meaning of citizenship in our country cannot be completely expressed without them.

POLITICAL RESPONSIBILITIES   In the field of voluntary citizen activity our *political* organization is a third important responsibility. The governments under which we live are established by constitutional agreements. Under these agreements we elect many officials; they in turn appoint others. We choose our elected officials and express approval and disapproval of their performance in government through political parties. These parties are not established by constitutions. They are created and kept going by the voluntary activities of citizens. The parties provide our candidates for offices and many of the officials who are appointed. The parties also greatly influence our policies, both foreign and domestic, and accept the responsibilities of power when in office.

No law requires the American citizen to be a Democrat, a Republican, or a member of any other party. But so long as we differ among ourselves on important (or unimportant!) public questions, the parties will be needed.

They in turn will continue to need citizens as working members. We shall have much more to say about this in Chapter 18.

The citizen has responsibility to vote in *all* elections—and this includes the primaries. And he should give some time and money to his party. No government can be better or wiser than the people it represents. In the United States the *voluntary participation of the citizens in the political process is a high responsibility of citizenship.*

THE PRIVILEGES OF CITIZENSHIP

All who live in the United States, citizens and non-citizens, are entitled to the equal protection of the laws. No nation is perfect, and we sometimes are guilty of discrimination and unfair application of the laws. But no nation distributes justice more equitably than the United States or gives to everyone a fairer opportunity to be heard. In general, the law falls evenly on rich and poor alike. One of the privileges of residence in the United States and of citizenship is and must be the right to a fair and speedy trial on those occasions when we are accused of violation of the law. We are also privileged, both citizen and alien, to go into court to win damages against someone who has injured us, or destroyed our property, or damaged our reputation. It has long been a matter of pride to Americans that the privilege of obtaining justice has been offered to all persons under our flag.

There are other privileges which are available only to citizens. These help to make American citizenship a prize worth almost any price. Only the citizen may vote in elections of government officials and take part, through party organizations, in the selection of candidates and the making of policies. Thus he, not the alien, shares in the power of government.

The citizen also has the privilege of seeking public office. Not all will be successful, but some must be elected to our legislative, executive, and judicial positions. There are also many appointive offices, usually requiring special training or certain abilities, to which only citizens may be appointed. Positions in key defense industries may also be reserved for citizens.

Another privilege of the American citizen may not occur to you at all, unless you wish to travel abroad—the privilege of holding a **passport** (a document authorizing you to travel in foreign countries). In fact, the Supreme Court has said that a passport is a "natural right" of free citizens, and unless you have violated some law, the Department of State will grant you one. In many countries citizens can obtain passports only with great difficulty or not at all.

Our citizens possess other privileges they have been willing to share with all who live here. First among these is freedom of worship, a great privilege with centuries of religious oppression behind it! Further, our people have not only the right of expressing their views but also the rights of silence and privacy. Last of all, we have the privilege of owning property—a little-appreciated right. To the Communist, private property is an evil, the cause of much of the evil of the world. To us, the opportunity to acquire and use property is one we have protected by the law and the courts. In Amendment V of our Constitution is included a provision forbidding the government to deprive any person of life, liberty, or *property* without due process of law. This provision, among others, makes life in America the dream of many oppressed people throughout the world.

SUMMARY

If someone were to ask you what it means to be an American citizen, you know that mere legal definitions of citizenship will not do. In order to understand how citizenship developed, both as an idea and as a reality, and to grasp the important point that it is still developing, ancient Greek and Roman experience as well as English history before 1776 are helpful. The American Revolution and the Constitution did not bring this history to an end. You have seen how more and more people have been included as citizens of our democracy, although some may not fully enjoy all the privileges of citizenship. You have studied the ways in which one becomes a citizen—birth, naturalization, derivation, and marriage. You have studied the responsibilities and privileges of citizenship in the United States. You will perhaps understand better now why it is that so many people from oppressed areas in the world rate American citizenship as a very high prize and would make almost any sacrifice to get it.

KNOW WHAT YOU READ

1. In what ways is a citizen different from a slave, alien, or subject?
2. Contrast the rights and responsibilities of the Athenians with those of people living in other parts of the world at the same time.
3. What was the *idea of citizenship* developed in ancient Athens?
4. Why did it mean a great deal to be a citizen in the Roman republic?
5. What classes of people were guaranteed rights in the *Magna Carta?*
6. When the early Americans spoke of their rights as "free-born Englishmen," what did they mean?
7. What is the importance of the fact that the men of the Mayflower made a covenant, or contract?

8. "Neither slaves, nor aliens, nor subjects of a despot could think of acting in such a manner." What is the importance of the *Fundamental Orders of Connecticut?*

9. In the years before the revolution, most colonists did not have one of the basic rights of citizenship. Which right did they lack?

10. Why is the Declaration of Independence important in the story of the development of the idea of citizenship?

11. What important parts of the idea of citizenship are found in (a) the Virginia Declaration of Rights; (b) the Massachusetts Constitution?

12. What changes made it possible for nearly all Americans to participate in government by voting?

13. Write out your best definition of loyalty. Make your definition so complete that it will answer any questions your classmates may raise about finding fault with our government, working against your elected leaders, or trying to change the ways in which we do things in our country.

14. Explain how changes may be made under our system of government by using our freedoms and not by using violence.

15. What does the law of the United States say about conspiracy to overthrow the government or teaching the overthrow of the government by force?

16. What is meant by *security?*

17. What is a security risk? Why is the problem of security so complicated today?

18. Summarize what is meant by the *idea of citizenship* in the United States today.

19. Who, according to the Constitution, are citizens of the United States?

20. Contrast the USSR and the USA views on the ownership of property.

21. What must a person do today to become a citizen by naturalization?

22. The rights of the naturalized citizen are not quite the same as those of the citizen-by-birth. Explain.

23. Your responsibilities as a citizen may be divided into two classes. What are the two? Illustrate.

24. What responsibilities of citizens are being carried out by such organizations as 4-H clubs? Veterans organizations? Professional organizations?

25. Name some of our greatest freedoms which we take for granted. Why do we do so?

26. Why are all citizens—even those who do not have children—expected to support public schools?

27. What does the Constitution say about religion? What does this mean?

28. How did Adams and Washington want churches to be supported? How are they supported?

29. Henry Jones is an enthusiastic member of a political party. He admits that being a good party member is hard work. Why is this so?

30. What privileges are shared by both aliens and citizens? What privileges are reserved for citizens only?

31. Why is it that civic-minded citizens join organizations? Name some of the organizations which work to make life better for other people.

WHAT DO YOU THINK?

1. Explain "Democracy does not work by itself; it is the citizen who must work."
2. Once an alien has earned the right to become an American citizen, should he then have the same rights as persons who are citizens by birth?
3. Should citizens whose children do not use the public schools be required to pay taxes for the support of these schools? Would you reason the same way concerning persons who do not benefit directly from lighthouses, roads, dams, old age assistance, public parks, and other services?
4. Does Jefferson's idea that "error of opinion may be tolerated where reason is left free to combat it" hold true today?
5. Twelve-year-old Marie was born in France. She now lives in the United States with her parents who have just become citizens by naturalization. Is Marie a citizen? Why?
6. A famous American has said that taxes are the price we pay for civilization. Do you agree with this?

PROBLEMS AND PROJECTS FOR YOU

1. Report to the class on the government of ancient Athens, showing particularly the activities and responsibilities of the citizens.
2. What rights did Saint Paul have as a Roman citizen which he would not have had had he not been a citizen?
3. Make an original poster urging citizens to vote and vote wisely.
4. Study the Declaration of Independence to find the "rights of Englishmen" which are mentioned or suggested in that document.
5. Investigate either of the following and report your findings to the class:
   (a) Americanization classes in your community
   (b) naturalization proceedings in your community
6. Interview people in your neighborhood to find out their ideas on why so many people do not vote. Set up a panel discussion on this question.
7. "For every right there is a duty." Make a list of 15 rights which you believe are important to you. After each of these rights, write the corresponding duties which also belong to you. See drawing on pp. 374–375.
8. In this chapter, the authors have discussed a number of rights and responsibilities of a citizen in general. From a study of this chapter, make a list of all of those rights which are yours now.
9. Make a list of the "social progress" activities which are carried on in your community. Compare your list with that of the textbook.

EXTEND YOUR VOCABULARY

city-state
aliens
citizens
body politic
Magna Carta
Mayflower Compact
compact
covenant

Fundamental Orders of
   Connecticut
commonwealth
constitutional monarchy
loyalty
security
naturalization
quota
citizenship by derivation

restrictive laws
ordinance
constructive laws
establishment of religion
social progress
civic-minded citizen
political responsibility
passport

YOUR NOTEBOOK: THE GOVERNMENT OF ——

1. Does your school district carry on Americanization programs for aliens? If so, who is in charge of the program? What training must the teachers have?
2. Who make the *ordinances* for the place in which you live?
3. Make a list of the organizations in your community through which "civic-minded citizens" may promote the welfare of their fellow citizens.
4. What percentage of the eligible voters in your state and community voted in the most recent state and local elections?

READ MORE ABOUT IT

Burns, James M., and Peltason, Jack W., *Government by the People*. Prentice-Hall, 1954. Chaps. 7–9

Gosnell, Harold F., *Democracy, The Threshold of Freedom*. Ronald Press, 1948. Useful and readable study of the citizen as voter and participant in the legislative process.

Irish, Marian D., and Prothro, James W., *The Politics of American Democracy*. Prentice-Hall, 1959. Chap. 7.

Konvitz, Milton, *Civil Rights in Immigration*. Cornell University Press, 1953. Advanced study of the problems of aliens coming to this country.

Merriam, Charles E., and Merriam, Robert, *American Government: Democracy in Action*. Ginn, 1954. Chaps. 2–5.
A fine study of the citizen and his government.

Ranney, Austin, *The Governing of Men*. Holt, 1958. Chap. 8.

Swarthout, John M., and Bartley, Ernest R., *Principles and Problems of American National Government*. Oxford University Press, 1955. Chaps. 5–6.

CHAPTER 16

Civil Rights and Liberties

In this chapter you will learn about

Civil liberties as tools of democracy

Voting

Freedom of speech, press, and assembly under Amendments I and XIV

Amendments II and III

Procedural rights

Civil rights and discrimination

In recent years there have been some well-publicized cases in Bulgaria and Hungary in which religious leaders have been forced to make long and strange "confessions." It is no secret that in Spain minority religious groups have suffered from hostile governmental policies, while in the Soviet Union the general absence of civil liberties and civil rights is well known. In some Latin-American countries, newspapers are controlled by the government. In many countries today, the government may do with its people just about anything its leaders wish.

The United States is one of too small a number of countries wherein individuals do have rights, where they may successfully defend their rights even against their own leaders. Here the citizens may, by established legal machinery, change the form or the leadership of their governments. The civil liberties of Americans are the tools of democracy. Without them we could neither change a government that became oppressive nor protect ourselves, as individuals, against it. Because we do have these liberties and rights, we should study them, understand them, and use them wisely.

The terms **civil liberties** and **civil rights** are frequently confused and frequently used interchangeably. In this book, when we speak of **civil liberties,** we mean the freedoms of Americans to *do* certain things—especially freedom to vote and freedom to speak, publish, assemble peaceably, and worship according to our preferences—all guaranteed by Amendment I (see p. 62). When we speak of **civil rights,** we mean personal protections against discrimination or arbitrary treatment by government—rights guaranteed to us by other amendments in our Bill of Rights.

We have already seen how democracy has developed in our republic by the passage of laws to give citizens more political rights—especially the right to vote. We have spoken briefly several times about voting, but we must now consider the privilege of voting more carefully.

PROCESS OF VOTING

The right to vote in free elections is the chief means by which Americans participate directly in the affairs of their government. Since the United States has a republican form of government, government itself is carried on by **representatives** of the people and by the appointees of representatives. Thus the ability of the people to *choose their representatives and to change them through free elections* is the basis of our free government.

Do you remember the distinction made in Chapter 15 between **citizens** and **non-citizens?** The requirements for citizenship are set by the federal government under provisions of the Constitution and by-laws enacted by the Congress. Only citizens may vote. It does not follow that *all* citizens may vote. The decision as to which citizens may vote was left, under the Constitution, among the powers **reserved** to the states (see Chap. 4). This has resulted in 50 different sets of laws regarding eligibility to vote—even to vote for national officials.

We have seen briefly, on pp. 83–84, how the privilege of voting has been gradually extended until, by the middle of the twentieth century, legal obstacles to voting by duly qualified citizens have been almost entirely removed. Criminals, insane people, and aliens are not allowed to vote.

In order to prepare yourself to be a voter, you should consult the officials of the election board in your city or town, since each state has different election laws. Copies of state election laws and handbooks for voters are usually readily available from such local officials. Some ways of electing our public servants are general, however. All states require certain qualifications: a *minimum age* (age of 21 in all states except Georgia and Kentucky, where it is now 18); *citizenship* in the United States; and *residence* of at least one year in the state and six months in the district.

Registration

Many states require, in addition, that potential voters pass a simple **literacy test.** This test most often consists of reading portions of the state and federal constitutions. Sometimes it requires also writing and "understanding" of what is read. In some cases a school diploma is accepted in place of the literacy test. Five states (Virginia, Alabama, Arkansas, Mississippi, and Texas) still impose a **poll tax** from $1.00 to $2.00 on anyone wanting to vote. Small as the tax is, it has worked to prevent some people from voting. This tax is not to be confused with a poll tax levied in many states on all citizens, whether they vote or not, to pay the cost of elections.

Once eligibility is established, voters are required to register. In each state, permanent lists of voters are kept. States are divided for voting purposes into election districts, which usually are small enough for effective control of records (if the roll books do not get too heavy!) Voters **register** in their own districts; that is, they sign their names on the roll of voters. The purpose of registration is to prevent fraud, since a voter's signature in the roll book on election day can be compared with the signature he entered when he registered.

Registration is either annual or permanent. In some states, a voter may register once and thereafter be eligible to vote in every election until he moves out of the district or until the boundaries of the district are changed. In other states, voters are required to register each year in advance of election day. In any case, the inspectors (representatives of the political parties appointed by law) at the polling place on election day have before them lists of eligible voters who have registered. As the voters arrive to vote, their names are checked off the lists. Thus the practice of stuffing ballot boxes, that is, one person voting more than once, can be held to a minimum, and persons unknown to the inspectors can be kept from voting.

Casting a Vote

All voting is by ballot, either filled in by hand or by pulling the levers of a voting machine. For many decades people have argued about the length of the ballot. Some believe that the **long ballot,** containing the names of many candidates for minor office, discourages voters from learning enough about the candidates to vote intelligently. The long ballot is defended by those who think that democracy is best served by having as many officials as possible elected directly by the people. Another view is that the so-called

384

short ballot (see p. 325) is preferable to the long. This ballot gives the names of candidates for only major offices, while minor officials serve by appointment. Thus it may be easier for the citizen to learn and remember the qualifications of the candidates for whom he is voting.

The **short ballot** now in use in many states for presidential elections, eliminates the names of presidential electors; the voter simply marks the name of his choice for President and Vice-President. However, the short ballot does not really eliminate the electors, since the constitutional provision for choice of the President and Vice-President by the electoral college has never been revised. Your vote for the presidential candidate of your choice is only a short cut to naming the electors pledged to him.

Voting is a matter of *procedure* only, until you know for whom and for what you are voting. The *substance* of the American election process is filled in by the political parties, which supply the candidates and programs for voters to decide on, as we shall see in Chapters 18 and 19. Voting is really the basic privilege of democratic government. It is a necessary civil liberty. But without other civil rights and liberties, voting itself would be useless as a tool of free government.

SUBSTANTIVE FREEDOMS

Guarantees to individual citizens written down in the Bill of Rights of the Constitution of the United States and in the bills of rights contained in the state constitutions have advanced democracy in our republic. Earlier in this book (Chap. 3, p. 75), we discussed briefly freedom of the press and freedom of speech, which are guaranteed in Amendment I of the Constitution. Freedom of religion is also provided in that amendment, as we saw in Chapter 15. These liberties of speech, press, and religion are necessary to the existence of all other liberties. We call them our **substantive freedoms,** while our safeguards against arbitrary actions by the government are known as **procedural rights.**

Amendments I and XIV

On the right to free speech and free press rest our newspapers, magazines, radio, television, and even motion-picture programs. The same right allows us to speak to one another and to groups. That is, Amendment I applies to all forms of communication, and forbids Congress to make any law interfering with the freedom of people to say or write what they think, or to listen to or read what they wish.

Amendment XIV (1868) forbids state governments to interfere with those rights, since the courts have decided that "liberty" as used in this amendment means the liberties mentioned in Amendment I. In other words, none of the American governments, from Congress to the smallest local legislature, is permitted to pass laws infringing our rights to speak and write freely. The freedoms of speech and press are tools of democracy. Only if men speak and write freely do men hear and read freely. And only by such free communication is it possible for our elected governments to know what we want and to pass laws providing it.

LIMITS ON FREEDOM OF SPEECH It must not be supposed, however, that the guarantee of free speech has no limits. Your good sense would tell you that it is wrong to shout "Fire!" in a crowded public place. The consequences of such speech could, of course, be disastrous. Government has a right to provide punishment for this kind of abuse of free speech, and does so. On the other hand, government may not prevent you in advance from saying anything you please, even the most irresponsible and false criticism of itself. In a famous case (*Near vs. Minnesota*, 1931) the Supreme Court declared that laws which would censor such criticism in advance are unconstitutional. Near published a paper in Minneapolis which severely attacked officials of the state government in Minnesota, charging them with bribery and corruption. Under a Minnesota law, he was ordered to cease publication unless he submitted his articles to state officials in advance of publication. The Supreme Court denied the right of the Minnesota legislature to pass such a law because it violated Amendments I and XIV.

You may well ask whether a person falsely accused in such articles does not have a remedy. The answer is that he does. He cannot prevent the articles from being published, but *after* they have been published he can sue the author and publisher for damages to his reputation (**libel**). If he can show the court that his reputation and income suffer from the articles, the court will award him damages (financial compensation). In certain cases, articles may be so vicious that the District Attorney will bring charges of **criminal libel** before a grand jury. A man who is convicted of publishing such articles may be sent to jail. The point here is that our freedom of speech cannot be stopped unless the public safety and morals are immediately and directly harmed by it; but individuals harmed by it can go to court for a remedy.

"CLEAR AND PRESENT DANGER" There is another very important limit on our freedom of speech. We may not advocate, or conspire to advocate, the overthrow of the government by force and violence. In the case of *Schenck vs. United States* (1919), the Supreme Court ruled that speech or printed matter urging citizens to resist the military draft is not protected by Amendment I if it constitutes a "clear and present danger" to the safety and welfare of the United States. This ruling of the Supreme Court was extended in the *Dennis* case, 1951, to allow for the punishment of speech or writing when

386

"the gravity of the evil, discounted by its improbability" justifies taking measures against it. Specifically this meant that Communists, or Fascists, may be punished for conspiring to teach the overthrow of the government by force or violence. In 1957, the Court further held that even such a conspiracy may not be punished unless it is intended to produce direct action. As a result of this decision, the convictions of a number of Communists under the Smith Act were reversed. The Court means that the "evil" must be "grave" indeed before free speech can be restrained.

Another case, *Terminiello vs. Chicago* (1949), shows what "gravity of the evil" does not mean. Terminiello gave a speech in a Chicago auditorium in which he inflamed the crowd to a fever pitch against another crowd outside which was protesting the meeting. He was arrested and convicted under a Chicago city ordinance for disturbing the peace. The Supreme Court set aside the conviction on the ground that the danger from Terminiello's speech was not great enough to warrant police interference.

These cases show that the Supreme Court does not make a binding rule on what is meant by a "clear and present danger," but that it will not allow any interference whatever with free speech unless the circumstances are very serious indeed.

FREEDOM OF ASSEMBLY AND RELIGION The "right of the people peaceably to assemble, and to petition the Government for a redress of grievances," also guaranteed by Amendment I, is closely associated with freedom of speech and press. The same limits apply. Organizing a mob to attack the local jail and release prisoners is not assembling peaceably, but holding a meeting for even the most unpopular purposes is permitted. Again, meetings may not be prohibited or broken up by government officials unless the public safety or morals are immediately endangered. The freedom of religion, with which Amendment I begins, has been discussed in Chapter 15. There was a time when human beings were oppressed for their religious beliefs. Even today many Americans might say that their freedom of religion is the most precious of the civil liberties and rights.

PROCEDURAL SAFEGUARDS

Amendments IV, V, VI, VII, VIII, and XIV taken together, provide basic protections to Americans in matters of law and justice—our **procedural rights**. What do we mean by procedural rights? We mean, in simple terms, those guarantees which require government to treat us all equally and only in accordance with the law. Let us examine them in order as they are stated in the various amendments.

TOOLS OF DEMOCRACY

Civil rights and liberties require constant use if they are to remain effective tools of democracy. Voters in primary elections, like these in Wisconsin, are exercising their right to help select the candidates who will run for President.

Another legal right is trial by jury. This precious right not only guarantees Americans accused of crimes or named in lawsuits a trial by a panel of their fellow citizens, but also imposes on us responsibility for serving on a jury if we are called.

Another important guarantee of civil rights is the protection of private property. If a town wishes to use someone's property in order to construct a road, or a dam, or a school, it must get the citizens' votes on whether the property should be used for that purpose, and it must then pay the owner fair compensation out of the public treasury. Each citizen, like this rural mailman at a town meeting in Vermont, has the right to express his views.

After free discussion, the matter is put to the vote. The ballots are counted by a Board of Civil Authority.

Informed voting on constitutional amendments is an obligation of citizens. It is the way citizens can keep their state constitutions up to date.

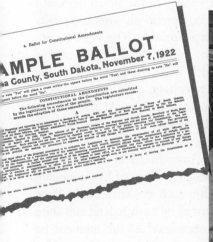

Amendment IV

The text of Amendment IV says:

The right of the people to be secure in their persons, houses, papers, and effects, against unreasonable searches and seizures, shall not be violated, and no Warrants shall issue, but upon probable cause, supported by Oath or affirmation, and particularly describing the place to be searched, and the persons or things to be seized.

One of the most common and, at the same time, most pitiful events in totalitarian societies, like Communist dictatorships, is the midnight knock upon the door followed by a visit from the secret police, a ransacking of the house, a beating perhaps, or an unexplained arrest and disappearance. These methods of intimidation and brutality are not new, though perhaps modern dictatorships have brought them into wider use than ever. The founders of the United States knew something about "unreasonable searches and seizures," and wished to make very sure that they would not happen here.

THE RIGHT TO PRIVACY   Amendment IV has far-reaching applications, through a long series of Supreme Court decisions, and its protections are extended by state laws. It covers, for example, the simple question of whether a federal officer can come into your living room to see whether you have done something illegal which some crank in the neighborhood says you have done. The answer is that he may not. Unless you invite him in, the officer will have to obtain a **search warrant,** that is, a document issued by a judge after the policeman has sworn that he has reason to suspect you (see p. 248). You are entitled to see the warrant before you admit the policeman. Under state constitutions you are entitled to the same protection from local police officers.

At another extreme, the same amendment applies to the much discussed matter of tapping telephone wires. Listening in secretly on someone's telephone conversation is an invasion of that person's privacy. The right to privacy is one of the important rights implied by Amendment IV. There has been much debate whether wire-tapping, which makes it possible for the police or the FBI to monitor or listen-in on telephone calls, is legal, even if by doing so the FBI can catch known criminals or traitors. At the present time, wire-tap evidence is not permitted in the federal courts, though it is permitted in some states.

When taken together with Amendment V, Amendment IV protects you from the use against you, in a *federal* trial, of evidence obtained by "unreasonable search or seizure." However, in many *states* such evidence can still be used. In a recent California case, a man was arrested by both federal and state officials at the same time for violation of narcotics laws. At the moment he was caught, he swallowed two tablets which were thought to be drugs. Not only had the officials entered his room without a proper warrant, but they

390

also had his stomach pumped to find out whether the tablets were in fact drugs, as they turned out to be. The Supreme Court held that the man could not be convicted in federal court on such evidence because it had been secured in violation of Amendment IV. The man's conviction for violation of the *state* law was allowed to stand.

As the courts have interpreted Amendment IV, it does not apply to vehicles or places of business, but only to private dwellings. Nor does it prevent a police officer from forcibly entering a private house, if his purpose is to make an arrest. Such exceptions are readily understandable and do not upset the sense of privacy and security in our homes which the amendment is intended to give us.

Amendments V and XIV

As a guarantee of our legal rights, Amendment V is in certain ways the most important protection available to Americans. Here is the text:

> No person shall be held to answer for a capital, or otherwise infamous crime, unless on a presentment or indictment of a Grand Jury, except in cases arising in the land or naval forces, or in the Militia, when in actual service in time of War or public danger; nor shall any person be subject for the same offense to be twice put in jeopardy of life or limb; nor shall be compelled in any criminal case to be a witness against himself, nor be deprived of life, liberty, or property, without due process of law; nor shall private property be taken for public use, without just compensation.

There are five different parts of this amendment. Each is important to an understanding of the ways in which government is limited in what it may do, so that your rights are protected.

GRAND JURY INDICTMENT AND TRIAL BY JURY The requirement that we may not be tried for a serious federal offense without the action of a grand jury is one of our most important guarantees of justice and equality before the law. Many states also make use of the grand jury in criminal cases under state law, though some use an information (see p. 229). In totalitarian countries a public prosecutor has power to bring charges and conduct trials in which the accused does not have the protection of a trial before a jury of his equals. Under Amendments V and VI, the United States Attorney may not have an accused person tried before a court of government officials. The same principle holds under the laws and constitutions of the states. In Chapters 9 and 10, we saw how accused persons are protected by the legal requirement for grand jury indictment before trial.

DOUBLE JEOPARDY Amendment V also protects us against what is known as **double jeopardy**. This means that, if Richard Roe has been found not guilty by a trial jury, he may not be tried again for the same offense. If, however, his offense involved the breaking of both a federal law and a state law, he may be tried for both, as in the California case we have discussed. He might be tried again if two federal laws were involved in his offense. Retrial after an appeal is not double jeopardy, because the second trial has been sought by the accused. The purpose of this amendment is not to let criminals go without punishment, but to make it as certain as possible that all of us are presumed innocent unless and until we are proved guilty. The burden of proof in American justice is on the prosecution—on the government. When Richard Roe is arrested, it becomes the government's job to prove him guilty, not his job to prove himself innocent. Thus Richard, as well as other accused Americans, is entitled to the benefit of whatever doubt exists.

SELF-INCRIMINATION   In recent years, the most widely discussed provision of Amendment V is that which says that we may not be required to testify against ourselves in a criminal case. At the time the amendment was adopted, the principal meaning of the clause was that the prosecution could not force an accused person to confess.

If you have ever read an account of a trial in a Communist-controlled country, you can see how important this protection is. "Justice" under communism is based on the "confession." Whatever means the secret police and prosecutors may use, they usually obtain confessions from everyone they accuse. In big-name cases, this confession will be long, detailed, and dramatic. Often the accused will even ask to be punished.

You may have read accounts of trials in our courts of persons who once confessed but in their public trials tried to convince the jury that they were innocent. While the confession is not sufficient evidence of guilt, it is considered strong evidence in most cases. Therefore, it is of great importance that an accused person be protected against being made to give information which might make him liable to prosecution or conviction. In any case, under Amendment V, an accused person does not need to confess and does not have to testify if he does not wish to do so. This keeps the burden of proof on the government. Under the criminal codes of many states, a plea of "not guilty" is mandatory (required) for certain offenses. That is, you *must* plead not guilty, and the government *must* prove that you are guilty, or else you cannot be convicted.

Court decisions have extended the meaning of Amendment V to make it cover more than actual criminal trials. The following example may help to give a clearer understanding of this issue of self-incrimination. The Smith Act of 1940 (see pp. 361–362) makes it a criminal offense to "conspire to teach or advocate the overthrow of the government by force or violence." In a series of cases, the Department of Justice proved that the Communist Party of the United States is a conspiracy as defined by the act. Under

Amendment V, a Communist being tried for violation of the Smith Act would not be required to testify against himself. In many cases, however, Communists have preferred to use their trials under this law to make speeches —that is, to denounce the American way of justice and life. If they had wished to do so, they could have refused to take the stand.

In Chapter 6, we saw how Amendment V protects the citizen against self-incrimination before committees of Congress. The refusal of a witness to testify before a committee is not confined only to cases involving alleged Communists. A short time ago a congressional committee investigating labor troubles in a midwestern state called in as a witness an official of the local union. This man was charged with forcing employers to pay him large sums of money. He refused to answer because he might incriminate himself.

A strong word of warning is proper here. The fact that a known Communist—or a known racketeer—uses the protection of Amendment V must not be allowed to confuse us as to the value of the amendment itself. Some people will abuse any privilege whatever. It does not follow that we should abolish all privileges. The privilege of owning and operating an automobile is constantly being abused. A person who votes according to his religious or national prejudices rather than the merits of candidates or parties is abusing the voting privilege. Few people would argue that these privileges should be abolished.

Likewise, the protection of Amendment V against self-incrimination should not be endangered because some people abuse it. Nor should it be assumed that a man who pleads Amendment V is guilty. It means, rather, that truthful answers to the questions he has refused to answer might incriminate him, that is, make him liable to prosecution or conviction. But being liable to prosecution is not by any means the same thing as being guilty. If the police knew that you had been at the scene of a crime, they might suspect you and bring charges against you. Therefore, though you were wholly innocent, you might refuse to answer questions about where you were in order to avoid prosecution and possible conviction for a crime you did not commit.

This is a protection which developed in English law three centuries ago. It has been preserved in England and America with great care. It remains a stout protection for the individual against what might become unjust and oppressive government. If a person *is* guilty of a crime, it is up to government to obtain the proof of that guilt, bring him before a jury, and convince the jury members that the accused did commit the crime. Until all this has been done, the accused must be considered innocent.

DUE PROCESS OF LAW Amendment V contains the well-known words "due process of law." This is a simple but important guarantee of the rights of the people. It means that government may not kill a human being, interfere with his liberty as defined by law, or take away his property unless it is done in the manner required by law. A man may be executed if a crime such as murder or treason is proved against him and he is convicted by a jury. He may lose his liberty by imprisonment for a crime of which a jury convicts him. He may be forced to turn over his property to the government for a certain sum of money if it is needed to build a highway. All this is not the same thing as giving a government power to condemn persons before they are tried, or to seize their property without compensation arbitrarily. Due process of law means that restrictions are placed upon the government, even in dealing with persons accused of crimes.

This, of course, is exactly the opposite of the procedures of a dictatorship, in which the secret police or the military can do just these things at the whim of the state. For example, one of the ways by which Hitler's dictatorship in Germany persecuted Jews was by confiscating their property either without legal procedures or by procedures which violated all the standards of decency and fair play in which free men believe. In the Soviet Union literally hundreds of thousands of people have been "liquidated" by the state simply because their existence was an embarrassment to the state. Under American law, on the other hand, Amendment V gives the individual full legal protection against brutal or arbitrary actions by the federal government.

Amendment XIV, adopted in 1868, makes procedural guarantees apply also to the state governments: "nor shall any state deprive any person of life, liberty or property, without due process of law." It is the protections of this amendment, as interpreted by the Supreme Court, which have played so great a part in the twentieth century in breaking down barriers of racial discrimination, since such barriers are found to deny some citizens the "equal protection of the laws." As a result, Americans are protected against invasions of their rights by any governmental agencies—local, state, or national—and have ultimate protection against such invasions by the federal law itself.

The courts have extended the meaning of "due process" in an important way by distinguishing between "**procedural** due process" and "**substantive** due process." *Substantive* due process means that your life, liberty, and property may not be molested except according to law. *Procedural* due process means that your life, liberty, and property may not be molested by use of laws which are themselves unconstitutional. In a famous case of 1925, the Supreme Court declared unconstitutional a law of Oregon requiring children under sixteen who had not completed the eighth grade to go to **public** school. The Court found the law unfair to people who wished their children to go to **private** schools—a violation of "due process of law." It should be said that the Supreme Court does not often presume to judge on the fairness or reasonableness of laws, preferring to leave such matters to legislatures.

394

PROTECTION OF PRIVATE PROPERTY   The final clause of Amendment V requires the federal government to make fair compensation to any individual or group whose private property is needed for public purposes. Property cannot, of course, be taken by government at all unless there is a law authorizing such an action. Amendment V guarantees that even when a law is passed authorizing the taking of private property for public use—in building a dam, in measures for soil conservation, in laying out public parks, in making military installations, or the like—the owners must be compensated out of the public treasury (eminent domain, p. 62). This protection of private property is fundamental to the security of our lives, as it safeguards our homes, our farms, and our places of business against arbitrary seizure by government.

Amendment VI

This amendment further provides for the procedural rights of persons accused of crime, as follows:

> In all criminal prosecutions, the accused shall enjoy the right to a speedy and public trial, by an impartial jury of the State and district wherein the crime shall have been committed, which district shall have been previously ascertained by law, and to be informed of the nature and cause of the accusation; to be confronted with the witnesses against him; to have compulsory process for obtaining witnesses in his favor, and to have the assistance of Counsel for his defense.

These procedures in criminal cases were not at all original with the Americans. They had been developed over centuries under the English **common law** (see pp. 223–224). The colonists had, of course, brought the common law with them when they settled the new world. All the original states of the Union provided their people with these safeguards in cases under the jurisdiction of the states. The point of the amendment to the Constitution was to make sure that the same protections would apply to persons accused of crimes under the laws which would be written by Congress.

SPEEDY AND PUBLIC TRIAL   To a person accused of a crime, the value of the safeguards of Amendment VI are obvious. To the ordinary citizen whose only connection with crime may be what he reads in the newspaper or a term of service on a jury, explanations may be necessary. To right to a "speedy" and "public" trial protects a prisoner from being locked up and forgotten simply because corrupt or tyrannical officials wish him out of the way—which is what happens under tyranny. Insistence upon speedy and public trials, therefore, developed in England from protests of the people against abuses of power by the king and his officers. Such abuses of these rights of a prisoner in the United States today are uncommon. The long delays in bringing people to trial with which we are familiar normally occur because time is required to prepare the defense and because the calendars of the courts are crowded with business.

TRIAL BY JURY The right to be tried by an "impartial jury of the State and district wherein the crime shall have been committed" protects an accused person from being taken to a place and among people where he is unknown, so that it would be difficult or impossible for him to procure sympathetic counsel and call friendly witnesses. Again, the practice of removing accused persons from the communities in which they live to remote places is a typical practice of tyrannical governments which the British long ago learned to guard against.

HEARING CHARGES AND CONFRONTING WITNESSES The right to be informed of the charges and to be confronted by witnesses against him protects the accused person from arbitrary conviction. Without such safeguards, he would be unable to prepare an effective defense. This right protects an accused person from the charges made by spies and informers who would be afraid to face him in open court, or whose testimony would not stand up under cross-examination.

BRINGING WITNESSES The right to bring into court witnesses favorable to his defense is another invaluable safeguard to the accused. It often happens that an innocent person could be saved from undeserved conviction by the testimony of witnesses who are frightened or who might themselves be implicated in the crime. Amendment VI makes sure that the accused may have the testimony of such witnesses whether or not they wish to appear. The court order compelling them to testify is known as a subpoena (see Chap. 10).

HAVING COUNSEL The right to have counsel is, again, an absolutely necessary safeguard for most people accused of crimes. The law is a highly complex system. Only specialists are, in most cases, capable of advising an accused person both as to his rights under law and as to how he should defend himself against the charges. More often than not the defense counsel is the key figure in a criminal case.

If a person accused of crime under federal law cannot afford a lawyer, the judge will assign one to defend him. This is also true generally in state courts. In some states accused persons receive the assistance of an official known as the public defender (see p. 250).

Amendment VIII

Since Amendment VIII contains important procedural rights which relate to criminal cases, it ought logically to follow VI. Amendment VIII is

"Can You See Me Now?"

from *Herblock's Special
For Today*
(Simon & Schuster)

copied directly from the English Bill of Rights to which we referred in Chapter 15:

> Excessive bail shall not be required, nor excessive fines imposed, nor cruel and unusual punishments inflicted.

EXCESSIVE BAIL AND HABEAS CORPUS The safeguard against excessive bail explains itself. If a prisoner could be held indefinitely in prison, before his trial, simply because he did not have enough money to get himself out, he might be handicapped in preparing his defense. Certainly it would not be equality before the law, because other prisoners held on the same charge might be able to raise the necessary bail. It is true that there are cases in which bail is set at a very high figure, and occasionally, under very special circumstances, bail may be refused. Normally such cases involve prisoners with a record of "jumping" bail (forfeiting the bail and running away) or of trying to escape from custody. In a typical case before our courts, bail is set at a reasonable figure and the prisoner is released to wait for his trial. Reasonable bail means an amount of money which the prisoner is capable of raising but which is so large that he will not wish to forfeit it by failing to appear in court. The privilege of **habeas corpus** (guaranteed in the Constitution, I, 9) is an essential part of bail proceedings (see p. 249).

CRUEL AND UNUSUAL PUNISHMENT   If you remember the story of the witchcraft trials in colonial days, you may recall that one old man was pressed to death with heavy stones. Amendment VIII forbids the government of the United States to use methods of torture to obtain confessions or to use cruel and unusual punishments of persons found guilty of crime. In practice this means that under our penal codes we may still send prisoners to solitary confinement, to hard labor, or even to death. But we may not punish them in a manner contrary to human decency.

Amendment VII

Amendment VII reads:

In Suits at common law, where the value in controversy shall exceed twenty dollars, the right of trial by jury shall be preserved, and no fact tried by a jury, shall be otherwise re-examined in any Court of the United States, than according to the rules of the common law.

A "suit at common law" here means an action in a court which is started by someone who wishes to gain ownership or control of money or property or to recover damages, as we saw in Chapter 9. This action may be brought by an individual against a group, by a group against an individual, by an individual against another individual, or by an agency of government against a group or an individual. Amendment VII protects the persons involved in the case against the possibility that a judge may be corrupt. If public trial before a jury were not possible, one of the contesting parties might bribe the judge. Jury trial is not required unless one or both of the parties want it. What actually happens is that many suits at common law are tried quietly before a judge or a referee appointed by a judge.

TWO SPECIAL GUARANTEES

Amendments II and III to the Constitution, so important to earlier Americans, may sound a bit strange today, but they still have significance for us.

Amendment II

Amendment II guarantees that "the right of the people to keep and bear arms shall not be infringed." The original purpose of this clause was to make sure that a militia of citizen soldiers would always be available for defense of the country. Actually the present system of National Guard volunteer soldiers and airmen is the direct descendant of the early colonial and national militias (see Chap. 27).

Your right to own a hunting rifle also comes from this clause. This does not mean that any and all types of weapons may be owned by just anyone. The Courts have held that the people's right to bear arms is not infringed by making rules for their ownership and use. The ownership of firearms is regulated by licensing systems under state laws. The purpose of such regulation is to make as sure as possible that weapons do not get into the hands of irresponsible people. Some of you who read this book may already have owned a "22," or even a larger weapon, which you purchased without any difficulty, but you would have found the situation very different if you had tried to buy a machine gun.

Amendment III

Amendment III, which forbids the quartering of soldiers in private homes in time of peace, states a guarantee which was dear to the Americans of the eighteenth century. If you had been a resident of Boston in 1774, you might have been compelled to take a British soldier into your home. This "quartering" of soldiers in homes was one of the causes of bad feeling between Americans and the mother country, leading to the Revolution. Congress and the state legislatures lost little time after the launching of the new government in adding this amendment to the Constitution. After so many years, the danger involved in the quartering of troops on civilians in peacetime seems quite unreal. Yet this constitutional guarantee is another of our important protections against our own leaders.

SOME PROBLEMS OF CIVIL RIGHTS

The civil liberties and rights which we have been discussing in this chapter, and which we refer to at many points in this book, are never cut and dried legal matters, nor are they universally practiced in the United States. In fact, they are continually raising serious problems. If you follow closely a session of Congress, you will frequently see discussion of civil rights in the proceedings of Congress and discover that from time to time various bills regarding civil rights are introduced and debated. Sometimes new civil rights laws are passed, to give the executive branch greater enforcement powers.

Voting

One civil rights issue is that of voting. There have been attempts for many years to prevent Negroes in certain sections of the country from exercising the privilege of voting. In Chapter 15 we discussed the use of literacy tests and the poll tax. A question not yet resolved is how much power the federal government has to back up a citizen's right to vote. The rules of voting, as we have seen, are in the hands of the states. According to Amendment XV, "the right of citizens of the United States to vote shall not be denied or abridged by the United States or by any state on account of race, color, or previous condition of servitude." The same amendment gives Congress power to enact laws to enforce this right. The problem arises in the interpretation of "on account of race." If a poor Negro cannot pay a poll tax, he is in no different condition from a poor white who cannot pay it. If a Negro businessman loses customers by going to the polls, it cannot be said that a *state* has denied him his voting privilege. Yet we cannot claim that our civil rights are complete so long as some of us are prevented by forces outside ourselves from voting in elections. The Civil Rights Law of 1957 gave the Attorney General greater powers to protect the right to vote and set up a Civil Rights Commission to investigate and report to Congress on voting infringements.

Discrimination

Another problem of civil rights is discrimination in employment. The federal government can and does, by executive order, require employers in the federal government to treat all applicants for jobs equally as regards race, religion, and other matters. But if a private employer refuses to give Negroes (or Jews or Protestants or anyone else) equal opportunity for a job, it cannot be said that either a state or the federal government is denying anyone his right to a job. There is, as a matter of fact, no federal law requiring employers to hire anybody, although Congress has several times considered enacting a law forbidding such discrimination and requiring "fair employment practices" in all businesses involved in interstate commerce. A number of states have already passed such legislation to apply to businesses carried on wholly within their boundaries.

Another problem that comes under the heading of civil rights is public education. We have already seen (Chap. 9) how the problem of segregation in the schools has perplexed the Supreme Court. The Interstate Commerce Commission has forbidden segregation according to color on buses, trains, ships, etc., which cross state lines. The courts have held that segregation in public parks and playgrounds is unlawful. Many states have outlawed segregation in restaurants and other public places. But there are still many places in the United States where schools and other public places remain segregated.

The Rights of All

We know that civil liberties and rights do not enforce themselves, and that courts cannot long preserve them unless the people wish them preserved. Such civil rights problems as those involving discrimination are no exceptions. These matters must ultimately be resolved in the minds and hearts of the people. Laws and courts can lay down the ground rules of fairness, but it is we who must understand and abide by them. You and I can bring our historic

400

struggle for full civil rights and liberties to completion by placing the idea of *liberty for all* at the top of our scale of values, remembering that so long as anyone's rights and liberties are denied or in danger, so too are ours, because anything that could happen to somebody else could also happen to us.

Throughout the whole development of democracy in America, one theme has been continuous and essential: the theme of faith in freedom and in the ability of the common man to govern himself. Democracy cannot grow up overnight. It requires a people who have the will to manage their affairs in their common interest and to make personal sacrifice for the greater good of all, and who are willing to take full responsibility for both the successes and the failures of society. Such a people must be intelligent and informed and unafraid to act on their best judgment. They must also be prepared to accept at times the judgment of others, no matter how mistaken it may seem. For these reasons the success of the American experiment in democracy can never be taken for granted. Our enormous wealth and strength as a nation give us a great measure of security against the overthrow of our freedom by external enemies, but the danger of internal decay and collapse can only be overcome if free citizens, faithfully and devotedly, bend their efforts to maintaining our free institutions and to improving them. That is the "eternal vigilance" which has been called the "price of liberty."

SUMMARY

Because civil rights and liberties are the tools of democracy—the absolutely necessary conditions of freedom—you will find them discussed and referred to in many places throughout this book. In this chapter, for convenience, we have considered them all systematically together. You have seen why it is proper to say that our rights and liberties are the tools which enable us to govern ourselves. Obviously we could not be free without the vote. But the rights to speak and write freely and to assemble peaceably are necessities if our votes are to have meaning and the opinions of the majority to be discovered. We must be free to criticize the government.

But you have also seen that none of these great freedoms is absolute and unqualified. Laws and Supreme Court decisions do limit our freedom, but you have learned from various cases that the Court leans almost always toward freedom in making its decisions, unless very serious dangers to the public safety and welfare are involved.

You have studied the "Bill of Rights" of the federal Constitution, which guarantees us fair treatment under the laws and requires government to treat us according to certain long-established procedures of fair play and equality.

401

These procedural rights underlie the others, because without them a tyrannical government could easily destroy the substantive liberties of speech, press, religion, etc. Finally, you have seen that there are a number of important unsolved problems in the field of civil rights—problems involving discrimination among our citizens on the basis of race, color, and sometimes religion. One reason for this is that not all of our protections against acts of Congress are binding against the states. In some states, laws and customs differ sharply from the pattern established in others. The solution to these problems lies not only in the decisions made by the Supreme Court in cases brought before it, or in laws enacted by Congress and the state legislatures, but also in the hearts and minds of the people. Only a people who wish deeply to treat one another equally will, in the long run, do so.

KNOW WHAT YOU READ

1. What are civil rights? Just how do they differ from civil liberties?
2. Why are civil liberties called "tools of democracy"?
3. What is the chief way in which most of you as citizens will take part in the affairs of your government?
4. You have often pledged allegiance to the flag of the United States of America and to the *Republic* for which it stands. What is the meaning of the word *republic*?
5. Before you become a voter, you will have to meet certain requirements. Who set up those requirements?
6. If you had been living in the United States in 1792, would you have been able to vote? Explain your answer. What individuals are excluded from voting?
7. What is *registration*? What is the purpose of registration?
8. What are the arguments for the long ballot? For the short ballot?
9. Why is freedom of speech so important to us? In what ways is it *limited*?
10. What rights are called *procedural*? What rights are *substantive*?
11. Mr. Trevett and his friends wish to organize a meeting to protest against the federal income tax. Is this one of their civil rights? Explain.
12. What is meant by "unreasonable searches and seizures"?
13. Is wire-tap evidence accepted in courts?
14. What is a search warrant?
15. May the officer at the customs station search your car without a search warrant? Explain your answer.
16. *List* and *explain* each of the protections guaranteed a person by Amendment V.
17. What kind of activity was made a criminal offense by the Smith Act?

18. Under what conditions may persons testifying before committees of Congress be allowed to refuse to testify? When may they be compelled to give testimony?
19. Why is Amendment V an important protection even though it is sometimes abused?
20. The federal government has announced that it is to build a dam in the valley where John Brown lives. His entire farm will be at the bottom of a new lake. What rights if any does John Brown have in such a case?
21. List and explain the procedural rights stated in Amendment VI.
22. What protection does a person get from Amendment VIII?
23. What is important about Amendment VII?
24. In what ways is the citizen's right to own arms restricted?
25. What power does the federal government have over voting in the states?
26. What problems of civil rights are involved in voting, employment, and education?

WHAT DO YOU THINK?

1. Do you believe that eighteen-year-olds should have the right to vote? Defend your answer.
2. In a recent class discussion Fred said, "Freedom of speech means you can say anything." Nobody disagreed with him. Was he right?
3. Do you believe in complete freedom of speech? In speech that is free within limits? What limits?
4. Study the cartoon, p. 397. What is the cartoonist's message? What do you think he believes is the basis of our civil rights?
5. Should any of the following not be allowed to carry on in their chosen professions if they make use of the Amendment V protection against self-incrimination: research scientists, college professors, teachers, lawyers, doctors, editors, news commentators? Why?

PROBLEMS AND PROJECTS FOR YOU

1. Visit a polling place on election day. Compare what you see there with the description of voting given in this book.
2. Study ballots used in elections in your state. Are they *long* or *short* ballots? Summarize in writing the advantages of both types.
3. Do you use the long or short ballot in elections in your school? Why? Does it serve its purpose? Write a letter to the editor of your school paper expressing your point of view on the preceding questions.

4. Topic for debate: Resolved that that freedom which is *limited* is not freedom.
5. Look up in Cushman's *Leading Constitutional Decisions* one Supreme Court case. Report to the class on
   (a) the background of the case
   (b) what rights were involved
   (c) the decision of the court
   (d) the meaning of the decision.
6. Neither Congress nor your state legislature may make a law infringing freedom of speech. Your freedom of speech may, however, be infringed by other people. Explain how this may be done.
7. Make a tape recording (or stage a playlet discussion) in which selected historical characters (*e.g.*, Alexander Hamilton, Thomas Jefferson, Abraham Lincoln, and others) meet with two or three students from your school to talk over the growth of democracy in our country.
8. If you like Gilbert and Sullivan, read *Pinafore* to note how it was determined that one man should be an officer in the Royal Navy while another man should be a sailor.
9. If your state makes use of the grand jury, watch for news items referring to it. Collect clippings for a bulletin-board display.
10. Interview a lawyer of your community to get his explanations of the meaning of "due process," both procedural and substantive. Ask for illustrations. Explain your findings to the class.
11. Look up *common law* in the *Encyclopaedia of the Social Sciences*. Give a three to five minute report in class, or hand in a composition on it.
12. One high-school student summed it up this way, "Procedural rights exist to protect substantive rights." Is this a good statement of the difference?
13. Which civil liberties have members of your own class exercised within the last week? List them.
14. Make a list of the civil liberties granted in your state constitution. Compare your state's guarantees with those of the federal government.
15. Using histories of Europe, or of the world, look up Magna Carta, the Petition of Right, and the Bill of Rights. Write a composition summarizing their contributions to the development of rights as we know them.
16. In Commager's *Documents of American History*, read the Declaration of Independence and the Articles of Confederation. What rights do you find in these documents?
17. Here is a partial list of liberties guaranteed in the Bill of Rights of the federal Constitution. Complete the list (you should have a list of sixteen or more liberties).
    (a) freedom of assembly
    (b) guarantee of due process of law
    (c) freedom from cruel and unusual punishments
    (d) guarantee of indictment by grand jury

404

18. Organize a panel to discuss the Report of the President's Committee on Civil Rights, entitled *To Secure These Rights.*

19. When televised trials were under discussion a few years ago, a federal judge had this to say:

> The reason courts are open to the public is not to provide recreation or instruction in the ways of government, but to prevent the possibility of star chamber proceedings where everything is secret. . . . The real question is whether television and radio interfere with the ascertainment of true facts.

Present and defend your own opinion on the questions involved in the televising of court trials. Be sure to consider all questions of *rights* involved in such trials.

20. In 1949 a one-time U.S. soldier was arrested on charges of dealing treasonably with the Japanese while he was their prisoner of war. The soldier was brought to trial 13 months later. He was found guilty and given a life sentence. Eighteen months later a U.S. Court of Appeals overruled the conviction on the grounds that the trial had been held in the wrong state. His retrial was then set for March 1955. The federal judge having jurisdiction dismissed the case on the grounds that the defendant had been denied one of his constitutional rights. Which right do you think was the basis for the judge's decision? Explain your answer, giving details.

21. Mr. John J. Lawyer wanted to travel in Europe. He applied to the State Department for a passport. His request was turned down on the grounds that "confidential information" which could not be disclosed showed Mr. Lawyer to be a Communist sympathizer. The State Department refused to tell where it obtained its confidential information. Mr. Lawyer took his case to court. The federal judge ruled that the plaintiff had been denied "due process of law." Why?

22. (a) John Doe is an employer. He says, "This is my business and I have a right to hire whomever I wish to hire. I don't like certain groups and I consider it an interference with my liberty to make me hire them."

   (b) In the same city there is a labor union which excludes people of a certain racial group from membership in the union.

   Are (a) and (b) examples of discrimination?
   Are they violations of laws of the states? Of the federal government? Of some of the states?

23. The following quotation states one of the most important understandings in all American government. What does it mean?
   "Civil liberties do not enforce themselves; courts cannot long preserve them unless the people want them preserved."

EXTEND YOUR VOCABULARY

civil rights
civil liberties
registration
literacy test
poll tax
long ballot
short ballot

stuffing a ballot box
substantive freedoms
Near vs. Minnesota
Schenck vs. United States
Dennis vs. United States
Terminiello vs. Chicago
"clear and present danger"

procedural rights
search warrant
wire-tapping
double jeopardy
self-incrimination
due process of law
bail jumping

YOUR NOTEBOOK: THE GOVERNMENT OF ——

1. List the voting requirements of your state.
2. Write the answer to this question: How are the people who work at the polls selected in your community?
3. Make a list of the civil liberties guaranteed in your state constitution.

READ MORE ABOUT IT

BARTH, ALAN, *The Loyalty of Free Men.* Viking, 1951.
The problem of loyalty and security vs. freedom of speech and thought—readable and stimulating.
BURNS, JAMES M., and PELTASON, JACK W., *Government by the People.* Prentice-Hall, 1954. Chaps. 7–8.
CHAFEE, ZECHARIAH, JR., *Free Speech in the United States.* Harvard University Press, 1948.
The standard book on this vital subject.
COMMAGER, HENRY STEELE, *Freedom, Loyalty, Dissent.* Oxford University Press, 1954.
Readable and provocative.
CUSHMAN, ROBERT E., *Civil Liberties in the United States.* Cornell University Press, 1956.
DAVIS, ELMER, *But We Were Born Free.* Bobbs-Merrill, 1954.
HAND, LEARNED, *The Bill of Rights.* Harvard University Press, 1958.
Beautiful work of a great jurist.
KONVITZ, MILTON R., *Bill of Rights Reader.* Cornell University Press, 1954.
A selection of leading constitutional cases with notes.
PRESIDENT'S COMMITTEE ON CIVIL RIGHTS, *To Secure These Rights.* Government Printing Office, 1947.
A great modern statement of our heritage of liberty and how it should be expanded.
RANNEY, AUSTIN, *The Governing of Men.* Holt, 1958. Chaps. 6–8.
RUCHAMES, LOUIS, *Race, Jobs, and Politics: The Story of FEPC.* Columbia University Press, 1953.
WOOD, VIRGINIA, *Due Process of Law.* Louisiana University Press, 1951.

CHAPTER 17

Public Opinion

In this chapter you will learn about—

The meaning of "public opinion"
Economic influences on public opinion
Cultural influences on public opinion
Regional influences on public opinion
Techniques of influencing public opinion
The media of mass communication
Thinking critically about mass media
Measuring public opinion
How the citizen can influence the opinions of others

As we have seen in Chapter 2, the power and responsibility of government in a democratic republic are in the hands of the citizens. It follows, therefore, that the opinions of the citizens will be the controlling influences on public affairs. In the long run, all free governments do what the people want them to do. An elected legislature or executive which seriously defies the will of the people is certain to be turned out of office before very long. The great question in a free society like the United States is, therefore, What is the will of the people? Politicians, critics, and propagandists, as well as ordinary citizens in the United States, are continually talking about the "people," and about "public opinion." What is "public opinion"? We must be on our guard and think critically about it, because it can be an exceedingly slippery and deceptive term.

THE MEANING OF "PUBLIC OPINION"

When a newspaper columnist or a politician talking on the radio tells us that "public opinion demands" that such and such a thing be done, when a speaker pledges himself to follow the wishes of the "people," or when a political party announces in its election platform that the "American people" will insist on such and such a program, we are confronted with something which sounds very simple but is in reality highly complex. In trying to understand what lies behind these common terms, we must remember that *there is not just one public but many publics*. This we discussed in Chapters 1 and 2.

Because of the many publics, the democratic process in the United States is not a way of expressing and acting upon clear-cut, universally held opinions. It is almost exactly the opposite. Democracy is a way of getting the public business done by compromise—that is, agreeing to accept less than we as individuals think is right and proper because others also agree to accept less than they think is right and proper (see pp. 37–40). Because of a natural and continuing difference of opinion in a democracy, we might say that democracy is a way of agreeing to disagree—and to compromise. If there were no disagreement, freedom would have no meaning. Our freedom of speech, for example, is valuable to us because we arrive at our opinions differently, in terms of different interests and different beliefs. We thus have different things to say. In this way, above all others, we differ from totalitarian countries like the Soviet Union, where there is only one point of view allowed on any important question, and where the people are forced to agree with it regardless of their private feelings.

The American "public" includes all of us. Since we differ as individuals and as groups, there is very seldom such a thing as "American public opinion" on any question. In Chapter 1, we saw how our different national backgrounds, our different religions, our different occupations, our different incomes, all contribute to the "uniqueness" of our country. They also affect our opinions and politics.

Here is an example with which many Americans are familiar. The consumers of food in a city like New York are naturally anxious to have the lowest possible prices. They may object to a government policy of buying the farmer's surpluses at high prices, using taxpayers' money, in order to keep prices for farm products high. Such a policy will result in high prices to the consumer. In a state like North Dakota, however, where most of the people live on farms or depend on farm income, a policy of keeping the price of wheat high will mean a good standard of living. A majority of these people may favor the very government policy which the New Yorkers oppose. We thus have two quite different publics, one in North Dakota, the other in

New York, both equally important parts of the larger "American public." A candidate for public office may talk about a "sound farm policy"; but for some of us a "sound farm policy" means one thing; for other "publics" it means another.

Economic Influences on Public Opinion

Our economic concern is to maintain our standard of living. The Communists have always insisted that economic differences are bound to bring about sharp and bitter struggles among classes of people (see Chap. 26). American experience has shown this is not so. In a free society, there are few such conflicts, and they are seldom bitter. In terms of our economic interests, therefore, what we have is not class conflict but only the differences which result naturally from our different occupations. Many of us work in factories and belong to labor unions; others of us live and work on our own farms; still others work as clerks and managers in business. And more of us are engaged in the professions in proportion to our population than in almost any other country.

These obvious facts are not very helpful, though, because, as we saw in Chapter 1, factory workers are divided into literally hundreds of different types, depending on which industry they work in, and so are farmers, businessmen, and professional men. Then too all of us in America are both producers and consumers. Often one policy may be helpful to us in the way in which we make our living, while another policy may appeal to us as consumers.

An interesting example of the way in which our economic concerns conflict with themselves is in the perennial American debate over the best way to produce and distribute electric power. Mr. Smith, who keeps the corner store, believes strongly in the American system of private enterprise—that is, he thinks individuals should own and operate business and that government should stay out of it. But Mr. Smith's electricity bills for both his home and his store seem to be going up all the time. He is faced with a conflict in his own interests, because a way to reduce his electricity bills may well be to have his city go into the power business and cut the costs of power production and distribution by reducing profits. Yet if he advocates that the city go into the power business, what happens to his belief in private enterprise?

Since most of us have similar conflicting interests, it is almost impossible to reach general agreement as to the best way to handle the power problem. There is, therefore, no such thing as "public opinion" regarding the merits of private as against public power. There are, instead, different publics with differing views.

Our individual occupations help determine our opinions on public questions. Those who work in related occupations have the same common interest. Assembly line workers in the automobile industry, for example, have

MOLDING AND MEASURING PUBLIC OPINION

Our newspapers, magazines, and books are a very important means by which public opinion can be both measured and molded. The free press is one of the strongest weapons of democracy.

In the U.S. Census, the government furnishes an important tool for measuring public opinion. The 1960 Census questionnaire includes questions not only on names, ages, sex, education, occupations, and incomes; it also asks the number of rooms in a house, whether it is owned or rented, the value of house or amount of rent, kind of transportation used to get to work. the number of household appliances in use.

One of the new techniques for making the census useful to many different segments of the population is such a Univac Console as this. Various kinds of information are inserted into it from which statistics can be drawn up of benefit to politicians, businessmen, and others who want to take the measure of public opinion in certain areas.

certain common interests with steel workers. They make up one "public," namely, workers in heavy industry. Farmers who produce grain have a common interest in high prices and good marketing facilities for their grain. They form one "farm bloc." At the same time, dairy farmers, who want low prices for the grain they feed their cows, form a somewhat different "farm bloc."

The same differences could be shown among manufacturers, who are also consumers as well as producers. Thus it is that our free society, contrary to Communist predictions, does *not* produce sharp "class" conflicts. Our opinions are influenced by our economic interests, but economic interest by itself does not determine what our opinions will be or exclude other factors in the formation of public opinion.

Cultural Influences on Public Opinion

In national elections there is always much talk about winning the vote of "cultural minorities." Many a candidate has been fooled by relying on this idea. Americans cannot be counted upon to vote solely on the basis of their cultural influences. There is no such thing as a Catholic vote, a Jewish vote, an Italian vote, or a Polish vote in the sense that *all* Catholics, or *all* Jews, or *all* Italian-Americans, or *all* Polish-Americans will vote the same way. Nevertheless, religious or cultural backgrounds do play some part in the formation of our opinions. In the period since World War II, for example, many people of Polish extraction who have relatives behind the Iron Curtain have been much interested in the foreign policy views of candidates for Congress. Italian-Americans might estimate the different political programs offered to them by the candidates, with conditions in Italy in mind. American Jews, watching the experiment of Israel, may wonder how candidates stand on American support for the new Jewish nation. Examples of this sort could be multiplied many times.

These varying backgrounds bear on only a few issues, however. They do not form public opinion; they only sharpen some of the opinions of some of the many publics. What the Polish-American in Buffalo or Milwaukee wants in foreign policy has no relation to that same man's views on public power, or social security, or price supports for farmers. An Irish-American may be continually suspicious of England, but that point of view will have nothing to do with his views on how to deal with unemployment at home or Communist aggression in Southeast Asia.

Over the years cultural differences have tended to lose their force in American communities. Nevertheless, the very freedom of the American way of life has kept alive what is best in cultural varieties. Our opinions as Americans must, assuredly, always take precedence over our particular opinions as

411

members of any special group, but the variety and vitality of the groups which influence us also contribute to the many different "publics" in America.

Regional Influences on Public Opinion

Our regional attachments also influence our opinions on public affairs. The "southern point of view" or "eastern point of view" or "midwestern point, of view" is subject to the same kinds of limitations as are economic and cultural points of view. In the southern states, for example, agriculture is the main occupation of a large proportion of the people. The southern states share a common tradition and inheritance and history quite different from those of other parts of the country.

All these things, and many more, such as states' rights, inevitably influence the Southerner's opinions. In both houses of Congress, we can speak of a "southern bloc." This does not mean that all southern Congressmen vote alike on every question. It does mean that on certain issues a large number of southern Congressmen agree.

The Midwest also has common tradition and experience which divide it from the East on some questions. On the matter of the coinage of silver or the establishment of a national bank for easy credit for farmers, for example, midwestern and eastern Americans have differed sharply. To the Easterner, it has sometimes seemed that his midwestern fellow Americans are so isolated by geographic distance from other parts of the world that they do not fully understand how international problems affect America. This regional difference has played a major part in determining the actual foreign policy of the United States on more than one important occasion, notably in President Wilson's neutrality policy regarding World War I, during his campaign for reëlection in 1916.

EVERY AMERICAN AND MANY PUBLICS Regional interests do not prevent us from belonging to still other publics and being subject to still other influences. We are not simply midwestern Americans, or Polish-Americans, or factory assembly line workers. For example, we may live in Milwaukee, be Americans of Polish extraction, work on an assembly line, and belong to the Catholic Church. Our neighbor may be an American of German extraction who works as a teacher in the public school and belongs to the Lutheran Church. Our neighbor on the other side may be an American of English extraction whose ancestors came to Boston in 1630, and who is a clerk in a bank. Our cousin may have married an American of Jewish background who lives in Baltimore and works as a chemist. Our brother may have married a girl of Italian extraction and gone into fruit farming in California.

In short, the typical American of the twentieth century is subject to various and complex influences. He belongs to the American public and contributes to American public opinion by actually belonging to several

412

different publics, each of which has its own opinion on matters of concern to it. With all these influences, forming so many different public opinions, it may not seem possible to arrive at *a* public opinion. But through negotiation, compromise, and adjustment, those views of the majority are reached which ultimately control the policies of our government.

TECHNIQUES OF INFLUENCING PUBLIC OPINION

Our opinions, then, are influenced by *what we are*. In our time, the techniques of popular persuasion are also used to influence us. The *mechanical* perfection of such techniques is higher than ever before. We now have not only newspapers, but also radio, television, and motion pictures, which can be used to show us how to think or what to think or why to think what we do think. These devices (or **media,** as they are called) of mass communication are *mechanical;* but the ways in which words can be manipulated in order to persuade us, as they come through the printed page, the loud-speaker, or the screen, are *not* mechanical and not new. We shall, in fact, do well to examine the ancient human techniques of persuasion before we deal with the mechanical means of communication.

Syllogism

The art of persuasion is very old. One of its most effective techniques, **syllogism,** goes back to the ancient Greeks. If you were to take up the study of logic, you would find the syllogism to be a very useful tool in deductive thinking. Here is an example:

(a) All men are mortal.
(b) John Jones is a man.
(c) Therefore, John Jones is mortal.

The first statement is called the **major premise.** The second statement is called the **minor premise;** the third is the **conclusion.** If the major and minor premises are true, then the conclusion will also be true. The syllogism is a perfectly good method of reasoning. We may follow its steps correctly, however, and come up with an answer, or conclusion, which is wrong if one of our premises is not true. Here is a simple example:

(a) All cats have nine lives.
(b) Blackie is a cat.
(c) Therefore, Blackie has nine lives.

In this example there is nothing wrong with the steps in reasoning. They are valid, or correct. If it is true that all the cats in the world have nine lives,

413

and if it is true that Blackie is one of those cats, then it should be true that Blackie has nine lives. The syllogism is not wrong, but the conclusion is false, because the major premise is false. Cats do *not* have nine lives.

We must then make an important distinction between **valid reasoning** and **truth.** It is a common trick in persuasion to argue in a valid manner but to state a conclusion which is not true. What conclusion is in Bob's mind as he opens his plea for the family car with the words, "Dad, you know, don't you, that *teen-agers today are good drivers?*"

In trying to influence public opinion, politicians, writers, and propagandists of all sorts make constant use of this device of valid but untrue reasoning. Often they are perfectly sincere. If we are not alert and do not think critically, we may easily be fooled by what appears to be a reasonable argument. For example, take the issue of public power. A man who wishes to have us oppose the private ownership of public utilities might argue as follows:

(a) Everyone who favors private ownership is anti-democratic.
(b) Candidate Smith favors private ownership.
(c) Therefore, Candidate Smith is anti-democratic.

A man favoring private ownership might argue this way:

(a) Everyone who favors public ownership is a Communist.
(b) Candidate Jones favors public ownership.
(c) Therefore, Candidate Jones is a Communist.

In both cases the steps taken in reasoning are correct, or valid. What is wrong is that in both cases the *major premise is false.* It is not anti-democratic to favor private ownership of power facilities, nor is it communistic to favor public ownership.

Emotionally Toned Words

Notice that these examples involve not only a trick of reasoning. They involve also the use of words which arouse strong feelings in American people. Americans are democratic by tradition and belief; they almost automatically react unfavorably to the word **anti-democratic.** Americans are also bitterly opposed to **communism** as standing for the very opposite of the liberties we all cherish. The word arouses our antipathy, again almost automatically. It follows that an argument built by the trick of a false major premise, and making use of such powerfully effective words as **anti-democratic** and **Communist,** may tend to exert a good deal of influence upon our opinions.

Students of rhetoric and propaganda call such words as "Communist" and "anti-democratic" *emotionally toned words.* It is really a very ancient kind of trick. Nowadays, as always, everyone finds himself reacting with emotion to the meanings certain words have for him. Different people, of course, react to different words.

There are also group reactions as well as individual ones. The more important words, from the point of view of influencing the opinions of others, are those which have an emotional appeal to the largest numbers of people. Thus, in early New England people were so single-mindedly devoted to Christian piety, as they understood it, that the use of the word *devil* or the word *sin* affected them powerfully. In the years in which the American republic was founded, some people feared that the violence of the French Revolution might spread to our shores. For them the word *Jacobin*, referring to the revolutionary party in France, was a word of similarly powerful emotional effect. In the same way, a word like *Communist* stirs a great deal of feeling among Americans today. If you think about it, you will discover that there are a good many words to which you react emotionally. A skillful propagandist will try to find out what the words are which so affect you and your neighbors and fellow citizens, and will use them to try to sway you for or against a certain idea or a certain individual.

Generalities

Another device of persuasion is the use of **generalizations** and **very general words** which mean many different things to many different people. One of the favorite tricks of the ancient Greeks was to play upon such words as *justice* and *right*. Not only the device itself, but also the same words are used in attempts to influence opinion today. Everyone is in favor of *justice*; everyone is in favor of the *right*. Simply identify your cause or your opinion with justice and right, and you are off to a good start in your attempt to persuade others. There are also, of course, expressions of a similarly general character which belong to the age in which we live. Everyone is in favor of "Americanism" and the "American way of life." As we have already remarked, everyone in the United States believes in "democracy." We all wish to be "forward-looking"; we are all against "reactionaries." You can readily extend the list from your own knowledge or from a look at the newspaper.

There is nothing wrong with these generalities in themselves. The difficulty is that they are so general that their meanings are vague. Let us take the word *justice*. It has had different meanings at different times. When applied to a specific case, *justice* may, for different people, mean exactly opposite things. In early Greece, to some men the word meant "the right of the stronger." To others it meant "equality before the law." To still others it meant "minding one's own business." To all, however, it meant acceptance of slavery. In the United States before the War Between the States, slavery was considered unjust in the North; but in the South, many people included slavery in their definition of justice. Today, the word *justice* could not in-

"BEWARE
THE AIRY SPEECH-MAKER"

Carmack in
The Christian Science Monitor

clude slavery. It has been well said that just men differ as to the meaning of justice; wise men differ as to the meaning of wisdom; good men differ as to the meaning of goodness. These differences are among the glories of liberty; but they pose some of the most important issues which must be adjusted and compromised through the processes of democracy. They also make it possible for people skilled in persuasion to use such general terms to influence our opinions.

Bandwagon Technique

There are many other devices of persuasion used in molding opinion. One, very common today, is called the **"bandwagon"** trick. The idea is simply that we should accept a certain opinion as our own because "everybody" is thinking along the same lines. Since "everybody is doing it," we should do it, too, lest we be left out.

This sort of appeal is often very powerful, because most human beings like the sense of solidarity and security which comes from agreement. Some of us, it is true, almost automatically prefer to "be different"; but the expert on public opinion knows that there are far more of us who wish to be like others. The "bandwagon" device of influencing public opinion often appeals subtly to this characteristic. In any case, we can be sure that to accept an

416

opinion or take a point of view on public matters because "everybody is doing it" is not making use of our faculties of critical judgment. Opinion formed on such a basis seldom represents the best wisdom of a people or a group.

Prestige Value

A variation of the "bandwagon," also frequently used in influencing opinion on public affairs, is the appeal to the **prestige** of someone who is very well known and enjoys a good reputation in his chosen field. In cigarette advertising, we may be advised to smoke a certain brand because a famous motion-picture actor has endorsed it. In public affairs we are often advised to accept a certain point of view or vote in a certain way because a prominent physician or banker or labor union leader does so.

Obviously, whether the opinion we are asked to accept is wise or unwise, we are not making use of our critical abilities if we accept it because of the prestige of an eminent person, who, as a matter of fact, may not know a bit more about the matter in question than we do.

THE MEDIA OF MASS COMMUNICATION

These, then, are some of the more common and important *human* ways in which public opinion is influenced. There is nothing new about them. Indeed, since they have persisted for centuries, they must still be useful and effective. In the United States today, they are perhaps more effective than ever, because so many more people can be reached; and reached so much more frequently than ever before.

While the use of the radio for the broadcast of speeches and of public meetings dates from just after World War I, the first national political conventions to be broadcast across the country were those of 1924. That date marks the beginning of the era of mass communication. Since then radio has become available to almost every American, and television has developed widely since World War II. It is estimated that the radio audience for major political speeches and conventions exceeds fifty million and the television audience may be over thirty million. One thing is certain. No one wishing to influence the opinions of his fellow citizens has ever before been able to address so many of them at one time.

Radio and Television

The broadcasts of political and other public occasions which are intended to shape public opinion are by no means the only uses of these media for influencing opinion.

COMMENTATORS   Tens of millions of Americans hear radio and television commentators every day. The commentator's position is new. Unlike the announcer, who reads news bulletins from the wires of the press services, the commentator expresses to a considerable extent his own opinion, or that of his sponsor, much in the manner of the editor of a newspaper writing on the editorial page or a newspaper columnist writing under his own name. We assume that press dispatches or news bulletins report the facts objectively. In the case of commentators, we often listen because we are attracted to the point of view they are expressing. There is nothing wrong with this, so long as we are aware of what we are doing and are careful to check opinions against facts.

STEREOTYPES   If we listen to more than one commentator, so that we are informed of more than one interpretation, our opinions will be the sounder because radio and television are available. On the other hand, if we rely on one commentator, as upon one editor or one columnist, we are cut off from currents of thought outside our own, so that our opinions become what are called **stereotypes**. Stereotypes are convenient pictures in the mind. They are fixed ways of thinking which become so much a habit that we are unaware of them. Thus, a commentator who is opposed to the United Nations may always refer to those who support it as "One-Worlders." Another commentator who favors the United Nations may always refer to the supporters as "Internationalists." The idea is that "One-Worlders" sounds as though you were somehow not a good *American*, while "Internationalists" is dignified and high-sounding.

Democracy has few more insidious enemies inside itself than stereotyped thinking. A little self-examination will quickly tell you whether you are the victim of stereotypes.

REPETITION   One of the most effective ways in which radio and television influence opinion is by constant daily repetition. In totalitarian countries this method is widely used. The citizen of the Soviet Union hears the same point of view day after day endlessly, and *never* hears any other. Opinions can be formed, after all, only on what information you have. If everything you hear is directed to the same end and the facts available point only to one conclusion, it is unlikely that much disagreement will develop unless conditions of life itself become unbearable. Americans can retain their independence of judgment and of opinion because they normally hear or read more than one side of the issue. In fact, the Federal Communications Commission, which regulates radio and television broadcasting, requires that stations give equal free time to political parties and represent important differences of opinion fairly in the public interest (see Chap. 8, p. 205). Of course, as we shall see (Chap. 17), stations sell time to political parties.

Newspapers

Newspapers are not regulated by government. They have imposed their own code of presenting all sides of the news.

Nevertheless, even the free press is no guarantee that Americans will have available all the important points of view, attitudes, and opinions with which we should be familiar in order to arrive at well-reasoned opinions of our own. Let us look for a moment at the newspaper industry.

On the whole, the record of our newspapers in presenting the news fairly and objectively is among the best in the world. A few American papers may slant the news to make it conform to a certain point of view, but in general we can rely on the news stories to give the facts as honestly as possible.

EDITORIALS AND SELECTION OF NEWS The point of view of a paper is not concealed by objective news reporting—nor should it be. One way in which the opinion of a paper is conveyed to its readers is by its editorial page. There the editors comment on the news and otherwise make their views on public questions known.

Another method is by the selection of the news to be published. Few newspapers have the resources to print even most of the news. American papers must make a selection, both of items to be covered and of the extent to which they are covered. Such a selection is necessary and proper. Some papers, however, select their stories so as to favor one side or another in a public controversy. The result is that the reader who depends on one daily newspaper may simply not see certain items which might give him a different view on a particular matter. The items he does see may be quite factual, but other facts may not be included at all. On the editorial page, the reader may find articles supporting the side which has already been weighted by the selection of news stories. Thus the reader's information is not adequate for him to arrive at a careful judgment.

NEWSPAPER CHAINS Even if you read both papers in your town, you may be getting only one point of view. The reason for this is that papers are owned and operated by small groups of people or even by individuals. Chains of newspapers cover many of our cities. Often there are no other papers in communities where a chain paper is sold. This may mean that one point of view on public questions may be very widely spread, while other points of view are not presented at all.

INDEPENDENCE OF NEWSPAPERS Newspapers are a business enterprise. Like other businesses, they must offer a product which is salable at a profit. The revenue of newspapers comes from sale to readers and from advertising. Since the latter source brings in much the largest share of the paper's income, a paper must bear in mind the views of its advertisers. Nevertheless,

419

American papers are **not** dominated by their advertisers, nor are they afraid to print articles with which advertisers disagree. For one thing, advertisers do not agree among themselves, so that a paper does not feel the steady pressure of a single point of view. For another, there is a strong tradition in the United States of newspaper independence. Editors in general are courageous people who are prepared to stand up and "be counted." American papers are predominantly Republican except in some of the southern states, where the Democratic party is virtually the only party. Yet the majority of the "Republican" newspapers usually present a fair portion of Democratic party news.

Regulation of Mass Media

The American public does have real protections against slanted news, dishonest reporting in the press, or a monopoly of the means of communication by people standing for a single point of view. Newspapers, for example, are regulated by a code self-imposed by newspaper publishers and editors. By disciplining themselves, newspapers protect themselves against government interference, on the one hand, and protect their readers, on the other. Freedom in journalism, as elsewhere, depends upon the acceptance of responsibility.

In totalitarian countries, the press is monopolized by the state. Ministries of public information dictate not only the point of view which may be expressed in newspapers but what the news shall be and how it shall be presented. No deviation from the policy of the government is allowed. In the Soviet Union, for example, a constitutional provision guaranteeing the people presses, paper, and ink so that the press may be free is rendered entirely meaningless by the complete government control of what may be printed.

In the United States, on the contrary, no one can tell a publisher what he shall print or what view he shall take. He is subject to no restraining laws except those against libel and slander. Even these laws do not interfere with what a paper prints *before* it is published. In a famous case, as we saw in Chapter 16, the Supreme Court of the United States held that no governmental authority can exert *prior* censorship on the press. This means that papers may print what they like, but must take the responsibility if they are sued for damages to reputation or indicted for libel (publishing knowingly materials which are false and scandalous). Thus it is that our American editors have developed their own code of self-discipline, their own rules as to what is honorable and fair. Violators of the rules are subjected to severe censure by the newspaper industry itself.

Radio and television, unlike newspapers, are regulated by the federal government to an important extent, as we saw in Chapter 8. The government has no power to tell broadcasters what they may say or what point of view they should take. In this respect they are as free as newspapers. But on controversial subjects or in political debate, radio and television stations are required by the Federal Communications Commission to allot equal amounts of free time to both sides, as we saw on p. 205. However, there is no *narrow* limitation on the amount of time a candidate or a party may buy if they have the money. We say "narrow" limitation because a station which allowed programs on behalf of one party or candidate, even if paid for, to dominate its air time would undoubtedly lose its license for violating the public interest. In general, it is true that political parties having the most money available for the purchase of radio or television time have a great advantage in influencing public opinion.

Motion Pictures

The motion-picture industry, which has grown to such enormous proportions since World War I, reaches almost all Americans. Motion pictures, of course, do not often deal with controversial subjects. Nevertheless, they can influence public opinion. An occasional picture may tackle a political problem or the kind of problem that stirs up popular feeling.

Public opinion can also be influenced through documentary films, short subjects, and selected news. Because motion pictures are entirely dependent on sales, however, the producer is not so much concerned with expressing a point of view through his film as he is with avoiding one. This is the reason so many of our films are love stories, detective stories, and westerns, which come out all right at the end. The goal is to entertain as many people as possible and to offend as few as possible.

THINKING CRITICALLY ABOUT MASS MEDIA

The total effect of these media of mass communication upon our minds is that we have more information about more subjects of interest and importance than people in the past ever had. But the possession of *more* information does not necessarily mean that we are better informed. Sometimes we may feel swamped by the sea of facts and opinions in which we are forced to swim. The greater our store of information, the greater is our need to train and use our critical faculties. At the beginning of this chapter, we discussed the methods by which the human mind is influenced to arrive at opinions. They are not new. Only the media are new. This is fortunate, because these ancient techniques of influence can be studied and understood. What is required of you, to be an effective citizen, is to think critically, to be alert to detect false reasoning and biased opinion.

We must not be misled into believing that all propaganda is "phony." Propaganda in itself is neither a good thing nor a bad thing. It is not possible to be completely objective about controversial subjects and, in spite of the enormous quantity of information available, it is not possible for us to know everything about a problem before we make a decision. Most political and social issues, about which we disagree, rest upon assumptions or convictions that cannot be verified scientifically. Thus they will always remain matters of opinion rather than knowledge.

What we can and must do is to weigh and sift the facts which come to us, try to gauge the sincerity of the views expressed, and, above all, try to see what the public interest is. This means that we should begin by identifying the "publics" to which we belong so that we can see their relation to other publics. Then we can determine whether the immediate interest of our particular publics will in the long run benefit more or fewer of the whole people. Only in this way will the mass of information we receive enable us to become truly informed.

It is necessary for a free citizen to have convictions and principles. It is equally necessary for him to understand that the convictions and principles of other citizens may be equally honorable and desirable. When we have reached such an understanding, we will see why our personal opinions are bound to lose out many times, and why we shall have to accept less than we think we should have. We shall also see that the contrary opinions of others will also lose out many times and they will have to accept less than they think they should have.

As we have seen, the opinion of **the** public is always a compromise among the opinions of the many lesser publics. The strength, integrity, and wisdom of "public opinion" will determine the strength, integrity, and wisdom of our government. One of the most demanding obligations of the free American as a citizen, therefore, is to make the fullest possible use of his information. He must think critically; he must press fairly and firmly to get others to accept his opinions; and he must learn to accept defeats as well as victories with good grace.

MEASURING PUBLIC OPINION

The citizen, in his attempts to form opinions on public questions, is bombarded by people skillful in the arts of persuasion. While it is important that free citizens should be well informed and prepared to state their considered views, it is not enough for the citizen to respond actively only when an election occurs. Yet perhaps this is just what is suggested to us by the emphasis being placed in recent years on public opinion polls at election time. Taking a "scientific poll" sometimes seems a little like taking a man's temperature and recording it on a fever chart. The comparison fails, however, because when the patient's temperature is 98.6 we say it is "normal," but there is no such thing as a "normal" state of public opinion. So long as we do not allow the percentages reported in polls to take the place of thinking for ourselves, they can be very useful.

Straw Vote Polls

Modern polling methods bear little resemblance to older "straw vote" techniques, used by the once famous weekly magazine *Literary Digest*. It ran straw votes on elections for years and had a record of coming quite close to accurate predictions. Its ballots were sent to people selected from the telephone books and various mailing lists. This meant that a very large number of people, whose names did not appear on such lists, were not reached. If these people voted in large numbers, the straw poll result might turn out to be quite seriously in error. In the election of 1936 just that seemed to happen. The *Digest* poll, at the end of the campaign, showed that Governor Landon of Kansas, the Republican candidate, would win by a comfortable majority. The result of the actual election gave President Franklin D. Roosevelt, the Democratic candidate running for reëlection, the most complete sweep since the second election of James Monroe in 1820. Shortly afterwards the *Literary Digest* went out of business.

Gallup Poll

In the same 1936 election, a young man named George Gallup, with a small group of·associates, also took a poll. Gallup analyzed the nature of public opinion as we have been doing in this chapter. Taking into account the various publics which compose the larger American public, he tried to get an accurate *sample* of each of these publics—or as many of them as possible—in each typical section of each state in each part of the country. He distributed only some 5,000 ballots (instead of the hundreds of thousands of straw votes distributed by the *Digest*). But each of the 5,000 had special significance, as representing, for example, Protestant wheat farmers in North Dakota, Catholic factory workers in Boston, Jewish clerks in New York, migrant fruit pickers in California, shopkeepers in Omaha, and so forth. This poll, almost unnoticed during the campaign itself, gained national attention immediately after the election, for it came within a tiny percentage of accurate prediction both of the popular vote and of the electoral vote, and even of the number of Congressmen who would be elected by each party.

The success of "scientific polling" in 1936 brought a new era in the study of public opinion. In the years following, Dr. Gallup himself has introduced improvements, and other experts like Elmo Roper have earned national eminence. Professors of social science have done exhaustive research on the techniques of scientific sampling and have trained many recruits for a new and growing profession. Pollsters, however, can make mistakes like anybody else. In 1948, they misjudged their own figures and predicted that Governor Dewey would beat President Truman. Similar mistakes of interpretation have occasionally been made in predicting the outcome of state and local elections.

Value of Polls

Scientific polling today is applied to almost every important question before the people. All elections are studied in advance by these methods; so are issues of public policy, and questions of relative popularity among public figures. From these polls, published in almost every daily newspaper and often the subject of radio and television programs, officials of government are able to obtain a much sounder notion of what the people are thinking than was formerly possible. Politicians running for office can obtain valuable indications of the kind of campaign with which they might be successful.

The expert in scientific polling will be the first to tell you there is always a margin of error in polls. Dr. Gallup says that on national questions and national elections, the margins may go to about 4 percent. Since we cannot know which way the margin of error is going, we can never be sure how a very close election will come out; nor can we be sure just how great a majority favors a particular policy or point of view. Thus we should not base predictions too firmly on the findings of such surveys or accept them without question as an accurate reflection of "public opinion."

The polls can help the citizen to evaluate public opinion if he does more than simply look at the percentages given in the tabulation. Other important information to look for is the exact wording of the questions asked, the number responding, the area or "public" surveyed, and the number who had no definite opinion. Frequently the number of the "undecided" is so great that no prediction is possible. In elections the candidate can reckon with the "undecided" as the group to whom he must address his strongest appeal. In attempting to lead national opinion, the President and the Congress can make a reasonable estimate of the number and sort of people whom they are not reaching or have not persuaded.

HOW THE CITIZEN CAN INFLUENCE THE OPINIONS OF OTHERS

The role of the citizen in forming "public opinion" is not fulfilled simply by making up his own mind on the basis of the facts available to him and the use of his critical judgment. The citizen who takes his citizenship seriously and who wants to participate actively and responsibly will wish to influence

424

How Private Opinion Becomes Public Opinion

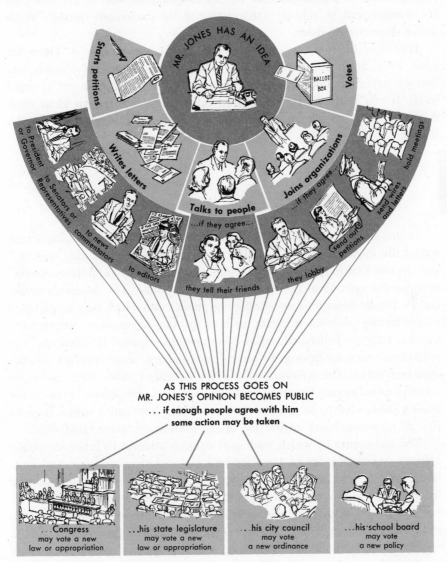

MR. JONES HAS AN IDEA

Starts petitions

Votes

BALLOT BOX

Writes letters

to President or Governor

to Senators or Representatives

to news commentators

to editors

Talks to people

...if they agree...

they tell their friends

Joins organizations

...if they agree...

hold meetings

send wires and letters

send out petitions

they lobby

AS THIS PROCESS GOES ON
MR. JONES'S OPINION BECOMES PUBLIC
...if enough people agree with him
some action may be taken

...Congress
may vote a new
law or appropriation

...his state legislature
may vote a new
law or appropriation

...his city council
may vote
a new ordinance

...his school board
may vote
a new policy

The freedom of the country depends upon the willingness of the individual—at the "grass roots"—to use his freedom as an individual. Starting with an idea, he can as an individual do many things, as shown in the first half circle of the chart. From these, the idea reaches wider and wider circles—through neighbors, through friends and associates, through organizations. Eventually, since our elected officials must respond to the wishes of private citizens (or risk not being reëlected), some action or legislation can result.

others to think as he does. This does not mean that we must all become propagandists. It does mean that we can maintain our way of life and even try to improve it by actively participating in the discussions through which public decisions are made.

How can the ordinary citizen influence "public opinion"? There are many ways. Study the drawing on p. 425 to see how private opinion may become public opinion—and may eventually influence government at many levels. If you at the "grass roots" start talking and acting, your ideas reach ever wider circles. Sometimes your idea can, as the chart shows, reach very far indeed.

SUMMARY

In this chapter you have studied three essential aspects of the democratic way of life in America. We have discussed the meaning of "public opinion," and the fact that in reality there is seldom any such thing as "public opinion" meaning the opinion of the whole American republic. The American public quickly breaks down into many different publics into which may be gathered people having common interests, such as income, occupation, cultural associations, religious beliefs, educational background, regional attachments. The individual American belongs to several such publics, some of which conflict with each other. The opinion of the *whole* American public turns out to be a compromise among the many publics; in such a compromise each of the smaller publics has to be satisfied with something less than it wishes in order that all may have some satisfaction or the promise of future satisfaction.

The techniques by which leaders of opinion attempt to influence public opinion involve the use of language and manipulation of logical and emotional tools. The citizen must understand what these techniques are and how they are used, and must use critical judgment in forming opinions.

Mass media of radio, television, and motion pictures now supplement the newspapers and magazines; together these media reach almost every American. With more abundant information also comes more constant bombardment of ideas and emotions. Therefore, the responsibility of the individual to think carefully, scrutinize what he hears and reads, and make critical judgments has grown in proportion.

Public opinion is measured by scientific sampling. Both leaders and you, the plain citizen, can learn much that is useful through surveys or polls of public opinion. The significance of the polls is not their accuracy but the dynamic quality of the opinions they are measuring.

Finally, there are ways in which you, the individual, can influence others —through direct contact with leaders, through local organizations, and through large national or state organizations concerned with political and civic affairs. "Public opinion" helps determine the general direction of events; it exerts ultimate control on the personnel and policies of government. But public opinion is made by the people, and the "people" are no more and no less than the individual citizen.

KNOW WHAT YOU READ

1. Explain: "There is not just one public but many publics."
2. Who make up the American "public"? Why then is there seldom an "American public opinion"?
3. List as many as you can of the economic groups into which our people are divided.
4. Explain how an economic issue such as public vs. private ownership may divide Americans into *publics*.
5. How may our opinions be influenced by our racial origin or religion?
6. What effect has the process of "Americanization" had on opinions based on cultural differences?
7. Give examples from the history of our country to show how regional groupings influence opinions.
8. What are the mechanical devices used in influencing public opinion?
9. What is a syllogism? Show how it may be misused.
10. Give some examples of emotionally-toned words. Why are they included among the "tricks of persuasion"?
11. List examples of "very general words."
12. Explain how the "bandwagon" device may be used.
13. Why should we be careful about accepting the opinion of persons who use the prestige device?
14. Explain why commentators may be very influential.
15. Some people claim that they get tired of having to listen to so much repetition. Nevertheless, advertisers and political parties continue to use this device. Why?
16. What is apt to happen to the opinions of Mr. Smith who reads only one columnist and listens to only one commentator?
17. How are newspapers, radio, and television stations regulated?
18. There are two principal ways in which a newspaper's opinions are expressed to the readers. What are they?
19. What is the importance of the fact that many newspapers belong to chains?
20. Newspapers are businesses. How does this affect the opinions they express?
21. What protection do we have against possible abuse of the powers of the newspapers?

22. Why is it that the movies so seldom are concerned with problems of real importance?
23. Many of us sometimes feel swamped by the sea of facts and opinions about us. What can we do about it?
24. Explain: "The opinion of the public is always a compromise among the opinions of the many lesser publics."
25. Explain the failure of the *Literary Digest* to predict the winner of the 1936 election.
26. Contrast the methods of the *Literary Digest* with Dr. Gallup's.
27. How accurate are the public opinion polls today?
28. Explain the process by which private opinion can become public opinion.

WHAT DO YOU THINK?

1. "What binds us together as one people is our *faith in freedom* and in the *democratic process of government*." Do *you* have faith in freedom? Which freedom? Do you have faith in the democratic process? Always?
2. One of the frequently mentioned techniques of the propagandist is the "bandwagon." How effective do you think it is?
3. What techniques is the "airy campaigner" in the cartoon, p. 416, using?
4. How do you explain the following figures? What, if any, importance do they have? A survey in an Ohio city in the late 1940's revealed that some people were "well informed" about the United Nations, some were "poorly informed." Of the poorly informed group, 88 percent did not complete high school, 75 percent were women, 58 percent were over 40 years of age, 47 percent had not voted in the 1946 election.
5. Some communities have PTSA's (Parent-Teacher-Student Association) instead of PTA's. Would you be in favor of including students in organizations of parents and teachers? Why?
6. Do economic interests determine what our opinions will be? How?

PROBLEMS AND PROJECTS FOR YOU

1. "Sometimes democracy is a way of agreeing to disagree." Write a one-page explanation of what this quotation means to you.
2. "There is seldom such a thing as American public opinion on any question." Make a list of exceptions to this statement, *i.e.*, occasions on which there was an American opinion on a question.
3. Write a statement of about 150–200 words explaining what *you* mean by a *sound* farm policy.
4. Analyze a President's State of the Union speech, or a party platform, to find the number of publics concerned. List them.

5. What is a *stereotype?* List some examples, or draw a cartoon.
6. Form a committee to interview an agreed-upon number of adults to find an answer to this question: Do people in general listen only to those commentators with whom they agree? Report your conclusions.
7. Organize a panel discussion on these questions:
   (a) Can the average citizen get all the facts on major issues?
   (b) Does he have a right to form convictions on major issues?
   (c) What responsibilities does he have?
8. If there is a radio or television station in your community, interview someone on its staff to find out to what extent broadcasting is regulated.
9. If you were to conduct a poll in your own school to learn who would win the next in-school election, what *publics* would you sample? How many persons in each public? Write out a plan for such a poll.
10. Take some strong opinion of your own—or of some person you know— and try to determine which influences have had the most to do with its formation.

> "The American electorate, which should be the most intelligent in the world, is plied with many spot-news dispatches, radio bulletins, television roundups. But the interpretation and the continuity—what does this mean, what does it portend, how does it tie into what happened last week, what comes next?—is quite often missing."

11. Do you agree? Why? Assemble clippings on one or more series of events to support your argument.
12. Report to the class on coverage of news stories in a newspaper, on radio and TV, and in a newsmagazine. Would you recommend or not recommend that the average citizen buy a newsmagazine? Why?
13. See question 4 under "What Do You Think?" Organize a survey in your own school on some current domestic or international issue. Write up the results for your school paper.
14. Make up, write out, and hand in three original syllogisms.
15. Make a list of all the "emotional" words you have encountered in one week.
16. *One* of the serious problems confronting our country today is how to provide and win support for our free public schools. Draw up proposals for ways in which your local PTA could help.
17. Review question 28 under "Know What You Read." Some students who have read this chapter think that the authors have been too optimistic about what ordinary citizens can do to influence "public opinion." What do you think? Write a newspaper editorial or a letter to the editor, in which you make a realistic statement of your views on the question of the citizen's power to influence the opinions of others. (Don't forget that *realistic* is not synonymous with *cynical*.)
18. Select three adults you know, and list all the "publics" to which each belongs.

EXTEND YOUR VOCABULARY

public opinion
private enterprise
farm bloc
cultural minority
subsidy
syllogism
major premise

minor premise
valid reasoning
emotionally-toned words
generalizations
propaganda
bandwagon
prestige value

mass media
stereotypes
libel
slander
controversial subject
scientific poll
straw vote

YOUR NOTEBOOK: THE GOVERNMENT OF ——

1. List the institutions and organizations of your community or area which try to influence opinion; *e.g.*, the name of your local newspaper(s), local industries which advertise via radio or TV, etc.
2. List the various publics mentioned in this chapter which are also found in your community.

READ MORE ABOUT IT

ALBIG, WILLIAM, *Modern Public Opinion*. McGraw-Hill, 1956.
A useful and informative text.
BURNS, JAMES M., and PELTASON, JACK W., *Government by the People*. Prentice-Hall, 1954. Chap. 10.
CATER, DOUGLASS, *The Fourth Branch of Government*. Houghton Mifflin, 1959.
Fascinating and readable study of the press in Washington.
GALLUP, GEORGE H., and RAE, S. F., *The Pulse of Democracy*. Simon and Schuster, 1940.
A readable study of public opinion polling.
IRISH, MARIAN D., and PROTHRO, JAMES W., *The Politics of American Democracy*. Prentice-Hall, 1959. Chap. 8.
KATZ, DANIEL *et al.*, *Public Opinion and Propaganda: A Book of Readings*. Dryden Press, 1954.
LIPPMANN, WALTER, *Public Opinion*. Harcourt, Brace, 1922.
A famous essay on the relation between public opinion and public policy.
See *Public Opinion Quarterly*.
RANNEY, AUSTIN, *The Governing of Men*. Holt, 1958. Chaps. 10–11.
SWARTHOUT, JOHN M., and BARTLEY, ERNEST R., *Principles and Problems of American National Government*. Oxford University Press, 1955. Chaps. 7–9.

CHAPTER 18

Politics, Parties, and the Citizen

In this chapter you will learn about

Government and political parties
What are political parties in the United States?
Political parties and the citizen
Money for politics
Advantages of party·membership
Responsibilities of party members
The process of nomination

Political parties are an important part of life in America. You may belong to a family of "rabid Democrats" or "rabid Republicans." If you do, you are likely to hear nothing but good things about one party and nothing but bad things about the other. Feeling about parties sometimes runs high, especially in election years. Strong feeling is not only unavoidable but healthy if it is based on a reasonable knowledge of the facts. Be on the watch for unreasoned prejudice, however. Whenever you are confronted by sweeping generalizations to the effect that "All Democrats are traitors" or "All Republicans are against the common man," just remember that about half of the voters support one party and half support the other. When so many tens of millions support a political party, whichever it is, it can only be because there is much good in it. Actually our two parties are indispensable to American democracy, as we shall see. But first we must understand what a political party—any political party—is.

431

GOVERNMENT AND POLITICAL PARTIES

No one can say when or exactly how political parties started. According to James Madison, they have their roots in human nature. We do know that there have been parties in England for several centuries. The English parties seem to have arisen out of the need felt by large numbers of people to organize and work together for common purposes, and to oppose, in parliamentary debates, others similarly organized.

If you belong to a fairly large club, or participate in your school student government, you can probably observe in your own experience the start, at least, of political parties. A permanent party does not usually develop when a group joins together simply for one special purpose; it becomes a party when its members discover that they agree on a number of important ideas and on continuing problems and issues. Once a party has come into being and scored some successes, it may continue with a kind of life of its own over many generations, even though the purposes involved in its founding are long since forgotten or its ideas greatly change.

In free countries, there are at least two and often more political parties. Elections can be really free only when people have a choice between alternatives and a way to express their choice. If you lived in the Soviet Union, for example, you would find your choice narrowly restricted. At elections you would be required to vote; but you could vote only for the candidates of the Communist Party. If you were opposed to these candidates, you would have no one else to vote for.

By contrast, if you have lived in a free democracy like France before 1959, you would have been bewildered by the large number of political parties discussing issues from many different points of view, and offering opposing candidates at elections. With so many parties, naturally each one was relatively small. As a result, no one party could ever win the majority in an election, but had to join with other parties to do so. Because of many shifts in such alignments, France had many changes in government—sometimes several in one year. This freedom placed a great burden on French statesmen to maintain stability in their country in spite of such shifts.

Political parties have been based on many different ideas and interests. Often these ideas and interests are economic. Thus there are parties of the working class in many countries, parties of small businessmen and shop-keepers, parties of farmers, and parties of noblemen and aristocrats. There are also parties based on religious or philosophical convictions—Catholic parties and Protestant parties, Marxist parties and parties devoted to other "isms." However, the United States has developed a different political system from those in Europe, and parties narrowly based on economic creed, religion, or social class have had little success.

432

WHAT ARE POLITICAL PARTIES IN THE UNITED STATES?

The two great American parties, the Republican and the Democratic, are at one and the same time the most original and successful products of our democracy and the despair of professional students of government. In most other democratic countries, the political parties are usually united by belief in certain special theories and programs which they urge upon the electorate and which divide them from other parties. The American parties, on the other hand, emphasize different specific programs but agree on basic principles. While political parties usually maintain points of view which restrict their membership to believers, American parties constantly strive for positions broad enough to appeal to the whole country. And while typical political parties, again, are tightly organized and keep firm discipline over their members, American parties are so loose and unwieldy, and contain so many differing views, that it is sometimes a kind of miracle that they do not fall apart. Yet the fact is that no attempts to organize a party in the United States along the narrow and specialized lines normal in other democracies have met with important success.

Minor Parties in the United States

An early specialized third-party movement was the Free-Soil party of the 1840's and 1850's. Based on the principle that the western territories under control of Congress should be closed to slavery and admitted to the Union only with constitutions forbidding slavery, this movement had the support of many distinguished northern citizens. But in 1856, most of the Free-Soilers joined in the formation of the Republican party, and the Free-Soil party disappeared entirely.

A more effective third party was developed by dissatisfied farmers and people of the western towns. The People's party, generally known as the Populists, was formed in 1892. The Populists agitated for stricter federal regulation of the railroads, and adopted other principles aimed at attracting lower-income groups. Their candidate for President in 1892 received over a million popular votes and 22 electoral votes. The Democrats were impressed enough to try to attract the Populists to their banner. They succeeded in getting Populist endorsement of their candidate, William Jennings Bryan, in 1896 and 1900. After that the People's party disappeared.

From time to time regular members of the major parties have become dissatisfied with the progress their parties were making and have split off to form third parties. The two outstanding examples are the Progressive party of 1912 and the Progressive party of 1924. In 1912 former Republican President Theodore Roosevelt, defeated in his bid for the Republican nomination against President Taft, organized a new party. This first Progressive party,

433

although it quickly developed a mass following, lost the election of 1912 to Woodrow Wilson, the Democratic candidate. The Progressive party soon died out, as many Progressives found President Wilson to their liking, and their leader, Roosevelt, became an "elder statesman" no longer available for office.

The Progressive party of 1924 was a similar movement. A large number of active citizens, dissatisfied with both major parties, formed a third party and nominated United States Senator Robert M. La Follette of Wisconsin for the Presidency. Their efforts fell far short of the 1912 record, though La Follette carried Wisconsin and received 4,822,856 votes. Like its predecessor, this Progressive party also rapidly dwindled into nothing. Many of its best-known leaders, however, were active in support of Franklin D. Roosevelt in 1932 and his "New Deal" in the following years.

The Socialist party, founded in the 1880's, was always small but very active. Its two leaders, Eugene V. Debs and Norman Thomas, were well known throughout the country. In 1932 the Socialist party platform called for a number of reforms and economic measures to combat the depression. Some of these, such as social security, unemployment insurance, banking and currency reforms, and strengthening of unions, were put into practice by the Democratic administrations of Franklin D. Roosevelt. The Democrats, by carrying out such measures in their attempt to overcome the great economic depression of the 1930's, deprived the Socialists of their chief attraction for the voters, and the Socialist party has almost entirely disappeared in recent years.

The American Communist Party, on the other hand, grew out of a split with the Socialists in 1917–1919 on the question of supporting Russian communism. While the great majority of American Socialists were deeply opposed to the anti-democratic, authoritarian leadership of Lenin (and later Stalin), a minority began to talk of a "proletarian revolution leading to a Soviet America." The average American, however, has shown not the slightest interest in the wares of the Communists—"miserable merchants of unwanted ideas," as Justice William O. Douglas has called them. The largest vote ever received by a Communist candidate for President was 102,991 in 1932, out of a total of almost forty million votes cast.

As an undercover conspiracy, the Communists are undoubtedly more dangerous to American democracy. As we saw in Chapters 15 and 16, the Smith Act of 1940 enables the Department of Justice to prosecute Communist leaders for participation in a conspiracy. It is important for you to understand that it is for *conspiracy, not open political activity*, that the Communists have been arrested. In this respect the Communist Party is not a political party and must not be confused with genuine political parties which openly advocate their point of view and try to win majorities at elec-

434

tions. Because so much of its work is secret, underground, and illegal, it is proper to say that the Communist Party is "un-American." It is not proper to say that an individual citizen who holds unpopular opinions is "un-American"—even if he thinks that Congress is a conspiracy to make life hard for businessmen!

Even such a quick sketch of minority and third parties as we have given shows not only that it is entirely "American" to hold and support unpopular ideas through political organizations, but also that many such ideas eventually become popular and are adopted. It is in developing new and different ideas which later become generally acceptable that the minority and third-party movements in the United States have served best. Third parties are, in short, among those "publics" we discussed in Chapter 17, whose voices speak for minorities and enable them to influence national policies through the political process. While minorities usually hold extreme opinions, if they are strongly enough held, sooner or later they are likely to result in workable compromises with the popular majority.

In a few cases, third parties operating only on a local level have been quite successful. In New York City, for example, a Fusion party of dissatisfied Republicans and Democrats kept Mayor Fiorello La Guardia in office during the 1930's. In Syracuse recently a Democratic candidate for county supervisor was elected by *seven* votes out of several thousand, because he had also been nominated by the Liberal party (*one* vote in the primary!), which gave him this tiny majority. Every vote counts!

The Democratic Party

The oldest of the two great parties which dominate American political life was at first called the Republican party. It was founded by Thomas Jefferson, James Madison, James Monroe, Albert Gallatin, and others who feared that the new government of the United States, in the 1790's, might lapse back toward monarchy. They opposed ceremonies of state, "aristocratical" tendencies, and centralization of government. In foreign policy, they preferred the friendship of France to that of England, and supported the French Revolution until the "Terror" of Robespierre frightened even the most liberal Americans. In domestic matters, they favored individual enterprise and agriculture and opposed banking and industry except as "handmaids" of farming. They emphasized strongly the individual and civil liberties. During Jefferson's Presidency (1801–1809), the name of the party became "Democratic-Republican," and in Jackson's time (1829–1837), the word *Republican* was dropped.

There was a long gap between the Presidencies of Democrats Buchanan (1857–1861) and Cleveland in his first term (1885–1889). It was in part owing to the War Between the States. In the 1850's the Democratic party was split between its northern wing, which was influenced by the anti-slavery

435

movement, and the southern wing, which was dominated by slaveholders. It took more than a generation for the party to recover sufficiently from this split to win a presidential election, though it did score victories in congressional elections as early as 1872. At the same time, it was the War Between the States and Reconstruction which, by vastly increasing sentimental attachment to the Democratic party, gave to the Democrats their almost complete hold on southern politics.

CHANGING POSITION Over the years a strange shift in position can be observed in the Democratic party. In its early days, it emphasized local government and wished to keep the activities of the federal government to a minimum. It favored what we have called "strict construction" of the Constitution (see Chap. 4), and even wished to limit the term of a President to four or eight years. It favored agriculture against industry, and small business against banking and big manufacturing. In the mid-twentieth century, however, the Democrats have tended to draw their chief support from big cities, have emphasized social welfare through the activities of the federal government, have favored "loose construction" of the Constitution, and succeeded in electing Franklin Roosevelt to the Presidency four times.

On the other hand, Democrats have been remarkably consistent all through their history in standing for free trade with foreign nations and for low tariffs; they have also appealed strongly to small farmers. Since the time of Jackson, they have used such phrases as the "common man," the "plain people," the "forgotten man," to attract the voters. A number of men of great wealth and power in industry and banking have nevertheless supported the Democratic party.

The Republican Party

The Republican party also has deep roots in the American past. It was founded during the 1850's, partly as a result of the controversy over slavery, though it was never an out-and-out abolition party. Its history may be traced back to the beginnings of government under the Constitution. The ancestors of modern Republicanism were the Federalists of the 1790's led by men like Alexander Hamilton, John Jay, and John Adams. The Federalist party claimed President Washington and elected John Adams, but during the so-called "Era of Good Feeling" under President Monroe, it almost entirely disappeared. In fact Monroe was reëlected in 1820 without opposition—the only President after Washington who did not have to campaign in the modern sense. However, the remaining Federalists joined in the 1830's with dissatisfied Democrats to form the Whig party, which elected William Henry Harrison in 1840 and Zachary Taylor in 1848.

Both the Federalists and the Whigs tended to favor the development of industry. They wanted tariffs to protect American manufactures and made

436

"Boy, Do You Look Silly"

Herblock in
The Washington Post, 1957

their chief appeal to the "middle class" of businessmen, professional people, and, of course, farmers. Like the Democrats, they were split in the 1850's by the slavery issue. The Whigs were not so dependent on their southern wing as were the Democrats, however, so that when they dissolved and joined with other groups to form the Republican party, their chief strength was in the North.

CHANGING POSITION Like the Democrats, the Republicans have also changed their views over the years. Their Federalist ancestors favored a strong central government and "loose construction" of the Constitution. In the mid-twentieth century, the party places much more emphasis on state and local government and holds to a more "strict construction." It was under Republican leadership that Amendment XXII was enacted, limiting a President to two terms.

However, the Republicans also have been consistent. Their emphasis on industrial development and their reliance on business leadership have not significantly changed, and many Republicans still favor trade restrictions which particularly benefit American manufacturers. As the Democrats appeal to the "common man," the Republicans usually offer a program to attract the "middle class."

These differences are often not so striking as are the similarities between the two parties. Despite their differences, it is important to repeat that the

437

Republican and Democratic parties of today do not differ on certain basic principles. Neither party has any desire to change our form of government. Both, despite differing emphases, hope for votes from all classes. Both are devoted to the preservation of our civil liberties. In other words, both are "democratic" and both are "republican." And differences on domestic program have not often prevented the two parties from working together in those times of greatest crisis during the almost endless strife which has beset the world since 1914.

POLITICAL PARTIES AND THE CITIZEN

The history of our two political parties shows that they are *national* in scope, and of course they are organized on a national scale. But the basis of party organization is at the local level—the famous "grass roots" of American politics. You and I are the "grass roots," and nobody knows it better than home-town politicians. You the citizen, when you register by signing your name on the voting roll book, signify the political party of your choice at the same time. You are not required, of course, to choose any party; but unless you do, you cannot be a party member and you cannot (in most states) vote in party primary elections.

As you have learned (Chap. 16), registration is by election district (precinct). The party members of a district usually elect two committeemen (often a man and a woman) to represent them on the county committee. These district or precinct committeemen often personally call on us to vote, ask us to support their ticket, and offer to transport us to the polls, if it is difficult for us to go there. Committeemen also try to persuade us to join their party and urge us to be active in party work. They are our neighbors, and our lasting opinions about political parties are often based on our opinions of these "grass-root" politicians.

If you wish to become an active party member, you should talk to your district committeeman. He will show you how to get started. And the best way to become influential in your party is to run for the office of committeeman yourself and persuade your neighbors to vote for you.

Ward or Town Chairmen

Between the district and the county committees is another level of organization known as the ward (in most cities) or the town (in rural areas). The various district committeemen choose the ward or town chairman who serves as leader of party activities in areas including several districts. The ward and town chairmen, in turn, usually choose from the committee membership the county chairman and serve as his principal advisers. The size of the county committee, then, depends on the population, and it may vary from twenty or thirty to many hundreds of members.

The County Chairman

The essential unit of party organization is the county committee. It is the official representative body of a party in the country. The county chairman in many ways holds the keys to American politics. If you follow public opinion polls, you will notice that it is the county chairmen all over the country who are polled to discover how strong a potential candidate for President is—and not merely the county chairmen of the candidate's own party. The county chairmen of the opposite party are almost as good judges of the candidate's drawing power with the voters. Why is this so? The best way to get the answer to this question is to call on the county chairman in your own home county. You will find him quite easy to talk with, and glad to "fill you in" on politics, both local and national. There is no substitute for such an interview, but we shall attempt here to give you some notion of what a county chairman does and how he gains his information.

The county chairman is the "leader" of his party, and is often called simply the "leader." The country chairman's duties are heavy anywhere, but in populous counties he has a full-time job. In such cases, he may be paid anywhere from $5,000 to $25,000 a year. He must, in the first place, be a man who likes people, likes to talk to them, and has a genuine sympathy for their problems. One of his chief tasks is simply talking. He meets people from every walk of life and with every sort of interest. He must at least give the impression of being interested in whatever concerns them. He must know personally as many people as is humanly possible. Most people are pleased to have an important person recognize them and call them by name. The chairman who has a knack of pleasing people in those ways is on the road to success.

Simply to please is not enough, however. In his party there will be various groups of people who disagree with each other on all kinds of matters. The chairman must strive to keep the respect and support of these differing groups. His chief purpose is to win elections for his party. Thus it is of the utmost importance for the chairman to keep conflicting groups working together for the good of the whole party.

THE CHAIRMAN AND "PATRONAGE"   Much of the chairman's conversation is with members of his party who are interested in becoming candidates for public office or who are already officeholders—in short, politicians. He must treat them all with respect, yet not indicate too great a preference for any until the party primary has determined the nominees. Usually the chairman himself plays the chief part in naming the candidates for the primary. For this reason, he must be constantly on the alert for promising "new blood,"

Organization of the Major Political Parties

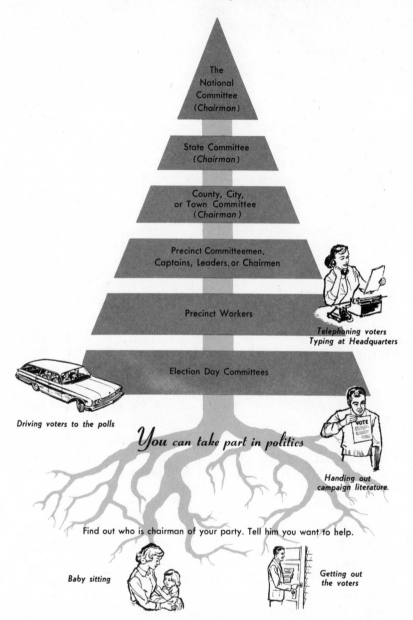

The
National
Committee
(Chairman)

State Committee
(Chairman)

County, City,
or Town Committee
(Chairman)

Precinct Committeemen,
Captains, Leaders, or Chairmen

Precinct Workers

Election Day Committees

*Telephoning voters
Typing at Headquarters*

Driving voters to the polls

You can take part in politics

*Handing out
campaign literature*

Find out who is chairman of your party. Tell him you want to help.

Baby sitting

*Getting out
the voters*

You can take part in politics. There is a place in a party organization for you. Some of you may be elected to public office; some may hold such responsible party positions as state or county chairmen. Most people, however, serve in the lower ranks of the party.

What can you, as average citizens, do? The following jobs may not sound exciting, but they may help you to get the kind of government you want.

(1) Find out who is local chairman of your party. Tell him you want to help.
(2) Some of the things you may do to help: check voting lists; type; duplicate, fold, stamp letters; hand out leaflets; put up posters; solicit campaign funds; drive automobiles; telephone voters; ring doorbells; sit with babies; arrange for meetings.
(3) Finally—be sure you vote, as soon as you are able to.

and must assess the weaknesses and strengths among the voters of the tried and tested politicians. Often he must make bargains, giving his support to this man in order to get the support of certain important people for another. He must try to gauge public opinion in his county so that his candidates for nomination have the best chance to be elected. Thus he must know not only people but also issues. From every scrap of conversation, from every bit of news in the paper, every expression of opinion on radio or television, and from the activities and expressions of the other party, the chairman tries to gather something useful to him in deciding what the voters are thinking and which candidates—from President to county commissioner—are likely to please them best.

He must, at the same time, pay careful attention to the state-wide interests of his party. He is the link between the local and the state organization. Often his policy or decisions may be "advised" by the state chairman, or by the governor's office if his party is in power. If there is a conflict of opinion between his county organization and the state organization, he may have some very tough problems. For example, suppose that the governor is about to appoint a high state official from Chairman Wilson's county. Wilson will be asked to suggest suitable names. Wilson thinks that Evans, a veteran supporter and financial contributor to the party, ought to have the job. The governor's advisers object to Evans because, as a businessman, he has had trouble with a labor union which the state-wide party is anxious to please. The governor's choice is Cunningham, who is well liked by the state Chamber of Commerce but not too popular in Chairman Wilson's home county. What is Wilson to do? Ask your county chairman what he would do under such circumstances. He will know well enough what you are talking about. Perhaps Wilson's best bet will be to say, "O.K. I'll take Cunningham, but see if you can't find something else for Evans." The chances are that Evans will get a job, since the governor and the state organization are dependent on Chairman Wilson and his kind throughout the state in order to get elected.

The problem we have just discussed is one of what is known as "patronage"—appointing people to public office who belong to and have worked for the party in power. Patronage helps to keep a party organization going and its members enthusiastic. Local patronage is most important. If the chairman's party is in power, he will normally be asked to suggest people for a great many positions—chiefly those positions appointed by a governor or a mayor or a board of county commissioners who are indebted to the county chairman for help in getting elected. In this way the chairman can make important friends, or "punish" enemies by ignoring their hopes for appointment to government jobs. If his party is out of power, his followers will be "patronage hungry" and all the more anxious to win next time.

FINANCING THE PARTY The chairman needs more than patronage to do a good job; he needs, above all, *money*. Many chairmen will say that they spend more time raising money than in any other activity. Thus a typical county chairman must make almost endless calls on business people, union leaders, and others who may make substantial contributions, and, as we shall see presently, he must help the party organization in many other ways of money raising.

CAMPAIGNING At election time, the chairman is the director of his party's campaign in his county. Individual candidates may have their own campaign managers, but the chairman is interested in the success of the whole ticket. He must work closely with all candidates and managers to avoid conflicts, watch for chances to turn the other party's mistakes to his own party's advantage, advise his party on issues, on publicity, on newspaper coverage, and on radio and television programs. Throughout the whole campaign he must be concerned all the time with keeping the party's best foot forward. When election day itself arrives, the chairman becomes the field general of the whole effort of his party in his county. He presents to the board of elections the names of the election inspectors who officially represent his party at the polls. He also appoints watchers to observe the polls and keep him informed on all details of the progress of the voting. He organizes groups of volunteers or paid workers who keep canvassing the districts to see that everyone in the party votes, and he directs a transportation corps to bring to the polls people who may be handicapped or just lazy. He even provides baby-sitters.

AFTER THE ELECTION When the election is over and the results are known, most people involved can sit back and rest awhile. Not so the county chairman. If his party has won the election, he must immediately begin to discuss patronage and other problems with the victorious officeholders and office-seekers. If his party has lost, he must immediately commence to "pick up the pieces," so that the party can start organizing its forces for the next election. In short, the county chairman's job never ends unless he dies, retires, or is defeated in a primary election.

The latter—a primary fight for control of his county committee—the chairman does everything he can to avoid! Winning elections is the surest way to avoid party fights and keep his party happy. Thus the county chairman starts by trying to win elections, and all his activities eventually come round to trying to win elections. You may be surprised now to learn that all the while we have been talking about the party "boss." Prosperity and civil service have pretty well eliminated the old-fashioned boss, like those who once dominated our great cities. The modern "boss" is the county chairman. You can decide for yourself just how much of a "boss" he really is.

The county organization, through district and ward or town leaders, is the citizen's real contact with his party. Any citizen may become a member of either party simply by declaring his preference at registration and voting in the party primary. Whether a citizen is influential in the party and whether his membership is valuable to him depend entirely upon himself. The vast majority of enrolled party members never take any part in the activities of the party except at elections. The relatively few who give time and money to the party inevitably become its leaders.

State Committees

The state organization of a political party is known as the state committee and consists of two members (often a man and a woman) elected by the party voters either from each county or from each election district within the counties. The state committee, in turn, elects the state chairman, who is the chief administrator of the party at the state level. The governor is the "leader" of his party in the state, and the defeated candidate for governor is the "leader" of the other party. The state committee formulates programs and policies in state elections and for sessions of the state legislature. It also helps to select candidates for state office. States with large populations and substantial party treasuries have secretaries, treasurers, and publicity directors to assist the committee and chairman.

National Committees

The national leader of the President's political party is the President himself; the national leader of the other party is the defeated candidate for President. The national chairman is the chief administrative official of the party and is chosen by the national committee, usually on the suggestion of the party's presidential candidate.

The national committee consists of two committeemen for each state (a man and a woman), chosen by the state committees. It is chiefly concerned with organizing the party to win national elections. Between elections it assists the party leader and the party's members in Congress to present the party's policies to the nation and to criticize the policies and point out the mistakes of the other party where it can. In the next chapter we will see how the national committee is organized to meet its responsibilities.

MONEY FOR POLITICS

If you ask any party official, at any level, anywhere in the United States what his hardest job is, he will tell you that it is raising money. The federal and state income tax laws do not allow the deduction of political contributions. The person who gives to a political party is simply out of pocket and often gets no reward or return for his money.

Where then do the parties get their money? The answer is that they get it where they can. Candidates are normally expected to make substantial contributions. Wealthy people are appealed to on the ground of civic responsibility. Some of them make large contributions in the hope that they may some day be appointed to an important state or national office or to a diplomatic post abroad. Quite often these ambitions are realized. A large number of individuals contribute money in order to gain a reputation within the party as deserving supporters. This may lead to nomination or appointment to office by a mayor or governor.

Money is also raised by smaller organizations within the parties, such as women's clubs, youth clubs, or clubs named after famous members of the party. They give endless picnics, clambakes, dinners, card parties, theater parties, outings, excursions, lectures, concerts, and dances, about which you read in the paper. These, of course, serve educational, cultural, and recreational purposes; but the chief purpose is usually to raise money. At the national level, both parties sponsor "$100-a-plate" dinners each year which are attended by politicians and supporters from all sections of the country. Many state party organizations follow the same practice. Receipts from such dinners are a major source of party income. Money from all these sources, as well as others, is absolutely necessary, for the expenses of the organization are many, as we shall see in the next chapter.

The law limits the amount an individual can give to national party committees to $5,000 in any one year and forbids corporations and labor unions to contribute. Even the contributions of wealthy people will not fully support national party organizations. In the last analysis, they must rely on the dollars of citizens. Additional contributions may be made to special organizations such as those set up for primary elections or to support particular candidates for election. Such money, however, may not be used for the regular work of the parties. The states have power to limit the amounts of money contributed for political purposes, but do not usually make restrictions.

Contributions to political parties come properly under the heading of genuine service to democracy. At every level of party work, a formal accounting of finances must be made: in national elections, the national committees must make an accounting to Congress; state organizations must file their expenses with a designated state official, often the secretary of state; local parties give their accounting to local election boards or to officials designated by law, such as the county clerk.

ADVANTAGES OF PARTY MEMBERSHIP

Membership in a political party—especially *active* membership—carries with it certain advantages as well as definite responsibilities. What are the advantages of active party membership?

444

A Vote in the Primary

The first and most important advantage, of course, is that by joining a party, you can vote in the primary and make your voice heard in the selection of party leaders and candidates for public office. If you do not participate in the primary, you lose much of the value of your vote, since you will have to choose among candidates selected by others, and you may not like any of them.

Not every office is filled by primaries. In many states, candidates for governor and other state offices are nominated in state conventions, while candidates for President and Vice-President are nominated in national party conventions. Even in these cases, however, the enrolled party member can vote in the primary (in some states a formal party meeting known as a caucus) for delegates to state and national party conventions. In this way, he can exercise an indirect but often very important influence upon the convention's choice of candidates. Since delegates have to be elected by the party members, they normally are responsive to the wishes of those whose votes will choose them or reject them. Even where delegates are hand-picked by the county chairman (as may happen when the rank-and-file party members have not taken an active enough interest to make their wishes felt or when the party has full confidence in its leader), the choices of the county chairman are not likely to be too far removed from the popular choice among the membership of his party. For the party chairman and other leaders with whom he works are equally dependent on the votes of the rank and file.

Contact with Politicians

A second great value in joining a party is that it brings you into direct contact with politicians, both professional party workers and elected officials or candidates for election. The United States, in most areas, has long since grown beyond the point where candidates for public office and leaders in political parties were your next-door neighbors or lived on the farm down the road. The simplest and most effective way to know officials and candidates in our time is to join a party and work with them. A party worker comes to know well not only the leaders in his own district and county, but also the state and even national leaders, who frequently go back to the "grass roots" in county organizations to keep their popular following.

Thus the active party member can decide for himself whether individuals are well or poorly qualified for office. And he can voice his opinions and exert some influence in the councils of the party. The outsider who simply waits until the election and then votes on the basis of prejudice or what he has heard in the campaign is not using his voting privilege to the full. Furthermore, he is throwing away his opportunity to play an influential part in democratic government.

POLITICS AND THE CITIZEN

The way you as a citizen can participate is to work at local party headquarters as these women are doing, folding letters, stamping envelopes, doing typing—all jobs which someone must perform. Volunteers, in addition, enjoy many opportunities to meet callers at headquarters, answer questions, and talk about issues and candidates.

Raising money for politics is another important way in which you can contribute to your party. Picnics, dinners, and such activities are fruitful sources for the money a party always needs. And they give voters a chance to see and hear the candidates.

Both Republicans and Democrats announce the meeting of a caucus of electors in a small town—another opportunity for citizen participation.

447

Formulation of Platforms and Programs

A third advantage of active party membership is the opportunity to formulate party platforms and programs. How does a political party know what positions it should take on public issues, where it should stand? The answer is simple. The party arrives at its stand by discussion, debate, and, often, voting within the membership of the parties. Therefore, the most effective way to make your opinions count is through active membership in a political party. You can express your opinions in your ward or town district; those opinions decide the views of the county organization. The state political parties depend upon what they learn from the counties about policies and programs most likely to be successful with the people. At the national level, parties must concern themselves with the views prevailing in the states and regions.

Thus your individual views are funneled through the various levels of organization and exert their influence all along the way. However, you will almost never find your party doing or thinking exactly what you want it to do or think. This is because the party represents many differing views. These are negotiated, discussed, debated, and compromised until, as we have often said, no one obtains all that he wishes, but most get some satisfaction.

You can, of course, influence the parties through membership in other organizations and sometimes simply by expressing your individual opinion to your neighbors and friends (see pp. 424–426). But party membership greatly increases the likelihood of your being heard and heeded. You have a voice in the selection of candidates and the formation of policies and programs, and your sense of belonging to the democratic process grows and brings with it its own special satisfaction.

RESPONSIBILITIES OF PARTY MEMBERS

Active work in service to the party has advantages, as you can see. With the advantages and privileges of party membership, however, go important responsibilities.

Work for the Organization

Party work is hard work, and there is a lot of it to be done at the "grass roots" level, as the chart on p. 440 shows. The first task is simply ringing doorbells in your own neighborhood or making telephone calls, asking for votes for your party's candidates or trying to persuade others to enroll in your party. The success of a political party most often depends on the kind of "leg-work" involved in such calling, and in tasks such as addressing envelopes and answering the telephone. When we say that a certain political party has a strong "organization," so that it will be hard to beat in a given election, we usually mean that the party has a large number of devoted workers who do doorbell-ringing and envelope-addressing, as well as a competent staff of paid workers for primaries, registration, and elections.

Give Time and Money

If he is on the committee, the party worker must be prepared to give a great deal of his time, usually at the sacrifice of something else he might like to be doing. He must be prepared to spend money, travel to meetings, and live in hotels. And committeemen are expected to contribute to the party's finances, as are all workers and all members in general.

Coöperate with the Party

Another responsibility which the party member must accept deserves special notice. As a party member, a citizen is responsible for the success or failure of his party, for its record, and for its reputation. The party, after all, is not something which exists "out there," or "over there," or down at the state capital or in the city hall or in Washington. The party is the people who compose it. It is therefore the responsibility of each member to do all that he can to make it an organization of which he can be proud and as nearly as possible one with which he agrees. Loyalty will require him to work at times for candidates he personally does not like, or with persons he does not admire. He will need to stand behind programs which are not as he would have written them. He will be compensated for his disappointments, however, by knowing that he is protecting his right to criticize and that he is making compromises for the sake of larger agreement.

THE PROCESS OF NOMINATION FOR LOCAL AND STATE-WIDE OFFICES

One of the most important of all democratic functions in the United States is not covered in the Constitution at all. This is the process by which we choose our candidates for public office. Since the framers did not foresee the development of political parties, they certainly could not foresee that the parties would take over and develop the function of *nomination*.

Local Offices

There are many varieties of the nominating process. The leaders of the political parties (usually the county chairmen) examine the qualifications of all candidates, check their records, estimate their ability to draw votes, and consider the extent to which the party may be indebted to them for past services. In this process of sifting through the list of people who are being considered for mayor or councilman or county commissioner, the leaders usually consult a great many district and ward leaders, as well as rank-and-file party members. Ultimately the leaders decide on a list (slate) of names to be presented to the party in the primary elections, which is where most nominations are made to fill town, county, or city offices. These candidates are known as the "organization candidates," and are assured of the support of the party organization.

However, those who have not been selected for the primary by this process may still try for nomination. Such candidates usually arrange to have petitions circulated among the party membership. This might be where you come in. If you think your party organization has been doing a poor job or is choosing poorly qualified candidates, it is not only your right but also your party responsibility to protest. Thus you could be helping someone whose qualifications you approve to get the signatures he needs. In such a case, you will yourself carry his petition from house to house in your neighborhood asking your friends to sign. If enough signatures are secured (usually the number necessary is fixed by law), the names of such candidates are added to the primary ballot. At the primary election, you and your fellow party members then have a choice between "organization" candidates and "insurgents."

Sometimes the insurgent candidates have sufficient influence and appeal to win. Nevertheless, in such primary contests the candidates of the organization have a great advantage. Sometimes, on the other hand, a whole ticket (list of candidates) of insurgents may get on the ballot by petition to challenge the leadership of the party. In such contests there is often a considerable amount of money invested and feelings run high. After the primary the great problem is for the victors, whether the old or a new group, to unite the party for the election campaign. In any case, the candidates having the highest vote for each office in the primary become the official candidates of the party at the regular election.

In most states the party primary is not the only way to get on the ballot for local office. In these states, independents, or party members acting outside their party, may set up organizations of their own and circulate petitions for nomination. If they secure the number of signatures fixed by law, the candidate is placed on the election ballot along with the candidates of the parties. In general most candidates for public office on a ballot are those first selected by the party leader and chosen by the party members by their vote at the primary (or caucus). The same process applies to candidates for Congress. The latter, though they are officers of the national government, are nevertheless local officials in the sense that they represent local constituencies, and they are chosen in the same way as other local candidates on the ballot are chosen.

450

State-Wide Offices

The various states differ in the way they nominate candidates for governor and other state-wide offices. In most southern states the principal contest is in the primary of the Democratic party, since nomination by that party is almost a guarantee of election. In these states, the candidates chosen by the leaders at the state level are frequently opposed by people who do not have party support. Under these circumstances, the non-organization candidates may put on very vigorous and financially well-supported campaigns, and they may be elected. Very often in the southern states the Democratic party organization will remain neutral in the primary. When this happens there may be several candidates, each building his own organization while the party as such takes no part. Again, circulating petitions and securing a fixed number of signatures are the means of getting the names on the primary ballot. If no candidate in the primary wins an absolute majority of the votes cast, a second, or "run-off," primary is held between the two or three highest-ranking candidates.

In many states, candidates for state-wide office such as governor and United States Senator are nominated in state conventions. Under this system the party members vote in the primary not for candidates but for delegates from their district to the state convention. Before such primaries, an individual who wishes, for example, to run for governor frequently puts on an intensive campaign to persuade the local party organizations to choose delegates favorable to him to work for his nomination at the state convention. If there are two or more vigorous and attractive candidates for the governorship, there may be two or more slates of delegates appearing on the primary ballot, each favoring a different candidate for governor. The party member, then, by voting for certain delegates rather than for others, knows that he is expressing a preference for a particular candidate for governor.

State Conventions

When the delegates meet in the convention, the county chairmen, who head their delegations, try to keep tight control over them. They want to be able to hold their votes as units in order to have a good bargaining position. Suppose in New York, for instance, an upstate chairman has no particular candidate he wants for governor, but he does have a candidate for lieutenant governor. Before the voting, he withholds his support and that of his delegation from any candidate. All the candidates need that block of votes, however; and this gives our upstate chairman friend a chance to bargain. In effect, he says to a candidate, "I'll give our support to you for governor—if you, in turn, will help me to get my candidate on the ballot for lieutenant governor."

451

The same chairman might, in other circumstances, want to defeat both candidates for governor because they are both from New York City. In that case, he might join with other upstate chairmen, to get a large block of votes for their own upstate candidate.

All this maneuvering takes place before the actual voting, which is done much as it is at the national conventions; that is, each delegation rises to cast its vote (as a unit) as its name is called on roll call.

It might, of course, work the other way around, with leaders from the city holding the bargaining position. The point is that not only in New York, but in all states which nominate by convention, there is a great deal of such bargaining and maneuvering. In general, it is to the advantage of local leaders to cast their votes for the eventual winner, who will be in a position to make appointments to state office from among the membership of the local organization. Or he can invest state money in the area in such a way as to build the prestige of the local organization as well as to improve the community. For this reason, it is a common practice, after the final ballot has been taken and a candidate has received a majority of the votes, for someone to move that the nomination be made unanimous.

Some states choose their nominees for state offices entirely by primary ballot. In these states active campaigns among those who wish to be nominated take place in the weeks just preceding the primary. In some states a voter may choose on primary day the party ballot he prefers (open primary). In other states, notably California, candidates may enter the primary of both parties.

To a great many Americans, such primaries and conventions are something they read about, rather casually, in the paper. Every citizen has an opportunity, however, through active political party membership, to participate at one or more stages in the process leading to a convention or primary election—to have a voice in the actual choice of candidates.

SUMMARY

Politics is the heart's blood of American democracy. You will often hear that politics is a "dirty business," or that some transaction or other is "just politics," as though that were a bad thing. It is true that there is sometimes graft and corruption in politics; there is also crime in private life. But politics is as "clean" as the citizens who participate in it. In this chapter you have been introduced to the American political parties—the third parties and minority parties as well as the great major parties. You have seen how the Democratic and Republican parties of the United States differ from political parties in most free countries because they aim to draw into their ranks everyone, not just a small number of people having the same ideas. You have examined the structure of the parties and followed in some detail the activities of the county chairman, who holds the key to party organization. The citizen's most direct access to democratic government is through the political parties. There are definite advantages to be gained through party membership. But the success or failure of the parties and of free government depends largely on the work of the citizens; so we have considered also the important responsibilities of party membership. The Founding Fathers, did not dream of one of the most vital aspects of the American political process—the process of nomination. Nomination is a function of the political parties, and you have seen how it works in local and state politics. In the next chapter you will learn about presidential nominating processes.

KNOW WHAT YOU READ

1. Why do you find more than one political party in a free country?
2. What are the advantages and disadvantages of a multi-party system?
3. In what ways are the major political parties of our country different from parties in other democratic countries?
4. Name three third parties from history. How successful were they?
5. In most countries there are parties based on Marxist ideas. How successful have Marxists been in carrying on parties in the United States?
6. Why is the Communist party not a genuine political party?
7. Even though they failed to become strong, third parties have been important in our history. Why is this so?
8. Outline briefly the history of each of the major parties.
9. On what basic principles do both parties agree?
10. What is a county committee? How is it chosen? What does it do?
11. What are the duties and responsibilities of a county chairman? What kind of person should he be?
12. What is patronage? Why is it so important?
13. How are the following party officials chosen: state committee, state chairman, national committee, national chairman? What are their responsibilities?
14. How do parties raise money? Why do they need so much money?
15. Why should John Q. Citizen be a member of a political party?
16. Why should a party member contribute money to his party?
17. Explain why a citizen who really wants to influence government in his state should become an active party member.
18. In those states that select candidates by direct primary, how does the would-be candidate go about winning his party's nomination?
19. What must a person do to be nominated for local office? For state office? For Congress? Why is nomination so important in southern states?
20. How are delegates to state conventions picked? Describe the procedure.

WHAT DO YOU THINK?

1. It is sometimes proposed that boys and girls entering senior high school should be assigned in equal numbers to "Democratic" and "Republican" parties. School elections and "student government" activities would then be based on political-type activity. What do you think of this idea?
2. How do you think more citizens can be stimulated to take an active part in political parties?
3. Study the drawing of the organization of a political party. Where do you think you could fit into the organization?
4. It has been proposed that political campaigns be financed by the U.S. Treasury. All parties would then receive the same amounts of money for use in influencing the voters. Who might favor this scheme? Who would oppose it? What is your own view?

PROBLEMS AND PROJECTS FOR YOU

1. Interview a person, not a chairman or committee member, in your community who is active in the affairs of his party. Find out what he does and why he is willing to devote so much unpaid time to politics. Report to the class. (Of course it may be even more informative if you can interview your favorite party's county or local chairman.)
2. Make an original drawing or poster on the subject of why citizens should take an active part in political-party work.
3. In Dixon and Plischke, *American Government: Basic Documents and Materials*, study the political party organization charts in Chapter 4. Make a written summary of the ways in which they are similar or dissimilar to the organization charted in your textbook.
4. The cartoon on p. 437 depicts a situation frequently faced by our two big parties. From our history name three candidates and issues which similarly affected our major parties.
5. Study the Populist platform of 1892. Report to the class on the extent to which the radical demands of the third party have since been carried out by the major parties.
6. In 1956 one of the major broadcasting systems sponsored two booklets on the election of that year. The following quotation is taken from one of these publications.

> In general the Republican party has tended to resist enlargement of the role of the government in regulating business, while the Democratic party has given a somewhat warmer welcome to government regulation of business.

Do you agree? List what you believe to be the real differences between the two parties.

7. Report to the class on any one of these chapters in *Capitol, Courthouse and City Hall*: "How Tammany Holds Power"; "City Politics: Free Style"; "Exit the Boss, Enter the Leader"; "People's Answer to Political Bosses"; "Why Participate in Party Politics."
8. Watch the newspapers, in an election year, for items about party finances. Make a bulletin-board display of clippings.
9. Read and write a book report on Joseph C. Harsch's *The Role of Political Parties U. S. A.* You may be able to obtain this booklet from your local League of Women Voters.

EXTEND YOUR VOCABULARY

grass roots   committeeman   politician
precinct   patronage   ticket

YOUR NOTEBOOK: THE GOVERNMENT OF —

1. Write here the names of your state committee members of the major parties.
2. By what methods are party candidates nominated in your state?
3. What is your precinct? What is the name of your county chairman?
4. Does your state use the open or closed primary?

READ MORE ABOUT IT

AGAR, HERBERT, *The Price of Union*. Houghton Mifflin, 1950.
    A stirring plea for responsible parties.
BINKLEY, WILFRED E., *American Political Parties: Their Natural History*. Knopf, 1943.
    Readable and reliable.
BROGAN, DENIS W., *Politics in America*. Harper, 1955.
    A cultivated Englishman looks at us, with humor and compassion.
BURNS, JAMES M., and PELTASON, JACK W., *Government by the People*. Prentice-Hall, 1954. Chaps. 9–10, 12–13.
CATER, DOUGLASS, "How to Tell a Democrat from a Republican," *New York Times Magazine*, September 20, 1959.
    Timely but timeless analysis of our parties.
IRISH, MARIAN D., and PROTHRO, JAMES W., *The Politics of American Democracy*. Prentice-Hall, 1959. Chaps. 8–9.
RANNEY, AUSTIN, *The Governing of Men*. Holt, 1958. Chaps. 12, 13, 15.

CHAPTER 19

The Working of Political Parties at the National Level

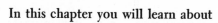

In this chapter you will learn about

Presidential primaries

National party conventions

Presidential campaigns

Does the campaign determine the election?

Non-voters in America

The party in power

The party in opposition

When the delegates to the Constitutional Convention debated for three days about whether the national executive should be one person or several, they never dreamed that the office would become the prize of a national sweepstakes in which America frantically engages every four years.

Starting in the spring of a presidential election year, when state primaries are held at scattered times, the drama reaches its climax on election day itself. In the interval, political parties move into high gear, people who ordinarily take little or no part in politics jump into the fray, and what the candidates say and do, what they wear and eat, what their hobbies are—every little bit of human interest or great thought about them—monopolize the headlines of the newspapers, the radio, TV, and almost every other part of American life.

Almost as soon as a new presidential term begins, people start to talk about whether the President will run again and who will be the candidates of the Democratic and Republican parties. Nomination and election campaigns for the Presidency are, in other words, almost always going on. No one can say just when a candidate actually begins to make his bid for a nomination, but in most cases those who aspire to the Presidency are really running all the time. The coming of the state primaries, however, is the signal for active candidates for nomination to busy themselves in campaigning for delegates to be chosen in party primaries.

PRESIDENTIAL PRIMARIES

There are three principal kinds of presidential primaries: those where delegates are pledged by state laws to support certain candidates; those where delegates are instructed, but not bound by law, to vote for certain candidates; and those where delegates are uninstructed and therefore open to control by state leaders. (In a few states, delegates are chosen at state party conventions.)

Primary Campaigns

Campaigning is intense in all three principal kinds of primaries. The voter has a chance to see and hear the major candidates, shake hands with them, even ask them questions. It costs a lot of money for candidates to reach the people that way. Consequently, candidates usually form national and state primary committees to raise money necessary for all the expenses of the campaigns—thousands of miles of travel, salaries for large staffs to make the arrangements and keep the public interest aroused.

In Minnesota and California, states with laws binding delegates to vote for candidates as instructed, primaries attract nation-wide attention as an indication of which way the political wind is blowing. Primaries in New Hampshire, Wisconsin, and Oregon, held early, with delegates instructed (but not bound) to vote for certain candidates, also excite keen interest. Large states like New York and Texas neither bind nor instruct their delegates. As a result, state party leaders who control blocs of delegates can use their influence to advance the cause of a particular candidate. In the 1952 Republican Convention, for example, Governor Thomas E. Dewey was able to provide General Eisenhower with 94 out of 96 New York delegates' votes, assuring Eisenhower's nomination and the defeat of Senator Robert A. Taft. In the same year, the control by Mayor Lawrence of Pittsburgh over the

457

Pennsylvania delegation enabled him to play a major part in nominating Adlai Stevenson at the Democratic Convention, even though Senator Estes Kefauver had won most of the primary contests, and Stevenson had not even been a candidate in the primaries.

"Favorite Sons"

Sometimes the voters of a state send delegations to national conventions prepared to back a so-called "favorite son," some respected citizen of the state. Frequently blocks of votes at national conventions are held out for such a candidate (who may have no other support). Then the party organization can shift its allegiance and votes to play a significant part in determining which candidate is chosen. In the Democratic Convention of 1924, the Alabama delegation, pledged to Senator Underwood, held out for 102 ballots while the rest of the convention was mainly divided between William G. McAdoo and Alfred E. Smith. Ultimately neither of the two leaders was able to gain the necessary votes (two-thirds at that time), and a "dark horse," John W. Davis of New York, was nominated on the 103rd ballot.

Uniform Primary Law

State party primaries play a major but not decisive part in presidential nominations. Many people feel that presidential nominations should be open to all voters through a general, nationally uniform primary law. Under such a law, all candidates would be required to file their candidacies in each state and campaign for the nomination on a nation-wide basis, just as the nominees do in the election. The candidate in each party having the highest total vote in the country, or carrying states representing the most electoral votes, would be the nominee of his party. There are obvious advantages in such a system. It would not merely bring the election of the President directly to the people, but would also guarantee their choice of nominees.

However, there are important objections to the proposal. One of these is that it would weaken the organizations of the political parties—organizations which are necessary instruments of political life and invaluable parts of the governmental process. Party leaders would receive less tangible rewards under such a system, since they would have little influence either upon national conventions or upon state delegations. You remember what this means to a county chairman. With substantially less reward for their time and energy, it is quite probable that the quality of the organization leaders would deteriorate, while the prestige of the parties would be lowered and their usefulness as breeding grounds for candidates would be diminished. Another objection is that the best candidates for the Presidency would often not campaign in the primaries, because they are not always anxious to run. If a uniform national primary law had been in effect in 1952, for example, neither President Eisenhower nor Adlai Stevenson would have been nominated.

NATIONAL PARTY CONVENTIONS

Every fourth year now, there takes place the perhaps gaudy but fascinating show of the political conventions. There are flags to bedeck the meeting place, there are parades of delegates, carrying state banners and yelling and whooping it up to create enthusiasm (or at least the appearance of enthusiasm), there are crowded hotel lobbies where delegates, hangers-on, reporters, and the general public meet before and after the formal sessions to talk things over and try to detect how the political currents are running. There is newspaper, radio, and television coverage, so that the entire country may be kept informed. And, finally, there is the formal presentation of the candidates, a great burst of oratory, and a driving, headlined start for the regular campaigns.[1]

These "fascinating shows" take place in the summer of a presidential election year. The choice of the city where a convention is to be held gets wide publicity; each state committee is duly notified in time to choose the allotted number of delegates. The delegates are either instructed or uninstructed according to the procedures already described. The two parties differ slightly in the number of delegates and in the voting procedure at the conventions. In general, there are two delegates for each Congressional District in the country, a member for each territory, and two delegates for each Senator. In addition there may be "bonuses" for performance in the previous elections. There are usually some delegates "at large," chosen by the state leaders.

Thus there are likely to be from 1,250 to 1,500 delegate votes at a national convention. In some cases, individual delegates are allowed only a half-vote, so that there are many more delegates at a convention than there are votes. The great size of the conventions means that the winning candidate must have 650–750 votes to gain a majority. Today both parties choose nominees by simple majority.

Getting Down to Business

The chairman of the national committee calls the meeting to order. After a prayer, temporary officers of the convention, nominated by the national committee, are announced by the chairman. The temporary chairman makes a "keynote" speech, lauding his party, perhaps attacking the opposition party, and predicting victory for his side. There may also be addresses by other national leaders, asking the party to pull together for victory and to promote this or that issue. The permanent chairman (often the Speaker of the House or the Minority Leader of the House) presides over the business sessions of the convention which follow.

[1] Roy F. Nichols, "It Happens Every Four Years," *American Heritage*, June 1956.

The membership of the convention is so large that it must be broken down into committees to do certain work. The national committee appoints such committees before the convention opens. Usually there is one member from each state on each of the four main committees.

The **Committee on Credentials** is one of the four important committees. It examines the eligibility of the delegates to sit in the convention. Usually this is routine, but sometimes two sets of delegates are present, each claiming to be the proper ones. Such a situation occurs when there is a split in the party in the state, each faction sending a delegation.

The **Committee on Rules and Order of Business** recommends that certain rules of convention procedure be adopted; it also regulates the order of business for the convention.

The **Committee on Permanent Organization** names the permanent chairman and officials for the convention. The chairman, escorted to the platform by the ceremonial committee set up for just such duties, in his first speech presents the issues of the campaign as seen by the party.

The fourth important committee is the **Committee on Resolutions,** which prepares the party platform and submits it to the convention. A rough draft of the platform is usually prepared before the convention begins. The Resolutions Committee, after the convention is called, works long and hard on getting the final platform into shape.

The Platform

The Resolutions Committee hears the recommendations of many people and pressure groups. Representatives of business and industry, labor unions, farm organizations, consumer organizations, minority groups, and a host of others appear before the committee and submit proposals for ideas, principles, and programs to be included in the platform. The committee works much like a legislative body. It is faced with many conflicting opinions and pressures. The members will disagree—often seriously—among themselves. Yet somehow they must write a platform with very broad appeal to the masses of voters and more or less satisfactory to all important groups within the party (see p. 11).

Usually the committee can agree on criticisms of the other party. A good portion of the platform actually consists of such criticisms. But the platform must also say what the party is for. If a party is in power this may be fairly simple to accomplish. It can praise the record of the administration and promise to continue and improve it. Always when a party is out of power—and sometimes even when it is in power—it must say what it will do if elected, either because it has no record to point to or because its record is under severe attack.

PLATFORM COMPROMISES   In writing the platform, the process of compromise must be effectively used. Two examples will illustrate.

The split in the Democratic party between northern and southern wings on the question of civil rights is one example. Writing an acceptable "civil rights plank" in the Democratic platform is usually the most difficult job of a Democratic Convention and its platform committee. Often they compromise by using in the platform very broad and general language which does not commit the party to any specific program.

Republicans, on the other hand, have a somewhat similar split between midwestern and eastern Republicans on the question of foreign policy. Thus there frequently develops a struggle over the "foreign policy plank" in Republican national conventions. Again, the issue must be compromised, usually by the use of broad and general terms without specific program commitments.

Normally the issues of program and policy are ironed out by the platform committee, and it is ready to report fairly early in the convention. Sometimes, however, the issues arise again on the floor of the convention and are bitterly debated there. In any case, party platforms are eventually adopted by majority vote of the delegates of the whole convention. These national party platforms may use very general language, or may sound "cynical" or "demagogic" at times. However, the national conventions are the voice of the American people—at least of the tens of millions who support the parties. Thus their platforms inevitably reflect the issues, conflicts, and even outright contradictions which are facts of American life. As we have said in Chapter 18, American political parties try to win the support of *all* Americans, not just a small number who may be in agreement. Their platforms will therefore have to contain "something for everybody." If they compromise some of the deepest differences within the parties, that is because these differences are deep in American life. They must be compromised if we are to have anything like national unity and harmony. Neither the parties nor their platforms are perfect, but neither are the American people. Their ability to compromise, however, is one of their strengths.

Convention Campaigning

While the delegates are being seated and the platform is being written, candidates are already vying for support of delegates. The representatives of the candidates endlessly confer with delegates and party officials. On the second or third day, the names of the various candidates are put into nomination by speeches upon the floor of the convention. After each name is offered, the candidate's followers put on a noisy "demonstration." Banners bearing the names of the states where he has support are borne about the hall; bands play; applause and whistling, as well as every other kind of noise one can

ONCE EVERY FOUR YEARS—

Long before a convention is actually held, people are busily at work making preparations. Public relations staffs in national headquarters write, telephone, interview, to arrange hotels and other facilities for housing the convention members. Restaurants must be prepared to cope with the influx of thousands of people who may all get hungry at the same time!

Television and radio equipment must be set up and tested so that people not in attendance can watch the "gaudy but fascinating" convention.

The convention hall must be provided with signs, loud-speakers, a speaker's podium—all the paraphernalia that will make the convention successful.

When the convention is under way, the excitement is tremendous. Speeches are greeted with loud applause, banners are waved, as delegates express approval of their candidates.

The planks of the party platform are discussed with newspapermen who rush to press to keep the country informed of events of the convention.

Then, once the party candidate has been chosen, he in turn gives a press conference to reiterate his advocacy of party policies and to promise to "put up a good fight."

manage to make, are kept up for as long as possible. It has even become a custom to use the length of these demonstrations as a sort of guide to the candidate's prospects and qualifications. The fact is that these demonstrations are often staged, that is, put on by people who are not delegates at all but paid noisemakers. This is a variation of the "claque" for an opera singer, who hired people to attend the opera and applaud his performance so that the manager would be duly impressed. Of course the demonstrations at national conventions have little effect on the balloting, though there may be a few delegates who are swept away by the desire to "get on the bandwagon."

Nominations

When all names have been placed in nomination, the balloting begins. It is done by states. As the name of a state is called, the leader of the delegation from that state arises and announces how many votes his delegation gives to each of the candidates. This means that the state delegations must hold frequent meetings to ballot among themselves. If they are simply following the lead of their charman, or if they were elected in a "binding" primary, it is an easy matter. Sometimes, however, their candidate "releases" them from supporting him, when he sees that his cause is hopeless; and sometimes the delegation is divided in its loyalties. In such cases, there may be intense political activity within the small groups from individual states. Many states have a rule requiring all their delegates to vote for the same candidate so that they must first vote among themselves to see which candidate has a majority (**unit rule**).

Often members of the delegation disagree as to just how many ballots it is casting for which candidates. These disagreements may occur on the floor of the convention, and a delegate will challenge the tally being given by his chairman. When this happens, the chairman of the convention instructs the clerk to call the roll of the delegation in which the dispute occurs. Each delegate is then called by name and gives his vote before the whole convention. This is sometimes a very tedious process, but it forestalls both errors and misrepresentation. It also gives individual delegates an opportunity to prove to their constituents back home that they remained loyal to a particular candidate, or that they are voting the popular preference shown in a primary. Perhaps some just wish to appear on television!

The balloting proceeds until a candidate has a clear majority and secures the party's nomination for President. As we saw in the case of the state conventions, it is common practice, after the balloting is over, for a resolution to be introduced and carried declaring the choice of the convention to be unanimous.

VICE-PRESIDENTIAL NOMINATIONS The final business of the convention is the nomination of the candidate for Vice-President. This normally takes

464

very little time. As you saw on p. 186, often he is chosen just to balance the ticket. More recently, the necessity for more careful choice of the Vice-President has been dramatized by the death of President Roosevelt and the illness of President Eisenhower. Normally both parties allow their candidate for President to choose his running mate.

When the presidential nominee has made his choice known, there may still be some other names placed in nomination—favorite sons or others who have deserved well of the party and are given a moment of honor and publicity. Sometimes there may be a serious contest, but more often the person designated by the presidential nominee will be chosen in one ballot. The convention is then ready to hear a speech by its presidential candidate, and, finally, to adjourn for a much needed rest and to prepare for the election campaign.

PRESIDENTIAL CAMPAIGNS

A presidential election campaign is the climax of the election process. The campaign covers, as far as possible, every nook and cranny of the country and deals especially in issues with which most of the people are concerned.

Over the years the methods of presidential campaigning have changed a great deal, mainly because of the enormous changes in transportation and communication. In 1896, for example, when newspapers were the chief means of communication, William McKinley, the Republican candidate, stayed at home and campaigned from his "front porch." That is, the managers of the campaign brought groups of people, at party expense, from different parts of the country and representing different interests, to call on McKinley and hear his views. Thus almost every day there was a front-page story from McKinley's home in Ohio. William Jennings Bryan, his opponent, chose to travel about the country by train, speaking from the rear platform.

Although McKinley was elected, Bryan's method caught on, and most candidates in recent years have traveled extensively by campaign train. Perhaps the most famous campaign by railroad train was that of President Truman in 1948, in which he made hundreds of "whistle stops." In our times the airplane has come into greater use but still has not entirely replaced the train.

Since the 1920's much campaign speech-making has, of course, been done by radio. Franklin Roosevelt was famous for his "fireside talks." Today presidential candidates rely heavily on television and reach millions of people with one speech. The voters not only hear the candidate, but see him at close range and have a chance to "size him up." This has meant that the listener must guard against being misled by the techniques of television advertising which are widely used.

NATIONAL COMMITTEE ORGANIZATION

Organization is of the greatest importance in election campaigns. A presidential nominee is usually supported by at least two organizations and often by three. The first is the national committee of his party (see p. 443). The job of the national committee is to bring the whole force of the regular, permament party organization into line for the nominee and stimulate it to the utmost effort.

The national committees of our two parties have offices in Washington. If you visit one of them—and you will be welcome—you will find a beehive of activity. Party workers—some paid and some volunteers—will be engaged in all sorts of tasks. Some will be reading newspapers from all parts of the country, clipping editorials, keeping track of the coverage given to the views and actions of the party's representatives in government and the party's speech-makers everywhere. Some will simply be hunting for evidence of blunders by the other party. If, for example, a state treasurer belonging to the other party is indicted for mishandling public money, someone in the national committee will follow the whole story in the papers and file away the clippings for future use in party speech-making.

Other party workers will be talking to citizens who have called at the national committee for any number of reasons: to recommend a friend for a job, to get help in negotiating a contract to supply some product to the government, to complain that the party is poorly led in his state or that the national committee is not paying enough attention to the party in his community back home. If you peek into the office of the national chairman at any time of the day, you will see him conferring with some party leader or other or with a government official who belongs to the party, and probably talking on the telephone at the same time.

Speaker's Bureau

Down the corridor is the Speaker's Bureau, where workers are, again, on the telephone dealing with requests for speakers coming in from every state. This is one of the most important and delicate jobs in the whole campaign. There are always plenty of party politicians prepared to stump the country for the party—as well as to bring public notice to themselves. Many state candidates must be fitted effectively into the speaking schedule. The nominee himself must be presented in a way to advance his own candidacy, as well as to help his running mates on the ticket at state and local levels.

Some speakers cannot be used in certain areas because they may be unpopular there for having voted for unpopular measures in Congress, or for other reasons. Clashes of personality may make some speakers more valuable in one place than in another. This kind of thing is actually very common, since both parties contain so many individuals and groups of differing interests, opinions, and prejudices. Here is another place where our old friend the county chairman gives valuable advice. All this calls for generalship of a high order in the national organization.

Campaign Literature and Speeches

On another floor at the national headquarters are offices where committee members are preparing copy for political advertisements and pamphlets. They serve under the Publicity Director, whose job is to use every means he can find to present the party, its leaders, and its ideas in the most favorable light to the country at large. This means that a staff of researchers is required to dig up the worst things that can be said about the opposing party and candidate, as well as the strongest points about the party's own record and candidate.

Basic decisions have to be made as to which issues and which achievements are to be emphasized, and in which areas various positive and negative points are to be stressed. Some literature must be designed to appeal to the whole country, while other literature may be addressed to certain regions or to certain groups.

The researchers must be aided by a staff of writers who can take the materials provided and present them in simple and forceful language, with the catchiest possible slogans and turns of phrase. A good memorable phrase, like "Keep Cool with Coolidge" or "I like Ike," has enormous value in keeping the name of the candidate favorably in the minds of the voters. This writing staff has to produce thousands of speeches, as well as radio shows, television shows, handbooks, and handbills.

Planning the Conventions

It is the national committees which are responsible for the enormous amount of work that goes into organizing the national party conventions held every four years. The national committee chooses the city where a convention is to be held, makes contracts with hotels to house the delegates, with printers for the convention program, with broadcasting companies for radio and television coverage, and handles all other arrangements for the convention, including talking with local officials about police and fire protection.

Expenses

As you can imagine, all this activity is costly. Money must be raised—and on a very large scale. (We saw how it is done in Chapter 18.) There are salaries and office expenses to be paid. One fifteen-minute national television

467

hook-up may cost $35,000 to $50,000. Since as often as possible the party wishes to present its candidate on more than one network, or even on all networks, the complete cost may run into hundreds of thousands for one appearance. Radio and printing costs run into additional tens of thousands, and salaries for temporary workers also swell the budget. The national party organization needs, therefore, to raise several millions of dollars. Money-raising is a continuous responsibility, but the work of the party cannot wait until finances are adequate. Planning, printing, writing, and scheduling of speakers must begin right after the convention has completed its work. Usually by Labor Day the campaign is well under way. It lasts about two months.

Public Relations

Public relations is a vital and endless job of the national committee. The committee knows that all the money spent for publicity will not be enough if the press is not favorable. Constant attention to newspaper, radio, and television reporters, presenting always the best face of the party, is a tremendous responsibility.

National party leaders live in a state of nervous anxiety all the time, lest someone blunder in a talk with the press. In 1954, for example, Republican National Chairman Leonard Hall had to "explain away" a speech by Defense Secretary Charles Wilson, who told a Detroit audience that he preferred "bird dogs," who take the initiative and provide for themselves, to "kennel dogs," who waited to be fed—this at a time of serious unemployment in Detroit's automobile industry, and during a congressional election campaign. During presidential campaigns the anxiety is greater than ever, since even one serious slip can injure a party's chances. In 1952, for example, Governor Adlai Stevenson caused the hearts of Democratic leaders to turn over when he answered a question from the editor of the Oregon *Journal* (Portland) as to whether he thought he could "clean up the mess in Washington." He said "Yes." It looked harmless enough. Surely he should not say "No." Yet this seemed to be an admission of charges raised by General Eisenhower and the Republicans that there was a "mess in Washington" which only the Republicans could clean up. The possibility of such slips as this, and more serious ones, keeps leaders and their public relations people constantly alert.

PERSONAL ORGANIZATIONS OF CANDIDATES

A second form of organization in presidential campaigns is the personal organization of the nominee. He must have a staff which in many ways paral-

468

lels that of the national committee. The national organization must concern itself with the entire ticket—not only the Presidency but also the Congress and state offices.

Staff Duties

The nominee's organization concentrates on putting him over with the voters. It plans his schedule of appearances, decides what issues are to be discussed and where, which leaders of the party are to be drawn close to the nominee and which are to be treated politely but distantly. It follows the campaign of the opposition and decides how to meet it, decides when to attack and when to defend. It follows the opinion polls constantly for guidance as to weaknesses and strengths in the nominee, his campaign, his party, and the issues. The staff includes political advisers whose job is to know the state of affairs in all parts of the country, advisers on foreign policy, writers, researchers, public relations men, radio and television technicians, money raisers, and a good number of "leg men."

Sometimes the nominee's organization is kept in close touch with the national party organization by a single individual who serves both as campaign manager and as national chairman. When the two offices are held by different men, close liaison must be maintained by staff people assigned to that task.

"ADVANCE MEN" One of the most important functions of the candidate's staff is to provide "advance men." They precede the nominee on his travels about the country and prepare the way for him. This means finding out which local politicians are most important and influential in their communities so that the nominee is sure to meet and spend time with the right people (again the county chairman plays an important part). It also means learning just which specific issues seem to mean most to the people the nominee will see and address when he arrives, so that his speech will hit the right note. A third function of the "advance men" is to make sure that all arrangements are in order for the nominee's appearance and that there will be a crowd. Size of crowds is always important, since people tend to estimate the possibilities of a nominee's success in terms of the size of his crowds, and to compare them with those of his opponent.

The "advance men" must work hard on drumming up crowds, but the basic responsibility for this job is in the hands of local party leaders and workers. For their part the local people are always anxious to have large and enthusiastic meetings, since this helps them to impress the candidate and the national leaders who appear with him and work with him. The nominee may be elected, and as President he may remember how well he was received in this or that community and who the leaders were—especially the county chairman!

VOLUNTEER ORGANIZATIONS

A third type of organization in presidential campaigns has been more and more frequent in recent years. This is a voluntary organization of "amateurs" who are devoted to a particular candidate. They may have been organized in the first instance to help him get the nomination, and sometimes they play important parts in the election campaign. They often draw enthusiastic individuals from both parties, and normally try to give the public the impression that their candidate has bipartisan backing or even that he is "above party." While it is true that there are always a large number of registered party voters who "cross the line" in presidential elections to vote for the nominee of the other party, it is a great mistake to suppose that any candidate can be elected without the tireless efforts of his own party. Volunteer, non-partisan or "independent" groups, like the "Citizens for Eisenhower" or the "Volunteers for Stevenson" in 1952 and 1956, can help their candidates greatly, but they are no substitute for regular party organization.

These volunteer organizations, like the other campaign organizations we have discussed, raise money, provide speakers, and distribute literature. Their most significant contribution to politics, however, has not been their "independence" but the large number of younger people they have drawn into political activity in the two parties. They have performed a great service in bringing in "new blood," often engaging the interest of alert and well-informed citizens who formerly took no part in party affairs. Both the Republican and Democratic parties are permanently enriched because so many of the "amateurs," imaginations fired by General Eisenhower and Governor Stevenson in 1952, joined their parties and helped to reinvigorate them.

DOES THE CAMPAIGN DETERMINE THE ELECTION?

When all these organizations are in full swing, we have an election campaign. We have endless speeches, rallies, personal appearances, "whistle stops," banners, placards, signs, radio and television shows, millions of words in the press, countless pictures, buttons on lapels, parades, torchlight processions, arguments and wagers among citizens, high feelings, a great wave of national excitement and anticipation, until the night before the election itself.

Suddenly there is a calm. On election day the voters go to the polls and, in privacy, record their choices for President and for the party they wish to govern the country. A few hours later it is over. There is a winner and a loser. For most Americans, there is an emotional letdown marked by a show of goodwill between the parties and the rival candidates. It has been a long, long grind. From Labor Day to November it has involved everyone; for months, even years, before that it has engrossed the attention of the politicians. But what has the campaign actually accomplished? Did it really decide the election? Or was the result determined in other ways which the campaign itself could not alter?

Opposing Views

Students of American politics give a number of different answers to these questions, and none is entirely accepted. One view is that elections are determined largely by economic factors. If the country is prosperous, the party in power will remain in power. If conditions are depressed, the party out of power will be given its chance to improve things. Another view is that Americans vote according to interest groups to such an extent that only a small number of voters, who may feel a special stake in the outcome, can make or break a candidate. Political scientists thus sometimes refer to a "Negro vote," or a "Polish vote," or a "Labor vote," or the "Farm vote." If an election appears to be very close, it is argued that the outcome will depend on how such groups decide to vote. Still a different view is that the outcome is determined by the size of the vote. Thus, since there are several million more registered Democrats than there are Republicans, it is held that the larger the vote, the greater the chances of the Democrats. Another view is that the number of "party-line" voters is so nearly equal that those who do not support a party—the so-called "independents"—decide the elections.

There is some truth in each of these views, but none gives nearly a complete answer, and each can be refuted by reference to particular elections. Thus the agricultural depression of the 1920's did not bring about the defeat of the Republicans. The unparalleled prosperity of the early 1950's did not keep the Democrats in power. In 1948 the intensive campaign of President Harry S. Truman entirely upset all advance predictions, as we saw on p. 424, and his election seems to have been the direct result of the campaign itself.

Facts for Analysis

There are a few solid facts upon which to base any analysis of American presidential elections. The southern states have been traditionally Democratic and usually give the Democratic candidate their electoral votes. Certain northern states have been similarly Republican, like Maine, New Hampshire, Vermont, the Dakotas, Nebraska, Iowa, and Kansas. In the heavily populated states, the principal Republican strength is in the rural areas, while the Democratic strength is in the big cities. Since in most of these states—New York, Pennsylvania, Ohio, Illinois, California—there is a near balance between rural and urban populations, elections are likely to be close.

The border states, like West Virginia, Kentucky, and Missouri do not necessarily follow the lead of the South and may at times turn the balance

471

one way or the other. Certain states like New Jersey and Indiana have a Republican tradition which the Democrats have found very hard to break. California was for many years a conspicuous example of the inability of the parties to depend on registration figures. In that state, Democratic registration is much heavier than Republican but, until the Democratic sweep of 1958, this fact seemed to have little bearing on the way the voters voted in national or even in state elections.

A different kind of fact, well known both to party politicians and to students of public opinion, is that a great name can upset all calculations based on economic, regional, interest, registration, or other considerations. No one can say how important was the magic associated with names like those of Franklin Roosevelt or Dwight Eisenhower. The fact is that they were elected by great margins in defiance of other factors which might otherwise have been decisive, and both tended to run far ahead of their parties in the total vote cast.

Thus any answers to the question whether election campaigns actually decide the outcome must be inconclusive. The evidence is that they play a very important part in influencing public opinion. It may be that a very high percentage of voters have already made up their minds before a campaign ever begins. But those who have not yet decided may well hold the balance of power.

Value of Campaigns to Citizens

Deciding the election is not the only value of presidential, congressional, and gubernatorial election campaigns. Perhaps even more important is their role in dramatizing issues, educating the people, and renewing interest in the democratic process and in government itself. The tempo and pressure of campaigns are so great that, for a few months at any rate, almost everyone is forced to reckon with the great issues of the day. All of us get some education on foreign affairs and have to face certain issues of domestic policy. We cannot help thinking about the problems of the farmer, the working man, the professions, business and industry. And, above all, we are made aware of the political parties and how indispensable they are in our democracy. We may be displeased by what we see and hear, but we are challenged to enter in and do something about it. Unfortunately, not enough of us accept the challenge.

NON-VOTERS IN THE AMERICAN DEMOCRACY

You have seen that politics and democracy itself begin with the individual citizen. Free government can never be wiser nor more successful than the citizens who compose it. A strong and effective democratic government depends upon the fullest participation by citizens who are at once alert,

**"LET'S NOT BE LULLED
TO SLEEP"**

Carmack in
The Christian Science Monitor

educated, and devoted. A great tragedy of the American democracy is that a very large number of citizens do not even take the trouble to vote.

The election of 1952 brought more than sixty million votes for President. President Eisenhower received the highest vote for a winner and Governor Stevenson the highest for a loser in the history of the country. These figures are very deceiving, however. There were more than ninety million people in the United States eligible to vote in that election. Only about two-thirds actually voted. In earlier elections there have sometimes been total votes amounting to less than half of those eligible. Under these circumstances, even so popular a man as Eisenhower can become President of the United States by the votes of no more than a third of the citizens. In recent years we have not had a President elected by an actual majority of the voters.

What are the reasons for this? Is it a common occurrence in democratic countries? The answer to the second question is an unqualified *no*. The United States has the poorest voting record among all the free governments of the world. In England, for example, about 80 percent of the voters normally cast their votes. In other countries the figures are even higher. In none are they so low as in the United States.

The reasons are not easy to discover. Experts have calculated that as many as 10 percent of the eligible voters are unable to vote on election day through

473

no immediate fault of their own. Some are ill and cannot get to the polls. Some are traveling and cannot reach the polling place at which they are registered. Some have changed their residence so recently that they do not meet state or local residence requirements for voting. In some southern states the obstacles to registration and voting discourage a large number of citizens. In some cases where one party has almost complete domination, many citizens may not vote simply because they think their vote makes no difference.

All these reasons will not account for nearly all those who fail to take part in elections. Scientific polling of non-voters shows that the most common reason for non-voting is that the citizen just does not care how the elections come out. To counter this indifference, those who do care must take on the added responsibility of "selling" democracy to their slothful fellow citizens. To do this, we must show the non-voter that his vote does count, that it does matter who wins, that it does matter which party holds power, that the condition of the country is his responsibility. If there must always be some who prefer to let "George do it," the answer must be to increase the number of Georges!

In the mid-twentieth century we have heard a very great deal about the dangers of communism and of fascism and the threat these totalitarian systems offer to our liberties. And they are real dangers. But they are not nearly so dangerous to our liberty as our own unwillingness to defend that liberty. The citizen of a free country who will not use his citizenship has always been the greatest danger to freedom. The Greeks learned this lesson more than 2,000 years ago. The Founding Fathers of our republic pointed it out over and over again. Our nation prides itself on its "individualism," its rugged character. It is political freedom which has made our individualism possible. Even our vast wealth in natural resources and human skill could not have brought us either the strength or the prosperity we now enjoy without political freedom. It is therefore our duty to ourselves to join in the enterprise of free government not only by voting in elections, but also by taking as active a part as our circumstances permit in the whole political life of the country. The road is not easy. No great good in human life is ever easy to get. But the rewards of participation in the experiment of American democracy are among the richest and most satisfying ever open to mankind.

PARTIES AFTER THE ELECTION

When an election is over, the victorious party, whether at the local, state, or national level, must assume the responsibilities of governing. Technically, of course, it is only the elected or appointed officials who exercise the authority of government. In a larger sense, however, the whole party has responsibility.

474

The Party in Power

A President has to make many thousands of appointments. Most of them will come from the ranks of his party. The quality of these appointments will have much to do with the success or failure of his administration. Party organization and personnel must therefore play a vital part in the President's administration. Obviously, as an individual a President can make only a small number of appointments from among people known to him personally. He is dependent upon advice, and most of his advice will come from the party leaders, both in the national committee and in the state and county organizations. Thousands of names are offered for his approval, and he has no choice but to trust the recommendations of the party. Governors, mayors, and county commissioners have the same problems on smaller scales.

Patronage not only keeps the party strong by "rewarding" faithful party workers with jobs, but greatly influences the quality of government. A national chairman, for example, who recommends too many poorly qualified people to the President will get his party quickly into trouble and will not last long in his job. So it is with state and county chairmen who make poor recommendations to governors, mayors, or county commissioners.

In Chapters 5 and 6 we saw how important a role the political party plays in legislatures. The majority party usually has enough votes to control the committees and to enact legislation, though it often needs some votes from the opposition to get its measures through. The majority party is nevertheless held responsible for the record of a legislature. Executives, whether Presidents, governors, or mayors, must work closely with their party group in the legislature, both for the good of the party and to enhance the possibilities of reelection. Both executive and legislature are under constant temptation to place the interest of the party ahead of the total interest of the country or the state. The choice a man makes is a measure of his caliber as an elected official. In a good many cases, of course, the vote for the larger interest often turns out also to be best for the party. At any rate, party responsibility inevitably includes facing such choices and making them wisely.

The party in power must always be in the business of public relations. The national committee never lets up in its efforts, through speeches, articles, radio and television shows, and news releases, to support the administration and the congressional group of the party, to cover up mistakes, correct blunders, and in general put the best possible face on all party activity. At the same time it keeps the opposition party under constant critical fire. To do this, it makes full use of the free press we considered in Chapter 17. Exactly the same kinds of facilities are, of course, available also to the party out of power, the opposition. As for the private citizen, he should be reading both sides, listening to both sides, watching both sides—and using his critical judgment to decide for himself.

The Party in Opposition

Unlike the British system, the American system does not provide for an executive leader of the party out of power. A defeated candidate for President or governor is known as the "titular leader" of the party, but he has no formal status or responsibilities. Informally, however, he may play a considerable role as a well-known public figure who is critical of the party in power.

Opposition, a necessary part of democratic government, is shared by the titular leader and the members of his party in the legislature. Usually the titular leader carries the burden of criticism for his party in set public speeches and news conferences. In the legislature, on the other hand, the opposition has the opportunity to make a voting record which it can take to the voters in the next election. Thus a minority party in Congress may offer a program of legislation which it cannot hope to pass but in which it believes and which may appeal later on to the voters. And it can record its opposition vigorously by voting against bills offered by the majority. It can and does criticize the proposals of the majority and of the executive. It is constantly alert to point out mistakes, uncover wrongdoing, "view with alarm." Like the majority, however, a minority opposition must take care lest it appear to put party interest above the broader public interest. Some measures of the executive and the majority are always supported by the opposition; some compromises are always made in order to serve the public interest. If the two parties are nearly equal in number in a legislature, it is likely that the laws actually passed will have support from both sides.

The opposition is naturally concerned about winning the next election and returning to power. It must therefore balance nicely the advantages and disadvantages of supporting this measure or opposing that, attacking this official of the majority or supporting the other. The whole process of opposition, in short, is a test of political skill and political responsibility much like that faced by the executive and the legislative majority. Both the Democratic and the Republican parties have uneven records in governing and in opposition. Their weaknesses and strengths are the weaknesses and strengths of American democracy. It may be that the large number of citizens who do not actively join either party serve to keep both more responsible than they would otherwise be. On the other hand, the uncertainty of elections is an even more important factor in maintaining stable and responsible government. The two great parties probably serve us best precisely because neither is ever sure of winning or of staying in power, and both are always and endlessly trying to win and to stay in the winning column. One thing is certain: as an active party member you will be far closer to the real power of government and have a better chance to make it what you wish it to be than you can if you remain "outside."

SUMMARY

The American system of nominating and electing a President—or a governor or a mayor—is unique among democratic nations. In this chapter you have examined the presidential nominating process in detail, a process developed out of experience. You have studied the state primary elections and had a chance to consider how effective they are in nominating presidential candidates of the two great parties. You have seen how our parties meet together once every four years in the national party conventions, not only to nominate presidential and vice-presidential candidates, but to take stock, to adopt a program, and simply to keep up old acquaintances in the party and make new ones.

The presidential campaign is the climax of America's four-year cycle of politics. You know something of the drama and emotion in such campaigns from your own experience. By learning about the "inner workings," you should have a better understanding of the whole process.

We have examined the question whether campaigns do decide elections after all. You should be able to form your own opinion on that difficult question. Once more you have seen that America's sorry record of non-voting lowers the character of our democracy. Here is a way in which you, as an individual, can do a great service—by entering, when the laws admit you, fully into the responsibilities of citizenship and persuading others to do the same. Party activities and responsibilities do not end with elections. The parties, after elections, carry on their jobs of governing or of opposition. Finally, you should understand better why it is that party membership, which is open to all citizens, can bring you into closer touch with the workings of your government, at all levels, and give you a richer opportunity to make America over in the image of your ideals.

KNOW WHAT YOU READ

1. Explain: "Nomination and election campaigns for the Presidency are almost always going on."
2. Explain each of the three types of party presidential primaries.
3. Why are the primaries so important in each of these states: New Hampshire? Minnesota? California? Wisconsin? Oregon?
4. In most states, all delegates are not selected by the voters of the parties in primary elections. How are they chosen?
5. Why do some people argue that presidential nominees should be chosen by primaries in all states? What are the arguments against this proposal?

477

6. In what sense are the conventions "gala occasions"?
7. Some critics of the convention system claim that the real business of the convention is accomplished by secret deals made in "smoke-filled rooms." How correct is this criticism?
8. Who make the plans for the nominating conventions? Who are the officers of the convention?
9. Explain how a platform committee works.
10. Why must a platform contain "broad and general terms" which commit the party to no specific policy?
11. A platform must contain "something for everybody." Why?
12. Describe a demonstration. What is its purpose? Is it effective?
13. Explain the steps by which a convention elects its nominee.
14. How are candidates for the Vice-Presidency nominated? Why are more and more people dissatisfied with the old ways of choosing candidates for this office?
15. In what ways has campaigning changed in recent years?
16. Summarize the work of a party's national committee in carrying on a campaign.
17. The presidential candidate must have his personal organization. What does it do?
18. How important are the voluntary organizations of "amateurs"?
19. Does the campaign determine the winner? Explain your answer.
20. Whether your answer to 19 is *yes* or *no*, what other values can you find in presidential election campaigns?
21. Why do so many citizens fail to vote? Why can non-voting be dangerous? Use cartoon, p. 473, in your answer.
22. What are the responsibilities assumed by the party which wins an election? By the losing party?

WHAT DO YOU THINK?

1. Here are four common statements about national politics.

    (a) Convention delegates are controlled by leaders.
    (b) Presidential nominations are "rigged" in smoke-filled rooms.
    (c) Demonstrations are just window dressing.
    (d) Party platforms are "hot air."

    Do you agree with any or all of these? Why?

2. Your text says that in listening to campaign speakers on television, you must "guard against being misled by the techniques of television advertising." What are these? Do you think they are all bad?

478

PROBLEMS AND PROJECTS FOR YOU

1. In Chap. 7 of Dixon and Plischke, *American Government: Basic Documents and Materials*, study the presidential preference primary ballots, the short and long presidential ballots, and the certificate of ascertainment. What did you learn by comparing these ballots? What points mentioned in your textbook are illustrated in the ballots and in the certificate?

2. Many people support a political party because it is the party their parents favored. Many others support a party because they feel that the party will do the most for them in dollars and cents. Conduct a poll among adults to find out why they favor one party or the other. Report to the class. More interesting results will be obtained if several of you conduct the poll and combine your information.

3. Find in *The Book of the States* the table "Voting Statistics: Selected Data on Persons Registered and Voting by States." Study this table to get information to help you to answer these questions and report:
   (a) Which states had the best records in percent of registered voters who voted in the most recent general election?
   (b) Which states had the poorest record?
   (c) In which states did voting in the primaries exceed voting in the general election?
   (d) In which states did the smallest percent of voters take part in the *primary* elections?

4. In 1957 the Democratic National Committee formed a permanent advisory Council to formulate national party policy between conventions. From back files of newspapers, learn as much as you can about the Democratic Advisory Council, and report to the class. Also report on Republican reactions to this new idea in party politics.

5. Using United States history references, make a list of slogans used in presidential elections.

6. Look in the *World Almanac* to find the platforms of the major parties for the last presidential election. Study these platforms to answer the following questions:
   (a) Do the platforms try to offer "something for everybody"? If so, for what groups?
   (b) Do the platforms use "broad and general terms"? On what issues?

7. Use a United States history textbook to find out why the parties nominated their vice-presidential candidates. For example, the Whigs in 1840 nominated John Tyler because he was a Southerner and a friend of Henry Clay.

8. One candidate for Congress in Ohio in 1954 did the following things in one Sunday afternoon:
   (a) umpired a few innings of a baseball game
   (b) attended a VFW picnic (40 miles away)

(c) attended a picnic of the Rumanian-American Club

(d) attended a Knights of Columbus picnic.

At each picnic he chatted with voters and made a short speech. Having run behind schedule, because the baseball game was late in starting, the candidate completely missed one picnic at which he was expected. In all, he drove over 200 miles in Sunday traffic and arrived home after midnight. What conclusions about campaigning can you draw from the above?

EXTEND YOUR VOCABULARY

presidential primary	delegates	Speaker's Bureau
bloc (of votes)	credentials	campaign literature
favorite son	platform	titular leader
uniform primary law	demonstration	

YOUR NOTEBOOK: THE GOVERNMENT OF ——

1. How are candidates for governor nominated in your state?
2. How are delegates to the national convention selected in your state?
3. If you are studying government in an election year, (a) list the principal issues in your state's gubernatorial campaign; (b) list the names of candidates for the chief state offices.

READ MORE ABOUT IT

BERELSON, BERNARD et al., Voting. University of Chicago Press, 1954.
A valuable symposium.

BURNS, JAMES M., and PELTASON, JACK W., Government by the People. Prentice-Hall, 1954. Chaps. 9–10.

HARTZ, LOUIS, Is There a Republican Majority? Harper, 1954.
Thoughtful and lively analysis of a current question.

IRISH, MARIAN D., and PROTHRO, JAMES W., The Politics of American Democracy. Prentice-Hall, 1959. Chaps. 8–9, 11.

KEY, V. O., JR., Parties, Politics and Pressure Groups. Crowell, 1958.
One of the best books on our parties and a very readable one.

LUBELL, SAMUEL, The Future of American Politics. Harper, 1952.
Lively "profile of the future" by a great student of American opinion.

MERRIAM, CHARLES E., and GOSNELL, HAROLD, Non-Voting. University of Chicago Press, 1924.
An older book—but still a timely problem.

RANNEY, AUSTIN, The Governing of Men. Holt, 1958. Chaps. 13–16.

CHAPTER 20

Taxation

In this chapter you will learn about

The power to tax

How our tax money is spent

Who and what are taxed

Who collects taxes

State and municipal taxes

Problems of taxation in a free society

In earlier chapters of this book we have considered many of the things governments do for the people: providing college education for veterans, keeping up highways and parks, delivering the mail, disposing of garbage, building bridges, inspecting foods, giving police and fire protection, and maintaining our national defense. Some people seem to think that when government does something for them, they get it for nothing. But everything governments do costs money, and the money must come from somewhere. The "somewhere" is the people of the United States.

All Americans who have occasion to spend money are taxpayers. When you buy school supplies at your neighborhood store, the clerk will probably add some pennies to your bill, with some remark like "That's for the Mayor." In that case you have paid a sales tax. But even if you did not, the store owner had to pay a property tax and a number of other taxes. A portion of these taxes he passed on to you, in the price of your school supplies. So you pay taxes whether you know it or not.

481

THE POWER TO TAX

Taxing the people is one of the best known and least popular functions of all governments. There is an old saying that "nothing is certain except death and taxes"; but it might make more sense to say that nothing is certain except death and life, which means much the same thing. For where there is human life and civilization, there is government. Furthermore, where there is government, there is taxation to pay for it. What matters is who has the power to tax, what tax money is used for, who and what are taxed, and how much.

From very early times it has been recognized that the power to tax the people—the power to force people to pay money into a government treasury—is the most important power of all government. Officials, whether self-appointed or elected, can issue orders and make laws, but they cannot carry them out without money. Thus the power to tax makes other powers possible. Not all governments raise and collect taxes in the same way.

One big difference between free governments and totalitarian governments is the way they raise their revenues. In a free society, taxes are levied by freely elected legislative bodies; in a totalitarian society, they are levied by decree. This point was dramatized in early English history in the struggle between Parliament and the king. If the king had power to raise money by royal decree, to force the people to pay money or goods into his treasury, he was a tyrant. But if Parliament had power to raise money by law, it could limit the authority of the king. Parliament came out on top in this struggle, and established the principle in Britain that only the people themselves, through their chosen agents, have the right to tax the people.

No Taxation Without Representation

This principle was one of the chief issues in the American Revolution, as you know from your American history. The cry "Taxation without representation is tyranny!" expressed the hard-won right of the people to be taxed only by laws passed by legislatures with freely chosen representatives.

After independence, the Articles of Confederation, which governed the states until 1789, were a failure from the first; under them the young nation almost fell apart. One of the chief reasons for this failure was that the Articles gave no effective taxing power to Congress. The Americans learned from this experience (see Chap. 3) that a national government which cannot tax cannot govern. At the Constitutional Convention of 1787 about the only thing the delegates were entirely agreed upon was that the new government must have power to tax the people directly. They might differ on *how* the power was to be applied, but not on *whether* the government should have it. Thus the new Constitution stated that Congress should have power "to lay and collect taxes, duties, imposts, and excises" (I, 8).

482

We have seen in Chapter 14 that *some* Americans are still taxed without representation. The residents of Washington, D.C., have no vote. Yet they pay federal taxes like anyone else. The same is true of aliens anywhere in the country. Children's earnings are taxable, though they are not old enough to vote. But this is only to say that the principle of "no taxation without representation" is no more absolute than the principles of free speech or universal suffrage.

Taxation for What?

In the past, there have been two main purposes for taxing the people in the United States: to pay for services provided by government, and to pay the cost of national defense. In recent times, as we shall see (pp. 486–489), people have realized that the taxing power of government can be used to change or affect the economic condition of the country.

When our nation got its start, people expected very little service from their government. Only as population grew and the nation expanded, did they expect more services, and taxes rose to pay for them. In 1802 President Jefferson, in his Annual Message to Congress, could ask, "What farmer, what mechanic, what laborer, ever sees a taxgatherer of the United States?" In our time one might well ask, "Who hasn't seen one?" What Jefferson meant was that the income of the government, from the sale of land and from taxes on imported goods, was sufficient to pay the debt built up during the Revolution, administer the government and the court system, and provide for the national defense. Local government was responsible for police, education, and roads.

Jefferson could go on to talk about the problem of what to do with the surplus the government would have available in a few years, after the national debt had been entirely paid! In the War of 1812 the nation again went into heavy debt. Yet the prosperity which followed the war soon refilled the Treasury, and by Jackson's administration in the 1830's a surplus actually did exist for a short time.

The growing needs of the people and the dreadful cost of the War Between the States finally put the national government into permanent debt and made the "taxgatherer of the United States" a more and more familiar figure. In our time the overwhelming majority of our families pay federal taxes.

HOW OUR TAX MONEY IS SPENT

Where in general does our federal tax money go? The chart on p. 484 shows how our federal tax dollar is divided.

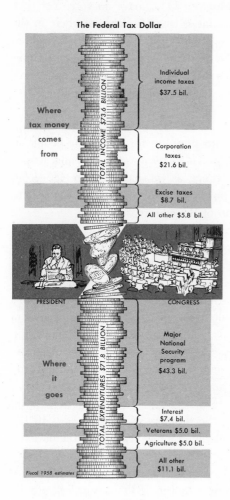

The Federal Tax Dollar

Where tax money comes from

TOTAL INCOME $73.6 BILLION

Individual income taxes $37.5 bil.

Corporation taxes $21.6 bil.

Excise taxes $8.7 bil.

All other $5.8 bil.

PRESIDENT   CONGRESS

Where it goes

TOTAL EXPENDITURES $71.8 BILLION

Major National Security program $43.3 bil.

Interest $7.4 bil.

Veterans $5.0 bil.

Agriculture $5.0 bil.

All other $11.1 bil.

Fiscal 1958 estimates

The proposed allocation of money from taxes and other sources of income is shown in the budget estimates for the fiscal year 1958. The government estimated an income of 73.6 billion dollars for the year and expenses totaling 71.8 billions, which would have resulted in a 1.8 billion surplus. Actually, expenses exceeded income, 71.9 to 69.1 billions—a deficit of 2.8 billion dollars for the year:

1958 BUDGET—INCOME AND EXPENSES

Income	(Billions)
Individual income taxes	34.7
Corporation taxes	20.1
Excise taxes	8.5
All other	5.8
	69.1

Expenditure	(Billions)
National security program	45.0
Interest	7.7
Veterans	5.0
Agriculture	4.5
All other	9.7
	71.9

Because expenditures were higher than income for the fiscal year 1958, the government had a *DEFICIT* and therefore had to borrow on the credit of the U.S. (authorized by the Constitution, I,8). Most of the government's borrowing is accomplished through the sale of various forms of bonds, which are purchased by U.S. government agencies and trust funds, commercial and mutual savings banks, insurance companies, state and local governments, individuals, and other miscellaneous investors.

Major source of income for the government is the personal or income tax. This is followed by corporate taxes, excise taxes, and "other" sources. The latter includes such things as inheritance and estate taxes and tariff revenues.

The largest percentage of the tax dollar is used for the national security or defense program, which includes the cost of foreign aid to our allies. The "all other" category includes such varied expenses as social security; aid to labor, commerce, public housing, and education; and development and maintenance of our natural resources. The cost of administering the government is also included in this group.

The next highest expense for the government is that of paying interest rates on money borrowed by the government. Aid to agriculture is in the form of monies for agricultural studies and subsidies for crops, and the money granted to veterans is used for pensions, medical services, and rehabilitation programs.

In earlier years, federal expenditures were thought to be limited by the Constitution to a very narrow range of activities. A long series of decisions of the Supreme Court has, by our time, established the constitutionality of taxation by the federal government for many purposes and also the principle of federal grants to the states. (See Constitution, p. 53.) Thus today, a large proportion of the money raised by federal taxes is returned to the states for the services and programs included in the chart under "all other," explained in the caption. These payments from federal to state treasury are known as **grants-in-aid**. Some people still fear that the federal government threatens the independence of state and local governments and of private citizens by taking on too many functions. But the contrast between the early days of our republic and today shows how much more we expect the federal government to do for us with the money it collects from us in taxes.

National Defense

The deep tragedy of human life in the twentieth century is shown clearly enough in the chart on the tax dollar. That tragedy is the fear of war. About 70 percent of our federal tax money is spent for national defense and veterans' benefits. Even though our national debt has reached an astronomical figure of some 290 billion dollars, it could be entirely paid off in about seven years if we could count on a world of permanent peace. The struggle for peace is expensive, not only in human life, but in wealth. Some of the money that goes into defense is not, of course, wholly lost, but by far the greatest part of it is. Missiles, for example, soon are out of date. We purchase all the protection we can because we must (see Chap. 26); but we purchase it at the expense of rebuilding the whole world for a new age of formerly undreamed-of comfort and abundance.

THE ARMED FORCES AND MATERIALS OF WAR How do we spend this money for national defense? (For the structure of our national defense system, see Chap. 27.) Defense money is spent in three principal ways: to pay the cost of our armed forces, to buy the materials of war, and to support our allies all over the world. The first two ways use up about 90 percent of our defense expenditures. They cover the wages and salaries paid to soldiers, sailors, and airmen, as well as to the civilian administration of the armed services, and the cost of every item used by some three million men, from nuts and bolts to bombers, from socks to air bases, and from rifle bullets to nuclear weapons. A single long-range missile, for example, capable of carrying hydrogen bombs, costs more than the whole national government of Washington's time. Yet we must have scores of them. As weapons grow more complex, they become more costly, and the men who operate them must be more highly trained. Thus there is no prospect of drastic reduction in the costs of national defense, unless efforts at world-wide disarmament should be successful.

485

AID TO ALLIES The third type of defense expenditure, aid to our allies, amounts to 10 percent or less of the total. In a world as interdependent as ours, no nation can maintain a position of strength without allies. The United States, with such an enormous share of the world's wealth and resources, has accepted a large share of responsibility for helping our allies to be ready to defend themselves. The largest share of our financial assistance to the free world goes for military equipment and other forms of military aid. Under our foreign military aid program, we make large annual gifts to many countries allied to us under the North Atlantic Treaty and the Southeast Asia Treaty (see Chap. 25). A much smaller sum is spent each year to help increase the industrial productivity of our allies and finance their purchases from us. A still smaller sum is given to many nations for "technical assistance," under what is called the Point Four Program, first announced in President Truman's State of the Union Message in 1949. This is the famous program of sending skilled technicians to help native peoples in underdeveloped areas to improve their own living standards. (We shall discuss this program, as well as the whole matter of foreign aid, in Chapter 25.)

Controlling the Economy by Taxation

Taxation, in addition to paying for government services and for defense, has another very important function which does not show up on the tax dollar chart. Federal taxation is a means of controlling the national economy. In early times, the total budget of the national government was so small and its taxes so few, that federal tax policy had little direct effect on the people.

There were important exceptions, however. In 1794 the farmers of western Pennsylvania rebelled against the federal tax on whiskey. There were some angry, armed demonstrations. Then cool heads quieted the farmers down and the federal troops, sent to the scene, were not needed. The reason for the rebellion was that the federal taxing policy was very effectively regulating the lives of these farmers—for the worse. An excise tax was collected on each barrel of whiskey, a commodity which was not considered a necessity. The farmers of western Pennsylvania felt that this tax was a direct one on their way of earning a living. They had found that transporting grain in its natural form over the Alleghenies to their eastern markets was very expensive. Their customers could not pay prices which would cover transportation costs. The farmers, therefore, distilled their grain into whiskey, barreled it, and shipped it in this cheaper form (for which they got higher prices) over the mountains. By taxing each barrel, the government was controlling their source of income and thus regulating their lives.

Special taxes, like the whiskey tax, have always regulated the lives of the people taxed. In our time many similar taxes on so-called luxuries (including

Prosperity to Depression

(as in the rise and fall of general business
conditions in the late 1920's and early 1930's)

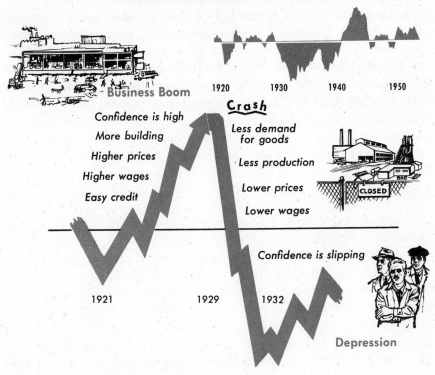

Business Boom

1920   1930   1940   1950

Crash

Confidence is high

More building

Higher prices

Higher wages

Easy credit

Less demand
for goods

Less production

Lower prices

Lower wages

CLOSED

Confidence is slipping

1921   1929   1932

Depression

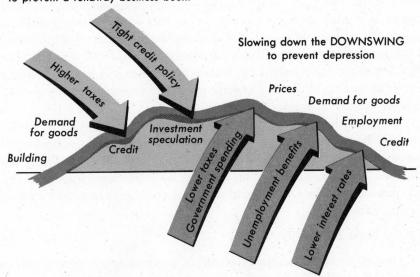

Slowing down the UPSWING
to prevent a runaway business boom

Tight credit policy

Higher taxes

Slowing down the DOWNSWING
to prevent depression

Prices

Demand for goods

Employment

Credit

Demand
for goods

Investment
speculation

Building   Credit

Lower taxes
Government spending

Unemployment benefits

Lower interest rates

The top half of this chart shows how an uncontrolled business cycle may run its normal
course of ups and downs. The lower half shows how government might use powers it now
has to bring the cycle under some degree of control.

487

whiskey) directly affect certain people. Taxes also control our economic life in other, more important ways. Today between one-fifth and one-quarter of the whole annual national income (all the dollars received by all Americans) goes through the hands of the federal government, while at least 8 percent passes through the hands of state and local governments. Government decisively influences economic life. If the national government, for example, reduces personal income taxes, the average person has more money to spend; more spending tends to bring greater production to meet the increased demand; and greater production may create more jobs and higher profits for business. More people have incomes high enough so that they must pay federal income taxes. Thus the government actually takes in more money than before.

Inflation and Deflation

Sometimes the demand for consumer goods becomes greater than industry can meet. In that case, people compete for the available goods, prices rise, and money buys less. This condition, where too much money is in circulation, is called **inflation** (money will buy too little). It brings great hardships to those whose dollar income does not rise—people on fixed salaries or pensions, for example—and sooner or later everyone suffers. Under these conditions the federal government may increase the income tax to reduce the amount of money people have to spend. This should reduce the demand for consumer goods and give industry a chance to catch up until there is a balance again between supply and demand. (See graphs, p. 487.)

If the supply of consumer goods becomes too great and the amount of money in the hands of the consumer too small, we have **deflation.** Consumers cannot buy goods, and prices drop. When this happens, government may reduce the income tax to leave more money in the hands of the consumer. Thus the federal tax policy plays an enormously important regulatory role. Needless to say, the matter is not simple. Economists and politicians disagree among themselves as to when to make changes in income tax policy and what changes to make. (See graphs, p. 487.)

The same thing is true of taxes on corporate income—that is, taxes on business. By lowering taxes, government can leave larger sums in the hands of business, with which to expand plant and production, thus producing more jobs and giving income to more people. By increasing corporation taxes, government can reduce the amount of money available to business for expanding its production.

Luxury Taxes and Tariffs

Through taxes on luxuries or tariffs on imported goods, government can directly affect other parts of the economy. A high tax on amusements can cut down attendance at theaters and ball games; a low tax can increase it. A low tariff on Swiss watches may enable the Swiss to sell their products at lower prices than American watchmakers can, since the cost of producing watches in Switzerland is lower than it is in the United States. This could ruin some American watchmakers. On the other hand, a very high tariff on Swiss watches (watchmaking is the chief industry of Switzerland) could ruin American relations with a friendly country.

Other Special Taxes

Another quite different way in which tax policy can regulate our lives is illustrated by the federal tax on gamblers. In most states professional gambling is illegal. Under federal law it is not illegal, but there is a law requiring gamblers to have a federal license. A license, since it must be paid for, is a form of tax. When the gambler applies for his license and pays the tax, his gambling becomes known. Then he is exposed to the law enforcement officers of the state or states where he operates. In this way, the tax can eliminate gambling as a profession (or drive it "underground").

Exemptions

American life is influenced in quite another way by the government's policy of **exemptions** (freedom from taxes). Thus the churches are encouraged by the exemption of church property from taxes; education is supported by the exemption of schools which do not operate for a profit; and many kinds of cultural activities are fostered by exempting non-profit organizations. Gifts (up to 25 percent of income) made by the individual to such enterprises—churches, schools and colleges, community chest, Red Cross, and countless others—may be deducted in figuring personal federal income taxes. Tax policy is thus used as a way to promote social welfare and social progress. Taxpayers, it is worth pointing out, may *not* deduct gifts to persons or to non-charitable organizations; and if you receive a gift of money or goods or win a prize, you must pay taxes on it.

These are only a few of the many ways in which the tax policy of the President and Congress can affect the economy of the United States, and even of the world. Taxation, once considered solely as a source of revenue to meet the costs of government, has thus become one of the most important powers of the government in maintaining stability and prosperity.

WHO AND WHAT ARE TAXED?

The anxious American taxpayer of the 1960's if asked "Who and what are taxed?" might say, "Everybody and everything is taxed." He would not be far

STOUT FELLOW

Justus in *The Minneapolis Star*

wrong. It is true that the federal government cannot tax state or local governments. But almost everybody else is taxed. Out of every dollar you earn, at least thirty cents goes for some sort of tax. The average wage earner today pays an income tax to the federal government (and most of us pay taxes to state government and local government as well, as we shall see). All of us are also taxed through the things we buy if we have any money at all. When you buy a package of playing cards and pay two cents in sales tax to your city and four cents to the federal government in excise tax, you are at the end of a series of taxes which began when your cards were in the original state of wood pulp. The owner of the forest paid property taxes; the lumber company paid corporate income taxes; the card manufacturing company paid corporate taxes; the distributor of the cards paid corporate taxes; his workers paid personal income taxes; the store where you bought the cards paid real property taxes; the clerk from whom you bought them pays income taxes. Some fraction of the money paid for the cards can be found in all these taxes back to the beginning of the process.

The Income Tax

The income tax is the most familiar of all our federal taxes. We are so used to it that we have come to accept it with no more than a moan and a joke. Yet our forefathers considered a direct federal income tax a violation of personal freedom, and the Supreme Court declared the income tax levied

490

during the War Between the States to be unconstitutional. Later, Amendment XVI to the Constitution (1913) gave Congress the power to levy income taxes.

The tax has reached almost all of us only within recent years. A large part of every week we work for pay goes to support the activities and services of our national government. Personal income tax was levied because other forms of taxation were not supplying the government with sufficient funds and because it was felt by many people that the burden of the cost of government should be more widely shared among the people. The personal income tax was justified on the ground that since all Americans benefit from the services of government and have responsibility for national defense, the costs ought to be spread among the people according to their ability to pay. Everyone who can afford it should pay something; those who are best able to do so should pay more—much more. Thus government sets its income tax rates according to a scale, with a small percentage of tax for the first few thousand dollars of income per year, and increasingly higher rates for greater earnings. From no income tax at all if you earn only a few hundred dollars, the rates rise to 87 percent if your income is in the hundreds of thousands. We sometimes refer, therefore, to the personal income tax as a **graduated** or **progressive income tax.**

Other taxes may hit only certain people or groups, but the graduated income tax involves everyone, except the very poor, in some direct participation in government. As the chart on p. 484 shows, it gives government the largest share of its income.

THE PERSONAL INCOME TAX   Every American with an income of $600 or more is required to fill out a form showing what his income for the year was, what items he may deduct according to law ($600 for each dependent, certain business expense, medical expense, etc.), and to compute his tax according to formulas provided by the forms. (See sample p. 492.) These returns must be filed by April 15 each year. Failing to file and falsifying returns are punishable by federal law. The rates rise gradually from 21 percent on the lowest taxable incomes to 87 percent on very large incomes. If a taxpayer works for wages or salary, a certain portion of his estimated yearly tax is deducted by the employer from each pay check. At the end of the year, he must pay the government any additional sum he may owe, or, if he has paid too much, the government sends him a refund.

Taxes are paid directly to the regional Director of Internal Revenue of the Treasury Department (see chart, p. 521). If the taxpayer does not receive a salary or wages, he must pay his tax in quarterly installments, based on his estimates of what he will make during the year. While this procedure is simple enough in outline, the tax law and the regulations of the Internal

491

Revenue Service have become more and more complicated. Many taxpayers need the help of experts in preparing their returns. The various offices of the Internal Revenue Service provide this assistance. Many private people also specialize in it, and a thriving business has sprung up in which tax experts advise taxpayers and make out their returns for them for a fee.

THE CORPORATE INCOME TAX   The corporate income tax works in much the same way. It is a tax levied by law on the *profits* of business enterprise. Companies are allowed to make full deductions for the expenses they incur in producing and selling their products. What is left over after expenses is known as profit. Corporation income is taxed at a flat rate of 52 percent on all profits above $25,000 a year.

There are certain important exceptions, however. For example, companies which produce oil and natural gas are given a **depletion allowance** of 27 percent because they are assumed to be investing capital in the search for and production of commodities which are constantly being used up (depleted). Thus their costs are greater than those of other companies, such as automobile companies, which can use the same plant over and over again. Such special benefits to certain groups often cause controversy in the Congress and among citizens generally.

At certain times of great financial need, the Congress has authorized what is known as the **excess profits tax.** This means that profits up to a certain point, depending on the income a company receives, are taxed at the rate of 52 percent (1959), but after that a still higher percentage of all profits must be paid in taxes to the Treasury. During World War II the excess profits tax was 95 percent. Because excess profits taxes tend to reduce seriously the amount of money business can invest for expansion, the Congress does not like to impose them, and they are not used in peacetime. The taxes business must pay are passed along in the price paid by the consumers of their products. Thus the individual pays the tax ultimately out of his earnings. This shows that there is no other source of tax revenue save the earnings of the people.

Tariffs

Under the first great American Secretaries of the Treasury, Alexander Hamilton and Albert Gallatin, taxes on imported goods (**duties**) provided the government with all the revenue it needed to raise by taxes. Today the tariff (customs duties) brings in less than 1 percent of the federal revenue. The tariff has become, in fact, a much more important device for regulating business and foreign relations than for raising money. The reason is that the United States has become by far the largest producer of manufactured goods in the world. Our foreign trade consists mainly of shipping finished goods to other countries in exchange for certain raw materials, such as rubber, tungsten, manganese, and tin, which we either do not have in this country or have only in small quantities. Since these imports are necessary to the welfare of the nation, or close to it, we do not levy a tax upon them. Those imports which are taxed are mainly luxuries of foreign manufacture (Oriental rugs, china, toys, cosmetics, furniture, etc.) or goods which we do not need but other countries need to sell, if they can (automobiles, bicycles, electrical appliances, etc.). The tariff today is mainly a "protective" tariff, protecting American manufacturers against competition from foreign makers.

The U.S. Tariff Commission, an independent agency (see chart, p. 163), was established in 1916, with six members (no more than three from one party) appointed by the President with the consent of the Senate. They serve for six years, one term expiring each year. This Commission investigates international trade conditions and reports to Congress and the President its advice on what rates of customs duties are fair to American importers.

Excise Taxes

Next to the income tax, the federal government today raises its largest revenue from the excise tax. An excise tax is an indirect tax on consumers, in the price of the goods they buy. The manufacturer is taxed directly by the government, but "passes on" his tax burden to his customers. Originally the excise tax was levied only on luxuries. With the tremendous rise in our standard of living, however, yesterday's luxuries become today's necessities. Thus the excise tax on gasoline seems like a tax on a necessity. Other important excises are levied on tobacco, liquor, beer, and wine, transportation tickets, television sets and home appliances, cosmetics, luggage, amusement tickets, fur coats, jewelry, and similar goods. Revenue from these taxes is very

493

large, producing almost 15 percent or more of the federal government's annual income. Look at a package of cigarettes or of playing cards, and you will see an Internal Revenue stamp over the opening. This signifies that the manufacturer has paid the excise tax, but the amount is included in the consumer's purchase price.

Other Taxes

INHERITANCE AND ESTATE TAXES Another federal tax is the one on estates. It raises only a relatively small revenue (about one billion dollars in 1953–1955), but illustrates the power of tax policy to regulate the economy. Large estates are taxed both by the federal government and by state governments (in 49 states).

The federal estate tax runs from 5 percent on estates of $5,000 or less up to 77 percent on estates in excess of ten million dollars. The tax is charged on the net value (after expenses) of an estate left by a person at his death. State governments tax the shares of such estates left to each heir (inheritance tax). These taxes explain the gradual disappearance from American life of great inherited fortunes. They are also one reason why a great deal of wealth is given away for educational and charitable purposes, which are tax free. The estate and inheritance taxes are intended, in part, to encourage such giving.

SOCIAL SECURITY TAX The social security tax, which produces 5 percent or more of the federal income, is a different kind of tax. Both employer and employee pay this tax. The money is paid into the Treasury, as are the proceeds from any other tax, and may be used for any purpose approved by Congress. Payments to retired persons under the social security system, as we shall see in Chapter 24, are authorized by Congress to be paid out of the Treasury but amount to less than the income from the tax.

WHO COLLECTS TAXES

There are various channels through which our taxes flow, depending on the kind of tax each is and for what it is intended. They are all part of the Treasury Department (see chart, p. 521), the non-tax activities of which we will discuss in Chapter 21.

Internal Revenue Service

The agency for collecting our federal taxes is the Internal Revenue Service of the Treasury Department. This agency, with more than 50,000 employees, reaches more directly into the lives of the people than any other. For make-up of the staff and other duties, study the chart, p. 521.

Unlike many other agencies, the Internal Revenue Service is *decentralized*, that is, its work is done mainly in various regions and districts throughout the country. The Commissioner, appointed by the President with the consent of the Senate, makes important decisions, under the laws, regarding methods of tax collection, estimates of revenue, methods of enforcement, and management of personnel. His Deputy and Assistant Commissioners carry out the tax laws of the United States on behalf of the President.

In the nine geographical regions, each headed by a Regional Commissioner, with 64 Internal Revenue Districts below them, are the many thousands of working personnel who handle the papers involved in what is the world's largest administrative operation, collecting our federal taxes. These workers mail out tax forms, audit tax returns, advise taxpayers, find errors and make adjustments, inspect businesses, issue revenue stamps (for excise taxes), and carry on a great number of other necessary activities.

Under the Commissioner and his assistants in Washington are some 2,000 employees who deal with nation-wide problems and handle specific matters referred to them from the regions. Taxpayers may appeal decisions about their taxes to the District Office. If they remain unsatisfied, they may appeal to the Regional Commissioner, and from there, if necessary, to the central office in Washington. Lawsuits arising out of such appeals are tried before the Tax Court, as we saw in Chapter 9. Employees in the central office are nearly all career civil servants, as are the district directors and most of the field force. The merit system of employment is even more important in the Revenue Service than in most other agencies of the government, since the collecting and handling of the people's money must be kept free of influence.

The Internal Revenue Service is also one of the law enforcement agencies of the United States (see chart, p. 262).

The Bureau of Customs

The external taxes of the United States are collected by the Bureau of Customs, also in the Treasury Department. Even though the volume of its business today is relatively small, the Bureau must conduct its operations at every port of entry into the United States. There are 51 district offices, including one each in Hawaii, Puerto Rico, and the Virgin Islands. All of us who have crossed a border, from Canada or Mexico, for example, have met the customs officer. He requires us, as he does all importers, to fill out forms declaring what we have bought in the country we visited, how much we paid for it, and whether we intend to sell it in the United States. Tourists are allowed, if they have been out of the country more than two weeks, to bring in without customs duty $500 worth of goods purchased abroad. Businesses must pay duties set by law with the advice of the U.S. Tariff Commission (see p. 493). Some of the customs duties are *specific*; that is, so much for every piece of merchandise. Other duties are *ad valorem*; that is, a certain percentage of value for each group of merchandise. In some cases, items carry both specific and ad valorem duty charges.

Evasion of these taxes is **smuggling,** a criminal act. The penalties for it are very severe. In this connection, the Bureau of Customs is one of the U.S. Law Enforcement Agencies (see chart, p. 262). To check imports, officials examine a part or all of shipments coming into the country to be sure they are properly marked with country of origin and that invoices represent true value.

STATE AND MUNICIPAL TAXES

At least 27 percent of the taxes we pay are for state and local government —amounting to more than forty billion dollars a year. State and local taxes are levied only by the authority of a freely elected legislative body. State taxes are authorized by laws enacted by state legislatures. State legislatures have the same taxing power within the borders of the states as does the Congress over the United States, except that the Constitution forbids one state to tax imports from another or from a foreign country.

The taxes of local government are voted locally by city and county legislative bodies, and in some cases by towns and townships, villages and boroughs. The taxing power of local government depends on the state legislature. What this means is not that state legislatures decide how much taxes shall be paid into city or county treasuries, but which kinds of taxes shall be allowed and what limit shall be placed upon them.

Kinds of State Taxes

The chief revenue of state government comes from sales taxes and licensing. Some states also tax incomes but at a much lower rate than the federal government. For example, one of the heaviest costs of state government is the building and maintenance of roads. Money for this purpose, as well as for others, comes from the tax on gasoline and other fuels and from the licensing of trucks and automobiles. The money is used in part by the state department of public works for the building and maintenance of state highways, and in part is returned proportionately (i.e., a percentage of the amount collected) to the counties for their use on highways and roads maintained by them. For example, in 1954 Massachusetts collected $53,077,000 from motor fuel taxes. Of this, $21,557,000 went into state highways; $7,114,000 into forest, park, and other state roads; $2,093,000 for state highway police and safety measures; $11,249,000 toward retirement of state highway bonds (paying debts); $6,259,000 for county and other local roads; $3,881,000 for city streets; $384,000 for service of local road bonds; and $540,000 for other purposes authorized by state law, not having to do with roads.

Another source of state revenue is licensing of hunters and fishermen. The states are responsible for maintaining public parks and state forest preserves, and for conserving natural resources. If you are a fisherman, the money you pay the clerk (city, county, or town) for your annual license goes to pay the costs of your state department of conservation. It is a form of tax. Other typical license fees charged by the states are those for barbers, tavern keepers, restaurants, drug stores, and amusement places. Important sources of state income are excise taxes on liquor and tobacco. In some states these form the largest source of income. An interesting exception is the state of Nevada. In this state gambling is legal, and the state government is almost entirely supported by the income from taxes on gambling.

There are many differences among the states as to state income taxes. Thirty-three states, like New York or Wisconsin, derive an important part of their revenue from the personal income tax, which is levied in much the same way as the federal income tax. Thirty-three states tax the incomes of corporations. However, unlike the federal government, the states have a serious problem of competition. Businesses may move to states where the state corporate tax is low. Since all states are anxious to attract industry as a source of growth, development, and employment for its people, tax rates may be frequently changed as one state competes with another in its attempts to attract industry. In 1956, for example, the governor of West Virginia made an extensive tour of northern states, like New York and Connecticut, trying to persuade businessmen to move their factories to West Virginia because, among other reasons, tax rates were lower. The same competition works at the local level. Twenty-five states levy a severance tax on businesses, that is, a tax for removing and selling natural resources like oil, metal, or timber.

What services do you get from your state in exchange for your tax money? Do you get a bargain? The table on pp. 289–291 lists some of the state programs from which you benefit. If you consider carefully what all these programs involve, you may decide that the money you spend in state taxes is one of the best investments you will ever make.

Typically a state government collects its taxes by means of a State Tax Commission. The administration is decentralized; local offices in the principal cities or districts do the actual collecting. The rates for taxes and the fees for licenses are voted by the state legislatures in revenue laws. The Tax Commission, responsible to the governor, carries out the tax law. In many states, the secretary of state through his licensing duties collects taxes (see p. 287). The license fees are paid into the state treasury.

State governments have authority to borrow money, as does the federal government. However, state constitutions limit the amount of borrowing allowed. Thus it often happens that a project to build new schools or roads or dams will require more borrowed money than is allowable under the constitution of the state. In this case an amendment will be submitted to the voters at an election. Most states have heavy debt loads from selling bonds to raise money for roads, schools, and other long-term necessities. Interest on the debt and money to pay bonds as they become due constitute an important item in a state's annual budget—and its bill to the taxpayers. Some debts, however, are assumed in projects which provide a source of income to pay them off. When you pay the toll to drive on a toll highway, the chances are that you are helping the state to pay off money borrowed to build it. States have other non-tax sources of income as well. Toll bridges, tunnels, and ferries, state businesses such as the sale of liquor (nineteen states), and fines paid in the courts are among these sources. One state, North Dakota, is in the flour business.

Local Government Taxes

While the federal government gets its principal income from the income tax and the states get theirs from sales taxes, local government is dependent normally on what is known as the general property tax. This is a tax on **real** property (land, buildings, and improvements) and on **personal** property (furniture, jewelry, stocks and bonds, etc.). Although the general property tax, as its name suggests, is supposed to fall on all property, some local governments make no attempt to tax personal property. Some tax easily assessed items such as livestock. Some tax personal property in excess of a fixed minimum, such as $1,000 or $5,000. Real property, however, is regularly taxed.

Under the authority of the state, local legislative bodies enact tax ordinances which establish the amount of tax money to be collected. Usually the rate is set by a local tax commission or board of assessors and is based on the value of individual or corporate property or on the extent, quality, and location of a taxpayer's land. A local official, known as the assessor, figures out the value of a home or a place of business. Assessments of real property may vary a good deal over the years as a piece of property deteriorates or improves.

In the counties where residents also pay a low-rate **personal property tax,** it is again the assessor who decides what the value of such possessions is and assesses the tax. But it is the tax on homes, land, and productive property like factories in the city or livestock on the farm which produces most of the revenue of property taxation.

Rates, too, are occasionally changed, as the community's financial needs change. Such changes are not often downward! Under law, many local governments grant exemptions or reductions to certain groups of people—for example, to veterans or to clergymen. Property owners may appeal their as-

Taxes are well used. Protection of our harbors by lighthouses manned by the Coast Guard is one service we buy.

OUR BEST BARGAIN

Jefferson's "taxgatherer" is known to practically all of us today. If taxes sometimes seem onerous, what we get for them is probably the best bargain of our lives.

The Bureau of Standards, by establishing and maintaining uniform weights and measures, ensures our getting full measure when we shop.

At the National Cancer Institute of the National Institutes of Health, government scientists explore cancer in animals to reach a better understanding of the disease in man—and a possible cure.

sessments if they consider the amounts unfair. Many local tax commissions hold annual "grievance" days for the purpose of hearing such appeals. Where the practice of holding grievance days is not followed, the taxpayer is always free to ask the assessor to reconsider. If necessary, the taxpayer can appeal to the county board, should he feel that he has not received fair treatment. If he is turned down, he can go to court and make a further appeal. With the exceptions mentioned, all privately owned land and buildings in a community are taxed. Thus if you live in an apartment owned by someone else, he pays the tax for the whole building, but he must then charge you enough rent to enable him to pay the tax.

There is no general rule regarding the method of collecting real property taxes. In some areas, a city resident pays a single property tax to a county collector, or treasurer, who then returns the appropriate share to the city. In other areas, city residents pay two different taxes, one to the city and one to the county. Township and village residents, again, may pay directly to a local collector or to a county treasurer, who returns the money to the local governing body.

As cities, towns, townships, and counties have grown and taken on more and more responsibility, the real property tax has tended to produce less revenue than is needed. There is, in any case, a limit to the amount of real property tax that can safely be levied. If the tax gets very high, businesses may move to other localities where the tax is lower. People may be discouraged from owning their homes.

The fact is that the property tax is to a great extent outmoded. It was devised in an era when most people lived on farms, when there were no apartment buildings, and when many modern services were unknown. As we shall see in Chapter 24, school taxes, whether separate or part of the general property tax, are based on property ownership, even though a large proportion of school children come from families which do not own property. The property tax today simply cannot produce enough revenue to meet the costs of local government. Thus other forms of taxes have had to be devised.

Local governments have had to go to state legislatures for further taxing power. In some cases, like Philadelphia, local income taxes have been authorized. The most common and lucrative of the newer local taxes is the sales tax, with which most city residents are now familiar. This tax, usually 1 or 2 percent, is levied on all retail sales except, in most cases, food or health necessities. The child of today who reports to his mother, "The ball cost 98 cents and 2 cents tax," is being introduced to the realities of local government at a much earlier age than were his parents. The tax may be levied on the gross receipts of a firm, such as a public utility. Then it is called a "gross receipts" tax. Sales and gross receipts taxes now produce a very high proportion of revenue in many cities. In some areas the tax is county-wide and collected

500

by the county treasurer. In these cases, a proportionate share is turned over to city treasuries and other local governments.

There is great variety among our 50 states. Some states share income tax money with their local governments. Other commonly "shared taxes" are those on incomes, liquor, and motor fuels. Local governments in most states receive grants from the states (see charts pp. 286 and 298) for such purposes as education, roads, public welfare. Sometimes this money is granted on a matching funds basis; for every dollar received from the state, the local unit puts up a dollar. Some grants are made on the "equalization" principle, which means that a poorer community may receive more aid than a rich one. It is common for the state to specify what the local government must do to receive the grant.

Special Taxes, Assessments, and Borrowing

In various states, local governments have been authorized to levy a number of different taxes, often popularly lumped together under the heading "nuisance." These include taxes on admissions, hotel rooms, restaurant meals, and so on. Though local governments may need the revenue, such taxes are so unpopular that the trend is away from them and toward raising the rates of other taxes instead.

The people through their local governments sometimes vote to tax themselves for special purposes—to erect certain buildings or to provide themselves with a new service, for example. More often, however, local governments, like the states, borrow money. The amount of such borrowing is limited by state laws. Local governments may sell bonds for schools, for sewage disposal plants, for water systems, for public buildings, and for other capital investments. In some cases, income from the investment pays off the debt. Thus water charges may be used to pay off water system bonds. Some local governments have income from publicly owned facilities like electric power plants.

Special districts (see Chap. 12), except school districts, often have income from their special functions—water supply, sewage disposal, sanitation, or public utilities. Authorities, like the Port of New York Authority, also frequently have an income from the services they perform. The Port of New York Authority collects for the use of its docks, tunnels, and other facilities, so that it can meet its operating expenses out of income and pay off its debts.

As we saw in Chapter 13, the problems of state and local financing have become so acute in a number of states that nothing less than a complete overhauling of the governmental and financial systems can solve them. But there are no easy solutions. Years of experience and experiment will be needed before we can find ways to make better sense out of our tax programs and public financing. Meanwhile, all of us can help by recognizing that the costs of government have risen because we expect more services from government, and because there are more of us making the demands. That is why our taxes have had to go up. Too often the hue and cry against taxes is raised by the very people who never cease demanding that the government do this, that, or the other thing.

SOME GENERAL PROBLEMS OF TAXATION IN A FREE SOCIETY

The basic principle of taxation under freedom is that only the freely elected legislatures shall have the power to raise money by taxing the people. No one in a modern democratic republic like the United States questions that principle today. Free men here and everywhere do debate the question as to which taxes are fairest and which will raise the most money. The two are not necessarily the same.

Ability-to-Pay Theory

The largest share of wealth in the United States today is in its business enterprise. Thus the problem is to tax business enterprise as painlessly as possible. One way to do it is to tax the incomes of the workers; another is to tax the profits of the company; a third way is to tax the dividends (earnings from stock) of stockholders. The federal government uses all three ways. This means that an executive on salary who also owns some shares of the company stock is taxed twice on his income from the company—once on his salary and once on his dividends. The corporation itself is taxed on its profits. Meanwhile a wage worker in the same company pays a tax on his weekly income—a much smaller tax.

The theory behind this inequality is that we should tax ourselves in accordance with our ability to pay, by means of **progressive** tax rates. According to this theory, the more we make, the more we can afford to pay and should pay; the less we make, the less we can afford to pay and should have to pay. This theory favors the "little man." It also discourages savings by the man with a larger income who might otherwise invest his money in a business of his own, thus creating more income to be taxed. Instead we tend to be more and more dependent on fewer and fewer large corporations.

Supporters of the theory deny this. They point out that there are other ways in which a man can start a business of his own. He can borrow from the government at low rates of interest for a long term. He can get preferential treatment under the tax laws if he is just starting out. For example, government insurance allows him to spread his tax payments over several years until he has recovered his initial investment. He can call on the agencies of

502

both state and local government for other kinds of assistance. But, these supporters continue, the government cannot operate without taxing pretty heavily those who can afford to pay.

There are other theories about it. Those who object to the ability-to-pay theory say that the government, especially the federal government, ought to cut down its services and thus reduce its costs. The trouble is that you cannot really find an important or expensive service which is not favored by a majority of the people. Democracy means government by the majority. Modern democracy tends toward more, not fewer, government services. As the chart of the tax dollar showed us (p. 484), the actual operating costs of government and of welfare are the cheapest items in the budget. If we could abolish war, we could drastically reduce our taxes overnight. Otherwise the best we can do is to avoid waste. In many cities and states, there are private organizations of taxpayers who exert pressure on government to do just that. These organizations make studies of the costs of government to reveal what they claim to be waste, and they lobby in the legislature for laws to exert tighter control on executive expenditures.

Sales Tax

One answer to the problems raised by the ability-to-pay theory of taxation is the proposal of a general sales tax. This tax falls "equally" on everybody— that is, everyone pays the same tax on the same article. A national sales tax would raise a tremendous revenue. It would remove a great part of the burden from taxpayers with larger incomes, and thus encourage new investment to create more wealth and greater prosperity.

OBJECTIONS TO SALES TAX The difficulty with this proposal, its opponents point out, is that it places the burden of government financing directly on those least able to pay. In other words, the family which has a low income would have to pay the greatest proportion of its income in taxes; the family with the largest income would have to pay the least proportion, since the basic expenses of food, shelter, and clothing are common to everyone. Thus if government levies a general sales tax on all purchases, John Poor, who has only a small income and spends every cent of it every month, is taxed on every cent he spends. His well-to-do fellow townsman George Rich is taxed only on a part of his money, since he does not have to spend it all to buy things.

This argument is stressed by persons opposed to the sales tax. They call it a **regressive** tax. This means that it is the opposite of a **progressive** tax (like the income tax)—it falls most heavily on those least able to pay. Since the John Poors outnumber the George Riches (and have more votes), the sales tax is not popular with politicians. Believers in the sales tax suggest that certain necessities, like food, be exempted to meet this kind of objection. This would be fairer to lower-income families, but would seriously reduce the revenues produced by the tax. A national sales tax remains a possibility, though most politicians are afraid to sponsor it as too unpopular.

Taxing according to ability to pay raises a further important question. To what extent do the American people wish to have economic equality among themselves? There is no doubt that the tax power of government can bring the people closer and closer to equal economic status, by placing heavy tax burdens on the rich. This is now in fact happening, very slowly but surely. In England during the ten years from 1939 to 1949, the tax policy brought about a state of near equality. Before World War II, England had a large number of very rich people, both industrialists and great landowners. In order to meet the costs of the war, Parliament had to tax these people almost to the point of taking their property away from them. In a few years almost nobody in the country had an income of more than $25,000. Many Englishmen argue that they are a stronger and happier people now than they were before. But if necessity had not forced such a tax system upon them, we can be quite sure they would not have chosen it.

In the United States, we have had a vital tradition of *equality of opportunity* in economic life rather than economic equality. Our philosophy has been that everyone should have a fair start, then let the best man get the most. It appears fairly certain that you cannot have both kinds of equality. There is perhaps no urgency for us to decide which we prefer. But it is certain that the costs of government will continue to rise (unless, which is unlikely, there is permanent world peace), that more tax money will have to be raised, and that it will have to come from our earnings. Future generations will have to decide how they wish to apportion the tax load. From present experience and understanding, the principle of taxation according to ability to pay seems closest to the spirit of our democracy.

SUMMARY

The power to tax is the fundamental power of all governments. Taxes provide government with the money it needs to get things done, so that all other powers depend on taxation. Under free governments, the people are taxed only by laws made by freely elected legislatures—that is, indirectly, by themselves—while tyrants impose taxes on the people. You have seen in this chapter how the taxing power developed in the United States and how it works. You have been introduced to the taxing procedures of the federal, state, and local governments. You have learned that all of us are taxed in one way or another, most of us in many ways. And you have seen how the money is spent—by the federal government for services and benefits for all of us

504

and for national defense; and by state and local governments for education and many other services and benefits.

Specifically, you have met a good many forms of tax: personal income taxes (federal and state), corporate income taxes, tariffs, excise taxes, inheritance and estate taxes, sales taxes, licenses, and property taxes, among others. You have seen also that neither the federal, state, nor local governments have sufficient income from taxes to meet all their financial obligations, so that all have to borrow from the people. National, state, and local debts are important facts of life in the United States. Mounting costs, increasing debts, and inadequate sources of tax money pose serious problems for Americans in mid-twentieth century. In considering these problems we discussed **progressive** and **regressive** taxes, "ability-to-pay," and "equality of opportunity." While it is an obligation an American cannot escape to pay his taxes, it is also a great privilege. For when you think carefully about what your tax money does for you and your countrymen, you realize that you are buying more and better services and benefits than Americans ever had before, and that you are helping to insure your own freedom.

KNOW WHAT YOU READ

1. Show how people of school age pay taxes whether they know it or not.
2. One of the chief differences between free government and authoritarian government is in the way taxes are levied. What is the difference?
3. Look up in the Constitution the exact wording of the taxing power. Why did the makers of the Constitution give this power to the federal government?
4. What Americans are now taxed without representation?
5. What services were offered by federal, state, and local governments in Jefferson's day?
6. List the principal items for which the federal tax dollar is spent.
7. Why does the federal government have to pay out so much in interest each year?
8. Explain why national defense expenditures must be so high.
9. In what ways do we spend defense money to aid our allies?
10. In what ways may government use the taxing power to *regulate* business? Ways we earn a living? The rise and fall of business conditions?
11. How can tax policy aid worthy organizations and activities?
12. Amendment XVI legalized a federal income tax. Congress then voted taxes as follows. Compare these rates with those of the present:

    1 percent on incomes in excess of $3,000 for single persons, and $4,000 for married persons
    surtaxes on incomes in excess of $20,000, running up to 6 percent on incomes in excess of $500,000.

13. How does the federal government collect the personal income tax? Why do so many taxpayers need help in computing their taxes?
14. What are the corporate income tax rates? How do they affect you?
15. Once the tariff was our principal source of federal income. What is the tariff's purpose now?
16. Define *excise tax*. On what things must excise taxes be paid today? Do you pay excise taxes?
17. What are the effects of the inheritance tax on conditions of life in this country?
18. Many of you have already paid a federal old-age-and-survivors-insurance tax. How is this money used?
19. Describe the organization of the Internal Revenue Service.
20. William Jones is planning a pleasure trip to Canada. He wants to know what he can expect to have happen when he encounters a customs officer. Tell him.
21. Which branch of state and of local government determines taxes?
22. What are the principal sources of state government revenue?
23. What kinds of activity are commonly required to be licensed?
24. To what extent do the states levy income taxes?
25. In what way do states compete against one another in tax rates?
26. What are the principal services performed by the states?
27. Explain how state governments "return" money to local governments.
28. What is the work of the state tax commission?
29. John Schmidt has just received his general property tax bill. How was the amount of his tax determined? How will he pay the tax? What may he do if he believes that he can prove that he was overcharged?
30. Why is the property tax *outmoded*?
31. What are the two principal reasons for increases in state and local taxes?
32. What is the *ability-to-pay* principle?
33. Explain the difference between taxes that are *progressive* and taxes that are *regressive*.
34. Explain how the use of ability-to-pay taxes affects *equality of opportunity* in the United States.

WHAT DO YOU THINK?

1. Do you think that the progressive income tax is promoting *equality* and destroying *equality of opportunity*? Explain.
2. It is sometimes argued that as long as we have progressive taxation, the fellow who pays little or no tax will vote to spend the other fellow's money. Do you agree? Is this a good argument in favor of the sales tax?
3. A United States Commissioner of Internal Revenue once admitted that most people grumble about the size of their income tax payments but, "they know deep down in their hearts that they're getting a bargain." What do you think he meant? Do you agree?

1. Look up the taxing power in:
   (a) The Articles of Confederation
   (b) your state constitution
   (c) the Constitution of the United States
   (d) your school student body constitution, if you have one

   Make a written report in which you compare and contrast the different statements. Explain the reasons for these differences.

2. Pretend that you are a resident of the District of Columbia and you are strongly in favor of getting the right to vote. Draw a "taxation without representation" poster. (See cartoon, p. 350.)

3. Review the problem of the surplus in the days of Presidents Jackson and Cleveland. How was the problem solved? Try to find out why a surplus is considered to be a problem. Report.

4. Look up the interest payments on the national debt for each of the last ten years. Draw a graph illustrating these figures.

5. Write or record an imaginary five-minute interview between Albert Gallatin and today's Secretary of the Treasury.

6. Read "Uncle Sam, Borrower" in Burns and Peltason, *Government by the People*. Report to the class on new things you learned from the reading.

7. Follow in your daily newspapers accounts of the costs of military equipment. Make a bulletin-board display of these, or make a written summary of the costs of new bombers, atomic research, carriers, etc.

8. Interview an employee of the Bureau of Internal Revenue on the subject of his experiences with mistakes—honest and otherwise—made in income tax returns.

> The owners and occupants of the following described parcels of real estate located in the city of Botolph, in the County of Exxes, and state of Franklin, and all other persons, are hereby notified that the taxes thereon remain unpaid and that said parcels of real estate will be taken by said city of Botolph on Tuesday, June 29, at 10 A.M.
>
> John Doe. About 8,000 sq. ft. of land on Colorado Blvd., being more particularly described in Section 52, block 52, Lot 3 of Assessors plans. Taxes $17.60.

9. What happens in your community when property taxes are not paid?

10. How big is the gasoline tax in your state? What uses does your state make of this tax?

11. Interview an assessor to find out the nature and difficulties of his work.

12. Write a feature article for your school paper, or your local paper, on the relationship of increased services of government (local, state, or national) to the increased costs of government.

13. In *The Book of the States* look up the chief sources of *state* revenue. Make a graph to show this information.

EXTEND YOUR VOCABULARY

levy (a tax)	depletion allowance	general property tax
grants-in-aid	duties	real property tax
surplus	excises	personal property tax
Point Four Program	estate tax	assessor
inflation	inheritance tax	assessment
deflation	social security tax	tax commission
ability to pay principle	Bureau of Customs	ability-to-pay theory
progressive income tax	specific duty	sales tax
excess profits tax	*ad valorem* duty	regressive tax
	smuggling	

YOUR NOTEBOOK: THE GOVERNMENT OF ——

1. In your state and/or community:
   What is the gasoline tax?
   The retail sales tax?
   Cost of a hunting license?
   Cost of a fishing license?
2. Does your state have a state income tax? If so, what are its rates?
3. What is the rate of a general property tax paid by your parents?
4. To whom may persons appeal if they feel that they have been over-charged on their property tax?

READ MORE ABOUT IT

BLOUGH, RAY, *The Federal Taxing Process.* Prentice-Hall, 1952.
   Authoritative discussion of the how and why of taxes.
BURNS, JAMES M., and PELTASON, JACK W., *Government by the People*, Prentice-Hall, 1954. Chap. 26.
SCHATTSCHNEIDER, E. E., *Politics, Pressures and the Tariff.* Prentice-Hall, 1935.
SWARTHOUT, JOHN M., and BARTLEY, ERNEST R., *Principles and Problems in State and Local Government.* Oxford University Press, 1958. Chap. 9.
SWARTHOUT, JOHN M., and BARTLEY, ERNEST R., *Principles and Problems in American National Government.* Oxford University Press, 1955. Chap. 21.
WALTZ, J., "Tax Dodgers' Dragnet." *New York Times Magazine*, April 15, 1956.
   Amusing but true account of how tax dodgers are caught by the use of tipsters.

508

CHAPTER 21

Government, Business, and the Citizen

In this chapter you will learn about

The free enterprise system
The Department of Commerce
The Department of the Treasury
The Federal Reserve System
The federal government in business
Business and the state and local governments

In April, 1956, General Motors announced that a lady in Bristol, New Hampshire, had bought fifteen shares of stock in the company to become the six-hundred-thousandth stockholder. This lady thus became a capitalist, a part-owner of one of our largest business enterprises, a participant in our free enterprise system of ownership. If this lady had been a citizen of the Soviet Union she could not have made the purchase for one very good reason: there are no such corporations in the Soviet Union, since ownership is in the hands of the government.

THE FREE ENTERPRISE SYSTEM

When Americans talk of their economic life they frequently use the term **business** as a kind of shorthand. Of course, not all of the American economy can be included under this head. The term is too limited to include agriculture, the professions, and government service itself. But **business** does cover much of the ground. In contrast to countries where business (producing, buying, and selling) is run more or less directly by government (**collectivism**), the American business system is known as **free private enterprise**. It may not be wholly free or wholly private, but the term is nevertheless very useful.

Free private enterprise is an economic way of life in which the **means of production**—plants, tools, materials—are owned by private individuals. George Brown owns the local machine shop personally. Schmidt and Green are partners in owning the grocery store. Very large numbers of people own the shares of General Motors, a corporation. Ownership is usually of these three types: individual ownership, partnerships, and corporations. Owners are sometimes called **capitalists**—that is, they own the **capital** (means of production) involved in a business.

Free private enterprise does not mean simply that you may own all or part of a business if you have enough money to buy it. It means also that owners are free to decide what they are going to produce and how much, where and how they are going to sell, how much they are going to charge, and how much profit they intend to try to get. They are free to take risks, and then to take the consequences whether favorable or unfavorable. This means that if Mr. Zimmerman wishes to use his time and money, as a manufacturer of bicycles, to produce a new model of bicycle, he is free to do so. If his company produces 50,000 bicycles and consumers buy them, he may make a fair amount of money—have a good year. If he sells only 20,000 of them, he may be forced to go out of business because he cannot afford to take such a loss. Free opportunity like Mr. Zimmerman's does not exist under collectivism such as is found behind the Iron Curtain.

Communists (who believe in an extreme form of collectivism) often argue that under free private enterprise such as ours, you, the consumer, are victimized by villainous capitalists who charge you too much, cheat you by persuading you to buy things you do not want, and are simply dishonest because they sell inferior goods. We know this to be contrary to the true facts of American life. This is not to say, however, that prices are never too high, that people are not sometimes "pressured" into buying, or that no inferior goods are ever sold as better than they are. The fact is that there is a minimum of such practices, because our whole free enterprise system is *regulated* in these different ways.

Kinds of Regulation

First, free enterprise is **self-regulated**. Businessmen are as honest as any other persons. For every dishonest transaction there are millions of honest ones. Think about your own experience in buying groceries or dealing at the drug store or the gasoline station. Businessmen have their own code of ethics, of decent behavior.

In many cities they have a kind of organization, to watch over their own activities, known as the Better Business Bureau.

Second, business is **regulated by the market** (that is, the buying public). Mr. Zimmerman, when he sold only 20,000 out of 50,000 bicycles, may have set his price too high. If prices are so high that the average customer cannot afford to buy the product, goods do not sell. The market drives the price down. If people do not wish to buy a certain product, we say there is no market for it. If they are anxious to buy something, we say there is a demand for it. To a considerable extent, supply (what business produces and how much) is regulated by demand.

The market also punishes businessmen who sell inferior products. If you buy a new jack and find, to your sorrow, that it bends and breaks when you have to change a tire, you will protest to your dealer. So will others who have bought the same kind of jack. The manufacturer will have to improve his product or he will lose his market. And, incidentally, your dealer will probably return your money and vent his anger on the manufacturer! In short, the market—the customers for all products in general or for a particular kind of product—must be pleased. The condition of the market necessarily regulates business.

Third, **governments regulate business.** When you drive in to a service station and buy ten gallons of gasoline, how do you know that you are getting 10 gallons, not 7 or 9.1? The pump could be wrong. If you buy 750 gallons a year and the pump is wrong by one-tenth of a gallon, you may actually pay for 75 gallons you never received. The government protects you from such a loss by sending a government official (a City Sealer, for example) to test the pump at regular inspections. If you look at the small print on a box of crackers, you will see that the exact weight is given. Federal law guarantees you will get full measure by standard weights on all products sold in interstate commerce. When you buy a box of painkilling pills, advertised to be harmless, do you have to rely on the advertising? The answer is no. Federal law requires the manufacturer to show on the box (no matter how small the type may be!) just what chemicals the pills contain. As you saw in Chapter 8, the Federal Trade Commission protects you against false and misleading advertising of products sold nationally. Many states give similar protection on products sold only within their own borders.

In general, businessmen must live up to rules made by government for the protection of consumers. Other regulations, such as those for the operation of trucks or the storing of inflammable liquids, protect the general

511

public. Still other rules protect workers—minimum wage laws, child labor laws, laws requiring fire escapes, and many others. Thus, by means of regulation, the American system protects the people against precisely those evils with which the Communists charge us, as mentioned above.

Kinds of Assistance

Governments do more than regulate the activities of individual businesses, partnerships, and corporations. As we have seen, businesses are *helped* by laws protecting them against unfair competition. They may also get help from government in many other ways.

For example, Mr. Bailey's delivery truck runs over roads built by government, state and local, and supported by federal funds. Mr. Bailey sells goods to customers who pay him in reliable money which is supplied by the federal government. A federal government worker, the mailman, brings Mr. Bailey's orders, payments, advertising, and trade journals. This is just the beginning of a list of ways in which governments help businessmen. Here are some others: protective tariff, lighthouses, the Coast Guard, patents, copyrights, loans, courts of law (through which businessmen may be able to collect money owed to them), weather forecasts.

If he is a small businessman, Mr. Bailey is also entitled to the assistance of the federal government's Small Business Administration, a special agency of the executive branch. Through this Administration, Mr. Bailey may be able to borrow money he needs to buy machinery or materials. He may also borrow money to rebuild his business if it has been carried away by a flood. The SBA will also help Mr. Bailey and other small businessmen to get government contracts.

Large businesses receive very substantial assistance from government. For example, cities may construct water or sewage disposal facilities to meet the requirements of a manufacturer, or may make a favorable tax assessment in order to attract him. A state may have a government department which actively promotes the sales of products of the state and attracts business investment. Federal money is granted to shipbuilders and air lines to subsidize their work. There are federal tax laws that "give a break" to businesses which risk their money in searching for oil (see p. 492). The national government is also a very large consumer of many of the services and products of business.

What we must understand here is that under our system of free private enterprise, businesses small and large are both *regulated by governments and aided by governments*. We call our system free because the people are free to own their businesses and compete for a profit. Mr. and Mrs. Smith are stockholders owning a small part of a big corporation which hires executives to manage for them. They receive **dividends** as their share of the company's

512

profits. Mr. Johnson wants to set up and run his own business and make profits for himself.

We must not forget that under our system we are free to compete for profit—but we may fail. For example, Mr. Roe puts his savings into a new firm to make waffle irons. Unfortunately there are already on the market several waffle irons superior to Mr. Roe's product. He fails and loses everything he has invested. Several thousand businesses fail every year—most of them small concerns. Some of them if managed more competently would have succeeded; others fail because they do not have enough capital to last until they become well established. Nevertheless, they illustrate the American's freedom of choice.

THE DEPARTMENT OF COMMERCE

There are a number of government agencies which assist American business and the free enterprise system. The Department of Commerce is the chief one. Some of the bureaus of the Department of Commerce go back to the earliest years of the republic. The present-day, cabinet-level Department was established by law in 1913. Under the Commerce Clause of the Constitution (p. 53), this law provided that the new Department should "foster, promote, and develop the foreign and domestic commerce, the mining, manufacturing, shipping, and fishing industries, and the transportation facilities of the United States." Other responsibilities have been added by law from time to time. The development of the aircraft industry and the growth of air transportation, for example, have been a source of new duties. The Department of Commerce serves as the President's chief administrative agency in handling the relations of the executive branch with business, and the Secretary of Commerce represents business in the cabinet. The Secretary, often himself a businessman, is appointed by the President with the consent of the Senate, and serves at the pleasure of the President. The chart, p. 515, shows how the Department is organized.

The Patent Office

Suppose you invented a carburetor which would enable an engine to run three times as long as other engines with the same amount of gasoline. How could you protect yourself against someone's stealing your invention and perhaps making a lot of money that should have been yours?

You can protect yourself by securing from the United States government a **patent**. This is a document which gives an inventor sole ownership of his invention under the law. To obtain a patent for your invention you write to the Bureau of Patents in the Department of Commerce at Washington, asking for appropriate application forms and describing your invention briefly. You then send the completed forms, with detailed specifications of your invention, to Washington.

If your invention is found, by comparison with other carburetors, to be original, you are given a patent, guaranteeing you sole right to your invention. You may make and sell your carburetors or you may sell your rights to a company.

This protection costs $60.00 ($30.00 with your application and $30.00 more for the patent), and it is good for seventeen years. At the end of seventeen years, your patent expires and cannot be renewed unless Congress passes a special act to cover your case. Your protection is available because the Constitution (I, 8) specifically gave Congress power "to promote the Progress of Science and useful Arts, by securing for limited Times to Authors and Inventors the exclusive Right to their respective Writings and Discourses." (See chart, p. 515, for details of the Patent Office activities.) We saw in Chapter 5 how authors are similarly protected by **copyright**.

You may also patent a design you have originated—that is, the specific shape of any article to be manufactured and sold, like a motorboat hull or a tennis racket. Patents for designs expire after fourteen years.

TRADEMARKS Businesses can protect the special names of their products by **trademarks** obtained from the Patent Office and good for twenty years. Trademarks can be renewed, however, simply by filing a new application. "Brisk," "Ken-L-Ration," "Nabisco" are examples. Trademarks are often worth very large sums of money, since they become identified with certain products in the public mind, and their protection is vital to business. Occasionally a trademark is granted by the Patent Office for a phrase so purely descriptive that the courts will void the trademark, declaring that anyone can use it. Some years ago the term *shredded wheat* was a trademark of the Shredded Wheat Company, but a series of court actions resulted in making the term common property. Now you can buy several different brands of shredded wheat.

You can get some idea of the volume of business the experts in the Patent Office handle from the fact that the 2,500,000th patent was issued in 1950. Because of this huge volume, it sometimes takes a very long time before an application for a patent is finally acted upon. This is why you so often see the phrase "Patent Pending" on an article.

Problems of patenting and trademarking have become so complex, as the number of patents and trademarks has multiplied, that the individual citizen often needs the services of a patent attorney. Patent attorneys are private citizens who specialize in patent law and procedures, both in the United States and abroad. Nearly all business corporations employ their services.

Department of Commerce

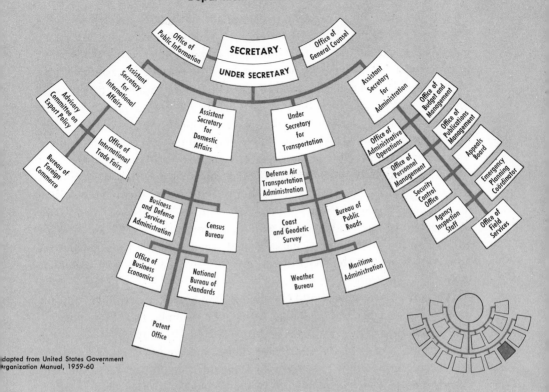

SECRETARY. Generally a businessman. Responsible for all operations and services of the Department and for advising the President on all matters pertaining to business and commerce. With Under-Secretaries and Assistant Secretaries, he makes the decisions and rules by which Department functions and carries out assignments from the President and Congress.

BUSINESS AND DEFENSE SERVICES ADMINISTRATION. Administrator (1953). Works through 25 Industry Divisions and related offices to carry out the Department's programs for defense production, industrial preparedness, and service to American business.

BUREAU OF THE CENSUS. Director. A fact-finding and statistical agency. Takes censuses of population; housing; agriculture; governmental units; drainage; irrigation; and manufactures, mineral industries, and business. See pp. 518–519. Prepares *Statistical Abstract of the U.S.*

BUREAU OF FOREIGN COMMERCE. Director (1953). Promotes trade (exports and imports), foreign investment, and travel.

MARITIME ADMINISTRATION (1950). Administrator. Constructs, reconstructs, or reconditions ships; sells, charters, or operates these ships. Maintains the National Defense Reserve Fleet; also four inactive shipyards. Operates Merchant Marine Academy, Kings Point, N.Y.

PATENT OFFICE (1802). Commissioner. Administers the patent and trademark laws enacted by Congress. Grants patents, determines priority of invention, classifies patents and trademarks. Staff of over 1,000 examiners. Maintains library of 69,000 books, 59,000 bound volumes of periodicals, over seven million copies of foreign patents. (See pp. 513–514.)

BUREAU OF STANDARDS (1901). Director. (See p. 516.)

WEATHER BUREAU (1890). Chief. (See p. 517.)

515

National Bureau of Standards

The Constitution gives Congress power to "fix the Standard of Weights and Measures" (I, 8). The purpose of this power is to make sure Americans have a set of common, uniform standards of all kinds of weights and measures in order to avoid misunderstandings in business transactions, specifications of products, and even conversation. Because federal law imposes penalties on dishonest sellers, you may be sure that when you buy a pound, it is 16 ounces; and when you buy a yard, you get 36 inches. Such measures were not always uniform. Many nations today, for example, use the metric system of measurement, which is not conveniently convertible into inches, feet, and yards. You may have noticed that an American track star who specializes in the 100-yard dash has to train himself specially to run the 100-*meter* race in the Olympic games. From early days the United States, under this power of Congress to fix standards, has worked continuously to develop accuracy and uniformity in all kinds of measurement. Since 1901 the National Bureau of Standards, now in the Department of Commerce, has been responsible for carrying on this work.

The advances of science and technology have brought increasingly difficult problems of weights and measures. What, for example, is a "horsepower"? How do we measure wave lengths and frequencies? How can you measure the heat resistance of a plastic substance? These and countless other questions are officially answered by the Bureau of Standards. The Bureau keeps standard examples of all such measurements—formula, model, or other device—which can be examined by state officials of weights and measures. It also coöperates with officials of other countries to exchange information about standards, weights, and measures.

Today the Bureau of Standards employs hundreds of scientists and technicians who conduct research and testing in such scientific fields as applied mathematics, atomic and radiation physics, building technology, cyrogenic engineering (refrigeration), data processing systems (business machines), heat and power mechanics, optics and metrology, radio propagation, physics and engineering, radio standards, weights and measures.

This work not only is useful in maintaining standards for the nation, but is also helpful to business and to other agencies of government. For example, if someone complains to the Federal Trade Commission, and the Commission is in doubt as to whether a certain product will actually do what is claimed for it, the Bureau of Standards will test it. The Bureau will do similar testing for private business if other testing facilities are not available. As in so many other fields of government activity, the tremendous expansion of the work of the Bureau of Standards, from the precise measurement of inches and pounds to research in nuclear physics, reflects the growth of American industry and technology.

516

Weather Bureau

Another agency of the Department of Commerce which is staffed by scientists is the Weather Bureau. Newspapers often poke fun at the "weatherman"—perhaps you do yourself—but analysis and prediction of the weather are highly important functions of our national government. In more than 300 branch offices and weather stations, the meteorologists of the Weather Bureau make observations of surface and upper air currents and wind velocities, and accumulate data on temperatures, precipitation, and other aspects of the earth's atmosphere which enable them to predict the weather.

If you lived in an area where there is a hurricane season, you would find the advance warnings of the Weather Bureau extremely important to your life. If you were in an outdoor business, the weather reports would obviously affect your schedule to a great extent. Stop to think how much weather observations and predictions mean to our air lines. If you like to indulge in harmless scoffing at weather predictions, you will be interested to know that modern science enables the Weather Bureau to be right more than 80 percent of the time.

Special Aids to Business

In the Department of Commerce are the **Office of Business Economics** and the **Bureau of Foreign Commerce,** which give direct assistance to business by providing valuable statistical information. The Office of Business Economics makes statistical studies of the market for all sorts of goods produced by American manufacturers for sale in the United States. From this Office you can learn how many boxes of crackers are produced and sold, how many barrels of oil are shipped by tankers, what the reserve supply of finished steel is. Such information as this is vital to businessmen in deciding such things as their production schedules, planning transportation, assessing potential markets.

The Bureau of Foreign Commerce makes studies of foreign markets for all types of products and thus directly aids American businessmen who produce for export. For example, the Bureau can tell you how many English bicycles are imported in a six-month period and what their prices will be, how many West German automobiles are planned for production in a given year, what the anticipated sales of electric refrigerators in Norway are, and so on. This kind of information is exceedingly valuable for all Americans engaged in international trade.

Federal Maritime Board and Maritime Administration

The federal government also assists the shipping industry. The Federal Maritime Board, having three members appointed by the President and the Senate, makes rules governing sea traffic and regulates rates and services.

The Chairman of the Board is also head of the Maritime Administration. For some of the activities of this Administration see chart, p. 515.

Because of the high wages paid to American workmen, private shipbuilders in the United States cannot afford to compete with the merchant shipbuilding of most foreign countries. To insure a great national merchant marine, Congress appropriates money to pay private companies the difference between the cost of building a ship at home and building it abroad. The Maritime Board allocates this money; the Maritime Administration administers it and enforces specifications of efficiency and safety in the building of ships. This policy of subsidizing the shipping industry not only directly benefits business; it also helps workingmen in the industry by keeping their wages at generally high levels. In addition, it helps the country by providing ships.

Federal aid to transportation is part of the general national policy of supporting free private enterprise. Air and shipping services involve great costs and risks and are not likely to be profitable without government support. In many other countries, shipping lines and air lines are owned and operated by government. Americans believe that competing companies in these fields provide the people with better service and lead to swifter technical and scientific advancement. It is our national policy to pay money out of the federal Treasury to keep these industries in private, competing hands.

Bureau of the Census

The Department of Commerce has another and quite different sort of responsibility—taking the census. In 1790 the first Congress ordered a census of population to be taken that year and every ten years thereafter, according to the provisions of Article I, Section 2, of the Constitution (see p. 50). The original purpose of the census was to determine the number of representatives to which each state was entitled in the House of Representatives and to determine the basis for laying direct taxes. In practice, taxes are not levied on the basis of population, but the apportionment of Congressional Districts still depends upon the census (see Chap. 5). In the intervening years many other uses of population statistics have been found. The Bureau of the Census in the Department of Commerce in our time takes the following regular censuses: population, every ten years; housing, every ten years; agriculture, every five years; manufactures, mineral industries, transportation, and retail, wholesale, and service trades, every five years; governmental units (federal, state, and local), every five years. (See chart, p. 515.) The enormous masses of data collected by the Bureau of the Census are of inestimable value to many agencies of government, including other bureaus of the Department of Commerce, and are highly useful to business.

You have undoubtedly found sample census statistics useful yourself. When you look up the population of a city in an almanac, the source of the figures is the Census Bureau. When a manufacturer of a new type of wind-shield cleaner wants to know how many gasoline stations there are, the census gives him the answer. When a university wants to know how many lawyers there are in order to estimate the best size for its law school, again the census statistics come into use. You can think readily of many more examples. If you are a young man approaching draft age, it will interest you to know that the Census Bureau supplies the military with accurate figures as to how many youths of draft age there are in the country at any given time. To gather all these statistics requires a permanent staff in the Census Bureau of some 2,500 workers, many of them statisticians, and thousands of part-time or temporary workers in the field.

Effect of the Department of Commerce

The Department of Commerce is the voice of American business in the federal government. As we have seen, the business community is actually many businesses competing and conflicting with each other. There are many things common to the interests of all businessmen, and these are the concern of the Department of Commerce. The assistance it renders to a particular business, like shipping, is intended to help not only that business but all business. Thus we may say that American business has a kind of lobby, an agency looking out for its interests, actively functioning by law in the executive branch of the government. You will see later (Chaps. 22 and 23) how the other great branches of American economic life—labor and agriculture—are similarly assisted by cabinet-level departments.

THE DEPARTMENT OF THE TREASURY

All business, public or private, is carried on, at least in part, by the use of money: paper currency and coins. The government of the United States has full control and supervision over the issuing of money, and itself handles a large portion of all money in use. The Treasury Department is in charge of managing this money. In Chapter 20 we dealt with one of the Treasury's functions: the collection of taxes. As you look at the chart of the Department's organization, you will see that the Internal Revenue Service and the Customs Bureau which collect these taxes are only two among numerous other bureaus. Two of them, the Bureau of the Mint and the Bureau of Engraving and Printing, are the direct source of the nation's money supply.

The Treasury Department began to function under Alexander Hamilton in 1789. Its staff consisted of Hamilton himself, an assistant, and a handful of clerks. As late as Jackson's time, the Department still operated with only a Secretary, an Assistant Secretary, a half-dozen auditors, a few clerks and district tax collectors. Today the Treasury has more than 80,000 employees and handles more money than any other agency in the world. It is administered by the Secretary of the Treasury, who, like other cabinet officers, is appointed by the President with the consent of the Senate and serves at the pleasure of the President. He must not be confused with the Treasurer of the United States, a subordinate official you will meet presently. The Secretary presides over an organization with such widely separate responsibilities as the coining of money, the collection of taxes, the Coast Guard, and the Secret Service. Our concern here is with those functions of the Department which have to do with the nation's business activities.

Bureau of the Mint

The Bureau of the Mint, headed by the Director of the Mint, manufactures the coins of common currency—the coins we carry and use in buying and selling. Article I, Section 8, Clause 5 of the Constitution gives Congress the power to coin money. By law Congress has given this responsibility to the Treasury Department. The Bureau of the Mint operates factories, known as **mints,** at which coins are made, at Philadelphia and Denver. The San Francisco mint no longer manufactures coins but serves as a storage facility. The Superintendent of each mint is authorized by law to purchase silver and other metals with which coins are made. The price of silver is fixed at 90.5 cents an ounce, but other metals—copper, nickel, and tin—are purchased from the lowest bidder. The metal is paid for in paper money and then coined and issued for public use through the banks of the Federal Reserve System, as we shall see on p. 525.

The Bureau of the Mint also operates two assay offices, at New York and Seattle, where the purity of metals is tested and evaluated, and has custody of the gold depository at Fort Knox, Kentucky. Until 1934 gold coins were minted in $20.00 pieces (double eagle), $10.00 pieces (eagle), $5.00 pieces (half eagle), and $1.00 pieces.

In 1934 a law was passed requiring people to turn in all their gold for paper money. Since that time all gold coins have been withdrawn from circulation; the government's supply of gold is stored. The Treasury buys all newly mined gold at $35.00 an ounce and keeps it in reserve. However, businessmen can purchase gold for use in foreign trade or for manufacturing purposes, such as jewelry, watches, or dental fillings.

Congress has power under the Constitution (I, 8) to regulate the value of money. Until 1934 gold was the basis of all American money. A dollar gold coin was set by law as equal to 25⅘ grains of nine-tenths fine gold. A paper dollar could be exchanged for gold. During the depression of 1929–1933, gold became scarce, because people hoarded it or shipped it out of the country. As a result Congress passed a law (Gold Reserve Act) which changed the whole system. Today a dollar is based on $15\frac{5}{21}$ grains of nine-tenths fine gold, but no gold coins are minted or allowed to circulate. The value of the dollar

Department of the Treasury

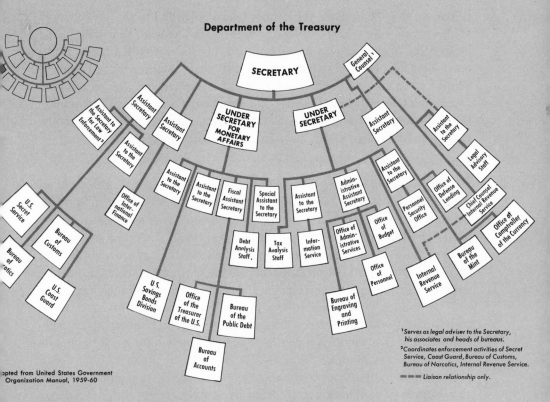

Adapted from United States Government
Organization Manual, 1959-60

[1] Serves as legal adviser to the Secretary,
his associates and heads of bureaus.

[2] Coordinates enforcement activities of Secret
Service, Coast Guard, Bureau of Customs,
Bureau of Narcotics, Internal Revenue Service.

— — — Liaison relationship only.

SECRETARY OF THE TREASURY (1789). Supervises the affairs of the Department. (See pp. 523–524.)

BUREAU OF ENGRAVING AND PRINTING. Director. Designs, engraves, prints U.S. currency, bonds, checks, engraved documents. (See p. 522.)

BUREAU OF CUSTOMS. Commissioner. Collects duties, prevents smuggling, supervises marine activities, enforces custom and navigation laws, coöperates with other departments responsible for enforcement of laws relating to incoming and outgoing goods. (See pp. 495–496.)

INTERNAL REVENUE SERVICE (1862). Commissioner. The Service is divided into 9 regions, 64 districts. The work of receiving and auditing tax returns, collecting money, investigating fraud, making refunds, selling internal revenue stamps, etc., is done at the District level. (See pp. 494–495.)

OFFICE OF THE COMPTROLLER OF THE CURRENCY (1863). Comptroller. Generally supervises

national banks. Comptroller is ex officio member of the Board of Directors of the FDIC.

OFFICE OF THE TREASURER OF THE UNITED STATES (1789). Treasurer. Receives, pays, accounts for the public money; furnishes checking account facility for all government agencies, pays Treasury checks, and related duties.

BUREAU OF THE MINT (1873). Director. Responsible for activities of the six Field Institutions (Philadelphia, Denver, San Francisco, New York, Fort Knox, West Point) in producing coin, manufacturing medals, guarding and processing bullion, carrying out the gold and silver policies of the U.S. (See pp. 520–522.)

U.S. SECRET SERVICE (1860). Chief. Suppresses counterfeiting, protects President, President-elect, Vice-President (at his request). Other duties relating to the money and obligations of the U.S., the FDIC, and the land banks.

U.S. COAST GUARD (1915). Commandant. Saves life and property, enforces maritime law. Serves with Navy in war.

521

is fixed by law. Thus, while you cannot take a dollar bill to the Treasury and ask for a gold coin or $15\frac{5}{21}$ grains of nine-tenths fine gold, your dollar *must* be accepted in any business transaction. It is known as **legal tender,** as are all other denominations of paper money and coins. Silver coins contain 90 percent silver, five-cent pieces are three parts copper and one part nickel, and pennies are 95 percent copper and 5 percent tin or zinc. These proportions of metal are used because of efficiency in making durable coins; the value is fixed by law, not by the amount of metal they contain.

Bureau of Engraving and Printing

The Bureau of Engraving and Printing operates the plants which print all paper money of three types: Federal Reserve Notes (see p. 525), U.S. Treasury Notes (only a few in circulation), and silver certificates ($1.00 bills). The Bureau also prints government bonds and notes and government checks. The Bureau is simply an agency of production, and has no control over the amounts or kinds of certificates it prints. In other words, it fills the orders of the Treasurer of the United States or of other government agencies.

The printing of money involves very skillful engraving in order to make counterfeiting as difficult as possible. The plates used in printing are carefully guarded. The paper itself is specially processed. You will notice, for example, the threads pressed into it. In spite of the difficulty, counterfeiting remains a great temptation to some people, and the Secret Service is constantly on the alert to protect us from being swindled by counterfeiters.

Office of the Treasurer of the United States

The Treasurer of the United States heads an office in the Treasury Department which functions as a bank for the government. This office receives, pays out, and keeps accounts of all public money; orders, issues, and redeems paper money; provides **checking accounts** for government agencies; and pays the principal and interest on **government bonds** and other obligations of the **national debt.**

Office of the Comptroller of the Currency

The Comptroller of the Currency is responsible for checking the operations and functions of all national banks. His office receives reports regularly from each bank in the national banking system (see p. 526), examines records, and makes frequent investigations to be sure that the national banks comply with the various laws governing banking. He should not be confused with the Comptroller General of the U. S. (see p. 117).

Responsibilities of the Secretary of the Treasury

Much of the work of the Treasury Department is technical and specialized, and most of its employees are career experts. But the Treasury also has very important responsibilities in the field of policy and decision-making. The

COWBOY SAM

Carmack in
The Christian Science Monitor

Secretary, or officials designated by him, must advise the President on all financial matters. The Secretary must maintain the credit of the United States, that is, protect the borrowing power of the government, either through policies he determines himself or by carrying out laws of Congress. And he represents the United States in international banking and monetary organizations of which the United States is a member.

Because money and credit are necessary for all government activity, the Secretary of the Treasury must be a man of sufficient imagination and understanding to deal with problems of great breadth and depth. He must see not only the immediate financial condition of the government and its future needs, but also the relation of federal finances to the states, to private business and commerce, and to world financial conditions. His power extends very directly to the regulation of economic life both at home and abroad. Thus if the Secretary decides to pay a low rate of interest on United States bonds, the effect may be that investors will look elsewhere for higher rates: private banks and other lenders may invest more money in private securities, and inflation may result. This is sometimes called an **easy money** policy, that is, you can borrow money easily at low interest rates.

If, on the other hand, the Secretary elects to pay high rates of interest on United States bonds, the effect may be to attract investors away from private

523

banks and securities, thus *tightening up* the money market. This is called a **tight money** policy, because you find it hard to borrow money and interest rates are high. Such a policy may remove too much money from circulation.

The Secretary, in short, must be a man of very shrewd judgment. And he must be well served and advised by those who work with him. Like all responsible officials of the executive branch, he must be politically sensitive and sophisticated. There are constant pressures upon him to make this or that decision. He must, therefore, know how to weigh alternatives, and strive to protect the interest of all the people as represented by their government.

THE FEDERAL RESERVE SYSTEM

The American banking system is unlike any other. In most countries there is a national bank, either owned and operated *by* the government or privately owned and operated *for* the government. This was the case in America during the colonial period when the Bank of England served both the mother country and her colonies. During the Revolutionary period, Americans began to distrust the Bank of England, feeling that their financial affairs were controlled autocratically from across the sea. After the Revolution many people retained their fear of a national bank and opposed setting one up in the United States. Actually a United States Bank was established under the leadership of Alexander Hamilton and played a major part in straightening out American finances from 1791 to 1811. A second national bank was established in 1816. President Andrew Jackson vetoed a bill to renew it, and its charter expired in 1836. Until 1913 the United States had no national banking system at all and money was issued by many banks as well as by the federal government. Thus, there was always danger of fluctuating values in our currency.

Many farmers, small businessmen, and laborers feared the concentration of financial power in eastern cities and opposed a national banking system. On the other hand, bankers, leaders of larger business, and many students of government urged that such a system be created to guarantee stability of American currency and regulate interest rates. By 1913 a majority in Congress had come to feel the need for such a system. The Glass-Owen Act was the result of a carefully worked out compromise between friends and opponents of a national banking system. This law provided for our present Federal Reserve System.

The basic principle of the Federal Reserve System is a partnership between government and private citizens. This was the great compromise. The Federal Reserve Banks, one in each of twelve districts into which the country is divided, are owned by private banks in each district known as **member banks.** But the Federal Reserve Banks themselves are regulated by a federal agency known as the Board of Governors of the Federal Reserve System. Thus we have private ownership with public control. The chart on p. 526 shows how the system is set up.

Federal Reserve Banks

The Federal Reserve Bank in each district sells stock to banks, which become members if they buy at least four million dollars' worth each. This money gives each Federal Reserve Bank the capital it needs to carry on its business. The money is lent to private banks and thus finds its way into circulation. The interest they receive from the loans increases the capital of the Federal Reserve Banks and pays dividends to the member banks, thus making the whole operation a profitable one. Federal Reserve Banks may not lend all their capital. A substantial amount of money—set by the Board of Governors—must always be kept in *reserve* in each of the twelve banks— hence their name.

The Federal Reserve Banks serve also as banks of deposit for the member banks. These deposits are the chief source of our common paper money, that is, the Federal Reserve Banks issue certificates known as **Federal Reserve Notes** to represent the deposits they are holding. The notes are backed by 25 percent of gold (though you cannot collect it!) and 75 percent of either U.S. government bonds or notes of private banks.

The member banks, which receive these Federal Reserve Notes, in turn put them into circulation by issuing them to their own customers. If you cash a check at your bank, you will probably get Federal Reserve Notes for any denominations from five dollars up. A dollar bill, printed and issued by the Treasury Department, certifies that the Treasury has an equivalent amount of silver on deposit. Most larger denominations of paper money are Federal Reserve Notes standing for deposits in Federal Reserve Banks. United States Treasury Notes in several denominations are also legal tender, but there is only a small quantity of these in circulation.

Both paper money and coins come into circulation through the Federal Reserve Banks. These banks order from the Treasurer of the United States (see p. 522) new coins or new printed money, and put it into circulation by distributing it to the member banks. These banks also withdraw old and worn currency from circulation and destroy it. About 90 percent of all the money involved in financial transactions is in the form of checks, notes, or other certificates. Thus the amount of cash in circulation at any one time is only about 10 percent of the money involved in business transactions.

While the Federal Reserve Banks are privately owned and get their income from private business transactions, they are controlled jointly by the

U.S. Banking System

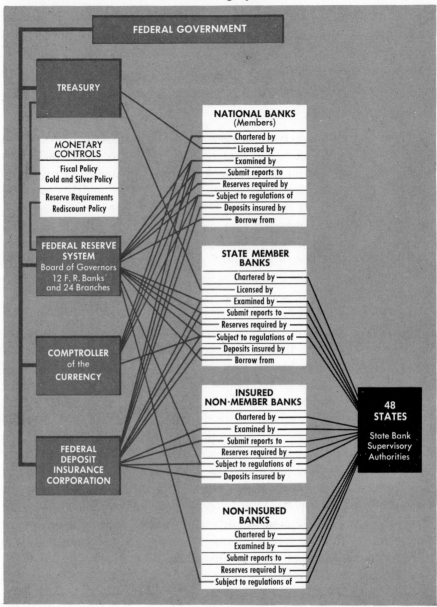

FEDERAL GOVERNMENT

TREASURY

MONETARY CONTROLS
Fiscal Policy
Gold and Silver Policy
Reserve Requirements
Rediscount Policy

FEDERAL RESERVE SYSTEM
Board of Governors
12 F. R. Banks
and 24 Branches

COMPTROLLER of the CURRENCY

FEDERAL DEPOSIT INSURANCE CORPORATION

NATIONAL BANKS (Members)
Chartered by
Licensed by
Examined by
Submit reports to
Reserves required by
Subject to regulations of
Deposits insured by
Borrow from

STATE MEMBER BANKS
Chartered by
Licensed by
Examined by
Submit reports to
Reserves required by
Subject to regulations of
Deposits insured by
Borrow from

INSURED NON-MEMBER BANKS
Chartered by
Examined by
Submit reports to
Reserves required by
Subject to regulations of
Deposits insured by

NON-INSURED BANKS
Chartered by
Examined by
Submit reports to
Reserves required by
Subject to regulations of

48 STATES
State Bank Supervisory Authorities

TREASURY. See chart, p. 521.

FEDERAL RESERVE SYSTEM

Board of Governors. Seven appointed members, no two from same District; 14-year terms. Chosen to represent financial, industrial, agricultural, and commercial interests. Has powers over money and credit (see pp. 525–527) and operation of the system.

Federal Advisory Council. One member from each Reserve District. Confers with Board and advises on general business conditions.

Federal Open Market Committee. Members of the Board and five representatives of the Reserve Banks. Makes regulations for open market operation of the Reserve Banks; that is, purchases U.S. securities from private holders, or sells at the highest bid.

COMPTROLLER OF THE CURRENCY. See chart, p. 521.

FEDERAL DEPOSIT INSURANCE CORPORATION. An independent agency; board of three directors (one is Comptroller of the Currency). Insures deposits (see p. 528), prevents unsound banking practices, related powers.

member banks and by the public. Each bank has a board of nine directors: three chosen to represent the member banks, three to represent business, agriculture, and industry, and three to represent the public. The latter are appointed by the Board of Governors of the Federal Reserve System, the others by the member banks.

Board of Governors

The seven members of the Board of Governors are appointed by the President with the consent of the Senate. By law they must come from different Federal Reserve Districts and represent different interests (chart, p. 526).

Under laws of 1913 and 1935, the Board of Governors has great power over our whole financial and economic system. As we saw, it determines how much **reserve** cash the Federal Reserve Banks must hold. It also sets the rate of interest at which the Federal Reserve Banks may lend money to member banks. This rate, called **rediscount**, in turn, regulates the rates which member banks will charge their customers. Thus the Board of Governors influences the whole credit system of American banking and business. See the chart, p. 526, for its relationship to the banking system.

Since it is an independent agency, the Board of Governors is not bound to support the policies of the President and the Secretary of the Treasury. Thus the President and his financial advisers must maintain close, coöperative relations with the Board. Normally no difficulties arise from this divided authority. The purpose of it is to prevent irresponsible political interference with our system of money and credit.

State Banks

National banks, all of which are member banks of the Federal Reserve System, are chartered by the federal government. They often have the word "national" in their names. There are thousands of banks chartered under the laws of the various states. Such banks may purchase stock in Federal Reserve Banks and become members of the Federal Reserve System if the Board of Governors admits them, but many do not belong. These state banks are nevertheless subject to federal banking laws as well as those of their states. They do not issue money, since money is now under the sole authority of the federal government. The interest rates they charge for loans are directly influenced by the Federal Reserve, since they could not afford to charge more than national banks and would find it unprofitable to charge much less. State banks are supervised and inspected by state departments or commissions of banking.

State banking departments also serve the citizens directly by protecting them against fraud or default by state banks. Recently, when the president of a local bank in one of our eastern states falsified the accounts to favor some of his friends, the state banking department closed the bank, collected money owed to the bank from many debtors, organized new management, and saw to it that depositors did not suffer from the mismanagement of the former president.

Federal Deposit Insurance Corporation (FDIC)

From time to time in American history up to 1933 there were bank panics. A bank panic occurred when depositors were frightened into trying to withdraw their money from the bank all at once. When this happened the banks did not have enough cash on hand to pay. They would be forced to close. Crowds would gather in front of the bank, jostling one another in a kind of stampede. If your lifetime savings were deposited in such a bank, you yourself might understand how these people felt. It would be almost like being trapped in a locked room when fire broke out.

In 1933, however, the Federal Deposit Insurance Corporation was established by act of Congress to insure bank deposits, up to $10,000 for each depositor. While the FDIC could not, of course, actually pay out in cash the equivalent of all the money at any time on deposit in *all* banks, it could if necessary cover the deposits up to $10,000 each in any one bank which failed or where a panic might start. Thus it serves to protect us all by removing the fear that our bank could not pay on demand.

The FDIC is an independent agency under a board of three directors. Two are appointed by the President, with the consent of the Senate, to serve terms of six years. There must be one from each major political party. The third member is the Comptroller of the Currency of the Treasury Department. The FDIC received its original capital from the sale of stock to the Federal Reserve Banks and the Treasury. Today its assets (more than two billion dollars) are accumulated from the charges it makes upon banks for their insurance—one-twelfth of 1 percent of the total deposits in each insured bank on some designated day each year.

THE FEDERAL GOVERNMENT IN BUSINESS

Thus far we have seen how the government of the United States assists the business enterprise of the people and how it produces, circulates, and regulates the money and credit with which business is done. Government is also *in* business—in fact, in many businesses. Government businesses include production of goods, supply of services, and contracting and purchasing as the largest of all consumers. Governments at all levels are in so many businesses that we can comment here on only a few examples.

Tennessee Valley Authority

An example of the government as producer is in the field of electric power. The Tennessee Valley Authority, the largest producer of public power, is an independent government corporation, as we saw in Chapter 8.

What does TVA do? It was set up for several different purposes to be achieved simultaneously. It was to build dams on the unnavigable Tennessee River to control floods and enable wastelands to be reclaimed for agriculture. It was to produce and sell electric power generated at the dams, to give farmers and business companies cheap power. It was to produce fertilizer from the nitrates of the Valley and sell it cheaply to farmers to raise the productivity of the Valley. It was to take other measures throughout the area (see the map, p. 530) to aid farmers and business, improve the land, and extend technical knowledge. TVA was to "make" enough money over the years to pay for the dams and power plants out of the sale of power, nitrates, and fertilizer.

ACHIEVEMENTS TVA set about its task with enthusiasm and energy. With sound policies of construction, engineering, and management, and a good personnel system, its commercial enterprises have been increasingly profitable. It has systematically repaid money to the Treasury. And in the generation since 1933, TVA has attained most of the goals set for it. The river is clear and navigable, the farms are electrified at low cost, the land is rich, the timber lands are reforested, and flooding is controlled. TVA makes money out of the sale of power and chemicals which it sells at low cost, so that old businesses in the towns and cities have revived and countless new ones have grown up. Even enemies of TVA salute its accomplishments.

CONTROVERSIAL ISSUES TVA was controversial at the outset, and the years of experience with it have not settled the issues it raised. Basic among the issues is the status of electric power. All are agreed that public utilities are "affected with a public interest" since all Americans are dependent upon the natural sources of electric power. Therefore, government, as agent of the people, must have some say about the production, distribution, and price of electricity. Should the power companies simply be *regulated* by government, federal, local, and state, or should they be *owned* by government? The country is divided on this highly important question. The result is that we have regulation over all utilities, including electric power, but public ownership of some and private ownership of others.

Those who favor private ownership argue that private ownership and operation of business has always been the American way. They claim it is unfair to require private power companies to compete with public power, which is used as a yardstick. After all, the private companies must pay taxes while public companies do not.

529

The Tennessee Valley Authority

where electricity from TVA dams is used

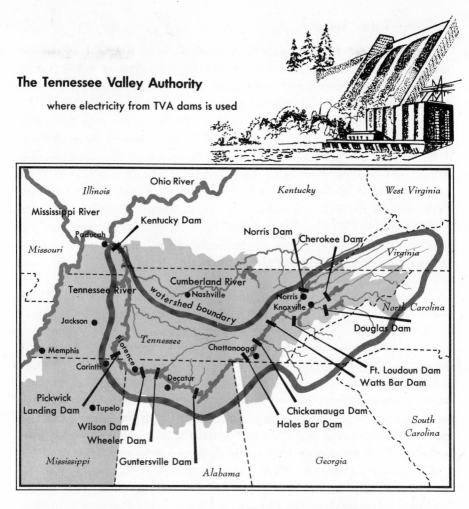

As shown on the map, TVA built dams on the Tennessee River to control floods and reclaim waste land for agriculture. It is by far the largest planned development of an "under-developed" area in the world. In addition to the conservation work it does, TVA produces chemicals and fertilizers in huge quantities and produces and generates electric power at the dams, giving farmers and business companies in the area cheap power. The wholesale price it set was intended to act as a yardstick for private producers of power. The great controversy between public and private power is by no means settled. Private producers complain they have to pay taxes and yet compete with TVA which is supported by tax money. Defenders of TVA argue that TVA pays back money to the government and that private companies could not plan and develop whole areas to the benefit of so many people.

Those who favor public ownership argue that power, which is a necessity, ought to be managed in the same way as the mails so that rates are uniform and as low as possible. Public ownership, they say, makes it possible to plan more intelligently to meet growing power needs. National defense, they feel, is better served if the government owns its own power instead of being dependent upon private companies.

530

Throughout the whole continuing debate runs the question of **planning** in the public interest. What should be done with a great natural power resource? Private business is properly anxious to make use of waterfalls and man-made dams to produce and sell power at a profit. Advocates of public ownership, however, favor multi-purpose dams higher than are needed for power, and much more costly—too costly for private companies. Such high dams as those of TVA serve the purposes of reclamation, flood control, and conservation as well as the production of power. In recent years there has been much talk of a "partnership" theory of resource development. This means that government would put up the money and private business would do the work under contract. An objection to this idea is that the taxpayers would be asked to give too much help to private enterprise. But it would have the advantage of maintaining the private enterprise system.

A much broader question is raised by TVA, however: To what extent is it proper for government to engage in business enterprise? Some feel that individual liberty depends on the rights of Americans to own and operate their own businesses. Others feel that there are a number of economic activities and industries—like utilities, railroads, communications, and finance— which ought to be owned by government in the interests of all the people because they touch directly the lives of all the people.

These differences are really matters of degree rather than principle. Few Americans now believe that general ownership of business by government is desirable, while few assert that no businesses ought to be publicly owned. The free political processes of persuasion achieve the best solutions to such problems. The American system in the middle of the twentieth century, with most business privately owned and managed, public regulation of those businesses which affect us all, and public ownership of a few, has given us one of the strongest and richest economies in the world, and a very considerable measure of individual freedom. TVA has contributed to this achievement. Congress and the people have before them today proposals for a Missouri Valley Authority and a Columbia River Authority similar to TVA. You yourself may before long have to make a responsible decision as to whether you approve or disapprove such projects.

Bonneville Power Administration

TVA is by no means the only example of the federal government in the power business. The Bonneville Power Administration is an agency of the Interior Department (see Chap. 23) which markets electric power generated at federal dams in the Columbia River Basin of the Pacific Northwest. It receives and sells power from such famous dams as the Bonneville, Hungry Horse, Grand Coulee, and McNary. Building and production are the tasks of either the Bureau of Reclamation in the Interior Department or the Army Corps of Engineers (see Chap. 27).

In all, the government produces power at twelve major dam sites in the Northwest. When all projects are completed, the government will have more than six million kilowatt capacity in this area. This power services the states of Washington, Oregon, Idaho, and Montana. The service is intended chiefly for rural consumers and domestic users not easily reached by the private power companies. Under the law, Bonneville and other federal power agencies (TVA, and Southwestern and Southeastern Power administrations in the Interior Department) must first meet the needs of public power agencies of the states and cities and of coöperative power-distributing organizations in their sale of federally produced electric power. However, private companies do buy and distribute a great deal of public power. The law also requires government to sell its power as cheaply as possible, and to require companies distributing it to charge reasonable rates to individual consumers. There is still a profit to the government, and this money is used to pay back the cost of building the dams and plants and the costs of non-profit-making conservation functions.

The Post Office Department

Government is also in the business of providing services. The oldest of all government businesses, the Post Office, is an example. Carrying mail has almost always been a public service directed by the government. You will remember that Benjamin Franklin was Postmaster General before the Revolution. The Constitution gave Congress power "to establish Post Offices and Post Roads" (I, 8), and the Postmaster General was one of the first offices created under the Constitution. We are a long way today from the era of stagecoaches and the "pony express." The volume of postal business has grown with the population and with advancing technology and continues to grow unceasingly. Many millions of pieces of mail are in transit every day, by carrier, bus, train, ship, and airplane. Private business could not possibly handle such a service except at exorbitant prices, and could not guarantee delivery and safety.

The Post Office Department today has more than half a million employees. Government, through the Department, contracts with private railroads and air lines for transportation, but Post Office employees do all handling of mail from the time you drop a letter in the box or mail a package at the Post Office counter until it is delivered. The mail rates are set by law, but the income of the Department is never adequate to meet its expenses, and Congress always has to appropriate money to cover its deficits. The whole American public is a lobby to keep steady pressure on Congress for low rates. Whether you realize it or not, you are a part of that lobby whenever you remark that you hope "they won't raise the price of a four-cent stamp." The chart shows how the Post Office Department is organized.

Post Office Department

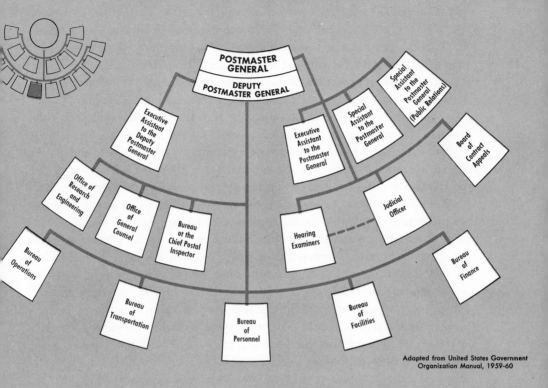

POSTMASTER GENERAL

DEPUTY POSTMASTER GENERAL

Executive Assistant to the Deputy Postmaster General

Special Assistant to the Postmaster General (Public Relations)

Executive Assistant to the Postmaster General

Special Assistant to the Postmaster General

Board of Contract Appeals

Office of Research and Engineering

Office of General Counsel

Bureau of the Chief Postal Inspector

Hearing Examiners

Judicial Officer

Bureau of Operations

Bureau of Transportation

Bureau of Personnel

Bureau of Facilities

Bureau of Finance

Adapted from United States Government
Organization Manual, 1959-60

POSTMASTER GENERAL (1789). Administers the Department. Appoints its officers and employees, except Deputy Postmaster General, Assistant Postmaster General, and those postmasters appointed by the President.

CHIEF HEARING EXAMINER. Acts as trial examiner in cases involving violations of postal rules, regulations, laws.

CHIEF POSTAL INSPECTOR. Advises his chiefs on needs and conditioning of the service; acts as Security Officer, Civil Defense Officer, and Defense Mobilization Officer for the Department.

GENERAL COUNSEL. Legal adviser to principal officers of the department; acts as legislative officer for the department, drafting bills, preparing reports, etc.

BUREAU OF OPERATIONS. Assistant Postmaster General. Makes policies and programs for work of personnel and for general management of post offices and branches.

BUREAU OF TRANSPORTATION. Assistant Postmaster General. Develops policies and programs for transportation and distribution of mailing, its exchange with countries, territories and possessions.

BUREAU OF FINANCE. Assistant Postmaster General. Develops policies, programs, procedures concerning the handling and accounting for the money involved in the business of the Department; also for the stamps, money-order forms, savings certificates, and for philately.

BUREAU OF FACILITIES. Assistant Postmaster General. Responsible for the real property and vehicles of the Department.

BUREAU OF PERSONNEL. Assistant Postmaster General. Responsible for development of an effective personnel program.

POSTAL SAVINGS SYSTEM (1910). Board of Trustees. Responsible for providing facilities for the deposit of savings at interest.

533

POSTMASTER GENERAL The Postmaster General is assisted and advised by the Deputy Postmaster General. The six bureaus, each under an Assistant Postmaster General, carry on most of the work. The Bureau of Chief Postal Inspectors sees that postal laws are enforced. There are today over 37,000 post offices in the United States. Postmasters in charge of them are classed according to the amount of their receipts. Classes 1, 2, and 3 are appointed by the President with the consent of the Senate from three applicants highest in civil service examinations. Their terms are indefinite. Class 4 postmasters, letter carriers, postal clerks, and others are appointed by the Postmaster General under civil services rules.

The Postmaster General himself is a member of the cabinet, and he is chosen like other members of the cabinet. He is the chief administrator of the Department and has also certain very important policy decisions to make. For example, he grants or withholds the **second-class mailing privilege.** This is a privilege available to periodical publishers enabling them to mail all their publications cheaply for an annual fee. The fees paid to the Department do not cover costs. The Congress thus subsidizes publishers in order to obtain the widest possible circulation of information, on the democratic theory that public information is an essential of good citizenship. If forced to choose between government without newspapers and newspapers without government, Jefferson said he would take newspapers. You may not agree, but you probably would agree that the United States would be a poorer country if you could not buy periodicals like *Time* or *Newsweek, Life* or *Look, Harper's* or the *Atlantic Monthly* or the *Saturday Evening Post* at your drugstore or newsstand or have them delivered at your home by the mailman. Yet the fact is that the costs of shipping such periodicals at regular express or air-express rates would be so enormous that they simply could not be distributed nationally. We, as taxpayers, help these and all other periodicals to stay in business, since Congress appropriates tax money to pay the deficits of the Post Office. This is an important part of the "price" for a free press.

The Postmaster General is responsible for seeing to it that this privilege is not abused by unscrupulous publishers who might use the mails to defraud or for sending out obscene literature. This is a very difficult assignment, since he must be careful that in protecting us, the public, he does not interfere with legitimate freedom of the press. He may not refuse the mailing privilege to a periodical simply because he does not like its ideas. If he attempts to do so, the publisher can take his case to court.

In recent years there has been much discussion of the use of the mails for unsolicited advertising. You have seen at your own home a great deal of advertising matter sent to you and your family (or simply addressed to "Occupant") which you did not ask for and may find a nuisance. We, the taxpayers, are paying to have this material delivered to us—since tax money is used to pay the deficits of the Post Office. This is another manner in which government assists private business enterprise. Many people feel that this is going too far. At the same time, to deny this advertising privilege might interfere with freedom of the press. Magazines and newspapers carry a great deal of advertising. You, the citizen, will need to think about this problem and decide where you stand.

The Postmaster General is frequently chosen because of his standing in the political party in power, rather than any particular ability to run the Post Office. But the technical work of the Department is directed by career officials under him.

THE GOVERNMENT AS CONSUMER

The federal government is the largest of all consumers. In this respect it not only contributes enormously to the volume of business done but significantly influences production, employment, and sales generally. Government makes contracts with private business for nearly all its supplies. The most obvious purchases, of course, are those required by national defense. Orders for airplanes, tanks, guns, missiles, uniforms, food, building construction, and so on, flow constantly into the factories of American business. Manufacturers plan their production schedules, estimate their needs for raw materials, estimate the size of the labor force they will need, and regulate their inventories of stock, according to their government contract obligations.

The civilian agencies of government, too, buy vast quantities of supplies. Thousands of automobiles and trucks, thousands of typewriters and other business machines, millions of reams of paper, dynamos for power plants, miles and miles of wire cable—there is almost no end to the list. These items are very important in the planning and production schedules of private business.

In recent years government economists in the President's Council of Economic Advisers (see Chap. 7, p. 178) have taken particular interest in the defense budget because of its influence on the level of employment in, for example, the automobile and airplane industries. National defense is not simply a question of having plenty of trained men and good equipment on hand; it is also a question of the economic strength of the country. Some economists and politicians are anxious to keep defense expenditures to the very minimum so that the public money will not be wasted or diverted from other projects; others are concerned that these expenditures not be reduced so hastily as to have an adverse effect on employment and business prosperity. We have here again a case requiring political understanding and ability to compromise by both legislators and administrators. Military leaders are never satisfied with the quality or quantity of their equipment; industry is always anxious for new and larger contracts. Taxpayers are always anxious for lower taxes and reduced expenditures. Some citizens believe that the way to peace is by reduced armaments, while others believe that peace can be secured only by means of defense preparations. In such a maze of conflicting ideas and interests, legislatures and administrators must find their way by compromise.

Another aspect of government consumption is the problem created by the placement of government orders. In some ways, it seems wise to concentrate orders for, say, trucks or tanks in one big company which can make them quickly and cheaply. But this may not be fair to smaller companies or to other big companies. In view of the disaster an atomic attack would bring on a great city like Detroit, it seems wise to scatter production of military cars and trucks as widely as possible. The industry itself is still heavily concentrated in the Detroit area. Thus it is no simple matter to decide just how the government shall do its ordering.

In general, the government asks for bids from any company that wants to supply a needed product. Preference goes to the low bidder, but the government is not required to accept his bid unless it is fully satisfied that his product will meet the necessary specifications. Thus purchasing authorities of the government in defense and elsewhere can use their discretion as to where they will buy and how much they will pay. This has meant in practice that purchasing and contracting officials are subject to very severe pressure from businessmen. In some cases, there has been bribery and corruption. Congress has provided severe penalties for corruption and bribe-taking in the government's consumption business. It has also provided that a businessman who works for the government must sever all his connections with business which may be related to his government job. If he returns to private business, he may not deal with his former government agency for at least two years after leaving it. These are provisions of the law known as the Corrupt Practices Act. That act was intended to protect our government against the fraud and corruption from which governments everywhere have always suffered.

 ## BUSINESS AND THE STATE AND LOCAL GOVERNMENTS

The relations between business and government at the levels of the states, counties, and cities are similar to those at the federal level, only on a much smaller scale. In many cases local businesses are themselves small, so that the smaller scale of government does not mean it is less important. A coal company in a medium-sized city, for example, that submits a low bid and wins the city's contract for coal is likely to find its books pretty well in

536

balance. Construction of roads is largely a local industry, so that local governments as contractors for road building play a major part in a major business. And regulation is no less regulation whether it is federal or state.

Most American businesses of any size are organized as **corporations**. A corporation is a legal entity which can act under the law in many ways like a person, an individual. It can buy and sell, contract, sue or be sued in the courts. It pays taxes, and it is subject to corporation laws. Corporations are created under state law. Thus the primary control by the public over business is exercised at the level of state government (see Constitution, Amendment X). It is state law which determines the field in which a corporation is allowed to function and prescribes the rules under which it must operate. If a group of businessmen wish to form a corporation and build plants to manufacture products for sale, they must first obtain a charter of incorporation from a state government. Each state has an official or group of officials authorized by state law to issue charters of incorporation. A charter need not be obtained necessarily in the state where the plant is situated. If the charter is issued in one state and the corporation does business in another, the corporation will need to get a license from the latter state. States may refuse to issue either charters or licenses. Thus a state government can do a good deal of planning as to what kinds of industry it wishes to encourage and where they shall be situated within the state, and what industries it may wish to discourage, by its policy of issuing or refusing charters or licenses.

State laws, in addition, deal with conditions under which people work (wages, hours, health, etc.), safety, business practices, and many other aspects of business. The states license businesses, professions, and individual artisans. And, as we saw in Chapter 11, the states regulate rates and other conditions of such businesses as public utilities, insurance, and state banking.

Counties and cities have important relations with business. They assess real property values and property taxes, as we saw in Chapter 20. In addition, they inspect milk, restaurants, hotels, theaters, regulate land to determine where businesses may or may not operate (zoning), and provide services such as police and fire protection to business on a community basis. Both state and local governments are important customers of many businesses.

Many local governments are also *in* business. Cities in most cases own their own water supply system, as do many towns and counties. Many cities own and operate their electric power systems, or bus systems, or subway systems.

When you look at the overall picture of America, you may well find it difficult to see just where business ends and government begins. But the limits are real. As we saw at the outset, the chief characteristic of American business is that it is for the most part privately owned. Government ownership normally occurs only in fields where private investment is unprofitable or, as in the case of atomic energy, the public interest requires absolute government control (see Chap. 8). In its relations to business, government at all levels acts as regulator, supporter, and customer. Government must encourage business because business is chiefly responsible for national strength and prosperity. Government must also protect the interest of farm workers, professional people, and housewives lest business become too dominant in our national life. And government must also protect businesses against each other. As we shall see in Chapter 23, government has a vitally important law enforcement problem in this regard. Above all, the relations between government and business are political. Government, in both its legislative and its executive branches, must constantly deal with business pressures for favors, assistance, contracts, etc., weigh opposing claims, mediate differences, serve the interests of the country, and protect the system of free enterprise itself.

SUMMARY

The American governments and the American economic system are so closely related that in order to understand either one it is necessary to consider them both together. In this chapter you have studied the meaning of **free private enterprise** as a way of doing business. You have also seen that American business is neither wholly free nor wholly private. Governments, at all levels, regulate business—make the rules under which business must operate. These rules are to protect us, the customers, and also to protect businessmen by making the conditions of competition as fair as possible.

We have seen that the federal government plays five different roles in the business life of the country. (1) It *regulates* business, through the Department of Commerce and certain independent agencies (see also Chap. 8). (2) It provides statistical and technical services *for* business. Here certain bureaus of the Department of Commerce have a place: Bureau of the Census, Weather Bureau, Bureau of Standards, and Maritime Administration. (3) The government *is in* business. As a producer, it operates the TVA; as a provider of service, it runs the Post Office Department. (4) The government gives direct and indirect *financial assistance* to business. The Treasury Department manufactures money. The Federal Reserve System regulates money, banking, and credit, and maintains the financial stability of the government and the nation. (5) The government is the *best customer* of business. Contracts for all kinds of defense supplies, as well as for supplies for civilian government, make government the largest consumer of all.

Finally, you have seen how business and government are related at the state and local levels of government. You should now be in a position to appreciate more fully your own relation to both business and government.

KNOW WHAT YOU READ

1. What is *free private enterprise?*
2. What criticisms of this system are made by its opponents?
3. In what three ways is free private enterprise regulated?
4. There are many ways in which businesses are helped by governments (local, state, and national). Make an extensive list of these aids to business.
5. Show how the Smiths, Mr. Johnson, and Mr. Roe all illustrated what is meant by *free* private enterprise.
6. What are the responsibilities of the Department of Commerce?
7. John Kovar has invented a new kind of glue. How does he go about getting a patent?
8. What is a trademark? Why is it valuable?
9. Why do you so often see the expression "Patent Pending"?
10. What is a patent attorney?
11. What is the work of the Bureau of Standards?
12. Why is the work of the Weather Bureau so important?
13. In what ways do the Bureau of Business Economics and the Bureau of Foreign Commerce help businessmen?
14. Summarize the work of the government agencies which regulate and assist the air transport industry.
15. How does the federal government assist the shipping industry?
16. In what ways are census data useful to business?
17. What is a *mint?* What policies does the Bureau of the Mint follow in buying silver, gold, and other metals?
18. What is the gold value of a dollar today?
19. If you were to visit the Bureau of Engraving and Printing, what would you expect to find going on there?
20. On United States notes you will find the signature of the Treasurer of the United States. What is his job?
21. What is the work of the Comptroller of the Currency?
22. Why is the office of the Secretary of the Treasury such an important one? What decisions must the secretary make?
23. Explain why the Federal Reserve System is a privately owned one.
24. What is the relationship of the Federal Reserve Sytem to national banks? To state banks?
25. Explain what makes the Tennessee Valley Authority controversial. Give both sides of the controversy.
26. What is the government's function as a consumer? Name the various ways in which it is a consumer.
27. How do the state governments affect business?
28. In what ways can we say that local governments are *in* business? Give examples.

WHAT DO YOU THINK?

1. It has been said that the Secretary of the Treasury has a voice in a greater variety of matters than any other member of the cabinet. He must help to decide such things as whom to tax and how much, whether and how to build federal roads, how much economic aid to give to what countries. Name three other matters in which he might have a voice. Why do you think this is so?
2. The government, as we have seen, has many connections with business, and helps the business community in many ways. Can you think of any types of business which do *not* benefit from the government's help? What might the disadvantages of government help to business be?
3. Read the controversy on the TVA. Do you agree with the arguments of those favoring public ownership or with those favoring private ownership of such projects? Defend your position.

PROBLEMS AND PROJECTS FOR YOU

1. Interview three businessmen in your community to find out what government agencies or departments they feel give them assistance (in supplying information, regulation of competition, etc.). Report to the class.
2. Make a study of activities of the Weather Bureau. Describe a particular service of the Bureau important to orange growers; the fishing industry; wheat farmers; seashore resorts.
3. You have just invented a device for a sewing machine to make it possible to cut as well as bind buttonholes. How do you protect your invention? Describe the process, using information in this book and in any other books available in your school library.
4. Make a study of the way the Census Bureau gets its population statistics. Include information about how field workers are trained. Does the Bureau actually count every nose—or does it make some estimates? What people in your community make use of the Census Bureau statistics?
5. Prepare a bulletin-board display of the various kinds of coins we have had in this country. The artists of the class can draw the coins from information available in your library. The librarian will help you to locate sources.
6. The chart, p. 526, on the banking system of this country mentions the "Rediscount Policy" of the Federal Reserve System. Do some research on how this "rediscount" policy works and what effect it has had on the business and the economy of the country generally. Draw a graph illustrating your findings.
7. Read in *Only Yesterday* by Frederick Lewis Allen (or any other book describing the period) about the 1929 crash and the bank panic of 1932

which led to the closing of all banks. Report to the class on the conditions that led up to the bank closing, and the measures taken to prevent such a thing from happening again in our country.
8. Write a history of the postal service, starting with Franklin's term as Postmaster General, and including such enterprises as the Pony Express, the stage-coach, etc. Describe each phase of the history, and have the artists in the class draw the different kinds of carriers that have been used in our country.

EXTEND YOUR VOCABULARY

business
collectivism
free private enterprise
self-regulation
regulation by the market
dividends
patent
trademark

weights and measures
census
mint
legal tender
checking account
government bonds
national debt
national banking system
tight money

member banks
Federal Reserve Notes
rediscount
public power
corporation
government corporation
private ownership
public ownership
Corrupt Practices Act

YOUR NOTEBOOK: THE GOVERNMENT OF ——

1. List in your notebook the businesses in your community that make use of Weather Bureau reports, and tell how.
2. List the banks in your community which are national banks, state banks, noninsured banks.
3. How many post offices are there in your community? Are the postmasters class 1, 2, 3, or 4?

READ MORE ABOUT IT

ALLEN, F. L., *Only Yesterday*. Harper, 1931.
Interesting history, business and social, of the United States from 1919 through 1931.
CLAPP, GORDON R., *The TVA, An Approach to the Development of a Region*. University of Chicago Press, 1955.
Thoughtful study by the second Director of TVA.
LILIENTHAL, DAVID E., *TVA, Democracy on the March*. Harper, 1953.
The first Director of TVA tells the story with enthusiasm.
SWARTHOUT, JOHN M., and BARTLEY, ERNEST R., *Principles and Problems in American National Government*. Oxford University Press, 1955. Chaps. 22–26.
SWARTHOUT, JOHN M., and BARTLEY, ERNEST R., *Principles and Problems in State and Local Government*. Oxford University Press, 1958. Chap. 10.

CHAPTER 22

Government & Labor

In this chapter you will learn about

Labor in a free society

Labor unions

Labor contracts

The Department of Labor

Federal Mediation and

Conciliation Service

Labor and the states

While it is certainly true that almost every adult in the United States works for his living—in store, office, or factory, on the farm, in the mill or the mine, or in the domestic tasks of the housewife—the word *labor* has a special meaning. It means in particular those of us who work for hourly wages. There have always been such workers, of course, but it is the industrial revolution that has brought the wage earner into special relations both with employers and with government.

LABOR IN A FREE SOCIETY

In the early days of our republic more than 90 percent of laborers worked on farms, many on their own land. Today, of the 67 to 70 million Americans who earn their living, only a small percentage work on farms. The vast majority work for wages in factories, shops, small businesses.

In Chapter 21 we saw how the principle of free private enterprise has persisted in American business life. Business freedom has helped to maintain political freedom. But if such freedom is to be general, the freedom of the farmer and the businessman must be matched by the freedom of the laborer. Much of the history of American economic life in the nineteenth and twentieth centuries has in fact been the history of the efforts of labor to maintain or to extend its freedom.

The original theory of free labor was that the individual workman should be free to choose his occupation or skill, free to make his residence where he chose, and free to bargain with his employer for the rate of his wages and the conditions of his work. This theory assumed that business would be small and individually owned. The laborer would personally know his employer, and could talk with him on a man-to-man basis. In the first American factories, like the iron foundries and cloth mills 150 years ago, the theory worked fairly well in practice. Emmet Miller, the "mechanic" who worked in Mr. Downer's iron foundry, knew his boss very well. Emmet lived on one side of the town and Mr. Downer in the big house on the hill on the other side. But they had gone to school together, and their children, in turn, were going to school as chums. They were on a first-name basis, except that sometimes Emmet called Mr. Downer "Boss." They talked over things like wages and hours personally.

When power-driven machinery replaced handicraft labor, factories expanded in size. Ownership of most of important industry was widely distributed among many stockholders. Workers tended to lose their individuality in the manufacturing process. Emmet Miller's grandson Jim is a steelworker skilled in handling blast-furnace work. The factory employs 6,000 workers who live in or near a great city. They work on eight-hour shifts. Jim knows only a dozen or so of the men on his own shift. The work is supervised by a foreman who works, like Jim, for wages. The administration of the factory is in the hands of businessmen who are specialists in various kinds of business skills—production, personnel, sales, accounting, finance. Jim never sees any of them, but they, too, work for a kind of wages called salaries.

Who are the owners? Well, Jim may be an owner himself, if he owns a few shares of stock in the company. The librarian in the public library of a city a thousand miles away is another owner. Several industrialists in New York and Chicago, several thousand housewives, some foreign "capitalists," college professors, baseball players, bankers, clerks, postmen, farmers, dentists, lawyers, and so on and on—these are the owners because they are the stockholders. Obviously Jim has no dealings with them. Emmet Miller knew his boss and got his job by asking for it, because Mr. Downer knew him, his ability, and his reputation. It is a different story with Jim. Jim had to fill out application blanks, provide references, take a physical examination, and sign a number of other papers. Jim has none of the personal contacts with the owner that his grandfather Emmet had with the boss.

As early as the 1840's William Cullen Bryant, editor of the *New York Evening Post*, supported the emerging movement for unions of workers in such impersonal factories. *Individual laborers* were being replaced by *labor*.

543

LABOR UNIONS

The history of organized labor in the United States is a long one. Behind the great and powerful unions of today (the Amalgamated Clothing Workers, the International Ladies' Garment Workers, the Railway Brotherhoods, the Brotherhood of Carpenters and Joiners, the United Steel Workers, the United Automobile Workers) there stretches a history of struggles for organization and recognition. Sometimes these struggles were marked by violence and bloodshed. All Americans must read of the Pullman Strike of 1894 with regret. As late as 1937 the Republic Steel Strike brought bitterness and bloodshed. The United States, however, was fortunate enough to escape such widespread class warfare as tore Europe apart in the nineteenth century in wave after wave of revolution. We avoided it because our great natural resources enabled us to maintain almost continuous prosperity, marred only by occasional periods of depression, and because our political system could adapt itself to changing conditions. As labor became aware of common interests in the economic system, like other competing influences, it began to exert influence on government. As a result, labor did not have to revolt in order to secure its rights and appropriate privileges. Violence and bloodshed there were, and occasional serious strikes. But these were sporadic and the economy always managed to recover quickly.

The American Federation of Labor

By the 1890's the American Federation of Labor (AFL) had organized more than a million workers into unions, mostly in the skilled crafts—cigar makers, carpenters, plumbers, barbers, masons. These were the workers least directly affected by economic depression. They were also the ones who met least resistance from business leaders when they attempted to organize. Workers in mills, shoe factories, foundries, railroad shops organized more slowly.

Unlike European labor leaders, who agitated for class warfare against government, Samuel Gompers, first President of the AFL, set a pattern for American unions by adopting a policy of "helping your friends, and punishing your enemies." This meant that the unions entered politics as a unified force only to support candidates friendly to their interests or to oppose those who seemed unfriendly. Labor did not form a political party. Individual workers, instead, participated in politics through the old established parties. Both parties, for their part, recognized the growing strength and numbers of union workmen, and gradually both made room for them and modified their programs in response to labor's influence. Occasional attempts by impatient union leaders to form political parties failed miserably because they were not really needed. However, as labor's strength increased at a rapid pace, the threat to form a labor party was at times a useful device to influence the programs and platforms of the Republican and Democratic parties.

The Congress of Industrial Organizations

The organization and policies of the AFL served the skilled workers well, increasing their wages steadily and improving their working conditions. Its principles of organization, however, were not suited to the great mass of unskilled laborers created by the assembly lines of mass production industries. To meet the needs of these millions, a new organization—the Committee for Industrial Organization—was established by some leaders of the AFL in the 1930's. The leader of this group was John L. Lewis, president of the United Mine Workers. Lewis promoted the idea of industrial unions to unite the workers of an entire industry whether they were skilled or unskilled. The CIO, as Lewis's committee came to be known, aided by the National Labor Relations Act (Wagner Act) of 1935 (see Chap. 8), succeeded in organizing into unions hundreds of thousands of workers in the mass production industries— automobile, rubber, steel, electric products, and others. These new unions claimed and won the right to bargain for the wages and working conditions, not merely of hundreds and thousands of workers as did the older craft unions, but of millions. The CIO (with its name changed to Congress of Industrial Organizations) declared its independence of the AFL, and at times fought with it for jurisdiction over workers. For example, at one time there were competing auto unions, electrical unions, and others. But by 1955 the two great union organizations, with more than fifteen million members, had again merged.

Unions and Management

By the time of World War II, almost all important industries had been organized, and management was dealing regularly with the unions. Serious resistance to union demands brought crippling strikes throughout whole industries, damaging to both business and labor, and sometimes to the economic health and strength of the nation. The strike, or the threat of a strike, is the weapon used by the unions to back up their demands.

Emmet Miller could meet his boss "man to man." If they could not agree, Emmet might pack his tools, move his family, and go to work elsewhere. Since there were not many Emmet Millers in early industrial days, Boss Downer would go a long way to meet Emmet's demands. The situation changed, however, when laborers became abundant. If one man would not take the wages and hours offered, another would. The boss held real power. Workers and owners or managers were not equally matched.

Jim Miller, today, belongs to the United Steel Workers. This union, with hundreds of thousands of members, can bargain with the managers on Jim's behalf. The union gives Jim a kind of equality with his employers; that is, each owner can find employees, but, on the other hand, employees can refuse to work. If negotiations break down, the union may strike and the factories

WHAT OF OUR BIG
COUNTRY?

Fitzpatrick in
The St. Louis Post-Dispatch

will have to shut down. When this happens both sides lose—the company its business, the workers their wages.

In recent years, both management and unions have learned rapidly that negotiation and compromise are much more advantageous for all concerned. The right of labor to strike remains, as does the right of management to close plants (lockouts), but the tendency in labor relations is more and more toward peaceful settlement of disputes and agreement to long-term contracts. The steel strike of 1959–1960 is an exception, not common practice.

Unions and the Courts

While, as we have said, Americans generally did not show violent resistance to union growth and influence, there was much resistance in the courts. For many years, business tried to restrain unions in the courts. Unions for their part tried both in the courts and through legislation to establish the rights of unions. The first tendency of the courts was to uphold the cause of employers by granting **injunctions** against unions. An injunction is an order by a court to "cease and desist" a particular action and has the force of law. Disobedience is punishable as contempt of court. The courts granted injunctions on the ground that a strike violated the rights of employers under

546

Amendment XIV—that is, taking away the liberty of employers without "due process of law." Thus unions could be effectively frustrated by this means.

Yet the conditions of labor made unions a necessity, and no legal device could indefinitely keep them in check. In 1932 the Congress passed the Norris-La Guardia Act, making such injunctions illegal under most circumstances. And in 1935 the Wagner Act established the rights of unions to organize and, if they had a majority of the workers, to bargain with management.

We have seen how this works under the administration of the National Labor Relations Board (see Chap. 8). The Taft-Hartley Law of 1947 modified the Wagner Act to outlaw the **closed shop** (a system requiring workers to join the union *before* they can obtain employment) but recognized the **union shop** (a system whereby the worker must join the union within a certain length of time *after* he has secured employment). The distinction may not seem important. But in practice it means that management retains the right to choose its employees, whereas under the closed shop the union would have this right.

The Taft-Hartley Law also protects companies against so-called sympathetic strikes. Thus members of one union under contract with a company may not strike to support another union which is striking against the company in order to obtain a better new contract. Union leaders are required, under the law, to certify that they are not Communists or members of other subversive organizations. This latter provision was introduced because the Communist Party had in some cases succeeded in gaining control of unions and was using them for illegitimate purposes. Most unions, however, have effectively "cleaned their houses" of subversive elements or expelled from their ranks organizations under control of the Communists. Today there is no question of the patriotism of our great labor unions.

Unfortunately like other important organizations in our economic life, unions have sometimes been taken over by dishonest men. In 1959, Congress amended the Taft-Hartley law to give additional protection to rank and file union workers against the possibility of their being cheated or misrepresented by corrupt leaders.

LABOR CONTRACTS

The contract between union and management is the heart of modern labor relations. A contract, any contract, is an agreement by two parties, having the power to make agreements, to do things agreed upon. Under our legal system, a contract signed by both parties in good faith has the force of law. A labor contract is an agreement between a company and the organization of its employees governing the relations between the company and the employees for a stated period of time. While the contract is in force, both sides are bound, under law, to abide by it. Thus strikes usually occur only when a contract comes to an end. The unions use the strike to influence a company to give them better terms under new contracts.

Collective Bargaining

Most contracts today stipulate a period of a certain number of weeks before the contract expires during which a new contract should be negotiated. Often unions bind themselves under contract not to strike during negotiation, even though such periods may extend beyond the day of expiration. When you read in the paper that a certain union is probably going to strike at a certain time, this usually means that the union is trying to influence management to agree with the demands it will make when its current contract expires. As you follow the newspapers carefully, you will see that such threatened strikes seldom occur. By far the largest percentage of union contracts are renewed, after negotiation, without strikes or interruption of production. The process that produces a labor contract is known as **collective bargaining.**

Collective bargaining works in general this way. The employees, below the level of management, are represented by elected leaders who meet with designated representatives of the company. In the larger unions, the bargaining committee is assisted by full-time paid employees of the union who have expert knowledge of the business and of economic matters in general. The company representatives are themselves specialists in labor relations and are assisted by staff experts. The bargaining sessions are devoted in great part to the discussion of highly technical matters. Rates of production, investment schedules, profits, the whole structure of wages and prices, the tax problem, and numerous other matters are exhaustively analyzed. The two negotiating parties settle what the contract will specify on each subject through an understanding of the facts and compromises of interest on both sides.

What the Contract Covers

A labor contract covers such things as the wage scale, the length of the work week, conditions of work (including safety, recreation, health), welfare benefits, retirement and vacation benefits, and pensions. Frequently when a union announces that its new contract calls for a general raise of ten cents or so an hour, it does not mean that the individual worker's wage will rise from, say, $2.00 to $2.10, but that the company has agreed to invest the equivalent of such an increase not only in the wage itself but in welfare, pensions, and such things, called "fringe" benefits. In the summer of 1955, a labor contract between the United Automobile Workers and the Ford Motor Company included, for the first time in a major industry, provisions for payments by the company to its workers during periods when the plants are shut down. Such payments, supplementing the payments of unemployment insurance from the state, give workers a year-round income for the first time. This plan is sometimes called the **guaranteed annual wage.**

A labor contract is a long and detailed document, as you can see. A *summary* of the contract between the steel companies and the United Steel Workers negotiated in the winter of 1959–1960 (after a long strike) took a whole page of the *New York Times.* Such a contract is a vitally important paper. Not only has it the force of law, like any other contract, but it is a symbol of the peaceful and successful process of collective bargaining and the freedom of American labor. During the past century and a half the American workingman has given up certain freedoms he once had as an individual to bargain with an individual employer, just as individual employers themselves have so often disappeared in favor of the corporations of our time. Through the union, however, workers have gained new freedoms and new strength and have achieved a new and important kind of individual security. The steel strike of 1959, indeed, raised the question whether the unions, like the companies, have become so strong as to need federal regulation to protect the public interest.

The Individual Worker and the Contract

What do membership in a modern union and work under a labor contract mean to the individual worker? Let us go back to Jim Miller. When he applied for his job at the steel mill, he did not belong to a union and had only studied steelworking for a few weeks at the vocational high school. As you saw earlier, he had to fill out application papers and follow other procedures before he got his job. Once on the job, the union seemed to be all around him. All his fellow workers were members. The agent of the local (branch of the union operating at Jim's plant) came around to see him and explained what the union was all about. Jim had been told when he was hired that he would have to join the union after thirty days and that his union membership dues would be taken out of his pay check. Jim was glad to learn about these things from the agent. He found that his dues would be $5.00 a month. This money would be spent to help pay the salaries of union officials and to build up the union treasury for many purposes, including a "war chest" to pay money to the members if they should go on strike.

As a union member, Jim would get a health insurance policy for himself and his family and could buy life insurance at low rates. In the small unit of the local he could talk about his job, and vote to elect union officials.

Through the union, Jim could make his grievances known. Thus, if he felt that his foreman was expecting him to produce too much in an hour of labor, he could complain to his shop steward—an official of the local. His complaint would be passed on to the union grievance committee and brought

549

LABOR IN OUR COUNTRY

The Department of Labor, through the Secretary of Labor, represents labor in our government. This department performs many services useful to the whole country. The consumer price index, compiled by the Department's Bureau of Labor Statistics, is valuable not only to labor, but also to the whole country, and represents the basis for many decisions of labor, business, and government.

Unions themselves have come a long way since they were organized to raise wages and improve working conditions. Now they provide health services to their members, such as the eye examination shown here, educational facilities, like the union sponsored sculpture class for creative union members, and vacation resorts at which union members can relax in pleasant surroundings.

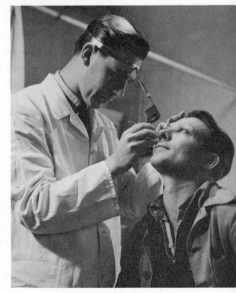

An indication of the coöperation of labor and management is the arbitration meetings at which they try to iron out their mutual difficulties. Here at left of table are negotiators for the United Steel Workers Union; at right, negotiators for the steel industry.

to the attention of a labor relations official of the company. Usually such grievances are worked out in discussions between company and union officials. If discussions fail, however, unions may even go on strike to back up their demand for settlement. Labor contracts in general provide for this kind of machinery to settle grievances and disputes.

As the end of a contract with the company approached, Jim's unit would hold meetings to discuss the wishes of the workers for the new contract. His elected representatives would explain his views and those of his fellow workers to the higher officials of the union, who, in turn, would sit down to bargain with the company managers. Thus, Jim learned, he would be a part of a great organization devoted to the interests of the workers in his field.

The Individual Worker and Politics

As a union member Jim will also learn something about politics. His union has an agency dealing with political education, which holds meetings and provides him with literature about political issues and candidates from the union's point of view. He will even be asked to contribute money in political campaigns. His union may endorse candidates he does not favor, but his vote remains his own business. Jim may conclude that in some ways he has less freedom than his grandfather, Emmet, had. He will also learn that he has more power and greater security. He may even decide that his greater power and security add up to a kind of freedom and independence Emmet did not have. He will know that his union membership gives him greater protection for his income so that he can own his home, feed and clothe his family, buy a refrigerator and a television set, and own a car. In other words, Jim's union membership helps him to obtain a steadily increasing share in the technical achievements and the prosperity of the industrial age. If Jim's union does not deal honestly with him—and some unions have not done so— he and his fellow union members will have to take responsibility, for union members, like members of all organizations, must be active in promoting the welfare and standards of their union. In this respect, unions are not different from political parties. Corruption flourishes only when the rank-and-file members are content to "let other people do it." When the members are alert to their own interests and accept their responsibilities, unions, like political parties, serve their members honestly and well.

Unions and the Government

The giant, successful unions of today present a new problem to which our governmental system must adjust—the problem of union responsibility. Through the dues they collect and the capital investments they make, unions often have in their treasuries many millions of dollars. The International Ladies' Garment Workers (ILGWU), for example, actually lends money to business and runs an insurance company. The unions are an economic power, therefore, not simply as representatives of the workers. And, of course, they also have great political influence at all levels of government. But they are not businesses and are not, therefore, required to incorporate under the laws of the states. Thus, if complaints regarding their practices are made, it falls to the courts to determine to what extent unions may be held responsible for honoring contracts, for the behavior of their members, and for the actions of their officials. The process may be a very long one because courts do not make laws, but only interpret them. Meanwhile the Congress may move in and enact legislation in addition to the Wagner and Taft-Hartley acts. But it has already been established in the courts that unions can sue and can be sued. This fact forces upon the unions self-discipline and acceptance of responsibility. In addition, the Taft-Hartley Law requires unions to file accounts of their organization and financing with the federal government. At any rate the unions are certainly gaining "maturity" and more and more surely commanding national respect. Their magnificent record during World War II and the Korean War amply shows that they deserve the high seat they have taken in the councils of the country. The daily press has begun to recognize the importance and the dignity of the unions and their leaders.

THE DEPARTMENT OF LABOR

While many American workers today belong to a union, there are still large numbers of hourly wage earners who are not organized. Workers in small companies do not need unions, nor do those in small individually owned services. In such businesses there may be normally only two or three to six or a dozen employees. Added together, these workers number many millions. It was to serve them as well as union workers, before the union movement had reached its present massive proportions, that the United States Department of Labor was established in 1913. That Department now impartially assists all American workers regardless of their status or affiliation.

In 1884, the new railroad industry was spanning the continent, the Rockefeller oil empire was mushrooming, and Andrew Carnegie's steel company was providing the basis for modern American manufactures. Congress responded to the growing demands of labor at that time by establishing a Bureau of Labor in the Department of the Interior. At first, appropriations of money were small and services limited. Government recognition of labor as a major pressure group deserving of being heard and supported was something new. Looking at the class warfare in Europe and fearing such words as *socialism*, many Americans were suspicious and even fearful of giving labor a place for itself.

The Bureau grew nevertheless. In a few years it became an independent department, but below cabinet level. In 1903 it was brought into the newly formed Department of Commerce and Labor, again as a bureau. By 1913 its usefulness had been settled beyond doubt, and the voice of labor was so much to be reckoned with that it was separated from commerce and set up as a full-scale Department. A modern Secretary of Labor is an outstanding figure of the federal government and presides over a department of more than 5,000 employees. Under law, the Department of Labor is charged with "administering and enforcing statutes designed to advance the public interest by promoting the welfare of the wage earners of the United States, improving their working conditions, and advancing their opportunities for profitable employment."

The Secretary of Labor is appointed by the President with the consent of the Senate and serves at the pleasure of the President. Like the Secretary of Commerce, he is expected to represent the special point of view of the people his Department is intended to serve—in his case the workers of the United States. He is the voice of labor in the executive branch and in the counsels of the President. Thus an essential characteristic of a Secretary of Labor is that he know the unions well and have their confidence. He must serve also the interests of unorganized labor. Some Secretaries have been drawn directly from union ranks; others have been lawyers whose practice involved them with labor. At least one was a businessman, but none has been an active industrialist at the time of his appointment. It is interesting to note that one Secretary, Frances Perkins, who served under President Franklin Roosevelt, was the first woman ever to hold an office of cabinet rank in the United States.

The chart on p. 556 shows the organization of the Department of Labor with its many agencies devoted to special activities.

Bureau of Labor Statistics

The Bureau of Labor Statistics, the oldest agency in the Department of Labor, is the principal resource of the government for the collection and publication of information about American labor. The word *labor* is here used very broadly. For under it the Bureau includes many functions, as the chart, p. 556, shows.

The Bureau's official publication is the *Monthly Labor Review*. Every month, as you probably know from your own newspaper, the Bureau also publishes its Consumer Price Index based on surveys of how much consumers spend. This Index shows whether the cost of living is rising or falling and how much. In recent years, a number of labor contracts have been based on the Consumer Price Index. Thus in the automobile industry, wages must

554

be increased by the companies if the Index rises, and may be reduced if the Index falls.

The Bureau of Labor Statistics keeps the figures on employment and unemployment that play a prominent part in public and political discussions of our national economy. In addition to making such popularly known reports, the Bureau makes many studies of a more specialized nature useful both to business and to labor—price statistics in fields like wholesale marketing, raw materials, semi-finished goods. It even makes studies of prices, wages, and supplies of raw materials and finished goods for certain very large cities which are the marketing and employment centers of geographical and industrial regions. The Bureau, of course, serves not only the public but many other agencies of government, federal, state, and local. It has made a brilliant record for full and accurate statistics, and has succeeded over the years in keeping itself remarkably free of partisan influences.

Bureau of Employment Security

As the depression of 1929 mounted, "unemployment grew steadily, until by the end of 1930 the number of jobless was figured at somewhere in the neighborhood of six million; apple salesmen stood on the street corner, executives and clerks and factory hands lay awake wondering when they, too, would be thrown off, and contributed anxiously to funds for the workless." [1]

Congress acted to relieve unemployment immediately by emergency relief measures. It also looked to the future in the hope of avoiding the recurrence of such a disaster. The Social Security Act of 1935 and the Fair Labor Standards Act of 1938 entrusted to the Department of Labor programs designed to encourage employment and regulate working conditions.

The Bureau of Employment Security administers and enforces certain provisions of the Social Security Act. Under the Social Security Act the states are entitled to receive grants of money from the federal government to administer their programs of unemployment insurance. This provision of the law is intended to encourage the states to insure their workers against unemployment. The Bureau prescribes the conditions the states must meet to be eligible, and awards the federal grants. Unemployment insurance, as we shall see, remains primarily the responsibility of the states. They are assisted by the federal government through the Bureau of Employment Security by both grants of money and technical advice.

Under the Wagner-Peyser Act, the Bureau provides the states with similar services in connection with their employment programs. The United States Employment Service, within the Bureau of Employment Security, was organized to do this work. Under the system, each state operates a local Employ-

[1] From F. L. Allen, *Only Yesterday*, New York, Harper & Brothers, 1931.

555

Department of Labor

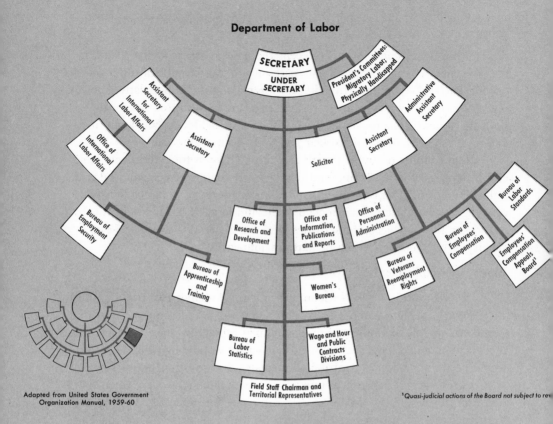

SECRETARY
UNDER SECRETARY

President's Committees: Migratory Labor; Physically Handicapped

Administrative Assistant Secretary

Assistant Secretary for International Labor Affairs

Office of International Labor Affairs

Assistant Secretary

Solicitor

Assistant Secretary

Bureau of Labor Standards

Bureau of Employment Security

Office of Research and Development

Office of Information, Publications and Reports

Office of Personnel Administration

Bureau of Employees' Compensation

Employees' Compensation Appeals Board[1]

Bureau of Apprenticeship and Training

Women's Bureau

Bureau of Veterans Reemployment Rights

Bureau of Labor Statistics

Wage and Hour and Public Contracts Divisions

Field Staff Chairman and Territorial Representatives

Adapted from United States Government Organization Manual, 1959-60

[1]Quasi-judicial actions of the Board not subject to rev

SECRETARY (1913). Under-Secretary, Assistant Secretaries. Administers laws to promote the welfare of wage earners.

BUREAU OF LABOR STATISTICS (1913). Commissioner. A fact-finding agency; collects and analyzes data on employment and manpower, productivity, housing construction, wages, industrial relations, accidents, price trends, costs, and standards of living. Publishes monthly Consumer Price Index (see pp. 554–555).

BUREAU OF APPRENTICESHIP AND TRAINING (1937). Director. Develops standards of apprenticeship for the training of skilled workers in industry; working with state apprenticeship agencies, tries to extend these standards widely.

WOMEN'S BUREAU (1918). Director. Works to promote the welfare of wage-earning women. Administers no laws but does make studies and recommendations on such subjects as equal pay, minimum wages, hours of work, civil and political status of women.

BUREAU OF EMPLOYMENT SECURITY. Director. Administers and enforces the provisions under which state unemployment insurance programs and state employment programs receive federal financial and technical assistance. U.S. Employment Service aids the states in establishing and maintaining public employment offices and makes grants for them.

WAGE AND HOUR AND PUBLIC CONTRACTS DIVISION (1942). Administrator. Enforces the Fair Labor Standards Act (see pp. 557–558) and the Walsh-Healey Act; requires minimum wage and 40-hour week; restricts child labor and convict labor; requires safety and health standards on government supply contracts over $10,000.

BUREAU OF VETERANS REEMPLOYMENT RIGHTS (1947). Director. Assists former members of the armed forces, rejectees, reservists performing training duty in the exercise of their employment rights.

556

ment Service, listing people who wish work and the skills they possess. When the housewife needs a gardener, or a contractor needs half a dozen men for a particular job, the local office of the State Employment Service is ready to help. The U.S. Employment Service assists the states in administering this service, and makes grants of money for the same purpose.

Wage and Hour and Public Contracts Division

The Wage and Hour and Public Contracts Division of the Department of Labor is more independent than the bureaus. See chart, p. 556, for its place in the Department and some of its duties.

The Administrator is appointed directly by the President with the consent of the Senate, and reports to the President as well as to the Secretary of Labor. It is his job, and that of his Division, to enforce the Fair Labor Standards Act. In particular, the Division sees to it that workers get not less than the national minimum wage prescribed by Congress. The minimum wage, set at $1.00 an hour, applies to all those workers "engaged in interstate commerce, or in the production of goods for interstate commerce, including work in any closely related process or occupation." The law also requires employers to pay their employees time and one-half for all time worked beyond forty hours a week. Thus the law places a "floor" under the wage system of the United States, and determines what the standard work week shall be. Of course, there are millions of workers not covered by the law because their labor is not connected with interstate commerce. But the law has influenced wages everywhere in the nation.

The Fair Labor Standards Act is also the federal law against "child labor," and is enforced in this respect by the Wage and Hour Division. For generations attempts have been made to amend the Constitution to abolish child labor. These efforts have consistently failed for lack of sustained political support. One reason is that some people are opposed to a constitutional amendment, or a law, that would prevent youngsters from starting their active careers as newsboys, for instance. If you have had a paper route to earn money on your own, you may be opposed to the amendment yourself. The courts have held that the abolition of child labor by federal law is unconstitutional if applied to all children. However, the Supreme Court has upheld the constitutionality of the Fair Labor Standards Act, because it applies only to interstate commerce, which Congress has full power to regulate. Thus we can have newsboys, messengers, errand boys, boys working on the farm, but we do not any longer have boys or girls under sixteen working in factories whose products go into interstate commerce, or in any other occupations connected with interstate commerce. The Fair Labor Standards Act may in fact be a better solution than the proposed amendment would

557

have been, since under the act the exploitation of child labor—a national disgrace in the nineteenth century—has largely disappeared, but the ambitions of young people are not frustrated.

Finally, the Wage and Hour Division enforces the federal law requiring private businesses doing contract jobs for government amounting to more than $10,000 to pay prevailing minimum wages in the area where the work is done. Usually the minimum wage actually paid workers is much higher than that required by law. Therefore, this part of the law simply means that the government will not support by its orders and contracts a firm that pays less than the going wage. This applies also to the work week, so that time and a half must be paid to workers employed on such contracts and orders.

The Fair Labor Standards Act, thought by some historians and economists to be the most important single piece of labor legislation in the United States, is nevertheless only one of the laws enacted in the interests of labor. The Department of Labor, as you can see from the examples of its work we have considered, is a remarkable illustration of what a free government can do for its people. The existence of the Department, as well as the many functions added to it over the years, is testimony to both the power of labor in the American community and the adaptability of our form of government to changing conditions of life.

THE FEDERAL GOVERNMENT AND MEDIATION

Outside the Department of Labor, the federal government provides an additional service to both labor and management. This is the Federal Mediation and Conciliation Service, an independent agency. Although this agency, established under the Taft-Hartley Act, has no enforcement power, it serves the whole country in a most important way. It maintains a staff of trained experts in industrial relations who can be called in to aid in the settlement of disputes between unions and business. Their service cannot be imposed on business or on labor but is available when requested by either. The purpose of the Service is to help maintain industrial peace, that is, to prevent strikes and lockouts in advance or to settle them quickly if they get started. More than one strike potentially dangerous to national safety or prosperity has been avoided by the quiet, effective efforts of negotiators of the Mediation Service.

The National Mediation Board, created in 1934, provides a more narrow service than the Federal Mediation and Conciliation Service. The Board mediates differences between railroads, the express and Pullman companies and airlines on the one hand and their employees on the other.

LABOR AND THE STATES

Labor relations and problems have always been of deep concern to the states—indeed long before the national government entered the labor field. While almost every important federal law involving labor has been opposed at one time or another on constitutional grounds, there has never been much question as to the authority of the states. The powers reserved to the states by the Constitution itself were ample basis for labor legislation.

Thus every state has many laws covering such matters as the qualifications of workmen (age, apprenticeship, standards), conditions of labor, safety, union organization, arbitration of disputes, unemployment compensation, and accident insurance. The laws differ widely among the states. Large industrial states have laws regulating the conditions of labor and supporting union activity very much like those of the federal government. Less populous states have never been as friendly to organized labor and have felt less pressure for labor benefits.

In recent years some states have passed and others have rejected laws aimed directly at the power of unions. These laws, known as "right to work" laws (that is, the right to work without belonging to a union), would make the union shop impossible unless the union's members were unanimous in their support of it. The federal law, on the other hand, authorizes the union shop if a majority favors it. Such laws are constantly being tested in the courts to determine whether they conform with the Constitution. There is no uniform attitude toward labor among the states, and the states by no means all conform to the standards set by the federal government.

Each state has a department of labor in many ways similar to the United States Department of Labor. That is, the department serves the governor and the executive branch as the voice of labor in state matters, provides statistical and other services, and enforces state labor laws. In a state like Michigan, the labor department is one of the chief agencies of the state government, since the Michigan labor force is very large in proportion to the total population of the state. In smaller, non-industrial states, the labor department is often a very minor agency of government.

Unemployment Insurance

Both unemployment insurance and employment service are the direct responsibilities of the states. The states receive financial support from the federal government, but money paid unemployed workers comes from taxes paid by employers (not by workers, except in a few states). Rates and periods of unemployment compensation vary among the states. Usually about one-third of a worker's wage is paid to him by the state during a maximum of 26 weeks of unemployment in any given year. State governments also require

559

employers operating within the state to carry insurance against injury or disability of their employees. Payments made to workers during periods of unemployment caused by injury are known as **workman's compensation.**

No one who has not experienced the awful sickness of the soul that comes with the inability to get a job and make enough money to support his family can fully appreciate the meaning of these state and federal measures of job security. The ordinary American worker at the beginning of the present century too often had this experience. In our time, it is increasingly uncommon. Partly, of course, this is because of continued prosperity. It is also owing to a change in our notion of what government should do for the people.

Fair Employment Practices

Another matter in which the states have taken a prominent part is known as "fair employment practices." This means that certain states have enacted laws forbidding employers in hiring workers to discriminate on grounds of race, creed, or color. In these states a worker who is discriminated against for any of these reasons may obtain a court order requiring the employer to comply with the law. Failure to comply can mean imprisonment. There has been too much difference of opinion on "fair employment practices" for Congress to agree on a federal statute. When a majority in a state feels strongly about it, the state has power to take action. Many northern and some western states now have statutes enforcing a policy of anti-discrimination; by executive order the national government is forbidden to discriminate in its employment policy.

State Mediation and Arbitration Services

In general, cities and counties either do not have labor problems requiring important legislation or do not have legislative power delegated to them from the state legislatures. Some larger cities have established their own mediation, conciliation, and arbitration services to supplement those of the states and the federal government in disputes of purely local concern. In particular, larger cities have an immediate interest in disputes regarding transportation—buses, trolley lines, subways, taxicabs—or essential services. Cities like New York or San Francisco are seriously affected by any labor unrest in their great international ports. Even in such local situations the state has a large interest and state laws and state mediation or arbitration services carry the major share of responsibility for labor peace.

Many minor disputes arising under labor contracts are submitted by the two parties to private arbitration. Many labor contracts call for the arbitration of grievances as a regular procedure. There are no overall figures, but it has been estimated that as many as 75 percent of all labor disputes are arbitrated by private persons who have special competence in labor relations or command sufficient respect upon both sides to render satisfactory judgments.

A private organization, the American Arbitration Association, is prepared to supply such arbitrators in most areas of the country.

Peaceful settlements of labor disputes, both by private arbitrators and by state and federal mediation services, are the real *news* about labor in the middle of the twentieth century. Unfortunately for all of us, it is the great strike that gets the headlines and influences us in forming our impressions of unions and management. A well-informed citizen will not be content with the sensational news of the moment. He can well take pride in the enormous accomplishments made in the past generation, by both labor and management, in understanding each other and in respecting the public interest.

SUMMARY

Free labor is the partner of ownership and management in our economic system of free private enterprise. In this chapter you have looked at the system from the point of view of labor. While almost all adult Americans work —at jobs or as housewives—we speak of **labor** more specifically as that very large group of people who work for hourly wages.

You have seen how the conditions of labor changed with industrial development, from simple laborer-boss dealings to the present-day union-management relationships. You should now understand, not only how unions came into being and grew, but what a union actually is. You have seen how important his union is to the worker's daily life—what it does for him, how it restricts him, and how it nevertheless increases his power and gives him a new kind of freedom.

You have seen what some of the great labor problems are and should be better able, as a citizen, to judge them. Unions today enable workers to be strongly represented in their relations with the owners and managers of business.

Labor, like business, is directly represented in the executive branch of the national government. The Department of Labor is responsible for aiding all laborers, whether or not they are union members. You have studied some of the ways in which the Department assists labor—important statistical information, employment security, regulated wages and hours to provide "fair labor standards" for workers in interstate commerce.

Finally, you have seen that the states provide important assistance to workers, including accident and unemployment compensation, safety measures, and regulation of wages and hours. You should now have a better understanding of the tremendously important part played by labor in our society, and be able to appreciate what free government means to free labor.

KNOW WHAT YOU READ

1. Which section of our people or public should you think of when you see or hear the word *labor?*
2. Emmet Miller was an *individual laborer*. His grandson, Jim, was a *part of labor*. Explain the difference.
3. Why has the labor movement in the United States been able to develop with little class warfare?
4. What political policy did Samuel Gompers recommend to the American Federation of Labor?
5. Why was the Committee for Industrial Organization established?
6. How successful was the drive in the 1930's to organize industrial unions?
7. Why has such a large part of our labor force joined unions?
8. Is it better for both labor and management if disputes can be settled without strikes?
9. What rights were given to labor by (a) the Norris-La Guardia Act; (b) the Wagner Act?
10. What changes in labor-management relations were brought about by the Taft-Hartley Act?
11. What is a labor contract?
12. How is a labor contract made? People often think of a labor contract as just an agreement on hours and wages. What else does it include?
13. What do membership in a union and work under a labor contract mean to a worker?
14. In what way are unions like political parties?
15. What does a large modern union do for its members in addition to bargaining for them?
16. What is meant by saying that unions are gaining "maturity"?
17. When and why was the Department of Labor created?
18. What is the chief responsibility of the Secretary of Labor? Must he be a member of organized labor?
19. Summarize the work of the Bureau of Labor Statistics.
20. Why are so many people interested in the Consumer Price Index?
21. In what ways might the Bureau of Apprenticeship be important to you or to other young people?
22. What is the work of the Women's Bureau?
23. Make a list of the activities and services of the Bureau of Employment Security.
24. What services do state employment services provide? How does the U.S. Employment Service take part in this work?
25. William Jones works in a factory which manufactures packing cases. Are his wages and hours affected by the Fair Labor Standards Act? Explain.
26. Fred, age 15, would like a summer job in an automobile assembly plant. What does the law of the United States say about his chances of getting such a job?

562

27. The ABC Construction Corporation wishes to bid for a government contract. What restriction will the government put on the corporation's wages if ABC gets the contract?
28. Explain how the Mediation and Conciliation Service works to keep down losses due to strikes.
29. Review the *reserved powers* of the states (page 99). Explain why the states' labor powers are reserved powers.
30. Why are the labor laws of the states so different? What matters do most of the states regulate?
31. Which states are most favorable to organized labor?
32. What are "right to work" laws?
33. What activities are carried on by state departments of labor?
34. John Smith needs workers and John Jones wants a job. Explain how a state employment office might help them both.
35. How do some states try to protect workers against job discrimination?
26. Most labor disputes do not result in strikes. How are they settled?

WHAT DO YOU THINK?

1. In an ILGWU office a few years ago appeared a poster carrying a picture of a bunch of bananas and the warning, "Stick to Your Bunch or You'll Get Skinned." What do you think of this argument for union membership?
2. Are there any unions which should not be allowed to strike?

PROBLEMS AND PROJECTS FOR YOU

1. Look up the number of stockholders and number of workers in each of our country's five largest business enterprises.
2. Report to the class on the Pullman Strike of 1894 or write a newspaper account of the strike as it might have been written at the time.
3. Make a list of all the different unions of which parents or students of your community are members.
4. Interview an adult who is a union member. Find out what union membership means to him or her.
5. Report to the class on the contents of an actual union contract.
6. In daily newspaper files study the facts about the steel strike of 1959–1960. Organize a panel discussion on the question whether the national government should have power to prevent or end such strikes.
7. Study the cartoon, p. 546, which appeared on May 24, 1946. Investigate events of that time, and report to the class the background of the artist's

message. How does the cartoon apply to the panel discussion of 6 above? Has there been a change in attitude of the two "big" interests toward each other and toward "our big country"?

8. Organize a committee to interview 5 employers and 5 union members to obtain their opinions on any or all of the labor-management questions mentioned in this chapter. It may be best not to mention names of the persons interviewed, but their views can be used in a panel discussion.

9. (*sociodrama*) Present to the class a scene from a collective bargaining meeting of representatives of labor and management. This can be particularly interesting if you get pro-labor students to take the part of management, and vice-versa.

10. Report to the class on labor's campaign against the Taft-Hartley Act.

11. Make an original chart of the organization of the Department of Labor.

12. Make up your own price index and keep it up to date for six months.

13. Look up the backgrounds of the U.S. Secretaries of Labor in the last twenty-five years. What do you learn about the kind of experience a person should have to qualify for this position?

14. Write a two-page summary of the early and unsuccessful attempts of Congress to regulate child labor.

15. Use the *Readers' Guide to Periodical Literature* to obtain information on "right to work" laws. Report your findings.

16. Visit your nearest state employment office to find out just how it operates.

17. Report to the class on the work of the American Arbitration Association.

EXTEND YOUR VOCABULARY

labor
Samuel Gompers
American Federation of Labor
craft unions
John L. Lewis
industrial union
National Labor Relations Act
  (Wagner Act)
jurisdiction
CIO; Congress of Industrial
  Organizations
bargaining; collective
  bargaining
arbitration
injunction
Norris-La Guardia Act
Taft-Hartley Act

closed shop
union shop
sympathetic strike
union local
guaranteed annual wage
socialism
Consumer Price Index
Wagner-Peyser Act
Social Security Act
Fair Labor Standards Act
unemployment insurance
minimum wage
mediation and arbitration
strikes and lockouts
right to work laws
workmen's compensation
fair employment practices

YOUR NOTEBOOK: THE GOVERNMENT OF ——

1. Does your state have a department of labor? What is it called?
2. How many unions maintain local offices in your community? Write here the names of any three.
3. Does your state have a fair-employment practices law? Who enforces it?
4. Where is the nearest state employment office?

READ MORE ABOUT IT

DERBER, MILTON, and YOUNG, EDWIN, *Labor and the New Deal*. University of Wisconsin Press, 1957.
How unions grew in the 1930's.
FAULKNER, HAROLD U., and STARR, MARK, *Labor in America*. Oxford Book Co., 1955.
Readable and authoritative brief history of labor in this country.
LEEK, JOHN H., *Government and Labor in the United States*. Rinehart, 1952.
A thorough and readable history.
LESTER, RICHARD A., *As Unions Mature*. Princeton University Press, 1958.
Thoughtful analysis and speculation about the future of unions.
ROSENFARB, JOSEPH, *The National Labor Policy and How It Works*. Harper. 1940.
SUFRIN, SIDNEY C., and SEDGWICK, ROBERT C., *Labor Economics and Problems at Mid-Century*, Knopf, 1956.
Standard reference book.
SWARTHOUT, JOHN M., and BARTLEY, ERNEST R., *Principles and Problems of American National Government*. Oxford University Press, 1955. Chap. 23.

CHAPTER 23

Agriculture and Conservation

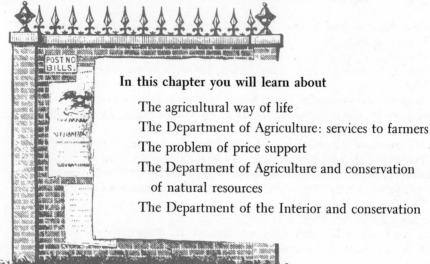

In this chapter you will learn about

The agricultural way of life

The Department of Agriculture: services to farmers

The problem of price support

The Department of Agriculture and conservation
of natural resources

The Department of the Interior and conservation

Industry and labor are not the only big-time producers in the United States today. Agriculture has kept up with them—or even ahead of them. It has had to, because it is the base on which the other two are built. For despite the amazing changes which have come over the face of America during the past century and a half, the agricultural way of life still holds strong attraction for millions of Americans, and the farmers of today not only supply us with our food, as they have always done, but retain enormous influence upon government at all levels, often far beyond their numbers.

THE AGRICULTURAL WAY OF LIFE

The importance of the farmers has increased at the same time that their numbers have decreased. In our time there are only a small percentage of farmers who are content simply to produce subsistence for their families. Farms vary in size from a few acres to many thousands, and from one individual farmer to corporation farms employing hundreds of laborers. Many farms are highly specialized. Thus there are wheat farms and corn farms, cattle farms and hog farms, cotton farms and peanut farms and tobacco farms, dairy farms and truck farms. The farmers who concentrate on one crop or one product supply all of us with our food and supply factories with raw materials. They sell their crops for cash, and spend their money for the necessities and luxuries of life, just as do workers in all other occupations.

The industrial revolution has not by-passed agriculture. Farm machinery of all sorts, from tractors to milking machines, has put farming on a mechanized basis. The American farmer of today is part of an interdependent economic system. He feeds not only himself, his family, and small communities, as he did 200 years ago, but a nation of over 180 million people—and a good part of the rest of the world as well. He raises five times as much wheat and corn to the acre as did his ancestors; he produces so much milk, from a proportionately smaller number of cows, that he sometimes baffles our efforts to consume it. He provides us with fresh vegetables the year round, and he has made meat production one of the largest industries in the world. The productiveness of American farming has in fact been so great that it is one of the chief reasons for the decline in the farming population—we just do not need so many farmers. But the declining number of the farmers led for a long time to declining political influence. Only within the past fifty years have they largely restored a balance of agriculture as against business and labor in the political process.

In the early years, when county courthouses, state legislatures, Congress, and even the Presidency (the first five Presidents were farmers) were dominated by men of the land, it was not necessary for farmers to organize *as farmers* in order to have an effective political voice. As the growing industries and cities attracted young men and women away from the farms, there followed a long period in which farmers were the truly forgotten men of America. As we saw earlier, they were exploited by the railroads. They were often dependent on banks charging high interest rates. They were nearly always short of money, and chronic economic troubles led them finally to organize in various sorts of pressure groups. Their political party—the Populist party—and their economic organizations like the Grange and, later, the Farm Bureau Federation were unsuccessful. Nevertheless, the reforms for which they agitated in banking and credit policies and in regulation of the railroads were achieved through the Democratic and Republican parties. In our time, farmers work through powerful organizations like the Farm Bureau and the Farmers Union and coöperative organizations for the distribution of dairy products and grains. They also play leading political roles in most county governments, many state legislatures, and in the Senate of the United States. The "farm bloc" in the House of Representatives (Representatives from agricultural areas, voting as a group in agricultural matters) also expresses the interests of the farmer. Above all, the farmer's direct interests are served and the agricultural way of life is supported and improved by the United States Department of Agriculture.

THE DEPARTMENT OF AGRICULTURE: SERVICES TO FARMERS

The various services provided to farmers under law by the executive branch of the federal government were first organized into a single executive agency in 1862, when the Department of Agriculture was established. At that time it was under a Commissioner who did not have cabinet rank. In 1889 it was elevated to cabinet status and the Secretary became the eighth member of the President's cabinet. Today the Department has more than 67,000 employees and is third largest in the government. It is, among other things, the largest research agency in the world.

The chart on p. 569 indicates how large and complex the Department of Agriculture is.

The Secretary of Agriculture is the voice of agriculture in the cabinet and in the executive branch. There are few more difficult assignments, for American agriculture is not one but many things, not one but many kinds of farmers, with differences depending on region, state, crops, size of farm, customs, and traditions. The Secretary must serve all impartially and serve the public interest as well.

Many of the people assisting the Secretary are career civil servants whose years of experience and technical knowledge are indispensable to the administration of the Department. Indeed, some of the Department's agencies are so specialized, as we shall see, that it is impossible for the Secretary to have more than a very general understanding of them. Yet the Secretary remains finally responsible to the President for every policy and every operation of his Department. He must advise the President not only on specialized and technical matters but on policies bearing directly on the welfare of the nation and on political success or failure of the administration. Thus, he must be an astute politician. He must be able to plan an agricultural policy which will suit the big wheat farmer in Kansas, the orange grower in California or Florida, the cotton farmer in South Carolina, and the small subsistence farmer in New England. At the same time, the policy must benefit all the people everywhere who depend on the farmers.

Department of Agriculture

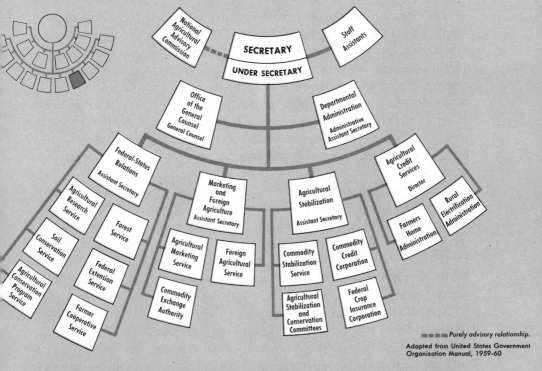

SECRETARY

UNDER SECRETARY

National Agricultural Advisory Commission

Staff Assistants

Office of the General Counsel — General Counsel

Departmental Administration — Administrative Assistant Secretary

Federal-States Relations — Assistant Secretary

Marketing and Foreign Agriculture — Assistant Secretary

Agricultural Stabilization — Assistant Secretary

Agricultural Credit Services — Director

Agricultural Research Service

Forest Service

Soil Conservation Service

Federal Extension Service

Agricultural Conservation Program Service

Farmer Coöperative Service

Agricultural Marketing Service

Foreign Agricultural Service

Commodity Exchange Authority

Commodity Stabilization Service

Commodity Credit Corporation

Agricultural Stabilization and Conservation Committees

Federal Crop Insurance Corporation

Farmers Home Administration

Rural Electrification Administration

▬ ▬ ▬ ▬ Purely advisory relationship.

Adapted from United States Government
Organization Manual, 1959-60

SECRETARY. Under-Secretary, Assistant Secretaries.

AGRICULTURAL RESEARCH SERVICE (1953). Administrator. Conducts research in agricultural products, farm and land management, livestock, home economics, new uses for farm products. Conducts plant and animal disease and pest control programs. Enforces the federal meat inspection laws. Operates the Agricultural Research Center at Beltsville, Maryland. Administers federal funds granted to state experiment stations. (See p. 570.)

FARMER COÖPERATIVE SERVICE (1953). Administrator. Studies management, financing, organization, merchandising, and efficiency for farmer coöperatives. (See p. 571.)

FEDERAL EXTENSION SERVICE (1924). Administrator. Works with the land-grant colleges, states, and counties in educational programs in rural areas. Works with county agents. (See p. 571.)

AGRICULTURAL MARKETING SERVICE (1953). Administrator. Studies problems involved in moving agricultural products from farm to consumer (storage, transportation, pricing, packaging, etc.). Studies the economic situation and the outlook for farmers. Administers school milk and lunch programs.

COMMODITY EXCHANGE AUTHORITY (1936). Administrator. Regulates grain and produce exchanges; protects investors against fraud, price manipulation. (See p. 572.)

COMMODITY CREDIT CORPORATION (1933). President. Carries out the support program through the personnel and facilities of the COMMODITY STABILIZATION SERVICE (1953). (See p. 575.)

FEDERAL CROP INSURANCE CORPORATION (1938). Manager. Provides farmers with low-cost insurance against losses of crops from causes beyond their control. (See p. 575.)

FARMERS HOME ADMINISTRATION (1946). Administrator. Lends money to farmers for purchase or improvement of "family-size" farms. (See pp. 575–576.)

RURAL ELECTRIFICATION ADMINISTRATION. (See p. 576.)

FOREST SERVICE. (See p. 578.)

SOIL CONSERVATION SERVICE. (See p. 579.)

569

The Agricultural Research Service

The Agricultural Research Service contains some of the oldest services supplied to farmers by their government. This agency, under the administration of the Assistant Secretary for Federal-States Relations, has more than 13,000 employees all over the country and in the territories, who conduct research and administer laws in such fields as agricultural chemistry, animal husbandry, dairy industry, insect control, plant industry, soils, and all kinds of agricultural engineering, such as how to use land in relation to forests and water, and how to plan. It enforces federal regulations to control and eradicate pests and diseases not only on crops, but also on dairy products, and on livestock.

The Service inspects all of our meat, both what is produced by our farmers and what is imported from other countries. It also conducts important research in the fields of nutrition and home economics, including studies of diets and the nutritional values of all foods, food planning, recipes and menus, and regularly publishes the results of its research in home management, labor-saving devices, clothing and textiles, used by homemakers, farmers, and industry.

AGRICULTURAL EXPERIMENT STATIONS The Agricultural Research Service represents the government in the Agricultural Experiment Stations of all the states. These stations, which have had federal support since 1888, conduct research in all sorts of agricultural problems that come up in the types of farming done in each of the states, and give their findings to the farmer directly through the **county agents** (p. 303). You may be familiar with the Experiment Station in your state. If you are not, it is worth seeing. The fields of carefully cultivated crops, the vineyards, the herds of fine cattle, the seedling trees, and the scientific laboratories characteristic of these stations are among the finest in the world. It is here that new seeds are developed and tested, new methods of cultivation tried out, soils tested, and all kinds of breeding experiments carried on. The Experiment Stations are jointly supported by the states and by the Department of Agriculture. Such experiment stations illustrate the American system of state and federal coöperation at its best.

FARMS AND LABORATORIES The Agricultural Research Service operates a number of farms and laboratories of its own. Among these the best known is the great experimental farm at Beltsville, Maryland. Here 12,000 acres are in constant use to learn how agriculture can be improved for the American farmer. Here, too, were first raised the famous Beltsville turkeys that many of us enjoy on Thanksgiving Day. These are smaller turkeys grown in response to consumer demand for birds to fit small ovens, refrigerators, and freezers.

570

Farmer Coöperative Service

The Farmer Coöperative Service is also under the administration of the Assistant Secretary for Federal-States Relations. It makes continuing studies of management, financing, organization, merchandising, and efficiency for the farmer coöperatives. Coöperatives are businesses owned by the farmers who use their services. The system of producer coöperatives gives farmers independence from middlemen who would otherwise have to be used for such services as storing grain and processing milk. Instead, farm members of the coöperatives get these services and share the profits among themselves. The Farmer Coöperative Service is used directly by three out of every five American farmers, since the coöperatives now have 60 percent of them enrolled.

Federal Extension Service

The Federal Extension Service coöperates with county and state agencies in many farm activities. Through this service the county agents make available to the farmers the results of the research done by the Department as well as by state departments of agriculture and the land-grant colleges. These colleges, established by law in 1862, are built on land given to the states by the federal government to provide both general and agricultural higher education for the children of farmers and for others who wish to make farming their vocation, and to carry on research in agriculture. Such famous institutions as Iowa State College at Ames, Iowa, and Michigan State University at East Lansing, Michigan, are land-grant colleges.

One Farmer and the Department of Agriculture

To illustrate some of the many ways in which the American farmer benefits from the services we have discussed, we can take an example of one farmer's problems. Farmer Davis owns 1,000 acres in one of the great farm states of the Middle West. He raises corn, oats, soybeans, and hogs. His annual yield of corn has been falling, to a point where he has become worried about it. He has a talk with his friend the county agent, who advises him that his soil may be losing some of the chemical content best suited for the hybrid seed he has been using. Farmer Davis learns from the county agent that a new hybrid seed has been tested at the state Experiment Station which may be the answer to his problem. Farmer Davis sends a sample of his soil to the Station for analysis and suggestions. The experts at the Experiment Station, after testing the soil, are able to recommend a new seed to him that has recently been developed in another state and has been sent to them for experimental planting by the Agricultural Research Service in Washington. They offer to plant several acres of Farmer Davis's corn land, without charge, to see how it works. In two years' time Farmer Davis is using the new seed in all his fields and getting a better yield than he ever had before.

Now he is having trouble with his hogs; they are not fattening as they should. The county agent advises him to write to the Agricultural Research Service where the division of animal husbandry may be able to help him. From Washington he receives the suggestion that he make a slight change in the diet of his hogs. Scientists in the field of animal husbandry at his state land-grant college have been working on this diet problem for some years. Farmer Davis may find that they have solved it.

When Farmer Davis begins to worry about the erosion of topsoil on one of his hillside fields, he gets help from the Soil Conservation Service, which we shall meet presently. Mrs. Davis, by the way, learned her new recipes for plum preserves and sweet corn pudding from a demonstration at Farmer Williams's home by a representative of the Extension Service. We must not forget Fred, Farmer Davis's twenty-year-old son, who has been learning about farming through the 4-H Club (sponsored by the Extension Service and the state department of agriculture) for ten years and is now a junior at the state land-grant college where he pays only a small tuition.

Marketing and Foreign Agriculture

A second group of functions in the Department of Agriculture is under the administration of the Assistant Secretary for Marketing and Foreign Agriculture. The **Agricultural Marketing Service,** with offices in most larger communities, does research and advises farmers, coöperatives, wholesalers, and processors on prices for commodities, on what is in demand, on the best kind of transportation, on preservation. It generally helps the farmer to distribute the produce of his farms.

The **Commodity Exchange Authority** regulates the grain and produce exchanges in much the same way as the Securities and Exchange Commission regulates the stock markets. At these exchanges wholesalers bid for the purchase of products like wheat, corn, cotton, and thus determine the market prices. The Commodity Exchange Authority protects investors by insuring that the future crops on which they bid will be delivered to them, and that the funds they bid for such crops will be protected. It also acts to prevent dishonest manipulation of prices on farm exchanges by brokers.

The **Foreign Agricultural Service** helps farmers to sell their produce abroad, by giving advice on available markets and helping farmers to prepare the papers necessary for international trade. It also collects data on foreign farming, and represents the Department of Agriculture in foreign relations having to do with agriculture, such as trade agreements on farm products. It does not, however, make foreign policy or send official representatives to international organizations. It only advises the Secretary on such matters.

THE PROBLEM OF PRICE SUPPORT

In recent years the most controversial aspect of American agricultural policy has been price supports. The problem arises from the fact that modern farming produces such huge crops that supply greatly exceeds demand and prices tend to fall. Government payments (subsidies) to farmers keep these prices at an artificially high level. Agitation for such supports by the government became intense in the 1920's when farm prices fell steadily in spite of industrial and financial prosperity elsewhere in the nation. The great depression of 1929 actually began many years earlier on the farms. In the 1930's and 1940's, various acts of legislation, especially the Argicultural Adjustment Act (AAA), committed the national government to maintaining the standard of living of American farmers as evenly as possible with other groups of the American community. A device known as **parity** was worked out to define the prices farmers would need to obtain in order to keep their standard of living stable. The idea of parity is simple. In 1910–1914 the average farmer received enough cash income from such basic crops as wheat, corn, tobacco, peanuts, and cotton to enable him to buy as many of the necessities and luxuries of life as the average man in other occupations. Parity means a high enough price on such crops in today's market to permit the farmer to maintain the same relative standard of living as in the 1910–1914 period.

Congress authorized the Department of Agriculture to keep the prices of certain basic crops up—at parity or near parity—by buying surplus crops which would otherwise have to be sold at less than parity prices. Thus wheat might be supported at 90 percent of parity, corn at 88 percent. That means, the Department buys wheat at 90 percent of the price which would give the farmer parity with the standards of the 1910–1914 period, or lends the farmer sums equal to the price of his crop. These surpluses are stored under government auspices. They accumulate unless or until a market can be found where they can be sold.

In some cases direct cash payments (**subsidies**) to farmers have been authorized without government purchase. That is, the government pays the farmer the difference between the market price he receives for his crops and the support prices established by law. Thus, if the support price of wheat is $2.60 a bushel and the farmer gets $2.40 at the market, the government pays him $.20 a bushel. The law specified that in order to be eligible for such support payments farmers had to limit the number of acres they planted to price-supported crops. Farmers vote annually on this matter in regional balloting conducted by the Agricultural Marketing Service. By this means Congress hoped to avoid overproduction and excessive drain on the treasury, and at the same time to keep market prices up by adjusting production of crops to demand.

573

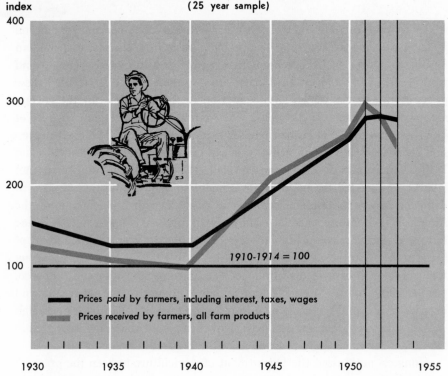

Why Farmers Want "Parity"
(25 year sample)

index

400

300

200

100

1910-1914 = 100

■■■ Prices *paid* by farmers, including interest, taxes, wages

■■■ Prices *received* by farmers, all farm products

1930   1935   1940   1945   1950   1955

The farmers of America can and do produce crops which are so huge that they cannot all be sold. As a result, prices tend to drop. Various laws have been enacted since 1933 to try to protect the farmers against their own overproduction and help them to maintain a standard of living like that of other Americans. For this purpose, the idea of PARITY has been worked out.

In 1914 farmers on the average received enough cash income from such basic crops as wheat, corn, tobacco, peanuts, and cotton to enable them to buy the same proportion of the necessities and luxuries of life as the average man in other occupations. A *parity* price means a price on such crops in today's market high enough to enable farmers to maintain a standard of living comparable to other occupations as in the period 1910–1914.

As the chart suggests, the farmer is more anxious for parity in some periods than in others.

The Special Case of Dairy Products

The Agricultural Adjustment Act of 1933 and subsequent acts also authorize the Secretary of Agriculture to fix the price of milk (hence of other dairy products) under certain circumstances. If the milk producers of an area get together and apply to the Secretary of Agriculture for a marketing order, the Secretary will appoint a Market Administrator for their area ("milkshed"). His salary is paid by the producers, and he negotiates with them and with state authorities, after public hearings, a fixed price to producers for fluid milk.

In 1960 there were more than 50 such milksheds covering most of the big cities and their metropolitan areas. Many states regulate the consumer price of milk as well.

The Farmer and Subsidies

This complex system has satisfied almost no one. Government has accumulated at times huge surpluses for which there has been no suitable outlet. City dwellers feel that they pay taxes to help farmers and pay high prices for food at the same time. Dairy farmers pay high federally supported prices for grain for feed. The farmers object to the restrictions on their enterprise and to the close supervision of their operations.

No one nowadays is prepared to let the American farmer suffer as he did in the 1920's. Nor has anyone come forward with a better solution to the problem. Our friend Farmer Davis finds it hard to decide what to think. He needs parity prices for his corn and hogs in order to maintain his standard of living. Unlike most businessmen but like all other farmers, Farmer Davis is dependent on wind and weather. Since he can never be sure how big a crop he will harvest, he plants as much as he can to protect himself against bad weather and bad years. Thus he does not like to be restricted as to how much he shall plant and what. And he does not wish to be dependent on government "handouts." His is a real dilemma. If he is like a majority of his fellow grain and cattle farmers, however, he will probably tend to favor government price supports when he sees prices for tractors and other farm machinery, as well as household necessities, rising.

Agricultural Stabilization

The price support and crop regulation functions of the Department of Agriculture are administered by the Assistant Secretary for Agricultural Stabilization. Under him are the **Commodity Credit Corporation,** to which are entrusted the federal funds appropriated for support; the **Commodity Stabilization Service,** which administers the funds and the crop control regulations; and the **Federal Crop Insurance Corporation.**

The latter insures the farmer at low cost for the money he has invested in his crops. Farmer Davis, for example, may not have enough money on hand in the spring to buy his seed and hire labor to prepare his land for corn. He borrows what he needs from the bank, and the Federal Crop Insurance Corporation insures him against the risks of loss from pests or from bad weather as his corn matures. If he has, unluckily, a poor crop, at least his loans will be paid at the bank.

Agricultural Credit Services

Farmers have available two very valuable loan services, administered by the Assistant Secretary for Agricultural Credit Services. The **Farmers Home Administration,** carrying out laws dating from 1937, lends money to farmers for the purchase or improvement of "family-size farms" (see chart, p. 569). Farmers who cannot obtain loans from other sources on reasonable terms may get their money from the government through this agency at low rates and

575

for long terms. They may also borrow money for investment in machinery and livestock and for the installation of water systems. The **Rural Electrification Administration** lends money to coöperatives, municipalities, or private business to provide electric power for farms that cannot otherwise be serviced. It also lends money to individual farmers for such improvements as wiring and electrical appliances. Before 1935, when the REA was established, 90 percent of American farms were without electricity. Now more than 90 percent have been supplied.

Between 1935 and 1954, REA was authorized to grant almost three billion dollars in loans, to build almost one and one-half million miles of power lines. No single feature of American agricultural policy has at once been so successful in its results and brought about such immediate and revolutionary improvement of farm life. Farmer Davis, for example, built his new grain silo and his cyclone fence with money borrowed from the Farmers Home Administration. REA brought him electricity back in 1938, not only lighting his home but making it possible to hook up the milking machine he bought in 1948 when farm prices were high above parity. Last year, when Farmer Davis bought his prize bull, he borrowed the money from the **Federal Land Bank** in his district. This bank is one of twelve governed by the **Farm Credit Administration**, an independent agency. **The Federal Land Banks** are run by the government and the farmers in partnership and are entirely owned by farmers.

The States and the Farmers

The heaviest part of the load of setting agricultural policy and supplying agricultural services to our farmers is carried by the Department of Agriculture. But nearly all its activities are supplemented by state departments of agriculture, which administer a large part of state tax money. The states operate their own experimental farms, forests, and laboratories and coöperate with federal projects. They do important work in suppressing plant diseases, controlling and eradicating pests and insects like Japanese beetles and corn borers, preventing hoof-and-mouth disease in cattle, exterminating weeds, and paying bounties for killing predatory animals like wolves and foxes. The states give scholarships to students for higher education at agricultural colleges, conduct fairs at which farmers can display their produce, and assist farmers in finding markets, especially in metropolitan areas. The county governments play their part, as we have suggested, in the combined federal, state, and county agricultural extension systems.

Continuing Problems of American Agriculture

American farmers have received more benefits from government than most other farmers of the world. Nevertheless, our agricultural problems are by no

FARMER IN THE DELL

Justus in *The Minneapolis Star*

means solved. People are still leaving the farm for the city, so that fewer and fewer Americans are following the agricultural way of life. Many farmers who do not wish to leave their farms are forced to do so because they simply cannot make enough money. Surpluses of farm products continue to pile up. The smallest farmers—those who simply try to support their families, or work on someone else's farm for hire—are still too often in a condition of real poverty. Agriculture, in short, presents to you, the citizen of the future, one of the most difficult problems the United States must face. It is to be hoped that through the democratic process we can find solutions as effective and workable as those that are being found for the problems of business and labor.

THE DEPARTMENT OF AGRICULTURE AND CONSERVATION OF NATURAL RESOURCES

The United States today takes justifiable pride in its program for the conservation of natural resources. Until early in the twentieth century, however, Americans probably wasted more of their natural resources than any other nation has done. In the nineteenth century huge forests in the West and Northwest were cut down with no thought of selective cutting or replacing the trees with seedlings or preserving the soil. Lumbermen made quick fortunes in timber and ignored the morrow. Forests were literally stripped bare. Mineral resources were also exploited at a rapid and nearly disastrous rate. The national domain (land owned by the government of the United States) was granted in huge quantities to private enterprisers, who took the riches from it and then moved on. More than 200,000 square miles were granted as subsidies to the railroads in the era of transcontinental expansion. About the only public land that was used in any sensible way was farmland granted to individual farmers under the Homestead Act of 1862. Under this law any farmer could obtain a quarter-section (160 acres) for a $10.00 fee and an agreement to farm and improve the land for five years. This acreage was developed into the great "breadbasket" of the Middle West. But much more land was almost laid waste by men who exploited it without any regard for the public interest.

Forest Service

As public interest in natural resources and the public domain grew, a movement for **conservation** developed to stop the exploitation of the land. President Theodore Roosevelt made conservation the cornerstone of his domestic policy and dramatized the problem for the whole nation by a White House Conference on Conservation in 1901. In 1906 some of the functions of the Agriculture and Interior departments were brought together in the Forest Service, with Gifford Pinchot, a great American conservationist, as chief. Under the leadership of Pinchot and his successors, the Forest Service, now part of the Department of Agriculture, has restored millions of acres by reforestation and water conservation. It manages the vast national forests, which, taken together, cover a territory almost as big as Texas, and regulates their use by the people. The National Forest Service coöperates with the forest services of the various states, by encouraging the states to conserve their own forests and extend them, by providing technical and scientific advice, and by coöperating in the endless task of the Forest Rangers in fighting forest fires. In our time the largest part of our 700,000 square miles of public land is in the national forest preserves and the national parks, which you may have visited.

The conservation of the land and its forests remains controversial. Some people would like to persuade the government to open these lands generally for grazing, timbering, and exploitation of mineral resources. A certain amount of such use is undoubtedly good for the land itself. In fact, grazing to keep down scrub growth is permitted by the Forest Service, as is cutting of timber by private lumber companies to thin out forests. The problem is to avoid past excesses while making constructive use of our public land.

578

Soil Conservation Service

The thoughtless timber stripping of the nineteenth century led to rapid erosion and the disappearance of the topsoil in which crops may be grown. In the twentieth century, poor farming practices added millions more acres to those already seriously eroded. The "dust bowl" of the Southwest resulted in part from drought and wind, but also from poor management of water reserves and poor use of the soil, such as failure to rotate crops. Smaller dust bowls developed all through the country. The efforts of the Department of Agriculture to cope with this problem were united in 1935 in the Soil Conservation Service. Coöperating with the Forest Service, with various agencies of the Department of the Interior, and with the states, this Service has been able to restore much land to fertility and save more from serious damage.

The country is divided, by state soil conservation laws, into almost 2,700 **Soil Conservation Districts** for the convenient management of conservation problems. Land owners of each District elect their chairman from among interested citizens. The work is directed by a team of federal technicians, who advise the residents of the District, and coöperate closely with state foresters and conservationists. These Districts are really "grass roots" efforts of the people and their governments. When Farmer Davis decided to sell his dairy herd, he planted his pasture land to trees. The Soil Conservation District agent, a federal employee, tested his soil for him and recommended that he plant spruce and larch trees. From his state forest service he bought seedling trees, grown in a state forest experimental nursery. His trees are now five years old. The old pasture is a young and vigorous plantation which helps control drainage of his whole farm. In another five years he will have a crop of Christmas trees to sell. Instead of abandoning and wasting his old pasture, as farmers of earlier years might have done, Davis has conserved and improved the natural resources of his farm, and made a good investment as well.

THE DEPARTMENT OF THE INTERIOR
AND CONSERVATION

Much of the basic work both in conserving and in managing our natural resources is done by the Department of the Interior. Headed by the Secretary of the Interior, it is one of the older divisions of the executive branch. It was established as a cabinet-level Department in 1849. It is charged with the development, management, and conservation of the natural resources of the United States, including the reclamation (restoring to fertility) of arid lands, the development of electric power, water supply reserves, and mineral deposits. It is also responsible for "conserving" one of the nation's rich human

Department of the Interior

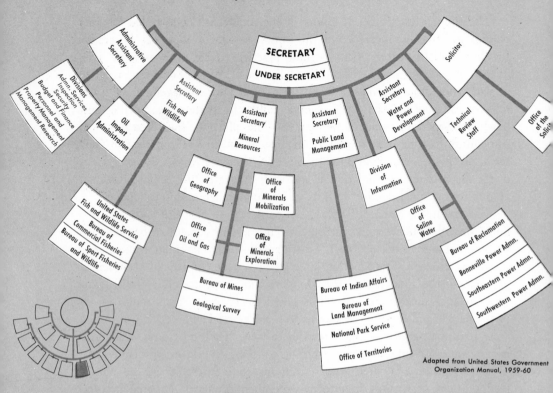

BUREAU OF LAND MANAGEMENT (1946). Director. Responsible for use and management of more than 150,000,000 federally owned acres. Regulates federal lands used by ranchers, administers publicly owned mineral resources. Its purpose is to make the best use in the public interest of renewable resources on public lands. Coöperates with the Forest Service and the Soil Conservation Service of the Department of Agriculture.

BUREAU OF MINES (1910). Director. Conducts research in mining and mineralogy, especially with oil and coal. Makes studies of oil and coal resources. Owns and operates helium plants in Kansas, New Mexico, Texas. Works to promote safe and healthful conditions in the mineral industries.

BUREAU OF RECLAMATION (1923; started as Reclamation Service in 1902). Commissioner. Aim is to transform arid and semi-arid lands, through irrigation, into productive lands. May transmit and sell electricity generated at Bureau projects, provide water for municipal or private use on a repayment basis, reduce flood hazards, and many other activities related to the problems of use of water.

FISH AND WILDLIFE SERVICE (1940). Director. Maintains about 580 field stations, including wildlife refuges, fish culture stations, field laboratories. Works to conserve migratory bird resources. Coöperates with states, with Canada, and with Mexico. Carries on marine fishery program to conserve sea food. Maintains stocks of game fish in national parks and forest preserves and 90 hatcheries.

NATIONAL PARK SERVICE (1916). Director. Promotes and regulates the use of national parks, national monuments, and reservations. Works to preserve historic sites, buildings, and objects of national significance. (See p. 585.)

BUREAU OF INDIAN AFFAIRS (1824). Commissioner. Aids the social, economic, and political advance of Indians and Indian tribes. Works toward the termination of federal supervision and special services. (See pp. 585–586.)

resources—the Indian population. As we saw in Chapter 14, the Interior Department has important responsibilities in governing the territories of the United States.

The Secretary, appointed by the President with the consent of the Senate, serves at the pleasure of the President. He is assisted by an Under Secretary and four Assistant Secretaries. Under them are more than 50,000 employees, working within a series of agencies. The chart on page 580 indicates the great variety of areas dealt with by these agencies.

Secretaries of the Interior have been drawn from various walks of life and have had widely different views about their responsibilities. Extreme examples might be Harold Ickes, who served under President Franklin Roosevelt, and Douglas McKay, who served under President Eisenhower. Both men were devoted to reclamation and conservation. Ickes, however, was a fiery believer in public ownership of electric power and mineral deposits and was committed to the expansion of the public domain. McKay, on the other hand, was committed to a "partnership" theory of the use of national resources—that is, part private ownership and part government. He favored private power development in many cases, and believed that other natural resources, such as grazing lands and timber, ought to be shared more fully with private enterprise.

These examples illustrate the difficulty of the Interior Secretary's position. He must preserve the public domain and develop its resources in the national interest. His policy will depend on his conception of what the national interest is. He must not be an enemy of the economic system of free private enterprise, nor must he dissipate our natural resources under his control by too easy a policy with private business. He must play a major role in the nation's program to provide more and more electric power, and in doing so he must strive to please both the advocates of public power and the advocates of private power. In making the best use of timberlands and mineral deposits, he faces similar problems.

Like so many other important officials, the Secretary of the Interior must be a politician, knowing how to work within the political process, yielding ground here to one group and there to another, compromising as wisely as he can, and holding firm to the principles of reclamation and conservation. Like the Secretaries of Agriculture and Labor, the Secretary of the Interior deals with matters of immediate practical concern to important groups of citizens in areas of strategic importance in national politics, like the Tennessee Valley or the Pacific Northwest. If his policies are successful, he may contribute greatly to the political success of the whole administration, but he may also start political controversies that will result in defeat of his party at the next election.

Bureau of Land Management

The Secretary of the Interior carries out his responsibilities through a number of agencies. The Bureau of Land Management, one of these, though established in 1946, goes back to the 1790's. As the General Land Office in the early years of the country, it was mainly concerned with selling public lands [1] of the western territories to settlers and private citizens. Today, as the chart, p. 580, indicates, its responsibility has grown enormously. In addition, it administers the laws regulating mining and leases mineral deposits to private operators. In its conserving and renewing of the resources on public lands, it coöperates closely with the Forest Service and Soil Conservation Service of the Department of Agriculture.

Bureau of Mines

The Bureau of Mines, as the chart shows, has a wide range of duties having to do with our present and future resources in fuel: oil and coal.

Research by the Bureau of Mines resulted in the discovery of the vast oil deposits in the offshore lands along the Gulf of Mexico. The submerged lands along the coast are often referred to as Tidelands, i.e., land exposed by the receding tide. Actually the offshore lands are permanently submerged, and they extend at some points, particularly along the east coast and in the Gulf of Mexico, for many miles from the coast. These lands constitute the "continental shelf." Control of the lands has been the subject of bitter political controversy. Do they belong to the national domain or to the states they border? While the Supreme Court several times decided that the offshore lands belonged to the nation, the Congress in 1953, under its power to dispose of public lands (see IV, 3, 2, p. 60), passed a law which turned title over the lands to the states with the provision that the title of the states did not extend beyond the original boundaries of the states and did not exceed the three mile limit. The states, in turn, will lease them to private oil companies and will receive the royalties. This law was strongly opposed by conservationists, who preferred federal regulation of oil production in all the offshore lands, and some wished the federal government to apply the royalties to public education. The law does, in fact, provide something of a compromise, since lands beyond the original state boundaries remain in the national domain administered by the Bureau of Land Management, and those lands, particularly in the Gulf of Mexico, are known to be rich in oil deposits.

The results of the researches of the Bureau of Mines are made available both to other government agencies and to private mineral and mining operators. In particular it assists other agencies in maintaining fuel and mineral

[1] Public lands came to the government in three ways: (1) seven of the original states turned them over when the government took on their debts (see p. 348); (2) they were bought (for example, the Louisiana Purchase); (3) the government acquired them by conquest (for example, in the Mexican War).

582

GOVERNMENT HELPS THE FARMER

The Department of Agriculture represents the farmer in government, at the same time serving the rest of the country by improving crops, conserving forests, controlling insect blights, and many other such activities.

The U.S. Forest Service uses a plane to spray DDT to protect Boise (Idaho) National Forest from pine butterflies.

Here a Soil Conservation Service planner works out with a Texas farmer ways to increase his crop yield per acre—by terracing, contour cultivation, rotation of crops, and use of soil-building crops.

reserves for national defense. The Bureau of Mines is also in business for the government. It owns and operates the helium wells and plants at Otis, Kansas, Shiprock, New Mexico, and Amarillo and Exell, Texas. (The supply of helium, the non-flammable gas used in airships, is so small that the national government must control it in order to be sure of an adequate supply for national defense.) Finally, the Bureau of Mines enforces safety regulations in coal mines. Its experts inspect the mines and have power to order safety measures to be taken by the owners, or even to close mines not in a safe condition. The occasional mine disaster we read of in the news is sufficient reminder of how important this work is.

Bureau of Reclamation

If you drive through the valley of central and southern California, you will see a delightful prospect of fruit orchards and extended fields of garden vegetables. If you live in an eastern city, you will eat fruit and vegetables from this valley in the winter season. What you may not realize is that many of these fruits and vegetables are grown on what was once arid desert lands. They have been "reclaimed" by irrigation. It is the United States Bureau of Reclamation which serves us all by working to reclaim our deserts.

Established in 1902, the Bureau of Reclamation differs from the Soil Conservation Service, with which it coöperates. The SCS wants to conserve lands already under cultivation. The Bureau of Reclamation wants to reclaim new land.

The Bureau is today in rather sharp conflict with the Department of Agriculture, which wants to reduce crop acreages in order to reduce surpluses of farm products. The Bureau of Reclamation, working with the Army Corps of Engineers, builds irrigation systems, works out techniques for controlling silt deposits in rivers, builds dams and reservoirs, and takes part in the development of electric power projects at multi-purpose dams. (See chart, p. 580.) The power projects themselves are administered, as we saw in Chapter 21, by other agencies of the Department.

Fish and Wildlife Service

The Fish and Wildlife Service is concerned with the conservation of fish and game. The chart, p. 580, indicates some of its activities in coöperation with states and private citizens, and, with Canada and Mexico, in the conservation of waterfowl. Lovers of wildlife have been interested in recent years in the successful efforts of the Fish and Wildlife Service to preserve the whooping crane from extinction.

The marine fishery program to conserve vital sea food includes administration of the laws respecting the Alaska fisheries and important research into marine life in all waters bordering on the United States. The Service's inland fishery program maintains stocks of game fish in national parks and forest preserves, and assists the states in their fish conservation and recreational programs. The Service strives to conserve American birds not only for their own sake but because they are very important to insect control. It determines the hunting season on all game in federal lands and sets the "bag" you may take.

National Park Service

The National Park Service of the Department of the Interior, established to carry out the National Parks Law of 1916, is concerned with conservation and recreation in parks. It also preserves "historic sites, buildings, and objects of national significance" by maintaining and developing a great many national monuments throughout the country, as well as the White House in Washington, D.C. To do this, it coöperates directly with state, local, and national governments.

The main job of the Park Service is to maintain the great national parks, such as Yellowstone, Yosemite, Grand Teton, and others. As you perhaps know from your vacation automobile trips, these parks contain some of the finest scenic beauty in the country. The Park Service not only conserves their beauty; it also tries to make them more available and pleasant for public recreation. This is a tremendous job. It means building and maintaining roads for automobiles and trail systems for horseback riders and hikers, engineering projects to preserve watercourses and waterfalls, selecting and developing campsites, leasing areas for camping and cabin-dwelling vacationers, and policing both for law enforcement and for fire-watching. Over fifty million Americans make at least some use of the national parks each year. It is good evidence of government efficiency that the parks are so well kept and so pleasant to use. It is a continuing responsibility of the citizen to help the Park Service in every way he can to keep our common property clean and beautiful.

Bureau of Indian Affairs

The relations between the Indian inhabitants of the United States and other Americans have always been complex and, at times, difficult. After the United States was formed under the Constitution, a great many treaties with Indian tribes were negotiated and signed. In most cases these treaties stipulated territory (reservations) which was to remain the sole possession of the tribes, or to be held in trust by the United States for the tribes. Until 1924 Indians remaining on reservations were not citizens of the United States. If, however, an Indian wished to leave the reservation and take up his residence in territory of the United States, he automatically became a citizen and accepted the responsibilities of citizenship.

In 1924 Congress by law naturalized all adult Indians, but exempted them from certain citizen responsibilities such as paying federal taxes so long as they live on the reservations. The United States, for its part, undertook in all the treaties, and by subsequent laws, to protect the Indians against all enemies and to respect the borders of their territories.

The Bureau of Indian Affairs was established as a bureau of the War Department in 1824 and transferred to the Department of the Interior in 1849. The Bureau administers reservations under the Commissioner of Indian Affairs. The chief function of the Bureau is really to make itself unnecessary, either through fostering the assimilation of Indians into the population generally or through encouraging the growth of independence and self-sufficiency of the tribes. Over the decades the load of the Bureau has gradually lightened as it achieved some successes in its purposes. It still performs many important functions, however. On reservations where financial and other resources are inadequate, it maintains schools, health centers, and other services. It assists Indians in learning the techniques of self-government and management. Indians who wish to leave their reservations are helped to find employment and make adjustments in the cities or on the farms. In addition the Bureau provides schools, hospitals, and such services to the Eskimo and Indian populations of Alaska. Their treatment of the American Indians—the original Americans—was for generations a heavy burden on the consciences of sensitive American settlers. Through the work of the Bureau of Indian Affairs we have gone a long way to clear that conscience.

SUMMARY

While American farmers are declining in numbers, their importance to the nation cannot diminish. They are the source of our food supply and of important raw materials for our factories. In this chapter, you have learned how the farmer has managed to gain great influence in political life and has won great benefits from the national and state governments. You should now understand not only what such benefits are but why they are necessary.

You have examined the Department of Agriculture and looked at examples of the many services it performs for farmers. You have seen how complex are the problems of marketing, subsidy, and surplus in the basic crops of agriculture. You should know now what "parity" is and be able to think critically about government's responsibility for the farmer's economic condition.

Next you turned your attention to the great problem of conserving our natural resources in land, water, forests, game, and minerals. You have seen how the Forest and Soil Conservation services work to preserve land and trees, in coöperation with state programs of conservation. In the Department of the

Interior you have met the bureaus which control or regulate many other natural resources, reclaim arid lands, improve irrigation, and produce electric power. You have seen here, once again, examples of the conflict between private business interests and advocates of government ownership and regulation. Thus you should have a sympathetic understanding of the role the Secretary of the Interior must play, as well as of his responsibilities. Finally, you were introduced to the work of the Bureau of Indian Affairs, which tries to "conserve" a great natural resource of human beings.

KNOW WHAT YOU READ

1. In what ways has farming changed during the last century and a half?
2. Why has the number of farmers declined?
3. Through what organizations have the farmers worked to take care of their interests?
4. Outline the section (pp. 568–579) on the Department of Agriculture.
5. Explain: "No other department carries on so many activities for the national government."
6. Summarize the work of the Agricultural Research Service.
7. What activities are carried on at Experiment Stations? How are they supported?
8. What are coöperatives? Who own the coöps? How are they aided by the Farmer Coöperative Service?
9. How does the Extension Service help the farmer?
10. Point out the different ways in which the Davis family was helped by state government.
11. How may the farmer's life and work be affected by each of these?
    (a) Agricultural Marketing Service
    (b) Commodity Exchange Authority
    (c) Foreign Agricultural Service
12. What is the principal reason for the existence of price supports? What effect do supports have on prices?
13. What does the government try to do through *parity?* How is this done? How, for example, could Mr. Davis get money through this system?
14. Mr. Davis and his fellow farmers do not agree on the worth of this system. What do they consider to be its advantages and disadvantages?
15. Your textbook mentions the Commodity Credit Corporation, the Commodity Stabilization Service, and the Federal Crop Insurance Corporation. What do the Davises and other farmers have to do with these agencies of government?
16. For what purposes might Mr. Davis borrow money from the Farmers Home Administration? From the Rural Electrification Administration? Federal Land Bank?

17. Summarize the work and achievements of the REA.
18. Define conservation.
19. What were the principal ways in which our country's natural resources were wasted in the nineteenth century?
20. Summarize the work of the Forest Service.
21. Explain how the wrong farming methods have been bad for our soil resources.
22. What is a Soil Conservation District? How does the Soil Conservation Service work with farmers and ranchers in the Districts?
23. Not all conservationists agree on the part to be played by the government and the part to be played by free private enterprise. Contrast the public ownership theory and the partnership theory.
24. What activities would you have to be carrying on to have any contacts with the Bureau of Land Management?
25. List the responsibilities of the Bureau of Mines.
26. Explain the difference in purpose between the Bureau of Reclamation and the Soil Conservation Service.
27. If you were a sportsman, you would be interested in the Fish and Wild-life Service. Why? Would people who are not sportsmen also be interested in this service? Why?
28. What work must be done by the Park Service to make it possible for millions of Americans to enjoy the national parks each year?
29. Explain why the chief function of the Bureau of Indian Affairs is "to make itself unnecessary." What does the Bureau do for Indians?

WHAT DO YOU THINK?

1. Should the United States government continue to subsidize farmers, or should this practice be dropped? Defend your answer. The cartoon, p. 577, may help your argument.
2. Do you favor public ownership or "partnership" in use of resources?
3. Do you think it a wise policy to allow Indians to become citizens only if they leave the reservation? Why?

PROBLEMS AND PROJECTS FOR YOU

1. Find out from your state department of conservation, or from your state government handbook, or both, what conservation activities are carried on by your state government.
2. Look up in a United States history book the agricultural decline of the 1920's. Explain to the class why agriculture was in a period of depression while other business was good.

3. Interview your county agent to find out the various ways in which he helps farmers. Report to the class.

4. Read the chapter in Dixon and Plischke's *American Government: Basic Documents and Materials* giving examples of the work of the various agencies of the Department of Agriculture. List the agencies mentioned in this chapter and after each write one or two sentences explaining what it does.

5. Write a letter to an editor or a member of Congress on the subject of "parity."

6. Organize a small committee to visit your nearest Experiment Station. The committee should then tell the class the most important and interesting things learned.

7. Why is Gifford Pinchot a man to be remembered? Write a short biographical sketch about him. Stress his achievements.

8. Some of our universities offer programs of study to prepare young men for careers in forestry. If catalogs are available in your guidance office or library, study them to find out what courses a student must take if he wishes to work in one of these fields of specialization.

9. Plan and deliver a report on just how a Soil Conservation District is organized and how it operates.

10. To dramatize the spread between what the housewife pays for food purchased and what the farmer receives for food sold, the Department of Agriculture announced in 1956 that even if the farmer were to give his wheat away, a loaf of bread would still cost the consumer about 14 cents. Why could this be so? Select three well-known foods and list all you can of the items going into the price your family has to pay. This would make a good subject for an original drawing.

11. In November, 1955, the annual session of the National Grange favored:

   (a) the cause of the family farmer
   (b) expansion of "right to work" laws
   (c) economic aid and technical assistance to underdeveloped countries
   (d) support of the United Nations
   (e) trade with Iron Curtain countries—except in strategic materials
   (f) expansion of the federal school milk program

   Explain, in writing, any three of these stands taken by farmers.

EXTEND YOUR VOCABULARY

farm bloc	experiment station	4-H Club
Populist party	farmer coöperative	price support
The Grange	land-grant college	subsidy
Farm Bureau	Federal Extension Service	parity
Farmer's Union	Agricultural Research Service	

support payment	national domain	public ownership
family-size farm	Homestead Act	national interest
Federal Land Bank	exploitation	tidelands
surpluses	crop rotation	helium
conservation	Dust Bowl	reservation
Gifford Pinchot	Soil Conservation Districts	assimilation

YOUR NOTEBOOK: THE GOVERNMENT OF ——

1. Write here the titles of your state government's agencies responsible for (a) agriculture; and (b) conservation. Who is the chief official in each of these agencies?
2. Is there a Soil Conservation District near you? Who are its officials?
3. Who is your county agent?
4. Where is your nearest Experiment Station located? Describe the projects in which it is engaged.
5. What is your nearest college of agriculture? What are its entrance requirements?

READ MORE ABOUT IT

BENEDICT, MURRAY R., *Farm Policies of the United States, 1790–1950*. Twentieth Century Fund, 1953.
The first in a series of three studies of the "farm problem."

BENEDICT, MURRAY R., *Can We Solve the Farm Problem?* Twentieth Century Fund, 1955.
The second scholarly study of a three-part series on the "farm problem."

BENEDICT, MURRAY R., and STINE, OSCAR C., *The Agriculture Commodity Programs*. Twentieth Century Fund, 1956.
The final of the series of three on the "farm problem."

GAUS, JOHN M., and WOLCOTT, LEON O., *Public Administration and the United States Department of Agriculture*. Public Administration Service, 1940.
A classic study.

HARDIN, CHARLES M., *The Politics of Agriculture*. Free Press, 1952.
Emphasizes the politics of agriculture and conservation; of genuine interest for the dedicated student.

UNITED STATES DEPARTMENT OF AGRICULTURE, *Yearbook of Agriculture*. Government Printing Office, published annually.
Indispensable reference books.

VAN DERSAL, WILLIAM R., *The American Land: Its History and Its Uses*. Oxford University Press, 1943.
An interestingly written and attention-holding book.

590

CHAPTER 24

Health, Education, and Welfare

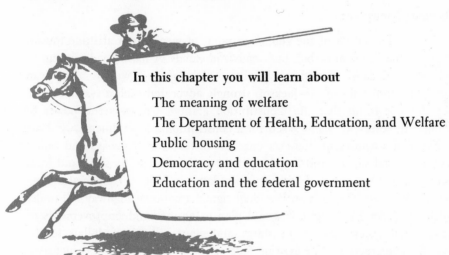

In this chapter you will learn about

The meaning of welfare

The Department of Health, Education, and Welfare

Public housing

Democracy and education

Education and the federal government

When you listen to an American politician making a campaign speech, you are almost certain to hear him say that his party is for the "welfare of all the people." If, for example, you were listening to a Democrat, you might suppose—if you had no experience of politics—that the "welfare of the people" is something only Democrats care about. As soon as you heard a Republican speaker, you would find yourself in a state of great confusion, since the Republican would lead you to suppose that the "welfare of the people" is really the concern only of Republicans.

There is an important point to be learned from this apparent confusion. **Welfare** means the conditions of life under which people live—shelter, clothing, food, health, education, opportunity. Thus any political party must be devoted to the welfare of the people. Parties differ only on the best means to promote the welfare of the people. In the United States there have always been differences of opinion both as to what means are best to promote the welfare of the people and as to what means the Constitution allows.

THE MEANING OF WELFARE

The Preamble to the Constitution sets forth promotion of the "general welfare" as one of the purposes of the Constitution itself. But the Preamble is not a grant of power to the government; it is simply a declaration of principles and aspirations. It does not settle disputes. Congress is granted (I, 8) the power "to provide . . . for the general walfare," by laying taxes on the people. This appears to be a simple statement, but as we have seen (pp. 96–97), it is in fact one of the most continually disputed articles in the Constitution. The issue is still disputed in Congress, between the political parties, and among the citizens generally.

Changing Viewpoint

A good illustration of the change in point of view in our attitude toward welfare is the problem of building roads and canals. A nation-wide system of highways and canals would surely promote the general welfare. American Presidents from Jefferson to Jackson strongly advocated such a system. Since they did not think that the Constitution granted Congress the power to establish it, several of them asked for a constitutional amendment.

No such amendment was ever enacted. Instead our highways and canals were developed slowly, and largely without national plan, by state and local governments. One hundred and fifty years later, in 1956, a Democratic Congress passed and a Republican President signed a national highway bill under which the federal government would plan extensions and improvements of the national system, advise the states, and grant billions of dollars to the states for construction. The existing federal tax on motor fuels was increased to provide the money for the road-building program. No one seriously questioned the constitutionality of the measures involved.

Another example of a changing point of view is education. In 1806, again, the President wished to establish a national university but could not do so because neither he nor Congress could find any authorization in the Constitution for Congress to act in the field of education. One hundred and fifty years later it is taken for granted that the federal government should support the educational system of the whole country. The issue is not *whether* the federal government should support education, but *to what extent* and *in what ways*. In the intervening years many decisions of the Supreme Court have established the increasing powers of Congress to promote the general welfare. And the demands of the people have become increasingly insistent.

Government's Role in Modern Times

In general, the federal government has moved gradually into ever broader welfare measures as the nation grew in size and population, while state and

592

local governments proved less and less adequate to meet the burdens they were once expected to assume. For example, today we expect government to care for the old through old-age pensions; in former times this was a matter for friends and family, if there were friends and family. Welfare used to be an individual matter, with government entering the picture only to protect the individual against unjust treatment by others. Today all of us, through taxes, share the cost of the welfare of everyone. In promoting welfare, the government takes responsibility for such things as the public health, relief of the needy, support of the unemployed, vocational rehabilitation for the injured and handicapped, and treatment of mental disorders.

There are many different opinions on this. Some believe that such government protection may weaken the character of the people. Others maintain that the federal government alone can assure that everyone gets fair and equal treatment, and that therefore more fortunate Americans should be taxed to help those less fortunate. The problem of what kinds of welfare and how much is to be the government's responsibility is likely to be a continuing one. Each citizen will have to decide for himself how much freedom he wishes to exchange for security.

THE DEPARTMENT OF HEALTH, EDUCATION, AND WELFARE

The poverty and human misery of the earlier 1930's focused public attention as never before on the needs of the aged, the handicapped, and the sufferers from disease. With understanding came irresistible demand for action. Congress attempted to meet this demand by passing the Social Security Act of 1935, by expanding the public health service, and by numerous other measures. By 1939, the federal government was carrying on so many health and welfare activities that a special agency had to be set up to bring some of them together. This was known as the Federal Security Agency. In 1953 the Federal Security Agency was joined with certain bureaus of other departments and raised to cabinet level as the Department of Health, Education, and Welfare. The education functions of the Department will be discussed on pp. 611–613, when we consider the whole problem of education. Here we will take up welfare and health responsibilities.

Welfare and Politics

Like other cabinet members, the Secretary of Health, Education, and Welfare is appointed by the President, with approval of the Senate. Unlike the Secretaries of Commerce, Agriculture, and Labor, the Welfare Secretary represents not *one* important group among the American people but *all of us*. He is subject to the innumerable political pressures arising from the many voices of America.

593

Department of Health, Education, and Welfare

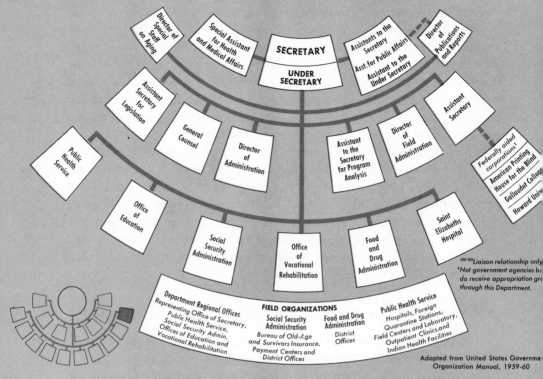

Adapted from United States Governme
Organization Manual, 1959-60

SECRETARY. Under Secretary, Assistant Secretaries.

PUBLIC HEALTH SERVICE (1798). The Surgeon-General is over-all manager. Service includes four bureaus: *Office of the Surgeon-General* (staff services for other bureaus); *Bureau of Medical Services* (services for seamen, Indians; research and aid to states on hospital programs; enforces quarantine regulations covering sea, land, and air traffic); *Bureau of State Services* (grants-in-aid to states for health programs); *National Institutes of Health* (research in causes, prevention, diagnosis, treatment of certain diseases). (See pp. 595–597.)

FOOD AND DRUG ADMINISTRATION (1907). Commissioner. Maintains 36 inspection stations. Inspects factories, tests products; checks drugs, foods, prepared meats, and cosmetics in interstate commerce. Controls issue of new drugs; checks retail drugstores. Conducts many research projects, including study of safeguarding food and drug supplies from atomic, biological, or chemical attack. (See pp. 597–598.)

SOCIAL SECURITY ADMINISTRATION (1946). Commissioner. Administers federal old-age and survivors' insurance, and approves grants to the states for aid to the aged, the blind, the disabled, dependent children. (See pp. 598–600.) Maintains *Bureau of Old-Age and Survivors Insurance* which assigns account numbers to individuals; keeps their records of earnings. (See p. 598.) Also includes the *Children's Bureau* (1912) which gives advisory services and grants to states. Gives special attention to juvenile delinquents, children of migratory workers, mentally retarded children, children in unprotected adoptions. (See pp. 600–601.)

OFFICE OF EDUCATION (1867). Commissioner. Studies education and trends here and abroad; administers grants to the states. (See pp. 612–613.)

Because he is responsible for the health activities of the government, the Secretary must take a position on such questions as health insurance, federal control of major health programs, and federal enforcement of uniform health practices. He must work closely with the medical profession and pay attention not only to its code of ethics and practice but also to its voice as a powerful lobby. He must heed the pressures of unions and other private groups and welfare organizations which may differ from the medical profession and private insurance companies on such matters as government health insurance. He must realize that there are different ideas of health and welfare in various parts of the country where customs and traditions differ, as do financial resources. Because he must advise the President on all questions having to do with health, education, and welfare, he will play a crucial role politically. And in the future he will be more and more concerned with problems of education, as we shall see presently. A controversial problem may have important political implications. This much, at least, is certain: the Secretary of Health, Education, and Welfare will have to be no less a skilled politician than any of his fellow cabinet members.

The chart on p. 594 indicates the size and scope of this newest cabinet department.

The Public Health Service

The Public Health Service, in the Department of Health, Education, and Welfare, is directed by the Surgeon-General of the United States, who is appointed by the President with the consent of the Senate. The Service was established in 1798 to maintain hospitals for the care of American merchant seamen. The chart, p. 594, indicates four of the Services' divisions and their duties.

BUREAU OF MEDICAL SERVICES Today the Service operates 16 hospitals and 25 clinics for seamen, as well as nearly 100 offices where seamen may consult doctors. These hospitals and offices are the responsibility of the Bureau of Medical Services. The Bureau also runs the famous Freedmen's Hospital in Washington, D.C., a general hospital founded originally to care for the health of ex-slaves.

Over the years the responsibilities of the Public Health Service have been steadily increased. One of its important duties is to examine immigrants to the United States and the crews of vessels and aircraft arriving at American ports from foreign countries. It must make sure that all such people are in good health before they are permitted to come into the country, so that communicable diseases, in particular, do not come in with them. You can see the importance of this work immediately if you imagine what would happen in San Francisco or New York if an immigrant family should arrive and be admitted into the city while carrying such plagues as cholera or typhoid fever.

Transportation is so rapid today that an epidemic of influenza in Japan can spread to the United States in a few days, as America learned in 1957. In order to make sure that bubonic plague does not reach the United States, for example, the Public Health Service destroys all rats found on ships entering American ports.

BUREAU OF STATE SERVICES The many programs in which the Public Health Service shares responsibilities with the states, or makes financial grants to the states, are directed by the Bureau of State Services. It advises the states on the best methods of disease prevention and control, public vaccination and inoculation programs, recruitment of medical and administrative personnel, and many other matters. It allocates to the states such funds as Congress may appropriate to support state health programs or national undertakings like polio immunization. The Bureau also represents the Service in coöperative health activities with foreign nations, especially those bordering on the United States and its possessions.

This bureau in coöperation with state health services, also determines quarantine periods for communicable diseases to prevent epidemics, and certifies the purity of the drinking water on trains and airplanes for the same purpose.

NATIONAL INSTITUTES OF HEALTH The Public Health Service includes the several National Institutes of Health. Sponsored by the federal government, but coöperating with state, local, and private groups, these carry on the research struggle against deadly diseases, such as cancer, heart disease, and nervous and mental disorders. Or they do microbiological research (study of germs and bacteria), test and license the sale of serums, vaccines, and certain other drugs, and do research in dentistry.

It is important to emphasize the coöperative nature of the National Institutes of Health. Such a spectacular success as the development of the Salk vaccine against infantile paralysis is an illustration. Dr. Salk himself was a professor in the medical college at the University of Pittsburgh, a private university, and developed the vaccine in the laboratories there. Much of the basic research into the polio viruses was done by members of the Harvard Medical School faculty, also a private institution. The experimental vaccination program involved the coöperation of the Public Health Service, state health departments, and municipal health officers. Production of the vaccine involved private commercial drug producers and federal inspection and licensing. The results of the test program were studied and evaluated by statisticians and physicians at the University of Michigan, a state public university. Serum was allocated to the states by the Public Health Service, allocated to local communities by state health services, and administered in public clinics and schools or by private physicians whose supply of serum was allocated by local health officers.

When you received your polio shots, you probably did not realize how much "government" was involved in making your injection possible. Yet your own case is a good example of government's relation to the public welfare. In the whole process of controlling and preventing disease, the Public Health Service and its National Institutes of Health play a major role. They do not seek to dominate, however, unless the Congress so directs by law or the public interest clearly demands it, as in the case of polio inoculation. Actually the Public Health Service is more likely to be criticized for *not* stepping more authoritatively into a situation than for doing so.

The relation between the nation's health and the national government is often a matter for controversy. The issue sometimes involves proposals of national health insurance. Many different types of insurance have been proposed. In general, one group prefers an extension of private health insurance such as Blue Cross and Blue Shield, while others favor some plan under which citizens would be insured through the national government. While national health insurance is frequently referred to by its enemies as "socialized medicine," there has not been much serious consideration in the United States of such all-inclusive plans as are to be found in England or the Scandinavian countries.

In its 64-million-dollar Clinical Center at Bethesda, Maryland, the Public Health Service does valuable research in serious diseases. There are a 500-bed hospital, extensive laboratories, and other facilities. All patients are volunteers, that is, people who are willing to be subjected to experimentation on the diseases from which they are suffering.

While the ancient dread disease of leprosy is rare in our time in the United States, the Public Health Service cares for those who do contract it, in the National Leprosarium at Carville, Louisiana. There patients are quarantined and treated, and studies are continually made toward improving the methods of control and care. The Service also operates two hospitals for the care of drug addicts.

The Food and Drug Administration

Early in the twentieth century, the United States was deluged with patent medicines. Every conceivable kind of concoction was being sold under labels intended to attract the unwary. People spent millions of dollars on worthless "cures." Although most of these were harmless, some patent drugs could do serious damage. Practically every country town carnival or fair had traveling "medicine men" who would sell you a cure for anything for fifty cents or a dollar. These quacks were colorful and sometimes amusing in their sales talk and advertising, but they cheated the public and kept people in ignorance about medical science. Since state inspection systems were inadequate or non-existent, there was need for federal control and regulation.

597

In 1907, therefore, Congress established the Food and Drug Administration, using the power to regulate interstate commerce as a means of protecting public health. Congress could do this since nearly all foods and drugs are sent across state lines.

Today the Food and Drug Administration, an agency of the Department of Health, Education, and Welfare, checks the production and importation of all drugs, foods, prepared meats, and cosmetics that go into the channels of interstate commerce. Factories are regularly inspected, products are tested in government laboratories, careful labels are required, and offenders are turned over to the Department of Justice for criminal prosecution. We have already seen that the Federal Trade Commission regulates business by enforcing fair trade laws, including honest advertising and honest standards of production. The Department of Agriculture inspects our meat. The Food and Drug Administration rounds out a nearly inclusive federal program to protect American consumers against fraud and against illness from substandard drug and food products.

Under state laws, most city and county governments inspect food which is locally produced and consumed, as we have seen, and maintain standards of sanitation for such places as drugstores and restaurants.

The Social Security Administration

Urgent public demand for greater old-age security and the nagging problem of unemployment led to the passage of the Social Security Act in 1935. This law, several times amended in later years, provided a basic old-age pension system for the United States. Today the pension system is administered by the Social Security Administration of the Department of Health, Education, and Welfare.

In its simplest terms, the social security system means that all workers covered by the law—more than 70,000,000 people are now covered—contribute a small percentage of their salary in wages to a national fund. In 1960, this amounted to 3 percent on the first $4,800 earned. Employers match the contributions of their employees, dollar for dollar, and are responsible under the law for handling all of the paper work and for forwarding to the Treasury the joint contributions of company and worker.

The Treasury deposits the money in a special account, known as the Old Age and Security Trust Fund. However, the records for each individual member of the social security system are kept by the Bureau of Old-Age and Survivors Insurance of the Social Security Administration. With more than 87 percent of all workers members, you can see that the Social Security Administration has a tremendous job of bookkeeping.

Under the terms of the law, when a member becomes eligible for his pension, the Social Security Administration directs the Treasury to pay his

MINIMUM AND MAXIMUM BENEFITS
DERIVING FROM SOCIAL SECURITY LEGISLATION

Monthly Salary	Old Age Benefit	1935	1939	1950	1952	1954	1958
54	Minimum*	$10	$10	$20	$25	$30	$33
399	Maximum*	85	60	80	85	108.50	127
	Family Benefit						
54	Minimum	x	10	15	18.80	30	33
399	Maximum	x	85	150	168.80	200	254

* Paid to retired worker   x Not provided for

Under the original Social Security Act of 1935 and subsequent acts or amendments, the amount of money that a worker can receive for himself and/or his family upon retirement or his death has gradually increased. For instance, in 1935, a worker who retired would receive anywhere from $10 to $85 a month depending upon what his monthly earnings had been and the amount deducted for social security from his pay check. However, nothing was provided in the original act for other dependents. In comparison, a retiring worker, under the 1958 stipulations, would receive anywhere from $33 to $127, again depending upon his monthly earnings before his retirement. In addition to this, he would receive anywhere from $33 to $254 for his dependents. The average pay for a retired worker with no eligible dependents is $66 a month.

monthly retirement benefits. Thus the family of a retired worker over 65 in 1959 received as much as $254 per month or as little as $33, depending on the amount he contributed, whether he was married, and how many dependents he had. If a member dies before retirement age is reached, his savings in social security, as well as the contributions made by his employer over the years, still come to the assistance of his survivors in the form of life insurance. That is, a worker's widow and surviving children are paid monthly benefits so long as the widow survives and the children are under 18 years old.

The responsibility of assisting needy old people who do not receive benefits under the system remains with the states. But the Social Security Administration, under federal law, makes large grants of money to the states for this purpose. The grants are based on statistical records kept by the Social Security Administration showing the needs of the various states according to population. The cost is thus shared by the states and the federal government. In addition, the Social Security Administration makes grants-in-aid (see p. 485) to the states for programs of assistance to the blind and to dependent children.

Some workers do not come under the Social Security Act. Self-employed people, such as doctors and lawyers, and federal employees are not covered, nor are men and women in the armed services. Other systems of pensions or retirement plans do protect some of them. For example, the Railroad Retirement Board, an independent agency, administers extensive federal welfare and retirement benefits for employees of railroad, express, and sleeping-car operations.

PROBLEMS OF WELFARE IN A FREE GOVERNMENT You may ask why so rich and strong a country as the United States should place such an enormous burden of direct "welfare" upon its government. Certainly the founders, whatever their political differences, would have unanimously opposed such an idea as old-age pensions for everybody. Social insurance, "from the cradle to the grave," is the basis of a "welfare state," that is, one in which individual security comes from the government rather than from the individual's own efforts. Such a nation would seem to be in sharp contrast to our tradition of individual responsibility. Yet today almost every leader of both political parties strongly favors the social security program.

There are several important reasons. One is that we have now in the United States a far higher percentage of old people than ever before, and the percentage is growing rapidly. In the census of 1950 more than 7 percent of the population was over 65. Safe estimates are that this figure will increase to 12 or 13 percent in three more decades. In the early years of the nation only a tiny handful lived to be 65 or over. This does not mean, as is sometimes said, that we are becoming an "old people." What it means is that our national age is increasing with the constant improvement of our national health. At any rate, we have now many millions of people too old to work who must be cared for. Local governments have not the financial resources to follow the old practice of sending them to the "county poorhouse." Nor have the states. In any case, only the federal government can insure equality in standard of living for older people.

The social security program is not a "handout" to the aged or the families of workers who die young. It is insurance. That is, the benefits paid are earned during the worker's productive years. People who live on social security income are not "on the government." They are on their own. Thus many people who fear the growth of a welfare state have come to accept the principle of old-age pensions, nationally administered, because the pensions result from the earnings of the people who receive the benefits. A worker who retires on social security is receiving the earned benefits of his years of labor.

CHILDREN'S BUREAU The Children's Bureau was first set up in 1912 to provide advice on problems of child welfare to the states. It was transferred to the new Department of Health, Education, and Welfare in 1953 and is now a part of the Social Security Administration. For many years the Children's Bureau was mainly a research agency, making and publishing studies, about work on child nutrition, educational psychology and methods, psychological and emotional adjustment, and the problems of caring for and training handicapped children. These studies are used by state and local agencies such as schools, health services, and welfare bureaus. Under the Social Security Act the Bureau now administers federal money appropriated by Congress for state programs of aid and care of homeless, dependent, and neglected children. Thus the Bureau is another example of the way the federal government backs up and supports financially welfare programs that remain to a great extent in the hands of the states and of local government.

PUBLIC HOUSING

One of the most important popular demands growing out of the great depression of the 1930's was the demand for government support of the building and purchase of homes. Before the depression, prosperous America had been able to build new homes and replace old ones at a fairly rapid pace. The construction industry has long been looked upon as a sort of "barometer" of the whole economy. If construction is booming, the nation tends to be prosperous. If construction sags, prosperity tends to dwindle. During the depression years, construction slowed down to a walk, homes rapidly deteriorated, slums grew to terrifying proportions, and low-income families were truly desperate for decent housing. Cities and states were much too poor to support programs of new construction and slum clearance. Private building almost disappeared, since most people simply did not have the money to invest in homes. Mortgages lapsed, and banks and loan associations went bankrupt.

The federal government was forced to move into this situation, and did so through a number of new laws. In 1934 Congress passed the National Housing Act and in 1937 the United States Housing Act, among others. Federal money was awarded to cities for slum clearance projects and for building low-cost housing for low-income groups. Private builders and buyers were provided with cheap insurance on their loans to encourage building and buying. Home loan banks and savings associations were reorganized and insured by the federal government. These building and insurance programs helped to improve both quality and quantity of the nation's housing. At the same time, they put hundreds of thousands of people back to work. Like many other government functions of the depression years, public housing was looked upon by many as a temporary expedient and inappropriate under a system of free enterprise. And it was not wholly successful, since in some cases slums were cleared before housing was available for those who had to move, and in other cases even the "low cost" of public housing was more than people could pay.

HEALTH, EDUCATION, AND WELFARE

The scope of the Department of Health, Education, and Welfare indicates a great change in point of view about government responsibility. Grants to states, administered by the Office of Education, go to our schools. The same office studies education here and abroad, and makes information available to educators and others who may be interested.

For research on causes and prevention of diseases, the Public Health Service of the Department maintains National Institutes of Health. Here a complicated electronic device is used in the study of neurological diseases and blindness to trace the central nervous system.

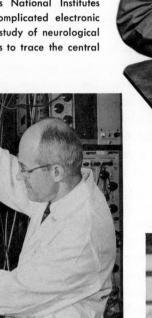

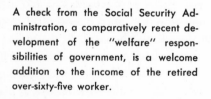

A check from the Social Security Administration, a comparatively recent development of the "welfare" responsibilities of government, is a welcome addition to the income of the retired over-sixty-five worker.

During World War II, very little public or private building of homes was possible. Housing again became run-down and inadequate. To aggravate the situation, the population was rapidly increasing, and there was a heavy influx of defense workers to the cities. After the war, homecoming soldiers wanted homes to come to. When they went away to war, they had perhaps been too young for homes of their own, but now they were older, getting married, and wanted to establish their families. At the same time, communities which had seen their houses deteriorate during the war years were anxious to improve them. Costs were high, however, and many who felt the need for better housing could not afford it.

Aids to Individual Housing Problems

The Veterans' Administration, as we have seen in Chapter 8, was authorized to insure low-interest loans to veterans wishing to build or buy permanent homes. And the Federal Housing Administration (FHA), also an independent agency, continued its program of insuring the mortgages (loans to buy homes, with the home itself as security until the loan is paid off) of non-veterans who wished to build or purchase.

Aids to Community Housing Problems

Under the pressure to provide low-cost government housing, Congress established a permanent Public Housing Administration to make financial grants to communities for slum clearance and low-rent, publicly owned housing units. Thus the government went "into the housing business," as an additional permanent type of welfare activity. The principle involved is still hotly debated. It seems evident, however, that public housing, like old-age pensions, grants to states for unemployment compensation, and other welfare benefits, has become a permanent activity of the federal government.

Housing and Home Finance Agency

In 1947 a number of government activities connected with housing were consolidated in the Housing and Home Finance Agency, an independent agency. The Administrator, appointed by the President with the consent of the Senate, is one of the leading figures in the executive branch. Under him are grouped the various boards and corporations having to do with maintaining the credit and insuring the funds of home loan and savings banks and associations, the Federal Housing Administration, and the Public Housing Administration. In 1955 the Federal Home Loan Bank Board was transferred from the Housing and Home Finance Agency. Under the Board a system of 11 regional Federal Home Loan Banks provides a credit reserve for private savings banks and home-financing institutions where most homeowners borrow money to make their purchase (mortgage).

There are supporters of public housing in both major parties, but it has become evident over the years that the Democratic party is more likely to favor expansion of public housing and the Republican party to stand for greater reliance on private building. The result of this difference is that there is no consistent national policy. As in so many other matters, the political process produces compromise legislation which may not satisfy anyone but assures us that extremes will be avoided.

DEMOCRACY AND EDUCATION

As a student, probably the most direct association you have with government is your own education. Education is by far the largest business of government today. If you are a public school student, you are studying in an institution established by the voters, paid for by the taxpayers, and administered by public officials. If you attend a private school, your institution is in certain important ways independent of government, but it is probably approved by your state department of education, and it is greatly assisted financially by tax exemption.

Education has been a principal concern of American leaders since the first colonies were developed in Massachusetts and Virginia. The New England towns set up schools in which children would be reared in the faith of their fathers and taught reading, writing, arithmetic, and other elementary subjects. For a time in the South, only the children of landowners received education, and there were no publicly supported schools. Public schools in some sections and private schools in others grew with the country. In the age of Jackson and after, Americans began to realize the need for educated and enlightened citizens who could exercise their freedoms wisely. Democracy and education were gradually understood to be inseparable.

The ways and means of providing education remained long in controversy. Even today there is disagreement on the question of how much control of education should be in the hands of government at various levels. Private instruction could not possibly meet the demands of a population both increasing and spreading out to fill a new land. Public, tax-supported schools were the most practical means of providing popular education. During the nineteenth century, common schools, as they were called, were built in thousands of school districts in all of the states. Today about 85 percent of all American children attend free public schools. In the past 75 years public high schools have been opened almost everywhere.

The American educational system grew unevenly. Dependent both for money and for leadership upon themselves, some American communities developed splendid school systems and required all children to be educated.

Others struggled with financial worries and resistance to universal schooling. Some communities very early admitted all children, regardless of race, creed, or color, to common school education and the opportunity for higher education. In others, a separation of children according to color has been traditional. In 1954 the Supreme Court declared segregation unconstitutional. As a result, there has been a trend toward universal, equal, non-segregated education.

Leadership in building a system of public schools came from Horace Mann (1796–1859) in Massachusetts. As secretary to the State Board of Education between 1837 and 1848, Mann established a uniform school year in the districts of Massachusetts, coördinated the curriculum into a state-wide system, paid tax money back to the districts from the state treasury, set up standards for the training of teachers, and established the first public normal school (teacher-training school). Mann's annual reports were read throughout the country and influenced educational developments in other states. No two state educational systems developed in exactly the same way, but that of Massachusetts under Horace Mann's leadership became a typical pattern.

The Public School Systems

The school systems of today have grown up under 50 different state education laws with no national planning or supervision. The basis of the typical system is the local school district itself, that is, the area served by a public school or group of schools.

These local school districts vary in different states. There are the **town** or **township** systems in certain parts of the country, particularly the New England states. In other areas the **district system** is used—quite small in size. Elsewhere, as in southern states, the unit is the **county system.** Sometimes there is a **city system,** though in certain areas it is included in the county system. In recent years there has grown up a **consolidated district system,** by which the states can provide better facilities to large schools located centrally. This sometimes requires students to travel long distances, but it may mean better buildings, equipment, and teachers than could be provided in smaller schools.

School districts are established under laws of the state legislature. Districting is intended to be in proportion to population so that as population grows or shifts, redistricting is often necessary. There is a traditional resistance to redistricting, however, rather like the resistance to reapportionment which we saw in Chapter 5. Nevertheless, the trend is toward larger districts today.

THE LOCAL BOARD OF EDUCATION   Each district is supervised by a board of education. In some cases city, town, or county school boards are elected directly by the people. In others, the boards are appointed by the legislatures. The boards have the power to receive tax money, approve the annual budget,

605

Organization and Purpose of a School District

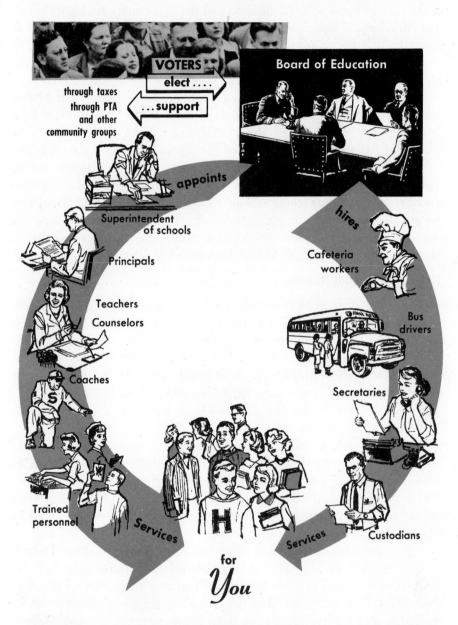

VOTERS elect.... Board of Education

through taxes
through PTA
and other
community groups

...support

appoints

Superintendent
of schools

hires

Principals

Cafeteria
workers

Teachers
Counselors

Bus
drivers

Coaches

Secretaries

Trained
personnel

Custodians

Services

Services

for
You

As used here, a school district means a unit of government which, by state law, is responsible for financing and administering a public school or schools. In most states the district is a special-purpose unit, or special district (see p. 309). In other states the unit may be the town, township, or county. (Delaware has a state-unit system.) Whatever the plan of organization may be, Americans tend to think of schools as local affairs. They wish to keep control of the schools as close to home as possible.

appoint the superintendent, and pass on matters of general policy. Through the boards of education, the people maintain control of their schools. Board actions are subject to state laws.

THE STATE COMMISSIONER AND BOARD OF EDUCATION   Just as the powers of local government are delegated by state laws to the municipalities, so the powers of educational administration are delegated by state law to the local school boards. Each state has a Commissioner, or Superintendent of Public Instruction, as he is sometimes called. He is elected in about thirty states. He is normally responsible to the board of citizens, sometimes called the State Board of Education or the Board of Regents. This Board is often appointed by the governor (32 states); members serve fairly long terms—six to ten years. The Board administers state tax money appropriated for the schools, approves the state educational budget, and generally supervises the entire school system. The State Board usually prescribes the curriculum of studies to be taught in the schools of the state both public and private. In some cases, state legislatures have directed that certain subjects be studied, such as American history or American government. In many states the State Board has other important duties, such as censorship, as we saw in Chapter 10.

The Commissioner is the chief administrative officer of education at the state level. Through his office, standards of teaching, curriculum, hours of study, and examinations are maintained for the whole state. While some states still prescribe textbooks and other teaching material, and all states have the authority to do so, there has been a tendency over the years to leave these matters to the discretion of local boards, administrators, and the teachers themselves.

THE SUPERINTENDENT   School administration is in the hands of professional people who are accountable to the school boards. Thus typically the superintendent is the chief executive officer of a school district. In a few places he is chosen by the school board or appointed by the governor, but in most places, he is elected by the people. He administers the funds, recommends the budget to the school board, recommends the appointment of principals and teachers, and is responsible for the maintenance of buildings and facilities.

Being a school superintendent is not an easy job. Like other important representatives of the people, whether elected or appointed, the superintendent has to deal with countless crosscurrents of opinion and endless individual pressures of citizens. In a single day, he may hear from one group of parents the demand that the children of North High School be forbidden to use automobiles because of accidents, and from another group urging that they be allowed to use them because transportation is so difficult. A little later he may be called on to hear a delegation of his teachers from several schools asking for a salary increase. At a luncheon meeting, he may feel heavy pressure from city officials to reduce his budget for next year, since they

607

are afraid of increasing taxes. When he comes back, the chief engineer may be waiting to tell him that Grade School No. 3 may have to be closed for two days because of a broken water main. At three o'clock, he has to make a speech to the Women's Civic Organization. Later in the afternoon, he has his regular meeting with his staff and the principals of the schools under his administration. At dinner, he is to make still another speech to the annual Parent-Teachers banquet, and later in the evening he may have to testify on various school matters before the Common Council of the city.

THE PRINCIPAL Principals are the chief officers in individual schools and, within their jurisdiction, exercise the same sort of authority as does the superintendent, and sometimes lead equally hectic lives.

Public Higher Education

All the states now maintain institutions of higher education. Some are for training of teachers; others are state universities with colleges of liberal arts and professional schools.

TEACHER-TRAINING COLLEGES In many states, colleges for the training of teachers are supervised by the State Board. In these colleges (formerly called normal schools) certificates are awarded to show the special competence of graduates for teaching in the public schools. This means that in addition to advanced study of the subjects taught in the schools, teachers' colleges provide their students with practice teaching and with instruction in educational methods and educational psychology. Graduates of other colleges and universities are normally expected to do certain additional work of this type in order to qualify for the teacher's certificate. However, many private universities have schools of education which meet the requirements of the states in their curricula.

STATE UNIVERSITIES While higher education in America has always been largely private (some of our private colleges and universities were founded before the Revolution), public demand for free or at least low-cost higher education grew with the growth of the country.

Jefferson conceived of a state university as the top of a pyramid of public education where the most promising youth would be educated for the tasks of democratic leadership. Those who could afford it would pay tuition; those who could not, but who qualified as scholars, should be sent to the university at public expense. At the university, according to Jefferson, would be taught all the "useful sciences." In it would be grouped professional schools to provide the state with its doctors, lawyers, engineers, and scientists. There, too, would be a center for continuing research into all phases of knowledge. From the university new knowledge would be diffused among the people. While Georgia already had a state university, Jefferson's plan for Virginia captured the imagination of the people, and it was widely imitated.

Stimulated by the opportunities available under the land-grant college plan (see p. 571), many states opened state universities in the middle and later nineteenth century. Today every qualified young man or woman has an opportunity to attend a state university at low tuition.

The cost to the student still remains high—too high for many—since it involves for most people travel, room, and board in addition to whatever tuition charges are made. For this reason, many states are extending public school opportunity to the thirteenth and fourteenth grades by establishing community colleges. These are junior colleges so situated as to minimize the costs for young people in their areas. They are usually financed jointly by state government and a local government unit—school board, city, or county. By 1958 there were 377 such colleges in 36 states.

Financing Education

SCHOOLS AND TAXES The largest single source of revenue for the public schools is a real property tax (see p. 499) sometimes called the **school tax**, paid by each property owner of the community. The funds so raised are supplemented by grants from the state treasury based on the number of school districts and the number of pupils in school.

Financing the schools has always been a serious problem. For one thing, the amount of school tax that can be collected has not kept pace with the growth of population. Nearly all communities have had to borrow large sums of money to maintain older buildings and to build new ones. In many cases these communities have reached either the legal limit of their power to borrow (as authorized by state law) or the limit of the voters' willingness to vote the necessary bond issues. In 1959, for example, it was estimated that by 1969 nearly 700,000 new classrooms would be needed to accommodate the vast numbers of new school children coming up with the great increase in population after 1940. At the same time, there is a growing shortage of teachers, largely because salaries are not sufficiently attractive. Thousands more teachers are needed now and for the future, with millions of dollars of increases in salary budgets. Educators and administrators everywhere wonder where the money needed for such expansion of schools and teaching staffs is coming from.

Another very serious aspect of the problem of financing public schools arises from the fact that some states have smaller populations and therefore cannot collect as much tax money from individuals and corporations as can others. This means that the opportunities for children are unequal throughout the country. In 1950, for example, Mississippi spent $85 a year per child on education, while New York spent $324 per pupil. Experience has taught us that equality of opportunity in education is essential to a healthy democracy. Thus most Americans today agree that ways will have to be found to make education equal throughout the country as well as to increase the money available to spend on it.

The American people annually invest about 2 percent of their income in all forms of education. But in order to do a satisfactory job now and for the future, something like 5 percent to 6 percent of income will be required. This means that education is the most pressing problem we face in the middle of the twentieth century. You may yourself have had the experience of going to an overcrowded school, with too little space for comfort, where overworked teachers had so many pupils that they could not give you or others the individual attention you should have had. If you fortunately missed such an experience, you should know that hundreds of thousands of your generation have no other experience of school. This problem must be faced now, but you, as an adult citizen, will find it still plaguing your generation. You will then have to think of what can be done for your own children. How the problem will be solved is still uncertain. But more and more people feel that the states, as we saw in Chapter 11, will have to reorganize their tax laws to permit a better distribution of tax money and to raise more of it.

Many educators (but not all) strongly feel that even the most sensible handling of the problem at the local and state levels will not provide sufficient funds for an adequate school system. Therefore they suggest that a major program of federal financial aid will be necessary. The federal government already assists through the school lunch program, low-interest loans for building schools and college dormitories, and subsidies for vocational education. Some people feel there may have to be a more direct program of financial aid by cash grants to the states, much the way the states now make cash grants to local communities.

COST OF HIGHER EDUCATION Public and private universities and colleges in America have served the people side by side for a long time. Private institutions actually receive substantial assistance from both state and national governments by their exemption from taxes. For example, colleges and universities do not pay real property taxes to their local communities, nor do they pay state or federal taxes on their income, as long as it is used strictly for educational purposes. Tax exemption amounts to a subsidy of vitally important dollars for institutions that otherwise depend upon gifts and student fees for their operation. In addition, some states award scholarships to public school graduates which may be used at either public or private colleges. This means that state funds again come to the assistance of higher private education. The G.I. "Bill of Rights" following World War II and the Korean War enabled thousands of veterans to attend private as well as public universities, and proved to be a substantial form of financial assistance to our private institutions.

610

The financing of higher education both public and private has become more and more difficult in recent years. Great expansion is needed to serve the constantly growing student population. Buildings are costly, and faculty salaries must be high enough to compete with salaries offered by business and other professions. The states have been forced to borrow large sums to maintain and expand their public colleges and universities, and private institutions have turned increasingly to philanthropic foundations for financial support. Such organizations as the Carnegie Corporation of New York, the Ford Foundation, and the General Education Board (Rockefeller) have given millions of dollars for teaching, research, and scholarship programs. Private business and industry are helping too, by gifts and scholarships as they recognize the importance of higher education for the training of scientists, administrators, and civic leaders, as well as a generally informed and enlightened citizenry.

Many educators, both in private and in public higher education, are beginning to feel, with public school educators, that ultimately there must be a federal program of aid to higher education. This will not only help the colleges and universities maintain themselves, but will also give our young people equal opportunities for education. While the college population has more than doubled during the past generation, there are still very large numbers of qualified young people who either cannot afford to finish their education or cannot afford even to go to college at all. Perhaps a federal program of competitive scholarships will eventually be worked out, or a system of grants-in-aid to the states established to meet this pressing need. On the other hand, some people still fear that a federal financial aid program might lead to government interference in education and eventually restrict the freedom of teachers to teach what they think is necessary. We can be sure, therefore, that future steps will be cautiously taken. But the success of state control of universities suggests that federal assistance might eventually be provided without undue interference with the educational process.

EDUCATION AND THE FEDERAL GOVERNMENT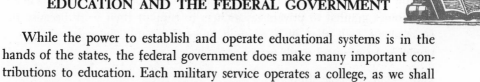

While the power to establish and operate educational systems is in the hands of the states, the federal government does make many important contributions to education. Each military service operates a college, as we shall see in Chapter 27. The Department of State has a graduate school, called the Foreign Service Institute, for members of the Foreign Service. The Department of Agriculture gives advanced training in problems of agricultural science in its graduate school in Washington. The Department of Health,

"YOUR FAULT!"

Fischetti; N E A Service, Inc.

Education, and Welfare maintains special colleges for the blind (American Printing House for the Blind in Louisville, Kentucky) and for deaf-mutes (Gallaudet College in Washington, D.C.), and Howard University for Negroes in Washington, D.C. Many other departments and agencies assist education through research contracts with colleges and universities or by grants-in-aid for research purposes. Examples are the Atomic Energy Commission, Department of Agriculture, Federal Aviation Agency, Public Health Service, Bureau of Standards, TVA, the Weather Bureau, all the military departments, and, of course, the National Science Foundation.

When government agencies make contracts with private researchers, the contracts specify the amounts of money to be paid and the results to be aimed at. These results, whether in the form of formulas, processes, or devices, become the property of the government. On the other hand, grants-in-aid are monies granted to private researchers to support their work because the government feels that such research is in the public interest, whether it produces a successful result or not.

U.S. Office of Education

In the Department of Health, Education, and Welfare is the United States Office of Education, in which are centered most other educational activities of the national government. This Office, under the Commissioner of Education, who is appointed by the President and Senate, was established in 1867 "for the purpose of collecting such statistics and facts as shall show the condition and progress of education in the several States and Territories, and of diffusing such information respecting the organization and management of schools and school systems, and methods of teaching, as shall aid the people of the United States in the establishment and maintenance of efficient school systems, and otherwise promote the cause of education throughout the country." Thus the Office of Education was at first a research and advisory agency, as were so many other government agencies.

Education, as we have seen, has always been a local and state responsibility in the United States, unlike the practice in many foreign countries where a national Minister of Education effectively controls the educational system of the whole country. The Office of Education, therefore, has worked with states, municipalities, and private institutions. Its research work, made available to all educators, helps to develop high standards of teaching and testing and frequently helps to introduce new and improved methods. For example, the Office of Education has adapted tests produced by the military departments to use in secondary schools, including tests of mechanical aptitude, spatial relations, speed of perception, code learning, language usage, word fluency, and mathematical reasoning. By sponsoring national and regional conferences, the Office of Education brings together for the discussion of common problems teachers with different kinds of training from many different schools.

In recent years as the federal government has gradually responded to the calls for federal financial aid to public schools, Congress has given the Office of Education new responsibilities. It now administers, on the basis of grants to the states, funds appropriated for loans for school construction and other funds for the support of vocational and technical training. Under the National Defense Education Act of 1958, it now also administers a small national college scholarship program. In the future, the Office of Education may well increase both in importance and in volume of business if the federal government takes on greater financial responsibility for our schools and colleges.

SUMMARY

In the course of American history our idea of welfare has undergone great changes. Once it was thought to be an individual responsibility. Over the years, however, there have been increasing demands for more welfare services from local and state governments and, in our time, from the federal government itself.

In this chapter you have examined the various ways in which government at all levels promotes the general welfare. You have studied the new federal Department of Health, Education, and Welfare. Here are located the Public Health Service, the Social Security Administration, and the U.S. Office of Education. You have seen the major role in protecting and improving the nation's health which is played by government through the agencies of the Public Health Service and the Food and Drug Administration. You have seen how the growing need for a national retirement plan is met by the social security system, which provides old-age pensions, based on the savings of workers, and assists the states to help the needy aged who are not covered by the system. You have also been introduced to agencies of the Department of Health, Education, and Welfare which help the states in programs of assistance to children, to the blind, and to other handicapped persons.

The problem of housing has also become a major concern of government since the days of the great depression. You have learned how the federal government, through the Federal Housing and Home Finance Agency, helps the states to build low-cost public housing, and helps individuals to build or buy their own homes. Finally, you have studied the American educational system —the biggest business of American governments. The public school system is the responsibility of state and local governments but receives important assistance from the national government through the United States Office of Education. You have learned something of the very serious financial problems facing us as we try to maintain an educational system of both public and private schools and colleges adequate for the needs of a growing population. Democracy and an educated citizenry are inseparable. You should have become aware from your study of this chapter that you will have, as an adult citizen, no more important task than to work with your fellow citizens to expand and improve our schools and colleges and to keep them open to free inquiry in the search for truth.

KNOW WHAT YOU READ

1. What is the meaning of *welfare*? (Note that differing meanings are given in the early pages of this chapter.)
2. Is roadbuilding a responsibility of the federal government or of the states? Whose responsibility was it in Jefferson's day? What important change does this indicate in our ways of thinking about the responsibilities of the federal government?
3. "The issue is not whether the federal government should support education. . . ." What *is* the issue?
4. Explain how our changing idea of responsibility for *welfare* is illustrated by public care for the aged.

5. Welfare can be a political issue. State two differing points of view on the use of federal tax money to support some of the people.
6. The Secretary of the Department of Health, Education, and Welfare is "subject to the innumerable political pressures arising from the many voices of America." Explain.
7. Make an outline showing the *principal agencies* within the Department of Health, Education, and Welfare, and the most important services they perform.
8. In what way did the Public Health Service help in the Salk vaccine program? Explain why this program may be called a *coöperative* one.
9. State two differing ideas on the question of national health insurance.
10. What is unusual about the Clinical Center at Bethesda?
11. Why do we now have *federal* regulation of medicines and drugs? What agency is responsible for this work?
12. As a consumer you are now protected by several agencies of the federal government. Name the agencies and the protections they give you.
13. Many of you have or soon will have your Social Security account number. What is the importance of the social security system to you?
14. Explain why the old-age-and-survivors insurance program (social security) may properly be called *insurance*.
15. Why is the operation of the Children's Bureau a good example of the way in which the federal government makes possible state and local welfare programs?
16. Why did the federal government move into *public* housing activities? How do the major political parties differ on this question?
17. Why do so many people believe that education and democracy are inseparable?
18. It would not be surprising if your community had a Horace Mann School. Why is he so important in the history of education?
19. What are the powers of a local school board?
20. What officials administer the schools of a district?
21. What does each of the following have to do with the public schools: (a) the State Board of Education? (b) the state legislature?
22. Why is the number of public junior colleges increasing?
23. Explain the work of teacher-training colleges. What are state universities?
24. Explain how the public schools are supported.
25. Why is the problem of support expected to grow more difficult?
26. In what ways does the federal government assist the public schools? What are the chief arguments for and against more federal aid?
27. Explain how governments aid higher education by tax policy.
28. Why has the financing of higher education become more difficult in recent years? What help have the colleges and universities received? In what ways might the federal government be asked to help?
29. What was the original purpose of the U.S. Office of Education? What work does the Office carry on today?

WHAT DO YOU THINK?

1. Are you for or against a national health insurance system? Why?
2. Do you believe that the federal government should go further "into the housing business"? Why?
3. Why do you think the building industry is a "barometer" of the economy of our country?
4. What do you think of the proposal that the educational benefits granted to veterans be extended to *all* qualified young Americans?

PROBLEMS AND PROJECTS FOR YOU

1. If you are interested in a career in medicine, you ought to know something about the National Institutes of Health. Report on the most interesting facts you are able to find about any of these institutes. (A limited amount of information about the Institutes can be found in the *Government Organization Manual*.) You may obtain booklets about the Institutes from the Superintendent of Documents.
2. (*debate*) Resolved: That the government of the United States should set up a national system of health insurance.
3. Write a composition on the work done by Dr. Harvey Wiley in the cause of pure food and drugs. Or—write a report on the work of the Food and Drug Administration today.
4. In *Capitol, Courthouse, and City Hall,* read "Shall School Systems Be Independent of Other Government Agencies?" Summarize the arguments pro and con. State your own conclusions.
5. Make a chart showing the government agencies involved in housing.
6. Interview some adults who are Republicans and some who are Democrats, to find out where they stand on public *vs.* private housing. Compare your results with your textbook's statement about party differences.
7. In Commager's *Documents of American History,* read 455 "Pierce vs. Society of the Sisters." What principles were involved. Do you agree with the reasoning of the Court?
8. Another great name in the development of free public education in our country is that of Henry Barnard. Write a composition on the career and contributions of this educator.
9. (*debate*) Resolved: That the federal government should maintain a program of financial aid to education. (The cartoon, p. 612, suggests some of political problems involved.)
10. Make a graph to show how the number of students in the schools has increased since 1945. Or—make a graph to show increasing college enrollments for the same period.
11. Report to the class on those parts of the report of President Truman's Commission on Higher Education (1946–47) which dealt with scholar-

ships and community colleges. See back numbers of the *Reader's Guide* or the pamphlet "Higher Education for Democracy," 1947 (D. C. Heath and Co.). The whole question of federal aid to students is discussed in the August–September 1955 issue of *Congressional Digest*, and in "Report to the President" (1957) of President Eisenhower's Committee on Education Beyond the High School.

12. A New York academy in the 1820's offered Latin, Greek, French, English grammar, criticism, algebra, trigonometry, geometry, engineering, rhetoric, natural philosophy, Euclid, Roman history, Greek history, United States history, surveying, mapping, composition, declamation, and bookkeeping. Compare this program of studies with that of your own school. How do you explain the likenesses and differences?

13. In a speech in 1955, Rear Admiral Rickover (who "built" the first atomic-powered submarine) pointed out to his audience that, "To maintain the present pupil-teacher ratio in the face of heavy population growth, the elementary and high schools will have to enlarge their teaching staffs by 500,000 in the next ten years, yet there is already a present shortage of 140,000 qualified teachers." Why is there such a shortage? What can be done about it? For answers to these questions interview adults in your community. Write an article for your school paper—or local paper—summarizing what you have learned and stating your own views.

14. In *The American High School Today*, James B. Conant maintains that conditions today require larger high schools with graduating classes of at least one hundred students, in order to ensure proper equipment and training. Find out whether there is such a "consolidated" high school in your area. Report on whether you agree or disagree with Mr. Conant's conclusion.

EXTEND YOUR VOCABULARY

welfare
old-age pensions
Federal Security Agency
Bureau of Medical Services
Freedmen's Hospital
Bureau of State Services
National Institutes of Health
Dr. Jonas Salk
vaccination
Clinical Center
National Leprosarium

Food and Drug Administration
pension system
Social Security Act
Old Age and Security Trust
   Fund
slum clearance
public housing
National Housing Act (1934)
United States Housing Act
   (1937)
Federal Housing Administration

Housing and Home Finance
  Agency
Horace Mann
curriculum
town, township system
district system
county system
consolidated district system
board of education
teacher-training colleges

state universities
school tax
G.I. Bill of Rights
Foreign Service Institute
American Printing House for the
  Blind
Gallaudet College
Howard University
U.S. Office of Education

YOUR NOTEBOOK: THE GOVERNMENT OF ——

1. Name your superintendent of schools.
2. How much does your state spend yearly per child on education?
3. Where is your state university located?
4. In your notebook, draw a map of the school district(s) in your community, locating on it every school.

READ MORE ABOUT IT

CONANT, JAMES B., *The American High School Today*. McGraw-Hill, 1959.
   The results of the Conant study of secondary education in the United States.
DAHL, ROBERT A., and LINDBLOM, CHARLES F., *Politics, Economics and Welfare*.
   Harper, 1953.
   A difficult but challenging study.
FOLSOM, MARION B., "Government and the Citizen." *Saturday Review of Literature*, January 17, 1959.
   A Secretary of Health, Education, and Welfare discusses the problems of his
   Department intelligently and readably.
FRIEDLANDER, WALTER A., *Introduction of Social Welfare*. Prentice-Hall, 1955.
   Traces the development of social welfare programs with a description of the
   present system in the United States.
RICKOVER, HYMAN G., "Let's Stop Wasting Our Greatest Resources." *Saturday
   Evening Post*, March 2, 1957.
   Very provocative article on American education.
SWARTHOUT, JOHN M., and BARTLEY, ERNEST R., *Principles and Problems of
   American National Government*. Oxford University Press, 1955. Chap. 25.
UDALL, STEWART L., "Our Education Budget Also Needs Balancing." *The Reporter*, June 25, 1959.
   Plea for a major federal effort to improve our schools, by an energetic Congressman.

618

THINK ABOUT

YOU AND YOUR GOVERNMENT

In the United States, the citizen and his government have a unique relationship. The special facets of that relationship are implied by the Notice of Jury Service used as the document to open this unit, You AND YOUR GOVERNMENT. Such a notice includes your "rights"—those specified by the Constitution, and those added by history and customs. But it also represents your responsibilities or duties—which, if neglected, will make many of the rights meaningless. The Jury Notice is short and simple; its meaning, however, is fundamental and lies deep in our history.

1. As a citizen of the United States you enjoy certain "inalienable rights." List them, with some of the background inspiring the Founding Fathers to include them in the Constitution. In a separate column, list the responsibility or responsibilities which each right gives you.

2. You are a member of a number of different "publics," as you have seen. Sometimes you will find your loyalty divided among these publics—in some cases even directly opposed one to another. How do you reconcile these different loyalties? Take one example and illustrate it fully, giving your steps in reasoning down to your final choice. Try to use something other than a strictly personal illustration—that is, use something that has community significance, if possible.

3. Even before you are able to vote, your United States citizenship requires certain actions from you. After you get the suffrage, certain new duties are added, if you are to take full advantage of that important right. What are these duties? Give specific examples of each general principle you list.

4. In Units II and III, you have studied the formal structure of the various parts of our government. You have also learned about the formal structure of our great political parties. As a citizen you should understand these things. But of even more importance is an understanding of your relation to the various parts of the government and to the parties. Make a list of what you think your relations to government will be (1) if you are a businessman; (2) if you are a college student; (3) if you are a parent; (4) if you are a member of a labor union.

Approval
Not Required.

SELECTIVE SERVICE SYSTEM
ORDER TO REPORT FOR INDUCTION

February 11, 1960
(Date of mailing)

Selective Service System
Local Board No. 50
123 Fourth Street
Centerville

(LOCAL BOARD STAMP)

| 50 | 26 | 42 | 16 |

(Selective Service Numbe

The President of the United States,

To __John__ __Middleton__ __Doe__
(First name) (Middle name or initial) (Last name)

Mailing address __56 Main Street__ __Center__ __Missouri__
(Number and street or R. F. D. route) (County) (State)

__Centerville__
(City, town, or village)
(Zone)

GREETING:

You are hereby ordered for induction into the Armed Forces of the United States, and to

at __Local Induction Center__ of __March__
(Place of reporting) (Month)

at __7:30__ A m., on the __1st__
(Hour of reporting) (Day)

(Member or clerk of Local Bo

for forwarding to an armed forces induction station.

IMPORTANT NOTICE

If you have had previous military service, bring your service records with you. If you wear glass
you. Bring proof of your relationship to the person you claim as a dependent if you intend to apply for

Bring your Social Security Account Number Card with you. If you do not have one, apply at ne
Administration Office.

This Local Board will furnish transportation to the induction station where you will be exam
for service, you will then be inducted into a branch of the Armed Forces. If you are not accepted
will be provided.

Persons reporting to the induction station in some instances are found to have developed di
being examined and may be rejected for these or other reasons. It is well to keep this in mind i
to prevent any undue hardship if you are rejected at the induction station. If you are employe
employer of this notice and of the possibility that you may not be accepted at the induction sta
then be prepared to replace you if you are accepted, or to continue your employment if you a

Willful failure to report promptly at the place specified above and at the hour and on the
violation of the Universal Military Training and Service Act, as amended, and subjects the viola
You must keep this form and bring it with you when you report for induction. Bring with you

If you are so far away from your own Local Board that reporting in compliance wit
hardship and you desire to report to a Local Board in the area in which you are now located
Board and make written request for transfer of your delivery for induction, taking this O

SSS Form No. 252 (Revised 5-23-58)   (Supplies of previous printings shall be used until exhausted)

YOU AND

AMERICA'S

PLACE IN THE

WORLD

Unit IV

CHAPTER *25*

The Meaning and Making of Foreign Policy

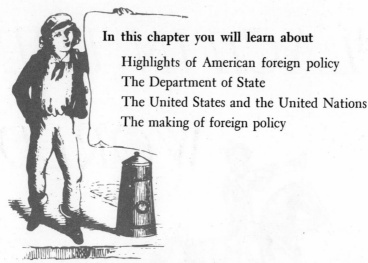

In this chapter you will learn about

Highlights of American foreign policy
The Department of State
The United States and the United Nations
The making of foreign policy

When the Continental Congress declared American independence in July of 1776, they spoke of the "separate and equal station to which the Laws of Nature and of Nature's God entitle" the people of the new United States. These words changed the course of world history, both immediately and in ways that could not have been foreseen. For, among other things, the words meant that henceforth there would be a new sovereign nation trading with foreign nations, making treaties and alliances, becoming involved in wars and striving for peace. The attitude of a nation toward other nations and toward the system used in conducting relations with them is what we mean by **foreign policy.**

Before the Revolution, the foreign affairs of the American colonies were handled by Great Britain and were a part of British foreign policy. As independent states, they had to band together to shape and conduct their own foreign policy. For example, once the Revolution was on, the United States

622

had to make her own arrangements for international trade and finance, and the difficult circumstances of the war required a search for allies.

The Americans sent Benjamin Franklin to Europe as an official representative of the new government, to arrange for loans from European banks, and to secure the military aid of France. That country, because of her rivalry with Britain, signed a treaty with us in 1778. The United States now had belligerent relations with Great Britain, an alliance with France, and commercial relations with such countries as Holland and Spain. She had a foreign policy.

The Americans learned the difference between conduct of foreign affairs in a tyranny and in a free government. The tyrant can direct the foreign policy of his country without consulting anyone unless he chooses. If he is successful, he remains "in the driver's seat." In a free government everyone must somehow or other be consulted. Decisions rest upon consent, much as do laws. Foreign policy is *suggested and executed* at the top. Specific decisions on specific matters at specific times are, of course, made by government officials, but the general lines of foreign policy cannot be decided without solid support of the people all along the line. And the people are free both to disagree and to speak their minds. They must be heeded. Thus from the first the American leaders had not only to grope for wise policies but also to persuade the people to accept them. They had to submit regularly and constantly to criticism and try to compromise the opposing views of important groups and regions.

HIGHLIGHTS OF AMERICAN FOREIGN POLICY

In spite of the advice of George Washington, political parties developed early in our history and disagreed on foreign policy. When John Jay made a treaty with England, people who strongly disapproved burned him in effigy. Alexander Hamilton was stoned in New York when he spoke in defense of the treaty.

The Monroe Doctrine

You may recall that in the early days of the republic we adopted a policy of avoiding permanent commitments in Europe. In the **Monroe Doctrine** (1823), we proclaimed that the independence of nations in the Western Hemisphere was a chief concern of the United States. European nations were told, in effect, to stay out, while Americans pledged themselves not to interfere in Europe. The Monroe Doctrine served as the basis of American foreign policy toward Europe until 1917, and still plays a major part in our thinking about our relations with the rest of the world.

623

World War I

When World War I broke out, President Wilson asked the American people to maintain an attitude of neutrality, but this proved to be impossible. Some Americans favored Germany, more favored France and England, and many others felt we should stay out of the war. In 1917, however, events forced President Wilson to ask Congress to declare war on the Central Powers.

The League of Nations

When the war ended, the President proposed a League of Nations. The League was established and most countries became members. However, public opinion in our country was divided.

President Wilson, knowing that he was dependent upon public opinion to carry out his ideal, stumped the country with a series of speeches trying to "sell" his policy and hoping that public opinion would not only agree with him but exert effective pressure on the Congress. But he failed to keep up good relations with Congress. After months of consideration and debate, the Senate refused to ratify the treaty which would have brought the United States into the League.

The election of 1920, called by Wilson a "great and solemn referendum" on the League, showed that the American people were not ready to throw their full weight behind such an organization as the League.

World War II

While the United States was very prosperous during the 1920's, Europe never entirely recovered from the war. Economic conditions grew worse in central Europe, particularly in Germany. The situation helped the fanatical German nationalist, Hitler, to seize power with a program of German expansion.

NEUTRALITY ACTS By the middle 1930's Germany, Italy, and Japan (known together as the "Axis") were on the march in Asia, Africa, and Europe. In the United States, anti-war opinion ran high. Many Americans felt that we had been drawn into World War I against our best interests. These people persuaded Congress to pass a series of **Neutrality Acts**, intended to prevent our ever getting into a situation in which we would have to fight. They were not favored by President Roosevelt, but they tied his hands in a way that could not have been done under a tyranny. Even his dramatic "quarantine the aggressor" speech in 1937 was not enough to turn the majority in Congress his way.

When war broke out in Europe in 1939, the United States had a "neutrality" policy. The countries fighting against the dictators could get American raw materials (but not war materials) only by sending their ships here and paying cash for the goods. Their enemies had the same privilege.

LEND-LEASE ACT Many Americans, however, felt that the United States should coöperate with the enemies of the Axis. Eventually, the administration was able to get the neutrality laws repealed and new laws passed favoring "all aid short of war." Most extraordinary of these was the Lend-Lease Act. President Roosevelt asked for authority to sell, exchange, or lease to any anti-Axis country any "defense article" or "any other commodity or article for defense." For three months a great debate raged in Congress and in the country. Then, in March, 1941, Congress gave the President the power he requested and the necessary money. The Lend-Lease Act was another one of those complicated democratic compromises we have studied—a kind of middle path between those who favored all-out support of the Allies in the war and those who wanted to stay out. Under the lend-lease policy, we gave billions of dollars in military aid to more than thirty-five countries.

FOUR FREEDOMS At this time, Roosevelt announced the "Four Freedoms" which became the war aims of the free world:

> In the future days which we seek to secure, we look forward to a world founded upon four essential human freedoms.
>
> The first is freedom of speech and expression—everywhere in the world.
>
> The second is freedom of every person to worship God in his own way—everywhere in the world.
>
> The third is freedom from want, which, translated into world terms, means economic understandings which will secure to every nation a healthy peacetime life for its inhabitants—everywhere in the world.
>
> The fourth is freedom from fear, which, translated into world terms, means a world-wide reduction of armaments to such a point and in such a thorough fashion that no nation will be in a position to commit an act of physical aggression against any neighbor—anywhere in the world.

These ideals were not new to the United States. What was new was making them the basis of *foreign* as well as domestic policy.

The Japanese attack on us at Pearl Harbor brought us actively into World War II against the Axis in December, 1941. By 1945, the Axis was beaten.

The Allied victory was disappointing in terms of accomplishing the Four Freedoms, however. The alliance with Russia did not persist in peace. The United Nations, with which we shall deal later, was launched in 1945 on a much stronger base than the League of Nations, and with full United States participation. Nevertheless, it could not prevent the outbreak of several "small" wars and of the Cold War between communism and the free world (see Chapter 26).

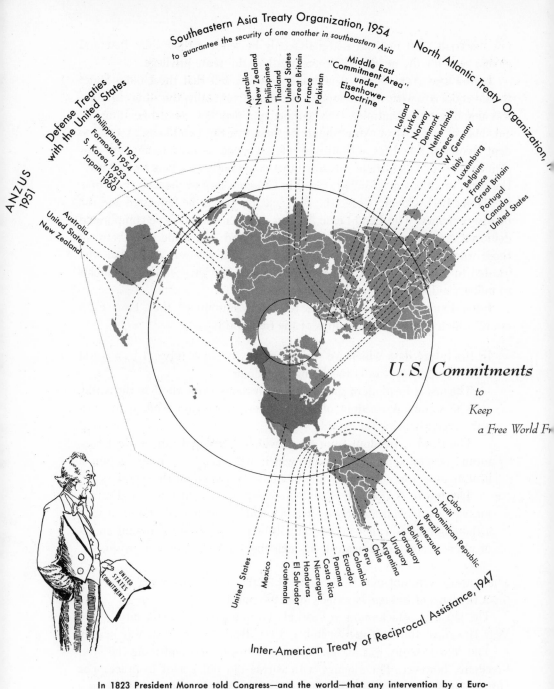

Southeastern Asia Treaty Organization, 1954
to guarantee the security of one another in southeastern Asia

North Atlantic Treaty Organization,

Defense Treaties with the United States

ANZUS 1951

Australia
New Zealand
Philippines
Thailand
United States
Great Britain
France
Pakistan

Middle East "Commitment Area" under Eisenhower Doctrine

Iceland
Turkey
Norway
Denmark
Netherlands
Greece
W. Germany
Italy
Luxemburg
Belgium
France
Great Britain
Portugal
Canada
United States

Philippines, 1951
Formosa, 1954
S. Korea, 1953
Japan, 1951, 1960

Australia
United States
New Zealand

U. S. Commitments

to

Keep

a Free World Fr

Cuba
Haiti
Dominican Republic
Brazil
Venezuela
Bolivia
Paraguay
Uruguay
Argentina
Chile
Peru
Colombia
Ecuador
Panama
Costa Rica
Nicaragua
Honduras
El Salvador
Guatemala
Mexico
United States

UNITED STATES COMMITMENTS

Inter-American Treaty of Reciprocal Assistance, 1947

In 1823 President Monroe told Congress—and the world—that any intervention by a European power to oppress or control the new countries of this hemisphere would be seen as "the manifestation of an unfriendly disposition toward the United States."

In 1947 President Truman told Congress—and the world—that "it must be the policy of the United States to support free peoples who are resisting attempted subjugation" (see p. 627).

This drawing indicates the promises we have made to carry out such policy. As it shows, our commitments are world-wide.

These agreements—along with our leadership in the Korean War, our foreign aid programs, and our continuing policy of working in the United Nations—are all convincing illustrations of our new foreign policy.

United States Postwar Leadership

By 1947 the United States, though war weary and partly disarmed, was forced to move directly to the leadership of the free world. Great Britain was economically exhausted, and in February had to withdraw both troops and financial aid from Greece. This friendly government was under attack by a Communist insurrection, and in great fear of the Soviet Union and Communist Yugoslavia.

THE TRUMAN DOCTRINE   On March 1, the Greek government asked the United States for help. (By this time the Communists were already in control of Hungary, Yugoslavia, Rumania, and Bulgaria—see Chapter 26.) President Harry S. Truman appeared before the Congress to ask support for Greece and Turkey against communism. On this occasion he stated a new policy (called the **Truman Doctrine**) which made the United States a protector of freedom not only for itself but for the world. Contrasting our way of life with that in dictatorships, he said: "I believe that we must assist free peoples to work out their own destinies in their own way."

The President asked Congress to authorize immediately a program of military and economic aid and to appropriate for it a sum of 400 million dollars. Only after two months of discussions, hearings, and debate, however, was the program enacted into law. A little more than a month later (July 26), the money was appropriated. Thus, through the regular legislative process, this important shift in our foreign policy was brought about.

THE MARSHALL PLAN AND POINT FOUR   In 1947, Secretary of State George Marshall proposed to help European nations to raise their production by a plan calling for our giving economic aid in the reconstruction of Europe. Congress voted the money for this European Recovery Program. Two years later, President Truman proposed, as Point Four in his State of the Union Message, that we send American technicians and specialists to help people in underdeveloped lands improve their standards of living. By the Point Four Plan, under the International Coöperation Administration (ICA), American experts have done such things as help farmers in India to increase their yield of wheat, improve sanitation in Iran, and show Arabs in the Middle East how better to conserve water. Today substantial sums of money are loaned to underdeveloped nations through a Development Loan Fund, and in some cases direct grants are made for economic development, such as India's five year plans.

NATO AND SEATO   Meanwhile, it seemed necessary to form military alliances to keep military strength up with the economic strength we were building. Consequently two such treaty organizations were formed: the

North Atlantic Treaty Organization (NATO), formed in 1949, and the Southeast Asia Treaty Organization (SEATO), formed in 1954. For member nations, see illustration, p. 626. Both of these are for **collective security** (that is, mutual defense), as authorized by the Charter of the United Nations.

THE EISENHOWER DOCTRINE In 1956 a brief war, involving the Suez Canal, shocking in its suddenness, broke out between Egypt and Israel, the latter joined by Great Britain and France. In its aftermath, President Eisenhower, in 1957, received the approval of Congress for a further extension of the American policy of protecting freedom and independence against Communist aggression by using military forces against Russian aggression if requested by any nation in the Middle East. Congress voted more funds to carry out this extension of American policy, called the **Eisenhower Doctrine.**

BI-PARTISAN SUPPORT OF AMERICAN POLICY Although there have been some members of both parties who have opposed each extension of our policy as discussed above, there has nevertheless been a substantial amount of agreement. During the Democratic administration of President Truman, Republican leaders Arthur Vandenberg and John Foster Dulles, as advisers to the President, played important roles in the conduct of foreign policy. During the administration of President Eisenhower, Democrats Walter George, Lyndon Johnson, and Adlai Stevenson gave vigorous support to the President. These leaders reflected a great degree of unity among the people.

THE DEPARTMENT OF STATE

When the Constitution was established as the basis of government in 1789, the Secretary of State, whose office was authorized by a law of the First Congress, was given responsibility not only for conducting foreign affairs on behalf of the President, but also for actually acting as the secretary of the government.

By the time of John Adams's administration, the Secretary of State had become not only the senior officer of the cabinet but in the many ways the most important. Because of the developments we have just seen, the office of Secretary of State has grown in scope and responsibility until now it is one of the most influential positions in the world.

The purpose of the Department of State is to advise the President and assist him in his duties as director of our foreign relations. Like all other cabinet-level departments, it both formulates policy and carries it out in the President's name. Thus the Department relieves the President of all but the most important functions of decision-making in the field of foreign affairs. It does not, and cannot, relieve him of responsibility.

The Secretary of State

The Secretary of State, appointed by the President with the consent of the Senate, is, as we have said, the senior officer of the cabinet, ranking next to the President and Vice-President on all ceremonial occasions. The chart, p. 630, shows how complex is the organization of the State Department.

The Secretary of State himself must be chosen more carefully, perhaps, than any other appointed official of the federal government. During the nineteenth century, some Secretaries were little more than party leaders deserving of reward from their party. A few have come to the office with little experience of foreign relations. However, most secretaries, and all recent ones, have been men of mature years and broad experience. Usually they have been lawyers with experience in matters of international law who have, in addition, been long active in various official capacities on behalf of the United States. The responsibilities of the office are so great that only the most level-headed men, skilled in the arts of negotiation and well adjusted to the political process, can expect to succeed.

The Secretary of State must be a man of fine imagination, so that he can at once propose long-range policies to the best interests of the nation and see what their implications for the future may be. Yet he must also have a gift for attending to detail. He cannot, of course, be familiar with every aspect of our innumerable foreign relations, which range from agreements with Canada about wild ducks to alliances for the peace of the world. Nevertheless, his general knowledge must be very great. He must be able quickly to grasp the significance of details brought to his attention by subordinates. He must be a master of both the spoken and the written word. He must be constantly on guard lest his tongue or his pen betray him into a blunder whose repercussions may be felt all over the world. The need for caution is so great that a modern-day Secretary of State feels an unending pressure upon him that could well break the spirit and the health of many men.

The Secretary of State is known everywhere, both for himself and as a symbol of his country. He must therefore be constantly alert to the appearance he makes and the impression he creates. Foreign governments study him for a possible hint or suggestion of how things are faring with the American government.

The Secretary faces not only the world outside, he also faces his own country daily. No public figure save the President himself is so constantly in the news or so constantly under criticism, friendly or unfriendly. His relations with the press, radio, and television, with citizen organizations, with his political party, with the opposition, and with Congress are all crucial both to the welfare of the United States and to the standing of the administration he serves.

Department of State

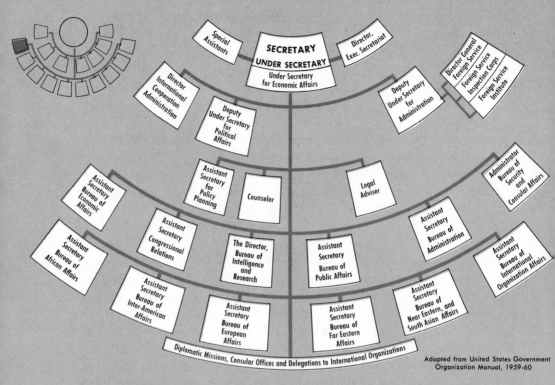

Special Assistants

SECRETARY
UNDER SECRETARY
Under Secretary for Economic Affairs

Director, Exec. Secretariat

Director General Foreign Service
Foreign Service Inspection Corps
Foreign Service Institute

Director International Cooperation Administration

Deputy Under Secretary for Political Affairs

Deputy Under Secretary for Administration

Assistant Secretary for Policy Planning

Counselor

Legal Adviser

Administrator Bureau of Security and Consular Affairs

Assistant Secretary Bureau of Economic Affairs

Assistant Secretary Congressional Relations

The Director, Bureau of Intelligence and Research

Assistant Secretary Bureau of Public Affairs

Assistant Secretary Bureau of Administration

Assistant Secretary Bureau of International Organization Affairs

Assistant Secretary Bureau of African Affairs

Assistant Secretary Bureau of Inter-American Affairs

Assistant Secretary Bureau of European Affairs

Assistant Secretary Bureau of Far Eastern Affairs

Assistant Secretary Bureau of Near Eastern, and South Asian Affairs

Diplomatic Missions, Consular Offices and Delegations to International Organizations

Adapted from United States Government Organization Manual, 1959-60

SECRETARY. President's chief adviser on foreign affairs.

UNDER SECRETARY. Principal deputy.

REGIONAL BUREAUS (Geographical Divisions). Six bureaus, each headed by an Assistant Secretary of State. One bureau deals with United States participation in international organizations. Others are divided into offices, each of which deals with economic matters, and with political and cultural information of a country or a group of countries.

BUREAU OF ECONOMIC AFFAIRS. Under Secretary for Economic Affairs. Director. Works with regional bureaus and policy-making officers of the Department to provide information and advice on economic aspects of foreign relations. Also has responsibilities in economic defense, international transport, and communication.

BUREAU OF SECURITY AND CONSULAR AFFAIRS. Administrator. Directs the security pro-gram of the Department; provides technical direction for the consular program. Includes Passport Office and Visa Office.

INTERNATIONAL COÖPERATION ADMINISTRATION (1955). Director. A semi-autonomous agency within the Department. Coördinates foreign assistance operations; conducts mutual security programs except military assistance. Maintains Operations Mission in most participating countries.

UNITED STATES MISSION TO THE UNITED NATIONS (1945). U.S. Representative to the United Nations and in the Security Council; representatives to the commissions of the United Nations. Carries out instructions of the President in UN affairs. Serves as channel of communication between the Department and the agencies and commissions of the UN. For organization of the United Nations, see pp. 636–643, and chart, p. 639.

630

Just as the burdens and difficulties of the Secretary of State's office are second only to those of the President, so too are the rewards. If he helps to maintain and strengthen the alliance of the free, adds to the list of nations friendly to us, lessens tension among nations, and offers constructive programs appropriate to the responsibilities of the United States as a world leader, he makes a contribution to the welfare of the world as great as are the problems it faces.

The chief assistant of the Secretary of State is the Under Secretary of State, who is normally chosen for the same qualities as the Secretary himself. The chart indicates other officials and their particular areas of duties.

Regional Bureaus (Geographical Divisions)

The chief operating bureaus of the State Department are divided geographically, and their work is coördinated by the Deputy Under Secretary. Each bureau is headed by an Assistant Secretary of State and handles both routine and policy relations of the United States with large foreign areas—Latin America, Europe, the Far East, the Near East, including South Asia and Africa, and the United Nations. Each bureau or division is, in turn, divided into smaller sections (sometimes called **desks**) in Washington to deal with our relations with major individual countries or groups of smaller countries. In the geographical bureaus, starting at the desk level, are hundreds of career officers of the State Department with expert knowledge of the countries with which they work. They deal with all sorts of economic matters such as foreign products that compete with American products, tariff regulations, and trade treaty administration, and collect political and cultural information. In general, their function is to know as much as possible about the countries in which they specialize, so that they can keep the Assistant Secretary in charge of their area always informed and up to date.

Numberless matters are involved in these country-to-country relations. The Bureau of Inter-American Affairs has a Canadian Desk. The officials who work in this office keep in constant touch with Canadian officials in the Canadian Embassy at Washington and with officials in the American Embassy at Ottawa. They read the Canadian press and pay close attention to political and economic developments in Canada. Thus Canadian development of electric power on the Niagara River, Canadian planning for use of the St. Lawrence, and Canadian customs and immigration regulations and policies are the "business" of the Canadian Desk. In such a vast project as development of the St. Lawrence Seaway, the Canadian Desk will obviously have a great concern. Its discussions with Canadian officials and its study of Canadian conditions and public opinion will be used to advise the Assistant Secretary on American policy regarding the project. The Assistant Secretary, in turn, will transmit information and make recommendations to the Under

Secretary and the Secretary. Thus the desk officials of the geographical areas in the State Department provide a basis for many important policy decisions, as well as simply collecting and exchanging detailed information.

The Assistant Secretary of a regional bureau is himself sometimes a career Foreign Service officer who knows his area well from years of first-hand experience abroad. Even if he is a "political" appointee—that is, brought in by the administration from private life—the Secretary and the President are nevertheless careful to choose a man with extensive knowledge of his area.

The Foreign Service

The policy-making officials of the Department of State are served by the geographical bureaus. Perhaps more important to them, however, is the reporting which comes from the Foreign Service itself.

The Foreign Service of the United States offers a career quite different from any other in the government. It is open to any citizen who can qualify by passing oral, written, and physical examinations, passing a security check, and satisfying the interviewing officials that his personality, the depth and breadth of his interests, and his ability to work with people make him a suitable representative of the United States abroad. The level of education required is high, at least the equivalent of a bachelor's degree. If a candidate has no foreign language at the time of his examination, he must learn at least one within a short time after his admission to the Service. Men and women who meet these standards for keen intelligence and attractive personality serve the Department of State at American embassies (under an Ambassador) in 78 countries or legations (under a Minister) in 3 countries.

An embassy is maintained in countries of large size and influence or in smaller countries of special importance to the United States. It is headed by an Ambassador. A legation is maintained in smaller and relatively less important countries and is headed by a Minister.

FOREIGN SERVICE OFFICERS If you were beginning a career as a Foreign Service officer, you would probably serve as a reporter, in Pakistan for example. Through the channels of your mission (the Embassy at Karachi) you would send to the Pakistan Desk in Washington information of all sorts, with emphasis on the political. You would read the daily papers and follow political and cultural periodicals closely, travel a good deal about the country, remember and report conversations with persons from other countries you meet socially, and, in general, keep your eyes and ears open.

In addition, you might act as assistant to one of the higher officials of your mission. You would be introduced, in the course of time, to the procedures of diplomacy, as you worked with your chief in negotiations and in ordinary social intercourse between the United States and the nation to

632

which you were accredited. Your promotion, automatic with satisfactory service, would normally involve your transfer to another country and a new post as a minor official—perhaps a Third Secretary—in another American embassy or legation. Over the years, you would move higher in grade and into more and more important responsibilities.

At the top you might become an Ambassador or a Minister or an Assistant Secretary in Washington. But even if you did not reach the top, there would still be many highly important diplomatic posts which you could, in the normal course, hope to get.

The vast majority of all diplomatic appointments of the United States are drawn from the career Foreign Service. In days when the United States was little concerned with diplomacy and American foreign relations were relatively simple, it was customary to reward political supporters, especially those who made large financial contributions, with ambassadorships. Today such appointments are occasionally made because the cost of living in diplomatic posts has become so great that often only rich men can afford to accept them. (Students of government are generally agreed that our scale of salaries and expense monies for the diplomatic corps is far too low.)

Payment of political debts by appointing wealthy men to such posts has become a handicap to the President and the Secretary of State that is hard to shake off. Experts are needed everywhere, and few people outside the Foreign Service can be expected to have the specialized training and experience necessary to manage well our direct relations with foreign governments. Therefore the present tendency is to try to find less critical positions with which to reward the heavy party contributors, and to appoint more career men (when they can afford it) to top diplomatic positions.

AMBASSADORS AND MINISTERS Ambassadors (Ambassador Extraordinary and Plenipotentiary) and Ministers (Envoy Extraordinary and Minister Plenipotentiary), as heads of American missions abroad, are appointed by the President, often on recommendation of the Secretary of State. Their appointments must be confirmed by the Senate. Ambassadors and Ministers are legal representatives of the President of the United States and speak with the official voice of the American government. They receive, of course, orders and advice from the Department at Washington, or, sometimes, directly from the President himself. They are charged with upholding the dignity of the United States in the country to which they are assigned, and must meet with the Foreign Minister or Chief of State of its government. They look after the interests of American nationals who may be living or traveling there. They attend to a host of detailed matters, from simply delivering official notes and attending diplomatic social functions, to advising Washington on every sort of important development that may be taking place and offering such advice as may be suitable to guide the formation and execution of American policy. They are assisted by a staff of lesser officials which may, in embassies like those at London, Paris, Berlin, or Moscow, be very large. When they are away from their posts, a secretary (called **chargé d'affaires**) takes their place.

ATTACHÉS American embassies and legations include other important officials who are not members of the Foreign Service. There is, for example, a military attaché, an officer whose duty is to observe military developments in the country to which he is assigned and report them both to the Ambassador (or Minister) and to the Joint Chiefs of Staff. Often there is also a naval attaché who has similar duties. Both may act as aides to the Ambassador (or Minister) on ceremonial occasions. Frequently there are an agricultural attaché (see Chap. 23) who is concerned with the international exchange of agricultural information and a commercial attaché representing the interests of American business. Officials of special missions such as those dealing with foreign economic aid (see p. 627) are also frequently attached to embassies or legations.

DIPLOMATIC IMMUNITY Diplomats abroad have what is called **diplomatic immunity.** This means that they are not subject to the laws of the countries to which they are assigned. Embassies and legations are considered as legally the territory of the nations owning them. These customs are recognized by all countries and are part of **international law.** International law also includes agreements made by treaties between nations and agreements to which many nations subscribe, such as freedom to sail on the high seas or to submit international disputes to a world court like the Permanent Court of International Arbitration at The Hague in Holland. The decisions of the United Nations, as we shall presently see, are a new kind of international law. But all international law depends on the voluntary agreements of nations.

Consuls and Consular Service

The immediate needs of Americans abroad are attended to by the Consular Service. Formerly independently organized, this is now a part of the Foreign Service. It maintains consulates in about 190 cities all over the world. The duties of a Consul and his staff are to deal with passports (see Chap. 15), visas (papers permitting entry into foreign nations), financial problems of Americans, legal questions such as the arrest of an American national under foreign law, and a great many routine details. In addition, consulates provide information about the United States and assist foreign nationals to enter and visit this country. If you are traveling abroad and need almost any sort of assistance, you should go to your Consul. He is your official representative in the city where he works.

The Consular Service is administered at Washington by the Administrator of the Bureau of Security and Consular Affairs. His duties also include investigating all Foreign Service personnel with regard to their loyalty to the United States and their reliability in dealing with secret matters. The latter is a very difficult function. A clumsy or over-zealous security official can upset the morale of the whole Foreign Service by poor judgment and unfounded charges.

Foreign Service Institute

The Department of State maintains a specialized graduate school known as the Foreign Service Institute (see p. 611), where advanced courses in the social, political, and economic problems of various areas of the world are given, as well as intensive training in foreign languages. New Foreign Service officials are often sent to the Institute for extended periods of study to prepare themselves for overseas assignments and to help them improve their standing in the Service. Occasionally, Foreign Service officials may be sent to private or state universities for specialized instruction.

Other Divisions of the State Department

The **Office of United Nations Political and Security Affairs,** under the Assistant Secretary of State for International Organization Affairs, provides a channel of communication between the Department of State and our mission to the United Nations at New York or our delegations at meetings of United Nations organizations elsewhere. (See pp. 637–642.) It helps to get personnel, administers the budget, and regularly gives advice on matters in which American delegations to the United Nations may be interested. The permanent Ambassador to the United Nations is directly responsible to the Secretary of State and to the President. He is appointed by the President and represents him at top-level meetings and conferences.

The State Department has a **Bureau of Economic Affairs** which works closely with the geographical bureaus and with the policy-making officers of the Department to provide specialized information and advice on economic aspects of foreign relations. It deals, for example, with such matters relating to our defense as defense allowances, procurement of supplies, raw materials from abroad, transportation of strategic goods, and statistics of world markets. It also advises policy-making officers on such meaty questions as tariff rates and import and export statistics. This bureau is under an Assistant Secretary of State, as is the **Bureau of Public Affairs,** which functions as the Department's agency of public information.

Finally, the Department maintains a **Bureau of Intelligence and Research** under a Special Assistant to the Secretary, whose duty it is to learn as much as possible about foreign countries which those countries may not wish us

635

to know. In this highly difficult and sensitive function, the Department works closely with Army, Navy, and Air Force Intelligence, and with the Central Intelligence Agency (see p. 178), to obtain as much information as possible and to put together what is learned in the most useful forms.

THE UNITED STATES AND THE UNITED NATIONS

Even before victory against Germany and Japan was in sight, the American, British, Russian, and French governments resolved that a new world organization should be formed that would profit from the mistakes made in establishing the League. Several preliminary conferences were held while the war was still going on, and the United Nations was founded in a conference at San Francisco, in September, 1945, shortly after the guns had ceased firing. New York City was chosen as the place for the U.N. Headquarters. On land donated by John D. Rockefeller Jr. on East River, a building was erected to house the U.N. Each member nation contributed proportionately to the cost of the building, but the money was advanced on a loan of 65 million dollars authorized by Congress. The building was opened in 1956.

The United Nations is a federation, as was the League of Nations, but it has far greater power and rests on a firmer foundation of approval in world opinion than did the League. The Charter of the United Nations pledges the member nations to avoid war and to preserve and extend freedom throughout the world. Its two principal bodies are the Security Council and the General Assembly. The Security Council, consisting of eleven nations, is responsible for maintaining peace. The United States, the Soviet Union, Great Britain, France, and China are permanent members of the Security Council, while the other six nations are elected annually from among the other members of the United Nations. The Assembly, which provides a world forum for the discussion of international affairs, is composed of equal representation from each of the member nations.

The Security Council

The Security Council holds at least one official session annually, but, through deputies, it is actually in almost constant session. It receives reports on actual or potential aggression anywhere in the world and decides what action the United Nations should take to put down or prevent such aggression. It has authority to negotiate with opposing parties, to raise armies on behalf of the United Nations, to police aggression, as in the Korean War, and to take any other measures it believes will advance the cause of peace.

Seven votes, five of which must be of permanent members, are necessary for passing any measure. Consequently, the veto power of a permanent member is powerful. This veto power by the permanent members over the Coun-

636

cil's actions and decisions has been the cause of widespread controversy. It was a necessary condition on which certain powers, notably the Soviet Union, would agree to enter the United Nations. In 1945 it seemed of little importance, since the five permanent members were the principal allies in World War II and had a deep common interest in preserving the fruits of their victory. However, the so-called Cold War had set in by 1946 (see Chap. 26), and the veto became a stumbling block to the carrying out of majority policy. It was exercised many times by the Soviet Union (and occasionally by the United States), not only to prevent United Nations action, but to prevent the seating of new member states in the United Nations.

Perhaps because of the veto powers exercised by the Soviet Union, the United Nations is not as strong an instrument for peace as the world had hoped it would be. Meetings of the Security Council have, in fact, often served to dramatize the bitter and perhaps irreconcilable conflicts between communism and freedom. Nevertheless, the Council has had some remarkable successes. For example, it played the chief part in preventing the spread of war in the Middle East during the building of the State of Israel. By its decision (while the Soviet Union had temporarily withdrawn), the United Nations repulsed the aggression of North Korea and China against South Korea. Even when the Council fails, however, it serves the interests of peace and understanding by showing where the fault lies for such failures.

The General Assembly

The General Assembly, on the other hand, has a growing record of success. In its annual debates, all nations have an equal chance to be heard. Under the U.N. Charter, the Assembly has power only to recommend action to the Security Council. If the nations in the General Assembly agree to an important policy, which is then vetoed in the Security Council, there is nothing to prevent the governments of the majority nations from acting to carry out the recommendations of the General Assembly. Thus the Assembly has become increasingly important. It is not yet "the Parliament of Man, the Federation of the World," but it is moving in that direction, without infringing seriously on the legitimate interests of the various member nations.

The United Nations and Cultural and Economic Development

There are several other important bodies attached to the United Nations. The Economic and Social Council deals with economic conditions throughout the world, working in many ways toward solution of trade, production, and distribution problems of world importance. It also works to advance cultural understanding among the nations and to raise the level of civilization. During the early years of the United Nations, the work of the Economic and Social Council was greatly overshadowed by the Security Council and

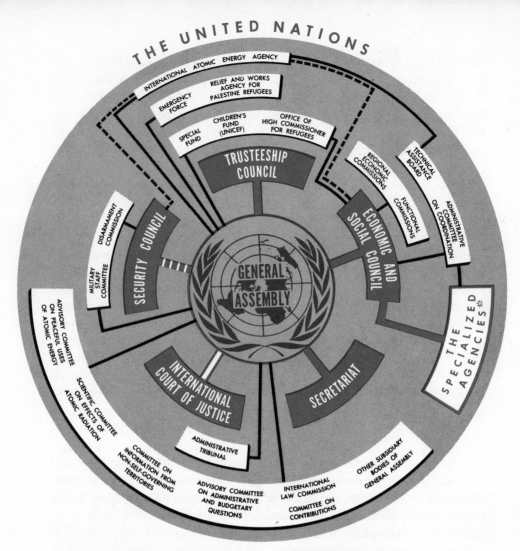

THE UNITED NATIONS

COMMISSION ON TRUSTEESHIP. Responsible for governing territories orphaned by war.

COMMISSIONS ON DISARMAMENT AND ATOMIC ENERGY. Includes peaceful uses of atomic energy. See Atomic Energy Commission, pp. 210–212.

INTERNATIONAL COURT OF JUSTICE (WORLD COURT). Rules on matters of treaties and international law when any branch of the UN requests it.

SPECIALIZED (RELATED) AGENCIES
International Labor Organization (brings labor unions of many nations into contact with one another)

Food and Agriculture Organization

United Nations Educational, Scientific, and Cultural Organization (devoted to interchange of knowledge and culture among nations)

World Health Organization

International Monetary Fund (see p. 642)

International Bank for Reconstructions and Development (World Bank) (see p. 642)

International Finance Corporation

International Civil Aviation Organization

Universal Postal Union

International Telecommunication Union

World Meteorological Organization

Inter-Governmental Maritime Consulate Organization

International Trade Organization (general agreement on tariffs and trade)

International Development Authority (lends money for projects in underdeveloped countries) problems of aggression. But the dream of the founders may yet be realized, and the Economic and Social Council one day become the most important body in the United Nations.

While the United Nations has often meant to the public debates on crucial issues and efforts to police aggression or stop wars, it may be that its work in pooling resources of nations that are well-to-do to assist the less developed and newly emerging nations to reach higher standards of living will be its greatest contribution to peace and to the welfare of mankind.

Officers of the U.N.

The chief administrative officer of the United Nations is the Secretary-General, who is chosen by the Security Council. The Secretary-General and his extensive secretariat administer the decisions and spend the money of the United Nations. They study problems of international tension and make recommendations to the Council and to the Assembly on any sort of international matter they think important. The Secretary-General himself functions as a kind of international "trouble-shooter" to heal international breaches and advance understanding among the nations. It is hard to imagine a more important or more difficult assignment. The whole world is deeply indebted to the wisdom, patience, and skill of the first two Secretaries-General, Trygve Lie of Norway and Dag Hammarskjold of Sweden.

The United States permanent Ambassador to the U.N. is appointed by the President with the consent of the Senate. In this case "permanent" does not mean that he always holds office but that he continues at the pleasure of the President while certain other American delegates may be appointed only for particular purposes. He serves as delegate to the Security Council unless, under special circumstances, the Secretary of State may himself choose to sit, or when he is represented by a deputy during routine sessions. The Ambassador to the United Nations is the administrative head of his mission, like an Ambassador to a foreign government. He maintains close contact with the President and the State Department, and acts as official spokesman for American policy in the United Nations. He normally leads the American delegation at the annual meeting of the General Assembly, and has the duty of making some of the most important policy speeches for the United States before that body.

In meetings of the General Assembly, the Ambassador is assisted by several other delegates, usually chosen from the Congress and from private life. These delegates are appointed by the President with the advice and consent of the Senate. Experts from the Department of State and the office of the Ambassador to the United Nations also assist and advise the delegation. All important matters before the delegation at the Assembly are fully discussed and "cleared" in advance with the President and the Secretary of State.

OUR FOREIGN POLICY AT WORK

Our foreign policy is made up of many elements—and is influenced by many things. In Washington, Secretary of State Herter meets the Foreign Ministers of France, Great Britain, and Germany at the State Department.

In preparation for service in a foreign post, young men take language instruction in the Foreign Service Institute at the State Department. They will be instruments of our foreign policy wherever they are stationed.

Abroad, our foreign policy takes many forms. ICA in Karachi, Pakistan, helps Pakistan with installation of a water and sewage project.

In Russia, we distribute a Russian language magazine, *America Illustrated*, prepared by U.S. Information Service to show a true picture of America. It is here being bought at a news-stand by a Russian woman in Moscow.

A joint Philippine-American malaria control program is carried on at the Institute of Malariology in the Philippines. The laboratory and equipment are financed by government funds provided by the United States.

Feeding children overseas also is part of our foreign policy. Here U.S. surplus wheat is shipped to Tunisia, with posters showing recommended daily portions of bread, cheese, and milk—all products supplied by the United States—written in Arabic.

The International Bank for Reconstruction and Development

Commonly called the World Bank, the International Bank for Reconstruction and Development was established in 1944. At first there were 44 members; by 1958 the number had grown to 68.

The purpose of the World Bank is to lend money to its members for repairing war damage and putting in or improving irrigation systems, for building power plants or modernizing transportation systems. In addition, it tries to encourage private capital to invest in different parts of the world.

The Board of Governors of the Bank consists of one governor from each member nation. It meets once a year. Actually, management of the Bank is carried on by a smaller body of sixteen Directors, appointed by the members, and a president, chosen by the Directors.

From its headquarters in Washington, D.C., the Bank has made over a hundred loans since it was established. The funds it uses (it has a capital of over nine billion dollars) come from the stock of member nations and from bonds. Most of the bonds were issued and sold in the United States.

THE INTERNATIONAL MONETARY FUND   At the same time that the World Bank was set up, under the United Nations, the International Monetary Fund was established. The aim of this fund is to get general agreement among all nations to the value of their currency. This makes world trade easier, because each country knows the exact value of the money of the country with which it wants to do business. Since members of the Fund have agreed not to change the value of their currency until the World Bank agrees to it, the Fund has served to stabilize international trade and has prevented the kind of fluctuations of currency which in the past have made for panics.

EXPORT-IMPORT BANK   An independent agency of the United States government, the Export-Import Bank of Washington, coöperates with these two international loan agencies to aid economic development. Established in 1934, the Bank loans money to facilitate exports and imports between this country and foreign countries, and it encourages the flow of private American capital to stimulate trade.

The United Nations and United States Foreign Policy

Since its establishment in 1945, support of the United Nations has been one of the bases of American foreign policy. The United States, regardless of which political party is in power, is a nation devoted to peace. This was dramatically illustrated by the decision of President Eisenhower to support the U.N. even when it meant opposing the policy of our close friends, Great Britain, France, and Israel, in the Suez crisis (see p. 628). The platforms of both the Republican and Democratic parties regularly pledge support of all measures for peace and support of the United Nations. Today most Americans believe that it is through the United Nations that we can exert leadership most forcefully and effectively, and through the success of the United Nations that we are most likely to achieve the peace and freedom that we so earnestly desire.

Foreign Policy Outside the U.N.

On the other hand, American Presidents realize that so long as communism and democracy divide the world and both are in the United Nations, the United Nations will often be unable to reach solutions satisfactory to the free world. Because of communism, which we shall discuss in the next chapter, some of the most important aspects of our foreign policy must be carried out in more limited groupings, such as NATO and SEATO. (See pp. 627–628 and chart, p. 626.) It is sometimes necessary for the leaders of states or their Foreign Ministers to meet and deal with each other directly, apart from the United Nations. In such matters the basic policy of the United States is not to undertake measures or agreements we would not be willing to defend before the General Assembly. Thus, in spite of its defects and failures, the United Nations remains, in American eyes at least, a great hope of the human race for a better and more civilized world.

As we have seen, American policy is necessarily deeply concerned to maintain good relations with Latin America. At times, we may have given the impression of wishing to boss our Latin-American friends. Many Latin Americans have resented what they called "Yankee imperialism." Nevertheless, we have always stood for the independence of the Latin-American nations. Today, by treaty, the United States strongly supports the Organization of American States (composed of all countries in North and South America), which is devoted to the exchange of information, economic assistance, and mutual defense (see chart, p. 626).

Foreign policy has appropriately been called the "shield of the Republic." Its basic purpose is to protect the safety and further the interests of the United States. As we have seen, it must continue to be defensive so long as aggression threatens anywhere. But in our times there are also unparalleled opportunities for leadership towards human betterment in peace. President Eisenhower, in 1954, opened the way for world collaboration in the peaceful uses of atomic energy (see pp. 210–212). American scholars, teachers, researchers, and students are exchanged with many nations under the Fulbright plan, which is administered by a committee of private citizens in coöperation with the State Department.

Our economic development policy also aims to improve conditions everywhere. Thus, the foreign policy of the American government, through the President, the Department of State, and other agencies, is to provide practical assistance to many nations struggling to achieve both free institutions and better standards of living.

THE MAKING OF FOREIGN POLICY

We have seen what great changes have taken place in the relation between public opinion and foreign policy since the early days of the United States. From preoccupation with purely domestic affairs (such as transportation routes or relations with the Indians), we have become involved in affairs the world over. These changes have brought about the development of a foreign policy which is extremely complex. As a result, the individual citizen could expect neither to understand fully nor, as an individual, to exercise much influence upon foreign policy. He could work through his political party. Experience showed, however, that votes were more easily obtained on domestic issues. Foreign affairs, therefore, seldom played an important part in election campaigns.

Foreign Policy Organizations and the Citizen

A sort of vacuum developed which has been filled in our day by the appearance of organizations specializing in foreign affairs and policy, just as labor unions, farmers' organizations, trade organizations, and other pressure groups specialize in the interests of their members. Such organizations as the Foreign Policy Association, the World Peace Foundation, the Council of Foreign Affairs, and research bodies in the universities and philanthropic foundations represent the interests and ideas of the people. These views are not ignored by officials of government, and often play important parts in the making of policy.

At the same time, business organizations, farm organizations, and labor unions have taken an increasing interest and exert important pressures upon government. For example, the National Grange in its eighty-seventh annual session in 1953 favored donating agricultural surpluses to distressed peoples, international wheat agreements, and reciprocal trade agreements (fixing tariffs at mutually desirable rates). The American Federation of Labor convention of 1953 favored a joint program with Mexico to deal with the problem of Mexican immigration to the United States. The CIO at that time went on record as favoring adequate national security "regardless of cost," and a reasonable balance of military aid and technical and economic aid. Representatives in Congress (especially in the Senate) have found it more and more important to give attention to foreign affairs, both to satisfy their constituents and to influence the executive branch.

Thus the people today speak with many voices on questions of foreign policy. And, as in all other matters of public policy, they have the ultimate "say" as to what the government shall or shall not do. They can most effectively express their views on foreign policy through one or more of these organizations and by writing to their Representative and Senators.

World affairs are no longer remote, and will never be remote again. Our survival as a free nation may depend in our time on the extent to which our citizens are enlightened and wise in supporting or correcting the foreign policy of their government. In this momentous task, we are assisted by extensive foreign correspondence in our daily press, and by radio and television, which give us consistently up-to-date information.

The President's Advisers

We have already seen that many voices are heard and heeded in the making of American foreign policy. It is important to understand what processes, officials, and bodies are involved. The general outlines of foreign policy are laid down by the President, and the most important decisions are made by him. Some Presidents have taken greater personal initiative than others. Franklin Roosevelt was said, for example, to have been "his own Secretary of State." Others have leaned more heavily on the Secretary, as did Harry Truman on George Marshall and Dean Acheson, or Dwight Eisenhower on John Foster Dulles and Christian Herter. But whether the President is a vigorous originator of policy or a "team man," the alternatives proposed to him for decision are the result of a careful and exhaustive process.

NATIONAL SECURITY COUNCIL The President in our time is advised not only by the Department of State but by several other governmental bodies and individual officials. One of the chief among these is the National Security Council. As we saw in Chapter 7, this is an advisory agency of the first importance, concerned with the safety of the United States. Since threats to the safety of the country come from foreign powers, national defense is inevitably tied in with foreign policy. The grand strategy of national defense includes not only the disposition of military forces but also the waging of political warfare, such as we conduct against the ideas of communism through periodicals distributed abroad and through the Voice of America, the official American overseas radio (see p. 215). This strategy must be coördinated with all other aspects of foreign policy. In the National Security Council, the Secretaries of State and Defense, as well as other officials, sit down regularly with the President to discuss problems and advise him. Thus the national security policy, as laid down by the Council and the President, becomes an important part of the foreign policy of the United States.

THE DEPARTMENT OF DEFENSE A second major source of information and advice to the President is the Department of Defense (see Chap. 27). The Secretary of Defense is a member of the National Security Council and through him the views and information of his Department are channeled to the President and the Council. At the specialized, professional military level, other important policy work is done. The President is, you will remember, the commander-in-chief of the armed forces. In this capacity he deals not

only with the Secretary of Defense and the civilian Secretaries of the armed services but also, at his pleasure, with the Joint Chiefs of Staff, the professional heads of the military. The Joint Chiefs, as we shall see, are responsible for all the technical aspects of military administration, but their point of view on defense policy is of vital importance to the country and can have a significant influence on foreign policy in general. Their opinions, for example, on the reliance to be placed on missiles, the proportion of ground troops to air squadrons, or the best location of air bases, are considerations vital to foreign policy. Their views need not be accepted by the civilian authorities, but they cannot safely be ignored.

PRESIDENTIAL OFFICE SPECIAL ADVISERS Within the President's own office there may also be important advisers on foreign policy questions. This is not a duplication of services of the Department of State. The Department is responsible for the actual conduct of American foreign relations. The President, however, needs people close to him who have specialized knowledge of such foreign policy questions as concern him most, and who can serve as channels of quick information from the State Department, the Defense Department, or elsewhere. Such individuals, because they work near the President and, sometimes, because of personal friendship with him, may actually have great influence on the making of foreign policy.

The Secretary of State remains the chief adviser to the President, and normally formulates a great deal of foreign policy himself, on behalf of the President (see pp. 629–630). In arriving at decisions, either for action or for advice to the President, the Secretary has at his disposal all of the services and agencies of his Department, such as those already described. The Bureau of Economic Affairs (see p. 635) and our Ambassadors and Ministers abroad, send

646

"THIS IS BIGGER THAN BOTH OF US"   Yardley in *The Baltimore Sun*

him a steady flow of information and counsel. He himself travels a good deal, meeting Foreign Ministers of other nations and observing conditions in areas of particular importance to the United States.

In addition, the Secretary has a Policy Planning Staff attached to his own office. This consists of experts in foreign policy matters who are also "idea men." They study our existing policy, originate new studies, and prepare memoranda or confer directly with the Secretary and Under Secretary on questions before them. The Policy Planning Staff, with no administrative responsibility, can be free to think, to examine, and to criticize. They only make suggestions to those who determine policy. Since they can be objective toward serious questions, they may have a better perspective than have the more responsible officials who must constantly heed political and international pressures. For example, the policy of "containment," to stem the aggressions of communism after World War II through a system of defensive alliances, was in considerable part worked out by the Policy Planning Staff under George Kennan.

Congress and Foreign Policy

The Congress also plays a very important part in forming foreign policy. Since the conduct of our foreign affairs requires money, the President and the Department of State are dependent upon appropriations by Congress. Thus, though the Constitution gives the President sole responsibility for the conduct of foreign affairs, and the Department of State is established by law to assist him, his policies must be generally satisfactory to Congress. For this reason, both the President, through his staff, and the Department of State maintain close relations with the Committees on Foreign Affairs of both

647

houses. Since members of Congress are close to the people and speak as the people's representatives, the President often finds it useful to consult certain congressional leaders quite regularly. In particular, the chairman of the Senate Foreign Relations Committee is an important figure in making foreign policy.

As we saw in Chapters 5 and 6, the committees of Congress very nearly control legislation, and the chairmen and ranking minority members of the committees are personally very powerful. The public speeches of the chairman of the Senate Foreign Relations Committee, his conversations with other Senators, and his close, day-to-day relations with leading members of the executive branch are of vital importance to foreign policy. The President and the Secretary of State must work with him harmoniously, both to consider his opinions carefully and to secure his approval of major decisions as a chief means of gaining congressional support. The ranking minority member also helps to provide supporting votes from the minority, and he may be chairman himself after a congressional election.

In concrete terms, what this means is that a decision by the President and the Department of State to give American money to friendly nations for military defense or economic improvement, cannot be made unless congressional leaders in foreign policy agree, and the proposal receives the votes of a majority of both houses. This gives the chairman, the ranking minority member of the House Committee on Foreign Affairs, and the leaders of the appropriations committees of both houses an important part in the making of foreign policy. In practice, compromise is often necessary. Foreign policy, as much as any other sort of policy, must be made within the political process. Thus on such a matter as foreign economic aid, one group or party may be very enthusiastic about it, while the other is more skeptical of its value. In that case, a President's recommendation for spending, say, four billion dollars may be scaled down by compromise to three billion in order to get any foreign economic aid at all.

The Constitution requires the consent of the Senate in the making of treaties (contracts binding on nations). Since much of our foreign policy is actually embodied in treaties, the President must watch his relations with the Senate carefully. More than once in our history political differences between the President and the Senate majority have resulted in disaster to our foreign policy. A very serious example of this was the failure of the Senate in 1919 to ratify the treaty which would have joined the United States to the League of Nations, as we saw on p. 624.

In order to avoid this sort of breakdown, more recent Presidents have taken special care to consult leading Senators from the earliest stages of important negotiations and policy decisions. The Senate, for its part, has responded by taking a deeper and better-informed interest in foreign affairs.

The keystones of modern American policy—economic aid to emerging nations, worldwide disarmament, treaties with many countries, defensive alliances with friendly free nations, and American participation in the United Nations itself—have all been established on a firm bi-partisan base, thanks to healthy coöperation between the executive branch and the Senate, as well as to broad support in public opinion. Thus in our time American foreign policy emerges from a process, both technical and political, which gives the fullest possible expression to the will and wisdom of the people.

Considering the state of the world, democratic citizenship has never meant so much. Squarely upon us falls the responsibility of determining by our thoughts and deeds whether our democracy shall be the best or merely the last hope of earth.

SUMMARY

Foreign policy means the attitude a nation takes toward its relations with other countries. At first the United States sought to "be left alone," that is, to avoid entanglements in the troubles of others, to avoid war, and to pursue our own course of liberty and happiness. The course of modern history has made this an impossible ideal. You have seen in this chapter how the United States has developed its foreign policy from isolation to collective security.

Under the Constitution, the President has sole responsibility for the conduct of foreign relations. Assisting him in this immense task is the Department of State, headed by the Secretary of State, the senior executive official of the government next to the President himself. You have studied the functions of the Secretary and the complex Department of State. You have seen how the Secretary is assisted by subordinate officials, by regional divisions which maintain our routine relations with specific countries and areas, and by the Foreign Service, the Consular Service, and other agencies.

The origin, structure, and function of the United Nations has been discussed. Through it, we have continued to develop a foreign policy reaching everywhere in the world.

The making of foreign policy is one of the heaviest burdens of government. You have seen how the President receives advice from the Secretary of State, the National Security Council, advisers in the White House, and from the Congress. You have seen how the Congress itself performs its vital political role in making and supporting our foreign policy, through committees, through appropriations, and through individuals, like the chairman of the Senate Foreign Relations Committee. Foreign policy can no more be "outside" the political process than can any other sort of national policy. Thus you have once more seen politics at work in democratic compromise.

America, once content to be isolated from the struggles and turmoil of the world, has been forced to accept ever greater world responsibilities, and you, as a citizen, must accept your important share in them. The stakes are freedom and survival.

KNOW WHAT YOU READ

1. Define foreign policy. What does it mean?
2. Summarize the beginnings of American foreign policy.
3. What part do we the people play in American foreign policy?
4. Why did the United States refuse to join the League of Nations after World War I?
5. Explain how Congress in the 1930's tried to make certain that we would not be drawn into a war.
6. What important changes in American foreign policy were made in the months between the outbreak of the war in Europe and the Japanese attack on Pearl Harbor (Dec. 7, 1941)?
7. When Great Britain in 1947 was forced to withdraw from Greece, how did President Truman react? What policy resulted?
8. What plans, programs, and agreements show our intention "to support free peoples"?
9. Why is the office of Secretary of State one of the most influential positions in the world?
10. What kind of person does a President usually look for to fill the office of Secretary of State?
11. The Secretary of State is often in the news and is frequently criticized. Why should anyone wish to take such a difficult job?
12. To act as chief advisor to the President and to act for the President, the Secretary of State must possess a great deal of information. From what sources does he obtain the needed information?
13. Who are the "high level" officials who assist the Secretary of State?
14. What are the *geographical divisions* of the State Department? What is their work?
15. What are some of the standards required for a career in the Foreign Service? What types of experience might a new member of the service expect to have?
16. Why have diplomatic appointments often been made from outside the Foreign Service?
17. What are the responsibilities of a United States Ambassador or Minister?
18. What services do attachés perform for Americans? Consuls?
19. Explain *diplomatic immunity*.
20. What officials make up the National Security Council? Summarize the work of the council.
21. Outline the organization of the United Nations.

650

22. What is the work of (a) the General Assembly; (b) the Security Council? In what ways has the General Assembly increased in importance?
23. How has the record of the U. N. been affected by abuse of the veto power?
24. List the principal agencies attached to the United Nations.
25. The work of the Secretary General is both important and difficult. Explain why this is so.
26. What is the work of our Ambassador to the United Nations?
27. Explain our relation to the United Nations.
28. What is the purpose of the World Bank? How does the International Monetary Fund aid world trade?
29. What is our policy toward Latin America?
30. How is our country now coöperating for peace with other countries?
31. Why is it so difficult for us as individual citizens to understand foreign policy and to influence foreign policy? How may we do both?

WHAT DO YOU THINK?

1. Do you think that the United Nations can keep the peace if nations maintain their sovereignty?
2. Is the Truman Doctrine an extension of the Monroe Doctrine, or a reversal of it? Explain your answer.
3. Should the post of Ambassador be given to a career diplomat, a specialist in a given area, or to a wealthy man who has been useful politically to the President? Explain.
4. What is the important point of the cartoon, pp. 646–647?

PROBLEMS AND PROJECTS FOR YOU

1. Read Washington's Farewell Address. To what extent is the United States following Washington's advice today? Present a panel discussion of this question, or write your opinion in the form of an editorial.
2. Consult one of your school's American history textbooks for a review of the development of American foreign policy from the Revolution to World War I. Outline these developments.
3. What do the publics which are interested in foreign policy want?
4. You have heard of the Monroe Doctrine, but do you know what the doctrine really was in the beginning? Exactly what did the President say in this message to Congress? Write out the exact words of the principal points of the message.
5. Report to the class on the divisions of opinion among our people on the subject of our relationships to World War I and World War II.

6. Shortly after World War II a poll taken in Cincinnati showed that a very small percentage of the voters had even a reasonably good idea of what the United Nations is. How do you explain this lack of information?
7. Name two outstanding Secretaries of State in recent American history and tell for what each was distinguished.
8. Report to the class on the work of any one of the bureaus of the State Department.
9. Military leaders, after retiring from office, have been known to complain that American foreign policy is influenced by other than military considerations. Why, under our form of government, is this to be expected?
10. Investigate and report on the growing importance of the General Assembly.
11. Report to the class on the work of any one of these organizations: UNESCO, The International Labor Organization, The World Health Organization, or The Food and Agriculture Organization.
12. Would you like to be an ambassador? For some idea of his daily work, consult the *Life and Letters of Walter Hines Page*, Vol. I, pp. 159–60.
13. Make a collection of editorials to help you to determine the foreign policy views of a newspaper or newspapers serving your community.
14. In this year's session of Congress, how much foreign aid did the President request? Is this too much or too little? Explain your answer.
15. Make a poster favoring, or opposing, the work of the United Nations.
16. Make a diagram to show the organization of a "geographical division."

EXTEND YOUR VOCABULARY

foreign policy	legation
Monroe Doctrine	ambassador
Western Hemisphere	minister
neutrality	chargé d'affaires
Neutrality Acts	attaché
Lend-Lease Act	diplomatic immunity
Four Freedoms	international law
Cold War	Permanent Court of International Arbitration
Truman Doctrine	consul
Marshall Plan	consular service
Point Four Program	passport
NATO	visa
SEATO	National Security Council
collective security	Economic and Social Council
geographical division	UNESCO
"desk"	WHO
Foreign Service	ILO
embassy	FAO

Commission on Trusteeship	International Monetary Fund
Trygve Lie	Organization of American States
Dag Hammarskjold	Joint Chiefs of Staff
International Bank for Reconstruction	Policy Planning Staff

YOUR NOTEBOOK: THE GOVERNMENT OF ——

1. On one page of your notebook, list all the organizations of your community which have views on foreign policy.
2. Here is an incomplete list of organizations which may be represented in your community: AFL-CIO, American Legion, Grange, VFW, League of Women Voters.
   (a) Complete this list.
   (b) After the name of each organization, write a brief statement of the foreign policy views of the organization.
3. Write in your notebook the names of your two U.S. Senators and your Representative in Congress. After each name, write a brief statement of what each stands for in foreign policy.

READ MORE ABOUT IT

ACHESON, DEAN, "The Illusion of Disengagement." *Foreign Affairs*, April, 1958.
Provocative analysis by a former Secretary of State.

BURNS, JAMES M., and PELTASON, JACK W., *Government by the People*. Prentice-Hall, 1954. Chaps. 21–22.

DAHL, ROBERT A., *Congress and Foreign Policy*. Harcourt, Brace, 1950.
Useful and unique.

KENNAN, GEORGE F., *American Diplomacy, 1900–1950*. University of Chicago Press, 1951.
Standard survey of our foreign policy.

KENNAN, GEORGE F., "A Chance to Withdraw Our Troops in Europe," and "How Can the West Recover?" *Harper's Magazine*, February and March, 1958.
Proposals for ending the Cold War, by a former Ambassador to Russia.

STUART, GRAHAM H., *The Department of State: A History of Its Organization, Procedure and Personnel*. Macmillan, 1949.
Authoritative reference book.

THAYER, CHARLES W., *Diplomat*. Harper, 1959.
A witty and informed former diplomat traces the history of diplomacy and reveals how diplomacy works in practice. Includes fascinating details of day-by-day operation of an embassy.

WRISTON, HENRY M., *Diplomacy in a Democracy*. Harper, 1956.
Interesting and readable.

CHAPTER 26

American Democracy, the Soviet Union, and International Communism

In this chapter you will learn about

The problem of communism

Principles of Marxian communism

The Russian Revolution

Soviet foreign policy

The Soviet Union and the Chinese revolution

How the Soviet Union is governed

"Co-existence" from the Soviet point of view

You have examined in Chapter 25 the ways in which American foreign policy is made and studied how it is applied. You will now find it useful to look out across the world and learn something about the chief problem our foreign policy has to deal with—the Soviet Union and its followers in international communism.

THE PROBLEM OF COMMUNISM

Most Americans know enough about communism to understand that it is a system of government and of economic organization which makes our kind of individual liberty impossible. We know too—at least we know if we read

654

the newspapers—that the Soviet Union is a strange new kind of enemy in a strange new kind of war called a "cold war." Too often this is about all we do know. Communism has become a kind of bad word used to make us angry. While abusive language may relieve frustrated feelings, it is no substitute for knowledge and reason. Democratic citizens are called upon to defend their freedoms with policies and programs, not angry shouts.

It is best to begin by facing the facts squarely. The Communists dominate about one-third of the world. Their industrial might, scientific achievement, and military strength rival ours. Communism prevails in China, where almost one-quarter of the world's people live. All of eastern Europe (Poland, Czechoslovakia, Rumania, Hungary, Bulgaria, Yugoslavia, Albania, and the Baltic States) and a large sector of Germany are in Communist hands. In France and Italy, the Communist Party is large and influential. In the Far East, Communists control North Korea and the northern half of Indo-China (Vietminh). There are vigorous Communist Parties in Indonesia, Burma, Malaya, India, and many other countries. In the Middle East nationalist leaders like Nasser who are not Communists nevertheless believe that friendship with the Soviet Union is a useful instrument of policy. Even in Latin America, Communist movements are stirring and making themselves felt. In short, communism divides the world with freedom geographically and struggles to control the world politically.

Because we are the strongest of the countries dedicated to liberty, we have become leaders of the free world. Thus we find ourselves constantly opposed to the Soviet Union. In the hydrogen age we are forced to live in what Sir Winston Churchill called a "balance of terror," always confronting the awful fact that each side possesses the means to destroy the whole world.

PRINCIPLES OF MARXIAN COMMUNISM

To understand the Soviet Union today, it will be necessary to go back to the Russian Revolution of 1917, to the Marxian system of the revolutionary leaders, and to look very briefly at earlier Russian history. Marxism, named for its founder Karl Marx (1818–1883), is a program for revolution against the capitalist economic system (see pp. 509–510).

The Marxian Analysis of Capitalism

In *The Communist Manifesto* (1848) and *Capital* (1867) Marx, with the assistance of his friend Friedrich Engels (1820–1895), argued that the system of private ownership of the means of production (factories, mines, businesses of all sorts) is doomed to destroy itself. This system, known as **capitalism**, Marx claimed, produces an ever larger class of people (**proletariat**) who do not own any productive property but make their living by selling their labor to property owners (**capitalists**). The owners, in turn, sell their products back to those who make them. By this means, argued Marx, the worker is cheated out of the fruit of his labor, since he is paid less than the value of what he produces and must then buy back what he has produced at a price which includes both his own wage and a share for the owner (profit). Marx reasoned that thus a small number of owners make ever greater amounts of money, while most people become workers struggling with one another for jobs.

This *contradiction*, as Marx called it, between capitalists and proletarians is the chief characteristic of modern times. It must end, said Marx, in revolutions in which capitalists have their property taken from them by the workers. Under worker control, productive property (factories, mines, businesses) will be owned and operated in common for the benefit of all. Marx's famous slogan for such a system was "From each according to his ability, to each according to his need." The name Marx applied to such a state of economic affairs is **communism**. Further, Marx believed that the proletarians would gain control of productive property by gaining control of the government and then using its power to abolish private property. In some very advanced countries, like Germany and Great Britain, Marx thought it possible that the workers would take power by peaceful means, but in general he predicted that capitalists would not yield their powers without a violent struggle, and therefore revolution would be necessary. The victory of the proletariat was in any case, he thought, inevitable.

Marx's fundamental philosophy was *materialistic*. As you see, he was chiefly interested in the economic system—the ways in which men produce, distribute, and consume the goods and services of life. This was because he assumed that everything has a material basis and everything is determined by material facts. He believed that the kind of social, political, and spiritual life we have is determined by the way we produce goods.

Marx and the "Class Struggle"

Marx also believed in a theory of the "class struggle." Throughout all history, so he taught, human beings have suffered and struggled with each other for shares of the necessities of life—food, clothing, and shelter. There has never been enough of these necessities, and thus the stronger have always exploited the weaker. According to the Marxists, "All history is the history of class struggles."

If you were a student in a Communist school, you would be expected to learn such lessons as these:

> that in earlier times feudal lords formed a class dominant over peasants and slaves,

that the nobility was overthrown by the capitalists,

that in the modern period capitalists form a class which rules over proletarians and farmers,

that the end to class struggle is coming,

that the capitalist system of production—the factory system of mass production—has shown that it may be possible to produce, for the first time in human history, enough of life's necessities for everybody,

that under capitalism, the workers will not get their share because the system is run by the capitalist class for the benefit of the capitalist class,

that the working class will not be satisfied with this system,

that the more advanced in production a country is, the more aware workers will be of the things they are lacking,

that the workers will some day seize power and begin a system of production and distribution for the benefit of all, instead of profits for a few.

This is the essence of Marxism.

Marx predicted that the "Communist revolution" would take place first in such countries as England, Germany, and the United States because it was in these countries that industrial development was most advanced. Russia, he thought, was so backward that she would be among the last to have a Communist revolution.

Marxian Errors

Why have Marx's predictions been so wrong? One answer often given by experts in economics is that Marx made certain technical errors in his analysis of capitalism. These questions need not concern us here. Another and much more important answer is that *Marx discounted the development of a democratic political system in the very countries which were most advanced industrially.* In England, for example, the voters, most of whom were people who had to work for a living, used their political freedom to elect governments which interfered with the economic system for the benefit of the workingman. Laws were passed to regulate competition among businesses, to support the growth of trade unions, and in many other ways control the development of the economy. The "upper classes" were not able to rule unchecked over the workers. Because Marx was so sure of his materialism he was sure that political democracy would be "taken away" from the people by the capitalists just as quickly as democracy became dangerous to their privileged position. The history of England and the United States will show you how wrong Marx was. The people of these countries liked their freedom and devoted themselves to making democracy work. These people are able to control their economic systems through representative government—without violence. *No free people has ever voted in favor of communism.* The fact is, on the contrary, that Communist Parties have come to power only

657

in backward countries or in countries, like Czechoslovakia, where Communists could seize power with the backing of the Red Army of Russia.

It is important to understand also that Marxian materialism means *atheism* (the belief that there is no God). Religious peoples have always opposed communism and have never accepted it except under force. In Poland, for example, the resistance of the Catholic church has caused the Communists to loosen their strangle hold on individual freedom. Protestant lovers of freedom have helped keep Communist influence at a bare minimum in such countries as those of Scandinavia. In the Soviet Union itself, the government continues to feel the pressure of religious people for freedom of worship. The official campaign against religion continues but never succeeds.

THE RUSSIAN REVOLUTION

You can see, therefore, that the Russian Revolution is a historical paradox: it was fought in the name of a theory which said that it couldn't succeed. When the Communists (Bolsheviks, as they were known in Russia) seized power in November, 1917, they took command of a state which had been autocratic from remote times. Russians had never known freedom of political action or freedom of thought until a coalition of pro-democratic forces brought about the downfall of the czar earlier in the same year. From March until November, under the so-called Provisional Government, Russia was very nearly in chaos. Her troops were being overwhelmed by the Germans and Austrians and Turks on the eastern front of World War I. Behind the surging battle lines, her cities were swarming with ill-controlled masses of cold and hungry people bent on destruction of the ancient tyranny but quite unable to agree on what should replace it.

Only the Bolsheviks, with their devotion to communism, had both a program and a disciplined party. Led by V. I. Lenin (1870–1924) and Leon Trotsky (1879–1940), both of whom returned from long exile and both of whom were dedicated Marxists, the Bolsheviks took advantage of the chaotic conditions in Russia to seize power by a military insurrection. Lenin proclaimed that Russia was henceforth a "Soviet Socialist Republic." **Soviet** is a Russian word for council or assembly of people. Soviets of workers and peasants had tried unsuccessfully to overthrow the czar in 1905. By the end of 1917, Bolshevik agents had successfully penetrated them and used them to overthrow the Provisional Government of Alexander Kerensky. Soldiers and sailors joined them, deserting the war effort. Trotsky, as Foreign Minister of the new regime, negotiated peace with the Germans. With the slogan "Bread for the Workers! Land for the Peasants!" the Communists struggled to assert their power over all Russia. A coalition of those who wished to retain the old ways of the czar and those who believed in political democracy fought to hold back the Bolsheviks. The civil war lasted almost four years, but in the end the Communists won.

Russia, except for a few larger cities, was one of the most backward countries in the world, with primitive agricultural methods and scarcely any industrial development. It was not the kind of place in which Marx expected the Revolution to occur. You can see that what took place there in 1917 was not a *Marxian* revolution. Lenin, indeed, doubted whether his party could retain power in Russia unless the Communists of Germany and other advanced European countries also made successful revolutions. In the first years of Bolshevik control, a new international revolutionary organization was formed to spread communism outside Russia. Native Communists, aided by by Russian agents, tried to overthrow the German government and for a short while actually seized power in Hungary. It was at this time, too, that the Chinese Communist movement began to develop. But the tide receded and by the early 1920's the Communists, though they had won some support in several countries, had failed to win control anywhere except in Russia. In many countries they had been driven underground. The Russian Communists built up a new tyranny far more absolute and brutal than anything known under the czars.

Joseph Stalin, who became dictator in the late 1920's after driving Trotsky into exile, instituted a series of five-year plans to bring rapid industrial and agricultural development. With all productive property in the hands of the government, central planning for industry and agriculture was possible on an unheard-of scale. Whenever central plans for production, building, or distribution ran counter to the interests or well-being of groups of Russian citizens, these groups had either to yield to the power of the state or be "liquidated." Mass murder became a technique of economic development, while terrorism against any who protested became the political way of life.

In the new Soviet system, class distinctions quickly developed. Members of the Party (the Communist Party of the Soviet Union) became the most privileged members of society, since no other political parties were allowed and all decisions were made and carried out by the Communists. The army, the secret police, the factory managers, engineers, scientists, and writers and artists who would use their skills for the benefit of the party made a new aristocracy. Workers and peasants remained at the bottom of the heap as before. Nevertheless, the Soviet Union grew in industrial and military strength, and by the outbreak of World War II had made remarkable advances in production of electric power, steel, and other essentials of heavy industry.

As the power of the Soviet Union increased, so did its prestige and influence among Communists throughout the world. The followers of Marx divided sharply among those who would and those who would not accept the leadership of the Russians. In nearly every country a party was formed of revolutionary malcontents devoted to bringing a Russian-type revolution to their own country. Such parties supported the Soviet Union without question or hesitation. The Soviet leaders laid down the "line" for these parties to follow and supplied them with money and professional revolutionists from Russia. The writings of Lenin and Stalin served as textbooks for Communists everywhere. Native leaders were sent to the U.S.S.R. for training in the revolutionary schools of the Soviet regime. Thus the world Communist movement became a valuable instrument of Soviet foreign policy, manned by people who were prepared to give allegiance to the Soviet Union above allegiance even to their own countries. The United States was no exception. While the Communists have never succeeded in building a party of any size or influence in this country, they have recruited enough discontented people to make trouble from time to time in various industries and for a while to infiltrate the federal government to a minor extent.

Soviet Foreign Policy

Just as you need to know something of both Marxism and the earlier history of Russia in order to understand the Russian Revolution, so too you will need to know something about the theory of communism and something about Russian history in order to understand Soviet foreign policy. People who assume that the Soviet leaders are not really Marxists but simply Russian autocrats, like the czars before them, will be likely to make serious mistakes of judgment about Soviet foreign policy. Similarly, people who assume that the Russians are simply dedicated Marxian Communists who place "world revolution" above the interests of the Soviet Union itself will fail to understand Soviet policy.

The chief thing that you should know about the Soviets, as you try to understand their international behavior, is that they are *both* Russian nationalists *and* Marxist revolutionaries. That is, their policies are seldom simply what they seem. Let us see how this works in practice.

Attempts at World Revolution

In the first years after the Russian Revolution, Soviet leaders tried to stir up revolutions all over the world, partly because they feared that Russia, as a backward nation, could not build communism alone, and partly because they felt obliged to try to promote world revolution in the interests of the "proletarians" of the world.

When it became apparent that revolutions were not going to succeed in Europe and that the Soviet Union would need to build her own strength in order to survive, all efforts were turned to internal development, and she

660

tried to "normalize" her relations with other countries. "World revolution" was not forgotten, but it was played down. Communists outside the U.S.S.R. were taught that they could best serve the working class by supporting the Russian effort to build "socialism" (as they called their system) in one country. In these years, about 1925 to 1935, the Communists outside the Soviet Union tried to persuade their own peoples that the Soviet five-year plans proved that "socialism" could solve the economic problem, while capitalism could not.

Search for Allies

After 1933, the rise of Nazi Germany presented the Soviet Union with an urgent need for allies. Hitler was a fanatical enemy of the Communists, though his own methods were at least as brutal as theirs. Soviet foreign policy accordingly changed. The U.S.S.R. called for "collective security against fascism." The rivalry between communism and capitalism was played down as every effort was made to reach agreements and alliances with Great Britain, France, and the United States, as well as with smaller nations like Czechoslovakia. From 1935 to 1939 Soviet policy was devoted to building political defenses against Hitler, and Communists devoted themselves to building "united fronts" with other political parties. Suddenly, however, in August, 1939, the world was astounded by the announcement that the Soviet Union had signed a treaty of friendship and non-aggression with Germany. Within a few days Germany attacked Poland. The Soviets also attacked Poland and later Finland.

Why did the Soviet Union so sharply reverse previous policy? The answer is to be found in the combination of national self-interest and desire to advance world communism which lies behind all Soviet Russian policy. The Soviet Union had evidently decided by the middle of 1939 that Hitler was going to attack Poland in any case, that the Western democracies were not sufficiently armed to prevent Hitler's conquest of Europe, and that the Soviet Union herself was not adequately armed to defend herself if Hitler should attack beyond Poland. Thus the smart course would be to make a deal with Hitler, if it could be arranged, and avoid attack. Meanwhile, if Hitler swept over Europe, democratic capitalism would collapse and communism would be nearer rather than farther away. Immediately after the Nazi-Soviet treaty was signed and the war commenced, Communists everywhere began to denounce the Western Allies as "plutocrats" and "imperialists"—the very nations which only a month before had been spoken of as democratic allies in the collective defense of freedom against fascism. American Communists, for example, denounced the war as an "imperialist war." America should stay out—"The Yanks are not coming!" they cried. Even when Hitler had overrun Europe, and England stood alone, the Russians and their Communist allies in other countries talked of British "plutocracy" and "imperialism."

In June, 1941, Hitler turned on his new "friends" and invaded the Soviet Union. Immediately the Communist line changed again. The war, they announced, was now for democracy and freedom against tyranny. England, France, and the United States were democratic comrades in the great struggle! In 1943 Stalin even announced the disbanding of the Communist International (the organization of world Communist Parties), since all the Allies were for democracy, and capitalism and communism could live peaceably together! As you can see, this change of policy requires no explanation. The Soviet Union was now fighting for survival and needed any allies she could get.

But the Marxian goals of world Communist domination were not forgotten even in the darkest moments of the war. As soon as the military situation permitted, the Soviets began to move in ways which would enlarge the Communist world. For example, the Soviet Union maintained relations with Japan, until it was clear that Japan would be defeated, even though the United States, Britain, France, and most of the other United Nations were at war with her. Then the Russians moved into Manchuria. The result of this strategy was that Soviet Russia became a victor entitled to be consulted in the whole postwar settlement of Asia. Korea was divided between American and Russian occupation armies, and Russian armies stood back of the Chinese Communists as they prosecuted their successful civil war against the Chinese Nationalists.

In the West the Soviet Union used her victories over Hitler—accomplished only with massive material support from the United States and the tremendous military effort of the Western Allies in the invasion of North Africa and of the European continent—to bring all of eastern Europe under Communist control. In a series of agreements made by President Roosevelt, Prime Minister Churchill, and Premier Stalin, the Allies made plans for the orderly restoration of freedom wherever Hitler's armies had brought the Nazi tyranny. Armies of occupation were to govern Germany and Austria, each of the major allies being assigned sections as its individual responsibility. Berlin and Vienna were also divided into sections to be occupied by Allied forces. Russian armies were to occupy Poland, Czechoslovakia, Rumania, Hungary, Bulgaria. In every case, the occupation forces were to remain only so long as might be necessary to put these nations back on their feet and to conduct free elections so that each of these countries would have its own democratic government.

Broken Agreements

One by one the Soviet Union broke nearly all of these agreements. The Polish government, returned from exile in London where it had functioned since 1939, was broken up and replaced by a Communist government backed by the Red Army. In Rumania, Hungary, and Bulgaria, Communist governments were soon established; no free elections were ever held in those countries. Czechoslovakia was an exception. The Czechs had a strong tradition of democratic freedom and outstanding democratic leaders in Eduard Beneš and Jan Masaryk. The Czech republic was restored. But it was surrounded by Soviet armies and subjected to Soviet pressures. In 1948 Czech Communists, supported politically by the Soviet Union, seized power. Beneš died while a prisoner in his own house, and Masaryk committed suicide. Thus Czechoslovakia joined the long list of "satellite" countries (countries under the control of the U.S.S.R.).

In Germany the Soviet leaders soon made it apparent that they did not intend to permit reunification unless the new Germany were under Communist control. With no free election they quickly established a German Communist government over their sector, with its capital in the Russian sector of divided Berlin. While the Western Allies worked to build up constitutional democracy in West Germany, the Communists put unrelenting pressure on the Germans under their control.

The Soviet Union regularly broke every agreement regarding the occupation of Germany. In 1948 they attempted to drive the Western Allies out of Berlin and force West Berlin to join East Berlin as part of Communist East Germany. They cut off highway and rail transport routes in order to deprive West Berlin of the necessities of life. The Western Allies replied by establishing a massive airlift which so successfully supplied West Berlin that the Reds abandoned their tactics for a number of years. Perhaps because of the stand made by the West in Berlin, no similar pressure developed in Vienna; then in 1955 all parties signed a peace treaty with Austria (but only after prolonged Russian bickering), and the armies of occupation were withdrawn from that tiny country. The Austrian agreements were the only agreements not repudiated in one way or another by the Soviet Union in her strategy of enlarging the areas of Communist (and Soviet) control.

One other country in Eastern Europe, Yugoslavia, was an exception to the ruthless postwar policy of the Russians. Unlike neighboring countries occupied by the Germans, Yugoslavia to a great extent accomplished her own liberation. As early as 1941, partisan armies of guerrilla soldiers fought the Germans from mountain bases in Yugoslavia. These armies were in contact with the Western Allies and received some military supplies, but their eventual success was mainly the result of their own heroic efforts. During the struggles against the Germans the Yugoslav partisans also fought each other. In this civil war, the anti-Communists led by Draja Mihailovich were defeated by the Communists led by Josip Broz, "Tito."

When they finally liberated themselves from the Germans, Tito became dictator of the new Yugoslavia and undertook to build socialism. Tito, as well as a number of his Communist colleagues, was close to the Russians and had lived in Russia in exile before the war. His policy was one of close collaboration with the Soviet Union. But when a new Communist international organization (Cominform, since disbanded) was formed with its "line" laid down in Moscow, Tito began to resist. In 1948, the Yugoslav Communists were expelled from the Cominform and denounced by the Soviet Union. Since that time Tito has acted independently on foreign policy. Usually he has been "neutral" in regard to matters dividing the Soviet Union and the West, but has maintained friendly relations with the United States and other Western democracies.

THE SOVIET UNION AND THE CHINESE REVOLUTION

Since 1949 the Russians have had a new and mighty ally—Communist China (correctly called the People's Republic of China). After a long civil war the Chinese Communists (led by Mao Tse-tung) finally defeated the Chinese Nationalists (led by Chiang Kai-shek) in the fall of 1949, and gained control over all of mainland China. The Nationalists retreated to the island of Formosa (Taiwan), where they have remained, with the heavy military and economic support of the United States.

Meanwhile Communist China, assisted militarily and economically by the Soviet Union, has been gaining strength and influence throughout the Far East.

In June, 1950, the Communists of North Korea treacherously attacked free Korea. When United Nations forces drove them back toward the Yalu in the fall of that year, the Communist Chinese intervened with massive armies. After more than two years of bitter fighting, the battle line was stabilized at about where the original boundary between North and South Korea had been. In the summer of 1953, a truce was agreed upon. The Communist Chinese, by their show of strength in the Korean War, served notice that they would thereafter play a major role in the politics of Asia. This posed a very difficult problem for the makers of American foreign policy. Soviet communism was prepared at any moment to create crises in Europe and the Middle East; Chinese communism stirred up trouble in Asia. Thus the free world of the West remains under constant threat of mortal danger.

Newly independent countries in Asia and Africa—India, Burma, Malaya, Ceylon, Indonesia, Ghana, Sudan, etc.—feel a constant pressure from the Communists. They are constantly being wooed by the Soviet Union or Communist China, while the West, led by the United States, strives to help them

JUDGING BY HIS ACTIONS   Carmack in *The Christian Science Monitor*

to remain free. This seemingly endless struggle for the minds of men, punctuated from time to time by aggressive military action, is what we call the "Cold War." Behind the Cold War, an arms race is going on which reminds us of the continuing threat that hot war will break out. Cold War, with the threat of nuclear destruction, has become the chief characteristic of foreign relations in the middle of the twentieth century.

HOW THE SOVIET UNION IS GOVERNED

One of the typical tricks of Communist propaganda is to use the words *democracy* and *democratic* to refer to Communist governments and Communist policies. Not long ago two young American students visiting in Hungary fell into an argument with some Hungarian students about freedom and democracy. The Hungarians argued that they were "progressive" and "democratic" because they accepted the teachings of Marx and Lenin and supported the policies of the Soviet Union. The Americans replied that this was undemocratic because in Hungary people who disagreed with Marxism or were critical of the Soviet Union were suppressed and there were no free newspapers or radio stations. At the height of the discussion, the police entered and arrested the Americans, clapping them into jail overnight. The charge? Making "undemocratic remarks"!

The Soviet Union, motherland of communism, employs the words *democracy* and *democratic* to describe Soviet life and the Soviet government. But you will be badly fooled if you take the Russians at their word. When democracy is understood as you have experienced it throughout your life here in the United States, and as it is defined and explained in this book, it is the very opposite of the kind of government established in the Soviet Union.

665

The key to understanding Russian government lies in the fact that there is only one political party—the Communist Party. The ideas and policies of the Communist Party are automatically law and policy in the Soviet Union. But not anyone can become a member of the Party; indeed only about 3 percent of the people are allowed to be members. To become a member of the Party, you must apply for membership first in one of the various youth organizations controlled by the Party. You must accept the discipline of your organization, attend all meetings, perform all assigned tasks, study Marx, Lenin, Stalin, and other Communist writings diligently in Party schools, and serve a long period of probation. Once you are a member, you are still not entitled to express your opinion on any except minor matters. On the contrary, you are "privileged" to be an "instrument of the Party's will," that is, your life is devoted to obedient carrying out of orders from the higher ranks of the Party. In the Communist Party all decisions of importance are made by the Central Committee, whose members are elected by the Party rank and file, but only after the leaders have given their approval to the candidates. The Central Committee, in turn, takes its cues from the Presidium, a small group of top leaders. Typically the Presidium itself has been dominated by one man—Lenin, Stalin, and now Khrushchev. You will find it useful to go back to Chapters 18 and 19 and compare American political parties with the Communist Party of the Soviet Union.

The form of government in the Soviet Union is, technically, republican. That is, the laws are made by an elected legislature (Supreme Soviet) consisting of two houses and are carried out by an executive branch which is appointed by the legislature. (See chart, p. 667.) Like the states of the United States, the Soviet Union is divided into smaller "republics" which have a large measure of authority over their local affairs and whose governments are modeled after the national system. But the Soviet governmental system, both local and national, is really only a "front" for the Communist Party. It is a system of organizations through which the Party works. The citizens are not given a choice of candidates in their elections. All adult Russians participate in elections and are free to campaign for their favorite candidates. This "freedom," however, is more apparent than real, for all candidates are either Party members chosen by the Party or non-Party citizens designated by the Party. The voter finds only one slate of candidates on his ballot. He can vote *yes* or *no*, but he cannot make a choice. Typically 95 to 98 percent of the voters vote *yes* on the ballot.

Since it controls the election process at the grass roots, the Party easily controls the whole country from top to bottom. All important officials at every level and in every activity are Party members owing allegiance not to the citizens but to the Party, and holding their positions by the will of the

Soviet Government under the Constitution of 1936

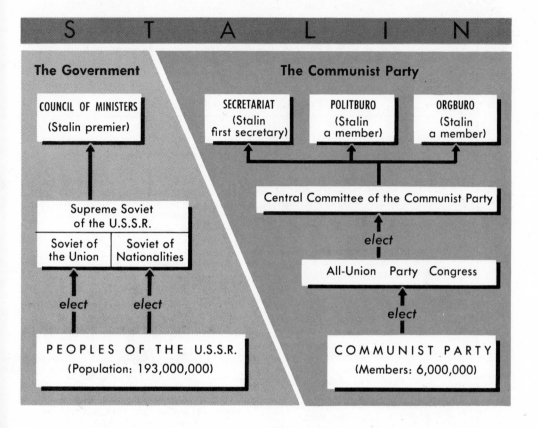

Party. Struggles for power go on, of course, *inside the Party*, especially in the Central Committee of the Party. (See chart above) The overall Party leader may be a dictator as powerful as Stalin or rather more limited like Khrushchev, but he is never secure against the sniping of political enemies jealous of his authority. The history of the Soviet government and Communist Party shows a long record of political murders comparable to those of ancient Oriental despots.

The Party and the government control all the means of communication in the Soviet Union. In the schools and colleges, on the radio and television, and through newspapers, magazines, and books, the Party is constantly and emphatically telling the Soviet citizen what he is to think about every matter that may come to his attention. Foreign periodicals are admitted to the Soviet Union only in tiny quantities. For example, the average Russian citizen goes through his whole life without ever seeing an American paper,

NEW YORK

Herald ~~Tribune~~

FOUNDED APRIL 10, 1841

Friday, October 17, 1958

A Hearing For a Master Spy

Col. Rudolf Ivanovich Abel of the Soviet secret service, convicted last year by a Federal Court in Brooklyn as the mastermind of a vast espionage operation, may be musing today on the comparative qualities of U. S. and Soviet justice.

There is no doubt of Abel's guilt. But there is a question whether our constitutional guarantees against illegal search and seizure were violated when he was arrested, on June 21, 1957, in Manhattan's Latham Hotel, and whether evidence that may have been improperly gathered at this time should have been admitted at his trial. Because of these questions, the Supreme Court agreed this week to review the case. (Abel is in Atlanta serving a thirty-year term.)

There was no appeal to a higher court from Stalin's chilling declaration (related by Khrushchev): "I will shorten you by a head." No constitutional guarantees saved the thousands in Communist lands who have disappeared in the night, or stilled the brutal staccato of Soviet firing squads. And, from their graves and their prisons, the muted voices of Hun-gary's known and nameless martyrs still, in the world's most eloquent silence, condemn the mockery of law in a lawless land.

The lesssons of his own case cannot be entirely lost on Abel, a brilliant man, widely read in the literary classics, fluent in five languages, electronics engineer, artist and musician. James B. Donovan, widely respected wartime counsel for the O. S. S., was named by the Brooklyn Bar Association to defend Abel, and, in the best traditions of the law, has carried his case to the highest court.

We don't attempt to prejudge the merits of Abel's appeal. But by its decision to review the case and to weigh the constitutional issues it presents, the court has once again demonstrated its concern for the protection of individual liberties, no matter whose. The questions raised are procedural: yet due process is at the very heart of law. Whatever its outcome, the court's review will serve as a reminder that the freedom of all of us is secure only so long as the freedom of each is protected.

magazine, or book either in English or in Russian translation, unless the government and the Party decide that for some reason it would be safe for him to do so. Thus American novels which happen to be highly critical of the United States might be translated and published, but books explaining American government or American foreign policy are rigidly excluded. Every effort is made to "jam" American and other Western broadcasts beamed to the Soviet Union. If you have a short-wave radio set, you need only to twirl your dials to get Radio Moscow clearly and distinctly, and you are free to listen to your heart's content. But if you were a young Soviet student anxious to hear American broadcasts, you would find only atrocious static when you dialed the call numbers of American stations.

It would be grossly inaccurate to deny that the Russians have made certain very great advances, even under their totalitarian government. One-party dictatorship has made central planning and decision-making possible on a scale far exceeding what a free people will stand for. Thus a backward country was industrialized in one generation. Famine, for centuries the worst terror of the Russian people, was abolished through mechanized agriculture and the opening up of millions of additional acres to cultivation. The country was electrified by the building of hundreds of power plants at damsites all over the vast area of the Soviet Union.

Totalitarian education not only served as a weapon in the endless war against the capitalist democracies but also lifted a nearly illiterate people to the highest levels of literacy. Emphasis on mathematics and science in school, college, and technical institutes has enabled the Russians to make advances which stunned the world in the 1950's. As the world moved into the space age, Soviet rocket, missile, satellite, and nuclear science placed the Russians in the forefront, able to match and sometimes to surpass all other nations. But when a Russian novelist produced one of the great books of the twentieth century, he could not get it published in his own country. When Boris Pasternak was awarded the Nobel Prize for *Dr. Zhivago* he dared not accept it. You may read *Dr. Zhivago* (and you should!), but young Russian students may not.

"CO-EXISTENCE" FROM THE SOVIET POINT OF VIEW

As you follow the news of Russian policy toward the rest of the world, you will become increasingly aware of the word **co-existence**. Ever since the end of World War II, all the while that they agitate and stir up crises everywhere to keep the Cold War going (see p. 665), and even while standing behind aggressors like Communist China, North Korea, and the Northern Communist Zone of Indo-China (Vietminh), the Russians have been talking about peace. The Soviet Union strives to persuade the world that it is the authentic voice of peace, while the American leaders chiefly, and other Western leaders to a lesser extent, are "warmongers." The Soviet Union, says its government, is anxious for "peaceful co-existence" with all nations, even capitalist nations. How are we to understand this kind of talk? What is the Soviet Union's real interest in peaceful co-existence?

Self-Interest of the U.S.S.R.

In part the answer to these questions lies in the facts you have learned earlier in this chapter. That is, the Soviet Union is looking out for her own self-interest and at the same time always intending to advance communism wherever possible. The Soviet Union was devastated by World War II. Remember that German armies occupied almost all of European Russia during the period 1941–1943, bombed to "saturation" Russia's industrial cities, and laid waste vast areas of farm lands. The Russians themselves pursued a "scorched earth" policy, burning over lands they were forced to abandon to the Germans. Thus Russia was faced, at the end of the war, with an enormous task of rebuilding. This task required a condition of peace, so that a maximum of manpower and of wealth could be devoted to it. Soviet Russia's rebuilding is now completed, and she has speeded up her programs of industrial and agricultural expansion to provide a better standard of living for her more than 200 million people. Thus a policy of peace suits the immediate self-interest of the Soviet Union.

You must not be fooled into supposing that the Reds will not fight, or will not risk war. In the fall of 1956, a democratic revolution against the Communist dictatorship broke out in Hungary. When the Hungarian Communist government was unable to suppress the revolution, the Russians did not hesitate to send in the Red Army. It was the tanks of the Soviet Union rumbling down the streets of Budapest, to the horror of free men everywhere, which put an end to the Hungarian uprising. Why did the Russians do it? It seems safe to answer that they risked world censure, and formal denunciation in the United Nations, because they believed that a free Hungary was too great a threat to their own security. There were stirrings of discontent in other satellites, especially in Poland, and even perhaps in the Soviet Union itself. A democratic revolution could not be allowed to overthrow a Communist dictatorship precisely because it might lead to an eventual overthrow of the Soviet dictatorship itself.

While the Soviet Union will evidently fight to prevent the triumph of democracy over communism, it does not follow that she will fight to spread communism. It is true that the Russians have supported, politically and with material assistance, the Chinese Communists, the North Korean Communists, and the Communists of Indo-China. It is important to realize, however, that in none of the aggressive wars of recent years have Russian troops been committed. As far as we can tell, the settled policy of the Soviet Union seems to be to stand behind Communist aggression so long as aggression is conducted by other Communists and so long as world war does not seem likely to occur. Her actions also seem to suggest that she will not involve herself too deeply, nor allow a small war to become a nuclear world war.

670

Past and Present Soviet Policy

What is the difference between the present-day Soviet policy and the policy she pursued before 1940? The objectives remain the same: protect the Soviet Union and spread communism as much as possible. But the conditions are different today. For the first time in human history, no nation can afford a risk of war to back up an aggressive policy, since for the first time world war would mean in effect world annihilation. In 1939 the Soviet Union, risking involvement herself, could stand by to watch Germany fight the democracies. Today a great war would bring devastation just as quickly to the Soviet Union as to any other area of the world. Thus no matter how deeply the Russians hate democracy, and the United States in particular, Soviet policy must in an important, though negative, sense coincide with ours—that is, the Soviet Union has no more desire to be incinerated than has the United States.

The "Cold War"

What then does "co-existence" mean, as the Soviet Union understands it? Not peace in the sense of happy and friendly relations among all peoples, with free going and coming, trade, and cultural interchange. But not war either. Co-existence means in fact cold war—keeping the democracies guessing and nervous all the time. Agitating, provoking, cheating, wherever and whenever it will help communism, but never quite allowing a big war to start. At the same time, we should note that the Reds have declared a trade war on us and have stated their intention of defeating us in world markets.

The Arms Race

What about the arms race? It seems reasonable to believe, on the basis of events, that the Russians would like to limit the arms race in two ways: (1) to keep it from reaching such proportions that a war must result, and (2) to avoid expending too much of her own resources on armaments. On the other hand, it seems equally evident from what has been going on that the Soviet Union does not really wish to end the arms race so long as the United States and the West can be forced to spend vast amounts of money on arms and build up ever greater public debts. The Russians, as Marxists, hope that a crushing burden of debt may bring internal collapse in the capitalist nations and open the way for communism.

In these ways a policy of "peaceful co-existence" as a mask for continuing the Cold War seems to suit the Russians. It may also be helpful to them in their endless efforts to persuade the uncommitted countries that the United States and her allies are warmongers, that capitalism and militarism go hand in hand, and that friendship with the Soviet Union is the best route to peace and prosperity.

671

SUMMARY

You should now be able to see fairly clearly the kind of problem communism presents to the United States today. You, like all your fellow citizens, will have to make up your mind as to what is the wisest policy for the United States to follow. In order to be critically responsive to the ideas offered to you by political leaders you will need to keep in mind the things you have learned in this chapter: the dimensions of the Communist problem, the principles of Marxism, the character and influence of the Soviet Union, the course of previous Russian foreign policy, the way in which the Soviet Union is governed, and the meaning the Russians attach to the idea of "co-existence." As a democratic citizen of a democratic republic, even though yours is the most powerful free land in the world, you must see that foreign policy decisions cannot be made so easily or so quickly in a democratic system as they can under Communist dictatorship. But vigilant citizens can compose their differences swiftly and patriotism can carry a free people a long way. If alert and thoughtful citizens put into high office men and women of imagination and courage, the United States and her allies can win the Cold War—no matter how long it may take—and the price paid for liberty will seem in the long run small.

KNOW WHAT YOU READ

1. Explain how Communism and freedom divide the world geographically.
2. Why has the United States become the leader of the free world?
3. What is Marxism? What is capitalism? Communism?
4. What does the Communist think is wrong with capitalism? What does he expect to do about it?
5. Why do we call Marx's ideas *materialistic?*
6. Explain what Marx meant by the "class struggle."
7. Marx predicted early "Communist revolutions" in some countries but not in others. Why were his prophecies wrong?
8. Why did the Bolshevik Revolution succeed in Russia?
9. By what methods were the Communists able to make their people accept economic planning?
10. To what extent did communism lead to a classless society?
11. Explain how Communist influence grew outside the Soviet Union.
12. Should we think of the leaders of the USSR as Russian nationalists or as Marxist revolutionaries?
13. Explain how it happened that the allied victory in World War II greatly increased the power of the Soviet Union.
14. What agreements did the Reds break in the postwar period?

672

15. What are "satellite" countries? Name some.
16. By what steps did China come to be a threat to the free world?
17. What is meant by "cold war"?
18. What requirements must a resident of the USSR meet to be a party member?
19. Outline the organization of the Communist Party.
20. "The form of government in the Soviet Union is, technically, republican." Why do we say "technically"?
21. In what ways does the Communist Party control the thinking of the citizens of the Soviet Union?
22. What real advances have the people of the USSR made under Communist leadership?
23. What do the Reds mean by "peaceful co-existence"?
24. What is a "scorched earth" policy?
25. Have there been any indications of dissatisfaction with Communist policy in the satellites?

WHAT DO YOU THINK?

1. How do you think Russian students reconcile occurrences in the world with the lessons they are taught about Marxism?
2. Why was the Communist Party able to keep its following in Russia even when it used "mass murder as a technique of economic development"?
3. Why do you think Soviet leaders were unsuccessful in stirring up revolutions all over the world in the first years after the Russian Revolution?

PROBLEMS AND PROJECTS FOR YOU

1. Write a paper contrasting the Soviet form of government with ours.
2. "The Russian Revolution is an historical paradox: it was fought in the name of a theory which said that it couldn't succeed." Explain.
3. Make up a list of ten agreements which Soviet Russia has made with various countries, and what has happened to them. A good source is the government book, *Soviet Political Agreements and Results*. Another useful book is *How Communists Negotiate* by C. Turner Joy. Use three parallel columns, with these headings, including dates if possible:

AGREEMENT   SOVIET ACTION   PERTINENT HISTORICAL BACKGROUND

4. Why does it take longer for a government to act in a democratic system than in a totalitarian one? Is this an advantage or a disadvantage?

5. Read the pamphlet *Democracy and Totalitarianism* (Your America Series, Grolier Society) or *Democracy and You* (Charles E. Merrill Co.). Draw a chart contrasting democracy and totalitarianism today.
6. In Carr, *Men of Power: A Book of Dictators* or in another book available in your library, read about *one* of the following, and report to the class on his background and rise to power: Mao Tse-tung, Stalin, Tito.
7. "The Soviet Union, says its government, is anxious for 'peaceful co-existence' with all nations, even capitalist nations." As a basis for making our foreign policy decisions, how is such a statement to be taken?
8. What steps did people of industrially advanced countries like England and America take which proved Marx wrong in his predictions of a coming "class struggle" in such countries?

EXTEND YOUR VOCABULARY

"cold war"
Karl Marx
Marxism
Communist Manifesto
Capital
Friedrich Engels
capitalism
proletariat
communism
materialistic
"class struggle"
atheism
Russian Revolution

Bolsheviks
V. I. Lenin
Leon Trotsky
Soviet
Alexander Kerensky
five-year plan
socialism
Communist Inter-
   national
armies of occupation
Eduard Beneš
Jan Masaryk
"satellite" country

Mao Tse-tung
Chiang Kai-shek
Central Committee of
   Communist Party
Presidium of USSR
Khrushchev
Supreme Soviet
Boris Pasternak
Nobel Prize
co-existence
Vietnam
Vietminh
"scorched earth" policy

READ MORE ABOUT IT

BELOFF, MAX, *The Foreign Policy of Soviet Russia, 1929–1941.* Oxford University Press, 1949.

BROWDER, EARL, *Marx and America.* Duell, Sloan, and Pearce, 1958.
   Advanced but important study of why Marx's theory has been disproved by American experience.

EBENSTEIN, WILLIAM, *Today's Isms.* Prentice-Hall, 1958.
   Brief excellent comparative studies of communism, fascism, capitalism, and socialism.

KHRUSHCHEV, NIKITA S., "On Peaceful Coexistence." *Foreign Affairs*, October, 1959.
   Readable article on the theme of Khrushchev's visit to the United States.

MOOREHEAD, ALAN, *The Russian Revolution.* Harper, 1958.
   The most readable recent history.

ROBERTS, HENRY L., *Russia and America: Dangers and Prospects.* Council on Foreign Relations. Harper, 1956.

CHAPTER 27

The Citizen and the Defense of Liberty

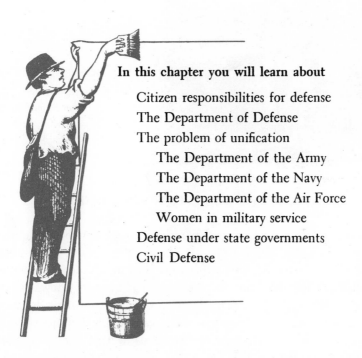

In this chapter you will learn about

Citizen responsibilities for defense
The Department of Defense
The problem of unification
    The Department of the Army
    The Department of the Navy
    The Department of the Air Force
    Women in military service
Defense under state governments
Civil Defense

    While foreign policy is the attitude taken by a nation toward the world, every nation needs some sort of military establishment to back its foreign policy. **Military establishment** is the term we use to mean permanent armed forces controlled by the national government and supported by public tax money. If all human beings and all governments were peaceful, there would be no need for armies, navies, and air forces. But so long as world conditions bring the threat of war and some governments have aggressive intentions, even the most peaceful countries must be prepared to defend themselves.

675

CHANGE OF WEAPONS?

Carmack in
The Christian Science Monitor

CITIZEN RESPONSIBILITIES FOR DEFENSE

It is a sad fact that the history of man has in large part been the history of his wars and his development of means to destroy himself. Every advance in the preservation of human life has been matched by advances in techniques of destruction. Thus the stone implement, the bow and arrow, explosive weapons, air striking power, and, finally, nuclear bombs for mass destruction have been developed as rapidly as have the means and techniques of healing and nutrition. In our time the human race seems to have reached a point at which it can either destroy itself or move into something like a promised land of material well-being.

The Militia

When the American colonies declared their independence of Great Britain in 1776, their chief means of defense was the citizen militia—farmers and artisans who took down their muskets from the kitchen wall, buckled on their powder horns and bullet bags, and joined together to fight for their homes. George Washington, as commander-in-chief, struggled for years to

676

build up a regular army that he could direct according to plan against the British forces. But even the most patriotic citizens who joined up with him could be expected to lay down their arms, regardless of the military situation, to go home and harvest crops, look after their families and business affairs, or simply to rest. The citizens fought with great courage and skill for their own homes, but they had no experience and little will to accept the rigors of military discipline far away. Even with the vital assistance of French professionals, and supplies and financial aid, it was little less than a miracle that Washington could finally defeat the British regulars and their hired allies.

When the war for independence was over, the citizen soldiers immediately returned to their homes and their peaceful ways, and the new nation was effectively disarmed. Circumstances have, ever since, required us to have a military establishment. But it has been very difficult for us to maintain sufficient armed forces to guarantee our safety. The War of 1812 and the Mexican War of 1846 were fought mostly with volunteers, since in those days only a small regular force was maintained, mainly to man western frontier posts and forts to protect settlers against Indian raids. The nation's first **draft** (required military service) came during the War Between the States, but from then until World War I, in 1917, the United States continued its old policy of relying on the militia for national defense.

Meanwhile, no substantial American navy was developed until the turn of the twentieth century. At that time Presidents McKinley and Theodore Roosevelt, recognizing that the United States was rapidly becoming a great power because of its unprecedented economic development, persuaded Congress to authorize large sums to construct and maintain a high-seas fleet. The world cruise of the "White Fleet," as the ships were called, in 1906 marked the emergence of the United States as a world military power.

During World War I, volunteers and drafted troops numbered some three million, and more than one million American soldiers were transported to Europe. By the end of 1918, American military power was among the strongest in the world. American yearning for peace and the traditional desire of the people to remain as far as possible isolated from foreign quarrels led us quickly to demobilize the army and infant air force and to disband the navy patrol fleet. At the Washington Conference, 1921–1922, the United States, France, Great Britain, Italy, and Japan, in a five-power treaty, agreed not to build for ten years ships over 10,000 tons. In the same treaty, Great Britain and the United States agreed not to build new bases in the Pacific.

Again in World War II, we had to build up a military establishment of more than 13 million men and women, construct the largest and most powerful navy in the history of the world, and build fighting aircraft not only for the

677

largest air force in the world but for the air forces of all our allies. Once again, when the war was over, the United States hastened to disarm, both because of peaceful instincts and because of the enormous costs of keeping the military establishment going. The war effort had cost more than 200 billion dollars of tax money and borrowed money. The national debt, negligible only a few decades earlier, went far over the 200-billion mark, and Congress felt the strongest public pressure to reduce the financial burden of the people, and to "bring the boys home."

By 1947 the danger in a policy of disarmament was already apparent. The Cold War between world communism and world democracy called for a policy of world-wide defense of freedom (the Truman Doctrine, see p. 627), and such a policy meant a permanent large-scale military establishment to maintain it. The great decision to arm, and to stay armed, in peacetime meant that a system of conscripting troops would become a regular feature of American life for the first time in our history. The militia (National Guard) and the professional military, though both are larger than ever, must today be supplemented by a steady flow of citizen soldiers into the army, navy, and air force of the United States. Most are volunteers, but perhaps prompted by the prospect of being drafted or enticed by good pay and education.

Selective Service System

The modern draft has, in a way, replaced the militia principle of earlier times. It is a new way of saying that every able-bodied adult male has an obligation to defend the freedoms he has inherited. This is, however, no longer the simple matter of taking down the musket from the kitchen wall and going out to defend your home. "Home," according to the poet Robert Frost, "is where, when you have to go there, they have to take you in." But in another sense the home of free men today is wherever men are still free—the home to be defended may be any home of freedom that is under attack. And so it is that the present-day citizen soldier, who has answered the call of his country under the selective service laws, is trained in the handling of the most advanced weapons, in the geography and culture and politics of far-away places, and sent, often enough, on tours of duty thousands of miles from his own community. To the youth of eighteen who is thus obliged to answer the call of military duty, the transition may seem abrupt and even unnecessary. But a little thought and a sense of perspective will show him that his service is an important part of a policy to protect for him and his generation the freedoms to which he was born. The Selective Service System was established in 1947, under the Universal Military and Training Act. This act requires all male citizens from 18 to 26 years old to register. They can be called for training when they are 18½ to 26.

The conscription (draft) of American youth for military service is kept as close to the people as possible. While there is a national Selective Service Administration, an independent government agency in Washington, most of the work is done at local centers. If you are a young man of eighteen, you must register with your local draft board. This board consists of three or more civilians who live in your area and are appointed by the governor of your state. The board will see that you have a physical examination and will collect other facts about you. When you are eighteen and a half, if you are physically fit, the board has power to induct you into the armed services to serve for 24 months. After your service, the law requires you to remain a member of a reserve military unit up to six years longer, retaining your same rank as soldier or officer. If you are a theological student (or have become a minister before you are called to service), you are exempt from service. If you object to military service for religious reasons, you may be assigned certain kinds of civilian work instead.

If you ask for deferment and it is refused by your local board, you may appeal your case to an appeal board. There is an appeal board in each Federal Judicial District. You may have your service deferred by action of your draft board if you have not finished high school, or if you are doing good work in college or graduate school. You may also be deferred by your board if you are doing certain civilian work which is considered essential, or if your board thinks that your service would bring too great a hardship on your family. In recent years so many men have volunteered in order to get their service out of the way early in their careers, that a high proportion of young men who are due for induction have been deferred. Thus the armed services have a nearly sufficient supply of young men coming in. A talk with the recruiting officers of the services in your area will reveal many interesting opportunities open to you if you should decide to volunteer instead of waiting to be called in the draft. Men over 26 are exempt from the draft, unless they have been deferred, in which case they are liable to be called until they reach the age of 35.

The Selective Service Administration in Washington, under a Director appointed by the President and Senate, supervises the Selective Service System, informs the state directors what quota of men is needed, and keeps records of the entire system. The power to induct or defer you, however, is in the hands of your neighbors, who are acting under the law on behalf of the President.

There is a serious question today whether the draft is the best way to supply a highly specialized military with trained manpower. Many people feel that high pay and other incentives would bring enough qualified young men into the services, and keep them there for some years, while drafted men must be released often nearly as soon as they are trained. Many Americans, it should be added, are opposed on principle to universal military service.

Civilian Control of the American Military Establishment

There was disagreement early in our history about the merits of standing armies and their size. But upon one thing everyone agreed: whatever military establishment there might be must be fully under the control of the civilian government. Careful provisions for civilian control were made in the Constitution by Article I, Section 8, Clauses 12, 13, 14, 15, and 16, p. 54. Congress, the civilian legislative body of the nation, was placed in a position superior to all armed forces. Even the power of Congress to maintain them was limited, however, by the provision that appropriations of money for military purposes could not be for longer than two years. In addition, and still more important, Congress was given the sole power to declare war (I, 8, 11). Finally, the civilian chief of state, the President, was made commander-in-chief (II, 2, 1), thus guaranteeing that all military officers would be subordinate to civilian authority. This latter principle governs all of the military branches established under the Constitution, since officers are subordinate to the civilian Secretaries who head the military departments. Our laws and policies are so scrupulously careful to maintain civilian supremacy that an officer of the regular army, navy, or air force who is appointed to a government post (except for certain specific military posts in the military departments) must resign his commission unless Congress makes a specific exception. This principle was called dramatically to public attention when Congress passed special acts to permit General of the Army George C. Marshall to accept appointments, first as Secretary of State and later as Secretary of Defense, and when General of the Army Dwight D. Eisenhower resigned his commission to run for President in 1952. Both men were already retired from active military duty, but so long as their commissions were in force, they were ineligible to hold office in any except a military capacity.

The American military establishment, so vigorously debated in the early years and an object of controversy for generations, came into being in 1789 when the first Congress set up the Department of War, with a civilian Secretary of War in the President's cabinet. The Navy Department was similarly established in 1798. The air force came into being as a part of the army in World War I. Experience in World War II showed that closer coördination among the services was necessary under modern conditions, and Congress, in a series of measures, responded to modern needs by establishing an overall Department of Defense, with a civilian Secretary in the President's cabinet. Subordinate Departments of the Army, Navy, and Air Force were placed under the Department of Defense, each with its own civilian administration.

THE DEPARTMENT OF DEFENSE

The Department of Defense today guides the destinies of a national military establishment numbering about a million civilian employees and nearly three million service men and women. Under conditions of emergency, the military establishment may also include the National Guard units of the various states and call into service many thousands of reserve officers. The military departments of the government are thus by far the largest and most costly.

The Department of Defense is a purely administrative and policy-making agency which reports to the President and assists him in carrying out his duties as commander-in-chief of the armed forces of the United States. The three service departments under it are the operating branches of our national defense.

The Secretary of Defense

The office of Secretary of Defense is so recent (1947) that we do not yet know what its long-range significance will be. The Secretary of Defense is a member of the cabinet, advising the President on all military and national defense matters. Through his membership in the National Security Council, and in his relations with the Secretary of State, he coödinates defense policy with foreign policy. He carries out the instructions of the President and the laws of Congress either through his own facilities or through the service departments subordinate to him.

The Secretary of Defense carries an enormous burden of responsibility. He must have the imagination to see the whole vast and sprawling system of defense in perspective and in relation to world-wide foreign and military policy. He need not be skilled in military affairs, but he must be able to choose subordinates who are so skilled and whose judgment he can trust. He must respond to and weigh wisely the different pressures he feels from the separate services, taking care not to favor one over the others at the expense of a well-rounded national defense as determined by the National Security Council and by Congress. And, finally, he must allow for the fact that military men talk from the point of view of their specialization. He must therefore prevent the military from being overemphasized and be sure that civilian supremacy remains secure.

In some ways the office of the Secretary of Defense is like that of the Secretary of State. It is so difficult and burdensome that the Secretary will find it impossible to please everyone. Yet the rewards of the office are great. For upon the defense of the United States and meeting the military responsibilities we have undertaken rests the security of the free world.

Department of Defense

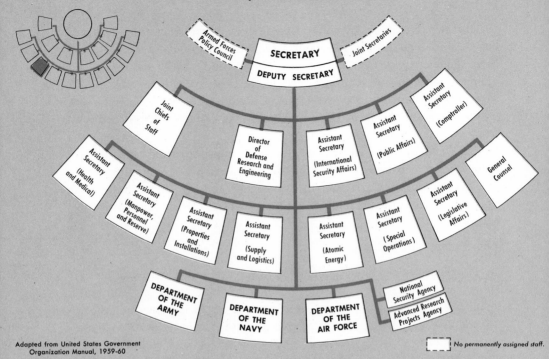

Adapted from United States Government
Organization Manual, 1959-60

☐ No permanently assigned staff.

SECRETARY. Advises President on military affairs. Assistant Secretaries of Defense administer these divisions: Comptroller (finance and accounting), Manpower and Personnel, Legislative and Public Affairs, International Security Affairs (Mutual Defense Assistance, NATO affairs, UN affairs, etc.), Research and Development, Applications Engineering (the engineering phases of development, design and production), Supply and Logistics (movement of men and supplies), Properties and Installations (property maintenance and management, family housing, etc.), Health, and Medical Affairs.

JOINT CHIEFS OF STAFF. Chairman: Chief of Staff, United States Army; Chief of Naval Operations; Chief of Staff, United States Air Force. Act as principal military advisers to the President, the National Security Council, and the Secretary of Defense. Bring together our best military knowledge and experience, develop policy, advise in making strategic and logistic plans. (See p. 683.)

DEPARTMENT OF THE ARMY. Secretary; Under Secretary, Assistant Secretaries, Counsel, Bureau Chiefs, Chief of Staff, Army General Staff, Special Staff, Technical Staff, Continental Army Command, U.S. Military Academy. (See pp. 685–687.)

DEPARTMENT OF THE NAVY. Secretary; Under Secretary, Assistant Secretaries, Chief of Naval Operations, Commandant of the Marine Corps, Commandant of the Coast Guard. The Navy also has bureaus of Aeronautics, Medicine, Ordnance, Ships, Supplies and Accounts, Yards and Docks, Naval Research, etc. (See pp. 687–689.)

DEPARTMENT OF THE AIR FORCE. Secretary; Under Secretary, Assistant Secretaries, Air Staff, 17 major commands (Air Defense, Research and Development, Continental Air Command, Strategic Air Command, Tactical Air Command, Security Service, Material Command, Proving Ground Command, Training Command, Air University, and the Overseas Commands). (See pp. 689–690.)

The Secretary of Defense is assisted, as you see on the chart, by the Deputy Secretary, several Assistant Secretaries, and a General Counsel. In addition he is advised by the civilian service Secretaries and by the Joint Chiefs of Staff, who are professional military men. The Deputy Secretary of Defense, like the Under Secretary in other departments, is the Secretary's right hand. He acts in the absence or incapacity of the Secretary and handles many important matters himself. He assists the Secretary, or acts for him, in the National Security Council, the cabinet, full meetings of the Joint Chiefs and Joint Secretaries, and represents the Department on numerous departmental and interdepartmental boards and committees, such as the Operations Coördinating Board.

The Assistant Secretaries of Defense administer the various divisions of the Department and report to the Secretary and Deputy Secretary. The names of these divisions can be seen in the chart, p. 682. Each division is, in turn, subdivided into specialized agencies to do particular jobs. The Assistant Secretaries work closely with each other to coordinate their work with the military officials of the services and with the civilian administrations of the service departments, and with outside agencies such as the Atomic Energy Commission. The General Counsel of the Department advises the Secretary, Deputy Secretary, and other officials on all legal matters. He is appointed by the President with the consent of the Senate.

The Joint Chiefs of Staff

The Joint Chiefs of Staff, composed of the military chiefs of the armed services and a chairman, also a high-ranking military man who is appointed by the President with the consent of the Senate, are responsible for recommending *military* policy to the *civilian* authorities and for coördinating all military operations. Their purpose is to bring together the best military knowledge and experience available in the country to work out and maintain wise military policy.

The Joint Chiefs are a subordinate body. They advise the Secretary of Defense, the President, and the National Security Council on the *military* aspects of foreign and defense policy. They do *not make* policy. For example, they do *not decide whether to defend* Formosa against attack by the Communist Chinese. They advise their civilian superiors on *whether it can be defended successfully* if a decision to defend it is made. If the decision is to defend it, and if it is then attacked, the Joint Chiefs would be responsible for drawing the military plans of the defense and, once the plans are approved by their civilian superiors, carrying them out through the chains of command down to planes, troops, and ships.

THE PROBLEM OF UNIFICATION

The American military establishment is not one unified organization. The Department of Defense coördinates all military activities, but it only supervises; it does not operate. Soldiers, sailors, and airmen, tanks, ships, and planes are the concern of the three service departments of the Army, Navy, and Air Force. During the 1940's there was much public discussion and considerable debate in Congress and in other parts of government on the question of amalgamating the army, navy, air force, and marines into one military organization with a single civilian administration and a single military command. There are some obvious advantages in such a system. World War II and the Korean War in 1950 to 1953 showed that modern warfare is not exclusively ground, air, or sea operations but *combined* operations, involving the closest working relations among all services and branches. Unified planning is required for the success of combined operations, whether on the attack or in preparing defenses. In addition, uniform specifications for equipment would save millions of taxpayers' dollars, and perhaps reduce the quantity of necessary supplies. Much money could be saved, and, perhaps, efficiency increased, for example, by maintaining a single air force, instead of the three to which we have become accustomed (Air Force, Navy Air Force, and Marine Corps Air Arm).

On the other hand, there are important objections to unifying the armed forces. Each branch has become so highly specialized that it is a complex matter to maintain efficiency. Thus no two branches could agree on a single type of night-fighter aircraft, since both Air Force and Navy have developed night-fighters for their particular and quite different assignments. By imposing one type on a single unified air force, the advantages of specialization would be lost. But if you did not impose one type of night-fighter, you would not really be unifying the air forces. In other words, opponents of unification argue that organization should be adapted to the jobs to be done, not the jobs to organization. The morale of the services is also involved. All branches have developed over the years fine traditions and service spirit. Distinctive uniforms and customs represent values inherent in the spirit of the different services which might be lost by unification. Finally, there is no doubt that each of the services feels a vested interest in its own independence.

The upshot of this extensive debate was a typical American compromise which, like the great compromise on national banking we studied in Chapter 21, satisfied no one fully, yet allowed something to each interested party. Congress reacted to pressures from the military, from civilian groups, and from veterans' groups, and to internal pressures from Congressmen previously associated with or prejudiced in favor of one or another service. It enacted laws to preserve the individuality of each service, but unified them all by making them subordinate to the new Department of Defense. Below the Department of Defense was established a Department of the Army, with a civilian Secretary and a full-scale civilian administration. A Department of the Navy was similarly organized. The air force was separated from the army and established as a parallel Department of the Air Force. The Naval Air Arm and the Marine Corps remained in the Department of the Navy. To coördinate military activities, the Joint Chiefs of Staff, already functioning under wartime regulations, was established by law; to coördinate administration and policy, provision was made for a commission of Joint Secretaries; and the Department of Defense, as we have seen, was established to coördinate and supervise the entire military establishment. In 1958 Congress acted to give the Secretary of Defense power to form combined military units, drawing personnel from each of the services.

The Department of the Army

The National Security Act of 1947 abolished the old War Department and assigned its functions of army administration and command to the new Department of the Army. The Secretary of the Army, who ranks below cabinet level, is appointed by the President with the consent of the Senate.

CIVILIAN ORGANIZATION   The Secretary must be a civilian, as must the Under Secretary, the two Assistant Secretaries, and the Counselor of the Department who are the Secretary's top assistants. Like the Secretary of Defense, the Secretary of the Army need not have specialized military training or knowledge. His duties require him, rather, to be an expert in the administration of very large-scale organizations. The first few Army Secretaries were businessmen or lawyers, but the office is so recent that no pattern has developed. In any case, the qualifications necessary do not differ appreciably from those of the Secretary of Defense, except that the Army Secretary's responsibilities are narrower.

The Under Secretary of the Army serves as the Secretary's principal deputy. He represents the Department on various boards and committees, relieves the Secretary of many time-consuming duties, supervises procurement, and coördinates the work of the operating divisions of the Department. The Assistant Secretaries have responsibiltities for finance and manpower, respectively, in addition to assisting the Secretary and the Under Secretary in handling such assignments as they may from time to time be given. The Counselor advises the Secretary and other officials of the Department on the innumerable legal aspects of army business. This means especially such matters as contracts for the procurement of supplies and the building of army installations.

MILITARY ORGANIZATION   The military aspects of the Department of the Army are administered by high-ranking army officers below the Secretary and his staff. At the top is the Chief of Staff, directly appointed by the President as commander-in-chief, with the consent of the Senate, who serves a two-year term. The duties of the Chief of Staff are to carry out the directives of the Secretary in all military matters. He is the operational commander of the army. All important orders to command posts and to commanders in the field are issued in his name through the military chain of command. In addition to his command duties, the Chief of Staff is responsible for explaining to the Secretary or to the Joint Chiefs of Staff the point of view of the army on all military questions of defense or attack. He plays an important part, also, in making decisions regarding types and quantities of armaments and other supplies, and recommends the number of men there should be in the forces and where they should be stationed. In his role as adviser, the Chief of Staff is frequently called to testify before Congress on matters of army policy.

The Chief of Staff is assisted by an elaborate organization of military officials. In particular, the work of the army is divided into four principal functions represented in the General Staff. These are G-1, Personnel; G-2, Intelligence; G-3, Operations; and G-4, Logistics (supplies and transportation). In recent years the Director of the Women's Army Corps has been added to the General Staff as an immediate subordinate of the Assistant Chief of Staff for Personnel.

THE CORPS OF ENGINEERS Among those offering technical services to the army is the Corps of Engineers with important duties in peacetime as well as in war. The Army Engineers build dams and reservoirs on public lands and waters, work closely with the Soil Conservation Service and the Bureau of Reclamation in many ways to conserve and improve the land, and play a major part in the vital work of flood control. (See Chap. 23.)

THE SOLDIERS The army's supply of professional commissioned officers is assured by the regular flow of graduates from the United States Military Academy at West Point. Here young men carefully selected by examinations and interviews undergo rigorous training and full-scale college education at public expense to prepare themselves for army careers. The army and the nation are proud of West Point, which numbers two Presidents among its graduates (Grant and Eisenhower). Large numbers of reserve officers are trained in college and university programs (ROTC) and in some high schools.

We may be equally proud of the many service schools operated by the army for specialized training of its personnel. In these schools men receive training valuable not only for army service but for later civilian life. The plain soldier, called an "enlisted man," is tested and interviewed upon his induction and, after basic training, is normally sent to one of these schools. See the table (p. 688) for the ranks and pay scales of commissioned and noncommissioned officers.

Army education has two purposes: to provide the army with the best possible supply of trained personnel, and to help soldiers to live useful and satisfactory lives after they leave the service. Thus the individual soldier may be trained in mechanics, accounting, business administration, radio work, or any of a large number of other specialties. His success as a specialist or as a leader of men is recognized by promotion from *private* into the ranks of the so-called non-commissioned officers (*corporal* up through various grades of *sergeant*). Unlike the commissioned officers who receive their commissions from the President, the non-coms are given their rank by the Department of the Army.

Perhaps the most important part of his education comes not from schools but from army life itself. When "G.I. Joe" from South Dakota meets "G.I. Joe" from Brooklyn, lives in barracks with him, goes through drill and maneuvers with him, and meets his sister and parents, a very important contact is made for both "Joes." And so it is with "G.I. Joes" from every corner of the land. Military service can broaden and deepen every young man's understanding of his country and its people.

The Department of the Navy

The Department of the Navy, originally a cabinet-level department of the national government under a law of 1798, was in 1947 made a military department subordinate to the Department of Defense. The navy grew very slowly, as did the army. Because a navy sails the seas, many Americans were afraid that an American navy would involve us in international disputes and wars. But our growing economic power and overseas commerce made a large navy necessary.

In the twentieth century we have spent billions upon billions of dollars for destroyers, cruisers, submarines, auxiliary vessels, and aircraft to support a line of capital ships (battleships and aircraft carriers) that had become by the end of World War II—and remains today—one of the strongest in the world. The prestige of the navy and its professional sailors has risen constantly. Naval vessels of all sorts, naval flyers, and the navy's shock troops, the marines, played so great a part in the war against Japan in the Pacific that they became a living legend. When it became apparent that modern striking power would be chiefly airborne, the navy not only developed a great air force of its own but built a whole new battle line of giant aircraft carriers to replace, for most purposes, the battleships of the past. With the coming of atomic energy, the Navy successfully built a fleet of nuclear-powered submarines. One of these, the "Nautilus," succeeded in sailing under ice across the Arctic Ocean. Both Congress and the public have been generous, even enthusiastic, in support of the navy, thus reversing the situation of early times.

CIVILIAN ORGANIZATION The Navy Department is today organized much like the Department of the Army. It is administered by the civilian Secretary of the Navy, who is appointed by the President with the consent of the Senate. The Under Secretary, two Assistant Secretaries, an Administrative Assist-

COMPARABLE RANKINGS OF COMMISSIONED AND NON-COMMISSIONED PERSONNEL OF THE MILITARY FORCES

(Army, Navy, Air Force, Marines, Coast Guard)

OFFICERS

Rank in Army, Air Force, Marine Corps	Ranks in Navy, Coast Guard	Monthly Base Pay[1]
General[2] (four stars)	Admiral[2]	$1200–1700
Lieutenant General	Vice Admiral	1063–1500
Major General	Rear Admiral (upper half)	963–1350
Brigadier General	Rear Admiral (lower half) and Commodore	800–1175
Colonel	Captain	593– 985
Lieutenant Colonel	Commander	474– 775
Major	Lieutenant Commander	400– 630
Captain	Lieutenant	326– 525
First Lieutenant	Lieutenant (junior grade)	259– 380
Second Lieutenant	Ensign	222– 314
Chief Warrant Officer	Chief Warrant Officer	265– 595
Warrant Officer	Warrant Officer	219– 390

NON-COMMISSIONED PERSONNEL

Army[3]	Air Force	Marine Corps	Navy	Monthly Base Pay
Sergeant Major	Chief Master Sgt.	Sgt. Major and Master Gunnery Sgt.	Master Chief Petty Officer	$380–440
1st Sgt. and Master Sgt.	Senior Master Sgt.	1st Sgt. and Master Sgt.	Senior Chief Petty Officer	310–380
Platoon Sgt. or Sgt. 1st Class	Master Sgt.	Gunnery Sgt.	Chief Petty Officer	206–350
Staff Sgt.	Technical Sgt.	Staff Sgt.	Petty Officer 1st Class	176–290
Sergeant	Staff Sergeant	Sergeant	Petty Officer 2nd Class	145–240
Corporal	Airman 1st Class	Corporal	Petty Officer 3rd Class	122–190
Private 1st Class	Airman 2nd Class	Lance Corp.	Navy Seaman	99–141
Private	Airman 3rd Class	Pvt. 1st Class	Apprentice	86–108
Recruit	Airman Basic	Private	Seaman Recruit	78–105

[1] Variations accounted for by years of service.

[2] By special acts of legislation, especially during wartime, Congress has conferred five-star ranking on specific generals or admirals, designating them as General of the Army or Admiral of the Fleet. There is no comparable ranking for the Marine Corps, which remains under the control of the Navy.

[3] Army ranks also include Specialists 4–9 corresponding to grades from corporal up.

ant to the Secretary, and a General Counsel are also civilians. Below them is the professional military administration of naval officers under the Chief of Naval Operations. The latter represents the navy on the Joint Chiefs of Staff. The Marine Corps, led by its Commandant, has a parallel system of organization and administration.

MILITARY ORGANIZATION   The Chief of Naval Operations heads a professional General Staff of high-ranking officers. They are responsible for all military aspects of the Department's work, for carrying out the policy of the civilian administration, and for coördinating the operations of the navy with those of the other armed services. The operating bureaus of the navy include: Aeronautics, Medicine and Surgery, Personnel, Ordnance, Ships, Supplies and Accounts, and Yards and Docks. These bureaus are responsible for building or contracting for vessels and munitions, maintaining the docks and yards of the United States, and building and maintaining airfields, training stations, and many other installations. At sea or at the naval bases are the various fleets whose commanders report to the Chief of Naval Operations.

THE OFFICE OF NAVAL RESEARCH   The Office of Naval Research (ONR), a bureau of the navy, is one of the most useful research agencies of the federal government. It carries on research in such specifically military matters as arms, aircraft, shipbuilding and design, and sound and transmission equipment, as well as in marine biology, oceanography, and even human relations. Much of its work is done by contract with private research organizations, universities, and individual scientists. Like the Corps of Engineers in the army, its work has continuing peacetime uses and values for all Americans.

THE SAILORS   Finally, the naval officer corps is constantly supplied with able young officers who graduate from the United States Naval Academy at Annapolis. This school, long one of the finest naval training colleges in the world, is known everywhere in the country for its fine tradition and its sports rivalry with West Point. Reserve officers, again, are trained in the universities. The navy also has many specialized schools which, like those of the army and air force, not only train enlisted naval personnel for their military tasks but give them a useful education for civilian life after navy service is completed. Navy "non-coms" (various grades of petty officers) are appointed in the same manner as the Army.

The ranks of officers in the United States Navy parallel those of the army and air force, though different titles are used. See table p. 688.

The Department of the Air Force

The youngest of the military branches is the United States Air Force, established as a separate Department in 1947. From a tiny beginning in World War I, the air force grew against the great resistance of skeptics who did not believe air power could ever take a leading part in warfare. Today it is high among the services in military importance. It played a crucially successful part in both World War II and the Korean War. In our time, the basic strategy of both defense and attack revolves around air striking power, including, of course, unmanned missiles. The dramatic history of the air force is symbolized by General "Billy" Mitchell, who was demoted in the 1920's for pushing vigorously but undiplomatically to build it up, yet has become a national hero today.

CIVILIAN ORGANIZATION   The structure of the Department of the Air Force resembles that of the other service departments. It is headed by the civilian Secretary of the Air Force, who is appointed by the President with the consent of the Senate, and a civilian administrative staff consisting of the Under Secretary, two Assistant Secretaries, an Administrative Assistant to the Secretary, and a General Counsel. Below the civilian authorities is the Air Force General Staff, under the Chief of Staff, which directs the military functions of the Department.

The Secretary of the Air Force, whose position in the government grows in importance with the rapid advances in air power as our principal military weapon, has responsibilities and functions like those of the other service Secretaries.

MILITARY ORGANIZATION The military operations of the air force are administered by the Air Staff under the Chief of Staff. Operating bureaus include Comptroller, Personnel, Procurement and Training, Operations and Materiel (military supplies including aircraft). Similar to the bureaus are the military air commands.

Details of air force military operations are not, of course, public information. But it is known that the Air Defense Command has radar screening for the whole North American continent, from Arctic bases down through the United States, while the Strategic Air Command is prepared to launch retaliatory attack upon an aggressor anywhere in the world. The Tactical Air Command prepares for air missions during actual warfare, as part of military operations at sea, on the ground, and in the air.

Officers of the air force are trained at the United States Air Force Academy in Colorado Springs, the newest of the service colleges. Formerly West Point supplied both army and air force professional officers. The new Air Academy is abundant evidence that the air force has come of age. Reserve officer training programs are conducted in universities. Enlisted airmen, like soldiers and sailors, are trained in specialized schools where they learn skills and trades useful not only to their careers in the air force but for their future lives as private citizens. As air force technicians gain in skill and usefulness, they may rise in the non-commissioned ranks as do non-coms in the army and navy. See table p. 688 for ranks and pay scales of officers and non-commissioned officers in the air force.

The endless research conducted by the air force, often in collaboration with private aircraft factories, industrial research laboratories, and universities, has not only steadily advanced the excellence of military aircraft and related equipment but also resulted in improvements and inventions useful in civil aviation.

Missiles and Space Exploration

The jet age quickly brought with it the development of weapons capable of hurtling great distances through the sky, carrying nuclear warheads and needing no human pilot. Such engines, launched from the ground, from submarines, or even from airplanes aloft, are called missiles. The Department of Defense and all of the service military departments have continuous and massive programs of research, development, and procurement of these weapons. There are many agencies and bureaus at work on missiles and on problems of space navigation, as the list on p. 213 shows. In 1958 a special independent agency, the National Aeronautics and Space Administration, was established to deal with all non-military aspects of space exploration and navigation. This agency is headed by a Director, appointed by the President with the consent of the Senate, and has a growing staff of technical experts. It works closely with the military departments on scientific matters and coördinates government with private research and development.

It is this agency which supervises the work of experimental rocket blasts at such famous points as Cape Canaveral and strives to meet the continuing challenge of Soviet space engineering.

Women in the Armed Forces

The contribution of women to the American armed forces has always been indispensable. The corps of nurses in both army and navy have long and heart-warming histories. For many years the women of the civilian Red Cross have worked closely with troops to relieve the rigors of military life and the suffering that comes with all wars. In World War II, large numbers of women were brought into the military services directly, on a volunteer basis. Women volunteers replaced men not only in secretarial work but also in driving trucks, assisting officers in command posts, and doing many technical jobs, thus relieving men for duty elsewhere. Today each of the services has a volunteer force of professional service women—the Wacs (army), Waves (navy and marine), and Wafs (air force). These women work side by side with men in nearly all military duties except combat training. If the United States should ever again be involved in an all-out war, it is possible that women would be drafted for service.

Non-Military Contributions of the Armed Forces

The army and navy are justly proud of their long traditions, and the newer air force is fast building up a proud tradition of its own. Not only have all of the services served well and honorably in any wars or defense activities we have engaged in during our history, but also their personnel has contributed to many non-military aspects of our life.

Army surgeons have discovered the cause and cure of such diseases as malaria and yellow fever. Navy men have done research which has advanced our knowledge of marine biology, oceanography. Flood control has been forwarded by engineers of the military. In fact, technical services of the various military have altered the face of the nation.

In addition, the training programs of the various services have given millions of Americans a better education than they might otherwise have

DEFENSE OF LIBERTY

Under our new Department of Defense, the Army, the Navy, and the Air Force still function as separate divisions. Between them they divide and share the duties of military defense of our liberties. The nerve center of this complicated system is the Pentagon in Washington.

In the Department of the Navy, the Marine Corps "hits the beach" in practice maneuvers, and jet planes of the Navy Air Force return to the aircraft carrier *USS Forrestal*—prepared to defend liberty in far corners of the world.

An Army anti-aircraft position, using a "radar trailer," defends liberty also—perhaps closer to home—though our soldiers are also prepared by training to take the offensive, if it should become necessary, by attacking enemy positions.

The Air Force itself is not only airborne; it also requires ground observer posts like this one in California.

obtained. Many of our commercial air-line pilots received their training in
the air force. Men and women in the service have learned skills and trades
useful to them in their civilian careers.

Military Courts

Each of the services operates a judicial system of its own. Military police,
or other officers, make arrests of military personnel charged with crimes and
the accused are tried in military courts. So far as possible, the accused receive
similar safeguards to those afforded by the civilian judicial system. Military
justice effectively keeps military and civilian affairs separated, though, of
course, military personnel off duty are subject to arrest by civilian police as is
anyone else.

DEFENSE UNDER STATE GOVERNMENTS

From colonial times until well into the twentieth century, the basic military manpower reserve of the United States was, as we have said, the militia.
The citizen soldiers of the militia were under the authority of the state
governments, with governors as commanders-in-chief. In our time, the National Guard, as the militia is known, has been to a great extent integrated,
under federal law, with the armed forces of the United States. This means
that the President may call the National Guard to service during wartime,
that it is supported financially by federal appropriations, and that it is provided with equipment and advisory officer personnel by the regular military
departments. But state governors are commanders-in-chief of the National
Guard units, when not in federal service, and commission the officers. In
peacetime the National Guard continues to be trained on the state level, with
local units in which citizen soldiers train for brief periods each year at bases
near their homes.

The National Guard today includes an air militia known as the Air
National Guard. It is militia duty, modern style, which takes your neighborhood grocer, bank teller, or cab driver to the annual training periods you read
about in the paper. Your father may be a National Guardsman who each year
trains with an artillery unit. Your neighbor may be the pilot of one of those
jet fighters you see zooming past your town in flight training. These are the
citizen soldiers of today.

Because the National Guard today is so largely concerned with national
defense, many states have established new military organizations known as
the State Guard to serve while the National Guard is on national duty. State
Guards, likewise composed of volunteer militiamen, are under the sole control
of state governments and take orders from the governor as commander-in-
chief. They may be called out at the discretion of the governor for the defense

694

of the state, to restore public order, or to undertake emergency tasks such as flood control. State Guards are not a part of the national military establishment.

CIVIL DEFENSE

The program of national defense is rounded out by the efforts of the people to keep themselves in a state of preparation for an enemy attack upon the American continent. Originally the program was directed by the Federal Civil Defense Administration, an independent agency. In 1958, a new law created the Office of Civil and Defense Mobilization in the Executive Office of the President. The Director of the new office, through his staff, coördinates civil defense work, maintains a national communications and alarm system, advises the state civil defense agencies on alarm systems, construction of shelters, education of citizens about civil defense needs, and many other matters. He makes grants to the states of federal money appropriated by Congress for civil defense work. In addition, the Office of Civil and Defense Mobilization conducts frequent conferences to bring together civil defense officials for the interchange of ideas and information.

Most civil defense workers are volunteers. They work as air raid wardens, ground observers, emergency police, and do many other important jobs. You may know from your own experience what a practice alert is like. You may also have noticed that too many people are unwilling to take them seriously. But if an actual atomic raid should come, evacuation of cities and adequate shelters for those who cannot escape would mean the difference between life and death for millions of people. If you are one of the many Americans who ask "What can I do?" to participate in democratic government, civil defense is a clear and immediate answer. You can serve yourself and your country by volunteering. But perhaps the best possibie "civil defense" will come with progress toward worldwide disarmament.

SUMMARY

Americans have a long tradition of opposition to war and to things military. For generations we had only the tiniest regular armed forces, and relied chiefly for national defense on the citizen militia of the states. You have learned in this chapter how our gradual involvement in world affairs and our growing economic strength led to our permanent military establishment.

Yet, as the Constitution provides, civilian government remains in full control. You have studied the relation of the citizen today to these forces, in the milita (National Guard) or through the Selective Service System.

695

We have seen in this chapter that the United States military establishment today is coördinated by an overall Department of Defense. You have seen how this Department works to supervise and coördinate the functions of the subordinate military departments. You have examined the structure and operations of the Departments of the Army, Navy, and Air Force. You should now have a better appreciation of the enormous scope of our military effort for defense and be able to see how valuable it is, not only for ourselves but for all free nations.

You have seen also how the state governments make their contributions to national defense through maintaining National Guard units, for the service of the states themselves and also of the nation in wartime. Finally, you have considered the problem of civil defense, and seen to what a great extent our survival in a future war would depend not only on our military but on our civilian efforts.

KNOW WHAT YOU READ

1. What is the meaning of *military establishment?* Why is it necessary?
2. Why has the United States found it necessary to maintain a large-scale military establishment?
3. Why must our country now carry on the draft (selective service) when we are not at war?
4. John Smith, Jr., is eighteen years old. With whom must he *register?* What may he expect to happen after registration?
5. Explain the extent to which civilians control the military establishment of our country.
6. Summarize the responsibilities of the Secretary of Defense. What officials assist and advise him?
7. What are the chief arguments for and against unification of the armed forces?
8. What is the work of the Joint Chiefs of Staff?
9. Explain how the problem of unification was "settled" by compromise.
10. What qualifications should a person have to be Secretary of the Army?
11. The highest ranking army man in our defense organization is the Chief of Staff. What are his duties?
12. First Lieutenant John Smith hopes some day to rise to become a four star general. What ranks must he first win if he is to be successful?
13. John's younger brother Joe is about to go into the Army. In what ways can he expect this experience to become a part of his education?
14. What official is the chief administrator of the Navy Department? What naval officer holds highest rank in the Navy's military organization?
15. List the ranks of officers in the United States Navy.

16. What kinds of activities are carried on by the Office of Naval Research?
17. In what ways is the civilian organization of the Air Force like those of the Army and Navy?
18. Compare the Air Force's military organization to that of the Army.
19. Summarize the educational and research activities of the Air Force.
20. Jane Jones too would like to serve in the Armed Forces of her country. What branches of the service are open to her? What types of activities might she expect to perform?
21. Fred is a senior in high school. He is also a member of the National Guard. Who is his commander-in-chief?
22. Fred is enthusiastic about flying. What aviation opportunities does the National Guard offer young men?
23. What are the responsibilities of the states in civil defense. What civil defense work is done by the Office of Civil and Defense Mobilization?
24. Explain how civil defense depends on volunteers.

WHAT DO YOU THINK?

1. Do you favor or oppose universal military training? Why?
2. Should our Armed Forces be further "unified"?
3. What do you think of this statement (made by an Air Force psychologist): "Today's generation is growing up with a lack of discipline in the homes and schools and churches. When they get into this airplane business they are plunged into an environment which demands discipline. They've got to be disciplined by the environment before it kills them."

PROBLEMS AND PROJECTS FOR YOU

1. Look up in a fairly comprehensive U.S. history book the contributions of both Theodore Roosevelt and Franklin D. Roosevelt to the building up of the U.S. Navy. Report.
2. From time to time young men, graduates of your school who are now in the Armed Forces, return to your community on "leave." Invite one or more to visit your class and answer questions about opportunities in the services.
3. As a study in civilian control, look up the facts of the disagreement between President Truman and General MacArthur. Summarize your findings.
4. Young men approaching military age should find out about the several "Reserve" plans available to them. Inquire at your local post office for the address of the nearest "advisor" who can give you this information. Tell the class what you learned about one or more reserve plans.

5. In one day in 1956 members of the Air Force did the following things:
   A wing of B-47's left Ohio for Africa.
   A squadron of F-84's left Virginia for Okinawa.
   An Air Force pilot flew a hospital case from Italy to Germany.
   Officers at Colorado Springs attended a class in public speaking.
   Instructors from our Air Force trained Brazilian pilots in jet fighters.
   What is the Air Force doing this year? Make a bulletin-board display.
6. It has been claimed that one of our defense shortages is a lack of scientists. Interview some qualified person in your community to find out what part scientists play in our defense.
7. Make a poster dealing with the subject of 6 above.

> Have that high school sheepskin in your hip pocket when you start to think seriously about your Army career. It may interest you to know that you must be a high school graduate to be eligible to take the Officer Candidate Test, and the Army's Technical Training Program gives preference to young men who are high school graduates in considering applicants for its classes. It's common sense that you are of greater value to your country, to the Army, and to yourself if you have completed your high school studies.

8. In the light of the above quotation, think very carefully about the subjects you have studied and the activities of your own high school career. Then write a composition on the subject, "Why I Should Finish High School."

   Or, you may prefer to set up a panel discussion of the pros and cons of the Army's attitude toward finishing high school. This may be a better discussion if you get on your panel young people who have not studied the same courses you have.
9. Present to the class a report on NATO. Consult the *Reader's Guide* for current material.
10. Recently it was reported that "in all of these states (the 32 states of the "skywatch" area) the problem of recruiting and holding the interest of volunteer watchers is one of serious proportions."
    If you are in a likely enemy target area, interview a volunteer worker of the Ground Observer Corps. Tell the class what you learn about this program.
    If unable to obtain information by interview, write to the Superintendent of Documents for the bulletin "Continental Air Defense." Report.
11. The U.S. Navy publishes a Navy Occupational Handbook which gives descriptions of every Navy job. This book also tells how naval training may be used in civilian life. Ask your guidance counselor for this book, or inquire at your local post office to find out the nearest Navy counselor. Report on jobs which interest you.
12. Write a composition on the work of Colonel Wm. C. Gorgas in Panama at the time of the building of the Canal.
13. Draw an original chart showing the organization of the Army, the Navy, or the Air Force.

EXTEND YOUR VOCABULARY

military establishment
militia
Washington Conference
National Guard
draft (conscription)
Universal Military and Training
  Act
unification
combined operations
Chief of Staff
logistics
commissioned officer
enlisted man
induction

reserve officer
procurement
Office of Naval Research
General "Billy" Mitchell
Air Defense Command
Strategic Air Command
missiles
National Aeronautics and Space
  Administration
Wacs
Waves
Wafs
Air National Guard

YOUR NOTEBOOK: THE GOVERNMENT OF ——

1. Is there a National Guard unit in your area? If so, what kind of unit is it? Where does it meet? How often?
2. Name the members of your local draft board.
3. Interview local officials, and write a description, with chart, of the civil defense organization of your community.

READ MORE ABOUT IT

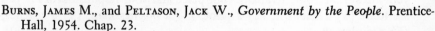

Burns, James M., and Peltason, Jack W., *Government by the People*. Prentice-Hall, 1954. Chap. 23.

Morgenthau, Hans J., "Can We Entrust Defense to a Committee?" *New York Times Magazine*, June 7, 1959.
Provocative discussion of a pertinent question.

Morgenthau, Hans J., *Politics Among Nations: The Struggle for Power and Peace*. Knopf, 1955.
"Realism" vs. "idealism" in foreign affairs and national defense—difficult but stimulating.

Stanley, Timothy W., *American Defense and National Security*. Public Affairs Press, 1956.
Readable and thoughtful.

Swarthout, John M., and Bartley, Ernest R., *Principles and Problems of American National Government*. Oxford University Press, 1955. Chap. 21.

THINK ABOUT

YOU AND AMERICA'S PLACE IN THE WORLD

In the early days of our republic, our policy was to avoid permanent commitments in Europe or elsewhere. In today's world we can no longer maintain such aloofness from the events in other countries or from their problems. Our foreign policy, setting a course to guide us through the currents of world events, must call on each citizen to take his place in the whole pattern. For that reason, this unit, which has discussed foreign policy, communism, and the defense of our country, is keynoted by a "Greeting from the President" draft notice. This symbolizes service to our country—though some of the service may be not in the armed forces but rather in a diplomatic post, or as an everyday citizen, taking an intelligent interest in and an active part in preserving the "self-evident truths" of our Declaration of Independence.

1. What part do you think your education plays in preparing you for the role you will play in the "defense" of our country? Try to think through your answer carefully. Evaluate your place and your responsibilities if you are to be (1) a scientist; (2) a pilot; (3) a businessman; (4) a teacher; (5) a diplomat.
2. America's stakes in world responsibility are "freedom and survival." Comment on this statement. What part can you as a citizen—even before you reach voting age—take in helping plan a foreign policy to meet the challenge to America?
3. Write an essay on the subject: "How American experience disproves the prophecies of Marx, Lenin, and Stalin."
4. Compare democracy and communism in standard of living; education; respect for the individual; in respect for agreements. Document your answer.

700

INDEX

Page numbers in *italic* refer to illustrations and captions

701

703

705

706

Mayor-council government, 316 ff., *319*; advantages and disadvantages, 321; council, 317 ff., *319*; mayor's functions, *319*, 321
Mediation, labor-management, federal services, 558; private services, 561; state, 560 f.
Mediation and Conciliation Service, Federal, 558
Mediation Board, National, 558
Medical services, local, 328 f.; Public Health Service, *594*, 595 ff., *602*; state, 290
Metropolitan area, 304
Midway Island, government of, 345
Military Appeals, U.S. Court of, 236, 694
Military establishment, 675; civilian control, 54, 680; *see also* Armed forces; Defense Department; National defense
Military power of President, 31, 54, 166 f., 169
Militia, 676 f., 694
Mines, Bureau of, *580*, 582; and state, 291
Ministers, 633 f., 646 f.
Minority rights, 32, 39; in dictatorships, 394; rule of democracy, 35, 393 ff.
Mint, Bureau of, 54, 520 ff., *521*
Misdemeanors, 222, 253
Missiles, 485; agencies, 213, 690 f.
Moderator, town meeting, 305
Money, easy policy, 523; tight policy, 524; *see also* Mint; Treasury Department
Monopolies, 259, 260
Monroe, James, 78 f., 181, 435, 436
Monroe Doctrine, 623
Motion pictures, and public opinion, 421
Municipal courts, 240, 253 ff.
Museums, local government services, 331

Narcotics, Bureau of, 262, *521*
National Aeronautics and Space Council, *176*, 179
National banks, 526, 527 f.
National committees, 443; organization, 466
National defense, and citizen, 676 ff., 694; civil defense program, 695; National Guard, 54, 398, 694; power of Congress, 53; taxation for, 483, *484*, 485 f; *see also* Armed forces; Defense Department
National forests, 578 f.
National Guard, 54, 90, 251, 398; and defense, 681, 694; functions, 694 f.
National Institutes of Health, 667
National Labor Relations Board, 207 f., 545, 553
National Park Service, *580*, 585
National Science Foundation, 212, 612
National Security Council, 166, *176*, 178; foreign policy advice of, 645, 681, 683
Naturalization, 6, 257 ff., *258*, 363; laws, 53; procedure, 366, 367
Naval Research, Office of, 689
Navigation, federal control, 59, *515*, 517
Navy, Department of, 680, 682, 687 ff., 692; "White Fleet," 677; rankings and pay, 688; reserve, 689
Near vs. Minnesota, free speech, 386
"Necessary and proper" clause, 54, 93 f.
Negroes, 400; equal rights, growth in, 18, 19; voting privilege, 399
Neutrality Acts, 624 f.
Newspapers, influence on public opinion, 417, 419; information source, 180

New Jersey Plan, 71
New states, admission to Union, 60
Nominations, methods of, 461 ff.
Nonprofit organizations, tax exemption, 489
Norris-LaGuardia Act, 547
North Atlantic Treaty Organizaiton, 486, 626, 627, 643

Offenses, 222
Offices, *see other part of title*
Old-Age and Survivors' Insurance, *594*, 598
Operations, Bureau of, 533
Operations Coordinating Board, *176*, 179
Opportunity, *see* Equal opportunity
Ordinances, 165, 316 ff., *370 f.*
Organic Act of 1950, 345
Organization of American States, 643

Panama Canal Zone, 344
Pardon, by governor, 285, 286; by President, 57, 165, 263 f.
Parity, 573, *574*
Parks, national, 94, 97; National Park Service, *580*, 585; state, 291
Parole, 264
Party conference, 120
Party whip, House, *121*; Senate, *129*
Passport, 377, 630
Patent Office, functions of, 513 f., *515*
Patents, Court of Customs and Patent Appeals, 237; power of Congress, 54, 513 ff.
Patronage, 195, 439 ff., 441
Payroll taxes, 494, 550, 559, 598
Peaceful persuasion, freedom to use, 35
Pendleton Act, 193
Personnel, Bureau of, 533
Petit jury, trial by, 62, 63, 229 f.
Petition, right to, 62, 75, 385 f.; *see also* Initiative
Philippine Islands, 341
Pittsburgh "Golden Triangle," 333
Plaintiff, 222, 223
Platform, party, citizen's role in forming, 11, 448; at national convention, 460 f.
Pocket veto, power of President, 52, 144
Point Four program, 643
Police, 248 ff., 329 ff.; state, 251, 291
Political parties, 11, 431 ff.; advantages of party membership, 444 ff.; citizen's role in, 438, 440, *446*; financing, 442, 443 f., 467 f.; foreign policy, bipartisan support, 628, 646; government, effect on, 432; local organization, 438 ff.; minority (third) parties, 433 f.; national organization, 443; operations, national level, 456 ff.; operations, state and local level, 449 ff.; opposition party, 476; organization of, *440*; party in power, 475; patronage, 439, 441; platform, 11, 448, 460; and President, 171; Presidential elections, 457 ff.; responsibilities of members, 448 f.; state organization, 443, 450; *see also* Democratic party; Republican party
Poll tax, 384
Polls, public opinion, 423 ff.; value of, 424
Population, distribution, *12, 13*; increase, 18
Posse comitatus, 301
Post Office Department, 532; chart, *533*; law enforcement by, 262; Postmaster General, *533*, 534

707

Searches and seizures, 62, 248 f., 390
Secondary boycott, 208
Secret Service, 177, 256, 520, *521*
Secretary, *see other part of title*
Securities and Exchange Commission, 206
f.; law enforcement by, 262
Security, and government, 257, 362 f.
Security Council (UN), 636 f.
Selective Service System, 678 ff.
Selectmen, 305
Self-incrimination, 62, 156, 229, 392 f.
Senate, action, 143; as continuing body, 51,
127; committees, 128, 131, 142; composi-
tion of, 50, 65, 127, 146; debate, limited,
130; floor leaders, 130; officers, 115, 127,
128, 129, 131; organization, 127, 129;
powers of, 51, 115, 125 f.; quorum, 52,
143; rules of, 52, 130; *see also* Congress;
House of Representatives; Senators
Senate Crime Committee, 154
Senators, choice of, history, 78; compensa-
tion, 52, 115, 127; election of, 51, 65, 71,
125; qualifications, 51, 65, 115, 127; *see
also* Congressmen; Senate
Seniority, 124, 137, 279
Severance tax, 497
Shays' Rebellion, 486
Sheriff, 300, 301, 302
Sherman Act, 259 f.
Silver, in coins, 522; price of, 520
Slander, 75
Slavery, Constitutional ban, 64
Slum clearance, local government, 331
Small Business Administration, 512
Small claims courts, 240
Small states, and Great Compromise, 71
Smith Act, 361 f., 392, 434
Smithsonian Institution, 212, 214
Social legislation, 592 ff.
Social Security Act, 53, 555, 594, 598 ff.;
benefits, 599; taxation, 494
Social Security Administration, 594, 598 ff.
Socialist party, 434
Soil Conservation Service, 579
Solicitor General, 256, 258; state, 251
Southeast Asia Treaty Organization, 486,
626, 627
Sovereignty, 92; of people, 99
Soviet Union, arms race, 671; Chinese Rev-
olution, 664; "co-existence," 669 f.; dicta-
torship in, 29; foreign policy, 660 ff.;
government, chart, 665 f., 667; Marxian
communism, 655 ff.; and Nazi Germany,
661 f.; policy, 671; satellites, 662 ff.
Space age, 213, 690
Speaker of the House, 50, 115, 120, 122
Speaker's Bureau, 466 f.
Special districts, 309, 310, 501
Speech, freedom of, 385, 386; guarantee,
62, 75; limits on, 75, 386, 387
Standards Bureau, 516
Standing committees, 123, 128
Standing vote, 143
Stare decisis, 223
State Department, 628 ff.; chart, 630; Economic Affairs, Bureau of, 630, 635; For-
eign Service, 632 f.; Public Affairs, Bureau
of, 635; Foreign Service Institute, 635,
640; Intelligence and Research Bureau,
635; purpose of, 628; regional bureaus,

630, 631; Secretary of State, 629, 631,
640, 646 f.; United Nations, 630, 635; *see
also* Foreign aid policy, trade
State governments, 270 ff.; activities, 289 ff.;
agriculture, services to, 576; apportionment, 276 ff., 277; attorney general, 284;
auditors and treasurers, 289; banks, 290,
526, 527 f.; business, 536 ff., civil rights,
80 ff., 383 ff., 385 ff., 395 ff., 399 ff.;
corporations, 537; concurrent powers, 98,
99 ff., 100; constitutions, 271 ff., 282;
courts, 234, 236 ff., 239, 394 ff.; defense,
694 f.; election procedures, 384 f., 399
ff.; employment, 555 f.; executive branch,
287 ff.; governors, 281 ff., 286; grants-in-
aid, 298, 299, 484, 485, 501, 612; health,
290 f.; housing, 331; interstate coöperation, 288, 289; labor, 559 ff.; law enforcement agencies, 251 ff., 263, 291; legislatures, 274 ff., 275, 277 ff., 280 ff.; local
government, 297 ff., 298, 334 ff.; nominations for offices, 449, 451; police, 251,
291; political organization, 441 ff.; powers,
99, 270; primaries, 78, 80, 377, 445,
449 ff., 457 f.; schools, 371, 605 ff., 606,
607; secretary of state, 284; taxes, 496,
609 ff.; universities 608; zoning, 334
State of the Union message, 170
State Tax Commission, 497
States' rights, 59, 63
Statutory law, *see* Law
Standing committees, of Congress, 122
Steering committees, 125, 131
Stock exchanges, regulation, 206
Straw vote, 423
Strict constructionists, 97 f., 436, 437
Subpoena, 62, 229, 249, 250, 396
Subsidies, 138, 575
"Suburbia," 332
Suffrage, *see* Voting privilege
Suits, civil, 222 ff., 247 f.; equity, 222
Summons, 223; and complaint, 246 f.
Superintendent, school, 607
Supervisors County Board, 300 f.
Supreme Court, appellate jurisdiction, 232;
appointment of members, 58, 231 f.;
checks on powers of President and Con-
gress, 30, 74; Constitutional provision for,
58, 59, 230; decisions, 53, 54, 55, 59, 60,
61, 64, 96 n., 103, 225, 231, 386, 387,
393, 490 f., 582; judicial review, 103, 231;
original jurisdiction, 232 f., 234; routine
of, 232; *see also* Courts; Judiciary
Supreme courts, state, 238
Suspended sentence, 253
Surgeon-General, 594, 595 f.
Surrogate courts, 240
Syllogism, and public opinion, 413 f.

Taft-Hartley Act, 207, 547, 553, 558
Tariff Commission, 162, 212, 493
Tariffs, 484, 488, 493; and parties, 436, 437
Tax Court, 236, 261, 495
Taxation, 481 ff.; ability-to-pay, 502 f.; chart,
484; controlling economy by, 486 ff., 487;
corporation taxes, 492, 494; estate taxes,
484, 494; excise taxes, 493, 494; exemptions, 489; expenditures, 117; external taxes, 495; gambling tax, 489; gift
taxes, 489; income tax, 53, 65, 484, 490;

709